THE

PHILADELPHIANS

A Story of Two American Families

jwcarvin

Nothing
in
Common

Cover design and maps by jwcarvin

Printed in the United States of America
ISBN 978-0-9768183-4-2

To Karen,
with appreciation
for her constant patience,
to Nancy, for teaching me
how to write my name, and
to David and Lisa, for
their help with the
final text.

Greater Philadelphia (Northside)

Germantown

Map 4: North Kensington
circa 1900 →

Lehigh Ave

Germantown Ave

6th St

Kensington Ave

W York St

Front Street

Map 3: Neighborhood
around Jimmy's Tavern
1877-1920

2nd St

Norris
Square

E. York St

Kensington

Front Street

Petty's
Island

Old Kensington

Master St.

Map 1: 1844 Riots →

Schuylkill River

Map 2: Canal St →
Area 1860-1880

West
Philadelphia

Philadelphia

Delaware River

Downtown

Market St

Statehouse
(Liberty
Bell)

CONTENTS

APPENDICES

Dominick F. Murphy & Hannah Donegan
1809 - 1878   1812 - 1893

Dennis F. Murphy
1834-1896

Hanna
1836-1924

James J.
1838-1874

Mary Ann
1840-1922

Edward V. Murphy
1843-1919

Dominic I Murphy
1847-1930

John A.
1849-1942

Joseph P. Murphy & Adele Miller
1845-1910   1849-1931

Adele G.
1871-1887

Anna Marie
1875-1951

Edward V.
1878-1964

Francis D.
1881-1959

Elizabeth H.
1883-1868

Maria A.
1885-1975

Mary R.
1888-1958

Loretto M
1890-1961

Walter L.
1892-1959

Raymond
1894-1975

Joseph D. Murphy & Stella Congdon
1873-1936   1872-1924

Stella Marie Murphy
1896-1976

Genevieve S.
1897-1897

Mary L.
1899-1899

Joseph E.
1901-1983

William Carvin & Mary Ann Morrow
1799 - 1864 1814 - 1863

Mary Ann Carvin
1832-1911

Catherine
1835- ?

James Carvin
1838-1862

Thomas J Carvin
1842-1906

Mary Carvin
1844- ?

Elizabeth
1846 - ?

William H.
1850-1929

George W.
1855-1891 Charles
1858-1930

Catherine Hagen & **Joseph J. Carvin**
1862-1893 1854-1834 & Kate Sherick
1872-1898

Joseph J Carvin Jr
1881-1919

Sarah (Sadie)
1884-1963

Florence C.
1888-1958

Charles W. Carvin
1897-1974

Preface

Many books have been written about the founding of America in Philadelphia. This is not one of them. It's not about George Washington cutting down cherry trees, and it's not always about wisdom, great accomplishments, or patriotic virtue. It aims to be about real people.

That said, no book could ever recount the accomplishments, faults and foibles of all of us; this book focuses on the efforts of two families – one well-to-do, the other less so – to realize the American promise of liberty.

Women may feel slighted by their almost complete exclusion, and with good reason: the men of this story acted as if they were running everything, not only taking charge of business, government and finance, but documenting their accomplishments in official records, newspapers and history books, while entrusting the future to their sons. They relegated their women to kitchens, pantries and nurseries, praising them with unwritten words that, while often sincerely felt, were rarely preserved for later generations. Attempts have lately been made to tell of the teachers, ministers and confederates among our motherly kin, and we can hope that there is more yet to be written about them. But this history – because heavily dependent on official records, newspapers, and history books – is mostly the story of men.

Just as limiting, and for similar reasons, this is mostly a story about white men. As such, it's the sort of history everyone studied while we were growing up, but to which youth, thankfully, is not limited today.

And be forewarned: these men shared a single ethnic heritage – Irish – a single religion – Roman Catholicism – and they all lived in the same urban environment – the city of Philadelphia. So this is most assuredly *not* a story about everyone. And yet, in a broader sense, it hopes to be. Philadelphia, after all, has always been a quintessentially American city, made of separate elements, but united under a single flag and a single goal: the realization of liberty. This is a story of how particular men, each with a vision of what it meant to be an American, tried to shape their country into what they thought it should be. Even if we've gotten some things wrong, the people described here, trying to achieve a common dream, parented the people many of us became. They helped make the world into which we were born, leaving us to try our own hands at the great endeavor they began. May we learn, by studying their lives, from their accomplishments and their mistakes.

1. Dominick F. Murphy

When one member of the Murphy clan died in 1936, his obituary stated that his family had been "engaged in the textile business in this country and Ireland for more than 200 years."[1] It was how all the Murphys wished to be remembered; they were proud of the family business, passed down from father to son, by which they'd become prosperous in the old country. Family tradition had it that an ancestor, a family patriarch, had once been Lord Mayor of Dublin.

But the story is also told that one of the Murphys (here supply a Christian name of your choice) once returned to the old country to investigate that tradition. Upon finding a bearded, almost elfin old man who served as Leinster's unofficial historian, the visitor was gratified to hear the old man say, in his heavy Irish brogue, that he'd known the Murphy patriarch well. He could see the family resemblance in the younger face before him. But as sure as he was of Jesus, Mary and Joseph, the ancestor had lived in Munster, not Leinster, and more importantly, he had not been the Lord Mayor of Dublin – he *had been hung by* the Lord Mayor of Dublin.

Whatever mix of good and bad gave rise to it, the Murphys who came to America cherished their success. They'd once made good livings by tending sheep, their wives and daughters spinning wool into skeins of yarn and handing it back to the men for weaving into cloth. In time, they'd come to engage other weavers to do likewise. Their success distinguished them from the more common immigrants of the day – the poorer, rougher, lower class of common laborers, and that was important, for identification with the lower class could mean being written off, told to move on, asked for proof, accused, blamed or arrested. Still, demonstrating that one was not of that class wasn't always easy: once ticket stubs had been discarded, there was little to distinguish first class from steerage.

Dominick F. Murphy (b. 1809) and his bride Hannah Donegan (b. 1812) were also proud to be members of the one, the true, the most holy apostolic Roman Catholic Church. Their British overlords hadn't let them own land, vote or teach school. Many Irishmen swore by the Mother of Jesus that the British had even outlawed the priesthood itself.[2] Oppression had split the Catholics of Ireland into two camps. Most followed Daniel O'Connell, a hero committed to an independent and strictly Catholic Ireland. The Murphys were among the followers of Thomas Moore, the bard whose dream of Irish Independence included sharing the country with Presbyterians. As a part of this faction, the Murphys were avid supporters of unity. (Living in the same country didn't mean you had to abandon your faith, as long as each faith respected the rights of the other.) Perhaps there was something about their interest in unity that made them optimistic about life in the United States of America.

Fourteen of the men who'd signed the Declaration of Independence were still alive when Dominick was born; he and Hannah had grown up hearing stories of the great American experiment in democracy. But given their prosperity, they had little incentive to leave Ireland until the late 1820's, when English manufacturers dumped cheap cloth on the Irish market and even prosperous Irishmen began wondering if things might be better in America, a "promised land of plenty," with "no tyranny, no oppression from landlords, and no taxes."[3] With their infant son Dennis (b. 1834), Dominick and Hannah made their way to the New World in search of democratic self-rule, religious tolerance, and economic prosperity.[4]

When their ship arrived in New York between 1833 and 1835, their first impression was that everything they'd heard about America was true. Yes, there were signs of division: notably, African slavery was still a fact of life, even in the north.[5] But President Andrew Jackson's Indian Removal Act had cleared the land for white settlement. There was no state religion, no laws against Catholicism, and more freedom than Dominick and Hannah were used to. After a few years in New York, they made their way to Kensington, a Pennsylvania township on the Delaware River about two miles north of Philadelphia. The country's birthplace and the smaller townships around it were known for the religious tolerance of their Quaker founders. Carding, spinning and weaving there were much the same as in the old country. It was said that a man could do well for himself weaving wool cloth or the cotton so abundant in the American South.

Spread out along the riverbank, Kensington was less crowded than New York, less crowded even than Philadelphia. Chestnut trees provided shady walks, houses stood apart from each other, the air was clean and there was rich farmland barely a stone's throw to the north. Of course, as the Murphys learned soon enough, not all the neighborhoods were so pleasant. Idyllic as it was in some ways, the township was a rough and tumble place in the early 1840's. While it had more greenery than much of the American West, it had a similar style of law enforcement: no police force, only a sheriff who, lacking funds to pay a posse, had to rely on volunteers.[6] Houses being made of wood and cotton being flammable, homes and mills alike were beset by constant fear of fire, and volunteer fire companies gave rise to street gangs that took responsibility for community welfare. One news reporter – Edgar Allen Poe – wrote for *Alexander's Weekly Messenger* in 1840 about "a delightful little war" in Kensington that year, in which residents fought against the building of a railway line they feared would bring sparks, burning coal and a threat of fire to their neighborhood. Poe described residents attacking the workmen who were trying to prepare the railroad bed, their weapons including stones "discharged from the fair hands of the damsels of Kensington." He described the "uproarious shout of triumph" and "high glee" when the residents succeeded in forcing the railroad company to stop work.[7] To the Irish of Kensington – the great majority of its residents – "rule-by-resident" embodied the American promise of liberty, the democratic ideal.[8]

And so, there was more rioting on January 9, 1843, when (to enforce justice as they saw it) a party of angry weavers started destroying property that belonged to those who'd agreed to work below the desired wage scale. "They tore out some material from a loom, broke the loom and other property, kicked the man's wife and trampled one of his children on the ground."[9] The meeting that ensued among the weavers at the Nanny Goat Market was only a stone's throw from Murphy's home. As a weaver himself, Murphy may have hoped the meeting would settle the problem, but it did not.[10] Some men, it seems, wanted to keep the advantages they'd worked for, while others wanted to share in them. Whether the former would be free to keep what they had, or the latter prove free to share in it, was an unresolved question that the land of liberty had yet to answer.

Kensington was growing; by 1850, it would be the twelfth largest urban settlement in the nation.[11] And as its population grew, small dwellings became prevalent – some no more than shacks or lean-to's in "courts and alleys running off secondary streets... in the rear of larger houses facing on the street, with access by means of narrow passageways between the front houses."[12] The Murphys' first home was such a place. A couple of months after a canvasser for *M'Elroy's Philadelphia Directory* stopped by to ask them questions, the directory listed Dominick as a weaver living at No. 4 Gay's Court, a short alleyway close to the center of Kensington.[13]

Gay's Court was so called after the property's owner, James Gay. A fellow Irishman, Gay would be Dominick's first employer in Kensington and would play a role in Murphy's later pursuits of the American dream.[14] But for now, the association with Gay was brief. By late 1842, the family had moved to Justice Court, a few blocks away, and Dominick, keen to keep the family business alive for his sons, had set up shop for himself.[15] Just as George Washington and Thomas Jefferson had called themselves "farmers" though others tilled their soil, calling himself a weaver didn't mean that Murphy worked his own loom. After learning from Gay how things were done in Kensington, he began employing others who wove on his account.[16] His was no sweat shop of drones governed by a factory whistle – he employed skilled hand-weavers like himself. Most of them owned their own looms; most worked out of their own homes.[17]

The quality (and therefore the value) of hand-woven cloth was largely a function of the weaver's skill, much of which was concentrated on keeping the tension of the weft yarn constant, especially at the edges of the fabric. If tension was too great, the weft yarn would pull the edge in toward the middle; if too loose, it would hang out beyond the edge or stick out above the surface. A good weave required constant tension, and if the fabric was wide, two weavers were required, one on each side of the loom, to pass the weft yarn between them. Dominick knew his fabric; a single glance at a piece of woven cloth was enough to judge the man who'd made it. To the handloom weavers who worked for him, Dominick provided raw materials, gave specifications, and paid compensation by the yard or the piece.[18]

Many of Dominick's weavers were Anglican Englishmen and Protestant Scots-Irish.[19] While he himself was in the religious minority, he was not, at first, subject to widespread prejudice. Protestants and Catholics had allied in forming the General Trade Union in the 1830's; when the Irish of Kensington struck for better wages, Protestants and Catholics had stood side by side, on both sides of the management-labor divide. Like Thomas Moore, Murphy wanted to unite all Irishmen, Catholics and Presbyterians alike, in a country where different religions could exist in harmony. And events seemed to justify his attitude – at least until May of 1844, when intolerance descended on St. Michael's Church.

The only Catholic church in the northern half of Philadelphia County, St. Michael's was located on the (southeast) corner of Jefferson St. and 2nd Street, in the center of Old Kensington's heavily Irish Third Ward. It was a simple structure compared to the palatial churches of later years, but it was the main Irish Catholic gathering place for miles around. No part of the Third Ward was more than about fifteen hundred feet from it, and Murphy's first homes on both Gay's Court and Justice Court were even closer to the center of Catholic life.[20] Dominick would later become one of St. Michael's trustees.[21] Based on the stories he'd heard, he fully expected to reap the rewards of American religious tolerance.

Dominick also believed in the value of education: it was what distinguished an Irishman of his class from common laborers and the other "low" Irish. Just a block southwest of the church, on Master Street between 2nd St. and Washington, was the well-regarded Master Street School. At least four of his sons attended it; the older three children were already pupils there in 1844.[22] As we'll soon see, the locations of the church, the school, and the Murphy residence in the early 1840's place the Murphys at the center of historic events caused by worsening relations between Catholics and Protestants.

> Increasingly, the role of the Irish in American society became a moral and political issue, for the growing numbers of "low-Irish" emigrants – poor, Catholic, often boisterous and disease-ridden – heightened all the tensions and anxieties which beset native Americans in the chaotic 1830's and 1840's. Because of their alien religion and peasant habits, all seemingly repugnant to native institutions and bourgeois

ideals, Irish Catholics provided easily identifiable targets for middle class reformers and beleaguered Protestant workers who joined ranks in a Second Great Awakening to purge the United States of everything sinful and foreign.[23]

Those Protestant families who'd come to the area earlier now called themselves "native" Americans,[*] and the increasing numbers of poor new European immigrants "foreigners." In 1837, facing the influx, a group gathered in neighboring Germantown and established themselves as "The Native American Association of the United States in the Township of Germantown."[24]

The vast majority of the nativists were Christians whose early martyrs had been persecuted by the Romans, so their own survival required vigilance, conviction, and a willingness to fight for what they held dear. The Pennsylvania legislature had therefore made study of the Bible mandatory in the public schools. Of course, the Bible used was the (Protestant) King James Bible.[†] In 1842, Philadelphia's Catholic Bishop, Patrick Kendrick, requested (in the name of religious liberty) that Catholic children be excused from reading the King James translation.[25] Alarmed by the request, local Protestant ministers began holding rallies designed to "save the Bible." As tensions and rhetoric grew, Catholic Alderman Hugh Clark suggested that Bible reading might be suspended altogether while a compromise policy was devised. When the principal of the Master Street School agreed, the suspension triggered outrage on all sides. Both the school and St. Michael's church became lightning rods for anti-Catholic sentiment. Protestant clergy formed the American Protestant Association; secular nativists formed the "American Republican Association."[26] Apart from heavily Irish West Kensington, every neighborhood soon had its own nativist association. In January, 1844, these associations adopted a set of principles upon which to defend the American way: (1) requiring immigrants to be residents for twenty-one years before gaining the right to vote; (2) making the King James Bible required reading in all schools; and (3) limiting any role in the making, enforcing and administering of laws to those (white) men (of European ancestry) who'd been born in the United States.[27]

Then, as rhetoric grew, the nativists advertised plans for a meeting to be held in the heart of the Irish Catholic neighborhood: their chosen location was the southwest corner of Second and Master Streets, between St. Michael's Church, the Master Street School, and a convent established for the Sisters of Charity of the Blessed Virgin Mary (known at the time as the "Nunnery"). The meeting's purpose was one "of considering the expediency of a proposed

---

[*] Of course, they referred to themselves as natives only after declaring themselves owners of land once inhabited by the indigenous Susquehannock and Lenape tribes.

[†] Chief among Protestant objections to the (Catholic) Douay Bible, prepared in the face of the Protestant Reformation, were its many annotations, explaining the text in such a way as to defend Catholic interpretations of God's Word.

alteration of the laws of the United States, in reference to the naturalization of foreigners" and "all friendly to the cause" were invited to attend.[28]

The southwest corner of 2nd and Master Streets was an empty lot next to the School. On this lot, the nativists – many from Philadelphia – erected a platform out of wood, from which a number of them addressed the sympathetic crowd. But perhaps as intended, the assembly also attracted local Catholic residents who didn't care for the speeches being made. Especially offensive was the speech by Samuel Kramer, editor of the anti-immigrant newspaper, the *Native American,* who claimed that the immigrants wanted to

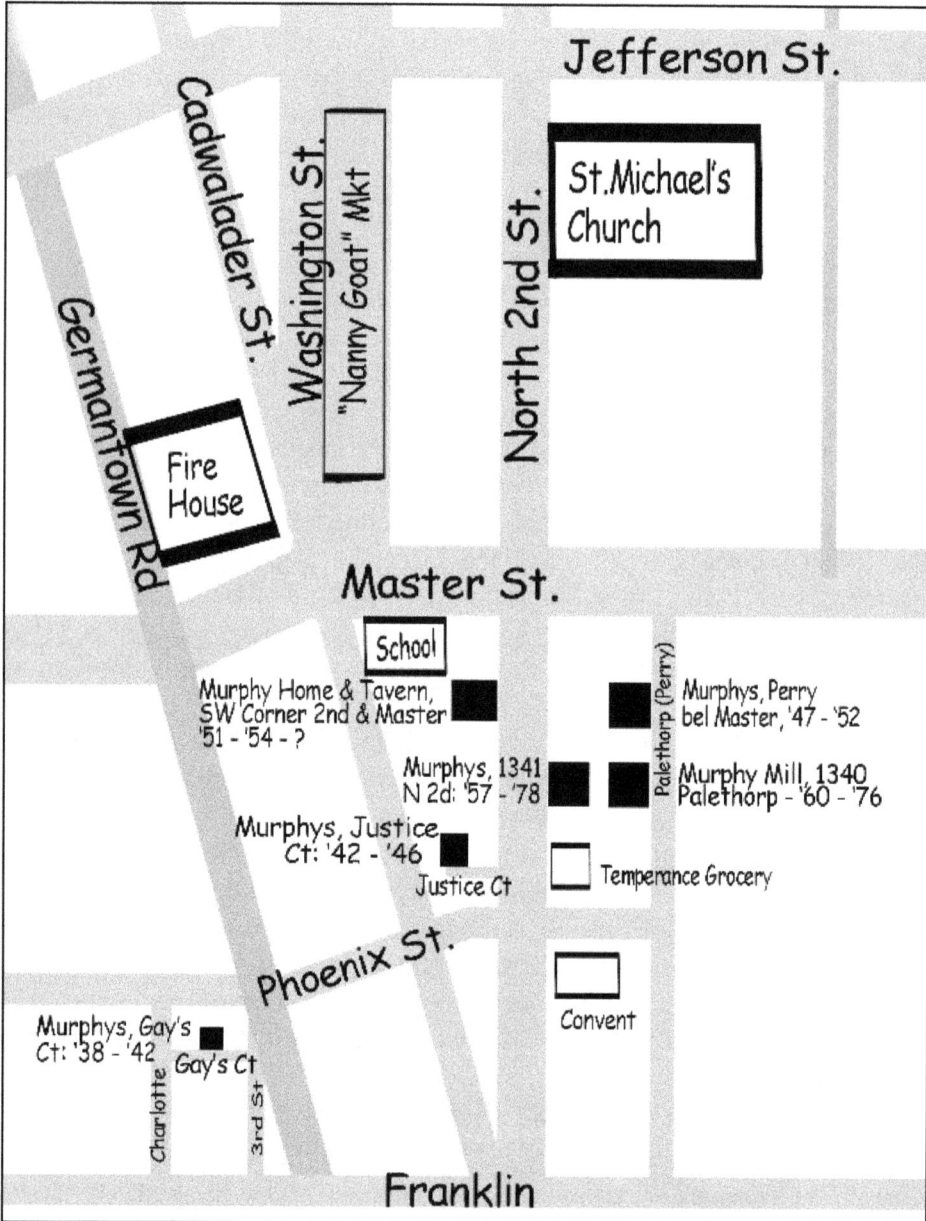

Solid black squares ■ *indicate locations of Murphy residences at different times*

change the American constitution or, even worse, sell the country to a foreign power – meaning the Pope. A Catholic resident called Kramer a liar. Rocks were thrown. Chasing Kramer off the stage, the locals made a bonfire of it.

A quiet weekend passed, but the following Monday, the nativist crowd gathered again on the same empty lot next to the school. This time, they numbered over four thousand people. Another stage was erected and speeches resumed amid taunts and insults from the Catholics who'd come out of their houses and gathered around them. When a harsh rainstorm sent nativists running for shelter under the roof of the nearby Nanny Goat Market, they were chased by the growing crowd of local Catholics. Jeers and taunts continued; rocks and bricks were thrown. Before long, there were guns fired, both from and toward the fire house. Catholics and nativists swarmed and rallied like troops on a battlefield. At the end of the day, at least a dozen nativists and an unknown number of Catholics had been wounded or killed. At least five Irish Catholic houses were "battered and ransacked, and one house having its door riddled with gunshot."[29]

The *Public Ledger* updated its coverage almost by the hour:

> 12 o'clock. – We have just returned from the scene of the riot. About 10 o'clock in the evening, a mob collected in the vicinity of Franklin and Second streets and commenced breaking into the homes on both sides of the street, destroying the furniture, demolishing the windows, and rendering the houses completely uninhabitable. The inmates of all the dwellings in the neighborhood fled with precipitation, abandoning their homes to the ruthlessness of the mob.
>
> This continued for some time without any resistance being offered. At length an attack was made upon a Seminary at the corner of Second and Phoenix streets, formerly occupied by the Sisters of Charity, and a number of persons were about tearing down and setting fire to the fence when some persons advanced from above and fired a volley of ball and buckshot among the crowd.
>
> This was followed by two or three succeeding volleys, when the crowd dispersed. Several persons fell severely wounded. A young man named Nathan Ramsay… received a shot through the breastbone, perforating his lungs, and he was carried from the ground to an apothecary store in Second Street, above the junction of Germantown Road…
>
> Several individuals who had left their homes during the day were afraid to return, some of them having left wives with small children unprotected. It having been rumored that an attempt would be made to fire the Catholic church on Second street, many of the residents retired from their homes to it,

with arms, determined to protect it at the hazard of their lives. Up to 12 o'clock no attempt on the church had been made. At that hour, individuals were seen leaving the neighborhood. The greatest consternation prevailed, no man knowing at what moment he would be shot down, nor by whom. [30]

The nativist mob gathered at Franklin, then "moved north on Second Street, attacking the homes of suspected Irish Catholics on both sides of the street." Nativist residents hung American flags in their windows to protect themselves, while the crowd broke windows and went into Catholic homes destroying furniture. "The inhabitants of the homes fled from the ruthlessness of the mob." After setting fire to the convent, the nativists proceeded north. When shots came from the Temperance Grocery Store, they sacked it.[31]

To say that the Murphys were keenly interested in the matter would be an understatement. Not only were Dominick's house, his mill, and his inventory of cotton goods all in harm's way, so were his wife and children. Given his connection to the Master Street School, his desire that his children be able to read from the Bible of the family's choice, and his future as a Church trustee, it's hard to imagine a man *more* likely to have been at the center of the action. And yet, none of the news accounts of the rioting mention his name, nor do later histories of the affair. We have to wonder why Murphy was not among those hospitalized, or those tried for criminal activity, or those called to testify at the trials that ensued. He may have been like Joseph Rice, "an Irishman who doesn't appear to have been involved in the rioting but rather was hiding inside his house with his family."[32] But a better explanation may lie in his station in life. Dominick Murphy was not the adventurous youth who'd arrived in America a decade earlier, but a thirty-five-year-old father of five concerned about the safety of his children. He was an employer concerned about his business, its flammable inventory, and the welfare of his employees. The handweavers he employed were not common laborers with nothing to lose, but skilled craftsmen, like himself, who "powered their looms with their own two feet." Dominick clearly had a stake in maintaining peace, a stake in good relations between opposing factions, a stake in preserving advantages he'd worked hard to acquire. His heart may have been with the Irish Catholic immigrants, but practical considerations kept him out of the conflict until cooler heads could prevail.

In any case, the hostilities were not yet over. Tuesday morning, the nativists called upon their friends to assemble in Kensington again: "Let Every Man Come Prepared to Defend Himself," read the posters found in public places all over town. Witnesses saw nativist Isaac Hare organizing an armed group at Phoenix and Second. A wagon of rifles was delivered to "Weaver's Row" between Germantown and Cadwalader roads, above Jefferson. The Nanny Goat Market and the firehouse were both soon up in flames. That night, organized militia arrived to restore order, pointing cannons loaded with grape and canister north and south from the Market. On Wednesday, with nativist numbers growing and houses burning, many Catholic tenants of the houses along Cadwalader, Washington, and Master, "and the various courts and alleys coming off of these streets," were "busy packing their belongings and fleeing the neighborhood. As the Irish moved out of their homes, the houses were soon fired by the mob…" And finally, late in the day Wednesday, with the Catholics driven out, St. Michael's itself, and its rectory, and the convent, were burned to the ground.[33] In the aftermath of the rioting, one immigrant commented, "They are worse on the Catholics in this country than… they are in Ireland."[34]

Burning of St. Michael's Church, on Wednesday afternoon, May 8.

West View, on Second street, with the Residence of the Rev. Mr. Donahue.

It was the deadliest riot the city of brotherly love would see for at least the next hundred years. Dreaming of religious tolerance and unity, the Murphys had felt the sting of hatred and exclusion. They'd observed violence erupt on account of where people had been born, the way they spoke, and the God in which they believed. They had to wonder whether their dream was possible, after all, and whether it made sense to rebuild their church from scratch. A Catholic history, written by a priest ninety years later, asserts that beginning the Sunday after the rioting finally stopped,

> [t]he Catholics straggled back to Kensington slowly, in small groups. Why did they return? Well, the neighborhood undoubtedly drew them, notwithstanding what had happened, for it was the only one most of them had known in America; but more than anything else, I think, they realized an answer must be made to the hatred and violence of the Nativists, not an answer of hatred and retaliation, but of the sweetness and Strength of the Catholic Faith. The good work begun would have to be carried on.[35]

By May 28, less than three weeks after the rioting, work began on the erection of a new temporary chapel on the site of the old rectory. The Church looked to all its members – and especially to the wealthier ones, like Dominick Murphy – to fund a more permanent one.

> Most of the families… were impoverished, for what they had saved by frugal living had gone into the homes destroyed by the Nativists. For a while, a long while for some of the families, no one was earning. So it is a mystery how they managed even to keep life in themselves.[36]

After the riots, the directories (1847-1852) listed the Murphy residence as "Perry below Master." Perry was the same street later known as Palethorp, and the move there reflects Murphy's commitment to the neighborhood of St. Michael's. His commitment became clear as he made his offerings to the church and provided jobs to its members.[37] The rebuilding of the church would take years, but the new structure would eventually be grander than the original.

> [B]efore the summer [of 1844] was out, nearly all of the men had steady employment. Some had gotten handlooms again and found manufacturers who would give them a regular allotment of work. [As a new church and rectory were built in '46-48], Irish immigrants pouring into Philadelphia heard the story of the renewed progress of St. Michael's, and lost their dread of Kensington. The fact of the new church and the likelihood of finding employment in this industrial section together proved a compelling attraction to many of them.[38]

The dream of religious tolerance had been shaken, but the dream of prosperity survived. Kensington grew from the ashes in no small measure on the strength of Dominick's contribution. But even as the Liberty Bell cracked and became "forever dumb," the Irish potato famine (1845-1850) triggered an even greater exodus from the old country.[39] Unskilled laborers began to flood Philadelphia and Kensington, and new arrivals skyrocketed:

> 1845:   8,416
> 1846:   6,477
> 1847: 18,726
> 1848: 24,463
> 1849: 25,169
> 1850: 27,553

By 1850, Hannah had eight children,[40] while Dominick's mill employed a hundred and twenty weavers. The Murphy mill was capitalized at a value of $3,000 – no small sum in those days – and it was one of only twenty-one textile mills in all of Philadelphia County employing over a hundred workers.[41] While some mills were turning to steam power, Murphy clung to the traditional method of hand loom weaving. The difference between the men and women he employed was apparent:

> The large handloom shops employed proportionally fewer women by far than did the powered mills...[42]
>
> In 1850, taking Philadelphia and Kensington together, there were nine manufacturers of cotton cloth in the area with over a hundred employees whose looms were powered by steam; there were three such manufacturers whose looms were powered by water (or a combination of water and steam); and there were nine whose looms were powered only by hand. Among the power loom manufacturers, the workforce was evenly split between men and women, but among the hand loom operations, the workforce was predominantly male. For example, the Kensington cotton mill operated by Dominick Murphy employed eighty men and only forty women. In such mills, the women, working as tenders, inspectors or bobbin changers, were paid about eight dollars per month, while the more highly skilled male weavers earned about twenty.[43]

As Murphy felt responsibility for employees, community, church, and family, his strategy of clinging to the traditional way of weaving cloth paid off. And with prosperity seemingly achieved, he began to think he and his sons might participate more fully in democratic self-rule – not through the unruly power of angry mobs, but through the political process.

His first step was to venture into the liquor business: in 1851, he opened a tavern at Second and Master, in the heart of Kensington.[44] If opening a tavern seems an odd way to enter politics, consider what E. L. Godkin would say about the liquor business in Irish communities a few years later:

> Liquor dealers are the medium and the only medium through which political preaching or control can reach a very large body of voters… The liquor dealer is their guide, philosopher, creditor. He sees them more frequently and familiarly than anybody else, and is the person through whom the news and the meaning of what passes in the upper regions of city politics reach them…"[45]

With the opening of the tavern, Murphy became one of the best-known people in Kensington. The nativist rally had been held on the vacant lot at Second and Master, between St. Michael's and the Master Street School, epicenter of the Bible wars. That address was now even more well known as the lot from which the riots had started. For about two years (1852-1853) Dominick operated his tavern at the infamous corner.

Any doubt about whether Murphy had politics in mind when he opened his tavern there is put to rest by the announcement of a "Democratic Meeting"

12

to be held at the Murphy home at the southwest corner of Second and Master, at which "business of importance" would be transacted.[46]

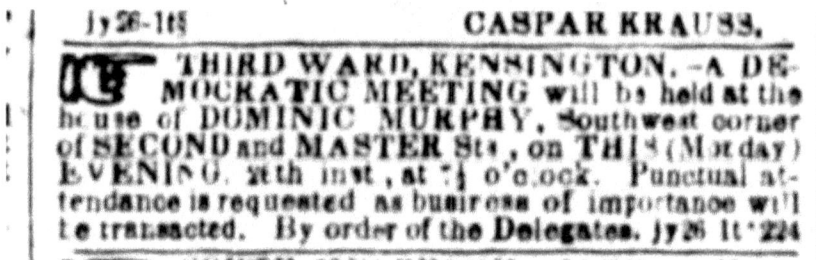

Jy 26-1t§   CASPAR KRAUSS,

☞ THIRD WARD, KENSINGTON. — A DE-
MOCRATIC MEETING will be held at the
house of DOMINIC MURPHY, Southwest corner
of SECOND and MASTER Sts., on THIS (Monday)
EVENING, 26th inst., at 7½ o'clock. Punctual attendance is requested as business of importance will
be transacted. By order of the Delegates. jy26 1t*224

The business of importance was not hard to guess. For one thing, the riots had convinced the archdiocese to organize its own school system. The cornerstone of St. Michael's Parochial School would be laid at the end of that summer, and the school would open for classes in September 1853. The reasons for building one of the first Catholic parochial schools in the country – to avoid further conflict over what Bible to read in the public schools – would be explained for Catholic and Protestant alike. A bit of separation between Catholic and Protestant would allow both religions their freedom, and so benefit both by ensuring peace between them.[47]

The riots had also revealed the need for a more effective system of law enforcement. Consolidation with the city of Philadelphia – unification of the neighboring populations under a single, county-wide government – was widely viewed as the answer.

> Consolidation was intended to unsnarl legal complexities that impeded police activity; to make an adequate police force financially possible; to end the reign of hoodlums… who battled each other for territorial rights on street corners, mauled and terrorized passersby, and covered walls and fences with graffiti; to send the fire companies back to fighting fires instead of – in shifting alliances with gangs – each other; and above all, to forestall any recurrence of the great riots of 1844.[48]

The idea of becoming a part of the larger city to the south carried big political stakes for the Irish of Kensington. Consolidation could make the Irish Catholic vote a permanent minority, swallowed up by the larger city. Dominick's views on the subject were already aligned with those of other local leaders with whom Dominick now worked, like his erstwhile landlord James Gay and the young lawyer, Lewis Cassidy.[49] Now they had to be explained and sold to the people at large. Namely, the city of Philadelphia had long been in the hands of Whigs, and more recently, of nativist Know-Nothings,* while Democrats held majorities

---

* The nickname given to the nativists who had formed a secret society, the members of which, when asked about their activities, responded, "I know nothing."

in outlying neighborhoods like Kensington. These outlying areas had been growing, due largely to the increase in the number of both Germans and Irish Catholics. And continuing immigration from Ireland meant that their strength would only increase with time. Uniting Germans and Irish, Catholics and Protestants, the immigrants could, together, have real power.

In January of 1854, not long after the meeting at Murphy's tavern, the Governor finally signed a consolidation bill. With the city's expansion to include the rest of Philadelphia County, Kensington and its large Catholic population were now a part of the new, much larger city. Elections to Philadelphia's City Council would now include the newly incorporated areas. In a nod to the founding fathers, the nativists arranged for the new Council to meet on the second floor of the old state house. [50] And Murphy promptly exercised his civil right, as a white male American citizen, to participate in the dream of self-rule. Along with his old landlord, James Gay, Murphy ran for the Common Council in the consolidated city's new 17th Ward.[51]

Reflecting Whig and nativist strength in the old city, the Whig Candidate, Robert T. Conrad, running as a "native American," won the city-wide mayoral election by a landslide[52] and immediately announced his intention to recruit a force of 900 men to police the now larger city. [53] It was welcome news to those who believed consolidation would restore law and order, but Conrad also announced that, to a man, everyone on the force would be of American birth.[54] Those who mistrusted nativist intentions braced for an anti-immigrant, largely anti-Catholic, crackdown.

On the other hand, since Kensington itself was largely Democratic, Dominick Murphy and James Gay were both elected – along with a third Irishman, C.B.F. O'Neill – to represent the heavily Irish 17th Ward of the newly consolidated city.[55]

Philadelphia, May 2, 1855.

To DOMINICK MURPHY.

SIR:—At a Municipal Election, held on the 1st inst., you were duly elected a Common Councilman of the Seventeenth Ward.

James McDonald,
Michael Devlin,
William Beaty,
Dennis Donovan,
E. C. Guyn,
Judges.

———

Now known by every man and woman in Kensington, Murphy found himself responsible to them as their democratically elected representative. Abandoned as soon as it had served its political purpose, we hear no more of Murphy's tavern after the election. But the man now came face to face with the practical realities of legitimate, democratic self-rule.

As the second largest city in the country, the newly consolidated Philadelphia faced more issues than ever before. Coming to the Council for decision were questions like whether to repair a particular culvert, pay a particular bill, install a gas lamp on a particular bridge, grade a particular road, clean sewer lines in a particular neighborhood. One frequent issue was how best to control stray dogs on the streets. Council considered motions, resolutions, petitions, ordinances, and amendments thereto. They were tabled, postponed, read for the third time, referred to committees, ruled out of order, and otherwise handled in accordance with proper parliamentary procedures. The large bicameral legislative body was expected to manage the city person by person, street by street, shed by shed. With ninety-eight members between them, the two houses "were cumbersome even as a legislative assembly... Their size and organization unsuited them for executive and administrative activity."[56] Amazingly, Murphy attended nearly all the meetings (usually at least one per week). The cumbersomeness of the process tried the patience even of the Whigs, who typically got their way; those in the minority, like Murphy, were outvoted at every meeting.

Meanwhile, with nativists comprising a majority on the Council, the new Mayor, Robert Conrad, made full use of his "all-American" police force to keep the undesirable in line. The Irish saw Conrad's police as "accustomed to beating up Irishmen and blacks." Among their more zealous endeavors, the police came down hard on violators of a new state law against Sunday liquor sales.[57] To the Irish, it was a direct assault on their liberty.

In his first Council meeting, Dominick was on the losing side of the vote to elect William P. Hacker as Council President.[58] Hacker appointed Murphy to the Committee on Markets, one of the worst assignments available.[59] During the year that followed, Murphy's Committee was charged with considering petitions to install, remove, or repair individual sheds and stalls, or to otherwise regulate specific vendors in the myriad little markets that dotted the city. Murphy appeared at meetings regularly and he voted on every matter that arose. But not once do we find him making a motion, presenting a petition, or speaking up in Council meetings on any specific matter. Perhaps he sat in silent awe of the cumbersome body of which he'd become a part. Perhaps, on some days, he simply fell asleep.[60]

In those days, Democrats generally opposed increases in City expenditures as aristocratic over-spending, feeling that working men could not afford the higher fees, licenses and excise taxes it took to fund them.[61] This did not keep Murphy from voting to approve the paving of Franklin street, running just south of where he himself lived. But when Murphy's Committee on Markets proposed an ordinance requiring anyone selling fruits, vegetables or similar goods to obtain a license from the City in order to continue doing so ($5 a year for a one-horse wagon, $10 for a two-horse wagon), Murphy voted against it. As a Democrat, his "limited government" philosophy was also behind his vote against a proposal to augment the city's fleet of horse-drawn fire trucks with a costly new steam fire engine called the "Young America." Despite Murphy's no votes, both measures were approved.[62]

There were of course times Murphy found it hard to hold his tongue. Petitions were being submitted (from opposing factions of citizens) for or against reductions in the size of Mayor Conrad's "American" police force. At a meeting in June, the petitions were all referred to the Standing Committee on Police, which Hacker had appointed.[63] The Council leaders knew the Committee's report would be contentious; when it was submitted, along with its request to approve funding of the department, the Council adjourned (until the following week) to give its members time to consider it.[64] We can imagine Murphy's reaction that evening as he read, by gas-light, at home, that the city's ills were clearly the fault of the immigrants:

> [O]ur American cities have within them… a dangerous source and element of pauperism and crime in the large masses of emigrants from foreign lands, who mingle with, and constitute so considerable a portion of, their inhabitants. These foreigners are very frequently marked by the prejudices, the ignorance and the vices…of the…institutions and governments under which they have been born and lived… They not unfrequently bring with them the hereditary and implacable feuds, the national hatreds, which, in their own countries, divide nations, and separate communities into embittered factions… Hence the known necessity which has frequently occurred, when large masses of these foreigners assemble to celebrate national festivals or rights, of employing a police force to guard the community against such outbreaks…
>
> Up to the year 1840, but one million of emigrants had arrived in our country. Since that time, the number of these strangers…who are brought annually to our shores, has swollen to from four to five hundred thousand.
>
> The largest portion of the positively vicious of the vast multitude – the paupers and criminals – remain to infest and burden our large cities…[65]

The Committee's report urged an increase in funding for the police department. Councilman O'Neill, Murphy's fellow Irishman from Ward 17, had been permitted to submit a minority report, which read in part:

> [T]he police, as at present organized, is not a preventive police.
> [T]heir conduct on duty is calculated to produce violation of the laws of the State.
> [T]hey make arrests without the shadow of authority.
> [T]hey imprison innocent citizens for the purpose of making them pay costs and hush money.
> [T]here is more crime against the good order of society committed by the police acting, or pretending to act as such, than there is by the same number of the worst portion of society…

O'Neill's minority report proposed to defund the police force, cutting its size in half.[66] In November, a compromise was reached, cutting the force's size to 650 men.[67] Murphy – never as confrontational as O'Neill – voted in favor of the compromise.

But Mayor Conrad didn't give up. In his January Message to Council, he insisted that 650 men were not enough, and in support of his argument to return the force to its former numbers, he included a table of 38,657 arrests made by the police during the prior year. His interpretation of the statistics was clear. There'd been only 22 arrests for murder and 10 for rape,[68] but 143 for selling liquor to inebriates, minors, or simply without a license, 184 for selling liquor on Sunday, and a whopping 11,234 for intoxication. There'd been 1,325 arrests for vagrancy, and 18,344 – by far the biggest cause of arrest – for that wonderful catch-all, "breach of the peace." Conrad's "American" police obviously saw liquor, intoxication, and rowdy defiance of the established order as public enemy number one. And who was responsible for that problem? Conrad's report included statistics to answer that question too. It broke down the prior year's arrests by country of the perpetrator's origin. The great majority of countries accounted for single-digit arrests, but blacks totaled four digits and Ireland five.

Of the above there were from

Ireland.	-	-	-	21,830	Portugal, - - - -	7
United States,	-	-	-	10 470	Doubtful, - - - -	7
Germany,	-	-	-	2.452	Hungary, - - - -	3
England,	-	-	-	1,231	Mexico, - - - -	1
France.	-	-	-	121	China, - - - -	1
Scotland,	-	-	-	110	Bavaria. - - - -	1
Italy,	-	-	-	53	West Indies, - - - -	1
Spain,	-	-	-	11	Poland, - - - -	2
Switzerland,	-	-	-	7	Russia, - - - - -	1
Prussia,	-	-	-	4	Blacks, - - - -	2,281
Sweden,	-	-	-	7		
Wales,	-	-	-	6	Total, - - - -	38,657

Clearly, argued Conrad, his nativist police were arresting Irishmen for drunkenness and defiance out of all proportion to their numbers. Blacks, too. And by carving blacks out of the American-born total, the figures made it appear that white Americans were relatively sober and law-abiding – or (as Irish and blacks would have stressed) simply less likely to be arrested. No one was heard to say that the high arrest rates for Irishmen and blacks suggested more about discriminatory police tactics than about crime; to Conrad and his supporters, the arrests proved the guilt of those arrested.

But Mayor Conrad didn't let the numbers speak for themselves. Stressing that they were "proof of the energy and activity of the police," he stated,

> To an enlightened and moral community, it is discreditable that the same army of inebriates, vagrants and

other constant offenders, should, month after month, outrage the moral sense of society without effectual restraint or correction... The most rigorous orders have been very frequently issued by this department for the suppression of vagrancy in its various deplorable and criminal shapes, and the police have manifested a commendable energy in their efforts to suppress it...[69]

Thus went the argument for a larger police force, needed to preserve nativist power in an increasingly "foreign" city.

Conrad's Whig Party, however, was declining in power all across the country. And with Irish and German numbers continuing to grow, prospects for immigrants began improving.[70] In the next mayoral election, with the support of Irish Catholics like Murphy and Lewis Cassidy, Democrat Richard Vaux beat Conrad, taking office as the city's new Mayor on May 13, 1856.[71] In addition to having his own constituency in West Kensington, Murphy's ally Vaux became one of the most influential men in Philadelphia. Vaux increased the size of the police force to as many as 1,000 men, and he did it by hiring scores of Irishmen. Arguably, as a result, rioting and gang violence subsided.[72]

Murphy was now poised for success in both politics and business. Of the 4700 looms operating in Philadelphia in 1857, over 2000 produced carpets, 2000 produced other textiles, and 700 produced hosiery. The city's fancy woolen hosiery was becoming as famous as that made in England.[73] Dominick didn't limit himself to a single product; he wove whatever the market could handle.[74] Although his first son, Dennis, took up a career in Washington, Dominick had five more sons to follow in his footsteps. The biggest threat to his business was not the competition, and certainly not lack of product knowledge, but the continuing rise of steam. More street railway lines were being laid, with steam engines pulling the cars.[75] The fetid, delicious, pestilent and inexorable pressure was powering more factories as well. Where steam moved warp and weft, the most important task of an operator – now more often called a "loom tender" than a weaver – was to watch for problems. In 1857, Freedley calculated the total power loom production of woolen and cotton goods in Philadelphia at $13,163,968, with only about a third that much – $4,746,000 – still produced by hand looms like Murphy's.[76]

Steam power lessened the need for skilled labor, while increasing opportunities for the less skilled.

Many of these workers were low-skilled immigrants, particularly Irish Catholics who settled in Kensington in large numbers in the mid-nineteenth century and made up a significant percentage of that neighborhood's mill workers.[77]

Not surprisingly, the new job of "loom tender" was increasingly held by women. As Philip Scranton noted in his economic analysis,

> The much more substantial presence of women workers in powered mills reflects their positions as loom tenders in addition to the standard service functions (…bobbin changing, warp dressing and drawing-in, and cloth inspection). Women power-loom operators posed a direct threat to male handloom weavers in districts like Kensington and Moyamensing…[78]

Murphy's and other mills in Kensington were slower to adopt steam power than mills elsewhere in the city for reasons rooted in culture and community:

> The Kensington steam-powered mills were established in a community that already had a complex set of manufacturing and social relations centered on handloom weaving. This material and cultural environment acted as a constraint on the use of power looms and women tenders…[79]

Conversion to steam power would mean utilizing more women, rather than preserving jobs for the skilled workforce of the past. Murphy's men saw themselves as craftsmen and family providers. They could also vote, while their wives could not: Murphy's hand-weavers were not just his employees, but his constituents, and he aligned himself with their interests, resisting the pressure of steam. Meanwhile, because there were Protestants among them, appealing to his male workforce meant appealing to both sides of the religious divide. Murphy's business decisions and political stances joined to support the practical economic self-interest of all eligible voters, rather than the less tangible causes of women's, Catholics', or immigrants' rights.

With his political life energized, strides being made toward acceptance of immigrants, and several sons in line to continue in the family business, Murphy could sense the realization of everything he'd come to America for: genuine liberty seemed right around the corner. But events that summer would spell the end of his political career. On July 17, the still new St. Michael's parochial school decided it would be nice for the students to take the new train for a Sunday-school picnic in the country. Some 600 of the school's pupils boarded at the Master Street depot and headed north, into the countryside. Unbeknownst to the passengers, a southbound train was coming directly toward them. They'd left late, but their engineer thought that with his boiler at full steam, with his regulator open, his Sunday School train could beat the southbound train. With no more than seconds of warning for the crew and none for the children on board, the two trains collided. The boilers exploded on impact, making a roar heard five miles away. "The sound of crashing woodwork, the hissing of steam, the screams and piteous moans of the victims succeeded the first deafening noise of the terrific impact." Over fifty students of the parish school met death in a single moment. The deadliest train wreck of all time cast its shadow into every corner of Kensington. No family in the Ward wasn't touched.[80]

Murphy and his allies had touted their success at bringing the rail to Kensington, including the depot on Master Street, a boon to the community and St. Michael's church in particular. But now, after the tragedy, grieving parents found fault with the government's decision to approve the rail line. Councilman Murphy represented the Ward where nearly all the victims had lived. Worse still, he had not enrolled his own children in the new parochial school, a failure that had tested his relationship with the Church even before grieving constituents complained that his family was not among the victims of the tragedy, but responsible for it.[81] Cash donations and fund-raising for the church were necessary penance, but could not extinguish nightmares of oncoming trains, nor silence the cries of maimed children that lasted long after the wreckage was cleared.

Meanwhile, pressure was building for other reasons as well. Vast plantations of fertile land, Eli Whitney's invention of the cotton gin, and the enslavement of African Americans had made cotton the biggest crop in America, and the northern textile industry had grown dependent on its profits. The Supreme Court's 1857 *Dred Scott* decision[82] confirmed that slaves were mere property which the federal government had no right to take from their owners. But among its other ramifications, the court decision threw the future of the western railroads into question, which led to a summer stock market slide, which led to the failure of a large national bank and fears of a general run. On September 26, the Bank of Pennsylvania closed its doors. The world-wide business panic that ensued tore into the Kensington textile industry.[83]

> While the ordinary shifts in the market might threaten handshop livelihoods even in steady times, the Panic of 1857 cut a swath through the Kensington textile trades. Suffering was severe, unemployment high, charities driven to the limits of their resources to supply the poor. Of 126 firms in 1850 Kensington, only 23 could be located in the 1860 Manufacturing Census... Of the six handloom firms with more than 100 workers in 1850, only one, Dominick Murphy, continued operations... The other large masters all seem to have withdrawn from the trade before the economic contraction...[84]

For some reason, Murphy's handloom business survived. But the number of his employees dropped from one hundred twenty in 1850 to only sixty in 1860 – more bad news for his employees and constituents.[85]

He might be faulted for not insisting on better management of the rail lines, but he could hardly be blamed for the panic. It didn't matter, however. Those in charge are blamed for bad news, whatever its cause. He found himself unable, or unwilling, to put himself in such a position again. When his term as Councilman expired, he chose not to run again. His political career had come to a swift and decisive end. Thereafter, his attentions turned away from public service, inward, to his own family, and to his own business.[86]

According to the 1860 federal census of manufacturers, his sixty employees were still mostly men (40 men to 20 women), as he still adhered to the old hand-loom model the craftsmen preferred.[87] The three thousand dollars of real estate he owned suggest that he'd purchased both his house on 2nd Street and the mill he ran on Palethorp, directly behind it.[88] More than one of his sons was now in the nation's capital, working for the U.S. Senate. In short, with a good business and a successful family, Dominick and Hannah were on the verge of making their America everything they'd ever dreamed it could be.[89]

Even after his Council term ended, Dominick was still well connected. Recent installation of telegraph cables and offices – installed by the railroads to prevent collisions – meant messages could be sent and received between major cities instantaneously. Working at the Capitol, Murphy's three oldest sons could send him telegrams faster than writers, editors, typesetters and printers could compose, print and distribute newspapers. So the one-time tavern-keep was still among the first to learn of important events. This proved especially helpful as events in Washington in the winter of 1860-1861 marked the country's deepening divide over slavery. Some believed that the threat of southern secession should be blocked by a threat of war to prevent it, believing that just as consolidation had been good for Kensington and Philadelphia, preservation of the Union, in the long run, would be good for both North and South. Others viewed it more like the Church had viewed public schooling – peace could be better maintained if opposing parties went separate ways, each side free to retain what it felt dear. But the opposing views had been hardening, so the outbreak of war was no sudden surprise. One might as well have been standing in a railroad bed, looking down a track that extended twenty or thirty years, watching an oncoming locomotive get nearer, week after week. The iron face of war grew larger by the week, metal on metal louder than rattling of sabers: stock prices fell; specie payments were suspended; the Crittenden Compromise failed; South Carolina and Mississippi seceded; Jefferson Davis withdrew from the Senate. By the time Abraham Lincoln took the oath of office, all chance of peace seemed lost.[90] The Senate struck the names of Southern Senators from its rolls. It requested that Lincoln copy it with dispatches from Fort Sumter. Thanks to his sons, Dominick learned immediately of every event that signaled the inexorable approach of war.

Racism was not confined to points south of the Mason-Dixon line, and even northerners were divided on the issue. To say that a black man should not be enslaved was far different from saying that he was the equal of a white man. Jean Louis Agassiz and Samuel George Morton, the influential proponents of polygenesis, were celebrated teachers at Harvard and the University of Pennsylvania. Their view that God had created black and white as separate species informed the understanding of educated people throughout the north.[91] The emancipation laws of most northern states hardly guaranteed instant freedom. New Jersey, for example, claimed to have ended slavery in 1846, but its law actually converted slaves into apprentices bound for life – the 1860 Census still listed eighteen slaves listed in New Jersey.[92] Pennsylvania, meanwhile, only prohibited slavery for children born after 1780; and even those, if born to slave mothers, were retained as indentured servants, bound as if slaves to the age of twenty-eight. Following Agassiz and Morton, a majority of northerners who supported the gradual elimination of slavery – or sending them to Liberia the way Catholics had started sending their children to separate schools – took as scientific fact that Africans were an inferior race. Accordingly, many northern state constitutions, like Pennsylvania's, still limited the vote to white people.[93] In the summer of 1842, a white mob in Philadelphia had attacked a parade of blacks marching to commemorate the abolition of slavery in the West Indies. In October of 1849, a two-day race riot in Philadelphia had left three whites and a black man dead, and twenty-five others in city hospitals.[94] And as a general rule, at least in Philadelphia, "Irish Catholics had little sympathy for the Abolitionist cause."[95]

Friction between the Irish and African-Americans has been attributed most often to competition for lower-end jobs.[96] However:

> Although Irish-Black violence can be attributed, in part, to competition for jobs within the unskilled labor force, Irish attacks on African-Americans were also demonstrations of 'whiteness.' As David Roediger has shown, "it was by no means clear that the Irish were white." For newcomers to America, following in the footsteps of native-born whites, the most obvious way to exert one's whiteness was to persecute African Americans.[97]

As Democrats, the Murphys saw themselves as champions of the underprivileged. But as prejudice against blacks ran even deeper than it did against the Irish, many of the Irish adopted it. Even for the few who may not have thought blacks inferior, the prospect of approaching war and the persuasive power of money brought a practical, self-interested dimension to their views about slavery. During the 1850's, "the merchants of New York City and Philadelphia... let it be known that the Northern merchant was the friend of his Southern customer."[98] In the 1860 Presidential election, Pennsylvania's statewide Democratic committee supported the pro-slavery candidate, John Breckenridge. "Other party chieftains, including the Richard Vaux-Lewis Cassidy axis and generally the labor and immigrant factions in the city... favored Stephen A. Douglas."[99] At the beginning of 1861, desperately seeking to avoid a divisive war, the Board of Trade petitioned the General Assembly to repeal any legislation that might be deemed unfriendly to the South. (If the Catholic Church could withdraw from the public schools in the interest of peace, didn't it make sense to allow the South to do likewise?) Resolutions were approved admitting the right of secession and calling on Pennsylvania to choose between fanatical New England abolitionists and "the South, whose sympathies are ours."[100]

Murphy had long been a part of the Vaux-Cassidy "immigrant faction" that supported Douglas, and there seemed no reason to break with them now. War threatened his business with southern suppliers and customers, on which the welfare of his family depended, and Douglas's desire to avoid war appealed to the long-time peace-maker in him. His advocacy for the right of states and territories to decide questions for themselves appealed to his support for a people's right to self-rule.[101] For all these reasons, Murphy was a Douglas man, not happy when Republican Lincoln was elected, all but guaranteeing war.[102]

When the call for troops went out, an "immense" crowd went through the streets of the city, "visiting parties whose loyalty was suspected and compelling them to display the Stars and Stripes." "Flag-raising and other demonstrations of loyalty and enthusiastic devotion to the Union and the Government became the order of the day."[103] When the annual July 4th celebration included a grand parade of Home Guards, people were thankful, at least, that if the war came northward, the city itself would be defended.

Most people initially expected that hostilities would be brief, but events quickly threw that into question. Soon, buyers could no longer get cotton. The warehouses emptied. And if cotton could be found anywhere, its cost was prohibitive. Then, the rout of Union forces at the Battle of Bull Run proved that the southern military could not be written off as easily as many had thought. Amidst great excitement in the city, pressure increased for people to take sides. Tempers flared. On August 22, a U.S. Marshall seized the bundles of the *New York Daily News* and *The Christian Observer* upon their arrival in Philadelphia, stopping circulation of those "disloyal" papers. In September, a Delaware Congressman who'd called the Lincoln Administration "a set of fools" was arrested for the disloyalty suggested by the statement.[104] On October 30th, fires at the cotton and woolen mills at 12th and Washington Street served as reminders of how vulnerable businesses like Dominick's were.[105]

Nothing could escape the impact of war. In response to the burning of St. Michael's during the riots of 1844, Bishop Kenrick had conceived and begun work on a magnificent cathedral that, after years in construction, was finally ready to open. At Logan Square on April 20, 1862, an immense crowd gathered for the opening of the Cathedral of Saints Peter and Paul, "the most spacious and costly cathedral in the country."[106] According to some, Kendrick had designed it specifically to withstand damage from anti-Catholic vandals or rioters:

> According to local lore, [the 1844 riots] greatly influenced
> the design of the building. The cathedral was built with only

very high clerestory windows that according to parish histories would inhibit vandalism. In order to protect the windows of the Cathedral Basilica from possible future riots, the builders would throw stones into the air to determine the height of where the windows would be placed.[107]

Some Irish Catholics saw war as a chance to demonstrate their credentials as loyal Americans. At the opening mass that Easter, Murphy and his fellow Catholics might have felt they were in a castle, constructed in the defense of their families, their culture, and their religious freedom, all of which seemed ever under attack. Scaffolding still in place, Bishop Kenrick told the crowd that Catholics were "of every clime and region, all molded into one harmonious mass by their creed," and "by no means dangerous citizens." "They [are] obedient and loyal to the mandates of the church," he proclaimed, "and [are] equally so to all proper authority. Other religions are divisive and tend to secession, disunion and death, but not so with the Catholic religion."[108]

Catholics did not, in fact, all agree about which "proper authorities" to obey. But as Dominick joined in celebrating the new Cathedral, his concerns about nativist violence had been joined by concerns about war. The Cathedral was not invincible. He prayed for tolerance, for peace, for business not to be harmed – in short, with Catholics now successful enough to be building such a magnificent cathedral, he prayed for the world and all the advantages it afforded him to remain as they were.

But it was not to be. The Panic of 1857 had left the economy in dire straits. Now the radical Republicans dipped into the pockets of northern businessmen to pay for their war. In the Revenue Act of 1861, they imposed a new tax on income – not on the poor, but on people of means like Dominick and his family.[109] In 1862, Congress increased the rate on higher incomes to 5%, added federal license fees on practically every sort of business, and imposed stiff excise taxes on manufacturers.[110] In 1864, they increased the tax rate again, to 7.5 per cent on incomes over $5,000, and to 10% on incomes over $10,000.[111] The taxes were unprecedented; many on whom they were laid viewed the whole scheme as highway robbery to support an ill-conceived war.

To implement their far-reaching revenue scheme, the Government divided the entire country into "collection districts." Lincoln appointed assessors and collectors in every one of them – the assessors to determine how much a man owed, the collectors to confiscate his property if he failed to pay. Each district's assessors, in turn, appointed assistant assessors. Dominick knew how to deal with the assistant assessor assigned to Old Kensington, a man by the name of John Budd.[112] He had to be friendly, to avoid irritating him, even to win him over with kindness if he could – even when Budd said he owed more than Dominick himself thought right. Some of his acquaintances spoke privately of offering bribes to their assessors, though none actually admitted to anything more than a friendly 'good-will gift" from time to time.

As it happened, however, and despite the tax burden, Dominick's worst fears about the oncoming war never materialized. The worst came in late June of 1863, when rebel troops brought battle to Pennsylvania. The Mayor of Philadelphia called on citizens to close their places of business and prepare to defend the state; earthworks were constructed on the roads leading into the city.[113] But like a hurricane that has veered off its predicted course, the rebels struck Pennsylvania a hundred thirty miles to the west, at Gettysburg. Philadelphia was never invaded; and while the cotton supply did become uncertain, the dire consequences Murphy had feared did not follow. Rather, the opposite occurred. The federal army needed tents, blankets and uniforms, and it needed them in vast quantities. The preferred material, at least for blankets and uniforms, was wool – and while most of it came from Texas, wool did not depend on southern supply, because an even better grade of wool was readily available from Ireland. This meant some changes for cotton manufacturers, but the slight differences between how wool and cotton were woven were more than familiar to a man whose family had been in the wool business in Ireland for generations, and who knew the best sources of Irish wool. War, it began to appear, might actually be *good* for business. The mobilization of the government's vast military machine meant sizable profits for those in a position to secure its contracts. And Dominick Murphy – so recently a member of the Common Council, still an ally of Richard Vaux, now the father of three sons at the pinnacle of power in Washington – had plenty of valuable contacts.

> By adjusting to lost southern cotton supplies and the concomitant rise in demand for woolen goods, most Philadelphia textile manufacturers survived the war decade in a substantially altered but extremely prosperous fashion… In his study of Philadelphia textiles, Philp Scranton found that the city's wartime manufacturers profited from government contracting, tariff protection, and their own flexibility.[114]

As the industrial heart of the Union, Philadelphia was "the largest staging area for troops and supplies north of the Mason-Dixon line, and the financial center of the North was the scene of great enterprise during the war… 'Wealth came suddenly and in large measure…'"[115] Or in the words of another writer:

> [M]any Philadelphia merchants prospered during the war— after an initial downturn for many of the textile establishments that had to retool from cotton to the production of wool… The contract system enabled businesses both large and small to participate in the general prosperity of the war years…[116]

As it happens, the records of the tax assessments on Murphy's manufactured products are still available. But their value in assessing the profitability of Dominick's operations is limited for a number of reasons.

To begin with, there was no requirement that manufacturers keep records or books of account. A manufacturer might ship out a month's worth of product the day before the assistant assessor arrived to visit him and might claim that he'd had no orders. Meanwhile, everything was to be taxed, from cigars, jewelry, perfumes, snuff, photographs and books, to shoes, blankets, tools, iron rods, barrels, carriages, steam engines and much more. The job of assessing such a variety of products required knowledge of market conditions across an enormous range of goods. But since there'd never been such taxes on manufactured goods before, every assessor, and every assistant he appointed, was inexperienced at the job. Finally, for those subject to tax on what they produced, there was an enormous feeling of being taken from, without consent; an enormous temptation to hide production, to avoid taxation.

An assistant tax assessor, working alone, with hundreds of homes and businesses to assess, and no required recordkeeping to audit, was supposed to assess the value of all the goods manufactured in his assigned division during a month. If he knew where to look, he might discover a certain amount of inventory, but how could he assess product already shipped or sold? It was a matter of taking a manufacturer's word or challenging what was claimed. Faced with such difficulties, the assessments made on Dominick's mill between 1862 and 1866 didn't begin until after one might expect, and once begun, they varied widely.[117] Perhaps the assessor was unaware of his operation; or perhaps he chose to ignore it. Perhaps he was sometimes persuaded that the recent member of the Common Council deserved an unofficial exemption. Between June of 1863 and December of 1866, the average amount assessed on Murphy's mill was about eighty-five dollars a month. But in many months he didn't appear on the rolls at all; in some, he was assessed less than ten dollars; in others, as much as four hundred dollars. Variations in production might explain some of this variation, but between July 1864 and August 1865, he went thirteen months during which his total assessment came to only $6.15. The figures reveal as much barter and bluff as actual legal obligation.

We also have the annual income tax to consider. In May, 1864, Murphy reported annual income of $887; a year later, no income at all; and in May, 1866, $1,672.[118] The variability in these assessments raises many unanswered questions, but keeping in mind the difficulties faced by assessors, we can only be sure that Dominick paid as little tax as he could.

The tax rolls confirm that Murphy wove with wool, presumably imported from Ireland, as well as cotton. During four years of war, prospects for peace rose and fell; Murphy's contacts kept him informed; wool did what cotton couldn't; and government contractors made ample profits. By war's end, Dominick had good reason to feel secure. [119]

Taxes Assessed on Murphy Mill, 1862-1866[120]

Month	Description	$ Assessed
March 1863	--	--
April 1863	--	--
May 1863	--	--
June 1863	Cotton manufactures	136.53
July 1863	Linseys	41.18
August 1863	Cotton linseys	151.52
September 1863	Cotton plaids	103.95
October 1863	Cotton linseys	61.74
November 1863	Cotton linseys	125.10
December 1863	Linseys	45.78
January 1864	Woolen Flannels	45.33
February 1864	Cotton linseys & woolen flannels	31.14
March 1864	Cottonades	13.14
April 1864	Cotton linseys	102.90
May 1864	Cotton goods	423.36
June 1864	Linseys (cotton)	374.61
July 1864	--	--
August 1864	--	--
September 1864	Linseys	6.15
October 1864	--	--
November 1864	--	--
December 1864	--	--
January 1865	--	--
February 1865	--	--
March 1865	--	--
April 1865	--	--
May 1865	--	--
June 1865	--	--
July 1865	--	--
August 1865	Cotton & Woolen linseys	385.08
Sept 1865	Mixed goods	220.86
October 1865	Linseys	92.88
November 1865	Linseys	67.50
December 1865	--	--
January 1866	--	--
February 1866	Woven goods	13.62
March 1866	Cotton goods	17.10
April 1866	Cottonades	29.94
May 1866	Linseys	30.96
June 1866	Linseys and flannels	120.96
July 1866	Linseys	61.50
August 1866	Cotton & Woolen Goods	316.70
September 1866	Cotton Goods	225.75
October 1866	Cotton & Woolen Goods	234.65
November 1866	Cotton & Woolen linseys	145.60
December 1866	Cotton & Woolen linseys	58.05

And then, of course, as final victory seemed imminent, Lincoln was shot. Shock gave way to grief; outrage spawned desire for revenge. Dominick and Hannah hoped that with Lincoln buried and the war soon over, they'd be able to let wounds heal, to extend the hand of friendship to those who'd been the enemy. They wanted to get back to the world that once had been, enjoying the success of children and the arrival of grandchildren.

As the war was ending, the two youngest boys, Dominic and John, began working at Dominick's mill. But oddly, two other sons – Edward and Joseph – returned home from Washington to work in tax collection for Andrew Johnson's Treasury Department. We will consider what their purpose was in due course; for now, it is enough to point out that except when the Senate was in session, the Murphy children and grandchildren remained in Philadelphia. Dominick and Hannah's household included themselves, three of their sons, both their daughters, and three grandchildren. Three more sons, three daughters-in-law, and three more grandchildren lived just a few blocks away.[121] Theirs was a thriving, prosperous family. After mass, with tables well-appointed and plenty of lamb and Irish stew, Sunday afternoons at the Murphy house were fascinating affairs. Strictly separated by gender, after-dinner discussions were loving, contentious, and always spirited.[122]

By 1870, employment at the Murphy mill was down to forty-five employees, still with "only handlooms to produce a changing mix of cotton and woolen goods."[123] As Philip Scranton points out, "With $10,000 capital in his 1870 firm, Murphy at 61 was certainly able financially to retire." But he did not retire. Scranton concluded that Dominick's decision "may have resulted from a commitment to assist his sons' entry into the textile manufacture."[124] His fourth son, Joseph, did indeed get into the business in 1869 or 1870, starting his own small mill (see Chapter Seven). And the reduction of employment at Dominick's mill in 1870 appears to support the transfer of business to his son.

In 1871, he was elected to membership in the Hibernian Society, an organization of prominent Philadelphia businessmen that stressed good relations among all Irishmen, regardless of religious faith.[125] Sadly, the bright outlook of the late 1860's met grim reality in the 1870's. Daughter Hannah's husband, John Kinney, abandoned her, leaving Hannah and her three children to move into the already-busy Murphy house.[126] Soon thereafter, tragedy struck son James's house in a series of terrible blows: a grandson, Frank, died in 1872, only five months old.[127] James himself developed a brain tumor. (Though his Senate work continued for a while, "he was in constant pain, which was only allayed by repeated hypodermic injections of morphine."[128]) Just a few weeks after James passed away,[129] his seven-month-old son died,[130] and two years after that, his six-year-old daughter died.[131] With death so frequent and close, post-war agony tested Dominick and Hannah in ways the Civil War had not.

Meanwhile, the Panic of 1873 resulted in one of the worst depressions in the nation's history. In 1875, disputes between coal operators and mostly Irish miners resulted in a violent strike. The Molly Maguires were blamed; anti-Irish sentiment increased once again.[132] In the spring of 1876, there was a strike at the mill now operated by Dominick's son Joe.[133] The 1876 Presidential election marked the national centennial with contested ballots and a constitutional crisis that only added to Murphy's stress.

It proved to be too much. The decade which had begun with five family deaths approached its end on a similar note, as Dominick himself succumbed to "cerebral congestion" – probably a stroke. He died on Sept. 17, 1878. A solemn high mass was said for him at St. Michael's Church. As befitted a church elder and benefactor who'd made great strides in shaping America to be the place he wanted it to be, he was buried with some fanfare at New Cathedral Cemetery. [134] As for Hannah, with the affairs of women not typically recorded in the newspapers or history books, we know only that after watching the successes and disappointments of her children and grandchildren for another fifteen years, she followed her husband to the grave.[135]

RETURN OF A DEATH
IN THE CITY OF PHILADELPHIA.
PHYSICIAN'S CERTIFICATE.

1. Name of Deceased, *Dominic Murphy*
2. Color, *White,*
3. Sex, *Male,*
4. Age, *69 Years*
5. Married or Single, *Married*
6. Date of Death, *7th September 1878,*
7. Cause of Death, *Cerebral Congestion,*

James McCaul, M. D.

Residence, *218 Oxford St, Phila.*

UNDERTAKER'S CERTIFICATE IN RELATION TO DECEASED.

8. Occupation, *Manufacturer*
9. Place of Birth, *Ireland*
10. When a Minor, { Name of Father,
    { Name of Mother,
11. Ward, *17*
12. Street and Number, *1345 N 2 St*
13. Date of Burial, *Sep 21 1878*
14. Place of Burial, *New Cathedral Cemy,*

Jos H Hooky, Undertaker.

Residence, *1245 N 2*

Notes on Chapter 1, Dominick Murphy

[1] *The Philadelphia Inquirer*, March 23, 1936, p 2.

[2] It is elsewhere said that the Penal Laws had never explicitly outlawed the priesthood; they had simply required priests to register, prohibited them from teaching or saying mass, and generally driven them underground (Kerby A. Miller, Emigrants and Exiles, Oxford Univ. Press, 1985, pp 21-25). Vile as the Anglicans were, by some accounts the Presbyterians (despite their own history as a persecuted people) were even worse. (*Ibid.*, pp 231-232.)

[3] *Ibid.*, pp 196 - 207.

[4] According to research by Murphy descendant Bill Colman, who visited St. Mary's Church in Cork, Ireland, in 1987, Dominick was the son of Dennis Murphy and Johanna Murnane, baptized in St. Mary's on the 6th of August 1809. Censuses and Dominick's death certificate corroborate 1809 as his year of birth (1878 Phila Death Certificate; 1840 U.S. Census, Kensington Ward 3, p 90; 1850 Census, Kensington Ward 6, Fam 1138; 1860 Census, Phila Ward 17, Fam 1454; 1870 Census, Phila Ward 16, Dist 50, Fam 1474.) Hannah Donegan's 1893 obituary states she passed in her eighty-first year (Phila *Public Ledger*, May 12, 1893) and the censuses appear to confirm that she was born in 1812. One source asserts that Dominick "landed with his wife and 2-year-old son about 1835, when he was 26" (Philip Scranton, Proprietary Capitalism: The Textile Manufacture at Philadelphia, 1800-1885, Cambridge Univ Press, 1983). Another supports 1835 as the year of their arrival in New York, adding that they moved to Philadelphia in 1837 (*Washington Evening Star*, March 27, 1896, p 3). But another asserts that he was born in Cork, Ireland, August 4, 1810, and came to America in 1833 (John H. Campbell, History of the Friendly Sons of St. Patrick and of the Hibernian Society for the Relief of Emigrants from Ireland, March 17, 1771 – March 17, 1892, Hibernian Society, Phila, 1892, p 467). The 1850 U.S. Census (Kensington Ward 6, Fam 1128) lists son Denis, age 17, born in Ireland, daughter Hannah, age 14, born in New York, and son James, age 12, born in Pennsylvania. Bill Colman theorizes that Dominick may have come to New York first, alone, and returned to get his wife and daughter later.

[5] In 1830, there were slaves in all Northern states except Vermont, including 2,254 in New Jersey, 747 in Illinois, 3,292 in Delaware, 102,994 in Maryland, and 6,119 in the District of Columbia. New York, Connecticut and Pennsylvania were relatively slave-free, with only 76, 25, and 403 slaves, respectively, in those states (Abstract of the Returns of the Fifth Census, Duff Green, Washington, 1832).

[6] Russell Weigley *et al*, Philadelphia, a Three Hundred Year History, W.W. Norton & Co. (1982), p 359.

[7] Poe's article appears in full in Kenneth W. Milano, Remembering Kensington & Fishtown, History Press, 2008, pp 80-81.

[8] In 1820, the population of Kensington was 86% Irish born (including both Protestants and Catholics). (National Register of Historic Places, "Buildings Related to the Textile Industry in the Kensington Neighborhood of Philadelphia," NPS Form 10-900-b, accessed at http://www.preservation alliance.com/wp-content/uploads/2014/09/KensingtonNR.pdf.)

[9] Kenneth Milano, The Philadelphia Nativist Riots, The History Press, 2013, p 44, quoting from Philadelphia's *North American* newspaper.

[10] The meeting put a temporary end to the trouble, but violence continued the next day. According to the *North American*, "A riot took place in Kensington at the Nanny Goat Market, north end, near Mud Lane. Rioters were armed with clubs, stones and firearms. The Sheriff organized a posse of two to three hundred... On approaching the mob, the posse was attacked viciously by a shower of stones and several pieces of firearms were discharged." (*Ibid.*)

[11] The population of Kensington rose from 13,326 in 1830 to 22,314 in 1840 and 46,744 in 1850. (*Population of Civil Divisions of Philadelphia County, 1790-1850*, accessed at philageohistory.org.)

[12] Andrew Heath, "Consolidation Act of 1854," Encyclopedia of Greater Philadelphia, accessed at https://phila delphiaencyclopedia.org/archive/consolidation-act-of-1854/; Weigley *et al, supra*, p 315.

[13] Prior to the riots, specifically between 1838 and 1842, the Murphys lived on Gay's Court (see McElroy's directories of 1839, 1840 and 1842, the latter listing on "4 Gray's Ct" an apparent typo). Gay's Court was described as "E from Charlotte n George" in the Street Names Section of the 1839 Directory. It was depicted on 1862 and 1874 maps as a short alley running between Charlotte and 3rd, just south of Phoenix – i.e., about three blocks southwest of St. Michael's church. James Gay himself was listed at "c 3rd & G T road" (the corner of 3rd St and Germantown Road) in the 1839-1843 Directories, and "3rd ab Franklin (K)" in the 1844 Directory. In the 1840 Census, Murphy was listed four names down from James Gay. Essentially, then, the Murphys lived on a small, unpaved court behind Gay's house. These entries confirm that they'd settled in the heart of Kensington by no later than October of 1838. (See Appendix 1 for dating of the directories.)

[14] The directories identify James Gay variously as merchant, conveyancer, and grocer at 274 N 2nd Street in the 1837 Directory, at 3rd St and Germantown Road in the 1839 - 1843 Directories, and at 3rd ab Franklin (K) in the 1844 Directory. Another source says he operated the Park Carpet Mill (Workshop of the World: A Selective Guide to the Industrial Archaeology of Philadelphia (Oliver Evans Press, 1990), p 233). He'd been elected a major of the Pennsylvania militia in 1835; in 1840, he ran (as an independent) for alderman; in 1841, he was nominated for Kensington Treasurer and for state assemblyman; and in 1852, he was nominated for a seat on the School Board. (*National Gazette*, June 11, 1835, p 2; *Public Ledger*, March 20, 1840, p 1, Aug 5, 1842, p 2, Aug 18, 1842, p 2, and April 15, 1852, p 2.) Assuming this was all the same man, Murphy likely worked in his mill briefly when he first arrived in Kensington and developed a friendship with the man who would later figure in his life. It was probably Gay who convinced Murphy to get involved in politics.

[15] The 1843 to 1846 directory listings have Dominick Murphy, weaver, living at Justice Ct, indicating he lived there by late 1842 (and, therefore, during the May, 1844 riots). Justice Ct was a little side street directly off N 2d (described in the directories' Street Names section as "rear 314 N 2d," the same street St. Michael's Church was on (see Map). A gentleman named Samuel Justice had lived at 314 N 2d (1837 and 1840 Directories), and Justice Court was presumably named after him. The precise north-south location of number 314 cannot be determined, since the system of regular street numbering was not in place until the late 1850's. Its n-s location on the Map here has been inferred. Murphy was listed as a weaver in the city directories until 1845, when he was listed as "carpet weaver."

[16] Scranton, *supra*, pp 192 and 221. While the 1840 Census doesn't state the occupation or business of the men counted (it doesn't even give the names of women, children and slaves), the 1850 Census calls Murphy a "manufacturer" and states that he owned real estate valued at $1,400, a rather substantial sum in 1850. The 1850 *U.S. Census Manufacturing Schedule for Philadelphia*, p 63, on which Scranton relied, asserted that Murphy's cotton mill then employed 120 people.

[17] Becoming a textile manufacturer in Kensington "did not necessarily require an initial capital investment in buildings, machinery or training... [T]he textile industry could subsist on individuals or families who worked out of their homes on their own equipment... These enterprises began with minimal capital investment, often out of homes or rented space, and machinery was acquired gradually as finances allowed... This system of cottage manufacturing, with items made equally both inside and outside of the factory, was successful..." (National Register, *supra*.)

[18] Edwin T. Freedley, Philadelphia and its Manufactures: A Handbook of the Manufacturing Industry of Philadelphia in 1857, (Edward Young, 1859), p 253, accessed at https://archive.org/details/philadelphiaitsm00freeiala/page/n8/mode/2up?ref=ol&view=theater. Freedley has an extensive discussion of the manufacture of textile dry goods in Philadelphia, covered at pp 232-263. "Handloom proprietors only had to rent a workshop or build a shed for their looms – a fraction of the cost of the larger, power-loom factories." (Scranton, *supra*, p 221; Milano, Remembering, *supra*, p 48; Workshop of the World, *supra*, p 233.)

[19] The Irish who immigrated before the potato famine of the late 1840's were of a different class than the "post-famine" immigrants who arrived later; they were a heterogenous group that included prosperous

Protestants. (Miller, *supra*, pp 193, 196, 263.) The bulk of the Irish textile employers were present to welcome the later (famine-era) immigrants to their mills. (Milano, Remembering, *supra*, p 48, quoting Scranton.)

[20] The Third Ward extended from Front Street in the east to 6th Street in the West, and from Montgomery Street down to Franklin Street, making it a square about three thousand feet across. Gay's Court and Justice's Court were both just blocks from the Church and the Master Street School. After the standardization of 1856 (see Appendix 5), the Murphy address was listed as 1341 N 2d – directly adjacent to the school – and they would live there for years to come. Some of their pre-standardization address changes may not have been a change of home, but simply a change in the way the address of the home was described. The 1850 Census listed Murphy as *owning* $1400 in real estate (presumably at "Perry bel Master," his directory address at the time.) Since one doesn't normally buy and sell as often as one might change a rented residence, it seems possible that the homes identified as "Perry bel Master," "801 N 2nd," "825 N 2nd" and "1341 N 2d" were all the same home, if not also the same home as the one on "Justice Ct."

[21] Campbell, *supra*, p 467.

[22] There were no parochial schools in 1844. The Master Street grammar and primary school – which had both a boys' and a girls' division – changed its name to the Harrison School in 1848. It was the largest school in Kensington, with 1197 students. A Catalogue of the all-boys Central High School reflects that four Murphy sons (James, Edward, Dominick and John) had attended Master/Harrison (General Catalogue of the Central High School, Philadelphia, 1838 to 1890, Phila Bd of Educ, 1890, accessed at the Internet Archive (archive.org/details/generalcatalogue00philrich/page/n5/mode/2up).) According to Kenneth Milano, all nine of the Kensington students who entered Central High in 1844 were graduates of the Master Street School (Milano, Nativist Riots, *supra*, p 36.) Given the family's proximity to the school, Milano's assertion and the Central High Catalogue, it seems certain that Dennis (age ten) and his siblings Hannah (eight) and James (six) were pupils at the Master Street School up to and including 1844, their younger siblings thereafter.

[23] Miller, *supra*, p 275-276.

[24] Milano, Nativist Riots, *supra*, p. 47; Weigley *et al*, *supra*, p 356.

[25] Milano, Nativist Riots, *supra*, pp 50-52.

[26] Weigley *et al*, *supra*, p. 356, and the records held at the Presbyterian Historical Society, accessed at https://www.history.pcusa.org/collections/research-tools/guides-archival-collections/rg-323. The A.R.A. was established in Spring Garden (just west of Kensington).

[27] Milano, Nativist Riots, *supra*, pp 53-54; Weigley *et al*, *supra*, p. 357.

[28] The proposed alteration of the laws was to conform them to the Nativist principles: the 21-year residency requirement, the reading of the Bible, and non-eligibility for public employment. The meeting "was to be held on an empty lot, measuring 100 by 150 feet, next to the Master Street Public School, site of the "Bible Wars" between Alderman Clark and the teachers of the district. The school was located on Master Street, about midway between 2nd and Washington Streets and about seventy yards east of the Nanny Goat Market (Washington Market)." Milano, Nativist Riots, *supra*, pp 57-58.

[29] *Ibid.*, pp 60-61, 71-72.

[30] *Public Ledger*, May 7, 1844, p 2.

[31] Milano, Nativist Riots, *supra*, pp 78-80.

[32] *Ibid.*, p 98.

[33] *Ibid.*, pp 101-113; Weigley *et al*, *supra*, p 357. Among other things, the registry of baptisms and marriages was destroyed in the fire.

[34] Miller, *supra*, p 276.

[35] Rev. William J. Boyle, The Story of Old St. Michaels, 1834-1934, Jeffries & Manz, 1934, accessed December 2020 at http://www.organistjohn.com/OSM_Docs

[36] *Ibid.*

[37] In the City Directory of 1846, Murphy's address is still listed as Justice Court, but in the Directory of 1847 – prepared in the latter part of 1846 (see Appendix 5) – he is listed as "Perry bel Master,"

putting him at the location later known as 1340 Palethorp Street, where his mill would be located for decades to come and where he'd later be identified as an owner, rather than a renter. (See Map, Appendix 1.)

[38] Boyle, *supra.*

[39] 1854 Philadelphia City Directory, p 18. The Liberty Bell had last been rung on Monday, February 23, 1846, to celebrate the birthday of George Washington; the major new crack exposed at the time rendered it "irreparably cracked and forever dumb" thereafter. (*Public Ledger*, Feb 26, 1846, p 2; "Liberty Bell Timeline," https://www.ushistory.org/libertybell/timeline.html). The number of new arrivals in Philadelphia peaked in 1852 when, though only eleven months were reported, it reached 31,394.

[40] Dennis, Hannah, James, Margaret, Edward, Joseph, Dominic and John. (1850 U.S. Census, Kensington Ward 6, Fam 1128.) The Census asserts that Hannah Murphy could not read or write. Whether this meant she could not read and write English, or was also illiterate in Gaelic, is unclear. The Murphy household is listed in the 6th Ward, rather than the Third, but this would not have required a family move. The 6th Ward had been created by a splitting of the old Third Ward in 1846, the dividing line between the two wards running down 2nd Street. A Murphy abode on Perry/Palethorp, or even on the east side of 2nd Street, would have been included in the new 6th Ward.

[41] Scranton, *supra*, p 192.

[42] Scranton, *supra*, p 193.

[43] *Ibid.*, pp 191-194. Scranton's Table 6.9 of area textile firms gives statistics from the U.S. Census Manufacturing Schedule of 1850 for Philadelphia. Scranton points out that many of the operations were not centralized factories with looms side by side, but what he calls "outwork enterprises" (i.e., where the handloom weaver worked at home). See also Freedley, *supra.*

[44] The 1852 and 1853 Phila City Directories list Dominick Murphy, 2nd and Master Street, with occupation "tavern." From 1854 to 1856, the Murphy residence was listed in the directories as 825 or 801 N 2d Street. Beginning in 1857 (after revision of the numbering system) they were listed at 1341 N 2d Street.

[45] E. L. Godkin in *The Nation*, Nov. 4, 1875, quoted in Alexander B. Callow, The Tweed Ring (New York; Oxford University Press, 1966) p 193.

[46] *Public Ledger*, July 26, 1852, p 2.

[47] Boyle, *supra.* See also Francis J. Ryan, "Roman Catholic Education," The Encyclopedia of Greater Philadelphia, accessed at https://philadelphiaencyclopedia.org/archive/roman-catholic-education/. (Catholics thought it better to run their own schools than be subject to the influence of Protestants in the public schools.)

[48] Weigley *et al*, *supra*, p 368. See also Heath, *supra*, asserting that the move to consolidation grew from the riots.

[49] The General Catalogue of Central High School from 1838 to 1890, *supra*, p 21, asserts that Lewis Cassidy was admitted in July of 1843 and attended until July of 1846 – his final year therefore overlapped with Dennis Murphy's attendance at the school. Cassidy was admitted to the bar in 1849 and went on to become Attorney General of Pennsylvania. Weigley *et al* (p 370) calls him the leader of the Irish Catholic faction of the Democratic Party.

[50] Charlene Mires, "Independence Hall," *The Encyclopedia of Greater Philadelphia on-line*, accessed at https://philadelphiaencyclopedia.org/essays/independence-hall/, and James Kopaczewski, "Nativism," accessed at https://philadelphiaencyclopedia.org/essays/nativism/.

[51] The City's governing Council was divided into two chambers, the "Select Council" and the "Common Council."

[52] Conrad received 29,507 votes to 21,011 for Richard Vaux, the Democrats' candidate. See Boyle, *supra.* Richard Vaux, the loser in the mayoral race, was a Democrat whose political connections were with Cassidy. (Weigley *et al*, *supra*, pp 370-371.)

[53] Consolidation increased the size of Philadelphia from the two square miles originally laid out by William Penn to nearly one hundred thirty. (Heath, "Consolidation Act of 1854," *supra.*)

---

[54] Weigley *et al, supra,* p 369.

[55] Murphy's election to the Common Council was on May 1, 1855. Journal of the Common Council of the Consolidated City of Philadelphia, May 7 to Nov 1, 1855, *Vol III,* p 21, accessed at https://babel.hathitrust.org/cgi/pt?id=nyp.33433010146607&view=image&seq=71. The new 17th Ward, along with the 19th Ward to its north, was largely fashioned from the Third and Sixth Wards of old Kensington, the 17th Ward running as far north as Oxford Street.

[56] Weigley *et al, supra,* pp 368-369.

[57] *Ibid.,* pp 369-370. The law applied to liquor sales in taverns, tippling rooms, oyster houses, and amusement parks.

[58] Journal Vol III, *supra,* pp 31-32, recounting Council action on May 7, 1855.

[59] *Ibid.,* p 73. The Committee on Markets had eleven members. It was the worst assignment because so many minor, private issues came before it, while few if any matters came before it of city-wide scope or of a controversial nature.

[60] The Council of which Murphy was a part did make some positive contributions to the City's future. For one thing, they approved measures that would soon lead to the creation of Fairmount Park. For another, they instructed the Commissioner of Highways to prepare a sensible and consistent system of street nomenclature to name and number streets in a methodical way, finally making it possible to use an address to find a person or a business (*Ibid.,* pp 334 and 414).

[61] Weigley *et al, supra,* p 370, pointing out that the Democratic battle cry against the Whigs began with "No increase of taxes!" and called for "frugal and economical" administration of municipal affairs.

[62] Journal Vol III, *supra,* p 227, setting forth the Report of the Committee on Markets, including the proposed Ordinance No. 29, "An Ordinance to Regulate the Hawking of Fruits, Vegetables, Etc, through the Streets, in Wagons," and Journal Vol IV, pp 428, 456-457, 484-489.

[63] After the referral, the Council turned to other business. An amendment to the recently-passed "Ordinance relating to horses, cows, sheep and other animals running at large" (which provided that each housekeeper would be allowed "one cow and no more to run at large on the public roads") was referred to the Standing Committee on Police. Consideration of an "Ordinance to regulate the speed at which cars may be conveyed and locomotive engines propelled over the railroads within the limits of the City of Philadelphia" was postponed (Journal Vol III, pp 184, 188-189, June 14, 1855). No doubt most of the councilmen had the police force on their minds.

[64] *Ibid.,* pp 192-194, June 14, 1855. The Report of the Committee on Police is at Appendix No. 13 to the Journal, p 41.

[65] *Ibid.,* Report of the Committee on Police.

[66] Journal Vol III, *supra,* Minority Report appended to Appendix No. 13 of the Journal, p 152.

[67] Unable to locate a copy of the relevant volume of the Journal, we base this assertion on the Mayor's characterization of it in his Annual Message to Council, presented at the January 31, 1856, Council meeting, Journal Vol IV, Nov 1, 1855 to May 8, 1856, p 286. According to that message, the figure of 650 was exclusive of Sergeants and Lieutenants.

[68] In addition to these, there were 16 arrests for adultery, 8 for bigamy, 39 for fornication and bastardy, 8 for fornication without bastardy, 1 for sodomy, 1 for incest and 4 for "seduction."

[69] Journal Vol IV, Appendix No 92, p 387, accessed at https://babel.hathitrust.org/cgi/pt?id=uiug.30112109694551&view=image&seq=1078.

[70] Murphy must have been gratified when Professor Knorr of Central High School addressed a meeting of the Common Council in 1856 and boasted to its members that all six of the Congressional Globe's reporters in Washington were graduates of the high school, and that two of them, Dennis Murphy and James McElhone, were "probably the most accomplished reporters living." *Daily American Organ,* Feb 15, 1856, p 2; also quoted in Franklin Spencer Edmonds, History of the Central High School of Philadelphia, J.B. Lippincott, 1902, p 296. See also Chapter 3, on Dennis Murphy, below.

[71] When Mr. Hacker retired from the Council after that election, Murphy was one of a new majority who voted against a motion to commend him for his service. Journal Vol IV, *supra,* Minutes of May 8, 1856,

p 632. Vaux's two years as Mayor and subsequent service in multiple capacities, culminating in a term representing Philadelphia in Congress, put him at the apex of politics in the city for the next thirty-five years. "Richard Vaux was an early local specimen of an American phenomenon, the gentleman in politics who, by connecting himself with working-class interest and organizations…establishes himself as a champion of the common man." Weigley *et al, supra*, p 371.

[72] Weigley *et al, supra*, pp 371-372.

[73] *Ibid.*, p 326.

[74] Freedley, *supra* p 253, listed Murphy as making "Checks in connection with Linseys, Cottonades, Ginghams, &c." Dominick's listing in the 1845 directory had called him a carpet weaver. Taxes in the 1860's were assessed on his cottonades and linseys.

[75] *Ibid.*, pp 372, 379. In 1855, the North Pennsylvania Railroad Company had established a steam-driven rail line that ran up Front Street from downtown to Germantown Road, and from there up Second Street. The route up Second Street through Kensington was on the way to points further north, to connect the city to the Lehigh coal region. (Boyle, *supra*.) There was a depot and station on Master Street just west of Second, just a block or two from Councilman Murphy's home. Horse drawn cars were not yet eliminated, however; steam powered cars were typically used along major routes, while horses continued to pull them on the side spurs.

[76] *Ibid.*, p 256.

[77] Jack McCarthy, "Textile Manufacturing and Textile Workers," *The Encyclopedia of Greater Philadelphia,* https://philadelphiaencyclopedia.org/archive/textile-manufacturing-and-textile-workers/

[78] Scranton, *supra,* p. 194.

[79] *Ibid.*

[80] Boyle, *supra.* See also *Timeline of Philadelphia History, 1646-1899,* accessed at https://www.ushistory.org/Philadelphia/timeline/ and "Great Train Wreck of 1856" on Wikipedia.org.

[81] A published list of the casualties contains the names of no Murphy children. Boyle, *supra.* As for Murphy not sending his children to the new parochial school, the teachers there made only half what their counterparts in the public schools made. Dominick and Hannah's eldest son, Dennis, had gone from the Master Street School to Central High; he had been admitted to the Philadelphia Bar. (Campbell, *supra*, p 467, dates the admission to November of 1857; listings in the city directories confirm it.) Public education had clearly served him well. So Dominick and Hannah continued to enroll their children in the Master Street School (now called the Harrison School), even if it did mean their having to read from the King James Bible.

[82] For the definitive treatment of that case, see Don E. Fehrenbacher, The Dred Scott Case (Oxford University Press, 1978). For the role of our mother's family in that story, see not only Fehrenbacher, but jwcarvin, *Alemeth* (Nothing in Common Books, 2017).

[83] Because of the invention of the telegraph by Samuel F. Morse in 1844, the Panic of 1857 was the first financial crisis to spread rapidly throughout the United States. "The Panic of 1857," Wikipedia.org, citing Johnny Fulfer, "Panic of 1857: A Story of Speculative Finance," *The Economic Historian,* 2018.

[84] Scranton, *supra*, pp 214-215.

[85] *Ibid.*, p 221, citing 1860 Manufacturing Census Schedule, p 404.

[86] Murphy's three-year term on the Common Council ended in the spring of 1858. Haunted by memories of the railroad disaster, he did not serve again. From that point forward, his politics were vicarious, living through his sons' careers.

[87] Scranton, *supra*, p 221.

[88] The street numbering system the Council had introduced while Murphy was a member was finally gaining a measure of acceptance, and the clarity it brought still benefits us today. In the Directory of 1858, for the first time, Dominick's home was listed with the numbered address it would bear for the rest of his life: 1341 N 2d. Whether that address represented an actual change from the southwest corner of 2nd and Master or was simply the address the Commissioner of Highways had settled on for the place Murphy had already lived in for years, is hard to tell. In any case, the new numbering system enables

us to know even without a map that this home address was literally back-to-back with 1340 N Palethorp, the address of his mill. (That numbered address first appears in the Census of 1860, but all signs point to its having been at that location years earlier.) The Murphys would live and work at those addresses at least until 1876.

[89] Of the five reporters of the U.S. Senate, three were now Murphy brothers (1862 and 1863 City Directories for Wash. D.C.) The first of these sources – compiled in late 1861 – shows the three Murphy brothers, Dennis, James and Edward, boarding together at "28 4-1/2 W" in the capital city. Hannah and Dominic's eighteen-year-old daughter Mary Ann had started teaching in Philadelphia; another son (Joseph) had become a reporter, and their two younger sons, Dominic and John, were doing well at the Master Street School, on track to follow their brothers' success. (See the 1860 U.S. Census Phila Ward 17, Fam 1454. Note that the value of Dominick's real estate was now matched by the same amount of personal property. Hannah Murphy's non-appearance in the 1860 census suggests a temporary absence, perhaps to visit an ailing father in Canada. (She would re-appear in the 1870 Census with her husband and go on to outlive him.) The 1860 City Directory lists "Murphy Dominick, cotton goods, 1340 Palethorp, h 1341 N 2d." In 1861, it's "Murphy Dominick, manuf. 1341 N 2d." In 1862 it's "Murphy Dominick, cotton, 1341 N 2d."

[90] "We must not be enemies," Lincoln pleaded in his inaugural address, "though passion may have strained, it must not break, our bonds of affection."

[91] Polygenesis was the belief that the various human races (white, African, Asian, "red men," etc.) had been created by God as separate and distinct species, with different attributes endowed by God, rather than evolving from a common ancestor.

[92] New Jersey State Library, accessed at https://www.njstatelib.org/researchlibrary/newjersey resources/highlights/african_american_history_curriculum/unit_5_antebellum_america/.

[93] See also, for example, Ohio Constitution of 1851, Art V, Sec 1. In 1865, Connecticut voters defeated a proposal to allow black suffrage in every Connecticut county but one (*New York Herald*, Oct 4, 1865, p 4).

[94] Weigley *et al*, *supra*, p 353.

[95] Dennis Clark, The Irish in Philadelphia: Ten Generations of Urban Experience, Temple Univ. Press, 1973, p 120.

[96] See, for example, Milano, Nativist Riots, *supra*, p 16.

[97] Greggory M. Ross, "Boxing in the Union Blue: A Social History of American Boxing in the United States During the Late Antebellum and Civil War Years" (2014), *Electronic Thesis and Dissertation Repository, 2043,* pp 193-194, accessed at https://ir.lib.uwo.ca/cgi/viewcontent.cgi?article=3423 &context=etd.

[98] Avery Craven, The Coming of the Civil War, Univ. of Chicago Press, 2d ed., 1974, p 291.

[99] Weigley *et al*, *supra*, pp 391-392.

[100] *Ibid.*, p 393.

[101] Of course, in Douglas's view, self-determination was essentially restricted to whites. He'd written that "this government was made by our fathers on the white basis ... made by white men for the benefit of white men and their posterity forever." (David Herbert Donald, Lincoln, 1995, quoted in "Stephen A. Douglas" at Wikipedia.org.) Douglas was opposed to forced abolition, and on that point, the Supreme Court's *Dred Scott* decision backed him up.

[102] In the 1860 Congressional election, Dominick's 17th Ward cast 1,975 votes for the Democrat, 1,252 for the "Peoples" party candidate, and 41 for the Constitutional Union party candidate (*Inquirer*, Oct 11, 1862, p 8).

[103] *Inquirer*, Jan 1, 1862, p 6, reflecting on the events of April 15, 1861.

[104] The Congressman had also said the Lincoln administration had "no sense among them," while calling Jeff Davis "a thorough gentleman, a soldier, and a statesman of the greatest calibre." (*The Inquirer*, Sept 13, 1862, under the headline, "Arrest for Uttering Treasonable Language.")

[105] Quotations are from *The Philadelphia Inquirer*, which ran a summary of major events in the city during the prior year at p 6 of its Jan 1 1862 edition.

[106] *Ibid.*

[107] "Cathedral Basilica of Saints Peter and Paul (Philadelphia)," at Wikipedia.org.

[108] *Inquirer,* April 21, 1862. Kenrick was right that nearly all the Protestant Churches had suffered schisms in the days leading up to the war, splitting along north-south lines, for and against slavery. And true enough, there'd been no similar schism in the Catholic Church. But many who'd been through the riots may have questioned his statement that Catholics were obedient to the mandates of civil authorities.

[109] The 1861 Revenue Act imposed a flat 3% tax on incomes – but only on the excess above $800 per year. A weaver making $20 or even $30 a month owed no tax. (Act of Aug 5, 1861, Chapter XLV, 12 Stats 292.) As a wealthier manufacturer, Dominick could see that it was him and people like him the Republicans were forcing to finance the war.

[110] Act of July 1, 1862, Chapter CXIX, 12 Stats 432.

[111] Act of June 30, 1864, Chapter CLXXIII, 13 Stats 223.

[112] Sections 2 through 38 of the 1862 Act, 12 Stats 433–446; *Inquirer*, Sept 1, 1862, p 4. See 1864 Directory, or 1863-1866 tax lists, for J. Fletcher Budd, Assessor, and John Budd, Assistant Assessor.

[113] *Inquirer*, June 16, 1863, p 4, and *Inquirer*, June 29, 1863, p 4.

[114] J. Matthew Gallman, Mastering Wartime: A Social History of Philadelphia During the Civil War, Univ of Penn Press, 1990, pp 263-264.

[115] Clark, *supra*, p 123.

[116] Richard A. Sauers, "Philadelphia: Economy of War," at *History Net.* https://www.historynet.com/philadelphia-economy-of-war.htm. Originally published in the September 2006 issue of *Civil War Times,* Sauers' article recounts instances of "fraudulent merchants eager to supply shoddy material in return for huge profits and bribery of government officials."

[117] To begin with, although a ten-dollar license tax was due, Dominick didn't even appear on the rolls during the months of September '62 through February 1863; he wasn't assessed the ten-dollar fee until March of 1863. Even then, he was assessed no tax on his *production* until June.

[118] See the Annual Tax List for Pennsylvania District 3, Division 9, for May 1864 ($887 income less $600 non-taxable = taxable income of $287 x 3% = $8.61 in tax assessed); and in Division 11 for May, 1865 (not listed) and May, 1866 ($1672 income less $600 non-taxable = taxable income of $1,072 x 5% = $53.60 in tax assessed.) In that final year for which records are available, he also paid a $2 tax on a piano.

[119] Before the war, Dominick had listed his business in the city directories as "cotton" or "cotton goods." In 1863 through 1866, the directory listed him simply as "manufacturer." In 1867, he'd been listed under cotton *and woolen* goods, and by 1870, he was listed as "woollengoods" alone. There is little mention of unadulterated cotton goods in the 1862-1866 tax records. In addition to occasional mention of woolen goods, they frequently refer to a cloth called "linsey" – a coarse broadcloth fabric made with a wool weft woven into a cotton warp.

[120] Monthly Tax Assessments Lists, Pennsylvania, District 3, Division 9 (through November 1864) and Division 11 (from December 1864), accessed via Ancestry.com.

[121] See 1870 U.S. Census, Phila Ward 16 Dist 50 Fam 1474. Dominick and Hannah's eldest daughter, Hannah, who had married a grocer, John Kinney, and had three children, were living with Kinney in the 1867 and 1868 directories at 1401 N 2d Street, just a block from Dominick's house. By 1870, they had moved into Dominick and Hannah's house at 1241 N 2d (though John Kinney did not move in with them.) Daughter Mary (now a schoolteacher) and sons Edward, Dominick Jr. and John were all still living at their parents' home as well. Dennis Murphy, his wife and his children maintained their permanent residence in Philadelphia (1870 Census Phila Ward 22 Dist 4, 2d enum, Dwelling 7, p 15, North Side of Armat Street in Germantown). James J. Murphy, his wife (Mary Ann Clarke, 1842-1882), their daughter Catherine (age 1) and a live-in domestic servant (Mary Hood, age 37) lived at 1323 Marshall Street in Kensington (1868 and 1870 Phila Directories; 1870 Census Phila Ward 20 Dist 64 Fam 37). Their son

Joseph, recently married, was also still living in Philadelphia (1870 U.S. Census Phila Ward 18 Dist 53, 2d enum, dwelling 1101).

122 Post-war interest in reconciliation may have helped change another aspect of the Murphys' lives as well. Their youngest child, John, was now past the age of attendance at parochial school. With that sore point in his relationship with St. Michael's eliminated, Dominick was soon elected a trustee of the Church. (Boyle, *supra,* and Campbell, *supra*, p 467). Neither source gives a date, but Boyle, writing his history of St. Michael's in 1934, lists trustees "of the last seventy years" in apparent chronological order, and Dominick Murphy's name appears second on the list.

123 Scranton, *supra,* p 221, citing 1870 Manufacturing Census Schedule, Phila, p 470.

124 *Ibid.* As Scranton observed, "The proportion of men to women employed (2:1) is constant in all three reports [1850, 1860 and 1870], suggesting the unchanging nature of the productive relations in place."

125 This organization should not be confused with the militant Catholic "Ancient Order of Hibernians." A group of Irish businessmen had founded an organization in 1771 called "The Friendly Sons of St. Patrick," which was later succeeded by "The Hibernian Society for the Relief of Emigrants from Ireland." (Campbell, *supra*, pp. 27-32.) Dennis Clark called the Society "a fairly select group of the more prominent Philadelphia Irish... one of the few Irish organizations in which the Irish Catholic and the Irish Protestant could meet in fraternal association." (Clark, *supra*, p 108.) Murphy joined it in time to attend the meeting at which President Ulysses S. Grant was also inducted into the Society as an honorary member (Campbell, *supra*, pp 226-227). Grant being a Republican and not belonging to any church did not prevent Dominick from breaking bread with him. For the date of Dominick's admission, see Campbell, *supra*, p 328. For his trusteeship of St. Michael's, see p 467. His involvement with the church and the Hibernian Society may seem the natural course of a moderate, practical, civic-minded man, now nearing retirement but with his old appetite for community involvement still showing signs of life.

126 A John Kinney does not appear in the 1870 or 1871 directories, or in the Murphy household, with Hannah, in the 1870 Census. Efforts to ascertain his death or other whereabouts were not successful.

127 Frank Murphy, age 5 month and 8 days, son of James J. and Mary A. Murphy, died Jan 15, 1872 of inflammation of the bowels and was buried in New Cathedral Cemetery. (Death Certificate of Frank Murphy, reviewed by Bill Colman.)

128 W. S. Garber, "Congressional Reporting," *The Shorthand Review,* Vol IV, No 5, May 1892, p 73.

129 James J Murphy, reporter, is listed in the Phila Directories on Marshall Street, in Kensington, in 1872 and 1873. He passed away on December 4, 1874 (Death certificate, original at Phil City Archives, FHL No's 1003700 and 2026535. The FHL film number refers to a microfilm copy of the source held by the Family History Library in Salt Lake City, Utah.) Cause of death "Necrosis of the visteal cerebreal."

130 Born in June 1874, little James M. Murphy Jr. died Jan 18, 1875, Death Cert at FHL No. 2026651, from congestion of the lungs, interred January 21, 1875 per Records of the New Cathedral Cemetery accessed at Ancestry.com. Having lost her husband and two of their three children, James's widow Mary and her lone surviving son, Charles, shared lodging with the children's nurse, Mary Ann Hood. (1870 U.S. Census Phila Ward 20, Dist. 64, Fam 37, and 1880 U.S. Census Phila Dist 689, Fam 109.)

131 *Public Ledger,* May 18, 1876. James's daughter's name was Katie.

132 Infamy attached to the Molly Maguires and to their alleged front organization, the Ancient Order of Hibernians

133 Lasting two months, that strike caused stress in more than one Murphy household. See Chapter 7.

134 *The Times*, Sept 19, 1878, p 3. According to an abstract of Gustavo C. Roman, "Cerebral Congestion: a Vanished Disease" (1987), the concept of "cerebral congestion" accounted not only for cerebral hemorrhage, but also for lacunes, *état criblé*, depression, maniac outbursts, headaches, coma, and seizures. (Abstract accessed at https://jamanetwork.com/journals/jamaneurology/article-abstract/586337.) Dominick's death left three widows: James's (Mary Ann Murphy) was left to live with her sole surviving child Charles and their nurse, Mary Hood. (1880 U.S. Census, Phila. Dist. 689, Fam. 109, at 824 Firth Street. [Digitally transcribed as "Fort" Street, but it must in fact have been Firth.]

Dominick's own widow (Hannah Murphy) and his widowed or abandoned daughter (Hannah Kinney) were left to live together with a brood of fatherless youngsters. The 1880 Census, Phila Dist 310, Fam 9, includes Hannah Murphy (68), Hannah Kinney (43), Mary A. Murphy (37, single schoolteacher), John A. Murphy (29, single son, mill hand) and three children in school: Mary C. Kinney (14), Anna R. Kinney (13), and John Kinney (11), living at 1342 N. 2nd Street (East Side). Dominick's obituary, which ran in the *Philadelphia Times* of September 19 and 21, 1878, invited guests to gather at his "former residence" of 1341 N. 2d Street – the home in which he and wife Hannah had been living for many years. The address appearing on the death certificate is 1345 N. 2d Street, two houses down from that long time residence. But the 1884 City Directory shows Hannah, widow of Dominick, back at the longstanding address of 1341 N. 2d. The reason for these minor moves between three neighboring addresses, or the simple errors they suggest, is unclear.

[135] Hannah died of heart failure due to influenza on May 8, 1893 (Obituaries in *The Inquirer*, May 11, 1893, p 6; *The Times*, May 12, 1893, p 5; and *The Public Ledger*, May 12, 1893).

William Carvin Naturalization Petition

"I, William Carvin, Do Declare on Oath, before the Marine Court of the City of New York, that it is *bona fide* my intention to become a citizen of the United States, and to renounce forever all Allegiance and Fidelity to any foreign Prince, Potentate, State or Sovereignty whatever; and particularly to the King of the United Kingdom of Great Britain and Ireland, of whom I now am a subject. I further declare on Oath, that for three years next preceding the time of making this Declaration, it was *bona fide* my intention to become a Citizen of the United States."

William ^{his} X _{mark} Carvin

Sworn in open court this 8 day of April, 1834,
John Barberie, Clerk.

Patrick Gregory, being duly sworn, doth depose and say that he is well acquainted with William Carvin, and that said William Carvin has resided five years within the United States, and three years next preceding his arrival at the age of twenty-one years, and has continued to reside therein to the time of making this application, and within the state of New York one year at least; and within that time he has behaved as a man of good moral character, attached to the principles of the Constitution of the United States, and well disposed to the good order and happiness of the same."

Patrick ^{his} X _{mark} Gregory

Sworn in open court this 8 day of April, 1834,
John Barberie, Clerk.

"I, William Carvin, do declare on Oath, that I will support the Constitution of the United States, and that I do absolutely and entirely renounce and abjure all allegiance and fidelity to every foreign Prince, Potentate, State or Sovereignty whatever; and particularly to the King of the United Kingdom of Great Britain and Ireland."

William ^{his} X _{mark} Carvin

Sworn in open court this 8 day of April, 1834,
John Barberie, Clerk.

2. William Carvin

While Dominick Murphy and William Carvin were both Irish Catholic hand loom weavers who immigrated to America at about the same time, no one in William's family ever claimed descent from the Lord Mayor of Dublin. Weavers who wove their own cloth lived in a different world than those who engaged others to do so, and they had incentives to leave Ireland well before men like Dominick Murphy did.

> ... In June of 1829, weavers in southern Ireland begged for relief. They were only making about five pence a day when they could get work, and on many days they could get no work at all. "We are in the most deplorable state of distress," a group of them wrote. "We are... deprived of any hope of existence, and see no prospect but in emigration..."[1]

But legal restrictions on emigration to the former colonies, imposed by the British in the early 1800's, had made transatlantic passage expensive, so the poor could only dream of life in America. Then, in 1827, faced with massive unemployment and poverty in its textile industry, Britain repealed the restrictions. Passage from Liverpool to New York suddenly cost only £2 or £3. The gates to America were flung open.[2]

Born when Philadelphia was still the U.S. Capital, William Carvin grew up in Ireland in the days of Jefferson, Madison, Monroe and the Adamses.[3] He'd heard tales of America's religious tolerance, of its democratic self-rule and other high-minded ideals. America, after all, had succeeded in ousting the British, something Ireland had never been able to do. But few things impressed William more than tales of American opportunity. From what he heard, a man could rise out of poverty in the new country, could give his family things unheard of in Ireland, so William saved until he could afford the £3 fare to New York (which, small as it was, was still half a year's wages), and he made the crossing in about 1829.[4] For the six-week ocean voyage, he and the other passengers in steerage were allotted two feet of space to stand in. They slept four to a berth. "[T]he filthy beds [were] teeming with abominations... [t]he narrow space between the berths... breathe[d] up a damp and fetid stench," the foul air "as dense and as palatable as seen on a foggy day from a dung heap." Since the fare didn't include meals, passengers cooked their own food on fires stoked below deck.[5] But William was fortunate: he completed the trip without succumbing to the cholera that took so many others.

Prior to 1850, the U.S. Census only listed the names of men; another sixty years would pass before most states registered marriages, ninety before they began registering births. Neither William nor Mary Ann Morrow, the woman he married in a year that history has forgotten, knew how to read or write.[6] Never mentioned in headlines, stories of important events or society pages, the poor only surfaced in court dockets and arrest reports. So even less is known of Mary Ann Morrow than of Hannah Donegan.[7] And even William's presence was too insignificant to be noticed: though he had come to New York by 1829, the 1830 Census failed to record him.[8] His and Mary's eldest daughter, Ann, was born in New York on the 20th of May 1832, when Mary was eighteen.[9] From his home on Greene Street, just below Washington Square, unable to find work as a weaver, William carried goods on a hand cart he pushed through the streets; lack of money kept them in New York even after the wealthier Murphys had left for Kensington.[10]

But despite his poverty, William had faith in the future. Andrew Jackson, champion of the common man, was President. Calling the Second Bank of the United States a corrupt institution that only benefited the wealthy, Jackson dismantled it. When Jackson was succeeded by Martin Van Buren – a Dutchman for whom English was a second language – William could hope that immigrants like himself had a real chance to make something of themselves. In 1837, when the refusal of some New York banks to redeem paper money triggered a depression and record unemployment, Van Buren's insistence that greedy bankers were to blame gave William faith. A powerful President recognized the problem. Common men had reason for hope.

By 1840, William and Mary had moved from Greene Street; they were living with their three children in the city's Sixteenth Ward, above Washington Square. The "huddled masses" had been growing: the 16th Ward, into which the city was sprawling, contained 42,936 people per square mile in 1840.[11] Competition was fierce, for everything from jobs to food and housing. Hopes for better times were diminished when the Whig William Henry Harrison was elected President that year, and quickly succeeded by his Vice President, the Virginia slaveholder John Tyler.[12] After ten years in America, William had still not found work in the trade he knew. As New York grew ever more crowded, thousands of Irish like him, at risk of being swallowed up by the place, made the move a hundred miles south to Philadelphia, a city said to offer more room to spread out – and where, rumor had it, there were more job opportunities than in New York. It was said that in the growing textile center there, men were willing to pay good money for quality fabrics of the sort William had the skills to make.[13]

And so, after a fourth child (a son Thomas) was born in New York on April 4, 1842, the family packed up what little they had and moved.[14] But the city of brotherly love showed little evidence of charity toward those in need. At least fifty-one street gangs vied for power in its streets, including the Killers, the Bleeders, the Blood Tubs, the Deathfetchers, the Hyenas, the Smashers, the Bouncers, the Flayers, and the Tormentors.[15] One Irishman wrote home describing the atmosphere in Philadelphia this way:

> "The people here think as little of killing others as you would of killing the mice in a cornstack… There's no such thing as men fighting here as they would about a Saintfield fair, for if you ever get into a fight here, you must either kill or be killed [with]… pistols and large knives, which they use instead of fighting with their fists."[16]

Arriving just as Kensington was being torn apart by the riots of May 1844, William found a place for his family about eight blocks east of St. Michael's Church and the Master Street School: a shed on a dirt path behind a larger home that fronted Frankford Road.[17] When the nativists began burning Catholic houses, William and Mary couldn't help but question the area's Quaker origins. Insistence that their children be taught from the Protestant Bible belied the religious freedom America had promised. In a matter of weeks, the Catholic neighborhood in which their children went to school was buried in rubble and ash. The divide was especially apparent at the First Presbyterian Church of Kensington, just one block north and east of St. Michael's church. Among the people who walked through its doors on Sunday mornings, William saw the faces of those who'd occupied the streets, shouted insults, thrown rocks, and fired guns. Many Irish spoke of revenge; bitterness festered in Catholic hearts.

William worked at home, weaving cotton yarn that had been advanced to him on credit; he picked up the yarn, received his instructions, and delivered his finished weaves, at what was surely Murphy's mill.[18] (It was the beginning of a relationship that would divide and unite the families for generations to come.) An 1842 article in Philadelphia's *Public Ledger* described the earnings of skilled hand-loom weavers, paid by the piece like William, this way:

> Since the early part of the past winter, the manufacturers have been paying three cents per yard for weaving what is technically called nine hundred check … A man employed upon this work, and who labors fourteen hours per day, as is usual with most of them, can weave, upon a fair average calculation, about twenty yards. It must be remembered also that his wife, or some other member of the family, or otherwise a hired person, is constantly required to attend him. According to this statement … it will require the constant exertion of two persons to earn sixty cents per day."[19]

A man and his helper making sixty cents a day would make $3.60 for a six-day week, or a little over fifteen dollars a month.[20] Both the new wave of unskilled immigrants spurred by Ireland's 1845 famine and the increasing number of steam-powered looms put downward pressure on wages, as owners paid women less than male hand-loom weavers.[21] As such mills converted to steam power, they often put skilled men like William out of work altogether, causing one historian to conclude that "women power-loom operators posed a direct threat to male handloom weavers in districts like Kensington…"[22] Bad as things already were, an 1848 strike pressured manufacturers to comply with a new state law restricting employment to ten hours per day, but some mills answered by cutting wages.[23]

William wanted more than anything to earn enough, to save enough, to go into business for himself. He wanted the sort of liberty that Dominick Murphy enjoyed, and like Dominick, he wanted something to leave to his sons. Like the other eighty men working for Dominick, William wanted higher pay, while Dominick wanted to keep costs under control. But the relationship between the two men was not determined solely by those conflicting interests. With public office on his mind, Murphy wanted to endear himself to the voters in his mill. Throughout the county, other manufacturers were abandoning their old hand-looms in favor of steam-power; by resisting that trend, Dominick was preserving his employees' jobs. William, he said, was lucky not to be working for even less in one of the new steam-powered factories, and William had to agree. While he may have wanted higher wages, he was grateful for Dominick's resistance to steam. It annoyed him, at times, that Dominick was the younger man; by all rights, his greater experience, his sheer number of years, should have counted for something; but working for a younger man was only an occasional annoyance. Their religion was a common bond, felt when they knelt at the same altar, when they said their confessions to the same priest. As Catholics, they were both in the religious minority. As immigrant Irishmen, they both experienced nativist prejudice. With so much in common, when Dominick promised the handloom weavers that one day they'd have businesses of their own, William wanted to believe him.

But William also had much in common with the other poor Catholics of Kensington; he had less to lose from conflict and confrontation, little to dissuade him from sharing the attitudes of hard-drinking ruffians and malcontents. On some days, hope for the future pulled him toward loyalty to the mill run by the younger man; on other days, a bitter taste of present indignities drove him away.

Both in conflict with the mill and dependent upon it, William and Mary's family continued to grow. Five years after their arrival in Kensington, they had seven children. Mary assisting William on his loom when she could, winding bobbins, replacing weft yarn when it ran out, passing the shuttle back across the shed to William at every pass.[24] And the older girls, Ann and Catherine, filled in when their mother could not, the women taking shifts between cooking and caring for babies.

It was convenient for William to drink at Murphy's tavern, and he preferred to drink there for the simple reason that it might give him a chance to befriend his boss, to build a relationship that could prove useful to his family. It was tempting to think of the possibilities. And Murphy, with an eye on Common Council, welcomed the men who worked in his mill. Alcohol loosed lips and made men bold, and as it did, talk naturally turned to the steam powered mills. William pointed out the poor quality of power-driven work compared to what he could produce; Dominick stressed the challenge such mills created for both of them, his commitment to the men he employed, his efforts to preserve their way of life. Both men stressed their belief in the Holy Mother Church, railing against nativist prejudice. At times, it seemed to William they could have been brothers.

They also shared attitudes about African Americans. In truth, the city's blacks had even less reason for hope than William did. In competition for jobs, Irish good fortune, limited as it was, came at black expense. It might have made some feel sympathy – maybe even guilt – but guilt could be avoided if a man believed he *deserved* a better job, whether because he was better qualified, or smarter, or more civilized. Little made an Irishman feel more civilized than boasting hundreds of years of history since Saint Patrick's day, and little made him feel greater resentment toward blacks than hearing a Know-Nothing say that the Irish posed a greater threat to native security than did the negroes, because the negroes had lived in America long enough to know their place, while the Irish got drunk, boasting about pride and always striving for independence.[*] Irishmen like William had more to lose than most blacks did. While nativist rhetoric could often be brushed off as the talk of extremists, in 1855, Pennsylvania's Committee on Vice and Immorality called for the grogshops to be closed altogether.[25] It was a shot across the bow of the one thing in life William looked forward to. A glass of beer after a long day's work was William's only pleasure, and nativist opposition threatened it with extinction. Dominick was fighting not only to preserve the craft by which William earned his bread, but for William's right to drink. Nor were all the nativists content to keep the Irish from drinking; some wanted laws to keep them from assembling altogether. Who else could a man like William support for a Kensington seat on Common Council?

Yet still, the two men eventually parted ways. After 1850, William disappeared from the historical record for several years. We know only that on Feb 1, 1853, Ann, the eldest of his children, became pregnant and married 24-year-old George Austin, a brass spicket maker, in the First Presbyterian Church of Kensington – that is, George's Protestant church, not Ann's Catholic one. The decision could not have pleased William and Mary, whose priests would not have recognized the marriage outside the Catholic Church. But the

---

[*] Some nativists were heard to say that no one on earth was as boisterous, impudent and vile as a drunken Irishman (Dennis Clark, The Irish in Philadelphia: Ten Generations of Urban Experience, Temple Univ. Press, 1973, p 49).

abandonment of William and Mary didn't stop there. William's oldest son, James, had always been a hard worker, with a good head on his shoulders. He'd always struck William as the sort of son who could take a family nest egg and build it into something that might be passed down for generations. Now, with Ann's marriage, both James and his brother Thomas had started hanging around the Austin brass shop, trying to learn the skills involved in molding brass; whatever their purpose, its effect was a further loss to William and Mary. Protestantism had taken their daughter, and now (it seemed) it was trying to take their sons as well.[26] Neither boy expressed interest in William's loom. Maybe the boys' futures didn't lie in weaving or in the Catholic church. Maybe their futures lay in brass.

Meanwhile, Dominick Murphy's workforce was getting smaller – from eighty men in 1850 to half that number in 1860.[27] And as William worried that he might be losing his sons, he became a casualty of Dominick's reductions. When the younger man informed the older that his employment at the mill was over, William's plans for the future were dashed. He and Mary moved out of old Kensington to faraway Gordon Street.[28]

Had William demanded a raise? Had too much drinking led to problems with his work? Had pints of stout emboldened him to speak publicly of "unfairness" to older men like himself? The reasons are lost to history.

But we do know that Philadelphia now had more textile mills than any other city in the world. The riverbanks along the Delaware were bursting with railroad and maritime business. Ship building, steel fabricating, importing and exporting were transforming the city into a major international port. Amid such progress, crowded shanties built along the banks of the Schuylkill had become a breeding ground for disease. Smallpox, yellow fever, malaria, scarlet fever, dysentery, and tuberculosis had killed many in the years since the cholera epidemic of 1848-1849.[29] While Murphy was on Common Council and William was out of a job, looking for work,

> …water was often filthy and in parts of the city sometimes too
> scarce to bathe in… Kensington drew from a stretch of the
> Delaware that by the mid 1860's received over thirteen million
> gallons of sewage daily. Pigs still scavenged for garbage in
> some of the streets and carved out their wallows… In the alleys
> of the old city and in clusters of jerry-built dwellings scattered
> around the urban periphery, blacks, immigrants and the poor in
> general huddled amid cockroaches, rats, and assorted filth,
> inviting new epidemics…[30]

Forced to take work at a lower rate of pay in one of the new power-loom factories, working in a multi-storied, brick-walled factory with iron bars on the windows to keep out burglars, muttering about the man who'd laid him off, working side by side with unskilled women and boys, William could only just get by. In 1860, he re-surfaced in the City Directory, living on Mascher

Street.[31] He still thought of himself as a weaver, even if tending a power loom, changing bobbins and tying ends didn't exactly deserve the name. Sunday was the only day of rest; the other six, he tended steam-powered machines under a factory roof for eleven or twelve hours a day, watching iron and hickory banging weft into warp, gears magnifying torque, dragging sheds of yarn through steel heddles, yard after yard, repetitively, ceaselessly, while the cotton, when thus tugged and pulled against metal, spewed an endless, invisible cloud of dust into the air. [32]

William had envied the power and wealth of the man who paid him, but he'd hoped to rise above his station as a laborer, to share a pint and find a joke that would make men laugh and earn him respect. But now, discarded by Murphy, trapped within factory walls, feeling the boilers hiss, his envy likely turned to bitterness. James, Thomas, Catherine and Mary had all been forced to take jobs in the mills too. [33] (Since there was no compulsory school attendance, the younger boys were left to their own devices.) There were no newspaper articles about meetings at his house, membership in societies, involvement at church, or service to the community. Without the notoriety of showing up in prison records, police blotters, or cemetery registers, without books, without the money to run charities or make large donations, the only thing for William to do, besides seventy hours of work a week, was to visit the neighborhood tavern. That, it seems, was enough to keep him out of the newspapers.

By decade's end, his household included eleven people. He'd built no equity in a home.[34] Next door to his rented shed lived Christopher Kelley and his household of nine; across the street lived John Fitler and his household of seven. [35] They lived without plumbing or running water, waiting for private moments in the outhouse they shared with their neighbors, and when they couldn't wait, they made do where they could. There was no central heat in winter; factory doors, closed to keep out the cold, trapped inside the tiny bits of cotton fiber people couldn't see.

The prospect of war meant something different for William than it did for Dominick. In November 1860, when Abraham Lincoln's election triggered southern secession, steam engines shut down for lack of coal. (The Army of Virginia had ransacked a rail shipment.) Cotton shipments became hit or miss. William and his family looked for work at whatever mill they could. And after Governor Curtin echoed Lincoln's call for troops to suppress the rebellion, working men had to decide if volunteering in the army – letting their women take their places in the mills – would be a better way to make a living.

Like many northerners, William believed slavery could be ended without going to war, while risking one's life for a black man made little more sense that doing it to preserve a country that broke promises. Disruption of the cotton supply meant lost production and a cut back in his hours. Now in his sixties, having seen better days, William gave no serious thought to enlistment himself. The war was for the wealthy, for the manufacturers like Dominick Murphy. If his older boys, James and Thomas, signed up, the household income would suffer from the loss of their pay. Balanced against that, thirteen dollars a month – the pay being offered to those who volunteered – might prove steadier income than mill work. It might help the family's finances. The boys might be able to save enough to have something to show for service, when the war was over. There was even talk of bonuses for those who enlisted. Mary didn't want the boys to sign up, but William felt the decision was up to them. (They agreed that, whatever the boys did, they should stick together.)

As it happens, both older sons volunteered that May. Thomas, the younger one, enlisted first, signing up with a volunteer infantry regiment; then James followed, enlisting in the Philadelphia Guards. (The "Guards," he said, had formed to protect homes and loved ones in case of invasion from the south; James was always thinking of the family.) Neither boy got a signing bonus (though later volunteers did, when the need for soldiers grew stronger). Mary went to Sunday mass, praying that the boys would come home safely. To ease her worries, James promised to look out for his younger brother, if he could.

On July 1, Thomas's regiment paraded in Philadelphia "to the great credit of its officers and the satisfaction of its friends," then left for Fort Monroe, a huge and powerful fortress that held out hope for safety.[36] The day after James enlisted, his Guards were off to Harrisburg for training; on Sept 10th, he was in the nation's capital, parading in front of Lincoln himself. Both boys seemed far from danger.

Still, Bull Run brought a dose of reality to the families of Philadelphia, and as the war continued, its impact was felt on prices and wages:

> Prices jumped an average of 75 percent over the course of the war. Taking this into account, real wages dropped by 20 percent. Knapsack strappers protested about low contractor pay in September 1861, while striking tailors attempted to coerce owners into adopting a uniform pay scale. In early 1862 Navy Yard workers, angered over a congressionally mandated pay cut, struck for a few days until the government recanted and actually increased their wages. In late 1863 arsenal shoemakers threatened to strike if they failed to receive a collective raise; their request was quickly granted to ensure uninterrupted production...[37]

William wasn't paid enough to be affected by the new federal taxes; he manufactured no products; he owned no gold watches, silver plates, pianos or other items of the sort the federal government now taxed. Yet he struggled. With older men going off to war, the factories were in need of help. Mary and their daughters joined William at one of the mills that were still operating. But as prices climbed, as rich men paid poor to take their places in the draft, William's resentment toward the wealthy grew. People started calling it a rich man's war and a poor man's fight, and as William heard of the money Dominick Murphy and others were making, his bitterness toward his old boss grew sharper.

William struggled to read his sons' letters from the front, if and when they came through.[38] The army's desire to keep its plans secret from the enemy meant keeping them secret from loved ones as well. With major troop movements reported only after the fact, William and Mary heard little about their sons. But they could see the hospitals being built. They could see young men returning home missing limbs or in coffins. Soon, the city was pock-marked with makeshift military hospitals.[39] Soon enough, there was even one on Master Street.[40] Civilian volunteers assisted in handling the wounded.

William and Mary learned only after the fact that their sons' regiments had moved into Virginia to join the assault on the rebel capital. On June 26th, 1862, *The Inquirer* reported that the troops under McClellan were "under arms and eager to fight;" on the 27th, that McClellan had met resistance and suffered two hundred casualties. On the 28th, its list of wounded and killed nowhere mentioned their sons' units; and on the 30th, it reported that the Reserves had seen action around Mechanicsville, with only "trifling" losses.

Trifling.

Their concerns increased as weeks passed with no word about either son. And then, on July 22, the *Inquirer*'s headlines quickened their hearts:

THE LATE BATTLES BEFORE RICHMOND
Official List of Casualties in General
McCall's Division

Such have been the difficulties in the way of procuring complete and correct lists of the casualties in the Reserve Corps, it is only lately that they could be compiled.

List of killed, wounded and missing in the engagements of June 26th, 27th and 30th, 1862…

It was unusual for the papers to list the names of enlisted men injured and killed; this list was several pages long, and it purported to be complete. General McCall himself had been wounded and taken prisoner. But page one only covered the first regiment of the first brigade. Turning to page two, William's hand was trembling… There – the Second Brigade. General Meade himself, wounded. William's heart was beating. First Regiment. Second. There, in the third column: the Seventh Regiment. Company A… Company B… Company G more than halfway down the page… James's Company G, the Philadelphia Guards – killed – only one man, Christopher Sloan – thank God! – only one man! But there, among the wounded, the name he hadn't wanted to see. James had been wounded… but not killed!

How badly wounded? What sort of wound? And where was he? In a hospital somewhere? There was no way to know. Even local army officers, even the provost marshal, could tell them nothing. It was being looked into. He'd be notified as soon as anything was known. The speculation was maddening. The only treatment for wounds was opium and amputation of limbs. Wounds to the head or chest were hopeless.[41] Another possibility was put forward: *Had he been taken prisoner?* Death rates at POW camps were worse than on the front lines.[42] Ignorance about James's fate and ongoing concern for Thomas meant many a sleepless night. Weeks passed without word.

On the 12th of September 1862, there was a tremendous downpour in Philadelphia. Cohocksink Creek – the dividing line between Kensington and the old City – overflowed. "Destructive Flood in Philadelphia" was the headline in *The Inquirer*. "Loss of Life. Ruin of Dwellings and Business Establishments."

> While the city bells were calling the people to arms yesterday morning, an invader against which no ordnance can prevail was sweeping through two wards of the city, carrying devastation in its train. The Cohocksink Creek… burst its bonds and deluged at least a thousand houses… About noon, the earthy barriers of some of the upper pools gave way, and a torrent of water at least four feet in depth… dashed with immense power against all obstacles, pouring into cellars like a waterfall, destroying frame tenements.[43]

The flood's course ran through tanneries, glue factories and print shops. Stray animals "floated through the streets." As a grim reminder that death doesn't only come from hostilities between men, the *Inquirer* reported that three children had drowned. The worst damage was in the poorer, low-lying areas a few blocks southwest and southeast of the Murphy mill, while that structure and others like it – built on higher ground – were unharmed. Complaints about filth and unsanitary conditions had been constant at meetings of the Common Council even before Cohocksink Creek overflowed; the Board of Health had warned there was a connection between poor sanitation and disease.[44] Now, the flood swept through Kensington with deadly after-effects of its own, even if ordinary citizens focused only on the amputations, the cholera, measles and consumption being treated in the city's makeshift hospitals.

Another six months passed. It was April of 1863 before someone contacted them, in the Army's behalf, conveying condolences that James had been killed nearly a year earlier. Officials explained why it had taken so long to report James's death, but as William saw it, it all boiled down to a government that didn't much care about the lives of boys like James. They were calling it a rich man's war; James and his friends had been lured into a system in which they meant nothing. Grief and resentment extinguished what little support William had once felt.

Meanwhile, the news only heightened their worry for Thomas. The last they'd heard, the 71st Pennsylvania was a part of General Meade's Army. In June of 1863, when the rebels entered Pennsylvania, Meade had gone out to find the invaders. On June 29th, *The Inquirer's* headline was "To Arms! Citizens of Pennsylvania!! The Rebels are upon us!" On the 30th, "The difficulty of obtaining correct information from the interior of the border counties of Pennsylvania is great." On July 1, "The Rebellion! Invasion of Pennsylvania!" On July 2, "A dispatch from Harrisburg, dated ten o'clock last night, states that a battle had been in progress during the entire evening, as heavy cannonading was distinctly heard in the direction of Carlisle. It was presumed that General Meade was engaged with the rebels somewhere in the vicinity of Gettysburg, but no news could be received from the supposed scene of conflict before morning." On July 3, "Cheering News!!! The Great Battle Near Gettysburg! Meade Victorious!"

In that day's paper, several officers were reported killed or wounded by name. But as to the masses, the description of casualties was unsatisfactory: "The chief loss was in the First Corps, which suffered severely in both officers and men."[45]

What could be gleaned from such a report? Wasn't a single loss of life severe? *Where can we get names?!* How hard it was to go to work, to thread tiny ends of yarn, barely visible, into the eyes of heddles by the hundreds. How hard it was to concentrate on delicate work against the pounding of battens that rocked and boomed like cannon fire.

The Inquirer's headline on July the 4th – "Heavy Losses on Both Sides" – was not reassuring. Every day, new maps made their heads spin. Advances. Retreats. Recaptures. Every one a possible clue to Thomas's whereabouts and fate.

Saturday: "The battle at Gettysburg last night was an extremely fierce and stubborn one. Heavy and determined assaults… the fighting being desperately severe, and the fiercest, possibly, of the war."

Sunday: the day of rest. *The Inquirer* didn't come out. There was nothing to distract one from the fear of not knowing.

Monday: "Waterloo Eclipsed!... Our killed and wounded up to Saturday night will number over eight thousand…" Long lists of casualties, but not a word about the 71st Pennsylvania. The Penn Relief Association made an urgent appeal for aid. "The wounded of the battles of Gettysburg must receive aid. Brandy and other stimulant, with old muslin for bandages &c., are much needed. We appeal to the citizens for their assistance. Let each one give something."

Tuesday, "Meade's Victory!"

Wednesday: news about Thomas's regiment at last! But it was not good. "In the battle of July 3, the Seventy-First … lost nine officers of fifteen taken in and one-hundred-and-one out of two-hundred-forty-six enlisted men. The Sixty-ninth and Seventy-first were on the extreme front, and in proportion their members suffered the worst."

Nearly half lost! They had suffered the worst!

Yet no way to confirm whether Thomas was still alive. Fragile hope slipping away, resisting restraint, trying to escape. Every day's paper devoured, satisfying nothing.

A few days later, Thomas walked in the door, very much alive.

As he explained in due course – right there, in front of them, in the flesh – he hadn't even been at Gettysburg. He'd been taken prisoner back in December; he'd been paroled. He'd spent months in Confederate prisons. From the looks of him, he'd been dragged through hell, but he'd been released on the 17th of July and now he was home. Joy filled the house. The reunion was sweet. But as soon as hearts were settled, concern shifted, first because Thomas's orders required that after his release from parole, he was to return to his unit for further action, and then because attention turned to their own failing health.[46]

In all their grief and worry, William and Mary had given little thought to themselves. But by the time Thomas came home in late July 1863, they'd both fallen gravely ill. Mary was in especially poor health. Though she downplayed her persistent cough, the children told Thomas it had been worsening. The *Inquirer* of July 6th promised that "Dr. Swayne's Compound Syrup of Wild Cherry" would cure weak lungs, coughs, night sweats and all pulmonary complaints. The next day's paper quoted Dr. A. H. Stevens, "Electrical Physician," as claiming to curie chronic diseases by "the use of Electricity alone, without any Medicine, or even any Pain." But Thomas had brought home no money; the war had cost the family two incomes; no one had money for food, much less for expensive cures.

Meanwhile, the 71st Pennsylvania Infantry was pursuing the rebels back into Virginia. Could Thomas really be expected to go south, alone, into enemy territory, in an effort to find them? Mary was too sick to work; William was finding it increasingly hard. If Thomas could get work at the Austin brass shop, or even at one of the mills, his very presence at home might help.

He decided not to report for duty. In fact, on September 6, he got married.[47] But the occasion did nothing to raise his mother's spirits, for Thomas had married outside the Church, a transgression that (if not repented) could doom his everlasting soul. And then, after birthing ten children, after helping William at his looms, after staving off a creek that had brought disease to their door, Mary finally passed away.[48]

One imagines William, Thomas and others as she lay dying – crying, maybe cursing, maybe getting a bit drunk after her burial. But the press of war left little time for mourning. On December 11, 1863, just 13 days after the death of his mother, Thomas was arrested, so as to be returned to the front lines. William's health quickly followed the same course as Mary's. Fevers. Cold sweats. The spitting up of blood. On January 28, 1864, less than two months after Mary died, William joined her. His death certificate called it "phthisis pulmonalis," a decaying of the lungs.[49] Mary Ann and William were buried in the cemetery of St. Michael's Church on November 29, 1863, and January, 30, 1864, respectively. There was nothing heroic or spectacular about either ceremony. William's interment cost $7.40. The newspapers saw no reason to mention it.

Nothing else is known of William and Mary. Illiterate Catholics living in the face of nativism, crowded conditions, disease, eleven-hour days and strikes for better wages were not the stuff of which long eulogies or obituaries were made. All they'd really wanted was what Dominick and Hannah Murphy had. But with poverty standing in their way, they'd been driven apart from prosperous men. The war to preserve the Union had taken their sons. Of all that they'd hoped their lives in America might be, the only things they'd really accomplished were the births of those children who'd survived. One can only hope that some of them, in some ways, made them proud.

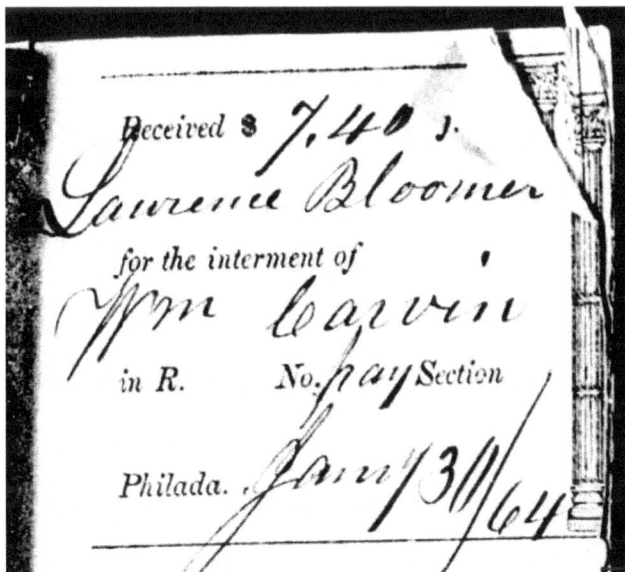

Notes on Chapter 2, William Carvin

[1] Kerby Miller, Emigrants & Exiles, Oxford Univ. Press, 1985, p 207.

[2] Ibid., pp 196 - 207.

[3] Although censuses suggest that William may have been younger (see 1840 U.S. Census, NY Ward 16, p 181; 1850 U.S. Census Kensington Ward 6, Fam 798; 1860 U.S. Census Phila Ward 19, Fam 3539), William's death certificate, dated January 31, 1864, states that he was 65, indicating a 1799 birth. George Washington died December 14, 1799; Philadelphia officially ceased to be the U.S. Capital on May 11, 1800.

[4] The name of William's ship and precise dates of sailing have not been discovered, but 1829 is the likely year of his passage, based on his 1834 naturalization record. Most ships bound for America departed from Liverpool. Kerby Miller points out that those who made the passage alone were generally poorer than those who traveled with their families. Until 1971, there were 240 pence to the British pound. If William earned five pence a day for 300 days of the year, his annual earnings would have come to six and a quarter pounds sterling, about twice the transatlantic fare.

[5] Miller, supra, p 255.

[6] When William filed his declaration of intent to become a naturalized citizen of the United States (Appendix 6), he made his mark with an 'X.' The 1840 Census indicates that neither William nor Mary could read or write. The 1850 Census indicates that Mary could not read or write, while the absence of a check mark in the column next to William's name suggests that he may have learned by then.

[7] The maiden name of William's wife, Mary Ann Morrow, is attested by the death certificate and funeral record of their son, William Henry Carvin, in 1929 (as attested to by William Henry's wife, Anna) and by the death certificate of their son Thomas. Among other mysteries, we cannot be sure whether William and Mary Ann Morrow met and married before or after William's arrival in New York. Early census records assert that Mary Ann Morrow was born in Pennsylvania, but her death certificate asserts she was born in Ireland. No record of their marriage, or any transatlantic voyage by her, have been found.

[8] On April 8, 1834, a witness swore that William had "resided five years within the United States, and three years next preceding his arriving at the age of twenty-one years" (Naturalization Petition) If accurate, that oath would place William's arrival in the United States in April of 1829 or earlier. Carvin being an uncommon name, finding William or Mary in New York should not be difficult, but a search of New York newspapers between 1829 and 1845 unearths only a single mention of a William Carvin – in the midst of over a hundred other men appointed as a "vigilance committee" in 1837 (New York's The Evening Post, March 27, 1838, p 3). Of course, given his illiteracy and Irish accent, he may have been one of the many Carvers, Garvers, Garvins, or others in the New York Census of 1930.

[9] The records consistently point to 1814 (or early 1815) as Mary Morrow's year of birth (1850 Census Kensington Ward 6, Fam 798; 1860 Census Phila Ward 19, Fam 3539; Death Certificate dated 11-29-63). The records conflict about the date of her daughter Ann's birth. Her 1911 death certificate (which gives her full name as Mary Ann) gives her birthdate as May 20, 1825, but her mother would have been only eleven that year, and the death certificate was based on information supplied by a non-relative who didn't even get the names of her parents correct. May 1832 is the date Ann gave in the 1900 Census (Phila Ward 29, Dist 0750, Fam 47), and seems more consistent with the birthdates of her siblings.

[10] In 1835, a William Carvin was listed as a carter in the City Directory for New York City. (Longworth's American Almanac, New York Register and City Directory, New York, Thomas Longworth, 1835, p. 148.)

[11] 1840 U.S. Census, NYC, Sixteenth Ward, p 187. The Census captures the family that emerged later perfectly, including one male between the ages of 30 and 40 (William), one female between 20 and 30 (wife Mary), one female between 5 and 10 (daughter Ann), and two children, one of each sex, under

the age of 5 (Catherine and James). By 1850, population density in the Sixteenth Ward had nearly tripled to 107,000 per square mile.

[12] John Tyler had succeeded William Henry Harrison in 1841 after Harrison died only 31 days into his term of office.

[13] "Finding themselves displaced by machinery, large numbers of skilled workers from all textile trades relocated to Philadelphia to ply their talents." (Nat'l Register of Historic Places, "Buildings Related to the Textile Industry in the Kensington Neighborhood of Philadelphia," NPS Form 10-900-b, accessed at http://www.preservationalliance.com/wp-content/uploads/2014/09/KensingtonNR.pdf.)

[14] Early censuses show Mary Morrow Carvin born in Pennsylvania, so she may have had roots in Philadelphia.

[15] Dennis Clark, The Irish in Philadelphia: Ten Generations of Urban Experience, Temple Univ. Press, 1973, p 114.

[16] Miller, *supra*, p 320.

[17] William and Mary's daughter Mary was born in Philadelphia in 1844 or 1845, so their move to Kensington must have taken place by then. As new arrivals, the Carvins may have been omitted from the 1843 and 1844 directories, even if present when those directories were compiled. A William Carv*er [sic]*, weaver, appears in the directories of 1845 through 1848 listed as "rear F road ab Phoenix," which is to say, in a structure to the rear of other houses on Frankford Road (just east of Front Street) above Phoenix. He had therefore moved to that address no later than October of 1844 (see Appendix 1). The 1847 Directory lists William Carver and William Carvin, both weavers, with Carvin's address as "F road bel Master." Since Master was one block north of Phoenix, "ab[ove] Phoenix" was the same as "bel[ow] Master." Finally, in 1849, it was Wm *Carven [sic]* at F road bel Master. Given the ambiguities, spelling difficulties and duplicates described in Appendix 5, it seems William Carv*er*, Carv*en* and Carv*in* were likely all the same person, included in the directories as living on Frankford Road no later than October of 1844, and probably earlier – i.e., likely before the riots.

[18] Philip Scranton, Proprietary Capitalism: The Textile Manufacture at Philadelphia, 1800-1885, Cambridge University Press, 1983, points out that many of Kensington's mills in 1850 were not centralized factories with looms side by side, but what he calls "outwork enterprises" (i.e., where the handloom weaver worked at home). The conclusion that William worked for Dominick Murphy is driven by a number of factors. Murphy's was one of the biggest mills in Kensington, and he employed only hand loom weavers like Carvin. (*Ibid*, pp 191-194; Scranton's Table 6.9 of area textile firms giving statistics from the U.S. Census Manufacturing Schedule of 1850 for Philadelphia.) Without convenient public transportation, people generally walked to work, and the Carvins' home on Frankford Road was just five minutes from the Murphy mill. "[B]ad streets and the absence or expense of transportation... obliged workingmen to live as close as they could to the scenes of their labors. The houses of operatives tended to cluster around mills and factories..." (Russell F. Weigley, *et al*, Philadelphia, a Three Hundred Year History, W.W. Norton & Co. (1982), p 374.) The William Carvins and Dominick Murphys both lived between Master and Phoenix streets, and the Murphy mill on Palethorp was between those streets as well. Carvin and the Murphy mill were separated only by the distance between Palethorp and Frankford. William's family was also in the parish of St. Michael's church, which the Murphys attended. Not only was it then the only Roman Catholic Church in the area, William and Mary Carvin were both buried in the St. Michael's Church cemetery (Historic PA Church and Town Records, Reel 961, Phila. St. Michael's Roman Catholic Church, Jan 30, 1864; PA Death Certificate for Wm Carvin, 1/28/64, FHL Film #1986423; Find-A-Grave Memorial ID #135435096, Mary Ann Carvin, Nov 29, 1863.) Seeing Murphy at church and hearing of his mill, Carvin certainly knew who Murphy was, and it's nearly inconceivable that Carvin didn't at least *seek* work in Murphy's employ. The other large handloom manufacturers in Kensington either had names suggesting they were Protestants, were farther away than the Murphy mill, or both. (According to Scranton, the other major handloom employers in Kensington in 1850 were the mills of (1) Blair and Bannister, (2) Thomas Harkness, (3) Daniel Hickey and (4) Thomas Mulcahey.) The 1846 directory lists no Thomas Harkness,

though it does list a Daniel Harkness, manufacturer, whose business address is given as N 6th Street, much further from Carvin than Murphy's mill. Blair appears in the 1846 directory as living on 2d below Master - a very close neighbor to Murphy – but Blair, Bannister and Harkness are all Scottish and English names; they may have had less interest than Murphy in employing Catholic immigrants like Carvin, and Carvin may have had little interest in working for an Englishman. We don't know if the Irishmen Hickey and Mulcahey were Catholics, but the 1845 Directory lists Hickey, manufacturer, at 612 N 3rd Street (without a (K) to designate Kensington) and doesn't mention Mulcahey, who first appears in the 1846 Directory only as a weaver himself, at Perry above Franklin. Both the Irishmen, therefore, were a farther walk from Carvin's home than Murphy's mill was. William's best chance of finding employment, and the place he surely ended up, was the largest and closest mill to where he lived – that owned by his fellow Irish Catholic, Dominick Murphy.

[19] *Public Ledger*, September 2, 1842, p 1.

[20] Scranton, *supra*, p 193, says that at rates prevailing in 1850, men in the mills earned about twenty dollars a month. Whether this represented an increase in typical earnings or simply a different method of computing an average is unclear. Estimates of average earnings vary, and variations may be explained by the fact that most of it was piece work, pay depending on the item woven, or by the fact that conditions of supply and demand changed over time. Weigley's history tells us that after earnings rose to $4.25 to $4.75 per week in 1843, they'd fallen again to $2.50 per week in 1846 (Weigley, *supra*, p 338). According to Edwin T. Freedley, Philadelphia and its Manufactures: A Handbook of the Manufacturing Industry of Philadelphia in 1857 (Edward Young, 1859), p 254, a male weaver who made twenty-five yards of cloth would make only about $3 to $4-1/2 per week.

[21] Post-famine Irish were generally poorer and less skilled than their predecessors (Miller, *supra*, pp 295, 298, 318). Scranton, *supra*, p 338, suggests a male average of twenty dollars and a female average of about eight dollars a month in 1850. Freedley, *supra* p 252, put a female weaver's wages at $4 to $5 in 1859, while young girls working as spinners or spoolers made $2 to $3 per week.

[22] Scranton, *supra* p 194. "There is some evidence that, for 1850 at least, power looms were not standard equipment in steam mills in those two areas [Kensington and Moyamensing], whereas more than a thousand of them were running in Old City and Manayunk, areas where handloom operations were virtually nil."

[23] Weigley *et al*, *supra*, p 338.

[24] 1850 U.S. Census, Phila Ward 6 (Kensington), Fam 798, enum Aug 8, 1850. Born in New York had been Ann (18), Catherine (13), James (10) and Thomas (7). Born in Pennsylvania by 1850 were Mary (5), Elizabeth (3) and William Henry (3 months).

[25] Clark, *supra*, p 49.

[26] Both boys listed brass finishing as their occupation when they enlisted in the army in 1861. According to the 1860 City Directory, the Austin brass shop was located at 1227 N Front Street, just a few blocks southeast of the Murphy mill and St. Michael's church, and so close to the Carvins as well.

[27] Scranton, *supra*, p 221.

[28] After the birth of William Henry Carvin in 1850, Mary gave birth to Joseph James Carvin, George Washington Carvin, and Charles Carvin, probably in 1854, 1855 and 1858, respectively. William appeared only once in the City Directory during the 1850's, that being in 1857, at an address on Gordon Street ("Gordon (R)," meaning Gordon Street in Richmond), on the Delaware River, north of Kensington, quite far from the Murphy mill. The move, which must have occurred before it was recorded in the 1857 Directory, would have increased walking time to the Murphy Mill to twenty minutes or so, if at Gordon's east end, or to an hour or more, if at Gordon's west end. Employment at one of the other mills, closer to Gordon, was surely the reason for the move. No William Carvin appears in the directories for the years 1850 through 1855. (The Wm Carver, weaver, who appears in Paschalville (West Philadelphia) in the 1856 and 1859 Directories, appears to be a different man, but even if he is the same as William Carvin, he has clearly gone far afield from Kensington and the Murphy mill.) Apart from their continuing to have children, nothing more is known of William or Mary in the

1850's. Why William dropped out of sight is not a matter of public record: he may have been trying to avoid public notice. But while canvassers for the city directory had their share of challenges (see Appendix 1), it was unusual to see a family overlooked year after year.

[29] Clark, *supra*, p 114; Kenneth W. Milano, Hidden History of Kensington and Fishtown, History Press, 2010, pp 107-109. Such diseases were concentrated among the lower classes, who lived in closer quarters.

[30] Weigley *et al, supra*, p 373.

[31] The 1860 city directory lists "Carwin, Wm., weaver," and "Carwin, James, brass worker" living at "Mascher n Norris." Thomas Carvin's CMSR lists his home address as "Mascher Street, about Norris," and "Masher Street, west side." Although closer to Murphy's Mill than the Gordon address, all these descriptions place the Carvin house a mile north of the Murphy mill, about a 13-minute walk away. By comparison, the Cotton and Woolens Manufacturing section of the 1861 Business Directory included John Dickey's Star Mill at Howard and Jefferson (11 minutes away), Irwin and Stenson's Columbia Mills at the corner of Columbia and Mascher (6 minutes), the Norris Manufacturing Cotton Co. at Norris and Frankford (6 minutes), Charles Greaves' mill at Otis between Frankford and Front Street (5 minutes), and others, all a shorter walk than the Murphy Mill. Since Murphy was still resisting the coming of steam, if William had been able to return to work for him, he'd have surely moved closer to that mill. We conclude that, no longer able to get work at Murphy's, William had taken work as a loom tender at one of the new steam-powered mills.

[32] Although Pennsylvania had limited the *required* workday to ten hours in 1848, work in excess of ten was still legal as long as it was "voluntary." Overtime work was most attractive to those hardest pressed for money. As of 1850, the average workday was still 11-1/2 hours. Massachusetts textile workers had argued in the late 1830's that a shorter workday (of only ten hours) would "lengthen the lives of those employed by giving them a greater opportunity to breathe the pure air of Heaven." ("The Movement for a Ten Hour Day," Digital History ID 3520, accessed at https://www.digital history.uh.edu/disptextbook.cfm?smtID=2&psid=3520#:~:text=",followed%20by%20Pennsylvania%20in%201848.)

[33] 1860 U.S. Census Phila Ward 19, Fam 3539, enumerated Aug 16, 1860.

[34] The 1860 Census includes no real estate value for William's household.

[35] See the adjacent listings in the 1860 Census.

[36] Samuel Bates, History of the Pennsylvania Volunteers, 1861-1865, Vol 2, Harrisburg, 1869, p 788. Thomas's regiment was the 71st Pennsylvania Infantry. Fort Monroe was known as the "American Gibraltar" because it boasted more big cannons than any fort in the union.

[37] Richard A. Sauers, "Philadelphia: Economy of War," at *History Net*. https://www.historynet.com/phila delphia-economy-of-war.htm.

[38] William must have learned to read a little at some point; he was no longer listed as illiterate in the 1860 census.

[39] When the war began, the closest hospitals to William's home on Mascher were the Protestant Episcopal Hospital at Front and Huntingdon and St. Joseph's Hospital on Girard Avenue. But that quickly changed. "In the course of the war 157,000 soldiers and sailors were treated in Philadelphia's hospitals. [There was] an established system of nearly two dozen military hospitals with roughly 6,000 beds. These military hospitals emerged as soon as casualties began streaming into Philadelphia." (J. Matthew Gallman, Mastering Wartime: A Social History of Philadelphia During the Civil War, Univ of Penn Press, 1990, p 130.)

[40] *Inquirer*, July 14, 1863, p 8.

[41] In the days before anti-biotics, in the unsanitary conditions of war, a wound to the head or chest was nearly always fatal.

[42] The death rate among *prisoners* in the Civil War would prove to be twice that among active soldiers. (Margaret E. Wagner, The Civil War Desk Reference, Ch 8, pp 583-4.)

[43] *Inquirer*, Sept 13, 1862, p 8.

---

[44] Sewage in the streets was not a new problem. On January 31, 1856, a petition from residents of the 17th ward (represented by Dominick Murphy) had been presented to the Common Council, "complaining of the nuisance existing in every street of said ward, arising from a neglect on the part of Nicholas Coleman, contractor…" to clean them. (Journal of the Common Council of the Consolidated City of Philadelphia, May 7 to Nov 1, 1855, *Vol IV,* p 278.)

[45] All quotations from *The Philadelphia Inquirer* on the dates indicated.

[46] Instructions to return to one's unit were new. Previously, a paroled soldier had to wait to be exchanged; unless and until that happened, he was supposed to refrain from returning to his unit or bearing arms. But in the course of the war, too many soldiers had got themselves captured on purpose as a way to get home and avoid further combat, so as of July of 1863, the protocols had just been changed.

[47] Philadelphia City Archives, 1863 Marriage Registrations, p 48. The occupation listed on his marriage license was "brass finisher."

[48] Mary died on November 29, 1863, according to an index based on original records in the City of Philadelphia Archives. ("Pennsylvania, Philadelphia City Death Certificates, 1803–1915." Index, FamilySearch, Salt Lake City, Utah, 2008, 2010. From originals housed at the Philadelphia City Archives. "Death Records.") Regrettably, at this writing, an outbreak of another contagious disease precludes a return to Philadelphia to view Mary's original death certificate, to determine her cause of death.

[49] William's death certificate at the Philadelphia City Archives indicates that he died at age 65 on January 28, 1864, of "Phithisis Pulmonatis [sic];" that his address was at Mascher Street, above Norris, in Ward 19; that he was a weaver, born in Ireland; and that he was buried January 31st at St. Michael's Roman Catholic Church. "Phthisis pulmonalis" was a nineteenth century term for tuberculosis, known as "consumption" because of the way the disease consumed the lungs with gradual decay. But these days, a diagnosis of tuberculosis is based on the presence of a specific bacterium, and in 1864, there was no such method of diagnosis. A doctor had only visible symptoms to go by, whether observed or simply heard about from surviving family members. The symptoms – worsening cough, fever, cold sweats, bloody sputum – were indicative of decaying lungs, so "phthisis pulmonalis" (decay of the lungs) went on the death certificate. But such decay could also have been caused by years of breathing cotton dust or various other conditions.

3. Dennis F. Murphy

As we've already seen, Dominick Murphy made a good life for his family in America. To overcome religious oppression, he'd had to wait until Catholics were numerous enough to share in political power; but even in the 1840's, his children were reaping the advantages of financial prosperity. Dominick's eldest son, Dennis, was a slightly built boy – some might even say sickly. Because his father believed in the value of education, he'd been enrolled in the Master Street School when he was four or five.[1] The youngster didn't go in for rowdy play with bigger boys, and he'd have happily read from either the Catholic or the Protestant Bible. But opposing factions of adults insisted he read the translation approved by their respective churches. When the riots broke out around him, his parents moved him from the Master Street School to the New Market School, a fifteen-minute walk away.[2] It was a first lesson in staying above the fray, to preserve the good things one already has.

In July of 1845, Dennis was admitted to Central High School, where admissions were competitive and the course of study rigorous.[3] Being selected to attend Central "was about equivalent to going to college in most respects."[4] The School was on Juniper Street, downtown, a couple of miles south of home.[5] A regular stagecoach carried passengers south from Kensington once an hour, and more often than not his father, who could afford the twelve-and-a-half-cent fare, let him ride the coach. (The walk – nearly an hour each way – would cut into study time.)[6]

Central had not escaped the city's Bible controversy:

> The school day commenced at 8:45 A.M., when the students assembled in three large rooms, one on each floor, there being no general assembly room prior to 1854. The Bible reading was conducted by the principal and two other members of the Faculty. At first Bibles were distributed to students, and the reading was responsive by verses, but this aroused prejudice, and one denomination petitioned that the students of their faith should be permitted to use Bibles of a certain edition. As a result the reading was thenceforth the function of the professor alone.[7]

Dominick wouldn't let his preference for the Catholic Bible stand in the way of his son's education, so as the professor read from the King James version, Dennis dutifully listened. He also enrolled in an after-school program that demanded careful listening, as it taught an entirely new way of recording what people said.[8]

In those days before magnetic or electronic equipment, gathering news required a skill at listening and writing that was the same skill needed for recording testimony in legal proceedings: the ability to take notes as fast and as accurately as possible, capturing words correctly even when several people were speaking at once. (Witnesses, policemen, lawyers, judges, and speech-making politicians rarely pause in their own discourse to listen to others, so rarely give reporters time to catch up.) For centuries, long-hand scribes had only been able to prepare summaries of what people said, rarely able to capture more than short phrases as direct quotations. But in 1848, a gentleman named Oliver Dyer organized a class to teach a new method, only recently invented in England, at Central High School after hours.[9]

Dennis and another student, John McElhone, did rather well in the course.[10] The difference between traditional longhand reporting and the new phonographic method is apparent from a sample of Murphy's later shorthand notes:[11]

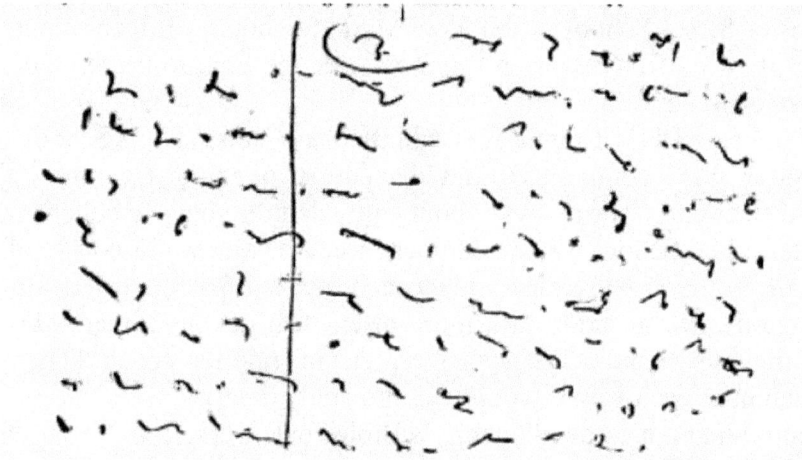

Writing such characters required an agile hand and an excellent ear. Dyer gave public lectures on the system in Musical Fund Hall on Locust Street, using Murphy and McElhone as examples of what could be done by the new method.

> [Dyer] would dictate to one of the boys and then the other would read from the notes that had been written. For a time this was looked upon as a trick until Dyer made a practice of inviting people from the audience to come upon the stage, make any address they wished, and have either Murphy or McElhone record it in stenographic notes and then repeat it word for word. This was convincing.[12]

Dennis was so good his name was used in advertising the new system. When the "Philadelphia Phonographic Society" announced its first annual meeting at the Franklin Institute, it pointed out that Master Dennis Murphy – described as "the most rapid writer in this country" – would be present.[13]

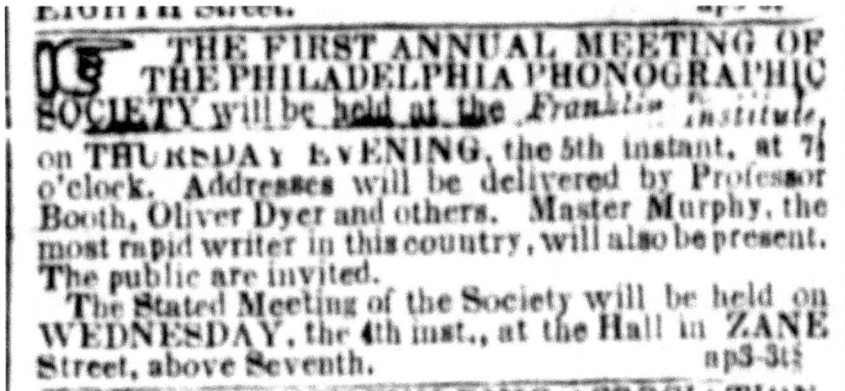

That spring and summer, the boys went with Dyer to report proceedings of the American Sunday School Union and the National Whig Convention.[14] Shortly thereafter, when Dyer was employed to report the proceedings of the U.S. Senate in Washington, he enlisted Dennis to assist him.[15]

There'd been political haggling over the reporting of Congressional Debates for years. Indignant that newspapers ignored some of their less newsworthy deliberations, Congress had started paying for reports of them in 1824.[16] They quickly learned that the way their words were reported was important to the public's perception of their performance. As a result, by 1848, the question of who should report their speeches had gained an importance the Founding Fathers had never imagined. And because their remarks were now being reported, the Senators opted not to admit (on the record) just how much it really boiled down to partisan politics. Yet the competition for who should report their words occupied their attention as much as treaties with foreign governments, the federal budget, and the propriety of slavery. It was later described as a "battle royal."[17] When a proposal was made to contract with a second, opposition newspaper, Senators questioned the benefits of having additional reports, ridiculed each other for caring so much about their reputations, and questioned the very possibility of accurate reports anyway.[18] A resolution to contract with a second newspaper had just passed in 1848 when fourteen-year-old Dennis Murphy came to town as an assistant to Mr. Dyer. The "official" reporting would now be done by two papers: The *Congressional Globe,* in the hands of Democrats Blair and Rives, and the pro-Whig *National Intelligencer*, where Murphy assisted Mr. Dyer.[19] At the opening of the session in December, 1848, the spectacle of the small boy taking shorthand notes caught the attention of such men as Daniel Webster and John C. Calhoun.[20] When Senator Calhoun "saw his frail body, he remarked that he 'would be better off outdoors, on a farm.'"[21] Another account asserts that in early 1850, Dennis was "seized with an attack of inflammation of the lungs" and had to return to Philadelphia for several months.[22] Dennis's illness might explain Calhoun's observation about his frailty. But sickly as he may have been, the boy was an excellent listener and a lightning-fast writer of the new syllabic system. When the *Intelligencer* relinquished its contract in March 1851, its contract was transferred to the *Globe*.[23] The *Globe* became the only journal publishing the debates of Congress, and declining Calhoun's suggestion that he spend time on a farm, the young Murphy went to work, with Sutton, for that publication.

Murphy and Sutton were in high demand. When the Senate was not in session, they reported the proceedings of the famous Methodist Church Property trial in New York and an extra session of the New York legislature.[24] In the spring of 1853 they reported the constitutional revision convention of Delaware, and a few months after that, the impeachment trial of Canal Commissioner Mather of New York.[25] Taking Murphy with him wherever he went, Sutton handled the business end of arrangements while relying on Murphy for the actual shorthand reporting. Murphy's speed and accuracy were such that, in the eyes of many, he outshone Sutton himself. In fact, some saw Sutton as "incompetent," and others that Dennis "was the real head of the corps long before Mr. Sutton gave up the position in name…"[26]

In his first decade in the Senate, Dennis reported speeches of Daniel Webster and Henry Clay, ratification of the Clayton-Bulwer Treaty,[27] and frequent debates regarding slavery, including those surrounding the Compromise of 1850, the Fugitive Slave Act (1850), and the Kansas-Nebraska Act (1854). He reported South Carolina Senator James Hammond's defiant declaration that "cotton is king" (1858)[28] and Jefferson Davis's farewell speech to the Senate (1861). Transcribing contentious debates in the Senate all day, every day, made for a remarkable education; Dennis learned that staying out of conflict was essential for one hired to transcribe the positions of all sides, so while perfecting his skills at listening and transcribing, he stayed above the fray, keeping his own views to himself.

After a few years staying in hotels, by late 1852, he'd settled into a room at Mrs. Elizabeth Holmead's boarding house, where he would make his D.C. home for years to come.[29] Congress was in session much less of the year than it is today, and the B&O railroad made travel between Philadelphia and Washington easy. Dennis did not squander his off-season time. Reporting trials, serving an apprenticeship in a Philadelphia law office, and reporting for newspapers in his hometown, his reputation continued to grow. An 1856 meeting of Philadelphia's Common Council made mention of his success,[30] and in 1857, after being admitted to the Philadelphia Bar, he began a law practice in that city.[31]

Senators complained loudly and often about errors and delays in the reporting of their words.[32] They debated whether partisan papers should be given privileges, or contracts, to report their own versions of what was said.[33]

They debated whether they should be allowed to see drafts, to have the opportunity to "correct" their own remarks as carried in official reports. New Hampshire Senator John Parker Hale's remarks were especially insightful:

> We hire reporters to report what is done and said in the Senate; but we shall never have precisely that so long as the practice is allowed of allowing members to revise their speeches. In these revised speeches I frequently find omitted things that were said, and I find put in things that were not said. This offer has been very kindly made to me by the reporters; but I told them to take what I say just as I say it. I do not want to make a speech afterward. If it is nonsense, let it be nonsense…
>
> I do not, like some other young gentlemen, come here to make a display of myself by talking…
>
> [W]hat I want is, that when we have a corps of reporters to keep a record of what is said, we should have what is said. I do not want to trust to the fertile imagination that may be licked into shape over the midnight lamp afterwards, and put in as being said on the spur of the moment….[34]

And so, long before television cameras entered the capitol, congressmen were performing for the public. Murphy wasn't just skilled with his pen; he was acquiring a breadth of knowledge one might only achieve by listening to the speeches of powerful men.

In Washington even more than elsewhere, people who can do favors are much sought after. Murphy quickly learned that by reporting the words of Senators, he was in a position to do them favors – even if only by correcting a reference, omitting a verbal stumble, or ruining an opponent's argument by failing to correct his gaffe. All Senators, Murphy learned, wanted him to safeguard their images as best he could. And to get him to do so, Senators were willing to do favors for him.

Of particular interest were the debates about whether the Senate should make direct payments to the individual reporters, such as himself. His ears must have opened wide the first time he heard the resolution that each reporter be paid the sum of $300 on top of the pay he received from his employer. Even a decade into the future, soldiers risking their lives in battle would be paid only thirteen dollars a month. At that rate, an extra three-hundred-dollar bonus would be the equivalent of two years' pay. Some Senators objected, as such extra compensation paid to the shorthand reporters would be paid with the public's money.

Senator Clemens: [I]t is the business of those who employ them to pay them – not ours… [T]he fact is that we pay the gentlemen

	who contract to publish the reports, and it is not our business to pay the reporters.
Senator Seward:	I regret that there should be any objection to this resolution…[W]e have been in the habit of bestowing a gratuity upon the officers who have attended upon us during our deliberations… The sums recommended by the committee are precisely the same as those which have been heretofore paid.
Senator Clemens:	I move to amend the amendment by adding the following: "And that the employees in the offices of the *Daily Union*, the *National Intelligencer*, and the *Republic* shall each be paid the sum of $300." I think, sir, that if we are to pay reporters who are not directly employed by us, but who are the employees of the proprietors of these papers, we might as well give extra compensation to each of the employees engaged in each of these offices.
Another Senator:	I would suggest to the Senator from Alabama that he ought to amend his amendment by including the employees of the *National Era*.
Another Senator:	And the *Southern Press*.
Senator Clemens:	But the *Southern Press* is dead, and there are no employees there.
Senator Mangum:	I think I may feel authorized to say that the two distinguished Whig presses named in that amendment desire no such gratuity.
Senator Clemens:	Then it is the first time I ever knew a Whig to refuse anything of the kind. [Laughter.][35]

After further debate, the Senators approved the gratuities, just as they had before. After receiving his first three hundred dollars, Dennis never forgot how important it was to make the Senators happy. He received a similar payment the next year, and the next.[36] At Dennis's recommendation, the *Globe* hired his brothers, James and Edward, and they joined him at Mrs. Holmead's boarding house.[37] Three of the six Senate Reporters were now Murphys, entitled to whatever gratuities the Senators saw fit to pay. Meanwhile, they watched the country's divisions grow steadily deeper, and war seem more certain with every passing year.

At the age of twenty-five, Dennis was admitted to practice before the U.S. Supreme Court.[38] Two months later, he was married to Miss Annie E. Chandler, a Philadelphia teacher.[39] The marriage was a good one; the following year, the first of his two children was born, and Dennis showed his political aptitude again by naming his son after his boss, Richard Sutton.[40] Twenty-seven when the Civil War finally broke out, no one that mattered thought he should volunteer in the army for just thirteen dollars a month – not when he could pay someone else to serve for him. Dennis merely watched as thousands of soldiers started pouring into the capital. The capitol building itself became a giant barracks; even the new Senate Chamber became a dormitory, a mess hall, and a medical office. And then, when the soldiers departed and Senators once again occupied the chamber, their reporter (who'd been raised as a Democrat) listened and reported as one Southern name after another was stricken from the rolls, leaving both houses of Congress firmly in the hands of Republicans.

Demonstrating a practical bent reminiscent of his father, Dennis resolved to maintain his status among the men on whom his life and income now depended. When the government sought to build its war chest by having Jay Cooke issue bonds, the new Mrs. Annie E. Murphy bought $500 of them.[41]

During the war, Dennis continued to put Congressional recesses to good use.[42] In 1863, he was admitted to the D.C. Court of Claims.[43] The Court of Claims was of more practical benefit than the Supreme Court; while the higher court limited itself to lofty principles, the Court of Claims heard lawsuits brought against the federal government. After fifteen years in the Senate, Dennis was familiar with Uncle Sam's weaknesses; its powerful men spoke (off the record) about its real strengths and vulnerabilities.[44]

Probably as early as 1864, Murphy left Mrs. Holmead's boarding house and made the National Hotel his D.C. residence.[45] Also residing at the National in the early spring of 1865 was the celebrated stage actor, John Wilkes Booth, whom he likely recognized.[46]

Then the tragic day came. Poor men and women were laid to rest in unmarked graves, but the President was embalmed some thirteen times as his slow funeral procession wound its way from the capital to his grave in Illinois. Twelve days after the shooting, with Lincoln's body not yet in the ground, Booth was tracked down and killed, never to stand trial. But in the zeal to mete out justice, eight others were brought to trial before a military tribunal. It began in Washington on the tenth of May 1865 – less than a month after the shooting – and Dennis, assisted by his brothers, reported it.[47]

Other eyewitnesses – including his own younger brother, Edward – might have been inclined to tell everyone about what they saw and heard behind those closed doors, but not Dennis Murphy. A brief sketch of the young reporter suggests that Dennis' store of knowledge was vast, but he was not given to idle talk. One of the reporters who worked for him, a man by the name of W.S. Garber, described him this way:

> Mr. D. F. Murphy is a small man of brusque manner and very few words, a fine classical scholar and linguist, a walking encyclopedia of general information, with a memory for facts and figures so tenacious that, it is said, he can give off-hand the date of the delivery and the volume of Congressional

Globe…and sometimes even the page, of almost every great speech or debate in Senate since 1848…

The marvelous lightness of his touch enabled him to write the longest conceivable outlines with great accuracy and without loss of time… I remember an occasion when one of the men in the office asked him how to write some word of many syllables, which he himself had failed in his efforts to represent shortly and satisfactorily. Mr. Murphy, with a graceful sweep of his pen, struck a form that reached half-way across the page.

'Is not that rather long, Mr. Murphy?' he suggested.

'It is a long word,' was all Mr. Murphy said as he handed him the paper."[48]

We find no record of Dennis's thoughts about the Lincoln conspirators' trial, or for that matter, any other issues of the day. Out of the limelight himself, he cultivated trust among the politicians he served by keeping his opinions to himself and his mouth shut. But eventually, Murphy's personal opinions on one matter did became known.

Despite being a Southerner, Andrew Johnson had opposed southern secession from the Union.[49] That alone was enough to impress Dennis, whose own views were unionist and anti-war. When the other Southern Democrats resigned from the Senate in early 1861, the Senator from Tennessee did not, becoming one of the few Democrats – and the *only* southern Democrat – left in the chamber. Murphy got to know him well, and he heartily approved when Johnson became Lincoln's running mate in the 1864 election. Naturally, that friendship became of particular importance when, with Lincoln's assassination, Johnson succeeded to the Presidency.

Sunday dinners at the Murphy house were fascinating: the assassination conspiracy trial, passage of the Fourteenth amendment, debates over the readmission of southern states. While Dennis was publicly quiet, he was not so tight-lipped with his father and siblings. His father, always concerned about the family business, complained mightily about the Republican war debt, its new system of taxation, John Budd's methods, and the many reasons for paying less at times, or even nothing at all. Dennis knew all about the Revenue Acts, of course. He'd listened to the debates, he'd recorded the words: he could recite them, page by page. The law required taxpayers to self-report what they owed; in theory, the assistant assessors were supposed to receive and examine the returns, question them if they saw fit, and turn them into the Assessor who, after approving them, would submit them to the Collector. But Congress had also given assistant assessors like Budd the right to visit homes and places of business, to enter and conduct inspections, and ultimately to decide for themselves the taxes owed; such decisions became final if not appealed within a few days. But so many taxpayers failed to file returns, the burden of compliance had shifted, as a practical matter, onto the assistant assessors, their on-site visits, inspections and assessments. The John Budds of the country had to visit every home and place of business, seeking the information on which to base their assessment of the taxes owed.

Dominick explained that he paid no tax when Budd didn't come by his mill. And that he paid a very small tax when Budd accepted his statement of how little he'd produced that month. Dennis reminded his father that it was *his* responsibility to report his production, whether he got a visit from Budd or not; there could be consequences if he was found to be hiding income. The older man's voice rose indignantly as he described the way Budd questioned him: calling his very honor into question.

The Revenue Acts had put hundreds of millions of dollars in play, so there was sure to be self-interested abuse; both Budd and the Murphys knew it. Since whiskey was subject to especially stringent regulation, it came as no surprise that fraud in the collection of the whiskey tax was soon in the papers.[50] The government was positive and optimistic, of course. "The Secretary of the Treasury is busy ferreting out those systems of expenditure so long indulged in by Congressmen for the benefit of their particular localities, with the intention of applying the corrective action which the public exigencies demand."[51] But in March of 1866, when news broke of more whiskey fraud in IRS Commissioner Orton's home turf of New York, the Treasury Department itself was said to be involved in the corruption. Ten arrest warrants were issued for payment of bribes to internal revenue officers.[52]

Everyone was talking about the opportunities for profitable dishonesty inherent in the tax collection system. But while ignorance of what was going on would mark you as a naïve fool, actual knowledge of wrongdoing would make you legally complicit, unless you reported it. As a result, everyone's public position was the same: they'd done nothing wrong themselves, and they knew nothing of dishonesty on the part of anyone they knew personally – yet somehow, despite that personal ignorance, they were quite certain of fraud on the part of just about everyone else.

Dennis didn't want to be accusing anyone, least of all his own father. He'd have rather seen men getting along. Well-schooled in cultivating trust from every quarter he could, he kept silent about his father's taxes, which he felt were, after all, really none of his business.

For many years, each Congress had created a committee to examine waste and fraud in government, calling it a "Retrenchment Committee." In July of 1866, Congressman Robert S. Hale moved to establish such a committee.[53] The joint committee he proposed had an enormous responsibility:

> Whereas the financial condition of the United States demands
> the exercise of a rigid economy… and whereas there is reason
> to believe that in many departments of the service abuses have
> for a long time existed, and still exist…:

> RESOLVED. That a joint select committee be appointed, to consist of three members of the Senate and five members of the House... to inquire into the expenditures in all the branches of the service of the United States, and report... what are the methods of procuring accountability in public officers or agents in the care and disbursement of public monies; whether monies have been paid out illegally... and for withdrawing the public service from being used as an instrument of political or party patronage; that said committee be authorized to sit during the recess of Congress, to send for persons and papers, and to report by bill or otherwise; and that said committee may appoint a clerk for the term of six months, and no more.[54]

Once the eight members of the Committee had been appointed, they proceeded to appoint the tight-lipped Senate Reporter, Dennis F. Murphy – now thirty-three years old – as their clerk.[55]

How these eight busy politicians and Murphy were supposed to inquire into the methods and expenditures of every single branch of government – a gargantuan bureaucracy, even then – in search of waste and abuse was not exactly clear. A lot depended on Hale himself, soon the chairman of the Committee. Would he be anxious to root out corruption in his home state of New York, where Tammany Hall still held sway, or would he want to avoid embarrassing political allies close to home?

Discussions among the men of the Murphy house often focused on the Committee and on corruption in collection of taxes.* Discussion eventually turned to the possibility that the family would be better off if it weren't subject to the whims of John Budd. If one of the family – perhaps one of Dennis's younger brothers – could be put in charge of local tax assessment, wouldn't they all be better off? Couldn't they then ensure that their own interests were protected, while keeping an eye on the actions of others? Dennis agreed to pursue appointments for his brothers, but such appointments don't happen overnight. And at the very time Dennis was reaching out to his Washington contacts, the heat on corruption in government was growing.[56] What he said, and to which politicians, are matters not found in the historical record, but within weeks, not one but two of his brothers – Edward *and* Joe –

---

* No one at the Murphy house doubted the absurdity of the task facing the Committee. The public expected it to do *something* to combat government waste and abuse, but what, really, was feasible? They could hold hearings, of course; they could summon witnesses. But corruption was rampant in all aspects of life. Without an apparatus of investigation, how would they decide who to call as witnesses? How avoid the appearance of unfairly concentrating their efforts on a particular state or region? Or on a particular branch of government? Or on officials of a particular political party? How could they make a serious effort in one area, without leaving themselves open to charges of "covering up" waste or abuse in another? Dennis's father and brothers sympathized but had no easy answers.

won roles as officers of the Treasury Department in Philadelphia. Brother Joe was appointed Assistant Assessor in Philadelphia's Third District; only two months later, brother Edward was appointed as Superintendent of Exports and Drawbacks for the Customs House.[57] The Murphys must have played their hands well in this sensitive environment; none of them were ever charged with a crime.

Still, none of them won awards for rigorous tax collection. The greatest recognition Dennis received for recovering illicit gains occurred in 1867, when the following report appeared in the *National Republican*:

> FULLY COMMITTED. – John Gilbert, the porter of the sleeping-car charged with the larceny of coupons from D. F. Murphy, clerk of the Congressional Retrenchment Committee, had a final hearing yesterday morning before Justice Walter.
>
> Mr. Murphy testified that he gave his valise in charge of Gilbert in Philadelphia, and paid him for his trouble; that on arriving in this city, and when at his hotel, he discovered that the valise had been opened, and five coupons, with nearly $13, abstracted. The coupons were rolled up with some others in a piece of paper. The five were taken out only, and the remainder not abstracted, but rolled up again.
>
> Mr. D. O'Brien testified to Gilbert having handed him the coupons, telling the witness that he had found them.
>
> Government detective John R. Cronin stated that he found a key upon the person of Gilbert, fitting the valise, and by which it was undoubtedly opened.
>
> The justice committed Gilbert, in default of security, to answer at court.[58]

If ever confronted by the fact that he never made a recovery for the Retrenchment Committee that large, Dennis certainly would have pointed out that he was no detective or investigator. As a clerk, he was simply charged to do what his Committee members instructed him to do. What, specifically, they instructed him, he kept to himself. For in twenty years of service, Dennis had learned that what politicians wanted most was to look good in the public eye; to avoid bad press. His tight lips must have pleased the members of the Committee, because his work for them went beyond its initial six-month limit; he was still working for the Committee two years later. And when Senator Trumbull, in the 41st Congress, questioned the creation of yet another Joint Retrenchment Committee, Senator Edmunds said he knew "of no committee that has… done more for infusing… some slight traces of honesty into administration than that committee has." Edmunds hoped such committees would be continued, and he got his way.[59] The new Committee was formed, and its members once again hired Dennis Murphy as their clerk.

But the Committee's hearings didn't satisfy the opposition news media. On January 20, 1869, the San Francisco Examiner ran a piece lambasting the Committee for its rather gentle (and inconclusive) investigation of corruption in the purchase of Alaska – "Seward's Folly"— and for the similar results it obtained when it investigated a contractor who'd furnished the Commissioner of Patents with stationery that – believe it or not – was *of inferior quality.* [60] Not always so sarcastic, the *Examiner* attacked "the men who run the Government through Congress, and who have been squandering the public money with unsparing hand and robbing the people to the tune of hundreds of millions of dollars." It cited corruption in the issuance of fraudulent immigration papers; it cited waste and poor work in constructing the Union Pacific Railroad; it cited scandal in the Port of New York involving drawbacks on export duties.[61]

The reporter's schedule got tighter in March of 1869 when Mr. Sutton finally retired and Dennis was formally put in charge of the other Senate reporters.[62] But busy as he now was, he did not resign his job with the Committee. His ability to keep secrets was nowhere in greater demand. But in the face of public and media outcry, it was increasingly incumbent on the committee to do *something*, so they held more hearings in New York in June. When complaints continued, they held still more hearings in San Francisco in August. For its trip to the west coast, the Committee was joined by Dennis and others who, though not specifically named, were of sufficient interest to be mentioned in the news media:

Movements of the Congressional Committee in Retrenchment

NEW YORK, August 13. – The Congressional Committee on Retrenchment, together with Senators Morrill and Cattell, of the Finance Committee, and D. F. Murphy, Senate Reporter, left Jersey City tonight on the Woodruff silver-palace car, for San Francisco via the New Jersey, Pennsylvania Central and Fort Wayne railroads. Several ladies accompany the party.[63]

It was a different era then, when relations between important men and traveling companions of the opposite sex warranted no more attention than that, even when the men involved were in charge of combatting government waste. But the San Francisco papers did describe a party given for Committee member Schurz, as well as the Committee's separation into two groups, Dennis and two members staying behind in San Francisco while the majority took a trip to see Yosemite.[64] The news media reported no exposure of corruption in government by the Committee. When it finally did issue its report, the report did not make the newspapers. And when the Committee expired at the end of the 41st Congress, its work would remain for others to tackle, at some later time.[65]

In the meantime, Congress was more concerned about its own struggle for power with the President, the origins of which dated back to 1864, when Lincoln and like-minded candidates, looking ahead to the need for reunification after the war, had run for re-election not as Republicans, but as candidates of the "National Union" party. To stress the need for unity, Lincoln had chosen southern Democrat Andrew Johnson to be his running mate.

But unity took a back seat to self-interest. The resignation and departure of so many southern Democrats three years earlier had left both House and Senate dominated by northern Republicans during the war. Lincoln's choice of Johnson in the name of national unity had made sense at the time, but the assassination left the Republican Congress anxious to make the south pay for its crimes. Having a Southern Democrat in the White House was not well suited to that purpose. Officially, differences between the new President and Congress centered around conditions for southern states' readmission to the Union. Lincoln himself had maintained that secession had no legal effect; in his view, the southern states had remained states; they were simply states in rebellion. But after Lincoln's death, the Republican Congress refused to seat southern Congressmen (Democrats) on the ground that their states had to be "readmitted" to the Union and could have no representatives in Congress until they met the North's conditions. Chief among these conditions was that they adopt new state constitutions outlawing slavery and that they ratify the 14th Amendment to the federal constitution.[66] Until then, said Congress, Congress would remain in Republican control and the South would be run by the federal Army.

Of course, underlying it all was a contest over the relative power of the political parties. Quick readmission of the largely Democratic southern states, as the President wanted, would strengthen his own party. Republicans were in no hurry to see that happen, as they scrambled to have northern territories admitted as new states, thereby increasing their own numbers.[67] And of course, the issue of black suffrage ran through it all – the freedmen, if they voted at all, would likely vote Republican, transforming a Democratic South into a Republican one. Naturally enough, the Democrats weren't anxious to let Republican-voting freedmen make that happen, but the Republican-dominated Congress was.

There were honorable, even courageous, things about Johnson. Campaigning against secession in his home state of Tennessee had not been easy. He'd received threats on his life, and he'd had to carry a gun to the lectern with him. When compelled to flee his home state after Tennessee voted to secede, he'd been shot at. Confederates had confiscated his land and his slaves, turning his home into a military hospital. He'd even led northern troops during the war.[68] For a brief time after he became President, even the Republican Congress had supported the pro-union, pro-unity man. But now, Johnson stood in the way of the Republican post-war agenda.

Through all the politicians Dennis Murphy had known during the administrations of five Presidents – Taylor, Fillmore, Pierce, Buchanan and Lincoln – he had kept his mouth shut, earning the confidence of politicians on whose trust he depended by keeping his opinions to himself. But Andrew Johnson had spent five years in the Senate during Murphy's time there. Not only were they well-acquainted, but Johnson's politics were also well aligned with those of the long-time Democrats in the Murphy family.[69]

In the eyes of many, the Republican Congress was being needlessly punitive against the South, standing in the way of the reconciliation Lincoln and Johnson had hoped for. Republican partisanship against Southern Democrats manifested itself in everything from major legislation to the passage of hundreds of private pension laws. These private laws granted civil war pensions to named individuals – individuals who, to a great extent, had connections to Republican Congressmen – notwithstanding that the government's own Pension Bureau had denied their claims. In January of that year, with relations between the Republican Congress and its Democratic President nearly at the breaking point, the House had asked its Judiciary Committee to consider grounds for impeaching the President.

It was not Dennis's style to inject his own political views into things. But for Andrew Johnson, he made an exception. His support for the beleaguered Johnson was an institutional thing, he explained, precisely *because* Johnson had been a Senator. And his support for Johnson was limited because he couldn't make personal attacks on Senators who were Republican. Publicly, Dennis's support for Johnson was revealed only by a couple of Washington press reports in the autumn of 1867.

In March of that year, Congress had adopted the Tenure of Office Act, declaring it illegal for the President to replace federal officials without Congressional approval. (Essentially, the Congress wanted to force the President to continue the employment of Republicans appointed by the Lincoln administration.) To test the constitutionality of that move, Johnson had suspended Secretary of War Edwin Stanton, replacing him with Republican war hero Ulysses S. Grant. The House Judiciary Committee was considering whether Johnson should be impeached for so doing when the Washington papers revealed Murphy's participation in meetings of the "Johnson Democratic and Conservative Club." In addition to the daily approval of pensions for their supporters, the Republican Congress (which was directly responsible for governing the District of Columbia) had voted in January 1867, to give blacks in the District the right to vote, a right they enjoyed nowhere else in the country. Some members of Murphy's Democratic and Conservative Club had a blatantly racist response.[70] And the following week, when the Club met again, that black vote – sure to be solidly Republican – was very much on their Democratic minds.

> The Chair [George Wilson] having been called up, made a speech, in which he asserted that the Democratic party would make a clean sweep at the next election; they would then blow their horns early, and be at the polls before the negroes would. He dwelt forcibly and severely upon both the engineers of the Freedmen's Bureau and of the City Hall, and

urged the necessity of defeating the City Council clique at the next election. The almighty negro had been the cry during the last four years, and what was he, after all? [A voice: "Ourang-outang; that's all."][71]

There's no record that Murphy approved of such bigotry, but also no record of him speaking out against it.[72] Just four days later, the House Judiciary Committee recommended Johnson's impeachment. Reflecting on the wisdom of being a member of such a partisan group, Murphy decided against it. Subsequent reports of the Club's activities make no mention of him, and after making an exception for Johnson, he never set foot in partisan politics again.[73]

On February 24, 1868, the full House voted to impeach. With his trial in the Senate looming, Johnson made nominations for a growing number of vacancies in positions like tax collector and postmaster, believing he had the right to nominate men whose views were compatible with his own, while Senate Republicans demanded he nominate people acceptable to them. The Senate kept rejecting Johnson's nominees. As the number of unfilled vacancies grew, the Senate was scheduled to adjourn, allowing its members to go home for the recess but leaving the country without a slew of governing officials. As the date drew near, the clash between the impeached Democratic President (still waiting to be tried) and his Republican Senate became a game of chicken, testing who would flinch first.

On April 16, 1867, the Senate debated whether to delay adjournment in the hope of filling the outstanding vacancies. The following day, an *Associated Press* report about the debate included a rather rancorous exchange between Senators Chandler and Fessenden. Chandler, said the AP's story, had accused two or three Senators of being so intent on going home for the recess that they'd declared they would "vote to confirm no matter whom the President should nominate."[74]

An indignant Fessenden, thinking he was being accused, asked Chandler to name such Senators. Chandler said he meant Fessenden. Fessenden denied the charge, and the two Republicans – though allied in their opposition to Johnson's nominations – became most uncivil toward each other, Fessenden saying Chandler "must not assume to be the leader on that side of the Chamber," and Chandler calling the desire to adjourn a desire for "mere personal convenience to the detriment of citizens," adjournment itself "neglect of duty." Fessenden invited him to look at the record to find his remarks. Chandler asked how he possibly could, as they were uttered in secret session.

Mr. FESSENDEN – My language was uttered in open session.

Mr. CHANDLER – What I allude to was in secret session, of which there is no record.

Mr. FESSENDEN – The Senator has no right to allude to me as having declared I would confirm improper persons.

Mr. CHANDLER – I did not allude to you. I told you I meant you. I would not have said so, if you had not asked me.[75]

The two Senators involved, allies of the same political party, were embarrassed by their short-tempered remarks, especially knowing they'd be printed up for the whole country to read. That very day, on the floor of the Senate, Senator Chandler criticized the Associated Press account, "in which I am made to say precisely what I did *not* say… Now, in order that there may be no misapprehension about this, I will ask Mr. Murphy to read from his original notes precisely what I did say to the Senate." Whereupon reporter James J. Murphy read back the notes taken the prior day by reporter Dennis F. Murphy.

By that time, Murphy's reputation was so strong that no one dared question his notes. That day's *Inquirer* had defended the Associated Press report, standing by those who wrote its stories while assuring the public that, in the interest of truth, mistakes by its reporters would be promptly corrected.[76] Having made that promise, when Senator Chandler had James Murphy read back the Dennis Murphy notes the following day, *The Inquirer* had little choice but to report it all under the heading "Correction."[77] An ugly and embarrassing split between Republican allies had been transformed, by Murphy's notes, into something that was the fault of neither politician, but of poor reporting by the press.[78]

Such was the power of having final say over what was released as the truth. In February of 1868, the House voted to impeach Johnson. After a Senate trial in which the President was subpoenaed but chose not to appear, he was narrowly acquitted when a few Republicans, led by Senator Fessenden, split with the rest of their party and voted not to remove him from office. But Johnson's victory was a Pyrrhic one. For his political career, the acquittal came too late. In July, at its National Convention at New York's Tammany Hall, under the slogan "This is a White Man's Country; Let White Men Rule," the Democrats snubbed their sitting President, nominating Horatio Seymour instead. Although Democrat Seymour campaigned as "the White Man's Candidate," he lost the election to the war hero, Grant.

Unlike Johnson's, the future of Murphy's career was yet to be decided. He had revealed his true Democratic leanings by supporting Johnson, but now that Johnson was gone, he faced a real test of his ability to survive in the divided city. But survive he did, by returning to his old formula, "speak little and be a trusted friend to everybody." As it turns out, the very partisan rancor that had divided the country over Johnson benefited Murphy in the long term, making him more careful than ever to be a friend to all powerful men, regardless of party. Dennis was back to taking care of Republicans as well as Democrats, even when divisiveness was the order of the day.

An example came during the 1872 debate on civil rights legislation, in which Murphy came to the aid of the radical Republican Senator from New York, Roscoe Conkling, who'd been accused of "tampering" with the Globe's reporting of the debates.

> "Mr. Conkling said this was… an effort to break down the character of the only record to which some senators had to look for justice, in view of the manner in which they are treated by certain journals of the country. He then caused to be read a note addressed to him by Mr. D. F. Murphy, chief of the corps of official reporters, stating that no request had been made by Mr. Conkling to exclude from the report any remarks he had made, and that he (Mr. Murphy) took down the debate, and was sure that he had omitted no part of the proceedings.[79]

The implication that he had omitted embarrassing material at a Senator's request was of obvious discredit to Murphy and to the *Globe* itself, but while politicians and the press were arguing over "fake news," Murphy's position as the final arbiter of fact had not been destroyed. And by sticking his neck out to defend Conkling, he must have endeared himself to the man. For all we know, Dennis had done favors for the Senators accusing Conkling as well. In a quarter century of private media criticizing the Senate's "official" (contracted-for) organ, nothing much had changed. Yet criticism from the private press was still a thorn in their collective sides. Perhaps the system was not as well designed as it could be. While it took them a year, the Senators, with Murphy's help, did come up with a solution: Instead of contracting with independent (and partisan) newspapers, Congress would henceforth be in charge of reporting debates itself.[80] While the House began hiring its own reporters and began paying them salaries of $5,000 per year as House employees, the Senate decided to contract with an individual it trusted: Dennis Murphy. Murphy "preferred having complete control over the corps of stenographers that he might select to assist him, and, upon his request, he was given a lump sum for doing the work, instead of a salary." Murphy's contracts with the Senate provided that he would be paid $25,000 per year.[81] On March 4, 1873 – the day of Ulysses Grant's second inauguration – the *Congressional Record* – Congress's name for its own reports of its proceedings –printed its first issue. It was well received, applauded for its accuracy and detail, and relied upon as a *verbatim* account of what elected representatives said and did. And no one man was more responsible for its creation than the man who would compose its Senate half, Dennis Murphy.

Having complete control over the jobs of his assistants gave Murphy unfettered control over what and how the remarks of Senators were reported, and that control went a long way to assuring their loyalty to him. Meanwhile, being personally in charge of Senate reporting made Murphy a *de facto* press secretary for the Senate. He became "the means of direct communication with the press representatives who swarm around the Capitol daily."[82]   But the *Congressional Record* was never entirely accurate, and in fact, it was never really intended to be. One 1878 account, written by a Congressional reporter, described the mayhem of Senatorial debate and argued that a "sense of propriety" justified the reporters' practice of re-ordering and regrouping the remarks that had been made.[83] But that wasn't all: the reporter was also justified in adding words of his own.[84] Much power, then, still lay in his hands. Turning endless banter into high oratory benefited no one more than the Senators themselves, by making them look more organized, less likely to interrupt, than they really were. But that was still not all. The reporter was also justified in *changing* what was said, simply in order to improve it. "He must understand perfectly everything he reports and must possess a knowledge of English so thorough that he will act as a delicate filter through which the language of the senator and representative will flow only to be purified and improved. To report correctly a grammatical error would be more apt to subject the stenographer to criticism than would be an apparent error in his notes."[85]

How much a reporter might be able to "correct" or "improve" a Senator's remarks may be suggested by the process employed: Murphy listened to the proceedings, taking down what he heard phonographically (in the written form that untrained eyes could not decipher); after returning to the reporters' room, he would hand his notes to his brother Edward and return to the Senate floor, leaving Edward to dictate the notes to a group of seven to twelve amanuenses.   The amanuenses would write out what Edward said in longhand. Once all their longhand accounts had been prepared, they would be returned to Dennis, who would "revise and prepare for the printer all the copy then ready... *every word of the copy being carefully revised by the tireless chief of the Senate corps.*"[86]

> [I]t is darkly rumored that many of the sentences uttered by the honorable Senators and members in the heat of debate do not evidence that "respect for the memory of Lindley Murray" which grammarians somewhat arbitrarily insist upon, and these the experienced Congressional reporter is expected to tone down and polish up until they can be safely entrusted to the pages of the "Record."[87]

> Mr. Murphy was exceedingly careful and particular about the character of the copy furnished to the printing office, and for many years insisted not only on taking all the notes himself, but upon reading over every page of copy before it was sent to the printer. While this delayed the manuscript, it ensured a degree of accuracy that made the reports of the Senate debates famous throughout the world. [88]

At day's end, we must marvel not only at the artistry, but the political acumen, Dennis applied to his task. If he'd been partisan, making the remarks of friendly Senators look good at the expense of their political opponents, he'd have been the cause of acrimony. Rather, he appears to have pleased all the Senators, regardless of party, putting the best face possible on everything they said, and thereby serving the institution itself. Such an approach pleased both individual Senators and the august body as a whole.

Murphy meanwhile negotiated contracts for other engagements and made money on all of them. In 1871 and again in 1874 he reported the general conventions of the Episcopal Church.[89] On November 26, 1872, he reported the Pennsylvania Constitutional Convention in Philadelphia, at which the delegates debated elimination of the word "white" from the definition of those eligible to vote (approved), equal voting rights for women (rejected), and the secrecy of ballots (various revisions made).[90] He was paid six thousand dollars for reporting Senate debates during the second session of the 43rd Congress, and an additional $1,636.12 for reporting the special session of March, 1873.[91]

And then there was the unprecedented constitutional crisis stemming from the Presidential election of 1876. New York's Democratic Governor Samuel Tilden was just one vote shy of the 185 necessary to be declared the winner; his opponent was 20 votes shy. The outcome depended on twenty contested electoral votes from four states. In response to bitter claims of fraud, Congress created a fifteen-person Electoral Commission to decide the matter. For tight-lipped, trustworthy Murphy, the sensitive and delicate proceedings presented another business opportunity. When the Commission proposed to grant all twenty contested votes to Republican Rutherford B. Hayes, the Democrats accepted the Hayes presidency in return for withdrawal of federal troops from still-occupied South Carolina and Louisiana (and other concessions). Murphy's work, for which he was paid twelve-hundred dollars, gave no hint of embarrassing deals, compromises, or sell-outs, no suggestion that the rival parties struck a deal, trading the Presidency for the political independence of the Jim Crow South.[92] Afterwards, Murphy's article on the legislative history of the law of presidential succession was well-received.[93]

As his reputation moved from Congress into all corners of Washington society, Murphy became a celebrity among members of his profession.[94] In a letter to a trade journal in January of 1879, a fellow reporter touted Murphy's choice of three-pointed pens:

My Dear Sir: — I observe in the September number, under the head-line of "Remarks Upon Mr. Murphy's Reporting Notes," that you say that "Mr. Murphy writes with a pen upon ordinary paper." That would of course convey the impression that he uses any kind of pen. That is not the fact. I enclose herewith a few specimens of the pens which Mr. M. uses. You will notice that they have three points… Mr. M has been using them ever since I have been with him, and I do not know how many years before… You will see by trying one of them how easily the light and heavy characters are made; and they never tire the wrist. Mr. M. also never uses anything else but a cedar holder, one of which I enclose.

The editors of the trade journal hastened to point out that they were diligently seeking a source of supply for the imported pens the famous Murphy used, and that they would notify their readers when the pens were available for purchase.[95]

With Dennis's financial success, he and his wife Annie decided to take up permanent residence in the nation's capital, building a magnificent house on C Street, one of the first two brownstones in that city. (It was reported that people "flocked" to look at the house because of its especially fine stonework.)[96] The society columns of the capital's newspapers grew fond of the couple, reporting their attendance at balls and receptions limited to the city's elite: presidents, vice presidents, cabinet members, senators, congressmen, foreign ministers, generals, admirals, Supreme Court justices, and other members of what the newspapers called the "crème de la crème" of D. C. society.[97] In 1884, Dennis was elected to the Hibernian Society.[98] The papers reported in advance the days on which Mrs. Murphy would be receiving guests, their summer visits to Cape May and Atlantic City, and the names of visitors staying at their home.[99] They reported Dennis's charitable activities, including a benefit concert for the Little Sisters of the Poor (attended by "the elite of the capital"), Dennis's election as chairman of a Senate Committee to aid the Irish Relief Fund, his donations to benefit Civil War nurses and, in 1889, his donation to relieve victims of the Johnstown Flood.[100]

As his earnings grew, Murphy began investing in corporations. The man with an encyclopedic knowledge of the past visualized a future in which technology would change the recorded word. He and five other men invested $50,000 to incorporate the Washington Typographic Company, Inc.; he was elected to the Board of Directors of the Capital Type-Writing Machine Company.[101] Like a twenty-first century athlete, he even did endorsements for the Columbia Phonograph Company, his name and words of praise appearing in that company's advertisements under the heading, "The Edison Phonograph in Congress."[102]

Dennis had achieved much of this success while his father, Dominick, was still alive, and though he hadn't joined the family textile mill as his father originally wanted, he never lost sight of his family obligations. He had risen to the heights of American society. As far as Dennis was concerned, America had proven that it was, indeed, a land of opportunity. (His own son Richard had already followed in his footsteps, becoming private secretary first to U.S. Senator Don Cameron and then to U.S. Senator Matthew Quay. [103] In 1888, Quay had become chairman of the Republican National Committee and was kingmaker for the Benjamin Harrison campaign.)

But of course, no matter how high one rises on the ladder of success, one can't keep rising forever. Mortality eventually makes itself known.

In 1886, the Murphys' beautiful home on C Street was threatened by plans to lay tracks on the street for a street railway. (Murphy signed a petition, presented to the Senate, protesting the plans.)[104] In February of 1890, a coconut mat was stolen from the Murphy's front porch.[105] Past triumphs could not forestall a changing world. But such signs were nothing like the one that occurred on Christmas Eve, 1890 when, stepping out of a streetcar, Murphy was struck by a team of horses pulling a cab, changing his life forever.

An Accident to Mr. Murphy.

D.F. Murphy, the veteran chief stenographer of the Senate, was knocked down this morning by a cab as he was attempting to reach the sidewalk from a street car at the corner of 13th and F streets. He was severely bruised. Owing to deafness Mr. Murphy was unable to hear the approaching vehicle and, as it appears that the driver of the cab made every effort to avoid the accident, he was not arrested.[106]

It was the first there'd been any public mention of Murphy's deafness. But severe as his deafness and the resulting accident may have been, Murphy did not lose his Senate contract – such was the trust that Murphy had earned; such was the power of the technology that, by the winter of 1891, had made his own listening and speed-writing skills less crucial. Debates in the Senate were now reported with the help of typewriters and phonograph machines. Like many inventions yet to come, the technologies Murphy had invested in reduced the need for unassisted human speed.[107]

Still, after the accident, the time had come for Dennis to rest on his laurels.[108] His health continued to worsen. Though elected President of the Washington Stenographer's Association in 1892, his increasing illness was likely apparent, as the following year, he was elected as the Association's "Honorary" President.[109] Later that year, Washington's *Evening Star* called him "the patron saint" of the reporting profession, writing that he was "without doubt the best known stenographer in the United States, and up to a short time ago, when he met with a serious accident... recognized as one of the most expert."[110]

From Atlantic City, he was able to write to David Brown, recalling his legendary start in phonographic reporting.[111] He placed an advertisement in the local papers about a home insurance policy he'd lost.[112] With his health getting steadily worse, he and Annie sold their elegant home on C Street and moved into apartments at the Cochrane Hotel.[113] There, on March 25th, 1896, he was "seized with a stroke of apoplexy" and died the next day.[114]

Annie spent September in Atlantic City without him, but she herself died the next month in Philadelphia.[115]

The obituaries were effusive in their praise. The *Washington Times* noted that Dennis had reported "[h]undreds of the most famous debates in American legislative history" and "had an acquaintance with public men as extensive as that of any other man."[116] Philadelphia's *The Times* called him "The King" of Stenographers. The *Evening Star* called him a "Famous Pen Wizard," adding, "Mr. Murphy was regarded as probably the foremost stenographer in the world. His long service, as well as his reputation for accuracy and speed, have made his name a household word among all shorthand reporters."[117]

At least six U.S. Senators attended his funeral.[118] Writing of Murphy and other trusted Senate employees, the *Evening Star* stressed that "their lips were sealed." From Murphy down to clerks, barbers and bathroom attendants, when the article asked why the Senate had kept such men in service so long, there was little doubt about the reason:

> The answer is plain… The Senate knew by experience that he could safely be trusted… [H]is retention was a matter of self-preservation, as it were, on the part of the Senate. To displace him with a new man who had not passed through a long apprenticeship would be a dangerous experiment… To all outward appearances the words spoken in their presence, in the common phrase, 'passed in one ear and out at the other.' … It was a matter of the highest moment that they should remain silent… With rare discrimination, they knew just what could be properly told, and beyond that they never went. They were as a rule wholly on the safe side, saying nothing whatever…

What was said about the old man who attended the Senate bathroom could have been said about Dennis Murphy just as well: "He knew just what to do, did it well, and never talked."[119]

Dennis didn't try to shape America to his own liking, into something he imagined it might be, because the life his father had made possible for him was quite good enough as it was. He was content to help the country's leaders look their best, and in that respect, at least, he was an extraordinary success.

THE EVENING STAR, SATU

SERVED THE SENATE

Trusted Employes and Their Long Terms of Service.

RECENT DEATH OF SEVERAL VETERANS

Repositories of Secrets That Will Never Be Known.

THEIR LIPS WERE SEALED

FAMOUS PEN WIZARD

Death of Dennis F. Murphy, the Senate's Stenographer.

HISTORY OF HIS REMARKABLE LIFE

Feats of Shorthand Writing Which He Performed.

LONG, BUSY LIFE

DENNIS F. MURPHY.

Notes on Chapter 3, Dennis Murphy

[1] Dominick Murphy was born in Cork, Ireland, on February 7, 1834 (*Evening Star*, March 27, 1896, p 3; John H. Campbell, History of the Friendly Sons of St. Patrick and of the Hibernian Society for the Relief of Emigrants from Ireland, March 17, 1771 – March 17, 1892, Hibernian Society, Phila, 1892, p 467.) The birth year of 1834 is corroborated in the 1860 U.S. Census Phila Ward 2, Fam 1737, the 1870 U.S. Census Phila Ward 22 Dist 4 (2nd enum), Fam 7, and the 1880 U.S. Census Wash, D.C., Dist 064, Fam 276, as well as in his death certificate, FHL No 2115022. Contrary is General Catalogue of the Central High School, Philadelphia, 1838 to 1890, Phila Bd of Educ, 1890, p 29, which asserts that Dennis was 12 years and zero months in July 1845, suggesting he was born in July, 1833.

[2] The conclusion that Dennis attended the Master Street School is based on several factors set forth in Chapter 1. However, the General Catalogue asserts that Dennis was admitted to Central from the New Market School, rather than from Master Street, like his younger brothers. Assuming that is not a mistake, Dennis probably attended the Master Street School until the May 1844 riots, and then (as a result of the disruption caused by the riots), spent the following school year at New Market before his admission to Central.

[3] General Catalogue, *supra*, p 29; Philadelphia's *The Times*, March 30, 1896, p 4. The course of study listed for 1850 included English Grammar, Literature, Rhetoric and Elocution; Algebra and Geometry; the History of Greece, Rome, and Pennsylvania; Moral Science, Mental Philosophy, Physics, Chemistry, Anatomy, Latin, Greek, Spanish and French. (Franklin Spencer Edmonds, History of the Central High School of Philadelphia, J.B. Lippincott, 1902, p 131 and Appendix G following p 386, accessed at https://archive.org/details/ historycentralh00edmogoog).

[4] Kenneth W. Milano, The Philadelphia Nativist Riots, The History Press, 2013, p 37.

[5] The school that is today called "Central" High School in Philadelphia began operating in 1838 on Juniper Street, downtown. The directories of the city in the 1840's included it, but they listed it simply as the "Philadelphia High School," as it was then the only high school in the city. In 1849, recognizing the school's strong curriculum, the Pennsylvania legislature gave the school the power to award degrees, explicitly stating that its degrees would be like those awarded by the University of Pennsylvania. (Edmonds, *supra*, p 130.) Early references to Dennis Murphy and the origins of stenographic reporting follow the practice of referring to the school as, simply, the Philadelphia High School. Central High was famous internationally. President James Polk addressed the students there on June 24, 1847 – Dennis Murphy, no doubt, was in attendance. (See the History Section of the school's website, https://centralhs.philasd.org/about-central-high-school/about-us/, and Edmonds, *supra*, p 124.)

[6] "Early Railroad Transportation," *Philadelphia History*, https://www.ushistory.org/philadelphia/ railroad.htm. The route went south along Second Street.

[7] Edmonds, *supra*, p 138. Central's principal at the time was John S. Hart, a licensed preacher who had attended Princeton Theological Seminary (*Ibid.*, p 101).

[8] The new method of capturing live speech, called "phonography," had been invented in 1837 by one Isaac Pitman of Bath, England; it consisted of transcribing the sounds of syllables rather than spelling words with letters, and it employed a sleek set of characters conducive to fast writing. In 1844, a book was printed in the United States setting forth the new method. (David Wolfe Brown, "What Has Half a Century Done for Shorthand?", *The National Stenographer*, Vol IV, No 9, September 1893, p 300, quoting Murphy. See also "Forty Years of Shorthand" from *The Phonographic Magazine*, Vol I, No 9, September 1, 1887, p 271, reprinted from the *New York Evening World*.)

[9] In 1848, phonography was taught by Oliver Dyer on an after-school basis (per Murphy himself, quoted in Brown, *supra*, p 295). Navigation and Phonography were not added to the regular curriculum until after 1849 (Franklin Spencer Edmonds, History of the Central High School of Philadelphia, J.B. Lippincott, 1902, p 131).

[10] McElhone went on to become the chief reporter for the U.S. House of Representatives.

[11] The sample reproduced here was Murphy's notes of comments of Senator Matthews in Senate debate on June 6, 1878. (*Evening Star*, March 27, 1896, p 3.) The vertical line through the middle was an indication by the amanuensis that the notes had been transcribed.

[12] *The Times*, March 30, 1896, p 4.

[13] *Public Ledger,* April 3, 1849.

[14] The American Sunday School Union convention was in May; the Whig convention (the one that nominated Zachary Taylor for President) was in June; Dyer had been engaged to report on it by the overtly Whig newspaper, the *North American.* (Murphy himself, quoted in Brown, *supra*, pp 294, 295, 300.)

[15] Henry M. Parkhurst, quoted in Brown, *supra,* p 286; *Washington Times*, March 27, 1896, p 2. Dyer was engaged by Richard Sutton of the *National Intelligencer* (then Washington's leading newspaper); Dyer had previously been an English parliamentary reporter who had "sat beside Charles Dickens in the gallery," apparently a reference to Dickens' time reporting on the debates of the House of Commons in the mid 1830's (*Washington Times*, June 29, 1902, p 34; *Evening Star*, Feb 14, 1915, p 9). Another description of young Murphy's early notoriety goes this way: "In June 1848, the Whig convention which nominated Gen. Taylor for the presidency met in Philadelphia, and Mr. Dyer was engaged by the *North American,* a leading Whig organ, to report the proceedings. He was assisted by a dozen of his high school class… The performance of these boys attracted the attention of Mr. Sutton, who was at the convention reporting for the *National Intelligencer*, the great Whig organ published in this city. It so happened that the Senate chanced then to have under consideration the question of obtaining full reports of its debates, and that year toward the close of the session arrangements were made for stenographic reports to be published at the public expense in each of the leading party organs in this city, the *Union* and the *National Intelligencer*. Mr. Sutton was placed in charge of the matter for the *Intelligencer*, and he chose Mr. Dyer as his leading phonographer. Mr. Dyer, at Mr. Sutton's suggestion, brought with him to Washington one of the boys who had been with him at the Whig convention, and young Murphy was chosen for this honor." (*Evening Star*, March 27, 1896, p 3.) A contrary and seemingly less credible version of the story is that Mr. Benn Pitman found Dennis and took "the little shaver" with him to illustrate the principles of phonography as he lectured. (W. S. Garber, "Congressional Reporting," *The Shorthand Review*, Vol IV, No. 9, May 1892.) According to Brown's article in *The National Stenographer*, Benn Pitman was the "accredited representative" of the inventor of the system, Isaac Pitman. According to Murphy himself, Mr. Dyer's lessons at the High School began in March 1848; by May, he was transcribing Mr. Dyer's shorthand into longhand, and by June, he was going with Mr. Dyer to report the Whig Convention in Buffalo. He was just fourteen years old at the time. Years later, asked for his thoughts about teaching shorthand in schools, the fifty-nine-year-old Murphy was strongly in favor. "I found the ability to take notes of lectures a great advantage to my standing at school," he wrote. "I should say that a beginning should be made by 10 or 12 years of age, while the muscles are in a plastic condition. Bad methods of longhand writing, previously formed, undoubtedly retard the mastery of shorthand." (Quoted by Brown, *supra*, pp 300-301.)

[16] The Constitution required both houses of Congress to publish a Journal to record their actions, but not the deliberations leading up to those actions. In fact, the Senate had met entirely in secret at first, i.e., in what came to be called "executive session." In 1794, the Senate had started allowing newspaper reporters into its chambers to witness (and report on) *some* of its proceedings – i.e., those not conducted in "executive session," to give the public a picture of what the Senators wanted the public to see. In those days, most newspapers were unabashedly aligned with political parties, and their reporters did what one might expect: they summarized debates to make the congressmen of their own party appear to have the better argument. These newspapers also chose which debates to report on, leaving out deliberations they didn't care to print. So in 1824, the Senate contracted with Joseph Gales and William Seaton, the publishers of the *National Intelligencer*, to publish all their debates; Gales and Seaton established the *Register of Debates*, attempting to include in it summaries of deliberations in all the public sessions, while at the same continuing to print, in their openly pro-Whig paper, whatever they saw fit. The

National Intelligencer allowed Senators and Congressmen to "correct" their draft summaries (and so effectively to revise them – or as some Senators claimed, to devise entirely new speeches) after the fact. But in 1833, hoping for reporting that was better suited to their own agendas, Andrew Jackson's Democrats contracted with Democrats Francis Blair and John Rives to publish *The Congressional Globe*. Beginning in 1834, the *Globe* began reporting debates on all matters, and doing the job so objectively that the Whigs called Blair and Rives "habitual falsifiers of debate." (*Reporters of Debate & the Congressional Record*, U.S. Senate, accessed at https://www.senate.gov/artandhistory/history /common/briefing/Reporters_Debate_Congressional_ Record.htm.)

[17] *Washington Times*, June 29, 1902, p 34. The main rivalry was between Murphy's employer, the *National Intelligencer*, and *The Globe*, run by Francis Preston Blair and John C. Rives.

[18] *Congressional Globe*, 30th Cong, 1st Sess, Aug 11, 1848, p 1065. Senator Benton argued, "each member receive[s] nineteen copies of his own speech, and no one ever read the speech of another, unless he made an attack on it." Mr. Foote referred to "the chariness felt by Senators to their reputation, which induced them to revise their speeches before they permitted them to be sent out to the world." When Senator King proposed that the reporters be sworn to make accurate reports, Senator Benton asked how reporters "could... be sworn to report correct speeches, when Senators themselves could not hear each other." To that, Mr. King's rejoinder was, "No reporter can take down every word, even when the Senate is in order; when it is not in order – and he regretted that it was now more disorderly than he had ever known it to be – it was impossible to come near it." That, at least, is what he was reported to have said.

[19] Dyer, in turn, reported to Mr. Sutton. (Henry M. Parkhurst, comments in *The American Reporter*, May 1852, quoted in Brown, *supra*, p 286.) This is also the account given by Murphy himself forty-five years later (Dennis Murphy to D.W. Brown, July 12, 1893, quoted in Brown, *supra*, p 300.) One source puts the employment of Dyer and his proteges at the *Intelligencer* as occurring in 1849, rather than 1848. ("Forty Years of Shorthand," *The Phonographic Magazine*, Vol I, No 9, Sept 1, 1887, p 271.)

[20] During a Senate break in 1849, when Mr. Dyer was engaged to prepare a phonographic manual in New York, he took young Murphy with him, returning to Washington when the Senate reconvened (*Evening Star*, March 27, 1896, p 3). Over a century later, in his *Historical Almanac of the United States* (1989), Senator and later presidential candidate Bob Dole wrote that the *Globe* hired fourteen-year-old Dennis in 1848 "on the recommendation of Senator John C. Calhoun." (Bob Dole, Historical Almanac of the United States Senate: A Series of "Bicentennial Minutes," Presented to the Senate During the One Hundredth Congress, U.S. Govt Printing Office, 1989, p 271, accessed at https:// babel.hathitrust.org/cgi/pt?id=msu.31293011524109&view=1up&seq=283.) Murphy was likely present in January of 1849, when Calhoun delivered his famous "Address of the Southern Delegates" for the cause of southern unity and the preservation of slavery, and Murphy's speed and accuracy may have caught Calhoun's attention, but Dole's assertion that Murphy was hired by the Globe, in 1848, on Calhoun's recommendation, seems mistaken. The other detailed accounts, including Murphy's own, make clear that Murphy began his Senate reporting with the *Intelligencer* in 1848; he did not start working for the *Globe* until 1851, after Calhoun was already dead. If the earlier date of Murphy's hiring by *The Globe* was true, it would mean Murphy left *The Intelligencer* almost immediately after arriving in Washington under Dyer's supervision – a rather bold thing for a fourteen-year-old to do. Dole appears to have based his mistaken assertion on the similar statement by Senator Hubert Humphrey in the *Congressional Record*, 86th Cong, 2nd Sess, May 18, 1960, p 10520.

[21] Remarks of Clifford Case, *Congressional Record*, 84th Cong, 1st Sess, Senate, January 21, 1955, pages 590-593.

[22] According to this account, at the opening of the Senate session of December, 1849, Dennis was employed on the corps of the *Union*, but in a few weeks he was seized with an attack of inflammation of the lungs and removed to his home in Philadelphia; that on his recovery in April, 1850, he returned to Washington and secured a position on *The Intelligencer's* corps under Mr. Sutton. (*Evening Star*, March 27, 1896, p 3.)

[23] Even then, confusion existed about which papers had been reporting the debates. See the conflicting remarks of Senators Bright and Gwin in *The Congressional Globe,* 33rd Cong, 1st Sess, May 11, 1854, pp 1156-1157.

[24] *Ibid.;* R. Sutton, Methodist Church Property Case, J. Early, New York, 1851; *Poughkeepsie Journal,* Nov 15, 1851, p 2. The church property case, *Bascom et al v Lane et al.,* was tried in New York May 17 – 29, 1851. The Methodist Church had been operating a book business that was worth some $750,000, and much of the profits were paid out to the church's ministers. When the Church split, in 1844, over the slavery question, the southern ministers "resigning" from the existing church and forming a new Southern church of their own, the New York based controllers of the book fund stopped paying the Southern ministers. The Southern ministers sued to get their share of the profits, and they won.

[25] *Evening Star,* March 27, 1896, p 3. Mather was impeached in 1853 due to various complaints about corruption, waste and neglect in the performance of duties, but acquitted by the New York Court for the Trial of Impeachments when the 18 to 14 vote to convict fell four votes shy of the number needed. See, for example, *New York Daily Herald,* June 16, 1853, p 8; *Buffalo Daily Republic,* August 18, 1853, p 2; *New York Times,* Nov 2, 1853, p 2, and https://www.nytimes.com/1853/08/24/archives/ court-of-impeachment-for-the-trial-of-john-c-mather-canal.html. "So far as relates to the canal lettings of '51," said one paper, "we believe Mr. Mather to have been guilty of gross corruption; but not more guilty, nor more deserving of punishment, than every other man who was connected with him in that Sub-Board by whom the fancy contractors were awarded their three millions of plunder." Otherwise, said the paper, it would keep an open mind. (*Buffalo Daily Republic,* Aug 12, 1853, p 2.)

[26] "Forty Years of Shorthand," *supra,* p 271; Garber, *supra,* p 72. But Dennis himself must have thought well of Sutton: when his son was born, he named him Richard Sutton Murphy.

[27] In that treaty of 1850, the U.S. and Britain promised not to build a canal across Central America without the consent and cooperation of the other.

[28] In his March 4 1858 speech, the Southern Senator challenged the north with the iconic argument, "No, you dare not make war on cotton. No power on earth dares to make war upon it. Cotton is king."

[29] Mrs. Holmead's boarding house was on 4-1/2 Street NW (off Pennsylvania Avenue). *The Daily Republic,* April 9, 1850, p 3, lists D. F. Murphy, Phila, at Brown's Hotel; the *Daily American Telegraph,* Nov 28, 1851, p 3, lists him at the United States Hotel; Alfred Hunter's The Washington & Georgetown Directory and Stranger's Guide-Book for Washington, and Congressional and Clerks' Register, Wash., 1853, accessed at http://name.umdl. umich.edu/AFJ8697.0001.001, has him at "Mrs. Holmeads, 4-1/2 St." In the 1862 D.C. City Directory, Dennis is listed as "bds 28 4-1/2 nw," while Mrs. Holmead herself is listed as "Holmead Elizabeth, boarding, 4-1/2 west, cor Penn av."

[30] Edmonds, *supra,* p 296. The mention was not by his Councilman father, as one might have guessed, but by Professor Knorr of Central High School, advancing Dennis's name, among others, as proof of that school's success.

[31] Campbell, *supra,* p 467, dates the admission to November of 1857. Dennis was listed in the 1859 Philadelphia Directory as "D.T.[sic] Murphy, attorney at law," with offices at 707 Sansom Street, though his permanent residence while in Philadelphia remained his parents' home. In 1858, he was one of two attorneys prosecuting a criminal case for the district attorney's office. (*Evening Star,* Dec 2, 1858, p 2.)

[32] See, for example, Missouri Senator Thomas Benton's comment on August 11, 1848, that he "had not seen any correct report of anything he had said for the last three months; what little he did say, he desired to have correctly presented to the world." (Cong Globe, 30th Cong, 1st Sess, p 1065); and see Cong Globe, 30th Cong, 2nd Sess, Jan 30, 1849, pp 395 *et seq* and the *National Union,* Jan 31, 1849.

[33] See, for example, Cong Globe, 32nd Cong, 2d Sess, March 1, 1853, p 933; and Cong Globe, 33rd Cong, 1st Sess, May 11, 1854, p 1156.

[34] Cong Globe, 32nd Congress, 1st Sess, Jan 22, 1852, p 347.

[35] Cong Globe, 32nd Congress, 1st Sess, Aug 30, 1852, pp 2469-2471.

[36] Cong Globe, 33rd Congress, 2nd Sess, March 2, 1855, p 1089.

---

[37] The three Murphy brothers boarded together in D.C. The 1862 Washington City Directory lists D.T. [sic] Murphy, J.J. Murphy, and E.V. Murphy, each with the occupation "official reporter Senate" and with residence address, "bds 4-1/2 west," the Holmead boarding house. (The same listing in the 1863 Directory gave "D.F." Murphy the correct initials.)

[38] *Evening Star*, Jan 18, 1859, p 3; and *Washington Union,* Jan 18, 1859, p 3, adding to its report of his admission, "Mr. Murphy has long been known as a very skillful reporter in the Senate of the United States." While admission to the Supreme Court bar made him eligible to try cases before that court, he never did so. It only took a nomination and a fee to be admitted; for some, it was enough just to be part of that exclusive club.

[39] *Public Ledger*, Oct 27, 1859, p 2; *Evening Star*, March 27, 1896, p 3. See also the death certificate of her son, Richard S. Murphy, PA Certificate 62307, June 22, 1907, and Pennsylvania Wills, 1896, Application for Probate of Annie E. Murphy, No 1641. Annie, the only daughter of the late Isaac A Chandler, was listed as a teacher in the 1856 Phila directory. They were married Oct 25, 1859, at St. Paul's Church, by Reverend John McAnany.

[40] Annie gave birth to son Richard Sutton Murphy in 1860 or 1861, and to daughter Annie Elizabeth Murphy in 1864.

[41] *Inquirer*, Sept 14, 1861, p 8.

[42] The 37th Congress was in recess between Aug 6 and December 2, 1861; then again for four-and-a-half months before its third session; and then there was an eight month break between the 37th and 38th Congresses.

[43] Wash D.C.'s *National Republican* of December 16, 1863, p 2. He continued to practice law in Philadelphia as well. The 1863 Septennial Census for Pennsylvania lists D.F. Murphy, attorney, in Philadelphia Ward 20.

[44] It also didn't hurt that Joe Casey, Chief Justice of the Court of Claims, had not only been a member of Congress from Pennsylvania, but was also a trained stenographic reporter like Murphy. The two men had a great deal in common.

[45] The 1863 D.C. City Directory recorded Dennis living with his brothers at Mrs. Holmead's boarding house and the 1867 and 1868 Directories recorded him staying at the National Hotel. Dennis was listed in the Philadelphia directories, practicing law on Sansom Street and with a residence of his own (no longer staying at his father's house), during 1864 and 1865, but as he is not listed in the D.C. directories for 1864 and 1865, this leaves unanswered where he was staying in D.C. when the Senate was in session. The National Hotel, on the corner of Pennsylvania Avenue and 6th Street, was closer to both his workplaces than the other large hotel in the area, the Metropolitan. We conclude that he was living at the National as early as 1864, but in no event later than 1866.

[46] Testimony of G.W. Bunker, Lewis J. Weichmann, and Bernard J. Early in William C. Edwards, The Lincoln Assassination – the Trial Transcript: a Transcription of NARA Microfilm File M599, Reels 8 through 16, *Google Books* (2012), pp 21, 77, 133 and 305. Most of the trial testimony can also be accessed at Ben P. Poore, ed., The Conspiracy Trial for the Murder of the President, Tilton & Co., 1865, via the Internet Archive, https://archive.org/details/conspiracytrialf01poor page/n5/mode/2up.

[47] The official reporters named at the outset of the proceedings were Pittman, Sutton, and D.F. Murphy (Edwards, *supra*, p 5). But while the older Sutton may have managed the contract, Dennis, assisted by his brothers Edward and James, with Joseph as amanuensis, did most of the actual reporting, just as they did in the Senate. Testimony of the witnesses was printed in some detail (though often summarized or paraphrased) daily in the Washington *Evening Star* from May 10 through June 29, 1865. One of those reports – that of May 16, 1865, on page 2 of the *Star* – referred to Major General Hunter, the officer in charge, directing Dennis Murphy and Ben Pitman to read back some of the testimony. Numerous sources confirm the role of Dennis, James and Edward Murphy, including Edward's own account in the *New York Times Magazine*, April 9, 1916. (See also the *Evening Star*, March 27, 1896, p 3.) Joseph Murphy's participation was asserted by the *Evening Star*, Dec 6, 1910, p 18.

[48] Garber, *supra*, pp 72-73.

[49] Albert E. Castel, The Presidency of Andrew Johnson, Regents Press of Kansas (1979), p 4. The whole Murphy family had ties to Southern-leaning causes. In addition to other indications herein, James reported the court martial of General James Briscoe, an army officer accused of passing war information to southern forces during the war (Wash *National Republican,* Oct 6, 1865). Dennis and James joined Sutton at "the Southern Loyalists Convention" in Philadelphia, after which, in 1866, they produced a pamphlet containing a report of its proceedings. (Wash *Evening Star,* Oct 8, 1866, p 2.)

[50] Whiskey tax fraud was discovered in Nashville in the autumn of 1865. In covering the "Whiskey Frauds," most of the press centered around whether William Orton, the former New York Port Collector and now Commissioner of Internal Revenue, would approve the one hundred thirty-thousand-dollar settlement proposed by the distillers. As some papers observed, the proposed settlement was "just forty thousand more than the assessed taxes on the articles they attempted to smuggle." Many expected the government to do better, with stronger punishment needed to discourage future frauds. Yet the settlement was approved, and after it, additional frauds continued to come to light. (*Chicago Tribune,* October 19, 1865, p 1. See also *Burlington Free Press,* October 17, 1865, p 2; *Raftsman's Journal* (Clearfield, PA), Nov 1, 1865, p 4; *Vermont Transcript,* October 27, 1865, p 2, and Nov 3, 1865, p 2.)

[51] *Chicago Tribune,* October 19, 1865, p 1.

[52] *New York Daily Herald,* March 15, 1866, p 5.

[53] *Congressional Globe,* 39th Cong, 1st Sess, July 2, 1866, p 3540. Hale represented New York's 16th Congressional District (the Bronx and Westchester County).

[54] *Congressional Globe,* 39th Cong, 1st Sess, July 18, 1866, p 3908.

[55] *National Republican,* Oct 29, 1867, p 3.

[56] In Philadelphia, no one was working harder to convince the public that he was protecting the public interest than John Diehl, Collector for the 2nd District downtown (*Evening Telegraph,* Aug 4, 1866, p 5).

[57] Joe Murphy appears on the tax rolls of District 3, Division 12, having made assessments for the month of September 1866. Edward's appointment as Superintendent of Exports and Drawbacks on December 21, 1866, was reported in *The Inquirer,* Dec 21, 1866, p 1.

[58] *National Republican,* Oct 29, 1867, p 3.

[59] *Congressional Globe,* 41st Congress, 1st Sess, March 10, 1869, p 42.

[60] *San Francisco Examiner,* January 20, 1869, p 1.

[61] *Examiner,* January 28, 1869, p 2; *Examiner,* February 19, 1869. The work on the railroad later exploded into the Credit Mobilier scandal. Drawback scandals were soon to become commonplace.

[62] *Evening Star,* March 27, 1896, p 3. Note that by 1869, Dennis had left the National Hotel and was boarding at the St. James Hotel, and in 1870, he was staying at the Metropolitan Hotel, while brother James was staying at the National and brother Edward at 423 Pennsylvania Ave. (See the respective D.C. Directories.)

[63] *The National Republican,* Aug 14, 1869, p 1. The ladies' names were not disclosed.

[64] After separating for the Yosemite trip, the Washingtonians reunited in Omaha for the return trip home. *San Francisco Chronicle,* Aug 15, 1869; *The Examiner,* Aug 24, 1869; *The Examiner,* Sept 15, 1869, p 2.

[65] On December 14, 1871, desiring to have their own Committee, the Senate established the Senate Committee on Investigation and Retrenchment. "The major targets of the investigations conducted by the committee were graft and corruption in the operations of the New York City customshouse." (*Records of the Committee on Governmental Affairs and Related Committees,* History and Jurisdiction, 11.1, National Archives website, accessed at https://www.archives.gov/legislative/guide/senate/chapter-11.html#Minor StandingExpCmts.) This committee was formed two months *after* work by Thomas Nast and *The New York Times* led to the formation of the "Committee of Seventy" to investigate corruption under New York's Boss Tweed and his Tammany Hall.

[66] Prior to ratification of the 14th Amendment, there was no federal obligation to grant *anyone* the right to vote. Who could vote was entirely a matter for states themselves to decide. The 14th Amendment,

if it became law, would create a federal guarantee that all free men have the right to vote. Johnson and others viewed this as an unconstitutional infringement of states' rights, pointing out that the condition was also arguably hypocritical, as many northern states, already seated in Congress, denied blacks the right to vote. And of course, women didn't have the right to vote; nor children; nor felons; etc. In effect, the Republicans were insisting that white southerners guarantee blacks the right to vote as condition of being allowed to vote on anything else themselves – although no such requirement applied to the northern states.

[67] Nevada had been admitted toward the end of 1864; Nebraska would be admitted March 1, 1867. Every Senator and Congressman from these two states was a Republican.

[68] "Andrew Johnson," Wikipedia.org, citing various sources.

[69] Until Johnson, no President since Murphy arrived in Washington had served in the Senate. Both Pierce and Buchanan had been Senators, but prior to Murphy's arrival in 1848.

[70] The first article appeared on October 29, giving notice that citizens of the city's 4th Ward had met and organized a "Democratic and Conservative Ward Club." The brief article simply mentioned that Murphy and another gentleman had been appointed to draft a constitution and bylaws for the organization. (*Evening Star*, Oct 29, 1867, p 3.) A week later, a second article reported that the Club had elected Mr. Owen Thorn, the owner of a D.C. newspaper, as its President, and that three names had been nominated to serve as the Club's vice president, including that of Murphy. The third man nominated, one George Wilson, was made vice-president. The group then changed its name because the President had "stood up to the radicals." Taking the chair, George Wilson stated that he "felt proud in presiding over white men." (*Evening Star*, Nov 7, 1867, p 3.) It was not the sort of statement Murphy himself would have made, but it does speak to the sentiment of many who were opposed to the radical Republicans in control of Congress.

[71] *National Republican*, Nov 16, 1867, p 3.

[72] The papers only reported that Murphy told the group his committee would have a constitution and bylaws ready for review at the next meeting, and that he was put on a committee to find a larger place for the Club to meet. (*National Republican*, Nov 16, 1867, p 3.)

[73] *National Republican*, March 14, 1868, p 3; *Evening Star,* January 30, 1868.

[74] According to the Associated Press report, Senator Howe, from Wisconsin, said the Senate shouldn't have to stay in session forever waiting for the President to nominate suitable men. "Let the responsibility rest where it belonged," said Howe. He did not want to extend the time "one minute beyond that day." Senator Cameron agreed – he thought the President wanted to throw responsibility for unfilled vacancies on the Senate. "He believed the President would appoint only the worst men willing to accept office... If the President sent in proper persons, he would vote to confirm them, but he should consent to no more compromises." Senator Chandler felt the Senate had an obligation to confirm postmaster positions and vacancies in customs houses, lest the postal service and customs operations came to a halt. The public, he said, would blame the Senate if that occurred, so he was prepared to stay until the President submitted acceptable names. Senator Davis, of Kentucky, spoke in Johnson's favor, saying that presidents had always appointed their friends to offices, and the Senate had no right to impose a requirement that all his nominees be "Radicals." Yates disagreed with Davis; in his view, the Senate had a duty to confirm the President's nominees when the President had been *elected*, because that was (indirectly) the expressed will of the people; but this did not apply in the present case, he said, where Johnson had *not* been elected by the people. *The Inquirer*, April 17, 1867, p 1.

[75] *Ibid.*

[76] *The Inquirer*, April 17, 1867, p 4. Under the heading CONGRESSIONAL REPORTS, the Inquirer opined: "Some of the United States Senators are dissatisfied with the Associated Press reports of the proceedings of that body. The difficulty seems to be that certain Senators are not pleased with the notice that is taken of their efforts, and their names are not so frequently brought before the country as they would desire. Occasionally the reporter of the Associated Press makes a mistake in assigning the remarks of one

Senator to another, which causes great dissatisfaction among the parties concerned. The Senator who gets the credit of these remarks is not anxious for the distinction; he who is robbed of the glory is mortified at the seeming slight. But whenever such cases occur they are promptly rectified in a succeeding report, and no great harm is done... [R]eporters for the press... execute their tasks with judgment and discretion... The Press, we undertake to say, is satisfied with those reports, and so is the country... Mr. BUCKALEW, of this State, it seems, however, is dissatisfied with them, and he has moved that the Committee on Printing be authorized to enter into a contract in the name of the Senate, with some proper person, to furnish a condensed or synoptical report of the proceedings and debates of the Senate, the same to be free to the press of the Country or to any authorized agency thereof... The expediency of this movement may be doubted. If the official synoptical report is to contain an account of every trifle that is said or done by every Senator it will be overloaded with a vast amount of nothing, which will fill up newspaper columns and make the reports tedious. Some journals may be willing to publish everything that is sent "officially" from Washington as an account of Senatorial proceedings, but many will strike out the unimportant matter, and in that case the actions of Mr. BUCKALEW may still be suppressed from the knowledge of the country, much to his grief no doubt."

[77] *The Inquirer*, April 18, 1867, p 4.

[78] As we will see, Dennis insisted on revising the transcriptions of his own reporting before they were sent out for printing and release to the world. So when the embarrassment here was shifted from a childish spat between Republican politicians to inaccurate reporting by the media, we might do well to keep in mind that Dennis himself had every reason to revise the transcript for the Senators' benefit.

[79] Washington *Evening Star*, February 7, 1872, p 1.

[80] *National Republican*, March 22, 1873, p 1. "Mr. [Henry B.] Anthony said... the Committee on Printing had entered into a contract with Mr. Dennis Murphy, the chief of the reportorial staff in the Senate, to continue the reporting of the debates. He then submitted a resolution designating Dennis Murphy as the official reporter of the Senate, and allowing to him and his staff at this session the rate of $1.07 per thousand ems, printer's measure, with 20 per cent. additional. He also said the committee had given instructions to the Congressional printer to print the same number of the *Congressional Record* as of the *Congressional Globe* at the past session, and that the *Record* be distributed as the *Globe* was distributed."

[81] *Evening Star*, March 5, 1874, p 1, March 27, 1896, p 3, and April 12, 1902, p 18; *Washington Times*, March 27, 1896, p 2.

[82] *Evening Star*, June 9, 1896, p 13.

[83] Personal Biographical Sketch of Edward V. Murphy, *Browne's Phonographic Monthly*, September 1878, p 12. "A Senator may be... soaring in the clouds of imagination and drawing a picture of the woe and desolation sure to fall upon the country if an appropriation for dredging and improving the Little Mudbigbee River is not made, when in comes the secretary of the President or the clerk of the House of Representatives bearing a message. Instantly the gavel falls...The message is received; and the senator resumes... Should the... reader of the Congressional debates be dragged from the dizzy heights into which he has ascended... into such miserable commonplaces as a message from the President announcing that he has approved and signed Senate Bill No. 1111 to incorporate a slaughter-house company in the District of Columbia? The feelings of the orator, the good taste of the reader, the literature of the age, and, above all, the sense of propriety of the reporter, forbid it."

[84] *Ibid.* "A Senator presenting a petition or report rarely states enough of its contents to convey an intelligent idea of the subject. He will say, for instance, "I present the petition of John Jones, and ask that it be referred to the Committee on Military affairs." This petitioner may pray for additional bounty, for restoration to the army, or possibly, for compensation for a mule seized by the U.S. troops during the 'late unpleasantness.' The reporters take the trouble to ascertain and state concisely and intelligently the contents of every such paper..."

[85] *Evening Star*, April 12, 1902, p 18.

---

[86] Personal Biographical Sketch of Edward V. Murphy, *Browne's Phonographic Monthly*, September 1878, p 12; *Evening Star*, March 27, 1896, p 3. Murphy's assistant reporter, W. S. Garber, confirmed that Murphy "revised all the copy before it was sent to the Government printing office." (Garber, *supra*, p 72.)

[87] *Washington Times,* June 29, 1902, p 34.

[88] *Evening Star*, March 27, 1896, p 3.

[89] *Ibid.*

[90] Debates of the Convention to Amend the Constitution of Pennsylvania (1873), pp 128, 131, 720-733, 785-805; accessed at https://babel.hathitrust.org/cgi/pt?id=miun.aew7549.0001.001&view=1up&seq=3; Campbell, *supra*, p 467; Russell Weigley *et al,* Philadelphia, a Three Hundred Year History, W.W. Norton & Co. (1982) p 442; *Evening Star*, March 27, 1896, p 3.

[91] *National Republican*, Mar 7, 1874, p 7, carrying the text of Session Law No 9, 43rd Congress, First Session, an act appropriating money for reporting. Approved January 28, 1874.

[92] Campbell, *supra*, p 467; *Evening Star*, Dec 23, 1878, p 1; *Evening Star*, March 27, 1896, p 3. The members of the Commission included not only future U.S. President James Garfield, but also the Honorable William Strong, justice of the United States Supreme Court and cousin of Alemeth Byers's step-mother, Eliza Strong Byers. See unnumbered frontispiece, *Proceedings of the Electoral Commission*, Library of Congress, accessed at http://memory.loc.gov/cgi-bin/ampage?collId=llec&fileName=001/llec001.db&recNum=2&itemLink=r%3Fammem%2Fhlaw%3A%40field%28DOCID%2B%40lit%28ec0013%29%29%230010305&linkText=1

[93] *The Critic*, Oct 11, 1881, p 2.

[94] Some reports of his fame and influence are so extreme as to test credulity. Thus, "So famed was he that when such eminent constitutional lawyers as George F. Edmunds and Roscoe Conkling made an appearance before the United States Supreme Court they would politely relieve the official stenographer of that body of his duties and have Dennis Murphy record their arguments." (Philadelphia's *The Times*, March 30, 1896, p 4.)

[95] "Style of Pen Used by the U.S. Senate Stenographers," *Browne's Phonographic Monthly*, Vol IV No 1, January 1879, p 31; the quoted letter being from Senate Reporter Henry J. Gensler.

[96] "Mr. and Mrs. D. F. Murphy are settled in their handsome house, No 314 C street northwest. Although Mr. Murphy has been so long connected with the Senate as the head of its official reporting corps, this is the first year his family have kept house in Washington." (*Evening Star,* Dec 14, 1876, p 1.) The house had its own stables. (*Evening Star*, Nov 20, 1893, p 10.) Both the Murphy house and the other new brownstone, built for the surgeon, Dr. May, were on C Street between 3rd and 4-1/2. "The novelty of a stone front was very catchy, and though there were plenty of brownstone fronts in New York, Philadelphia and Boston, there were none here until these houses were built." (*Evening Star*, Oct 3, 1896, p 14.)

[97] *Evening Star,* Feb 12, 1872, p 1; *National Republican*, Feb 14, 1873, p 1; *National Republican*, Jan 24, 1874, p 4; *National Republican*, Feb 21, 1876, p 4; *Evening Star,* Aug 23, 1884, p 2 (Mr and Mrs *and daughter…*); *National Republican*, March 15, 1877, p 1; *Evening Star,* Jan 22, 1880, p 1; *Evening Star*, Feb 5, 1880, p 1; *Evening Star* Jan 26, 1881, p 1.

[98] Campbell, *supra* at p 467.

[99] *Evening Star*, Dec 31, 1877, p 1; *National Republican*, Jan 1, 1877, p 4; *Evening Star*, Aug 16, 1879, p 1; *Sunday Herald*, April 25, 1880, p 1; *Evening Star*, July 10, 1880, p 1; *Evening Star*, Feb 7, 1881, p 1; *Sunday Herald*, July 12, 1891, p 10.

[100] *National Republican*, April 6, 1874, p 8; *Evening Star*, Jan 29, 1880, p 4; *National Republican*, May 16, 1883, p 2; *Evening Star,* Jun 15, 1889, p 5.

[101] *Evening Star*, May 17, 1883, p 4; *National Republican*, May 17, 1883, p 6; *Evening Star*, Jan 18, 1889, p 8.

[102] Murphy's letter to the President of the Company, which was printed in the Company's advertisements, included such statements as, "[B]y the use of the phonograph at least twice as much copy can be turned out in a given time and in better shape than by the use of the most skillful short-

hand amanuensis. So indispensable has the phonograph become to the business of my office that the wonder of myself and associates now is how we were able heretofore to get along without it." (*Evening Star*, January 9, 1892, p 1.)

[103] *Philadelphia Inquirer*, June 22, 1890, p 8; *Washington Evening Star*, Aug 4, 1943, p 12.

[104] *National Republican*, April 13, 1886, p 1.

[105] *The Critic*, Feb 22, 1890, p 3.

[106] *Evening Star,* Dec 24, 1890, p 14; *Evening Star*, March 27, 1896, p 3.

[107] Garber, *supra*, p 74.

[108] On April 29, 1891, Dennis gave his daughter Annie in marriage to a veteran of the civil war, an Army Captain whose military career was far from over (*Sunday Herald*, April 26, 1891, p 12). Enlisting as a private, Morris Cooper Foote was a lieutenant by the time the Civil War concluded (1890 U.S. Census, Veterans' Schedule, Westchester County NY, David's Island.) A Captain at the time of the marriage, he went on to participate as a Major, 21st Infantry, in the Battle of San Juan Hill; to serve in the Philippines; and to be promoted to Brigadier General (N.Y. State Archives, Abstracts of Spanish-American War Military and Naval Service Records, 1898-1902, Series No. B0809, Abercrombie-Zalinski; *Houston Daily Post*, Feb 11, 1903, p 1; *New York Times*, Dec 8, 1905, p 11; *Omaha Daily Bee*, Dec 26, 1905, p 5.)

[109] *The Stenographer*, Vol II No 11, March 1892, p 447; *Evening Star*, February 6, 1893, p 10.

[110] *Evening Star*, May 27, 1893, p 10.

[111] Brown, *supra*, p 300. (Murphy to Brown, July 12, 1893, from the Hotel Brighton in Atlantic City.)

[112] "All persons are cautioned against receiving or negotiating the same." *Evening Star*, Nov 20, 1893, p 10.

[113] Completed in 1891, the new seven-story Cochrane Hotel on Franklin Park had been called a "first-class" hotel by the Washington Post, with white marble floors, oaken doors, and "distinguished people in every walk of public life" resident in the neighborhood. "[A]ll the apartments of the Cochrane have been elaborately and sumptuously furnished, the carpets being principally moquette, Axminster, and Wilton, while cherry, mahogany, and antique oak predominate in the woods used for the furniture… Every precaution has been taken against fire and other accidents… in the corridor of each floor is a large fire gong and appliances for extinguishing flames…" (The Franklin Square Hotel, Streets of Washington, March 12, 2010, accessed at http://www.streetsofwashington.com /2010/03/franklin-square-hotel.html.)

[114] *Evening Star*, March 27, 1896, p 3. In his will, he left twelve thousand dollars each to his sons, smaller sums to his sisters Hannah Kinney and Mary A. Murphy, some to the church, and the rest to his wife. (PA Wills and Probate Records, 1683-1993, Phila Will No 529, 1896, accessed at Ancestry.com.)

[115] *Evening Times*, Sept 15, 1896, p 5; *Inquirer*, Nov 1, 1896, p 18. (Place of death the Hotel Stratford; date October 30, 1896.)

[116] *Washington Times*, March 27, 1896, p 2.

[117] *The Times*, March 30, 1896, p 4; the *Evening Star*, March 27, 1896, pp 3 and 6. The services were at St. Aloysius Church in the capital; his body was then sent to Philadelphia for burial in New Cathedral Cemetery.

[118] *Evening Times*, March 27, 1896, p 2; *Evening Star* March 30, 1896, p 3; *The Times*, March 30, 1896, p 4.

[119] *Evening Star*, April 11, 1896, p 17.

4. Mary Ann Carvin

Dennis Murphy and Mary Ann Carvin were nearly the same age. Both were Irish Catholics; both were the oldest children of immigrants who called themselves weavers. Both their families had come from New York and now lived just blocks apart in Kensington. Yet two lives could hardly be more different. Dennis was privileged, well-schooled, well-connected, and much celebrated.

Mary Ann was not.

In 1848, Elizabeth Stanton and Lucretia Mott organized a convention in Seneca Falls, New York, producing a document modeled after the Declaration of Independence: "We hold these truths to be self-evident: that all men and women are created equal..." But the Declaration was only a declaration, more dream than law. Typical of the women of her day (especially women of poorer families), William and Mary Carvin's daughter was not well known in Philadelphia, in Washington, or anywhere else outside of home. Recorded history barely mentions her.

Born in New York on May 20 (probably 1832), she was called Ann to distinguish her from her mother.[1] Ann was followed by siblings born when she was three, six, ten, and twelve (about the time the family arrived in Kensington), then two more when Ann was fourteen and eighteen. So there was always a baby that required attention. Ann did not attend school; she was needed at home to cook, sew, wash clothes, clean house and care for younger siblings. She could neither read nor write.[2] When she was about twenty, she herself became pregnant by George Austin, son of a well-to-do widow who had no intention of abandoning his Presbyterian faith. He agreed to marry her on the condition the wedding be at the First Presbyterian Church, right around the corner from St. Michael's.[3]

Ann's church forbade marriage in a Presbyterian Church: it was non-sacramental, so not blessed by God and therefore of no effect. (To be sanctified in the eyes of God, the ceremony had to be performed by a Catholic priest.) Any woman who would take a man as her husband without the sacrament was a woman willing to live in sin. But being with child, Ann was already a fallen woman in the eyes of her church, so on February 1, 1853, she married George at the First Presbyterian Church of Kensington.[4] Apparently, love (or necessity) mattered more to Ann than religious theory. Their first son, John, was born a few months later.[5]

Ann's disobedience cost her the ability to attend mass and to receive her church's holy communion, not to mention eternal damnation (unless she acknowledged the sinfulness of the marriage and repented of it). Going to First Presbyterian thereafter must have strained her relationship with her parents.

Ann continued to bear children: son John was followed by son George in 1856, followed by daughter Mary Emma in 1859. Meanwhile, Ann's mother Mary continued to bear children of her own: her sons Joseph, George and Charles were born about the same time as Ann's children; mother and daughter were nursing their children practically side by side. And by 1860, in addition to raising her own three children (and whatever help she may have provided in the care of the younger siblings her mother kept producing), Ann earned extra money watching the three-year-old child of a neighbor.[6] Her life, one might conclude, was all about children.

George stopped shaping pots and joined his brothers in the brass foundry business; brass spickets were used in kegs and barrels for liquids of all sorts, and for a time, the Austin family business did well at it. At some point during the late 1850's, not only George, but even Ann's brothers, Thomas and James, worked there.[7]

But then came the war. When Ann was pregnant with her fourth child, she learned that her brother James had been killed. Her mother died that November. Days later, her brother Thomas was arrested. Weeks after that, her father died. With both parents now dead, Ann was left to decide where her younger siblings, now orphaned, would live.

There were seven of them. Catherine, Mary and Elizabeth were old enough to fend for themselves, but the four younger boys – the oldest of them not yet fourteen – were a different story.[8] With four children of her own, taking her siblings in would be all but impossible. But none of the local orphanages would be able to take all four boys together.[9] The children were having to deal with the loss of both parents. Separation from each other at such young ages was unthinkable. So Ann convinced George to take all her younger siblings in. The Austin house became home to ten children, eight of them age 13 and younger: Ann's own – John (12), George (8), Mary Emma (5), and Thomas (newborn) – and her four youngest brothers, William (13), Joe (10), George (9) and Charles (6).[10]

Some situations simply speak for themselves.

The loss of two of her children likely caused Ann to cherish those who survived even more.[11]

By 1865, J. & S. Austin & Bro. was taking on new partners; by 1869, it occupied two lots back to back.[12] But by 1867, there was a falling out. Leaving his brothers' brass business for good, George moved Ann, their children, and her younger siblings out of the familiar neighborhood in Old Kensington to a newer neighborhood about a mile to the north, near Diamond Street, west of Norris Square. In the 1870 Census, he declared himself a general laborer. He never worked in his family's brass business again.

There in the new neighborhood, Ann gave birth to another daughter, Ida.[13] By 1870, her son John and her three younger brothers were all contributing to the household income, while her husband George was listed in the Census as a laborer, probably explaining why he wasn't listed in the directory for the next several years. Ann's hard life as a caregiver to the younger children continued, but perhaps with their help, she may have finally learned to read and write.[14] George got work as a teamster beginning in 1878 – perhaps driving a horse-drawn streetcar – and through that employment, likely met fellow teamster Thomas Smiley, who married their daughter, Mary Emma. The Austins and Smileys lived together for several years.[15] Then, in 1884, George died, leaving Ann with no husband, no pension, no history of earnings, and no marketable career skills.[16] Ann managed to keep the house for years to come, sharing the house with her son-in-law. It became her family's hub. She raised daughter Ida there until Ida married in 1887, and Ida and her husband moved into the house across the street.[17] And when her daughters bore children – at least six of them between 1880 and 1892 – Ann found herself helping care for their infants too.[18]

Nor was it only the children Ann cared for. When her brother Thomas needed someone to care for him in the early 1890's, Ann filled the need. For several years – probably until 1897, when he found another wife to care for him – she kept house for Thomas, cooking, cleaning, and laundering his clothes.[19] Ann then moved in with her daughter, now Ida Morris; soon after, her son George joined them.[20] And in 1910, when Ann was nearing 80, she lived with son George, just around the corner.[21]

While nothing is known about Ann's life apart from the bare skeleton just recounted, it's clear she was a caregiver and a unifier; she held her family together, making her life in Philadelphia the best she was able to make it. Her influence on her younger siblings was surely substantial. When she died of apoplexy at St. Joseph's Hospital on December 7, 1911, the newspapers took no notice of her death. The official certificate – based on information from her son-in-law – got the name of her father wrong. She was buried with her late husband at the Oddfellows Cemetery.[22]

Beyond that, everything is speculation. But we can be excused, perhaps, if we wonder what she thought of life in Philadelphia. She'd been twelve when the rocks were thrown, when the Nanny Goat Market rang with cannon fire, when men were shot and St. Michael's Church was turned to rubble. We can wonder what she thought of the civil war that took the life of her brother James, or of the shell shock that addled Thomas's brain, making him all but another child for her to look after. Or of the church that had thrown her out for conceiving new life, or of the men her husband and Tom Smiley picked up and dropped off from their streetcars in the city of brotherly love. And we can't help but wonder what she thought of all the babies she raised, and what her hopes were for the sort of futures they might have.

Notes on Chapter 4, Mary Ann Carvin

[1] The month and day, May 20th, are from her Pennsylvania Death Certificate, No 118653, dated December 7, 1911. Her death certificate gives the year of her birth as 1825, but the informant on the certificate, her son-in-law Thomas G. Morris, seems unreliable as a source for an event so many decades earlier. Censuses consistently gave her birthplace as New York, not Ireland, but it doesn't seem her father had immigrated to New York as early as 1825. The 1840 Census of her father's household (U.S. Census, NY Ward 16, p 181) includes two young girls, one (likely Catherine) under age 5 and the other (likely Mary Ann) between 5 and 10; if that Census was accurate, Ann was born between 1830 and 1835. The 1900 Census gives her birthdate as May of 1832, an assertion accepted here because more specific than years suggested by other censuses and most consistent with other information, including the birth dates of her siblings.

[2] The conclusion that Ann did not attend school is based on the assertion in the 1860 Census (when Ann was likely 28, though listed as 26) that she could neither read nor write (1860 U.S. Census, Phila Ward 17, Fam 660). Arguably contrary is the 1880 Census, in which boxes to be checked if a person could not read or write were left blank (1880 U.S. Census, Phila, Dist 365, Fam 4). Perhaps, Ann had taught herself to read and write in the interim.

[3] The 1850 and 1852 City Directories show Mary Ann Austin living on Hope Street, below Master, putting her house three short blocks west of the Carvins at Frankford Av below Master. The 1850 U.S. Census, Kensington Ward 6, Fam 782, lists Mary Ann Austin, age 49, as a head of household owning $1500 in real estate; her son John, age 21, as a brassfounder; daughter Catherine, age 18; son George, a 17-year-old potter; son Samuel, a 15-year-old brassfounder. Mrs. Austin's real estate was more than the worth of her simple residence; perhaps it included a business property, likely inherited from her late husband.

[4] Historic Pennsylvania Church & Town Records, Historical Society of Pennsylvania, lists the Feb 1 1853 marriage between Mr. George Austin and Miss Ann "Cravan" [sic].

[5] The conclusion that Ann and George conceived their first child prior to the wedding is based on the February 1 1853 date of marriage, and census records that point to the birth of their son John during the first half of that year. (The 1870 Census shows him as 15, but the ages in that part of the census are skewed towards multiples of five, suggesting unreliability. The 1880 Census records his age as 26 as of June 1, suggesting birth between June 1, '53 and May 31, '54, based on which conception could have occurred before or after the marriage. But the 1860 Census, Phila Ward 17, Fam 660, enumerated June 13, 1860 (the closest census in time), shows him already seven years old, indicating he was born between June 13, 1852, and June 12, 1853 – in which case clearly conceived out of wedlock.)

[6] Likely years of birth for Ann's children were John (1853), George (1856), and Mary Emma Austin (1859), and for her mother's children, Joseph (1854), George (1855) and Charles (1858) Carvin. At the time of the 1860 Census, living with Ann and George were three of their own children (John, 7, George, 4 and Emma, 1) and a neighbor's child, three-year-old James Hamilton (1860 U.S. Census, Phila Ward 17, Fam 658 and 660).

[7] One advertisement under Brass Founders in Philadelphia's 1869 Business Directory said the proprietor made "every description of steam, water, and gas cocks, whistles, oil cups and gauge cocks, water gauges, etc …" as well as "brass castings made to order." George's brothers may have built up a business started by their father (1850 U.S. Census, Phila, Kensington Ward 6, Fam 783). When James and Thomas Carvin joined the Army in 1861, each gave his occupation as a brass worker. City Directory listings for the Austins over the years are as follows:

  1850: Mary Ann Austin, Hope bel Master
  1852: Mary Ann Austin and John Austin, brass founder, Hope bel Master.
  1855: John Austin, brass founder, 136 New Market
  1857: John Austin, brass founder, 400 N 3rd

1859: John Austin, brass founder, living at 720 N 3rd

1860: The Directory lists all three Austin sons (John, George, and Samuel) as brass founders, and under "Brass Founders and Manufacturers." the Business Directory lists "J & S Austin & Bro" at 1227 N Front Street. (The "& Bro." part of the name confirms that George was last to join his brothers in the business.) The residential directory lists George living at Howard near Master, and the Census (Phila Ward 17, Fam 660) lists him as a "brass spicket maker."

1861: Geo Austin, brass founder and brass cock maker, living at 1347 Howard and working at 1227 N Front.

1863: John Austin, brass founder, living at 720 N 3rd, and Samuel Austin, brass spigot maker, at 610 Thompson

1865: "John Austin & Co. (George Gilbach, Godfrey Metzger and John Austin)" listed as "brasscockmanufrs" at 1242 Hope (which may be same address as 1852's "Hope bel Master"); John Austin, "brasscockmaker" living at 1232 Howard, while George Austin, founder, working at 1242 Hope, is living at 1347 Howard (across street from brother John).

1866: "John Austin & Co" (w partners Gilbach & Metzger), brasscock manufacturers, at 1242 Hope; John Austin, brass cock maker, living at 1232 Howard; George Austin, brass founder, living at 1347 Howard.

1867: "John Austin & Co, Brass Founders," at 1238 Hope, listed under Brass Founders in the Business Directory; John Austin living at 1232 Howard, George Austin, brasscock maker, living at 1345 Howard.

1868: George Austin, brass finisher, and William Carvin, sawyer, both listed in new neighborhood further northwest, at 2043 N 7th.

1869: "J. Austin & Co" listed in 1869 Business Directory in old neighborhood, at both 1242 Hope and 1241 Howard (back-to-back addresses).

1870 Census: George Austin house at 2123 Leithgow, w 4 Carvin children (7 min walk from 2043 N 7th). George's occupation listed as laborer.

1871 - 1874 Directories: no obvious Geo Austin households …

1872: "Austin & Mousley," brass founders, at 1241 Howard; John Austin, brassfounder, living at 1306 Howard.

1873: Wm Carvin (age 23) at York & Mascher.

1875: John Austin, brass founder, at 1230 Howard; George Austin household and Wm Carvin at 2122 N 5th Street, very close to 1870 address at 2123 Leithgow.

1877: Geo Austin still at 2122 N 5th. Jimmy Carvin, in his early 20's, listed still living with Austins there.

1878: Now George Austin, driver, and Wm Carvin, cooper, are at 2106 N 5th while Geo Carvin, Cooper, is at 2027 Emerald and Jimmy Carvin (w/o h) is at 2139 Emerald. A very short move for George Austin.

1879: Geo Austin still at 2106 N 5th. Geo Carvin close at 2017 Orianna, Jimmy now at 2137 Emerald.

1880 Census: Geo Austin (occ: Teamster) family at 2111 N 5th St. (Short move across the street). Now including Emma and Thomas Smiley family. Directory lists George as "carman" at same address.

1881: Geo Austin, driver, at 2111 N 5th St.

1882: Geo Austin, driver, at 2111 N 5th St. His son, John Austin, now bartender at 2401 N Front.

1883: Geo Austin, driver, at 2111 N 5th St. His son, John Austin, bartender at 2401 N Front.

1884: Geo Austin, driver, at 2111 N 5th St. His son, John Austin, bartender at 2401 N Kensington (same as 2401 N Front).

1885: George now deceased. His son, John Austin, bartender at 2400 N Kensington. Widow Ann is not listed, but her son-in-law, Thomas Smiley, driver, is still listed at 2111 N 5th St, so she surely remained there as well.

1886 - 1890: Son-in-law Thomas Smiley, driver, listed at 2111 N 5th St.

1890: Son-in-law Thomas G. Morris, printer, who married daughter Ida in 1887, now listed across the street at 2112 N 5th.

1891: Thomas G. Morris, weaver, a block away at 2330 Lawrence; Ann's brother Thomas Carvin now a bartender at 2425 Mutter; but no Austin relations are left at 2111 N 5th St.

1892: Ann Austin, widow of George, listed at 2425 Mutter Street, with brother Thomas Carvin.

1893 - 1898: Ann Austin listed in no directories. Unclear when it was that she moved in with her daughter Ida Morris again – perhaps when brother Thomas remarried in 1897.

1899: Ann Austin, widow of George, and Thomas G Morris, fireman, both listed at 1614 N 27th St

1900 Census: Ann Austin, age 68, living with her daughter Ida, son-in-law Thomas Morris (fireman), and son George (driver) at 1614 27th Street

1902: Thos Morris, inspector, at 1624 N 28th

1905: Thos G Morris, inspector, at 2831 Oxford (right around the corner from 1624 N 28th)

1908: Thos G Morris, assessor, at 2831 Oxford

1910: Thos. G. Morris at 2831 Oxford Street. Census: Thos is a city court magistrate. Ann living with son George at 1609 N 27th St.

[8] Ann's sisters, Catherine, Mary and Elizabeth, were twenty-eight, nineteen and seventeen in 1863. An unmarried Catharine Carvin is listed in the 1868 City Directory at 46 Norfolk Street, far out in West Philadelphia, but assuming that was Ann's sister, it's the last we know of her. (A Catharine Carvin was working as a domestic in a home on New York's Park Avenue in the 1870 Census, and another died in Philadelphia on January 10, 1886. Whether either of these Catherine's was Ann's sister is speculative.) Ann's sister Mary married a James McIlvaine and will be considered again in Chapter 8, but after 1864, she disappeared from the historical record. No mention is found of Elizabeth Carvin after the 1860 Census. Perhaps her sisters took the names of husbands; perhaps they left Philadelphia; perhaps they worked themselves into early graves. The only reason anything is known about Mary Ann herself stems from the fact that she and George took in her younger Carvin siblings after she was married; were it not for Census records establishing that relationship, her 1853 marriage to George Austin, and the taking of his name, would have effectively erased her from historical memory altogether.

[9] The local orphanages were St. Joseph's Asylum, St. Vincent's Home for Destitute Infant Children, and Girard "College." As one example of the limitations, Girard would only take "poor white male orphans between the ages of six and ten." (Holly Caldwell, "Orphanages and Orphans," Encyclopedia of Greater Philadelphia, accessed at https://philadelphiaencyclopedia.org/archive/orphanages-and-orphans/; also, "Girard College Civil Rights Landmark Historical Marker," at http://explorepahistory.com/hmarker. php?markerId=1-A-369.)

[10] See more in Chapter 10.

[11] The 1900 Census indicates that Ann had six children, of whom only four were still living that year. (1900 U.S. Census Phila Ward 29, Dist 0750, Fam 47). Her children John (1852-1929), George (1856-1910), Mary Emma (1859-1937) and Ida (1869-1917) all survived well past 1900, so it is apparent that Ann had another child, likely born in the 1860's who had passed away by the time of the 1870 Census; and that Thomas Austin, listed as age six in the 1870 Census, also passed away, apparently prior to the 1880 Census.

[12] The company became "John Austin & Co," brasscock manufacturers, at 2242 Hope Street; its principals were George Gilbach, Godfrey Metzger and John Austin. The business was still at that location in 1872, when a new partner made the firm name Austin & Mousley.

[13] Ida was born in April of 1869. (See 1900 Census, Phila Ward 29, Dist 750, Fam 47.)

[14] The 1870 Census in Philadelphia was so flawed that President Grant ordered a second enumeration. The obvious errors and discrepancies between the two enumerations require resort to other sources of information to determine the real Austin household. For example, the first enumeration lists two George Carvins in the house – one was clearly George Austin. Since one's age was given as 13 and the other as 14, the two were clearly confused. (Compare 1870 U.S. Census, Phila Ward 19 Dist 58, Fam 243, to 1870 U.S. Census, Phila Ward 19 Dist 58 (2d enum), Dwelling 2128.) What emerges is that Ann's brother William, now probably twenty, worked as a sawyer; her son John, eighteen, as an apprentice to a plumber; her brother Joe, sixteen, in a cotton factory; and her brother George, thirteen, driver of a horse and wagon. By the time of the 1880

Census, Ann may have learned to read and write, as there are no boxes checked on the Census form indicating inability to do either).

[15] For the 1879 or 1880 marriage, see the 1900 U.S. Census Phila Ward 31 Dist 800 Fam 140, indicating Thomas and Emma had been married twenty years. After renting in the new neighborhood, moving across 5th street above Diamond at least twice, George appears in the 1880 Census as head of the household at 2111 N 5th Street (See 1880 Census Phila Dist 365, Fam 4). Mary Emma and Thomas Smiley lived with them, as did son John, daughter Ida, Ann's younger brother William Carvin, and a boarder they took in. George and Thomas Smiley both worked as teamsters, John as a bar tender, and William as a cabinet maker.

[16] George Austin died on July 20, 1884 (Phila Death Certificate, FHL No 1003710.) He was buried in the Oddfellows Cemetery.

[17] Ida married Thomas G. Morris on February 7, 1887 (*Inquirer*, Feb 9, 1887, p 5).

[18] Emma Austin Smiley gave birth to a son, Thomas W. Smiley Jr., in 1880; to a son, George, in 1882; and to a daughter Mabel, in 1888 (1900 U.S. Census Phila Ward 31 Dist 0797 Fam 45 at 2181 East Tucker St, and Phila Ward 31 Dist 0800 Fam 140 at 2614 Coral Street.) Ida Austin Morris gave birth to a son William in 1887; to a daughter Anna May in 1890; and to a daughter Florence Isabelle in 1892 (1900 U.S. Census Phila Ward 29 Dist 0750 Fam 47 at 1614 N 27th St).

[19] Despite Thomas's unpredictable post-war behaviors (see Ch 8), Ann lived with her brother on Mutter Street, above York, in 1892 and thereafter. She may also have lived with him at 1230 Hope Street in 1890, and on Mutter in 1891, though (as a woman) she was not listed in the Directory in those years. Only the 1892 City Directory lists both Anna Austin and Thomas Carvin living at the same address – 2425 Mutter Street – but the 1891 through the 1896 Directories all list Thomas living in the 2400 block of Mutter Street (north of York), first at 2425, then at 2427, then at 2429, then back to 2427. As is often the case, apparent moves to such contiguous addresses may have been more a matter of mistake, or settling on appropriate numbers, than physical movement from one home to another. It being uncommon for the directories to list women unless they were heads of their own households or maintaining a business, and there being no evidence of Ann Austin living elsewhere, the likeliest scenario is that Ann kept house for Thomas from 1891 or 1892 until 1897, or that she lived with one of her daughters. If Thomas's common-law wife Mary lived with them for any of this time, she may have been ill, as she died in March 1897.

[20] Ann, widow of George, appears in the 1899 Directory at 1614 N 27th St, same address as her son George and as her son-in-law, Thomas G. Morris. She is listed in the 1900 Census as a part of their household (Phila Ward 29, Dist 750, Fam 47 at 1614 27th Street, household of fireman Thomas G Morris.) See also Directory of 1900 under Ann Austin and Thomas G Morris. Ann presumably moved to the next block with the Morrisses (directory listing for Thomas Morris at 1624 N 28th St) in 1902, and again around the corner with them (directory listing for Thomas Morris at 2831 Oxford) in 1905. It appears that Thomas progressed from being a fireman (1899-1900) to being an inspector (1902-1905), an assessor (1908) and a magistrate (1910).

[21] George Austin and his mother Mary were listed in the 1910 U.S. Census, Phila Ward 29, Dist 0678, as Fam 103 at 1609 27th St.

[22] 1911 PA Death Certificate for Mary Ann Austin, No 118653. The certificate gave the informant as Thomas G. Morris, 2831 Oxford St., whom the Directory now listed as being of Morris and Wagner, a magistrate's office. The certificate incorrectly gave her father's name as James Morrow (her mother's maiden name).

5. Edward V. Murphy

Edward Murphy, fifth of eight children, third of five sons, born February 15, 1843,[1] was technically a middle child, but from the beginning, he felt destined to be a leader. He grew up hearing the accomplishments of his older brothers, Dennis and James. He could not remember the 1844 riots or even their immediate aftermath, but his parents and older brothers talked about them as if they defined the world. (He'd missed something important by not having been there to witness them.) At the Master Street School, his teachers remembered his brothers with pride. By the time their father was elected to Common Council, it was clear that great things were expected of him, yet equally clear that he could never surpass the bar they'd set for his success. So when he was admitted to Central High School in February of 1856, he was only doing what was expected. He studied phonographic reporting, like his older brothers. And when he graduated from Central at the age of seventeen, his brother Dennis, in his twelfth year of reporting for the U.S. Senate, made sure he was introduced to the powerful men there.[2] But Edward knew he would always be in his brothers' shadows unless he found some calling of his own.

He'd spent a lot of time with his two younger brothers, Joseph and Dominick, Jr. He'd been their natural leader, for the attention and respect adults gave his older brother, Edward got only from them. Respected as they were, his older brothers were small of stature; Edward was a giant by comparison. And his confident, sociable nature led him in a different direction than the one they'd followed.

> Mr. Ed Murphy was entirely unlike his brothers. They were rather small men; he was considerably above normal height. They seldom had anything to say to anybody, and when they had, generally put it in the fewest possible words. Ed was genial and sociable, with a talent for story-telling and recitations which he liked to exercise.[3]

He was easy to notice. Geniality often made him the center of attention. With no shortage of self-confidence, he chomped at the bit to prove himself more than a mere younger version of his brothers.

Still, after graduating from Central, Edward went to Washington, moving into Mrs. Holmead's boarding house with his older brothers. The plan – not so much of his own making as something fate had arranged for him – was to join them in their reporting for the Senate.[4] (It was either that or go to work for his father in the textile mill, and he definitely didn't want to be hidden in that shadow.) But Edward didn't find himself rubbing elbows with Steven Douglas or Charles Sumner; he wasn't allowed to listen to the great debates his older brothers did. He found himself confined to the reporter's room, transcribing his brothers' notes in longhand when Dennis or James brought them in, or reading them aloud for transcription by others. Getting little practice with his pen, he never achieved his brothers' speed at phonographic writing. And so, behind the scenes at the Capitol, his desire for greatness went unfulfilled.

The approaching war promised more drama and glory than anything in the stuffy chambers of Congress, but as much as war attracted him, he couldn't see himself loading and firing on command, marching shoulder to shoulder, the way other boys were being trained to do. Edward was accustomed to standing out. Maybe, if he could see the war up close, he could use his reporting skills to tell whatever story he saw in it. From Dennis, he secured an introduction to General Winfield Scott. That introduction and his reporter's credentials were enough that Scott gave him a pass, and with it, he followed the army into Virginia. There, in July of 1861, he witnessed the Battle of Bull Run first-hand, watching General Beauregard humiliate the Yankees, making boys in blue turn and run by the thousands.[5] He wrote first class battle reports, telling of the action in prose he was proud of. But when his stories were printed in the D.C. and Philadelphia newspapers, they did not bear his name. Getting no credit for his work, he questioned its value.

And so Edward looked about for some other way to make his mark in life. He didn't see himself gaining influence by silent service to powerful men; he dreamed of *being* a powerful man. He was tall, after all. Good looking. (Vain.) Ambition gave birth to political aspirations.

A fellow reporter would later put it this way:

> [A]n irrepressible conflict was impending, and the country was on the verge of a mighty revolution... It was in such tumultuous times that [Edward] entered upon his career in life. They were times of high excitement, not adapted to study and reflection, when men were governed by their prejudices and their passions... At the age of seventeen he made his first public political speech and for several years following took an active part in every political campaign in his State. His position gave him an opportunity of becoming familiar with the great men of the day, of studying the political history of the country, and opened up to his ambitious eyes the hope of entering political life and securing popular favors.[6]

Philadelphia's 1862 elections were especially divisive.[7] Faithful to his family's politics, Edward campaigned for Democrats, but in the face of

Republican appeals to patriotism, the Democrats lost their municipal races.[8] They hoped that at least their candidate for Congress, John Kline, would win in the Third Congressional District, which included the Democratic strongholds of the 17th and 19th Wards (old Kensington). Edward's father being the recent Councilman from the 17th Ward, Murphy support was important to Kline's race, and on Wednesday, the day after the election, the Murphys had cause to celebrate, as Kline had won by a vote of 8200 to 8148.[9] However, that Friday, the judges of the Board of Return ruled that Kline had in fact lost; that his Republican opponent, Leonard Myers, had won the seat in Congress. Kline's people objected, claiming that the tally sheets – on which Kline totals had been crossed out and new numbers inserted that switched votes to Myers – constituted clear evidence of fraud. However, stating that they had no authority to consider claims of fraud, the judges ruled Myers the winner.[10] Republican Governor Andrew Curtain certified Myers' victory, and the Republican House of Representatives awarded him the Congressional seat. As young Edward Murphy saw it, the world was not only divided, it was also profoundly corrupt. But there was a valuable lesson to be learned, for one inclined to learn it. By comparison to the brutality of Mayor Conrad's police force and to the armed conflict now underway over slavery, tampering with votes may have seemed a more civilized form of exercising power.

Edward read law in a Philadelphia law office and at the Columbus University of Washington. In addition to his Senate work and legal studies, he corresponded for various newspapers "during several important political campaigns."[11] He also found time to marry, taking a young, well-to-do German bride by the name of Cecelia Haas.[12]

The descriptions of Edward's political career that have come down to us were based on assertions by Murphy himself. They may, therefore, reveal less about him than about what he thought of himself. Consider the following laudatory account from *Browne's Phonographic Monthly*, written by a man who wasn't there, a dozen years after the events it describes:

> Before he was 22 years of age, the candidate of his party for Congress being ill, almost the entire conduct of the campaign in his district in Pennsylvania devolved on Mr. Murphy, and, though the candidate was defeated, he polled a much larger vote than had ever before been cast on that side.[13]

In fact, Edward's efforts fell far short of such success. The Democratic candidate for Congress in the election of 1864 was Charles Buckwalter, seeking to take the seat that had been awarded to Leonard Myers in 1862. The assertion made in the article was technically correct – Buckwalter did get more votes than ever before – but the increase was entirely due to population growth in the 3rd Congressional District; his Republican opponent also received more votes. In fact, this time around, Murphy's man was defeated by a larger percentage margin than Kline had been two years earlier, 10,793 to 10,129.[14] But the account had come from Edward himself, and he could tell it any way he wanted.

The biographical sketch of Edward continued singing his praises:

> Two years later... though he had not attained the age requisite for a Representative in Congress, he was offered a large complimentary vote for that position in the nominating convention with a view of bringing him forward for the following election, when he would have been eligible. This compliment he declined in order to secure the unanimous nomination of a friend who had borne the brunt of many hotly contested campaigns.[15] He was twice urged by delegates in legislative conventions to accept a nomination for the Legislature in a district where a nomination was equivalent to an election, but he declined the honor.[16]

By that account, the man otherwise said to have ardent political ambitions was repeatedly doing the "honorable" thing by foregoing them.* At the same time, perhaps more objectively, the article described Edward's "impulsive and ardent nature," and his "mercurial temperament that rose and fell with the waves of the commotion that surged around him." One has to wonder if those "urging" Edward to seek office intended to honor him as much as he perceived.

A mercurial temperament, in any case, was more than enough for Dennis to keep him in the reporter's room, assisting from behind the scenes, rather than putting him out on the Senate floor. We can easily believe the assertion in *Browne's* biographical sketch that Edward "found more delight in listening to the arguments and rhetoric of the great debaters than in assisting in the drudgery of transcribing their utterances." But being out on the floor, listening to the debates himself, was not what Dennis assigned him to do. And given Edward's ambitions, "it is not surprising that he developed more love for the rostrum and public honors than for the untiring and herculean labors of the reporting profession."[17] For whatever reasons, Dennis assigned him to the very tasks that bored him. Ultimately, whether his political opportunities were genuine or creatures of his own self-image makes little difference: either way, Edward wanted more fulfilling ways to follow his dreams.

---

* The writer for the *Phonographic Monthly,* a dozen years later, must have relied on Edward himself as his source. The idea that Edward was urged to accept a nomination that would guarantee him election but "declined the honor" seems inconsistent with all else we know about him. According to the same source, Edward was "reluctantly compelled to abandon his legal studies" because of "the pressure of professional duties." But did he really discontinue his study reluctantly? The same source elsewhere credibly described Edward as having "more taste and talent for acquiring knowledge from men and the world about him than from books." That, too, may have contributed to his abandoning his legal studies.

In addition to his work for the Senate, in 1865, he got a Master's degree and was appointed private secretary to James B. Fry, the U.S. Army's Provost Marshal General.[18] The duties of the Provost included the arrest of deserters, spies, draft dodgers and disloyal civilians – an odd role for someone whose entire family, including Edward himself, had managed to avoid military service. But in April of 1865, his duties as secretary to Fry put him squarely, at last, in the limelight he loved.

The President's assassination was just the sort of drama to which Edward had long been attracted. As it turns out, the Provost's office was charged with taking preliminary testimony from witnesses and with arresting conspirators. So as a part of his new job, Edward began taking such testimony. Then, when the Military Commission hired Pitman, Sutton, and Dennis Murphy as its official reporters to record the testimony at the trial of those accused of conspiring with John Wilkes Booth, Edward again assisted his brothers.[19]

He was still a young man at the time. Nearly fifty years later, when he was the last alive of those who'd been present for the proceedings, the country's continuing interest in the assassination and his own love for the spotlight led him to give an interview to a reporter for the *New York Times Magazine* about his role in the trial. Characteristically, he made sure to tell the story as highly dramatic tragedy. He began by setting the scene, describing the old Penitentiary building in which the prisoners were held and the proceedings conducted, pointing out that under it lay the body of Booth himself. He described the seating arrangement, the long hours of work put in by the reporters, and of course, the proceedings themselves, as he remembered them. Most importantly, he emphasized his conviction that in several cases, the evidence supported neither the verdicts nor the hangings that resulted. His 1916 analysis of the testimony, set forth in Appendix 2, puts his "ardent" nature on full display. *The Times Magazine* summed up his story this way:

> Hardly more than a boy at the time of the trial, Mr. Murphy firmly believed that a great injustice was being done; that lives were being unjustly forfeited to quest the thirst for vengeance which seemed to have taken possession of the entire country. Passing years have not dimmed Mr. Murphy's recollections of the trial, and he entertains today convictions as strong as those he felt in his youth... [O]f the eight persons tried for complicity in the murder of Lincoln, but two, he believed, should have paid the penalty of death. He said further that Mrs. Surratt went to her death on perjured testimony.[20]

The view that only two of the accused should have received the death penalty may simply reflect a common Democratic perspective; or Edward may have been a sensitive soul, loathe to impose death for any crime. But the claim that Mary Surratt was put to death on "perjured testimony" was a fascinating one, and it sheds much light on the kind of man that Edward was.

The testimony he claimed was perjured was that given against Mrs. Surratt by two witnesses – Lewis J. Weichmann and John Lloyd. In an odd twist of fate, one of them – Weichmann – was a person Murphy already knew well. Though born in Maryland, Lewis Weichmann had spent his youth in Philadelphia; in fact, he'd been a classmate of Murphy's at Central High School, where the two Catholic boys had become friends. But their one-time friendship would not survive the trial, and it would certainly not survive Murphy's accusation that Weichmann had perjured himself.

Weichmann testified that after leaving Central High School, he had met and befriended John Surratt; in 1864, he'd gone to live with John at the eight-room boarding house in Washington run by John's widowed mother, Mary Surratt. The Surratt family sometimes saw the famous actor, John Wilkes Booth, perform at the theater; in fact, John Surratt aspired to an acting career himself, and he had spoken to Booth about the prospect of performing with him in Richmond. Surratt's younger sister, Anna, had a photograph of Booth (quite a celebrity at the time) in her room. The famous actor sometimes visited the Surratt's boarding house, where he was alleged to have discussed a plot to abduct the President and others. Weichmann testified that he never heard such a plot discussed.[21]

Weichmann's circumstantial testimony against Mrs. Surratt would have posed no great problems for her had it stood alone.[22] Its real significance came from considering it together with the more damaging testimony of John Lloyd, who had rented the Surratt family tavern and farm in Surrattsville. In his crucial testimony against Mary Surratt, Lloyd contradicted himself repeatedly. He testified that some five or six weeks before the assassination, John Surratt had asked him to conceal two carbines, some ammunition and other items, saying he would come back for them in a few days; despite having earlier told investigators that Mr. Surratt had hidden the items between the joists under a room of the house, he had in fact hidden them there himself, with Surratt's help; the Monday before the assassination (later in the trial changed to Tuesday) he'd met Mrs. Surratt when their buggies crossed paths at Uniontown; she'd told him to get the things out (he was "not altogether positive" she had called them "shooting irons") since someone would be coming for them soon; on the day of the assassination, about 5 p.m., Mrs. Surratt was at the tavern when he returned; she gave him a package which he took upstairs and found to be field glasses (though on subsequent examination, he said he wasn't sure he took them upstairs, because he was quite under the influence of liquor at the time); Mrs. Surratt told him at the same time to get out the "shooting irons," as someone would be by later that evening to get them; he did retrieve two carbines from under the floor and put them in his bedroom; Booth and accused co-conspirator Herold then came by late that night, saying they'd shot the President and "For God's sake, make haste and get them things" (first, Lloyd testified that Booth had made the statement; then, that Herold had made it); when he was first questioned about knowledge of Booth or the conspirators the following day, he denied any knowledge of their activities, and denied that the two men had come by the prior night, for fear of recriminations by the conspirators; four days after the assassination, he was arrested and accused of being a part of the conspiracy himself; only the day after his arrest did he first tell the authorities certain parts of the story he now described, implicating the Surratts; and in the course of the week, spanning several conversations with different investigating officers, he only gradually told them more.[23]

Another witness, Mr. Lloyd's sister-in-law, Mrs. Emma Offutt, testified that on the day of the assassination, she had accompanied Mrs. Surratt to Surrattsville, that Mr. Lloyd was extremely drunk the evening of the assassination, and that Mrs. Surratt had given *her* the package that contained the binoculars, rather than giving it to Mr. Lloyd.[24]

Mrs. Surratt's attorney, Frederick Aiken, succeeded in getting Lloyd to admit that he'd been arrested and accused of complicity at first. He obtained an admission from an officer who'd held Lloyd prisoner that even after Lloyd was arrested and repeatedly questioned, he did not at first implicate Mrs. Surratt.[25] Mrs. Surratt's attorneys wanted to impeach the testimony of both Weichmann and Lloyd by offering proof that (1) they had southern sympathies themselves and were more aware of Booth and the plot than they let on, and (2) that after being arrested themselves, they'd only turned on the Surratts when forced by investigators to implicate others or face criminal charges themselves. But the military prosecutors repeatedly objected to these attempts to plumb the motives of the prosecution witnesses. Every time the military prosecutors objected to such questioning, the Court refused to allow it.

In this light, let's consider again the testimony of Murphy's boyhood friend, Lewis Weichmann. When Mrs. Surratt's attorneys attempted to inquire into Mr. Weichmann's motives for implicating the Surratts, what little testimony they were able to elicit went like this:

Q.   By whom were you called on first to give your testimony in this case?

A.   I was called on by the War Department.

Q.   What member of the War Department?

A.   I was called on by Judge Advocate Burnett, I believe.

Q.   Were you arrested?

A.   I surrendered myself up on Saturday morning at eight o'clock to Superintendent Richards, of the Metropolitan Police Force. I stated to him what I knew of Payne, Atzerodt and Herold visiting the house. I stated also what I knew of John Surratt; that I saw these men in private conversation.

Q.   What was your object in being so swift to give all this information?

A.   My object was to assist the Government.

Q.   Were any threats ever made to you by any officer of the Government in case you did not divulge?

A.   No, sir: no threats at all.

For reasons we shall see, Weichmann's testimony that he'd experienced "no threats at all" would loom large in Murphy's view that he'd perjured himself. Meanwhile, Weichmann proceeded to describe how, first thing Saturday morning, he had "turned himself in" to the Metropolitan police, told them what he knew, and (as he portrayed it) was so anxious to help the government that morning that he practically directed their investigation. Continuing to probe Weichmann's motives, Surratt's attorney continued:

Q.   Did you ever say to anyone, about the time or previous to your surrendering yourself to Superintendent Richards and going to the office of Colonel Burnett, that you were fearful of an arrest?

A.   I myself had a great deal to fear. Being in this house where these people were, I knew that I would be brought into public notice.

Q.   I am not asking what you had to fear—

A.   But as far as myself was concerned, as being cognizant of anything of this kind, I had no fears at all; for I was not cognizant. When I surrendered myself to the Government, I surrendered myself because I thought it was my duty…

Weichmann never admitted, at the trial, that he'd been arrested; he repeatedly emphasized how cooperative he'd been in helping the government build its case. Nor did he ever answer the question posed to him, whether he'd ever told anyone that he feared arrest. He simply said he had a lot to fear from his circumstances as a boarder "in this house where these people were."

Surratt's lawyers might be faulted for not insisting on direct answers to their questions, or for not calling other witnesses to prove their position. But given how the trial did play out, after the testimony by Weichmann and Lloyd, the only hope for Mrs. Surratt was to show that they were southern sympathizers with knowledge of Booth's plans, and that they were induced to save their own skins by giving the government evidence against the Surratts. And this being the case, any fair reading of the transcript of trial makes clear that the tribunal did not permit Mrs. Surratt's lawyers to pursue that line of questioning.

In the aftermath of the trial, arguments raged about the methods and conclusions of the Tribunal. On July 17, *The Washington Star* published a letter from Weichmann denying assertions that he'd perjured himself, had collected a substantial government reward for his testimony, and had been "placed in irons" and threatened by the Secretary of War.[26] Philadelphia's *Inquirer* of July 26, 1865 then devoted 80% of its front page to printing a more detailed, more impassioned rebuttal by Weichmann, who denied that he'd been "arrested as a conspirator," but went on to admit that he and others had been imprisoned – "committed as witnesses," as he put it – imprisonment, he said, being "merely the customary precaution on the part of the Government to secure a witness."[27] One of Mrs. Surratt's lawyers later wrote a magazine article explaining his belief that Weichmann and Lloyd had perjured themselves to escape accusations of conspiracy, and describing how the military court had deprived him of the right to impeach their credibility on that account.[28]

John Surratt, meanwhile, was never tried before the military tribunal, because he was in Canada at the time. But the government paid Weichmann to travel to Canada to get him.[29] And when he was finally tried before a civil court (where the rules of evidence were more strictly adhered to) there was a hung jury; John Surratt was never convicted of any crime.[30]

All of this has been the subject of many books for and against the fairness of the Tribunal, for and against the guilt of John and Mary Surratt. We needn't add to that debate here. What's pertinent to the Edward Murphy story is that he had more than the evidence brought forth at trial on which to base his conclusion that his boyhood friend, Lewis Weichmann, had perjured himself. Amazingly, his conclusion was also based on first-hand observations he himself had made shortly before the trial. Murphy, as it turns out, was not only a reporter at the trial, not only a boyhood friend of a critical witness, but also a potential impeachment witness himself! Specifically, Murphy – then personal secretary to the Provost Marshal General – had been going about his work in the War Department one morning soon after the assassination when he had occasion to visit Colonel Burnett's office. As Murphy described it many years later in the *New York Times Magazine*,

> Seated in the room, I observed my old schoolmate, Weichmann, whom I at once cordially greeted. Upon leaving, I was followed into the corridor by Colonel Burnett, who proceeded to question me about Weichmann, my relation with and my knowledge of him. Amazed at the character of the examination, I inquired the reason. Colonel Burnett replied: "You will learn in good time." The following morning in front of the White House I saw Weichmann in manacles being escorted by an armed guard of soldiers to the War Department. The next day I learned that he was charged with being in the conspiracy to murder the President.[31]

In other words, Murphy had seen Weichmann under arrest – in manacles, no less, and under an armed guard – and claimed he knew that Weichmann had been charged in the conspiracy. Yet Weichmann's testimony at trial was designed to suggest he had never been arrested, charged, or imprisoned; that in fact he had been a most helpful, entirely voluntary government witness. Murphy's startling later assertion about what he'd seen, before the trial, directly contradicted Weichmann's testimony given at the trial. Had Murphy testified to that effect in open court, it would have supported the claim that Weichmann could have fabricated his testimony to avoid prosecution. It certainly would have contradicted Weichmann's efforts to imply that he'd never been charged or arrested, and therefore, his general credibility.

On the other hand, it's hard to imagine a court reporter, absorbed in listening to testimony and taking shorthand notes of it, standing up in the middle of a trial and contradicting a witness on the stand from his own knowledge!*

And yet, strange as all that is, the relationship between Weichmann and Murphy had not yet fully played out, even then. Another encounter between Weichmann and Murphy occurred during a break in the proceedings. As Murphy later told the *New York Times*,

> I observed closely his testimony and the manner in which it was given, and became convinced that he was perjuring himself to save his own neck. When the daily recess for luncheon took place, after Weichmann had been on the stand all morning, he approached me and asked what I thought of his testimony. I replied that I was satisfied that he was falsely swearing away the life of an innocent woman, whom he had repeatedly told me he loved as a mother, in order to save his

---

* Did Murphy tell his brother Dennis what he'd seen? Did he tell Surratt's lawyers? If he'd offered to give up his reporting duties in order to become a witness, would the Tribunal have allowed him to? How it might have played out will never be known, as Murphy said nothing when it might have mattered.

own worthless carcass, and that I would hold no further communication with him.[32]

Weichmann's testimony was not yet over – he would later be called back to the witness stand. For a court reporter to accuse a witness of perjury in the middle of that witnesses' testimony goes far beyond the bounds of professional behavior. It certainly illustrates the "ardent" and "mercurial" temperament that convinced Edward's brothers it would be risky to have him reporting debates in the Senate. But making his accusation of perjury privately, to the witness – while *not* coming forward with what would have been crucial testimony on the record – is beyond baffling. It is most disturbing. Most shocking. Ironically, given Murphy's conclusion that Mrs. Surratt did not get a fair trial, the unfairest cut of all may have been his own failure to state, on the record in 1865, what he so ardently told the *New York Times Magazine* in 1916.[33]

Mrs. Surratt was hung with the others just outside the Penitentiary Building on July 7th. Weichmann's admission that he had in fact been "committed as a witness" and imprisoned before giving his testimony against Surratt was printed at the end of July. Murphy's work as private secretary to the Provost Marshal General continued until Congress reconvened on December 4, 1865, at which point he returned to reading and transcribing his brothers' phonographic notes of Senate proceedings. But oddly enough, the saga of Edward's dealings with Lewis Weichmann was not yet over. Unbeknownst to him at the time, Weichmann had been "rewarded" (Murphy's later word) for his testimony with a federal appointment (as clerk in the Philadelphia Custom House) by William B. Thomas, a Philadelphia businessman who'd been a founder of the Pennsylvania Republican party and (therefore not surprisingly) a Lincoln appointee.[34] Treasury Secretary Hugh McCullough, who'd approved Weichmann's appointment, was also a Republican and Lincoln appointee. Given the spoils system so prevalent at the time, it seems unthinkable that a radical Republican government would award a federal job to a man who served as an accomplice in the Lincoln assassination – unless it was, as Murphy claimed, a "reward" for his cooperation with prosecutors. Murphy clearly felt that way in the autumn of 1866 when he discovered Weichmann at the Philadelphia Custom House, in the employ of Collector William Johnston. What happened is best described in Murphy's own words:

> Passing through one of the offices in the Custom House during the brief incumbency of ex-Governor Johnston of Philadelphia as Collector,[35] I happened to see Weichmann there. On reaching the Collector's Office I expressed my surprise to him. Having been installed in office but a short time previous, [Johnston] had had no opportunity to acquaint himself with the personnel of the staff. He was amazed to

learn that Weichmann had found lodgment there, denounced him as a perjurer, and immediately sent a letter to Secretary of the Treasury McCullough removing Weichmann and nominating another in his stead.[36]

Once again, Murphy's statement omits much. Of his own knowledge, Johnston had no basis to consider Weichmann a perjurer; he could only have read about the claim in the newspapers, or from Murphy himself. One assumes that Murphy urged Johnston to dismiss Weichmann on account of it. In any case, according to Murphy, Johnston travelled to the capital, called on Secretary McCullough personally, and threatened to quit unless Weichmann was fired.[37] One can imagine how the Republican McCullough perceived the Democrat's demand that he fire a Lincoln appointee on the ground that he'd perjured himself – *due to over-reaching by the Republican government* – in the recent conspiracy trial. The government had put people to death on the basis of Weichmann and Lloyd's testimony. If government pressure had gotten them to perjure themselves, the government was responsible for an injustice of major scandalous proportion. One can imagine Johnston being thrown out of McCullough's office for such effrontery, but he was not. Rather, as a result of that-face-to face meeting, McCullough *did* approve Johnston's firing of Weichmann. The result seems utterly inexplicable[38] – unless Johnston was able to threaten McCullough with more than just his own resignation. The inference that the Democratic ex-Governor, Johnston, had some sort of dirt on Republican McCullough is hard to dismiss.[39]

The wrangling over Weichmann's appointment to a clerkship was not unusual, given the wrangling over other appointees, from cabinet members to tax collectors, that would soon lead to the President's impeachment.[40] Politicians naturally wanted to reward their supporters with government jobs, and their supporters expected such rewards. But the job of Port Collector was attractive even to men of great power and pre-existing wealth – men like Johnston (a successful lawyer and former Governor of Pennsylvania) and William Thomas (one of the wealthiest businessmen in Philadelphia). There were two possible reasons that such a job could attract a rich man. For one thing, the Collectors were not paid fixed salaries, but a percentage of taxes collected and fines imposed; such amounts could be large.[41] For another, there was the possibility of self-enrichment by (to call a spade a spade) graft.

Reports of corruption in federal office were popping up everywhere. Nashville's "Whiskey Frauds" had been in the papers even as Mary Surratt was hung. Ten Treasury Department officials had been arrested in New York for taking bribes. In May, 1866, a letter from Internal Revenue Commissioner Rollins to the First District Assessor in Philadelphia noted a "failure on the part of the Revenue Officers to exercise that vigilance which is called for in the suppression of fraud" and warned that "in any district in which these frauds continue, [the Secretary of the Treasury] will consider it his duty to see that such changes are made in the officers of the district as may give promise of greater energy and fidelity."[42] And only weeks before Edward Murphy discovered Weichmann in the offices of the Philadelphia Port Collector, fraud in tax collection was discovered in Philadelphia.[43]

For four years Dominick had been griping about the taxes he paid to pay for a war he'd never wanted. Whether it was Edward himself or some other member of the family, someone suggested that when it came to federal taxation, it might be smart to be a part of the system rather than merely subject to it.

The biographical sketch in Browne's called President Johnson "an old personal friend," [44] a bit of a stretch, probably based on a claim Edward himself had made. But there's little doubt that the President was familiar with the Murphy family, due to his years in the Senate with Dennis and the family's political support against the "Republican radicals." Given that history, it's not surprising that on December 21, 1866, the President appointed Edward to a key role in federal tax collection: the office of Superintendent of Exports and Drawbacks for the Port of Philadelphia.[45]

A Philadelphia Appointment.
Edward V. Murphy, for many years one of the Senate official reporters, was to-day appointed Superintendent of Exports at the port of Philadelphia, vice Deihl, removed.

Johnson's appointment of Murphy required Senate approval at a time when the Senate was rejecting nearly all the president's appointments. Yet it did confirm Edward for the Port job, ultimately (we can assume) due to Dennis Murphy's influence among Senate Republicans.[46] Father Dominick was pleased; but once again, Edward was in his older brother's debt.

The office of Superintendent existed only in major exporting cities; in smaller cities, the Superintendent's responsibilities were handled by the Port Collector himself. In a sense, the Superintendent was a sort of "Co-Collector." When Edward took the job in late December of 1866, his office was on Dock Street, a block east of the Custom House where the Port Collector had his office. And as we've seen, the Port Collector at the time was the former Pennsylvania Governor, William F. Johnston.[47] Christmas of 1866 must have been a happy one for the mercurial young Murphy. A great deal was going his way. He'd obtained an appointment to a potentially lucrative position. He'd ousted Weichmann from his clerk's job at the Custom House. And around his father's dinner table, he could at last talk about his own important office, rather than simple employment assisting his older brothers.

When the Tenure of Office Act went into effect at the beginning of March 1867, President Johnson's recess appointees all across the country were slated to lose their jobs.[48]

The result was mayhem. Office holders across the country scrambled to hold on. A piece published in the *Evening Telegraph* on March 4, the day the Act went into effect, was headlined A POLITICAL COMMOTION IN THE CITY – THE "TENURE OF OFFFICE" BILL PLAYS HAVOC WITH THE FEDERAL OFFICE-HOLDERS. Alliances, promises and understandings were traded hour by hour. Party affiliations, while important, may not have been as important as trust among men who'd cooperated with each other's pursuits of personal gain. For whatever reason, men went to great lengths to hold on to their tax collection jobs, even allying with members of opposing political parties to do so.[49]

Murphy's role in the March 1867 job-scrambling at the Port is not known.[50] But his own job's more lucrative potential may have been put in jeopardy by all the personnel changes it caused, especially once his friend and fellow Democrat William Johnston was out of the Port Collector job. Once Johnston was out, Johnston's Republican replacement restored Lewis Weichmann to his job there.[51] No man wants to work with someone he's accused of perjury and gotten fired. Even more, he doesn't want enemies around if he's entertaining thoughts of fraudulent income on the side.

Though often aimed at whiskey distillers, accusations of corruption also targeted other sorts of revenue collection. The *Evening Telegraph* took notice in July of "the amazing and recently discovered frauds on the Government" through the evasion or non-collection of taxes on a variety of articles, demanding that a thorough investigation be made."[52] Part of the problem was that corruption ran up the ranks, bottom to top: the following year, Internal Revenue Commissioner Rollins himself, along with other high-ranking Treasury Department Officials, were tried for their own complicity in the frauds.[53]

The duties of Edward's office as Superintendent of Exports and Drawbacks put him in a perfect position to commit fraud if he was so inclined. Drawbacks had been an important element of import taxation since the eighteenth century, when an importer, having paid a tax on imported goods, was eligible for a refund if he subsequently exported the goods.[54] The drawback concept had now been extended to the internal revenue taxes of 1862. To prevent the internal tax imposed on manufactured goods from encumbering exports, the law provided that an exporter could claim a refund, or "drawback," of the internal revenue tax he'd paid at the time of manufacture. The only proof required to support this drawback consisted of three documents: a certificate showing that the tax on manufacture had been paid, an affidavit providing details of the export, and a certificate from a Custom House clerk verifying that the goods had in fact been exported.[55]

Any tax collector could skim off the top of funds collected; any assessor could extract kickbacks from taxpayers in return for favorable treatment. Drawbacks provided a much simpler means of self-enrichment: a successful application for drawback resulted in the Treasury's issuance of a check to the claimant. Many such checks were made payable to "bearer." And all that was required to support such a claim were three pieces of paper.

Rumors of the New York drawbacks frauds reached Washington in the latter part of 1868, and testimony at the trial revealed the extent of the operation. "Conspirators so skillful were not likely to neglect the important point of having a friend in Washington," asserted one newspaper. That "friend in Washington" turned out to be a man who'd previously been in charge of the Treasury Department office responsible for auditing drawback allowances. "[S]o implicitly did the Johnsonian administration trust him that he was selected to ferret out the frauds, if any, and bring the perpetrators to justice."[56]

So: why was Edward Murphy appointed Superintendent of Exports and Drawbacks in the Port of Philadelphia? He had no background in taxation. He did have some legal training, but no license to practice law; and his real expertise was in shorthand reporting. Since he liked being at the rostrum, if he had sought the appointment because he wanted to eliminate corruption, we might expect to see him running for elected office; we might at least expect newspaper reports of speeches quoting him about his desire to eliminate corruption – but we find no such evidence. Since he sought the appointment just as the controversy between President Johnson and Congress was approaching the breaking point, just as other tax collection appointees (from both parties) were scrambling to keep their fingers in the action, it's hard to imagine why he wanted the office, unless it was for the money, fame, or power it might bring. As an admirer would later write, Edward's position gave him "almost unlimited facilities for making money."[57]

There is no evidence that Edward was corrupt. But to regularly pull off tax fraud, one needed a number of people to be involved – real or fictitious manufacturers (or exporters) to serve as claimants; real or fictious certificates from Treasury clerks, attesting both to the payment of tax and the fact of export; and Treasury officials with the power to approve (or the negligence to overlook) fraudulent claims. The New York operation had been exposed because one participant became disgruntled that his share of the proceeds was too small. Such an outcome would have been far less likely if everything were in the family.

Between father Dominick's business activities, brother Joseph's recent appointment as Assistant Assessor (see Chapter 7), and brother Dennis's role as clerk to the Retrenchment Committee, there were several Murphy family members available for such an endeavor. And Edward already had an ally in former Governor William Johnston, who now served (albeit briefly) both as Port Collector and as acting Revenue Collector in the First District. It was a perfect gang to engage in corruption for profit if they were so inclined.

President Johnson's appointment of Edward strengthened the Murphy family's political support for him: Dennis joined the Johnson Democratic and Conservative Club in D.C., and Edward took the rostrum as chairman of the Philadelphia County Democratic Convention.[58] But pressure to root out corruption was becoming stronger by the day. From a nearby desk in the Customs House, Lewis Weichmann scrutinized everything Edward did. In the spring of 1868, a Republican Senator introduced a bill to abolish the office of Superintendent of Exports and Drawbacks.[59] And in September, Edward lost his wife Cecelia. Edward decided that appointment to federal office had proven more volatile – and less glamorous – than he'd once imagined. Two weeks after Johnson's own party failed to renominate him for President, Edward resigned as Superintendent of Exports and Drawbacks.[60] According to the flattering biographical sketch in *Browne's Phonographic Monthly*, he left the job "poorer in pocket than when he entered it, though at that time, peculation and speculation were the order of the day."[61]

Perhaps, Edward had flown too close to the fire. When Secretary of the Interior Orville Browning offered him a position as Indian Superintendent for the Northern Superintendency, Edward turned it down.[62] Instead, in February of 1869, he willingly returned to work with his brothers at the *Globe*.[63]

Nothing had changed in the Senate reporting corps. "Edward did not attend most of the Senate sessions himself but, having mastered the reading of his older brothers' notes, he dictated their content to other phonographic amanuenses, who in turn, transcribed them in longhand."[64] It was nothing like the celebrity of running for political office, or even the power and potential income of being Superintendent of Drawbacks and Exports. But he may have resigned just in time. In 1871, New York's Boss Tweed began his fall from power over widespread bribery, frauds and kickbacks. In 1872, a large group of government officials, including Senators, Congressman, and Vice President Schuyler Colfax were exposed as having major roles in the Credit Mobilier scandal, in which wealthy men made enormous profits through fraud in the building of the Pacific Railroad.

The Senate still took long recesses. During them, Edward served as private secretary to southern Senator James L. Alcorn, reported the general convention of the Episcopal Church, and reported the Pennsylvania Constitutional Convention of 1873. [65] But back in the Senate, he had to stifle his ambition to be in the limelight. His work there remained in the shadow of his older brothers, reading and dictating their shorthand notes.[66] It was not the glorious life he'd envisioned. Jealous, even resentful of playing second fiddle to Dennis, he decided to marry a Canadian woman, one Mary Ann Montgomery, but the *National Republican's* announcement of the upcoming wedding mistook Edward for his more famous brother, reporting that it was Dennis, not Edward, getting married. One can imagine the embarrassment for the bride, the criticism Edward must have directed at the reporter for the *National Republican*, and the reaction of Dennis's wife, upon reading the news that her husband was soon to be married.[67]

As we saw in Chapter 3, in 1873, Dennis secured the contract to produce the new *Congressional Record* in his own right. From that point forward, all the reporters in the Senate, including Edward, didn't merely work under Dennis's supervision, they were his employees.[68] Despite the indignities of his subordinate role, Edward continued to assist, and when brother James Murphy's brain tumor finally took his life in December of that year, Edward moved up a rung on the latter, with more frequent opportunities to be on the floor himself.

Meanwhile, great changes were automating the phonographic reporting business. First came the typewriter, which eliminated the need for amanuenses to write out the debates in long hand, and relieved typesetters from having to decipher their penmanship. The typewriter was soon joined by Edison's recording cylinder: the reader of the shorthand notes now recorded his voice onto the cylinders, which could be listened to later and replayed as often as necessary for quality purposes. The press, the public, and the politicians all wanted this evening's dramatic speech printed by the thousands in tomorrow's Congressional Record, and by the tens of thousands in tomorrow's newspapers. Both the typewriter and the recording cylinder made it easier to edit, revise and convert the words of Congressmen into type-set text as quickly as possible.

In 1876, James O. Clephane, a shorthand reporter who'd been instrumental in the invention of the typewriter, and Ottmar Mergenthaler, a clock-maker who'd recently immigrated from Germany, developed yet another machine that would revolutionize printing. Called the linotype machine, it threatened to make the manual setting of type obsolete by setting a whole "line o' type" at once. No longer would a human typesetter have to arrange single characters, one at a time, by hand.

While new technologies improved preparation of the Congressional Record, Edward's wife Mary began to bear children.[69] But tall, handsome Edward still longed for the limelight, finding outlets for his affable social style after hours and taking to the rostrum like a politician on the campaign trail. In 1878, he was a part of the "entertainment" for the St. Peter's Library Association.[70] Soon afterward, he founded the Senate Reportorial Banquet Association, inviting all current and former Senate reporters to an annual reunion and dinner.[71] At the Association's banquet in 1884, he was honored as the organization's founder. His speech on stenography as a learned profession was replete with manly[*] humor:

> [W]hat limits can be placed upon the possibilities of a calling in which it is admitted that to be thoroughly proficient, one must have an intimate acquaintance with science, mechanics, literature, politics, law, and theology, to say nothing of the languages, living and dead! Even in its

---

[*] While Edward and his colleagues focused on reporting the debates of the Senators, one member's proposed amendment to the Constitution – guaranteeing women the right to vote – was referred to the Committee on Privileges and Elections, where it languished. (Aaron Sargent of California introduced Senate Resolution 12 on January 10, 1878. Four years later (January 9, 1882), the Senate voted 35 to 23 to establish a Select Committee on Woman Suffrage, to consider the amendment, later referred to as the Susan B. Anthony Amendment. Four years after that, in February 1886, the Committee finally reported the bill, but on January 25, 1887, the Senate rejected the proposal on a vote of 34 to 16 – more than a two-to-one margin.)

infancy, its members have attained conspicuous places in the executive councils, in legislative halls, on the bench, and at the bar – more particularly, as I am reminded, *at the bar.* [Great laughter.]

I am credibly informed that some have devoted their mighty energies to the study of art, and "draw" beautifully. One gentleman, indeed, is said to have drawn "four kings" with such consummate skill as to have astounded an assembly of his fellow artists, who paid most extravagant sums to induce him to exhibit the pictures, that they might enjoy the felicity of "seeing" them. [Renewed laughter.]

But gentlemen of the profession, not content with these accomplishments, are branching out into other fields... "The art preservative" is to be revolutionized, and Typo's occupation, like Othello's, gone. In the near future, two or three hundred words a minute will be the ordinary task of the great machine, which is to astonish the world and make its inventors and owners personalized gold mines. Then shall the Congressional reports appear in full within a minute and a half after adjournment... [laughter and applause.][72]

Edward was not joking about machines that would bring men riches. If we accept his claim that he was "poor of pocket" when he left the Superintendent's job, he wasted no time looking for other ways a shorthand reporter might become a wealthy man. His 1893 election to the Board of Governors of the Stenographer's Association surely brought no salary with it; nor did his authorship of occasional articles about stenography as a learned profession.[73] But he did begin investing in District real estate.[74] And when Dennis passed away in 1896, Edward and fellow-reporter Theodore Shuey succeeded to the lucrative reporting contract Dennis had negotiated with the Senate.[75] Edward promptly hired two new reporters to assist him: his sons, Edward V. Murphy, Jr., and James Wilmot Murphy.

Still, none of these sources of income provided Edward the bulk of his wealth. Rather, back in 1884, when he'd told his banquet audience that "great machines" involved in typesetting and reporting would make its owners "gold mines," he knew personally of what he spoke. Edward had invested early in both the linotype machine and the new Edison cylinders. The linotype began printing the daily news for the New York Times, and by 1895, the National Printing Company had become the Mergenthaler Linotype Company. Dennis and Edward Murphy were both major stockholders.[76] Meanwhile, as Edison's cylinders became the centerpiece of the Columbia Phonograph Company, with a monopoly on their sales in Washington, Edward was again an early major investor.[77]

As one newspaper put it:

> Edward Murphy fell in with Merganthaler and since then he has probably done more than any one man to bring about the condition of things that has resulted in a revolution in the art preservative of all arts.[78]

Now identified as the Senate's "official" reporter, Edward rose to the podium again in 1897, this time to display the rhythmic oratory he'd always enjoyed delivering.

> Two of the greatest inventions of this marvelous age owe their existence largely to him [Andrew Devine]. While he did not invent the great linotype machine, which has revolutionized 'the art preservative of all arts,' he did discover, in connection with our good friend Clephane, in a humble workshop in the city of Baltimore, that surpassing mechanical genius who was to achieve this triumph and give to the world that for which its greatest inventive minds had struggled, and struggled in vain, for well-nigh four centuries. I hazard nothing in saying that had it not been for the enthusiastic fervor, the ceaseless energy and the prophetic foresight of James O. Clephane, aided by the cool, wise, level-headed judgment and… the almost princely generosity of Andrew J. Devine and of a few others… the linotype never would have been born, and Ottmar Mergenthaler, whose name now stands by the side of that of Gutenberg, would have been "to fortune and to fame unknown." By means of this wonderful invention, printing has been multiplied to an incalculable extent, and the humblest student is enabled to purchase at trivial cost the priceless literary gems of all the ages, which were heretofore accessible only to the wealthy and the great.[79]

Edward didn't mention that he himself was one of those "few others" who'd invested in the new technology; in fact, he said nothing of being a major stockholder in both the Mergenthaler Linotype Company and the Columbia Phonograph Company as he touted their glories to his audience – an audience comprised of precisely those who, as producers of huge quantities of the written word, were the primary target audience of those companies. Edward had finally found his place in the world, at the intersection of government service and private profit, generating sales for his companies.

The Merganthaler Linotype Company would go on to dominate the linotype industry throughout the twentieth century. At age 57, Edward was President of the Washington Linotype Association.[80] Using his Senate position to advantage, he endorsed (presumably, for compensation) a shorthand reporting school.[81] His wife and even his daughter Minnie, eldest of six, began appearing in the social columns of the Washington papers.[82] Elected a director of Mergenthaler, he took to the podium whenever he could.[83]

But despite the efforts of many Retrenchment Committees over the years, government service was still a breeding ground for corruption, fraud, and private profit. In 1905, the Government Printing Office placed a $231,000 order for 72 typesetting machines with the Lanston Monotype Company, a smaller rival of Merganthaler.[84] Claiming that officials in the Printing Office owned stock in Lanston, Merganthaler blew the whistle, taking its complaints to a new President, Teddy Roosevelt. Roosevelt halted completion of the contract and appointed a commission to investigate the matter. The Lanston and Mergenthaler companies appeared before the commission represented by their respective lawyers and principals – namely, in the case of Mergenthaler, not only by its President, Philip T. Dodge, but also by its major stockholder and director, Edward V. Murphy.[85]

The Typographical Union was cool to the new technology: it favored the old, manual methods of typesetting that meant more jobs (and more dues-paying union members to contribute to its own financial well-being).[86] But the matter was otherwise regarded as a contest between the Lanston and Merganthaler machines. In effect, the government purchasing decision between the two business rivals was to be made by trial. There was testimony from customers like the Riggs National Bank, the Baltimore Sun, and big book printers like Doubleday, all agreeing that the Mergenthaler was the better machine. (Not only did it set a whole line of type at once, it took only one man to operate it, while the Lanston machine took three.) A jury of experts at the St. Louis Exposition had awarded Merganthaler its grand prize as the better machine.

Testimony revealed the seedy underside of government contracting. For one thing, the Public Printer had placed the 72-machine order not from his federal office, but from the home of the President of the Lanston Company, after making several visits to that gentleman's home. For another, after Printing Office personnel indignantly denied owning any stock in the Lanston Company, it turned out that their wives did. A key witness admitted to having been entertained by both Lanston and Mergenthaler, but denied that Mergenthaler had gotten him his appointment to the jury that had given Mergenthaler the prize. There was testimony that the Riggs National Bank officer who testified for Merganthaler had been told of the Lanston order before it was placed; and that the key witness mentioned above had discussed the matter with Mr. Roosevelt's private secretary and intimate advisor, Mr. William Loeb.

Higher-ups were clearly involved, but someone had to be blamed. Scapegoats had to be found. Ultimately, two key witnesses in the case, who'd been lobbied hard by the rival companies, were ordered to tender their resignations or show cause why they should not be fired for insubordination.[87]

The most biting cross examinations were not entirely to determine if improprieties had been engaged in – either by the companies or the government – but to determine which sort of technology the government thought was better, and therefore would buy. As the trial went into its third week, the stock prices of Merganthaler and Lanston rose and fell based on that day's testimony and predictions of which company would be found to offer the better product.[88] When Roosevelt publicly announced that the contract with Lanston would be honored, the price of Lanston stock went up. When the Commission's written report was released, concluding that Mergenthaler's technology was better, the price of Mergenthaler stock went up. [89]

Thus ended the matter of the seventy-two machines. Mergenthaler would go on to dominate the printing industry in America for the next hundred years. The Columbia Phonograph Company would go on to be a dominant player in the recording industry.   By 1908, Murphy would renegotiate his firm's contract for Senate Reporting to $30,000 per year.[90] Before he died, the man reported to have left his federal tax collection job "poor of pocket" had not only become a major stockholder and director of Mergenthaler Linotype and the Columbia Phonograph Company, but a director of the Riggs National Bank.[91] Edward Murphy had become a wealthy man.

Still, even in the face of his financial success, Edward longed for notoriety and longed to publicly press the rightness of a cause. And so it was that, in 1916, at the age of 73, he pled the innocence of Mary Surratt and inveighed against the perjury of Lewis Weichmann for the *New York Times* magazine. More people read Edward's words in that article than had ever heard his podium speeches, ever read his stenographic papers, ever given a thought to his role in shaping the words of Senators in the Congressional Record. In an odd sort of way, it was if, stating the case for Mary Surratt, Edward had finally found the national audience he'd always craved. The testimony he gave on that occasion may have come too late to help Mary Surratt, but it may have helped Edward achieve the national pulpit for which he'd always longed.

He died on July 16, 1919, while on a train from Albany to his summer home in Canada.[92] It wasn't quite the fanfare that had been paid to Lincoln, but for the first time in its history, the Senate adjourned to mark the passing of one of its employees.[93] Although Edward's last will and testament does not directly reveal the value of his estate, its terms suggest that it was substantial.[94]

Edward had wanted the fame his brothers had attained. He'd been frustrated that his worth was undervalued by others. If he didn't spend his final days bitter or resentful, he owed his contentment to the wealth that government service had provided him. At the end of the day, Edward Murphy no doubt believed himself a success.

Postscript

In 1896, when Edward hired his sons, Edward V. Murphy, Jr. and James Wilmot Murphy to assist him, these two Murphys became the fourth and fifth members of the Murphy family to work as Senate Reporters.[95] After beginning work in 1896, James was made Assistant Reporter in 1903 and Official Reporter in 1904.[96] He served the Senate for sixty-five years, carrying on in the tradition his father and uncles had begun half a century earlier, and bringing the continuous Senate service of the Murphy family to 112 years – from 1848 to 1960 – two-thirds of the country's existence up to that time.

On June 20, 1948, Senator Alben Barkley gave a speech on the Senate Floor honoring the hundredth anniversary of the Murphy family's long history of service to the Senate.[97] When James Murphy finally passed away in 1960, the Congressional Record was filled with accolades for him and his family's service.

"Our spoken words are fashioned into their everlasting form by our devoted reporters," said Senator John Pastore. "[H]e shared our thoughts expressed upon the Senate floor and often dressed them so that our minor errors of quick speech might not cloud the permanent record for posterity."[98] Senator Hubert Humphrey asked, "How can any of us really measure the value of… careful editing, which on more than one occasion saved us from a dangling participle, split infinitive, or misplaced literary illusion?"[99]

Senators rarely admitted, in public, to any more serious lapses in judgment than dangling participles or literary allusions. But Majority Leader Lyndon Johnson said, "Under his deft touch, the technicalities, the contradictions, the subtle nuances and the bewildering phrases arrange themselves in a neat and orderly fashion. They fall into place in such a way that they have coherence and logic and reason."[100]

Majority Leader Mike Mansfield called the younger Murphy "a tradition in the life of the Senate;" the leonine Everett Dirksen called him "beloved;" William Proxmire called him "dedicated;" John Pastore called him a "friend." [101] Senator Clifford Case observed, "Innumerable times have his deft pencil and agile mind saved Senators from slips which spring from heat and excitement common in *ex tempore* debate…" And then, perhaps more tellingly, "Perhaps it is fortunate for us all that he has foresworn memoirs."[102]

After noting the combined service of all five Murphy reporters, Senator Hubert Humphrey observed, "In honoring our late associate and friend, James W. Murphy… we are actually honoring the entire Murphy clan for their tradition of service to the United States Senate."[103]

The accolades accorded to the last of the Murphy reporters, and to his family's tradition of service to the Senate, were many and strong. But perhaps most insightful of all, Senator Wayne Morse made an observation about James Wilmot Murphy that could have described all five Murphys who had served the Senate:

"He was a trusted friend, whose passing… leaves each of us the richer for having known and loved him."[104]

Notes on Chapter 5, Edward V. Murphy

[1] *National Stenographer*, Vol IV, No 9, Sept 1893, p 381; *Evening Star*, Feb 14, 1915, p 9.

[2] Biographical Sketches of E.V. Murphy in the *National Stenographer*, Vol IV, No 9, Sept 1893, p 381, and *Browne's Phonographic Monthly*, Sept 1878, p 11. Edward graduated from Central on February 13, 1860, with an A.B. degree.

[3] W. S. Garber, "Congressional Reporting," *The Shorthand Review*, Vol IV, No 5, May 1892, p 73.

[4] *Evening Star*, Feb 14, 1915, p 9; *The Evening Public Ledger*, July 17, 1919, p 1; 1862 Washington City Directory; according to Senator Chamberlain, Edward's Senate service began on Feb 13, 1860. (Congressional Record, Senate, July 18, 1919, p 2831.)

[5] Obituary of Edward V. Murphy, *The Public Ledger*, July 17, 1919.

[6] "Personal Biographical Sketch of Edward V. Murphy," *Browne's Phonographic Monthly*, Sept 1878, p 11.

[7] Campaigns descended into attacks on one's patriotism. Running under the "National Union" banner, former Whigs and Republicans charged that if you voted Democratic, you were voting "for the success of the Rebellion" and "permanent disruption of the union." *Inquirer*, Oct 7, 1862, p 4.

[8] See the *Inquirer*, August 30, 1862, p 8, and October 11, 1862, p 8. Among others, Democrat Daniel M. Fox lost to Alexander Henry in the October 1862 mayoral election (1863 City Directory, p 907; *Inquirer*, October 15, 1862, p 4) and the Irish-Catholic Lewis Cassidy lost his 1862 race against William Mann for District Attorney. Mann had resigned his commission as Colonel in the Reserves to campaign for re-election, before the men he'd recruited ever saw action. (See Chapter 6, below, and J. R. Sypher, History of the Pennsylvania Reserve Corps, Elias Barr & Co., (1865), pp 79-80; McElroy's 1863 Phila Directory, p 910.)

[9] With Murphy help, Kline carried the 17th Ward by 1647 votes to 830. *Inquirer*, October 16, 1862, p 4.

[10] *Inquirer*, October 18, 1862, p 8. Governor Curtain certified Myers as the winner to the House of Representatives. Testimony regarding the contested election was heard before two city aldermen (*Inquirer*, Feb 11, 1863, p 4). One source (https://staffweb.wilkes.edu/harold.cox/rep/Congress%201862.pdf) gives the final count as 8285 for Myers and 8243 for Kline.

[11] "Personal Biographical Sketch," *supra*, pp 11-12. The law office where Edward read law was that of Vincent L. Bradford, Esq. The 1863 Septennial Census for Pennsylvania lists Edward Murphy, Reporter, in Phila Ward 17.

[12] We know no more of Cecelia S. Haas than we do of the other women in our story. She was born in 1844 to a grocer, Frederick Haas, and his wife Rigma (1850 Census, Phila, Northern Liberties Ward 4, Fam 483.) The date of Edward's marriage to her is not known, but it must have followed Cecelia's listing in the 1864 Philadelphia City Directory as a 'gentlewoman' living with her father (now 'bookkeeper') at 1546 N 6th Street.

[13] "Personal Biographical Sketch," *supra*, pp 11-12.

[14] *Inquirer*, October 12, 1864, p 1.

[15] In the 1866 election, the Democratic candidate in the 3rd District (and therefore, the "friend" alluded to) was once again Charles Buckwalter, but this time, with the war over, Buckwalter defeated Republican Myers by 1870 votes to 1793 (*Inquirer*, Oct 11, 1866, p 1).

[16] "Personal Biographical Sketch," *supra*, p 11.

[17] *Ibid.*

[18] Biographical Sketches of E.V. Murphy in the *National Stenographer*, Vol IV, No 9, Sept 1893, p 381, and *Browne's Phonographic Monthly*, Sept 1878, p 11.

[19] "Personal Biographical Sketch," *supra*, p 12. The official records of the Military Tribunal show the reporters as Benn Pittman, R. Sutton and D. F. Murphy, (see William C. Edwards, The Lincoln Assassination – the Trial Transcript: a Transcription of NARA Microfilm File M599, Reels 8 through

16, *Google Books* (2012), p 5) but much like their practice in reporting for the Senate, Dennis was assisted by his brothers, James and Edward, with Joseph acting as amanuensis.

[20] *Lincoln Trial Court Reporter Tells His Story,* New York Times Magazine, April 9, 1916. The proceedings of the trial have been described elsewhere, including by David Miller DeWitt, in *The Judicial Murder of Mary E. Surratt,* John Murphy & Co, Baltimore, 1895, now available on-line at Project Gutenberg, http://www.gutenberg.org/ebooks/36188, and by more recent analyses which dispute DeWitt's (and Murphy's) interpretations and conclusions.

[21] Weichmann testified that he and John Surratt were close – "intimate" was the word he used – and that they shared meals, the same room at the boardinghouse, and even the same bed, for some months. No one disputed the fact that John and Mary Surratt had been among the majority of Marylanders whose sympathies were with the South; such people generally viewed Lincoln's war as a wrongful invasion of sovereign states. Given the general weakness of Weichmann's testimony against Mary Surratt, one can't help but feel that Murphy's claim of perjury rested largely on the presumption that Weichmann was in fact in sympathy with Booth, probably knowing more of Booth's plans than he admitted. Weichmann claimed that neither Booth nor John Surratt ever said a word or intimated the existence of any plot to assassinate the President (Edwards, *supra*, pp 85-86); if he had admitted hearing such plans from them, it would have made him presumptively complicit in the wrong himself.

[22] The Surratts owned enough property in Maryland, including a farm, that the place was called Surrattsville. After her husband died, Mrs. Surratt rented the farm to John Lloyd and moved to Washington, where she ran the family's boardinghouse. There was evidence that the Surratts, Weichmann and Lloyd all had southern sympathies, but that Mrs. Surratt was a kind woman whose kindnesses extended to Yankee soldiers as well as to her southern friends. Weichmann's testimony consisted of the assertion that Mr. Booth visited the Surratt boarding house frequently to call on John Surratt; that if John Surratt was absent, he would ask for Mrs. Surratt; that at times he (Weichmann) had seen Booth and Mrs. Surratt speaking to each other in the parlor of the boarding house, though he knew not about what; that a couple of weeks prior to the assassination, Mrs. Surratt had sent him (Weichmann) to the hotel where Booth was staying, to deliver a message that she wanted to speak with him privately; that on the Tuesday prior to the assassination, Mrs. Surratt had asked him to go to a stable to get Mr. Booth's buggy (which he often let her use for trips to Surrattsville) so that he could drive her there; that Booth, saying he had sold the buggy, gave Weichmann ten dollars to rent another; that on that day, he (Weichmann) did drive Mrs. Surratt out to Surrattsville in the buggy he'd rented; that when they encountered Mr. Lloyd coming in a carriage the other way, there was a brief conversation between Lloyd and Mrs. Surratt which he (Weichmann) did not hear; that Mrs. Surratt had a package with her, placed in the bottom of their carriage which, to Weichmann, felt like saucers; that again on the day of the assassination, he had driven Mrs. Surratt out to Surrattsville, and that Mrs. Surratt had had a conversation with Mr. Lloyd that afternoon – which conversation, again, Weichmann had not heard. (Edwards, *supra*, testimony of Lewis J. Weichmann, pp 76-104, 122-123, 290-306, 401-403.)

[23] Testimony of John Lloyd, Edwards, *supra*, pp 107-121, 123-124, 1153-1155.

[24] Testimony of Emma Offutt, Edwards, *supra*, pp 245-247, 1155-1166.

[25] Testimony of George Cottingham, Edwards, *supra*, pp 531-533.

[26] *Evening Star*, July 17, 1865, p 1.

[27] *Inquirer*, July 26, 1865, p 1. See also the *National Republican*, July 26, 1865, p 2.

[28] John W. Clampitt, *The Trial of Mrs. Surratt*, North American Review, Sept, 1880, pp 223-240, accessed at https://archive.org/details/trialofmrssurrat00clam/page/n1/mode/2up.

[29] *Evening Star*, July 17, 1865, p 1.

[30] *Ibid.*

[31] Excerpted from Appendix 8.

[32] *Ibid.*

[33] Perhaps Murphy's claim was invented, an example of what the *Phonographic Monthly* would call his "love for the rostrum." (1878 "Personal Biographical Sketch," *supra*, p 11.) Or perhaps his older

brother, Dennis, committed to silence as a way to maintain the trust of important men, insisted that Edward keep his observations to himself, protecting the impartiality of the reporter's role. We know for certain only that Edward came to have strong feelings on the subject, that he felt the Military Tribunal had overstepped its bounds in convicting Mary Surratt, and that his sympathy with Mary Surratt was consistent with the views of his father and siblings, as Democrats whose party had long been more sympathetic to the South than their Republican counterparts. Murphy's views about the injustice done to Mary Surratt could not have been softened when President Andrew Johnson denied that the petition for clemency (signed by five of the nine military judges) ever reached him; nor again when a writ of habeas corpus, issued by a federal court, was quashed by order of Attorney General James Speed. ("Mary Surratt," Wikipedia.org.)

[34] Thomas had amassed a substantial fortune by converting his family's water-driven flour mill into a number of steam-powered mills. When the Confederate army invaded Pennsylvania, he had organized his mill and Port employees into a regiment, and after three days' training, took them by train to participate in the action around Gettysburg, where they fared poorly. Scott Mingus, *Colonel William B. Thomas Commanded York County's Defenses During the Gettysburg Campaign: Part One*, blog posted November 28, 2009, accessed at https://yorkblog.com/cannonball/colonel-william-b-thomas-comma/.

[35] William F. Johnston (1808-1872), a Democrat-turned-Whig who'd been Governor of Pennsylvania between 1848 and 1852, was a political moderate who'd been a free-soiler and opponent of slavery but thought it unconstitutional for state officials to enforce the federal Fugitive Slave Act. He was an Andrew Johnson appointee who'd assumed the role of Philadelphia Port Collector on September 1, 1866. ("Governor William Freame Johnston," PA Historical and Museum Commission, http://www.phmc. state.pa.us/portal/communities/governors/1790-1876/william-johnston.html; *Evening Telegraph*, August 21, 1866, p 3). In the confrontation between Johnson and the Republican Congress, Johnston lost his job as Port Collector the day the Tenure of Office Act went into effect – March 4, 1867. Since Murphy says he came by a "short time" after Johnston took office, and since Johnston still had time during his brief term of office to lobby for Weichmann's removal, Murphy probably found Weichmann there in September, or at latest October, of 1866.

[36] Appendix 8, below.

[37] *Ibid.*

[38] The resignation of a Democrat would normally have been welcomed by the Republican authors of the Tenure-in-Office Act.

[39] Could Johnston have known something about McCullough that McCullough preferred to keep quiet? McCullough was never implicated in scandal and won a reputation as an honest man – but it might be noted that, according to Wikipedia.org, the main source of information about him is his own autobiography.

[40] Much attention has been given to the conflict regarding Johnson's suspension of Edwin Stanton, whose position as Secretary of War posed an enormous challenge to Johnson's plan of post-war reconstruction. The Republican Congress had installed military officers to govern the South, refusing to recognize the governments of the largely Democratic southern states or allow them their former representation in Congress. As Commander-in-Chief of the military, Johnson might have had some control over such a military government, but his Secretary of War, Edwin Stanton, a holdover from the Lincoln administration, was a radical Republican who, like Congress, favored imposing conditions on re-admittance of Southern states.

[41] "Because they were originally paid based on a percentage system that factored in both customs collected and fines levied for those who attempted to evade payment, these appointments were very lucrative… New York's Collector was the highest paid official of the federal government; as Collector from 1871 to 1878, Chester A. Arthur's compensation exceeded the modern equivalent of $1 million annually." ("Collector of the Port of New York," Wikipedia.org, citing Ballard C. Campbell, Disasters, Accidents & Crises in American History, Facts on File (2008), pp 152-153.)

[42] E. A. Rollins to John W. Frazier, May 21, 1867, reprinted in the *Evening Telegraph*, May 23, 1867, p 5.

[43] See Chapter 3, *supra*, pp 57-59. John H. Diehl, Collector of the Second Revenue District, had been responsible for "the seizure of forty or fifty different establishments which were engaged in distilling without any license whatever, and in the institution of some hundred and thirty suits against as many different parties, for making a fraudulent return of the capacity of their stills." On that same day, Albert Barnes Sloanaker, commissioned by President Johnson, took office as Collector for the First Internal Revenue District in Philadelphia. His appointment reportedly put an end to "the grievous trouble" associated with that office. Sloanaker's predecessor had retired "as gracefully as the circumstances of the case would warrant." (*Evening Telegraph*, Aug 4, 1866, p 5.)

[44] "Personal Biographical Sketch," *supra*, p 11.

[45] *The Inquirer*, Dec 21, 1866, p 1; *Washington Times*, July 17, 1919, p 21; the *National Stenographer*, Vol IV, No 9, Sept 1893, p 381; "Personal Biographical Sketch," *supra*.

[46] Although we have not found direct evidence of Edward's confirmation by the Senate, he must have received it, as Congress was in session (the second session of the 39th Congress had convened on December 3, 1866) and he was not among the recess appointees whose commissions expired on March 4, 1867, by operation of the Tenure-of-Office Act.

[47] In other words, at the very time Murphy "happened to be" at the Custom House, discovering Lewis Weichmann there and complaining to Johnston about his presence on Johnston's staff, Murphy himself had been appointed (or was in the process of being appointed) to essentially that same Custom House. Conveniently, Murphy didn't mention this to the *New York Times Magazine* in 1916.

[48] The Tenure of Office bill had been introduced in the Senate only weeks prior to Murphy's appointment by the President; as the rift between Congress and the President grew more intense, Dennis Murphy had followed the bill in the Committee on Retrenchment, to which it had been referred. Section 3 of the Act allowed the President to make interim appointments while Congress was in recess, but provided that when Congress reconvened, the appointments would expire; the incumbents could carry out the duties of office in "acting" capacities, but only until the Senate had confirmed other appointees. Two months after Edward's appointment as Superintendent, Johnson vetoed the Tenure of Office bill as an unconstitutional infringement on his prerogatives. On Saturday, March 2, Congress overrode Johnson's veto and the Act went into effect at noon two days later. (*History of the Impeachment of Andrew Johnson, Chapter V, The Tenure of Office Act*, Avalon Project, Yale Law School, accessed at https://avalon.law.yale.edu/19th_century/john_chap_05.asp. The website misstates the date of Johnson's veto as Monday, March 2, 1867; in fact, March 2, 1867 was a Saturday.) Section 3 of the Act: "The President shall have power to fill all vacancies which may happen during the recess of the Senate, by reason of death or resignation, by granting commissions which shall expire at the end of their next session thereafter; and if no appointment by and with the advice and consent of the Senate, shall be made to such office, so vacant or temporarily filled as aforesaid, during such next session of the Senate, such office shall remain in abeyance without any salary, fees or emoluments attached until the same shall be filled by appointment thereto, by and with the advice and consent of the Senate, and during such time all the powers and duties belonging to such office shall be exercised by such other officer as may lawfully exercise such duties and powers in case of a vacancy in such office."

[49] In the First District, the Senate reversed itself as to confirmation of J.W. Frazier, Johnson's appointee as Assessor, rejecting a nomination it had approved only days earlier. Then, about an hour before the Act took effect, the incumbent Collector, A.B. Sloanaker, appointed radical Republican George Kelly as his chief and sole Deputy, the effect being that when the noon hour struck, it was Kelly who assumed the responsibilities of the acting Collector in Sloanaker's stead; but within a few days, Kelly (as if he had some sort of pre-arrangement with Sloanaker) submitted his resignation. But Kelly's tendered resignation was not accepted by Washington. As *The Telegraph* put it, "Mr. Kelly then determined upon trying the effect of a flank movement, after the manner of the strategic Sloanaker. So on the 15th instant, he appointed as his chief and sole Deputy the Hon. William F. Johnston, sometime Governor of the Commonwealth, and sometime Collector of Customs of the Port of Philadelphia." (The same

William F. Johnston who had dismissed Lewis Weichmann at Murphy's behest before losing his office at the Customs House.) But on March 18, two weeks after the political shuffling began, Kelly revoked Johnston's commission as his chief deputy and headed to Washington, apparently to secure a better future for himself.

The vacancies attracted job-seekers the way mass carnage might attract hyenas. At the Port, where Murphy was now Superintendent, Collector Johnston was out (and briefly at the First District), but there were two claimants to act in his stead. The Port's Surveyor and Naval Officer, both of whom had roles in customs collections, were replaced by their deputies. And Sloanaker, fresh from his duties as First District Collector, now opened a "law and collecting agency" on the second floor of the Custom House. (*Evening Telegraph*, Monday, March 4, 1867, p 5; *Evening Telegraph*, March 19, 1867, p 5.) No one was willing to turn his back on the opportunities these jobs provided.

[50] Since Murphy's own appointment had been confirmed by the Senate, his position was not directly affected by the Tenure of Office Act.

[51] Appendix 2.

[52] *Evening Telegraph*, July 16, 1867, p 2.

[53] "The Revenue Frauds," *New York Times*, Sept 26, 1868, p 2.

[54] In colonial days, the colonies had few natural resources to export. "One way in which Americans could make large profits... was to participate in the carrying trade, in which the more expensive products from the British and French West Indies (such as sugar) were bought by Americans and resold to Europeans... By 1798, the New York Customhouse was refunding as Drawbacks more than one-third of all duties collected." Douglas L. Stein, *Drawback Forms and Certificates,* American Maritime Documents 1776-1860, Mystic Seaport Museum, at https://research.mysticseaport.org/item/l0064 05/l006405-c019/.

[55] "About 1862, a law was passed imposing an internal revenue tax on articles manufactured, with a provision that if any of the articles were afterwards exported, an amount should be paid to the exporter equal to the amount previously paid as tax. This was called a 'drawback.' In order to have a drawback claim recognized, an exporter is required, in the first place, to procure a certificate from a Collector of Internal Revenue, showing the amount of tax paid on the articles which were to be exported. After this was obtained it was necessary to make an affidavit in regard to the goods for export, stating their destination, the name or names of the owner or owners, etc. When the export was made the exporter applied to the Drawback Department of the Custom House for a certificate, or outward-bound manifest, as it is designated, certifying that the goods had been exported, and giving certain information about them and the vessels that carried them. It was the duty of a clerk to make out the manifest and to attach his initials or name to it as evidence of its genuineness, in order that it might subsequently be endorsed by one of the deputy collectors. Upon the internal revenue certificate, the affidavit and the custom-house manifest being procured, they went to the Auditor's office at Washington, going from there to the United States Treasurer, who issued a check for the amount of the drawback claim." (*Evening Telegraph*, Nov 12, 1869, p 1.)

[56] *Buffalo Morning Express*, Nov 17, 1869, p 2.

[57] "Personal Biographical Sketch," *supra*.

[58] *Inquirer*, Sept 4, 1867, p 2.

[59] *Inquirer,* March 24, 1868, p 1, and March 28, 1868, p 1. The bill, introduced by Edwin D. Morgan of New York, was referred to a committee chaired by Morgan himself, and the Committee reported favorably on the bill, which was ultimately enacted. There does appear to have been some wiggle room in the end date of the position. On Sept 15, 1868, the Secretary of the Treasury ordered the discontinuance of the office, but then postponed the discontinuance until March 4, 1869. (Journal of the House of Representatives, 40th Cong, 3rd Sess, GPO 1869, p 112, Jan 6, 1869, and p 156, Jan 14, 1869.)

[60] The *National Stenographer*, Vol IV, No 9, Sept 1893, p 381. Cecelia Murphy, daughter of Frederick Haas, 1538 N 6th Street, had died two months earlier, on July 19, 1868. (Phila death certificate, FHL No 1008635; the *Inquirer*, July 22, 1868, p 5; *Evening Telegraph*, July 20, 1868, p 5.)

[61] "Personal Biographical Sketch," *supra*. Again, one wonders what the source was for the statement regarding Murphy's lack of wealth at the time he left office, if it wasn't Murphy himself. Whether he really left "poor in pocket" is for the reader to decide. If he did, he appears to have been among the few who did so.

[62] *Ibid.* Browning was among the founders of the Illinois Republican party, so again we must ask why Browning would have offered Democrat Murphy such a post. The answer may be that on the death of Stephen Douglas, Browning had been appointed to Douglas's vacant Senate seat, where he'd gotten to know the Murphy reporters. Not only that, after Lincoln's assassination, Browning had been a supporter of Andrew Johnson; it had been Johnson who'd appointed Browning as Secretary of the Interior in 1866. Once again, it seems, despite having no background in Indian affairs, Edward Murphy had been offered a substantial federal office as a result of political alliances in Washington that crossed party lines.

[63] Was he still in grief, after the death of his wife? Burnt out? Wanting to avoid further political turmoil? Presumably based on Edward's own description, "Personal Biographical Sketch," *supra*, p 11, states that 'he had mingled in the turbulent scenes of political life and in them found neither contentment nor riches."

[64] "Personal Biographical Sketch," *supra*, p 11. W. S. Garber confirmed that Edward read and dictated Dennis's notes to the amanuenses, saying that the practice allowed Dennis to return to the floor; "the notes were in this way transcribed nearly as rapidly as they were taken in the Senate." (Garber, *supra*, p 74)

[65] "Personal Biographical Sketch," *supra*, p 12. Alcorn was something of a southern moderate, having supported the Fourteenth Amendment and suffrage for freedmen. But like all those elected to Congress from southern states after the war, when Alcorn was elected to the Senate in 1865, he was denied his seat, since Mississippi had not yet succumbed to the yoke of Republican reconstruction. Alcorn had instead been elected Governor of Mississippi in 1869, then resigned in 1871 when, elected once again to the Senate, he'd been allowed to take the seat.

[66] The "senior" Murphy brother had found it necessary to be relieved of that task in order to spend more time on the Senate floor and more time revising the amanuenses' longhand notes before they were printed. Edward had "thoroughly mastered his brother's system of shorthand in order to qualify himself to dictate the original notes… Such proficiency has he acquired in this line that he reads the notes of a running, disconnected debate of an intricate legal, theological, or other technical argument (not a word of which he has heard) with the same facility that an ordinary reader reads plain manuscript or print." *Ibid.*

[67] Mary Ann was the daughter of Dr. John Wilmot Montgomery of Ontario, Canada. The *National Republican*, Sept 26, 1874, p 4, announced that she and *Dennis* Murphy were to be married October 1, 1874: "The Murphy-Montgomery wedding will also take place next Thursday at Trinity church. Mr. D. F. Murphy is the principal stenographer of the Senate, and his long list of eminent friends have much reason to congratulate him, for all Washington cannot produce a lovelier bride than Mary Montgomery will be." But see "Personal Biographical Sketch, *supra*, p 12, correctly identifying Mary Ann Montgomery as the bride of Edward Murphy, not his brother Dennis.

[68] On repeated occasions between December of 1879 and February of 1883, editions of The *Evening Star* listed only one Official Reporter of Debates in the Senate – Dennis F. Murphy – while listing others, including Edward V. Murphy, as his "assistants." (The others were Theodore Shuey, Henry Gensler, R.S. Boswell, and D.B. Lloyd.) The paper also listed reporters for the House of Representatives, including John J. McElhone, Dennis's classmate at Central High, and David Wolfe Brown, who contributed much information about the Murphys to the *National Stenographer* magazine. See, for example, the *Star* of Dec 6, 1879, p 3; June 12, 1880, p 3; Feb 26, 1881, p 3; Feb 10, 1883, p 6.

[69]   Minnie Cecelia Murphy Carnahan (1875-1958); James Wilmot Murphy (1878-1960); Josephine G. Murphy (1880- ?); Edward Vincent Murphy Jr. (1883-1945); John W. Murphy (1891-1931); and Isabelle Murphy Wilson (1893-?).

[70]   The entertainment consisted of musical performances by some and "readings" by Edward and three others. The fundraiser was at the Carroll Institute on G Street (*Evening Star*, Feb 22, 1878, p 4).

[71]   *Evening Star*, Jan 28, 1884, p 4.

[72]   *Evening Star*, Jan 28, 1884, p 4. He was survived by his wife, Mary Ann Hannah Murphy (1853-1933), and [up to] six children.

[73]   Edward's article for *The National Stenographer* magazine, titled "Stenography as a Skilled Profession," argued that stenography should be considered among the learned professions like medicine and law (*Evening Star*, Feb 6, 1893, p 10; *The National Stenographer*, Vol IV, No 9, Sept 1893, pp 301-307). In 1903, he published another paper titled, "The Limitations of the Stenographer," presented at the annual convention of the National Shorthand Reporters' Association in Cincinnati (*Evening Star*, August 19, 1903, p 2).

[74]   In 1885, Edward sold a 100-by-120-foot investment property on the corner of H Street and 6th Street NE to one B.H. Warner for $3,600; Dominic sold his adjoining property to Warner and others for $2,160. In 1909, Edward sold another property on D Street NW, between 21st and 22nd for $1500 (*Evening Star*, Dec 26, 1885, p 5; *Washington Post*, Dec 14, 1909, p 12.)

[75]   *Evening Star*, March 30, 1896, p 1; *The Philadelphia Times*, March 31, 1896, p 10.

[76]   When Dennis Murphy passed away in 1896, he owned $74,800 dollars in Merganthaler stock, more than 40% of the value of his estate, according to the filed Inventory and Appraisement of his estate. (Per Bill Colman.)

[77]   Edward D. Easton (a stenographic reporter, like Edward) founded the Columbia Phonograph Company in 1882; it was named after the District of Columbia where it was headquartered.

[78]   *The Times*, March 30, 1896, p 4.

[79]   *Evening Star*, Dec 21, 1897, p 3. Andrew Devine, one of the reporters for the House of Representatives, had resigned his position to become Vice President of the Columbia Phonograph Company; Edward's remarks were delivered at the farewell dinner given in Devine's honor.

[80]   In 1899, at the Grand Army Hall in the nation's capital, Edward, as President of the Washington Linotype Association, addressed other stockholders of the Mergenthaler Linotype Company: "[T]here are very nearly 500 holders of stock in the company in this city. Their holdings are approximately a third of the entire capitalization of the company, having increased very rapidly in the past year." (*Washington Times*, May 5, 1899, p 4.)

[81]   *Evening Star*, Sept 20, 1900, p 13.

[82]   *Evening Star*, January 30, 1901, p 7.

[83]   In June of 1903, he was one of the speakers at a presentation at his old alma mater, Central High School (*Inquirer*, June 11, 1903, p 4). In August, he delivered the dedicatory address at a ceremony honoring Revolutionary War shorthand reporter Thomas Lloyd (*Inquirer*, Aug 23, 1903, p 5).

[84]   Teddy Roosevelt appointed a commission to look into government waste called the Committee on Department Methods, which was popularly known as the Keep Commission, after its chairman, Assistant Secretary of the Treasury Charles H. Keep.

[85]   *Washington Post*, June 29, 1905, p 10; *Washington Times*, June 29, p 12; *Evening Star*, June 30, 1905, p 2; and Washington Times, July 8, 1905, p 5.

[86]   *Evening Star*, July 12, 1905, pp 1-2, and July 13,1905, p 2; *Washington Times*, July 14, 1905, p 5.

[87]   *Evening Star*, July 14, 1905, p 1 and July 15, 1905, p 2 and p 5; *Washington Times*, Sept 8, 1905, p 7. Edward F. Riggs had served on the Board of the St. Vincent's Orphan Asylum and as a delegate to the Second National Congress of the Catholic Church with Edward's brother Dominick. (*Evening Star*, May 11, 1893, p 5; *Evening Times*, May 16, 1901, p 2 and June 3, 1901, p 5.)

[88]   *Washington Times*, July 17, 1905, p 5, and July 18, 1905, p 5.

[89]   *Washington Times*, Aug 7, 1905, p 5; *Evening Star*, August 31, 1905, p 15.

[90] *Evening Star,* March 8, 1908, Part IV, p 3.

[91] *Evening Public Ledger,* July 17, 1919, p 1; *Washington Herald,* July 18, 1919, p 3; *The Inquirer,* July 18, 1919, p 1. In 1910, Edward and his family lived at 2511 Pennsylvania Avenue (1910 U.S. Census, D.C., Washington Precinct 3, Dist 0043, Fam 73). The household included Edward's wife Mary, son John, daughters Minnie, Josephine and Isabelle, and Mary Wills, a 45-year-old black servant from Maryland. The Mergenthaler Linotype Company had been very profitable (see *Evening Star,* Nov 17, 1915, p 18) and became the dominant manufacturer of type-setting equipment for all publishing in the United States for most of the twentieth century. The report in *The Herald* that Murphy had until lately been a director of the Columbia *Graphophone* Company seems mistaken – possibly an ironic typographical error – as that British company was not incorporated until 1917; the Columbia *Phonograph* Company, after its stenographic start, would rise to the top of the entertainment recording industry, and appears to be the corporation of which Murphy had been director. The Riggs National Bank, headquartered in D.C. with offices right across the street from the U.S. Treasury building, was known for its involvement in government affairs. It had lent the Government millions of dollars to pay for the Mexican-American War, the purchase of Alaska, Admiral Peary's expedition to the North Pole, and expansion of the U.S. Capitol Building. In 1909, its president had presented to Congress the economic plan that resulted in establishment of the Federal Reserve. In the later 20th and early 21st centuries, it became known for its involvement in money-laundering scandals, including the transfer of Saudi money prior to the Sept 11, 2001, terrorist attacks, the hiding of the fortune of Chilean dictator Augusto Pinochet, and the embezzlement of oil revenues from Equatorial Guinea. ("Riggs Bank" at Wikipedia.org.) Riggs' Assistant Cashier and later Director, William Flather, was the Riggs officer who had testified for Murphy's Mergenthaler Company; he later became a director of the Bank.

[92] *Evening Public Ledger,* July 17, 1919, p 1; *Washington Evening Star,* July 17, 1919, p 7, 15 and July 18, p 7, 8; *Washington Times,* July 17, 1919, p 21 and July 18, p 3; *Washington Herald,* July 18, 1919, pp 3, 9. Oddly, unless only accurate as to his last few years, the obituary in the *Evening Star* states that "he had no society affiliations, being strictly a home man."

[93] The adjournment in Murphy's honor was on the motion of Henry Cabot Lodge. (Congressional Record, Senate, July 18, 1919, p 2831); *Washington Post,* July 19, 1919, p 5.

[94] *Washington Post,* Aug 5, 1919, p 2. The Post's estimate that Edward's estate included personal property worth over $140,000 is surely an understatement of his real net worth. Edward's Last Will and Testament left stocks and bonds to his wife and each of their six children, a thousand dollars to his widowed sister Hannah Kinney, five hundred dollars to his brother John A. Murphy, a hundred dollars each to St. Anne's Infant Asylum, St. Joseph's Male Orphan Asylum, and the Little Sisters of the Poor, and the rest of his estate to his son James and nephew Charles as trustees, from which the Trustees were to pay income to his sister, Mary Murphy, sufficient to give her seven hundred dollars per year, and thereafter – the rest of the estate to be paid for the care of his wife, and after her death, to be divided among his children. (Washington D.C. Wills & Probate Records, Boxes 0630 Hayden to 0638 O'Donoghue, Jan 11, 1919, accessed via Ancestry.com.)

[95] This count does not include the year (1865) in which Joseph P. Murphy assisted his brothers in their Senate work.

[96] *Evening Star,* April 23, 1904, p 23.

[97] Cong Record, 80th Cong, 2nd Sess, June 20, 1948. Since June 20 1948 was a Sunday, it is possible that the photocopy of Senator Barkley's speech in the author's collection reflects an incorrect date. However, the speech, titled "A Century of Senate Reporting," printed beneath a Congressional Record masthead by the government printing office, clearly reflects June 20, 1948, as the date of Senator Barkley's speech. (It also includes the number "797212-26320").

[98] Cong Record, 86th Cong, 2nd Sess, April 25, 1960, p 8629.

[99] Cong Record, 86th Cong, 2d Sess, May 18, 1960, p 10520.

[100] As quoted by Bob Dole in *Historical Almanac of the United States Senate*, G.P.O. 1989, p 272, accessed at https://babel.hathitrust.org/cgi/pt?id=msu.31293011524109&view=1up&seq=284 and at Cong Record, 100th Cong, 2d Sess, April 29, 1988, p 9509.

[101] Cong Record, 86th Cong, 2d Sess, April 11, 1960, p 7842 and April 25, 1960, p 8629.

[102] Cong Record, 84th Cong, 1st Sess, Jan 21, 1955, pages 590-593.

[103] Cong Record, 86th Cong, 2d Sess, May 18, 1960, p 10520.

[104] Cong Record, 86th Cong, 2nd Sess, May 4, 1960, p 9407.

6. James C. Carvin

After the Kensington riots of 1844, William and Mary Carvins' oldest son James had seen as much bloodshed as any six-year-old.[1] Though it seems he attended the Master Street School until he was twelve, his own parents could barely read, and his academic accomplishments were nothing like those of his classmates, the Murphy children.[2] When his father took the family north to Gordon Street, there was no school nearby. Of course, his father's lower earnings at the steam-powered mill meant that all but the youngest in the family had to go to work anyway, and James was an obedient boy. In the 1860 Census, he was listed as a weaver, along with his siblings Catherine, Thomas and Mary.

Their brother-in-law, George Austin, was like a favorite uncle, the Austin brass shop a favorite place to visit.[3] In those days, tacks and teapots, buckles and buttons, spoons, frames, and delicate parts for mechanical things like compasses and pocket watches were all made of brass.[4] Brass's allure was greater than cotton's; the mix of copper and zinc was hard, but when it was hot, it could be molded into any shape imaginable. Fire and heat could hold a young man spell bound, though breathing fumes of brass had never been good for one's health.

> The Birmingham historian, William Hutton, writing in the late 18th century, summed up the "curious art" of brassfounding as being "… less ancient than profitable and less healthful than either." In both respects he was accurate, as brassworkers contracted pulmonary and respiratory diseases from the dust and fumes emitted in the various processes. This led one industrial historian to comment in 1866 that "Brass casters are unanimously short-lived."[5]

But James was an obedient boy whose parents had taught him that "hardness endured is happiness secured." So he accepted the long hours, low pay, steam and cotton dust in the cotton mills, even as he longed for the full time work and freedom he imagined could be his at the Austin shop. When not doing his duty at the looms, he hung around the molten metal, willing to expose himself to the noxious fumes if that meant learning a lucrative trade.[6]

Traditional brass-making could be done in an attached shed, or even in the brass-molder's home. But in the mid-nineteenth century, many of the brass foundries were employing ten, twenty or even more workers at a single location. And just as in the textile mills, mechanization was reducing the skill required, allowing the employment of women and putting downward pressure on wages:

> During the 19th century, stamping and piercing, such as in the manufacture of buttons, medals and ornamental work, became increasingly mechanized, which resulted in a larger female workforce. These unskilled jobs generally paid significantly less than others in the trade.[7]

The Austin mill also faced competition from larger firms like David Siner's foundry on Randolph Street. As war loomed, talk turned toward belt buckles, bugles and parts for guns, toward cartridge casings and cannons. Even officers' fancy buttons were made of brass. James could hope that armed conflict might mean an increase in business at the Austin shop, a full-time opportunity for someone like him. But as war approached, a "Committee of Safety" was formed for the defense of the city, drilling young men to prepare for service.[8] When Lincoln's call for an army prompted Virginia to secede, its departure put Philadelphia practically at the border between north and south. On April 18, 1861, a regiment from Massachusetts passed through the city, brass buttons on their coats, brass insignia on their caps. Philadelphia's quota of 90-day volunteers was quickly filled.[9] Then, on May 3, Lincoln called for 42,000 three-year volunteers. Recruiting stations sprang up throughout Philadelphia.

There was talk of glory, of course, especially from reckless boys like James's brother Thomas, but at 5 ft 7-1/2 inches tall, light-complexioned, sandy-haired and blue-eyed, James himself had no interest in glory. Some were predicting that war would disrupt the cotton supply, putting the whole family out of work. As days passed, George Austin predicted that army contracts would likely be going to larger, steam-powered foundries, run by men with connections to powerful men. Recruiters, meanwhile, were saying than an army private would be guaranteed a place to sleep, plenty of food and drink, and thirteen dollars a month to spend as he pleased, or to send home, if that's what he wanted. Everyone believed the federal government would pay lifetime pensions to any veterans disabled by the war, as it had in the past. Still, neither James nor George responded to the call for volunteers, clinging to hope that the Army might pay them to make brass.

On the morning of May 8, 1861, a band was playing; fire engines were ringing their bells; spectators packed the streets, cheering an artillery regiment that was preparing to head south.[10] On May 10, a committee from City Council gave hero's welcomes to two bigwigs who'd arrived by train: Colonel Robert Anderson (the commander who'd just surrendered Fort Sumter), and Mrs.

Abraham Lincoln.[11] Flags in windows were everywhere, testaments to the patriotism of all who displayed them and the cowardice, or southern sympathies, of those who did not. And amid all the hoopla, James' reckless younger brother Thomas enlisted.[12]

His decision took them by surprise. Mary, their mother, paced back and forth with worry for the safety of her son. Her husband William, observing said Thomas was old enough to make his own decisions, said he'd have no more to say about the matter. James announced that he would postpone his dreams of making brass, that he too would leave the mill to enlist. But when he went down to join Thomas, he was too late. Thomas's company had been filled. Mary worried that James and Thomas would not be together.

On May 26th, James and a group of his friends listened to a pitch by John C. Chapman, who was organizing a company of Philadelphia militiamen. Commissioned as a Captain by Governor Curtain, the forty-year-old Chapman seemed to know what he was doing. Military service was important, he said. There was a real possibility that Pennsylvania could be invaded, overrun by enemy troops, and it needed companies to defend the home front. For that reason, he was calling his company "The Guards." If a man cared about his loved ones it was his duty to protect them, and Chapman needed such men to join him. His words were more than many could resist.[13] Edward Selby, William Cain, David McDowell, Patrick Cahill and Christopher Sloan all enlisted in Chapman's company that day, and James, always conscious of duty, decided to join them.

Looking ahead to what he'd do when his service was up, he gave his occupation as "brass-moulder."[14]

The next day, the "Guards" were off to Harrisburg, the boys talking of a quick and glorious fight, their enlistment the beginning of greatness. While they waited for uniforms and equipment, they began to train in the service of Pennsylvania. One pace – no more – behind the man in front. Shoulders square. Head erect. Eyes fixed forward. Face right. Face left. About face. Forward, march, halt, face right, forward march again, several times a day.

On June 26th, Chapman announced that the Guards and nine other companies had been grouped together to form a regiment, the Pennsylvania 7th Reserve infantry regiment. The men of the ten companies voted to elect Elisha B. Harvey – a forty-two-year-old lawyer from Wilkes Barre – to lead their regiment in the defense of Pennsylvania. Harvey was a smart man who knew much about conflict from his years in a courtroom. (All he lacked was military experience.)[15] Such lack of experience was not uncommon: of the thirteen colonels put in charge of Reserve regiments that June, only two had seen actual combat; two more had received training in militia roles but lacked combat experience. The rest lacked even basic training: three were lawyers, one owned a manufacturing business, one was a merchant, one a medical doctor and farmer, one the proprietor of the *Philadelphia Sunday Mercury*.[16] Respected men all, but innocent in the ways of war.

A few men feared the possible consequences of this inexperience. On July 4th, 1861, while James's regiment was still training in Harrisburg, Corporal Patrick Cahill slipped away and went home. His departure triggered a flood of condemnation. Patrick had shirked his duty. He was a coward. He was less than a man, and certainly less than the rest of them.

A few of the boys got homesick. Many missed girlfriends back home. No one spoke kindly of Cahill. Then, when the army was smashed by rebel forces at Bull Run only 30 miles west of D.C., word spread that Washington was in peril. Pennsylvania's Reserves were needed to aid in its defense. A series of urgent telegrams swept across the wires; the 7th Reserves were ordered to Baltimore.

Many questioned the order. Baltimore was sympathetic to the Southern cause. Lincoln himself, on his way to be inaugurated, had been forced to sneak through the city, fearful of assassination. In April, a mob of a pro-southern Marylanders had thrown bricks at the first union troops to pass through the city, leaving four soldiers and twelve civilians dead.[17] Some questioned the order to Baltimore on legal grounds, doubting the constitutional authority of Pennsylvania to send its militiamen – organized to defend their home state – into belligerent territory elsewhere.[18] And one man, David McDowell of West Chester, became the second Guard to desert the company. Those who remained expressed disdain for the cowards who'd stooped to desertion.

Colonel Harvey later described the move into Maryland this way:

> "Our orders at Harrisburg were to report to the commandant at Baltimore, General Dix. Our journey towards Baltimore, during daylight, was one constant scene of cheering. People – men, women and children – were loud in their demonstrations of patriotism and joy. When we reached the State line, we concluded to prepare for any emergency. We felt we were hovering between two authorities – passing from Pennsylvania State authority to the United States authority; and during this transit, I concluded I would be the authority, and the regiment cheerfully accepted it. We ordered the train to stop, and the men out. Ammunition was distributed, and the men loaded their pieces. We then moved on the train to within four miles of the city, and there stopped until daylight.

> "We next moved into the city and stopped at the Bolton Station. The men got out of the cars and formed a line on the side of the street, where we remained for five hours, awaiting orders. Immediately on our arrival in the city, we reported by telegraph … At about 10 o'clock, a.m., a dispatch was received … directing us to procure something to eat, and then

proceed to Washington as soon as we could obtain transportation … The mayor or Provost Marshal, attentive to our wants, sent Mr. S. Robinson of that city with a police force to conduct us to some grove to take refreshment. We formed, and under the pilotage of a policeman, started, as we supposed, for the grove aforementioned. After half an hour's march through the city, the head of our line halted at the Camden Depot!

"I inquired if this was where we were to get our breakfast and the three last meals not yet had. I was met by the policeman, who informed me that he had been ordered to conduct us to that depot, that we might be moved on to Washington at once.

"Just then some of the managers of the railroad came up, and insisted on our going ahead, as the train was already in waiting. I informed them that we should not leave Baltimore until the men had one full meal … I then marched the regiment back to the Bolton Depot. The Quartermaster, Judge Lane, and Mr. E Robinson had just returned, and the men enjoyed one good meal. I next authorized Mr. Robinson to make arrangements and contract for the transportation of my regiment – nine hundred men, baggage, horses, and equipment, to Washington; — and to move precisely at nine o'clock, p.m. Mr. Robinson soon returned, having made the arrangements. At seven o'clock we moved the regiment once more from the Bolton Station to the Camden Station, and were there informed that the cars placed on the track were for us and were ready. We loaded up.

"There were twelve cars. We filled them full, leaving four companies still on the platform! The superintendent, managers, &c., came along blustering and scolding us for not getting ahead. I remonstrated with them about the accommodations provided, but only received in return threats that if we did not load up in the twelve cars, they would move the trains and leave us behind. In addition to this, they refused to take the cars containing our horses, surplus arms and ammunition. Our contract called for nine o'clock as the moving hour; it was then eight o'clock. I at length went to the head of the train, detached the locomotive, and placed Captain John Jameson on the platform with three companies to prevent the re-attachment of the locomotive or the moving of the train… until I should give the proper order….

"… When I got back, a Mr. White, clerk of the road, and a man calling himself president of the road, were present, who informed me that they had just received a dispatch from Honorable Simon Cameron, ordering me forward at once, and that we were to proceed in twelve cars, leaving the horses and baggage behind … I therefore demanded a certified copy of the Washington dispatch. They refused to give it to me, saying that I had no business with it. I replied that I had something to do with rogues in my life, that they might write almost anything and call it a dispatch! This made a little flurry.

"Just at this moment stepped in a man who, in a loud voice, proclaimed himself assistant quartermaster of the United States, and demanded information as to who was interfering with and preventing transportation! I looked at him a moment, measuring his metal, and then replied, it was myself. He responded that he would not have country colonels interfering with his business, and blustered considerably …

"I thereupon said to this blustering major, that I had possession of the locomotive and cars, and that he must show me better authority than he had yet shown to induce me to change my determination. I then wrote a dispatch to General Cameron, Secretary of War, stating our condition – their refusal to take us comfortably, and to take our horses and baggage. They soon presented us with a reply, purporting to be from Secretary Cameron, ordering us forward. I ordered a certified copy of it, which they refused. I then left the office and returned to the cars, and waited till nearly nine o'clock, still refusing to move, when the aforementioned United States major, or quartermaster, came to me, and said they would furnish three more cars, that we might leave at nine o'clock. This was done, and we finally took our departure for Washington, where we arrived about one o'clock next morning."[19]

Questions about the authority of Pennsylvania to send troops into another state became moot when the 7th Regiment was mustered into the United States Army, officially a part of the Pennsylvania Reserves Division under the command of General George McCall. Now federal troops, they could legally be sent anywhere, Pennsylvania Reserves or not. Ordered to Tenallytown, Maryland, a part of the defensive ring surrounding the federal capital, the men built shelters and received instruction in the use of their weapons. On August 21, they paraded in front of President Lincoln and his newly appointed commander, George McClellan.[20]

On August 24th, they were sent to Great Falls, fifteen miles northwest of the capital, to guard the fords across the Potomac that separated Maryland from Virginia.[21] On the morning of September 4th, cannon fire from the Virginia side of the Falls suggested that a rebel attack might be imminent, but when the rebels withdrew rather than attack, the men "grieved because all prospects of a battle had now vanished."[22] A week later, they paraded in front of Lincoln again: this time, the President, his Secretary of War, General McClellan and other generals assembled to review the parade. Governor Curtain gave Colonel Harvey a blue silk flag fringed with yellow, Pennsylvania's coat of arms encircled by thirteen golden stars and the number 7, indicating the Seventh Reserves. Curtain appealed to the soldiers to risk their lives for the sake of nothing less than Christianity, civilization, and God himself:

> Our peaceful pursuits in Pennsylvania have been broken. Many of our people… have been forced to bear arms… All our material wealth, and the life of every man in Pennsylvania, stands pledged to vindicate the right, to sustain the Government, and to restore the ascendancy of law and order… Our people are for peace. But if men lay violent hands on the sacred fabric of the Government, unjustly spill the blood of their brethren, and tear the sacred constitution to pieces, Pennsylvania is for war – war to the death!
>
> [F]olly, fanaticism, rebellion, murder, piracy and treason prevail over a portion of this land; and we are here today to vindicate the right, to sustain the Government, to defend the Constitution, and to shed the blood of Pennsylvanians, if it need be, to produce this result….
>
> …[Y]ou have been willing to volunteer your services in defense of the great principle of human liberty. Should the wrong prevail, should treason and rebellion succeed, we have no government. Progress is stopped, civilization stands still, and Christianity in the world, for the time, must cease – cease forever. Liberty, civilization, and Christianity hang upon the result of this great contest.
>
> God is for the truth and the right. Stand by your colors, my friends, this day delivered to you, and the right will prevail… If you fail, hearts and homes will be made desolate. If you succeed, thousands of Pennsylvanians will rejoice over your success, and on your return, you will be hailed as heroes who have gone forth to battle for the right…. May the God of Battles in His wisdom protect your lives, and may Right, Truth and Justice prevail.[23]

The 7th and two other regiments were formed into a brigade under the command of General George Meade, and on the 9th of October, the Division abandoned the last pretense of being purely defensive when it marched into northern Virginia, setting up camp in Langley. McCall's Pennsylvania Reserves were now the right wing of the Union line. And as winter approached, they dug into camp there, doing battle with the cold and wet weather to come.

The men had bound themselves to fight for three years, but in October, the colonels who had organized them, egging them on with appeals to their courage and honor for the sake of their families and God himself, began to depart. The Fourth Regiment's Colonel Robert March resigned his commission and returned to Philadelphia "on account of physical disability engendered by over-exertion in camp." [24]   In November, the Second Regiment's Colonel William Mann resigned and returned to Philadelphia to run for political office.[25]   In December, the First Regiment's Colonel Biddle resigned his command to take a seat in Congress.[26]   Such was their sense of duty that they resigned their commissions and left the battlefield before ever coming under fire. Unlike the troops they'd recruited, they were under no obligation to remain.

And so the men hunkered down for a cold, tented winter. Facing the harsh conditions, more of the men followed the example set by their colonels. On December 18th William Haverland went missing; then Sergeant William Cain. Disdain for the deserters grew louder, even while men secretly wondered if they, too, should desert. Ordered to do so, men axed down trees, crisscrossed fields with snake-rail fences, burned logs to cook their food, to dry out rain-soaked blankets and to keep their coffee hot, while they tried to stay warm themselves. The winter snow was silent, white and pure; they waited uneasily for spring, when fairer weather would once again bring war.

In early March, the Army was reorganized into four corps. The Pennsylvania Reserves and all of McCall's division were assigned to the First Corps, commanded by Irwin McDowell, the career soldier so thoroughly humiliated at Bull Run.[27] Sitting in ice and rain, the soldiers heard of ironclad ships that, while indestructible themselves, had left men dead beneath the waves at Newport News and Hampton Roads.

Then, in the middle of March, the rebel forces unexpectedly pulled back. The northern Army of the Potomac crept forward to follow them south. Most of James' fellow Guards would have preferred remaining in Pennsylvania, to guard their city and their families, but some were now saying they'd rather not go home until they'd tasted the glory that would be theirs if they could take Richmond. With that in mind, they marched toward Alexandria, cold rain forcing them to stop for the night.

> After much patient labor, we succeeded in getting our fires started, and towards night, hot coffee was served. Such was the violence of the storm that it was impossible to put up our tents; most of the men spent the night in cutting wood and standing around the fires. At one time the heavens opened their flood-gates and poured down a torrent of water, stifling the wind and flooding all below; the fires were instantly

extinguished and the patriots were aroused to a full appreciation of their condition. Not to be thus conquered by the elements, they set up wild shouts and huzzas, making the woods and hills for miles around echo with their noise, actually outdoing the storm, and putting the men into a good humor.[28]

As the generals debated how best to proceed, voices within the regiment cried out for action. On a cold and rainy night in mid-April, they took a train to Manassas Junction, site of the infamous humiliation where they witnessed "skulls, cross bones, hands, feet and whole skeletons of their fellow soldiers who had fallen at Bull Run," and foraged on the farmers' poultry yards and milk houses.[29]

In mid-May, when the rebels abandoned Fredericksburg, the Reserves moved still further south, occupying that defenseless city. Taking control of the last rebel city before Richmond excited them. Battle could not elude them forever. With an attack on Richmond itself ever more imminent, the Tenth Regiment's Colonel McCalmont joined the other colonels who had resigned their commissions. "He was eminently successful; but when the time came for the well drilled regiment to be led in active campaigns, Colonel McCalmont was obliged, on account of his broken health, to allow that honor to his junior officer."[30]

Meanwhile, McClellan had been claiming all winter that his Army was outnumbered.[31] On June 8th, finally giving in to his pleas, the government ordered McCall's Pennsylvania Reserves to reinforce him. Marching south, boarding vessels about ten miles below Falmouth, the Reserves steamed down the Rappahannock River, arriving at Whitehouse Landing, on the Pamunkey, on the 14th of June.[32]

It should have been comforting to unite with the rest of McClellan's army, but it was not.

> When George McCall's Pennsylvania Reserves arrived at White House Landing that June, their first impression of the war on the Peninsula was not quickly forgotten. Piled on a wharf were scores of rough pine coffins awaiting shipment to the North, and several of the shed-like buildings lining the shore bore such signs as UNDERTAKERS AND EMBALMERS OF THE DEAD. PARTICULAR ATTENTION PAID TO DEAD SOLDIERS.[33]

On the 19th, the Reserves were ordered west to Mechanicsville, a small village only five or six miles northeast of the Confederate capital. Once there, they formed the extreme right wing of a Union line that stretched out east of the city.

They stopped on their westward march on the heights above Beaver Dam Creek, a ten-foot-wide stream with banks that rose sixty feet on either side.[34]

The riverbed was deep and swampy, both sides crawling with Virginia Creeper. The heights offered a clear view of any approach from the west, while the creek bottom waited to trap men in its mud. With the right wing

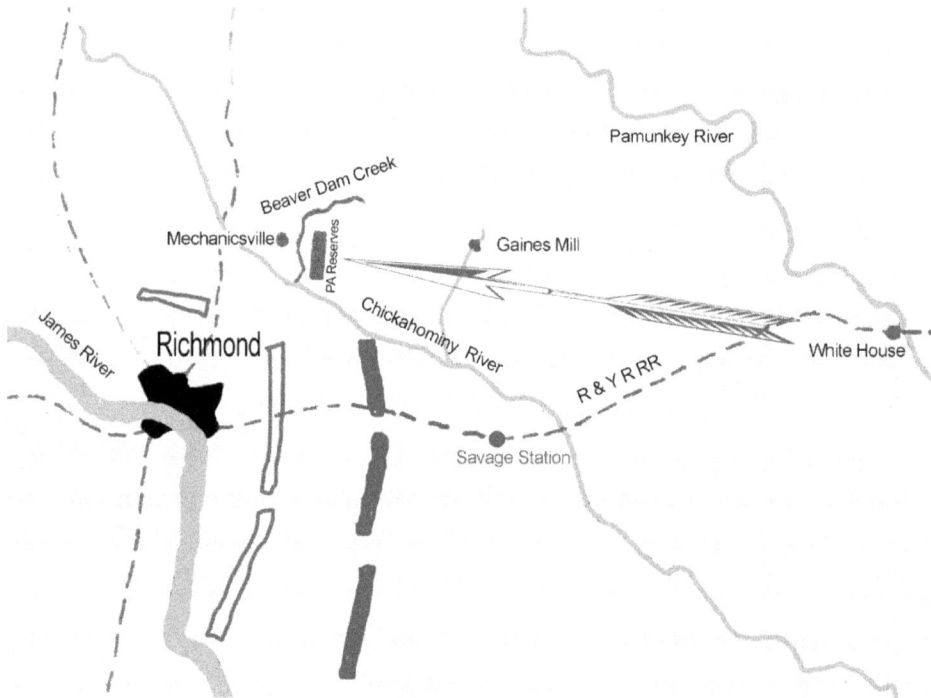

Pamunkey River

Beaver Dam Creek

Mechanicsville

PA Reserves

Gaines Mill

James River

Richmond

Chickahominy River

R & Y R RR

White House

Savage Station

established, "[t]he two most powerful armies that had ever faced each other on the Western Continent now stood like two giants, armed for the death struggle."[35] On the Union side, among the northernmost regiments of the entire Union line, Seymour's brigade was on the left, where the Creek flowed into the Chickahominy; Reynolds' brigade was upstream, on the right. To the great disappointment of many in the 7th Pennsylvania regiment, they and the rest of Meade's brigade were stationed in the rear. The men of the 7th had yet to see action. Some of Chapman's Philadelphia Guards hoped it would stay that way, while others were hungry for a taste of glory.

In front of the line of rifle-pits the ground descended for a distance, varying from seventy-five to one hundred and fifty feet to the creek, which was difficult to ford and wholly impracticable for artillery; beyond the creek there was a swamp that could not be passed by horses or artillery, and formed a serious obstruction to infantry. Two roads led from Mechanicsville through this swamp, one crossing Beaver Dam Creek at Ellerson's mill near the Chickahominy, and the other, crossing one mile further up the stream, led to Cold Harbor.[36]

Thursday, the 26th, came on still and motionless. Midday passed without incident. Late in the afternoon, word passed back to the 7th that a great number of rebel soldiers had pushed through the village of Mechanicsville; gunfire could be heard; soon, rebels could be seen on the other side of Beaver Dam Creek, back lit by a sun that was now in their eyes. First, the rebels attacked Reynolds, on the right. "[T]he command was given, and from the woods, out from the swamps, down the roads, along the entire front, with shriek and yell, flashing fire, thunder, and curling smoke, forward they came…"[37] Reynolds held firm; the rebels got nowhere on the right.[38]

Then more rebels could be seen advancing on the left, toward Ellerson's mill.

> [A]s soon as the enemy was seen advancing against that point, the Seventh Regiment, commanded by Colonel Harvey, was ordered to the extreme left of the Third Brigade to protect the left flank, in case the enemy should attempt to cross the creek below the mill…[39]

Their time had come! Fear that glory might pass them by gave way to a different, more heart-pounding fear that the real work for which they'd been trained might prove harder than they'd imagined. Yet James had taken an oath of service to his government. At the age of twenty-four, he had vowed to do his duty.

> Six companies were posted in the rifle pits, and four were sent forward across the meadow, along the creek, as skirmishers to receive the enemy.[40]

Posting skirmishers in front of the line would slow the enemy attack, keep them at the soggy creek bottom, within range of federal artillery, within sight of the federal riflemen looking down on them. But the skirmishers themselves had to give up the safety of the heights, taking what cover they could from the muddy creek bottom. John Chapman's "Philadelphia Guards" was one of the four companies sent as skirmishers to receive the enemy in the low-lying meadow. And no sooner had the skirmishers reached the bottom than the enemy advanced as expected.

> Between four and five o'clock in the afternoon, General Lee launched a heavy column down the Ellerson mill road … and maintained a furious attack until night, repeatedly attacking in the most terrific charges … The companies thrown forward as skirmishers made the most obstinate resistance …[41]

In the fighting at the muddy creek bottom, the 7th suffered four casualties. Robinson's Company lost two men: Henry Albert, who was killed on the spot, and Samuel Long, who was mortally wounded. John Chapman's Guards lost two as well: nineteen-year-old Christopher Sloan, who'd enlisted the same day James had, was felled on the spot.

And James himself was wounded.[42]

Due in large part to the delay caused by the skirmishers, the rebels' attempt to take the Union left failed; they withdrew from Beaver Dam Creek at about 9 p.m., after night had fallen. After that, "[n]othing could be heard in the black darkness of that night save the ghastly moans of the wounded and dying."[43]

General McCall was preoccupied preparing for a resumption of action at dawn. "My attention was now directed to the cleaning of the arms and the issuing of ammunition," he wrote, "to be in readiness for the resumption of the combat in the morning. This consumed our time till one o'clock a.m. of the 27th."[44] The general was right to get ready for the next day's battle, but as it turns out, such preparations were unnecessary. Although the Union had won the day (thanks to the skirmishers), McClellan – convinced as always that he was outnumbered – decided to order a retreat, pulling the federal troops back from Beaver Dam Creek to another creek, further east at Gaines Mill.[45] The skirmishers Henry Albert and Christopher Sloan were buried in place. Samuel Long and James Carvin were taken by makeshift stretchers and ambulance wagon to a field hospital in the rear, at Savage Station, on the Richmond and York River Railroad.[46] They likely arrived there on the morning of the 27th.

Once it was apparent that (despite his victory) McClellan had decided to pull back rather than press his advantage toward Richmond, the confederates swarmed across Beaver Dam Creek in pursuit, taking prisoners as they went.[47] There was a massive battle that day at Gaines Mill, and before midnight that evening, McClellan announced his decision to withdraw his Army south to the James River, abandoning his assault on Richmond, beginning a strategic retreat in the face of what he insisted was a superior Confederate Army. Federal soldiers spent the 28th caring for the wounded and disposing of the dead on the Gaines Mill battlefield, while depleted regiments moved south, across the Chickahominy, toward the James.[48] While Confederates could carry their wounded back to Richmond, the Federals were not so lucky.

> The Yankee wounded from Gaines's Mill who had been carried back across the Chickahominy were in worse straits, for with the White House base abandoned they could not be transported to Northern hospitals for advanced care. Instead they were crowded into a huge field hospital at Savage's Station on the York River Railroad, where surgeons labored around the clock to treat them. A New Jersey man having his wound dressed there matter-of-factly noted in his diary, "Four tables amputating all day."[49]

Wounded on the 26th, James had been among the first to arrive at Savage Station, before the great numbers from Gaines Mill were brought in on the 27th. Nothing was known in those days of microscopic germs or the dangers of infection. Medical care for the wounded was limited to amputation, to prevent gangrene, and doses of opium, to ease pain. The wounds to James's chest and abdomen could not be treated with amputation. His treatment was therefore limited to giving him opium. Thankfully, one of the first to arrive at Savage Station, he hadn't waited long for his first dose. But his comfort would remain only so as long as the supply lasted, and heavy casualties from Gaines Mill were quickly exhausting that supply.

The top brass ordered a withdrawal, an abandonment of the attack on Richmond. By 2 a.m. Sunday, the 29th, as a part of that withdrawal, McClellan's headquarters at Savage Station were being broken up.[50] The recently promoted Confederate General, Robert E. Lee, ordered his troops to pursue the retreating Yankees. McClellan's soldiers formed a rear guard to protect their retreat. But since Lee in fact had smaller numbers, he could not overrun the Yankee rear; he could merely engage them, advancing at whatever speed their retreat would allow. So the battle moved slowly toward Savage's Station that Sunday, the Yankees giving ground gradually, the rebels advancing yard by yard, only as far as the Yankees let them.

Meanwhile, the rebels' big 32-pound Brooke gun was moving slowly eastward from Richmond on the York River Railroad – directly toward Savage's Station. The gun was "shielded by a sloping casemate of railroad iron and nicknamed the 'Lady Merrimack.' It easily outranged any gun the Yankees had on the field, and as a rebel soldier told his wife, "During our progress… [it] would be turned loose on the enemy to their great dismay."[51] "Rolling, black clouds of smoke rose high over Orchard Station and Savage's Station on the railroad as the Yankees began destroying everything they could not carry away. Witnesses groped for words to describe the immensity of the destruction."

To keep supplies from falling into rebel hands, those still healthy among James's comrades set fire to hardtack boxes, beef, pork, coffee, vinegar, and whiskey. They destroyed rifles "by smashing the stocks against trees and throwing the barrels into the fires." Some of the last trains, full of ammunition, were set fire before they could be unloaded, exploding and producing "a rain of flaming debris," before the car was sent north, rolling down the incline toward the Chickahominy and the pursuing rebel forces.[52]

The movement of Union wagons south toward the James River made it clear to those in the field hospital that they were going to be left behind. "They saw many of the surgeons being called back to their regiments and the army's ambulances going with them – going empty so as to be available for the next battle."[53] Those able to walk out of the hospital, by themselves or with assistance from a fellow soldier, attempted to follow the retreating army. But some 3,000 wounded men, too ill or too badly wounded to move, were left behind to be taken prisoner – and left to whatever care the Rebels (short of opium for their own men) might choose to provide. One officer from Maine wrote home that leaving the wounded behind made his blood boil: "Their cries are yet ringing in my ears."[54]

Once his commanders had a moment to take stock, they counted James as wounded and as absent, but they provided no further information about him.[55] How could they have? The Union Army knew nothing about the fate of those they'd abandoned. Elisha Harvey's 7th Reserves had left the area. McClellan and the other top brass had retreated to safety on the James River. Not only James, but the entire assault on the Confederate capital, had been abandoned. And that's as far as history records the fate of private James Carvin of the Philadelphia Guards.

Over seven months later – on February 6th, 1863 – Harvey's 7th Regiment of Pennsylvania Reserves was ordered to Washington, D.C., to be stationed there and at Alexandria, where they would remain for more than a year to come. No one in the regiment could have known of James's fate until word came back from Rebel forces. And identifying Yankee wounded, nursing their wounds, reporting the names of those Yankees who'd died, was obviously not the Rebels' highest priority.

Seven weeks after James's death, the *Inquirer* of July 22, 1862, published a list of the wounded, dead and missing in the failed campaign against Richmond. Under the 7th Regiment, Company G, the list included J. C. Carvin – as one of those wounded.

COMPANY G—KILLED.
Christopher Sloan.
WOUNDED.

Capt. W. W. White,	Irvin Reich,
Serg. Edward Fontaine,	Wm. H. Meyer,
Serg. Charles Bastine,	Alvin White,
Corp. A. C. Bernard,	Charles Sands,
Corp. Luke Mullen,	H. Clay White,
Francis Short,	Henry Weager.
J. C. Carvin,	

It was not until a Special Muster Roll on April 10, 1863 – nearly a year later – that Carvin's records first included the notation, "Died at Savage Station July 1st 1862 from wounds received at Battle of Mechanicsville." A casualty sheet, certified by Captain John R. Barret, reads "Nature of Casualty: Death," and "Cause of Casualty: Wounded at battle of Mechanicsville June 26, 1862." "Clothing account sent 2nd Auditor. July 21."

Notwithstanding that report, confirmation of the death, and of its date, may not have been received that April. It could have been an assumption, based on the observations of those who'd carried James's stretcher and tended his wounds. There is no record of where his remains were buried.

How long should an army wait before an assumption of death should be made? How long before such an assumption is reduced to writing and communicated to a soldier's family? In James's case, it took a year to clear his clothing account. Of course, there was a war on, and commanders naturally gave priority to the needs of those healthy enough to fight.

James had followed orders. He had done his duty, obeying the call of his government. He had thought, perhaps, that if he could look out for his reckless brother, he might someday leave the cotton mill for a prosperous life in brass. Whether his enlistment served the needs of Christianity, civilization, or God himself, and even whether it helped to unify a divided country, we cannot say.

Notes on Chapter 6, James C. Carvin

[1] Born in New York in 1838 (1860 U.S. Census, Phila Ward 19, Fam 3539), James had been six when the bloody riots of 1844 erupted outside his front door, eighteen when the great train wreck of 1856 killed so many children from St. Michael's. His civil war muster roll gives his age as 23 as of May 27, 1861 (7th Infantry, Pennsylvania Reserves, Company G, Dept of Military & Veterans Affairs, Rec Grp 19, Series 19.11, Penn Historical and Museum Commission, accessed via Ancestry.com.) The 1838 date given here is based on the ages in those records, although the 1850 Census (Kensington Ward 6, Fam 798), which lists him as a ten-year old, is contrary.

[2] The 1850 Census lists him as attending school, and it must have been the Master Street School: St. Michael's parochial school had not yet opened, and both the other public schools in Kensington – the Palmer and New Market Schools – were smaller and farther away.

[3] For the Austin brass business, see chapter 4, above, and notes thereto.

[4] Brass pins had long been used in the weaving of wool, and since 1837, there'd been dependable molding machines to make other shapes consistently. Vin Callcut, "Brief Early History of Brass," accessed at https://www.copper.org/publications/newsletters/innovations/2000/01/historybrass.html; "History of Metal Casting: A Brief Timeline," accessed at http://www.metal-technologies.com/docs/default-source/education/historyofmetalcasting.pdf?sfvrsn=8.

[5] *Ibid.*

[6] James was listed as a weaver in the 1860 Census, but when he entered the military in 1861, he claimed brassworking experience. (CMSR of Pvt. James Carvin, Co G, 7th Pa. Reserves.)

[7] Doreen Hopwood, *Brass-Making: "The Brass Industry and Brass Workers in Birmingham," West Midlands History*, accessed at https://mhfonline.weebly.com/uploads/2/9/1/1/29114567/history_west_midlands_sample_magazine.pdf.

[8] J. R. Sypher, History of the Pennsylvania Reserve Corps, (Elias Barr & Co., 1865), pp 68-69.

[9] The following day, another regiment followed the first. J. Matthew Gallman, Mastering Wartime: A Social History of Philadelphia During the Civil War, Univ of Penn Press, 1990, p 101.

[10] *Ibid.*, p 102.

[11] *Ibid.*, p 105.

[12] Thomas Carvin CMSR, combined 69th and 71st Pa Infantry, Nat'l Archives; also Samuel Bates, History of the Pennsylvania Volunteers, 1861-1865, Vol 2, Harrisburg, 1869, p 713.

[13] The 1861 Phila Directory contains John Chapman, dealer, 7 Blackhorse alley; John Chapman, restaurant, 632 Shippen; John Chapman, clerk, 326 Culvert; Jonathan Chapman, machinist, 517 N 10th; Jonathan Chapman, commercial merchant, 205 Church alley; and Jonathan Chapman, commercial merchant, at 1216 Chestnut. Chapman's own CMSR indicates he was 43 at the time he entered military service.

[14] James Carvin CMSR and Bates, *supra.*

[15] Sypher, *supra*, pp 84, 318-319.

[16] Sypher, *supra*, pp 69-71, 80-90. Charles Biddle had seen service in Mexico; John McCalmont in Florida. Horatio Sickel and Seneca Simmons had military training, but no combat experience.

[17] Maryland, a slave state, may have seceded from the Union had Lincoln not ordered the arrest of state legislators to prevent it. (Carl Sandburg, Abraham Lincoln: The War years, Vol 1, Harcourt Brace, 1939, pp 273-276; "Affairs in Baltimore," *New York Times*, May 29, 1861, p 1; Michael Shearer, "Abraham Lincoln Crushes Civil Liberties in Maryland," Abbeville Institute, June 6, 2019, accessed at https://www.abbevilleinstitute.org/blog/abraham-lincoln-crushes-civil-liberties-in-maryland/.)

[18] Sypher, *supra*, p 76.

[19] Sypher, *supra*, pp 97-100. Col. Harvey's account of his doings makes it sound as if his insistence paid off, his command rewarded with adequate train cars. But according to Col. Harvey's account, twelve cars were originally provided, and after they were loaded full, four of the ten companies

remained on the platform. Six companies had therefore loaded into twelve cars – two cars per company. Then three additional cars were provided, and they left for Washington – which is to say, all ten companies were on 15 cars, or 1-1/2 cars per company. Clearly, a compromise had been reached as to the number of cars to be provided, as the cars were now significantly more crowded. Furthermore, Harvey's account does not reflect whether the horses and all the equipment made the trip – one suspects, to fit all 900 men into the 15 cars, sixty men per car, the horses were left behind. Yet Harvey's account reads as if his hard bargaining had resulted in his winning the day. (His report would not be the last war report of a distinctly self-serving nature.)

[20] *Ibid.*, pp 101, 109.

[21] *Ibid.*, pp 113-114. On September 2nd, McCall's dispatch to McClellan reported that the nine hundred and two men of Colonel Harvey's 7th Reserves, armed with improved rifles and muskets, in good condition and very well drilled, was performing picket duty at Great Falls. (*Report of McCall to McClellan*, Sept 2, 1861, in Sypher, *supra*, p 112.)

[22] Sypher, *supra*, p 114.

[23] *Ibid.*, pp 116-117. The parade speeches took place on the 10th of September.

[24] *Ibid.*, p 83.

[25] *Ibid.*, p 80. Mann was the sitting district attorney for the city of Philadelphia. According to Sypher's flattering description, the political race Mann entered – which resulted in victory of the Murphy ally, Democrat Lewis Cassidy – was "a sphere yielding, perhaps, less distinction, but requiring equal devotion to the Union."

[26] "It seems to me," said Biddle, "to be incompatible with the character of a representative and a legislator to be a paid officer, subject to the orders of the Executive, and present in his place only by the revocable leave of a military superior." (*Ibid.*, pp 69-70.)

[27] *Ibid.*, p 158.

[28] *Ibid.*, pp 170-171.

[29] *Ibid.*, pp 167-168, 172-173.

[30] *Ibid.*, p 188.

[31] Stephen W. Sears, To the Gates of Richmond: The Peninsula Campaign, First Mariner Books, 1992, pp 162, 190, 203, 217; Sypher, *supra*, pp 204-205.

[32] Sypher, *supra*, pp 192 – 195. The plantation on the south shore at White House Landing was the home of Martha Dandridge Custis before she married George Washington.

[33] Sears, *supra*, p 163.

[34] *Ibid.*, pp 201-202; Sypher, *supra*, p 209; William C. Davis, The Battlefields of the Civil War, University of Oklahoma Press (2000), p 64.

[35] Sypher, *supra*, 197-199.

[36] *Ibid.*, p 206.

[37] *Ibid.*, p 211.

[38] Sears, *supra*, p 204.

[39] Sypher, *supra*, p 212.

[40] *Ibid.*

[41] *Ibid.*, p 213.

[42] The official reports of the battle don't mention which four companies of Harvey's 7th Pennsylvania Reserves regiment were sent forward as skirmishers; nor do the later histories. But no soldiers from Companies A through E were killed at Beaver Dam Creek, nor were any from companies H through K. Robinson's Company F, from Luzerne County, and Chapman's Company G, the Guards from Philadelphia, each sustained two severe casualties, making their service among the skirmishers all but certain.

[43] Seldon Connor to brother, June 26, quoted at Sears, *supra*, p 207, fn 19; Sypher, *supra*, p 214.

[44] Sypher, *supra*, p 217.

[45] Sears, *supra*, p 211; Sypher, *supra*, p 217.

[46] Sypher, *supra*, p 217; Sears, *supra*, p 214.

148

[47] Sears, *supra*, p 212.

[48] *Ibid.*, pp 253-254.

[49] *Ibid.*, p 254.

[50] *Ibid.*, pp 259-60.

[51] *Ibid.*, pp 269-270. "With measured, thundering regularity, the railroad battery dropped its heavy shells into the woods and fields on the Yankee front. Before its aim was corrected, several reached as far as the field hospital."

[52] *Ibid.*, p 263-264.

[53] *Ibid.*, p 264.

[54] Sears, *supra*, p 271, and Thomas W. Hyde to mother, July 6, quoted in Sears at p 264. As it happens, among the rebel troops advancing toward Savage's Station that day were William Barksdale's Mississippians, pushing through the woods just south of the Williamsburg Road; among them was a young Alemeth Byers, a member of our mother's family. A fictional account of his arrival at Savage's Station, and his conversation with a delirious James Carvin there, is given in the novel Alemeth (Nothing in Common Books, 2017, ISBN 978-0-9768183-8-0, pp 319-321).

[55] James Carvin's pay records for May and June, 1862 – completed in early July – marked him as "absent" and then, "wounded, in Gen'l Hosp, left June 27, 1862." Pay records for the next six months, September through February of 1863, read the same way – there is no further reflection of his fate in them.

7. Joseph P. Murphy

Dominick and Hannah's fourth son, Joseph Patrick Murphy, grew up in the aftermath of the 1844 riots.[1] He attended the Master Street School; he took communion at the altar rail of the reconstructed St. Michael's church; some of the boys who came to mass looked at him with envy, and he at them only glancingly, the way people of means often look at those in need. Joe's well-known father ran the business that put bread on their tables. By the time Joe was ten, his father represented all of Kensington as a member of the Common Council; his brothers worked alongside the most important men in the country; he himself faced life with great expectations.

But having gone their own ways in the world, his older brothers had left no one to safeguard the family business. Nothing seemed worthier than taking up the enterprise that had made the family's blessings possible. Financial success was the goal to which all Americans aspired, and as an American, Joe was unabashedly interested in preserving his family's economic wellbeing. Indeed, if he could turn the family business into something even greater than his father had, future generations of Murphys would remember him well.

Joe attended the Christian Brothers' school at St. Michael's.[2] About sixteen when the War began, working in the mill after school, he caught only occasional glimpses of amputees entering and exiting hospitals nearby.[3] But he did see civic leaders use pomp and circumstance to gain support for war – honoring heroes with marching bands, standing on public platforms, doling out honorary swords with scabbards and golden tassels. Such ceremonies made a lasting impression: Joe could see how leaders shaped (or even bent) the opinions of others to suit their own goals and ambitions. Perhaps before he was even conscious of it himself, Joe acquired the skills he'd later need to be a leader of men.

On the third of April, 1865, the news of Richmond's capture brought rejoicing in the streets, the blowing of steam whistles, the ringing of carriage bells. Cracked as it was, the State House bell could nonetheless be heard for miles around. In front of Independence Hall, gongs were struck, firemen paraded. That night, candles, torches, and fireworks brightened the sky.[4] Now that the killing had stopped, leaders presented the war as a glorious thing, a national and philosophical triumph. Those who'd fought, died and killed were enshrined in granite and marble, heroes in the collective memory. And once the hoopla had cleared, once honor and respect had been bestowed and the collective memory fixed, the war was declared a thing of the past. A part of history. In its wake, people were declared its beneficiaries, free to go about the great business of living, free to make use of the unlimited opportunities that freedom itself afforded to all Americans.

It's been said that Joe served an "apprenticeship" with his father before the war and that, in 1866, with the war over, he "began a weave shop of his own, most likely with financial backing from his father."[5] But the truth is not so simple. If we imagine him watching his father operate a hand loom like a young, awe-struck Pip watching at the forge, we've got the wrong idea. Joe had already learned phonographic reporting from his brothers; he had practiced that skill reporting local trials and news stories.[6] He'd spent a year (1865) with his brothers in Washington, where he assisted them on the Lincoln conspirators' trial.[7] He'd been sixteen or seventeen when the 1862 Revenue Act became law, and he'd seen John Budd, the Assistant Tax Assessor, call upon his father's mill. He'd heard his father rail against taxes Republicans had levied to fund *their* war, and he'd listened to the older men talk – his father about prosperity, his brothers Dennis and James about the powers that be in Washington. And when conversation turned to corruption in the Treasury Department, his apprenticeship was nothing like that among the weavers, tanners, printers and blacksmiths of the old world: his own apprenticeship, if that's what it was, had a more modern, post-war focus. It wasn't about how to operate a hand loom, but about how to prosper financially, given the new relationship between government, markets, and commercial business enterprises. Joe learned shorthand reporting, worked with his brothers in Washington, and eventually became a tax assessor.[8]

The federal income tax and the new excise taxes on manufactured goods were supposed to be temporary wartime measures. But when the guns stopped pounding, the vast war debt had not been paid off. Many in government saw good reason to continue the vast systems of revenue that war had spawned. In 1866, with internal revenue taxes still in effect, news about scandals and corruption in their collection was everywhere. Brother Dennis's Retrenchment Committee, charged by Congress with exposing the problems, was charged by the press with ignoring them. Pressure on the Treasury Department to crack down on corruption was growing. In north and west Philadelphia, there was no love lost between the Murphys and Republican Leonard Myers, who'd been awarded his seat in Congress amid their protestations of fraud. Assistant Assessor John Budd sometimes assessed the Murphy mill and sometimes didn't. Tensions were also growing between Congress and the President over federal appointments. When Republican Thomas Allen was appointed to the Third District Assessor's office in 1866, he was able to appoint his own partisans as his assistants.[9] Yet for some reason, despite their opposing political affiliations, the Murphys' past opposition to Myers, and the absence of anything one might call relevant experience, Republican Allen appointed twenty-one-year-old Joe Murphy as one of his assistants. And he did so at almost the same time President Johnson appointed Edward Murphy to the Superintendent's position at the Custom House.[10]

For Joe Murphy, it would prove a very different kind of apprenticeship. Like John Budd, he was now able to question the monthly returns submitted by all the taxpayers in his division. This included the excise tax on all goods manufactured domestically, the income tax owed by higher-earning individuals, and the special taxes imposed on luxury goods like watches and pianos. Potentially, there were over a thousand taxpayers to assess out of a much larger population. Visiting factories and homes to determine what every resident and proprietor owed, Joe wielded enormous influence, especially in the industrial and residential neighborhoods along the Delaware River that were known, collectively, as Fishtown. With every taxpayer who sought to curry his favor, he was reminded of the power he held.[11]

He was not in a position to decide the taxes due from his father; that responsibility remained with John Budd. But a month after Murphy's appointment, Allen replaced Budd with a man more to his liking, leaving Joe in a position to keep an eye on how the new man treated his father's tax liabilities.[12] The only question is whether he was tempted to do more than that. With brother Edward now Superintendent of Exports and Drawbacks, the two were able to work with each other, if they chose, for the benefit of both.

At just this time, an older man by the name of John J. Miller entered Joe's life. Miller, who lived in the same neighborhood as Joe's office,[13] had worked as a customs inspector for the Treasury Department, but by the late 1860's was engaged in a commercial enterprise of an unknown nature.[14] Miller's wife was a Clothier, a family of some note that had been in America since colonial days.[15] His daughter Adele was just what Joe wanted.[16] After a brief courtship, the young couple were married and Joe moved into the Miller house.[17]

Neither Joe nor his older brother Edward had shown affinity for bookkeeping matters, but as we've seen, "peculation and speculation were the order of the day," and tax officials had "almost unlimited facilities for making money."[18] And somehow, just like his brother, Joe managed to accumulate significant wealth in those years. Whether the brothers and their soon-to-be father-in-law were able to avoid the temptations their offices afforded them will likely never be known.[19] But the brothers' stint as federal tax men didn't last long. Edward and Joe both resigned their federal offices just as the drawbacks scandal in New York was coming to public attention and public scrutiny was turning toward Philadelphia's tax collectors.[20]

As we saw in Chapter 1, Dominick Murphy had first listed himself in Kensington as a weaver. Able to operate (and repair) a handloom himself, his allegiance had been to the trade he'd grown up with, even while others were turning to looms powered by steam. But young Joe had received an education; through his "apprenticeship" as a tax assessor, he'd been exposed to alternative products, processes and personalities, each with a different scheme for making money. As a result, he felt more comfortable keeping an eye on the market, competitors, prices, costs, and margins – on the books of the business and the methods of government – than on the looms themselves. He was not, in the end, a mere weaver like his father, but a modern American businessman, keenly focused on how best to put his money to work. As the decade came to a close, he started listing himself in the city directory as a "manufacturer."[21]

His new cotton mill, like his father's, relied on the old hand loom technology:

> Though only 25, he had $15,000 invested and he was spinning
> his own yarns, using a 5-horsepower engine. Weaving,
> however, was still done on handlooms, with a total of nineteen
> men and twenty women employed by the firm.[22]

An early challenge to Joe's sense of business and opportunity came from the manufacturer's association. At the end of every season, the association's members selected one of their number to cut wages, to set a prevailing wage for the following year.[23] (Freedom for manufacturers meant doing what it took to maximize profits, especially if the means were legal.) In 1875, it was Joe's turn to do the cutting of the wages. Still only 31 years old, seeing the practice in terms of dollars and cents, Joe went along with his older peers: at the end of the season, he cut the wages of his employees.

Impatient to better themselves after losing ground in the war, the weavers were in no mood to let wage cuts continue. It was a free country; involuntary servitude had been abolished; their labor could be freely given or withheld. And so, on January 20, 1876, they passed a resolution "providing for the appointment of a committee of three to wait upon the men who are working for Joseph Murphy at a reduced rate. Also, a resolution that the meeting would not resume work at Murphy's unless he will guarantee twenty cents per spread in the warps. He is now giving only fifteen cents."[24]

Faced with this assertion of freedom by his workers, Joe responded with more freedom of his own: he hired men who were willing to work at the reduced wages. A week later, *The Inquirer* reported that the weavers had met again, and this time, they'd adopted resolutions "for the formation of a union on a firm basis for self-protection." "Only three men were working at Murphy's mill, the others having refused to return at the reduction."[25] Apparently, the experienced assessor had underestimated his employees' determination.

But in those days, strikes were not protected by law. After the panic of 1873 cut into its profits, the Baltimore and Ohio Railroad had cut its workers' wages by ten percent; when workers de-coupled locomotives and declared that no trains would leave unless the pay cuts were rescinded, President Hayes sent in federal troops to get the railroads running again; the President's message had warned "all persons engaged in or connected with said domestic violence and obstruction of the laws to disperse and retire peaceably to their respective abodes."[26] It was not a good time for organized labor. In Joe's case, the strike eventually ended without having done any permanent damage to his fortune. The mid-1870's turned out to be a great time for Philadelphia's manufacturers.

On July 1, 1874, America's first public zoo opened at Fairmount Park, featuring animals from all over the world.[27] In early 1876, regular railroad passenger service north to New York joined the service south to Washington. And then, opening on the tenth of May, the American Centennial Exposition showcased the newest inventions of industry.

> With the opening of the great Centennial Exposition of 1876, the city re-emerged nationally. No longer the center of politics, religion, intellect, arts and letters, even of finance and commerce, Philadelphia presented itself as Technology – Queen of the Engine. Let New York handle the finances and set the fashions, let Boston cling to its fading reputation as schoolmarm of the nation. Philadelphia was warming to business...[28]

The Exposition introduced Philadelphians to the typewriter. It introduced them to Bell's new invention, the telephone.[29] (Could a person profit by simply talking into a box?) Among the more striking attractions was the huge Corliss engine that gave heartbeat and pulse to the rest of the Exposition:

> Finally, President Grant and Emperor Dom Pedro grasped the valves that started the immense Corliss Engine in Machinery Hall, perhaps the greatest wonder of the Exposition. By means of cogs and underground shafts, this creation... supplied the power to drive some 800 other machines at the fair. Its two cylinders, each forty-four inches in diameter with a ten-foot stroke, propelled a flywheel thirty feet in diameter and weighing fifty-six tons through thirty-six revolutions a minute, governing 1400 horsepower of energy. With the Corliss Engine beginning to hiss with steam and turn its wheel, the fair was open. People cheered and threw their hats into the air...[30]

But impressive as the Corliss Engine was, the exhibit most fascinating to Joe Murphy was neither it, nor the typewriter, nor the telephone; it was the positive-motion looms set up near the engine in Machinery Hall.

Even when powered by steam, traditional weaving relied on paddles that sent shuttles and their little cargoes of weft yarn flying freely through the open sheds of warps. But as with any object flying through space, control was a problem. Whacked too hard, the shuttle would pass the fabric's edge; whacked too soft, it might never reach it.[31] The positive motion shuttle brought control and uniformity.[32] Looms could weave wider fabric than ever before, and with tension under control, costs could be reduced.

Weaving wide fabrics… by the hand loom hitherto has been a most arduous undertaking; three men were required, one at each end, to drive the shuttle with heavy hammers, a third to stand between them and aid them in beating the lay. It was labor of the severest sort, and those engaged in it became prematurely old. Contrast this with the colossal [new] machine which scarcely requires the attention of the single young girl in front of it…[33]

Combined with the immense power of steam, the control made possible by the positive motion shuttle could guarantee a product that was both uniform and inexpensive. That same year, Dominick Murphy stopped operating his old mill at 1340 Palethorp. Taking advantage of Dominick's connections and customer lists, Joe was soon operating two small handloom mills.[34] When Dominick died the following year, one might expect he left a substantial estate. (Legally, it passed to Hannah.) But as the estate's Administrator, Joe swore that it was worth less than a thousand dollars.[35]

If his father left him nothing, and if he'd earned nothing but his wages as a tax assessor, it's hard to understand where Joe got the money for his business. Yet somehow, Joe found himself with enough capital not only to survive, but to expand, as if he'd been waiting for the freedom to do things his own way. Focused on costs, prices and profits, he began thinking how best to modernize his equipment. The way Philip Scranton summed it up – that he "made his exit from the handloom trade"[36] – was an understatement.

His building at 531 East York was on a normally-sized residential lot, but the adjoining property at 529 was a larger lot with a larger commercial building.[37] And if three high-paid, strike-prone men could be replaced by one lower-paid girl, then steam driven, positive motion looms had to be good for the profit margin. By 1879, Joe had added twenty-two power looms to his seventy-five handlooms. The addition left him running out of space, looking for a way to expand.

The *Inquirer* of July 19 1879 reported the building of a new mill:

Another Mill.—Mr. Joseph P. Murphy, manufacturer of cotton and woolen goods, has commenced the erection of a new mill property at Fourth and Cumberland streets. The building is to have a front of about 46 feet and a depth of 200 feet, and is to be four stories high, exclusive of the basement story. The old mill on York street, east of Frankford avenue, is found inadequate for present purposes.

The new building was complete by the end of the year.[38] According to Scranton,

The York Street mills were a spatial constraint, being four stories high but only 54 by 30 and 54 by 37 feet... In 1879, Murphy made his exit from the handloom trade. He purchased a lot at Fourth and Cumberland at the western edge of the Nineteenth Ward and erected a five-story factory 200 by 45 feet... On its completion in December of 1879, Murphy installed 400 power looms. By 1882, he employed 546 workers, which was consistent with a two-loom system on fancy goods (shawls, spreads and worsteds) or even a single-loom arrangement, given that no spinning or dyeing was set up in this facility.[39]

Four hundred power looms! Five hundred and forty-six workers! Still, the old mills on York Street and the new one on Cumberland were not enough: Joe opened yet another mill, over a mile to the south – quite an accomplishment for a man who had reported his father's estate as worth less than a thousand dollars.[40] If not from his stint as a tax collector, where had the money come from?

The noise of the steam-driven looms was deafening. Steel reeds beat lays relentlessly as picker sticks drove shuttles back and forth. Workers couldn't hear the boys next to them. With the tension of warps and the packing of wefts left to the machines, small fingers – well suited to the threading of heddles, the tying of knots and the snipping of threads – did all the work that was left.

Here a handloom shopman [Dominick Murphy] provided his son with the skills and means to pursue the traditional craft, but the son reached gradually outward to engage the technology and productive structures that promised larger-scale profit and accumulation. Joseph Murphy... seems to have stepped out of the capitalism of competence into that of ceaseless expansion. That transition was not a matter of one decision but the project of a lifetime and the product of a long string of linked choices, which he evidently made with an accuracy that eluded many others. To move to larger quarters, to bring in that first set of power looms, to buy land and build a mill, to abandon spinning his own yarn, to specialize in woolens and high-ticket worsteds, each of these decisions took Joseph Murphy another step away from the social and productive relations of the workshops in which he had been schooled.[41]

In abandoning old traditions of the weaver's craft, Joe Murphy was anything but alone. The Second Industrial Revolution was reaching a crescendo. The electric arc-welder. Moving pictures. Aluminum. Coca-Cola. Something called an automobile. In Philadelphia, cable cars were supplanting horse-car lines, the wealthy were getting telephones, and Chestnut Street, downtown, was being lit by electricity.[42] It was a great time to be a manufacturer.

> Textile workers immigrating to Philadelphia [in the 1880's] were no longer handloom journeymen but factory veterans seeking factory jobs…. In the nativist riots of the 1840s one Kensington shop master, fresh from bitter conflicts with weavers over the price of work, distributed arms to his men in the face of external threat. The complex and tenacious bonds exemplified by that incident were by the eighties being replaced by the transactional motif so basic to "modern" capitalism… Scrapping his handlooms in December 1879, Murphy symbolically signaled that the last stages in a transition fifty years in the making had arrived.[43]

Joe moved his family of six, along with three in-laws and a live-in servant, into a new house at 123 Susquehanna Avenue, facing the beautiful Norris Square Park, and he started building a big new home of his own at 2529 North 6th Street – a "prestigious" neighborhood which, by Kenneth Milano's count, boasted twenty-four households from the Boyd's Blue Book list.[44] The neighborhood was not only prestigious, but far less "Irish" than the Murphy's prior haunts. In fact, the house next door to their new home was the residence of the wealthy widow Margaret Kiker, a staunch German Baptist who had inherited a substantial family meat business from her husband. One can't be sure that Margaret Kiker's reasons had anything to do with Murphy's religion or nationality, but almost immediately after Joe Murphy bought the lot at 2529 North 6th Street, Margaret Kiker left the house next door, moving several houses further north, as if she refused to live next door to the brash and successful Irish Catholic.[45]

We will see more of the tension between Murphys and Kikers in due course. But for all we know, when he moved to North 6th Street in 1880, Joe Murphy knew nothing of any resentments Margaret Kiker may have held. His focus was on his business. By 1883, he'd opened weaving operations at two more locations.[46] Over the next two years, he helped organize a new national bank – the Ninth National Bank of Philadelphia – and was elected to its board of directors.[47] In 1885, he was elected President of the Grover Cleveland Association.[48] By the late 1880's, he had over 500 looms and 900 workers, producing "cotton, wool and worsted goods of all descriptions to the value of $1,500,000 annually."[49]

Nine hundred workers! A million and a half a year! In 1883, there were labor strikes at J. Granlee & Sons' woolen mills, at Brighton Woolen Mills, at Watt & Sons, and at other uptown woolen mills.[50] When the weavers and beamers of Kensington struck over a ten per cent reduction in wages, one story noted that "[a]t the mills of Joseph P. Murphy, Fourth and Cumberland Streets, the places of the striking beamers have been supplied. Some of the men originally employed in the places of strikers have been induced to quit. Mr. Murphy does not know how long he will be able to keep his new hands."[51]

Murphy's weavers struck again on April 20, 1885, for "an advance of 25 cents on the cut of seventy picks. They have been getting seventy-five cents." [52] Less than a month later, about eighty-five of them struck, demanding nine dollars a week, claiming that only a few of them made more than six.[53] Four months later, when a meeting of mixed shawl weavers from mills across Kensington gathered to demand a general wage increase, a "particularly large delegation from Joseph P. Murphy's mill" was reported to have been present. Murphy claimed he was paying more than other mills in the city, but three hundred looms in his mill "were left to rattle and run unattended" as a hundred and fifty weavers quit.[54]

Murphy could sometimes be convincing. For example, he was able to convince some of his workers that while profit margins could absorb cost increases in one product, they could not do so in others:

'My gingham weavers wanted an increase,' he said yesterday, 'but I showed them that that was virtually impossible, as I am paying now as much if not more for that grade of goods than any manufacturer in the city. We settled our difficulties very amicably, and the mill will resume work on Monday.'[55]

The gingham weavers' happiness lasted well into the following year. An article in *The Inquirer* described work stoppages at several other mills, while about Murphy's mill it reported only that "Forty additional looms are now in operation at Joseph Murphy's mill at Fourth and Cumberland streets."[56]

But the power of labor doesn't only depend on the profit margins available; it also depends on the level of skill that workers have to offer. At the end of March, "ten dissatisfied boys" of Murphy's mill demanded an increase from $2.50 to $3.00 a week. The strike did not cause trouble. "[W]hen the employer refused to raise their wages, all of them struck. The matter was settled by permanently discharging all who went out, and filling their places by others at the same salary the strikers had been getting."[57] The boys learned what Murphy already knew: it pays to understand one's place in the market.

Characteristically for the time, labor troubles continued to plague the Philadelphia textile industry. Determined to keep costs under control, the ninety-six members of the Manufacturers' Association threatened to shut down in the autumn of 1886, locking out the employees of all the firms, including Murphy's.[58] On that occasion, the threat of lockout seems to have worked. But Murphy's battles weren't only with his employees. In 1886, Bromley and Sons, one of the biggest textile companies in the city, filed a lawsuit against Murphy and two others, "trading as The New York Carpet Company, Limited," for infringement of their patented design for carpet rugs.[59] Men say it's tough to run a business with employees striking and competitors suing. Still, the following April, Murphy was among the area's textile manufacturers who formed their own country club.[60]

In late October President Grover Cleveland issued a proclamation declaring the prosperity of the country and designating November 24th as a day of Thanksgiving to the Almighty.[61] The Murphys had much to be thankful for; business was good; Adele was pregnant again; their eldest children, daughter Adele and son Joe, were teenagers. But Murphy paid little attention to his daughter's complaints of a headache while cutting up her turkey breast; he hardly noticed her mild cough as she ate; the next day, he signed a judgment note for $5,000 he owed to a creditor.[62] But the young Adele's headache and coughs were followed by fatigue, nervousness, muttering, delirium, a fever that wouldn't stop. By December 14th, the teenager was dead from typhoid fever.[63]

Given the perturbations of the human mind, stress and grief may have caused a refocusing of Joe's energies at that point from business to politics. A month after declaring the country's prosperity, President Cleveland declared that the civil war debt had been paid off, the Treasury now had a surplus of over a hundred million dollars, and the government no longer needed the revenue that tariffs brought in. He therefore called for their repeal.[64] High tariffs were inflating the price of the imported wool Murphy's mills used for woolens and worsteds, making his quality line less competitive even while helping the price of domestic wool to rise.[65] Murphy made the pitch to his workers: by hurting business, and by shutting down factories, high tariffs indirectly held down their wages. Cleveland's tariff reductions, he urged, were in their interest as well as his own.

The zeal with which Joe took up the cause of tariff reform (and Grover Cleveland as its champion) was enough to make one think he'd taken up the cause of laborers everywhere.[*] When five thousand working men turned out for a rally of Democrats in Kensington, rockets sizzling, Roman candles exploding, clubs marching and bands playing, "the employees of Joseph P. Murphy, one of the biggest cotton and woolen manufacturers in the city,

_____

[*] Cleveland, who first took office in March 1885, was also widely regarded as an anti-corruption man; Murphy's support for Cleveland put him publicly behind opposition to graft and government corruption.

created the greatest enthusiasm." [66] Elected chairman of the campaign, the immigrant's son made a speech infused with a new brand of nativism. Speaking for Democrats generally, he said: "We are unalterably opposed to the importation of Chinese, Hungarian and Polish labor to compete with American labor."[67]

Campaigning against the new foreigners in October 1888, Joe served as Marshall of a Democratic Campaign Committee that paraded down Broad Street at night, carrying torchlights and setting off skyrockets and roman candles.[68] The Democrats put forth Murphy's name as their candidate for a seat on the Select Council, expecting to beat the Republican candidate in the general election, but Murphy announced he wouldn't accept the nomination.[69]

Benjamin Harrison, the Republican nominee, won the national presidential election that November, putting Cleveland out of office, but though Murphy had declined office himself, he did not abandon his efforts for tariff reform. At the 1889 state Democratic Convention, when the name of Grover Cleveland was mentioned and the crowd of seven hundred delegates began to cheer, Joe Murphy "stood on a chair and, waving a white handkerchief round his head, seemed to forget all else but that he was cheering for 'tariff reform's champion.'"[70] The following night, "Every seat was taken and throngs crowded the aisles to listen to the speeches of the Democratic leaders of tariff reform." With many state governors, ex-governors, senators and other notables in attendance, Adolf Eicholz introduced Joseph P. Murphy, the chosen presiding chairman, as "one of the largest manufacturers in the Kensington district and one of the ablest of our tariff reform leaders.... Cheers greeted Mr. Murphy's name, which were continued long after he rose to fill the duties of his position."[71] Murphy "stepped to the front of the platform and gave a gentle tug at his low-cut vest, which displayed an expanse of white shirt front."[72] After stridently attacking the Harrison administration, he predicted that "when [the] country summons [Grover Cleveland] again to the helm, he will guide safely the ship of state into the harbor of prosperity."[73]

Murphy continued pressing the cause of tariff reform, insisting that an end to tariffs on imported wool would enable more profits, save businesses, and create more and better jobs for workers. At the 1889 Convention of the Democratic Societies of Pennsylvania, he gave a speech honoring Thomas Jefferson ("our eternal founder"), 'Old Hickory,' and President Cleveland, while calling the Republican platform of 1888 "worm-eaten and decayed."[74] The following week, urging Democrats (including his own employees) to get out the vote, he was elected vice president of the new Philadelphia Tariff Reform Club.[75]

But while Murphy was busy campaigning for tariff reform, the high cost of imported wool continued to squeeze his profits. Murphy had kept his eight hundred employees busy making woolen goods in preparation for a cold winter, but as the year came to a close, the winter had not materialized. To aggravate this condition of affairs, lap robe weavers employed at the mill struck on the 24th of January for a raise from 5-1/2 cents to 8 cents per robe. Murphy offered an increase of one cent per robe, but his offer was refused; the weavers did not return to work.[76]

Two weeks later, the front page of *The Times*[77] headlined what must have been a surprise to nearly everyone:

MORE WOOL FAILURES

JOSEPH P. MURPHY MAKES A GENERAL ASSIGNMENT.

LIABILITIES PLACED AT $500,000

The Big Manufacturer Carries a Germantown Yarn Concern Down With Him in the Crash.

Murphy's lawyer said that his assets were likely worth $500,000 and his debts $600,000, explaining that the failure had been caused in part by "the mild weather of the last and present winters. He manufactured a line of goods that needed severely cold weather to sell well. They were principally woolen shawls, blankets, cloakings, cheviots, flannel shirtings and the like."[78] Murphy himself did not blame the failure of his company on the mild weather, nor on the striking weavers, but on high tariffs. His wool supplier said that Bradstreet, the credit rating firm, had dropped its rating of Murphy "because he refused to make a statement to them," but otherwise had only good words for their customer.[79] *The Times* called Murphy "one of the most progressive of the woolen manufacturers of Philadelphia" and said he "ranked high as a citizen in the northeastern section of the city." But Murphy's lender, Charles A. Furbush, was quoted as saying, "[W]e have practically been keeping Mr. Murphy for the last five or six years. We did not hesitate about loaning him large sums of money, because he always seemed to have good security. Our suspicions were aroused as to the state of his affairs about six months ago, and since that time we have been trying to get back as much of the money as we could... Lately he has been shirking his creditors. We tried to find him on several occasions, but he excused himself on the plea of sickness."[80]

Despite the headlines about "failure," Murphy was far from out of business altogether. For one thing, he maintained common cause with his employees, telling them his assets were worth $700,000, his liabilities $600,000 at most. An article in the next day's *Inquirer,* headlined "The Two Wool Failures," was subtitled "Much Sympathy Is Expressed for the Embarrassed Firms."

> At a meeting of the employees of Joseph P. Murphy, held during the day, a resolution was adopted extending their sympathy and earnest co-operation to their employer in his business troubles.[81]

Murphy's employees were reportedly "unanimous in their good feeling toward their employer," one group who'd been thrown out of work saying, "Mr. Murphy was always a good man to work for. He is always ready to help us when we are in trouble and helped any number of old and decrepit pensioners who depended on his mill for their small wages."[82]

Murphy was definitely not out of the game. That summer, having made a compromise settlement with his creditors,[83] he vacationed in Atlantic City. A social item in *The Inquirer* captured his mood:

> Joseph D. [sic] Murphy, the Kensington manufacturer, who recently failed, was one of the audience at Shauffler's garden to-night and seemed as happy as when he guided a large Democratic club at the inauguration of Governor Abbett.[84]

What the newspapers were calling his "failure" only seemed to increase Joe's presence in the public eye: most of the press he generated in 1891 and 1892 told of his continuing Democratic political activities. He served as Marshall in the inaugural parade for Pennsylvania's Governor Pattison. He remained active in the Democratic Club. He was a delegate to the National Democratic Convention, which nominated Grover Cleveland and made possible his re-election as president in November of 1892.[85]

While Murphy was thus engaged in state and national politics, *The Times* reported on a lawsuit brought against him by receivers of a company who had dyed his wool.[86] Then, a year later, a headline in the *Inquirer* sounded all too familiar:

JOSEPH P. MURPHY AGAIN FAILS

The Big Mills at Fourth and Cumberland in the Sheriff's Hands.

This time, the Sheriff took possession of Murphy's mills. "The theory of the cause of failure most generally accepted was the one justified by the bank report – a business too extensive for the amount of capital invested, and an inability to fully meet the engagements upon which Mr. Murphy's failure of February, 1890, was settled...attributed to his having again extended his business further than was warranted by his capital."[87] Six weeks later, the company that had spoken so highly of Murphy in 1890 won a judgment against him for $25,958.73.[88]

Murphy seemed unconcerned. On March 3, 1893, he traveled to Washington to celebrate the second inauguration of Grover Cleveland, where he served as marshal of the Union Democratic Club; the following week, he stood for election to the City's Democratic Committee.[89]

Twelve days before Cleveland's inauguration, the Philadelphia and Reading Railroad, overextended in its aims for expansion, went into receivership. Other failures followed; a deepening panic caused runs on the banks; Republicans blamed it on Cleveland's win; farmers blamed it on Republicans; socialists, communists and organized labor blamed it on capitalism itself. More railroads and banks began to fail. Stock prices tumbled. Pennsylvania's unemployment rate reached 25%, New York's 35%, Michigan's 43%.

The Panic of 1893 led to even greater tensions between management and labor. When the American Railway Union called a national boycott of all trains pulling Pullman passenger cars, most trains west of Detroit came to a standstill, but President Cleveland obtained a court order prohibiting interference with any train carrying U.S. mail. When the order was ignored, Cleveland sent in federal troops to stop the boycott. The union's president, Eugene Debs, was convicted of violating the order and sentenced to prison, but only after many were killed and there was much damage to property. But in September of 1893, Murphy was elected as an at-large delegate to the State Democratic Convention, and in October, he was among the many (Republicans and Democrats alike) who celebrated the opening of remodeled headquarters for the Young Men's Democratic Headquarters. [90]

Murphy had appeared in the city directories for years as "Joseph P. Murphy, Manufacturer" (or some similar designation reflecting his sole ownership). But the days of sole proprietorships were being supplanted by the age of incorporation and limited liability. Joe handled his continued financial problems like a modern businessman, settling with creditors, continuing in business with new principals (presumably creditors) who shared in the running of a limited liability business now separate from Murphy's personal finances: "Joseph P. Murphy, Ltd."[91] In February, 1894, another judgment was entered against him, but undeterred, but Murphy remained active in Democratic politics, winning re-election as President of the Union Democratic Club that fall. [92]

In August, 1894, with Cleveland back in office, tariffs were reduced, but not nearly as much as free-traders had hoped.[93] By the end of 1894, Murphy was being called a manufacturer of "dress goods," higher-end products that used even more imported wool.[94] If nothing else, Joe had become adept at profiting from *whatever* it was that government made possible.

And so his political work continued. In 1895, as President of the 19th Ward's Union Democratic Club, Murphy endorsed Robert Pattison and the Civil War hero Sylvester Bonnaffon, but both candidates lost.[95] Such negative outcomes didn't put bread on the table. Then, in August of 1895, about a hundred and fifty of his weavers went on strike yet again.[96]

> The cloth weavers employed by Joseph P. Murphy at Fourth and Cumberland streets, yesterday went on strike. They claim that they have had their wages reduced nearly 33 per cent. Mr. Murphy said the schedule of wages was changed to make it even with what other manufacturers are paying. He also said the reduction did not amount to 10 per cent. and is only on a few kinds of goods. About 150 weavers went out.

The ultimate resolution of that strike isn't known, but when Republican William McKinley was elected in late 1896 and tariffs were reimposed, Murphy's profit margin disappeared yet again.[97] In September of 1898, the Joseph P. Murphy Co. finally collapsed, throwing some two hundred remaining workers out of jobs.[98]

But as we've seen, Murphy was a thoroughly modern businessman. The effort to separate business and personal finances had worked. Murphy told the press he was confident things would be straightened out and that creditors would be paid in full.[99] Despite the business failure, Murphy could still afford a live-in servant in 1900.[100] And that same year, he set up two sons in business: Joseph Dominick Murphy and Edward V. Murphy appeared in the Kensington woolens business under the name "Murphy & Bro.," an arrangement that further shielded Joe himself from creditors while passing wealth to his sons.[101] By May of 1903, the Joseph P. Murphy Company had been declared a voluntary bankrupt with liabilities of $456,605.34 and assets of only fifteen dollars.[102]

Of course, fifteen dollars in corporate assets hardly paints a picture of Joe's personal finances. After some twenty years living on North 6th Street, the Murphys sold their home and moved to Germantown, where they remained until shortly before Joe's death several years later.[103] The newspapers make no further mention of him in these latter days of his life: if he was ill or incompetent, the historical record gives no evidence of it. He seems, rather, to have simply taken a back seat, a retirement of sorts, with a consulting role to his sons.[104]

In December of 1910, he died of a sudden heart attack; after a solemn requiem mass was said for him at the Church of the Holy Angels, he was interred in the Murphy family plot at Holy Sepulcher Cemetery.[105] He and Adele had not been empty-nesters; the household Joe left behind included six of their ten living children. The home was owned outright, free and clear of debt.[106] He had already left a business to his two older sons, and despite the business bankruptcy, he'd found ample means to provide for those who remained at home. He'd built the business into something greater than his father had ever envisioned, and he had enough money left that his widow lived for another two decades (and his children continued to live thereafter) on money he'd left them for that purpose.[107]

Maybe there was nothing inappropriate about such movement of wealth; maybe the bankruptcy laws worked as intended, supporting the capitalist ideal that a man should be free to make compromises with his creditors and pass wealth on to his family. If Joe had suffered discrimination on account of his religion, there's no record of it. He'd fully participated in the politics of representative democracy. He'd achieved great prosperity for his family. In short, he'd succeeded in every aspect of the liberty for which his parents had come to America. But though the papers described him repeatedly as one of the city's leading businessmen, and though the employees who struck against him were sometimes said to sing his praises, there were few reports of philanthropy or public service.[108] If he gave much away to others, he did so anonymously. His life, as reflected in the news accounts, had been devoted to furthering his business, to capitalizing on the opportunities his country gave him, and to supporting the political issues and candidates that favored his own prosperity.

Whether there should have been more to his aspirations, we leave for others to judge.

Notes on Chapter 7, Joseph P. Murphy

[1] Records establish Joseph's birth date as February 15th. Phila Death Cert No 126666 gives his birthdate as February 15, 1845, as do Philip Scranton, Proprietary Capitalism: The Textile Manufacture at Philadelphia, 1800-1885, Cambridge Univ Press, 1983, p 221 and A Biographical Album of Prominent Pennsylvanians, Vol III: Financiers, Railroad Officials, Merchants, Manufacturers, Inventors, Publishers, and Other Practical Men of Affairs, The American Biographical Publishing Co., Phila., 1890, pp 221-222. To the same effect are the 1850 Census (age 5) and 1880 Census (age 35). Contrary are the 1860 Census (which has him at age 16) and the 1900 U.S. Census, Phila Ward 19, Dist 0398, Fam 20, which gives his birth year as 1846.

[2] The Christian Brothers had opened their Catholic high school at St. Michael's, known as the "Select School," beginning July 20, 1858. It later took the name "Christian Brothers Academy" and later still became the college preparatory division of La Salle College (Website of LaSalle High School, accessed at https://www.lschs.org/about-la-salle/history.) Whether Joe Murphy took the examinations for entrance to Central High School is unclear, but the records of that school do not mention him. Perhaps he'd been unable to pass its stringent examinations. Or perhaps Central was too academic for him, despite its emphasis on practical, business education for the working class.

[3] He may have also spent time reporting local trials, or war news for newspapers. His work as a reporter is reflected by the occupation given in the 1860 Census and also by a reference in an obituary to the effect that at war's end, he had assisted his brothers in reporting the Lincoln conspirators' trial (*Evening Star*, Dec 6, 1910, p 18). The draft enacted in March of 1863 required men age 20 to register and, if chosen (by lottery), to serve. But a drafted man could avoid service by getting someone else to take his place, or by paying a three hundred dollar "commutation fee," unpopular exceptions that caused the war to be branded "a rich man's war and a poor man's fight." While it's possible that Joe Murphy (or his father) paid a commutation fee to avoid service, the law only applied to those between twenty and forty-five. Joe was likely too young to be drafted, and the lists of those drafted in 1863, published in *The Inquirer* on July 24th and July 27th for the 17th and 19th Wards respectively, did not include him.

[4] *The Inquirer,* April 4, 1865, *seriatim.*

[5] Scranton, *supra*, p 221; A Biographical Album of Prominent Pennsylvanians, Vol III, American Biographical Publishing Co., 1890, pp 221-222, accessed at https://www.familysearch.org/library/books/records/item/439278-a-biographical-album-of-prominent-pennsylvanians-vol-3-.

[6] The 1860 Census (Phila Ward 17, Fam 1454) shows him with the occupation Reporter, like his older brothers; since he didn't learn stenographic reporting at Central, he must have learned it from them.

[7] *Evening Star*, Dec 6, 1910, p 16.

[8] Scranton appears to have gotten his information on Joe Murphy's youth from the Biographical Album, *supra*, and unidentified 1888 biographical sketch. But one wonders if those sources presented an idealized picture of their subject. While it certainly seems plausible that a young man would learn something of his father's cotton mill and start out small, the idea of a humble apprenticeship at his father's side must be reconciled with the occupation of reporter given in the 1860 Census, with Dominick's own financial picture, with Joe's 1865 reporting in Washington, and with Joe's appointment as Assistant Assessor after the war.

[9] When J. Fletcher Budd resigned as Tax Assessor for the Third Congressional District in 1866, he was first replaced by Peter Keyser, but barely more than a month later, Thomas Allen was confirmed by the Senate to replace him (*Inquirer,* July 24, 1866; *Evening Telegraph*, August 10, 1866, p 3). Keyser assumed the duties of Assessor on August 10th, 1866. Allen's replacement was reported in the *Inquirer*, Sept 29, 1866, p 1. There was an assistant for each of the District's seventeen divisions.

[10] Allen's own appointment was not made until the last week in September, and Joe Murphy appeared as Assistant Assessor of Division 12 on the tax roll for the month of September, likely prepared in October or November. More evidence of the timing of Murphy's appointment comes from the 1867

City Directories, prepared in the autumn of 1866 and showing Joe Murphy with the occupation Assistant Assessor. Clearly, the appointment of Murphy by Allen occurred no earlier than the last week of September and no later than the end of 1866. Dennis Murphy, with his growing influence on both sides of the political aisle in Washington, likely had a hand in both appointments.

[11] The tax rolls on which his name appears as assistant assessor show in great detail the taxes he assessed and the variety of taxpayers on which he assessed them (National Archives and Records Admin, Record Group 58, Internal Revenue Assessment Lists for Pennsylvania, Series M787, Roll 18, District 3, Monthly & Special Lists, Sept-Dec 1866, Division 12).

[12] Assistant Assessor John Budd was replaced by Jackson D. Liner in Division 11 beginning with the returns covering the month of October 1866.

[13] As shown by later directories, the entry for Joseph D. [sic] Murphy in the 1867 Philadelphia City Directory clearly refers, in fact, to Joseph P. Murphy. His new office address was 443 Girard Avenue, by the river. The building is shown on an 1875 map (see G. M. Hopkins' City Atlas of Phila, Vol VI, 1875, Plate P, accessed at http://www.philageohistory.org/rdic-images/view-image. cfm/GMH1875v6-plate_P). John J. Miller's home address at 1029 Hanover St, where Murphy began to call on Miller's daughter – Columbia Street today – was a four-minute walk away. Edward's office was at 237 Dock Street, downtown.

[14] Born in Kensington Sept 13, 1821, John J. Miller spent seven years as a bank note engraver, then worked as a shipping clerk on the Reading Railroad; in 1848, he entered the grocery business *(Evening Star*, Sept 13, 1908, p. 10; 1850 Phila Census, Richmond, Fam 783). By 1856 or 1857, he worked as a clerk and "U.S. Officer" at the Philadelphia Customs house (1860 Census Phila Ward 19, Fam 2435; Phila City Directories of 1855, 1857-1859, and 1861-1862). Curiously, a biographical account on the occasion of his 87th birthday said nothing of his work at the customs house; after noting that he briefly worked in Washington in the early 1860's, it then glossed over the period between 1862 and 1875 by saying that he "entered upon a business career" in Philadelphia until the Jay Cook failure of 1873. The 1865 through 1868 City Directories listed him as a "bookkeeper;" by 1870 and 1871, he was a "commercial merchant"; and in 1872, he had an office downtown, engaged in the "oysters" business, which had expanded to two downtown locations by 1874. On his 87th birthday, the newspapers celebrated his 33 years of service to the Life Saving Service, i.e., back to 1875, when the relationship between the Service and the Treasury Department was still informal (the Service was not officially made part of the Treasury Department until 1878). He continued with the Life Saving Service in Washington until his death November 12, 1908 (*Washington Times*, Sept 14, 1907, p 6; *Evening Star,* Sept 13, 1908, p 10 and Nov 12, 1908, p 4.) By all such accounts, he was an honorable man, but his business in the years 1867-1869 remains unclear and apparently not an enterprise for which he was anxious to be remembered.

[15] According to her 1931 death certificate, Adele was born February 28, 1849. Her mother was Ann Elizabeth Clothier (b 1821 or 1822). Her maternal great grandfather, Samuel Clothier (1750-1804) was the subject of a biographical sketch as the head of a family in the first U.S. Census in 1790. Her great-grandmother, Barbara Bruner, was the daughter of one Henry Bruner, upon whose farm (at what is now 10th and Poplar Street) the Battle of Germantown was fought back when it was nothing but farmland. Space does not permit a detailed recounting of all that is known about Adele's ancestry, except to say that her grandfather was Samuel Clothier (1783-1832) and her grandmother – despite contrary assertions based on a much-quoted but flawed file of the Germantown Historical Society – was Ann Baker (1789-1870).

[16] Scranton cites the 1870 Census of Manufacturing for the 249 Oxford address and the assertion that Murphy had two mills at the location. Confirmation comes from the 1870 Philadelphia City Directory which lists Joseph P. Murphy, woolen mfr, at 249 Oxford (as distinguished from his home address – John Miller's address – at 1029 Hanover (now Columbia) Avenue. By November 11, 1870, when the second enumeration of the Census took place, Joe and his bride had moved out of her parents' home to 1101

Hanover Street, a block away, where they boarded in a household headed (coincidentally) by another man named Murphy, a ship joiner (1870 Phila Census Ward 18 Dist 53, 2d enum).

[17] Joe and Adele were married on June 23, 1868. (A Biographical Album of Prominent Pennsylvanians, Vol III, p 222.) The 1870 City Directory shows them living at the Miller house, 1029 Hanover St. Their first child was a daughter, also named Adele, born February 2, 1871; she turned out to be the first of many; for the next two decades, another child was born every two or three years until their eleventh, born in 1894. (Adele Gertrude (1871-1887); Joseph Dominic (1873-1936); Anna Marie (Rowey)(1875-1951); Edward Vincent (1878-1964); Francis Dominick (1881-1959); Elizabeth H. (1883-1968); Maria Agnes (1885-1975); Maria Regina (Pascoe)(1888-1958); Loretto Madelaide (Colman)(1890-1961); Walter Leo (1892-1959); and Raymond (1894-1975).

[18] "Personal Biographical Sketch of Edward V. Murphy," *supra*.

[19] Philadelphia was certainly not immune from tax frauds similar to those perpetrated in New York. The attitude of the public about corruption seems to have been more tolerant than it is today. In August of 1868, Edwin Brock, the former Deputy Collector for the Third District in Philadelphia, was released from prison, having received a pardon from Andrew Johnson despite having been convicted of executing bonds for the removal of distilled spirits from warehouses with the intent to defraud the government. Numerous others had been implicated in the fraud with him. Yet Johnson's pardon had been recommended by the city members of the Legislature, Congressmen, a number of the Grand Jury who indicted him, and ten of the jury who'd convicted him – "they believing that the prisoner had sufficiently suffered for his crime" (*Evening Telegraph*, Aug 26, 1868, p 8). As we've seen, a drawback claim only had to be supported by three documents; men with the occupations of Edward Murphy, Joe Murphy, and John Miller would certainly have been in a position to create fraudulent claims, had they been so inclined. Two plausible scenarios present themselves. In one, the Murphys were honest – vigilant in rooting out corruption in tax collection and ensuring the proper collection of taxes. In the other, they were less so. Having Dennis in Washington as clerk to the Retrenchment Committee, Edward in Philadelphia as Superintendent of Exports and Drawbacks, Joe assessing taxes in an industrial and shipping neighborhood by the Delaware River, Dominick manufacturing goods on which taxes were paid, and John Miller, former customs collector and current commercial businessman, available to help, had all the makings of an air-tight family operation – but there is no evidence of actual corruption on the part of any of them, and a charitable spirit might give them all the benefit of the doubt.

[20] Rumors of the New York drawback frauds reached Washington in the latter part of 1868 (*Buffalo Morning Express*, Nov 17, 1869, p 2). But the reasons for Edward's resignation may have had nothing to do with the additional scrutiny on drawbacks – see the account of his resignation in Chapter Five and its footnotes. The reasons for Joe Murphy's departure from office are also unclear. After December 1866, we no longer find tax assessment lists for the Third District, denying us the chance to pinpoint the last month Joe Murphy was responsible for assessments. The City Directory of 1868, published April 1 and compiled based on information available earlier that year (see preface to the 1867 Directory) reflects that Joe was still Assistant Assessor until at least February of 1868. But we find no City Residential Directory for 1869, leaving us unable to know whether it, too, listed him as Assistant Assessor. The 1870 City Directory, compiled in the early months of that year, lists Joe Murphy as a manufacturer. Within that two-year 1868-1870 window, the exact date of his departure from his tax job is unknown. One possibility is that because President Ulysses Grant had appointed a new Third District Assessor (a Mr. Elliott) by April of 1869, Elliott brought in his own assistants (*Evening Telegraph*, April 16, 1869, p 3). Joe's departure, like Edward's, may have had nothing to do with the increased scrutiny being given to corruption.

[21] The 1870 Directory listed both Joseph P. Murphy ("woollen mfr") and John J. Miller ("com mer") living at 1029 Hanover Street, while giving Joe's business address as 249 Oxford (East Oxford Street, in Fishtown), about a five-minute walk from his new home. Scranton reports that Joe "commenced in a small way; for in 1869 he had only nine looms, and his total source of employees did not exceed twenty-five." (Scranton, *supra*, p 221; A Biographical Album of Prominent Pennsylvanians, Vol III,

American Biographical Publishing Co., 1890, pp 221-222, accessed at https://www.family search.org/library/books/records/item/439278-a-biographical-album-of-prominent-pennsylvanians-vol-3-.) Seemingly unaware of Joe's stint as a federal tax assessor, Scranton suggests that he must have gotten financial backing from his father, and indeed he may have, regardless of what he may have accumulated as tax assessor.

[22] Scranton, p. 222. The 1873 and 1874 City Directories show Joseph P. Murphy's occupation as "carpet mfr" and "woolens," respectively, both giving his address as 427 E. York Street, an address revealed in the 1877 Directory to be a home address. Scranton, meanwhile, at p 222, has the mill moving directly from Oxford Street to 531 E. York. The 1876 Philadelphia Directory lists Joseph P. Murphy, "woolens," living at 427 East York Street.

[23] See *The Inquirer* of March 14, 1876, p 2, which reports the workers' assertion: "It has been an invariable rule for some years for manufacturers to reduce wages upon the last chains they give the weavers to work for the season, so that the next season commences with a reduction: now, as the season is about to terminate on this fabric, James P. Murray is the one selected by the manufacturers to reduce the wages for the present season, and so fix it as a standard price for the next."

[24] *The Inquirer*, Jan 21, 1876, p 3.

[25] *The Inquirer*, Jan 28, 1876, p 3. The Knights of Labor, most famous for its activities in the railroad industry, began in Philadelphia in 1869 as a secret society of city garment workers. See https://philadelphiaencyclopedia.org/archive/knights-of-labor/

[26] https://en.wikipedia.org/wiki/Great_Railroad_Strike_of_1877; https://millercenter.org/the-presidency/ presidential-speeches/july-18-1877-message-regarding-railroad-strike

[27] *Inquirer*, July 1, 1874.

[28] Russell Weigley *et al*, Philadelphia, a Three Hundred Year History, W.W. Norton & Co. (1982) pp 471-474. The Annual Report of the Pennsylvania Railroad, released that March, listed the new terminals, new tracks, new freight cars and new passenger services it had put in service during the prior year. Over ten thousand tons of iron and steel rail had been laid, forty-three locomotives built, nearly three thousand new coal cars put in service, a hundred and fifty new passenger cars added, several iron bridges built in and around the city (*Inquirer*, March 7, 1876, p 2).

[29] *Ibid*. Because of its slow evolution, the typewriter was previously known only to specialists like Dennis and Edward Murphy.

[30] Weigley, *supra*, p 466.

[31] In an article that appeared in 1876, the Scientific American magazine observed that even with the new power looms, "the principle on which they work remains precisely the same. The shuttle, in fact, becomes a mere projectile, entirely out of the control of the weaver during its passage across the warp." ("The Great Textile Invention at the Centennial Exposition: the Lyall Positive Motion Loom," *Scientific American* magazine, Vol XXXV, No 12, Sept 16, 1876, p 180.)

[32] Lyall's invention of the positive motion loom was actually a few years old already; see "Lyall's Positive Motion Loom," *Engineering Weekly* magazine, Sept 3, 1869, p 159, accessed at https://www.hand weaving.net/document-detail/5566/lyalls-positive-motion-loom-engineering-weekly.

[33] *The Great Textile Invention, supra*, p 180.

[34] Scranton, *supra*, p 222. Dominick and the Palethorp mill are listed in the City Directories of 1875 and 1876, but the Palethorp mill is no longer listed beginning with the Directory of 1877. Joe's mills were at 529 and 531 E. York Street. He also moved his family to a new residence a block away from the mills, at 609 E. York (1878 City Directory).

[35] Administration #798, on October 5, 1878, per Bill Colman. "The whole of the Goods, Chattels, Rights and Credits of the personal estate he died possessed of, in the aggregate, do not in value exceed the sum of one thousand dollars to the best of his knowledge and belief." Unless that oath was a lie, Dominick must have transferred his wealth to his wife and/or children prior to his death. Whether any of the children pressed Hannah for loans or capital contributions to their businesses is not known.

[36] Scranton, *supra*, p 222.

[37] G. M. Hopkins' *City Atlas of Philadelphia, Vol 6*, 1875, Plate R.

[38] The 1875 Hopkins Map, *supra*, Plate S, labels the unimproved lot on which the new facility was built at the southeast Corner of Cumberland and 4th Street as "M. Price." Michael E. Price was one of the principals in the firm of McMillen, Price and Wheeler, "produce." (1875 Directory). Apparently, the unimproved land had been used by Price to grow vegetables or to operate an open-air produce market. An 1888 map shows the map-maker's outline of Murphy's "Cotton and Woolen Mill" on the same property, occupying half a city block. (Baist's *Property Atlas* of the City of Philadelphia, 1888, Plate 21).

[39] Scranton, *supra*, p 222.

[40] The address of the newest mill was 1310 Lawrence Street. The 1881 Business Directory called Murphy a "Manufacturer of Cotton, Woollen and Worsted Goods" on both Lawrence and Cumberland.

[41] Scranton, *supra*, pp 222-223.

[42] Weigley, *supra*, pp 484 485.

[43] Scranton, *supra*, p 223.

[44] Kenneth W. Milano, Remembering Kensington & Fishtown, History Press, 2008, p 89. The Murphy family was described in the 1880 Census (at 123 Susquehanna) as Joseph P., 35, cloth manufactor [sic]; Adele G., 26, keeping house; Adele G., 10, at school; Joseph D., 6, at school; Anna M., 4, at home; and Edward W., 3, at home. The Miller family, living with them, was described as John J., 61, father-in-law and clerk at Washington, U.S. Treasury Dept; Annie E. Miller, 56, mother-in-law, at home; and Joseph R. Miller, 35, brother-in-law and clerk, Government Printing Office. The live-in servant was German-born Louisa Pfaefer, 22.

[45] While the exact date of his move is not known, Joe Murphy was counted in the 1880 Census, enumerated June 4, 1880, still living at 122 Susquehanna Avenue; he was then listed in the 1881 City Directory, presumably compiled in late 1880, living at 2529 North 6th Street. From that, we can conclude that he moved into the new house at some point in the latter half of 1880. His very temporary rental on Norris Square suggests he was building his new home. He probably purchased the lot, and began construction, in late 1879 or early 1880. (It was two blocks from a new church, St. Edward the Confessor, which the diocese had bought from the Episcopal Church in 1865.) The Murphys would live there on 6th Street for the next twenty years.

Antonne Kiker, meanwhile, was a German-American. (The name Kiker is a possible variant of Kiecker, Germans who hailed from Kieck, near Potsdam.) Though his family had immigrated from Germany, Antone himself had been born in the Philadelphia area in 1783, the year George Washington resigned his commission as General of the Continental Army. A butcher by trade, Antone had expanded into other aspects of the food business, running a restaurant, an oyster bar, and a grocery business. The 1870 Census reported his real estate as being worth $10,000 (U.S. Census, Phila Ward 20, Dis 68, Fam 145) and the nine members of the Kiker household at that time included daughter Mary Kiker, age 17, who would later marry Charles Sherick. When Antone died on April 11, 1873 at the age of 90, his residence was at 2527 N 6th Street (*Inquirer*, Apr 14, 1873, p 5). His death certificate gave his occupation as butcher; he was worth some $12,000 in real and personal property, which passed to his much younger widow Margaret (*nee* Hackett, c. 1820-1900) upon his death. (See https://www.findagrave.com/memorial/83373468/anton-kiker#view-photo=54295255.) Widow Margaret continued living at 2527 N 6th St at least through compilation of the 1880 Directory, which lists her still living there. But the 1880 Census, Phila Dist 376, Fam 190, enumerated June 8th, shows her at 2537 N 6th. So she must have moved between early in 1880 and June 8th of that year. She didn't move far – just a few houses up the street – but the move meant she would not be Murphy's immediate neighbor.

[46] In addition to his four-story building at 4th and Cumberland and his new location at 1310 Lawrence Street, the 1882 City Directory reflects the addition of a facility at 1713 Waterloo Street. Murphy also had an operation on the northwest corner of Cumberland and Third St, although he shared that building with four other firms and used the space primarily for storing stock. *The Inquirer* of August 30, 1883 asserted that Murphy, "proprietor of the large worsted and zephyr mills at the southeast corner of Fourth

and Cumberland streets," also had several looms in operation on the fifth floor of the building at Cumberland and Third. On August 29, 1883, when a fire in that building made the news, the total loss came to $50,000. (J. Thos. Scharf, History of Phila, 1609-1884, Vol I (1884), accessed at Ancestry.com, Phila History, Firemen, Fire Companies & Large Fires.) Murphy estimated his loss at $4,000. The property at Cumberland & 3rd is listed alongside the one at Cumberland & 4th in the 1887 City Directory.

[47] *Inquirer*, Dec 12, 1883, reported that "William Pault, Joseph P. Murphy, Hon. Nathaniel Niles, Richard Wood, James G. Kitchen, Hon. Jacob Tome and others are making arrangements for the establishment of a new national bank in this city, with a capital of $500,000." Murphy was elected to the Board of Directors (*Inquirer*, June 26, 1885). The Bank opened for business on August 3rd at Frankford Road and Norris Street. (*The Times*, August 7, 1885.) *The Inquirer*, 12 Jan 1887, reported Murphy's re-election to the Board. The founding of the bank by a group of Kensington textile manufacturers, in the wake of the scandalous failure of the Shackamaxon Bank, is recounted in Kenneth W. Milano, Hidden History of Kensington & Fishtown, History Press, 2010, pp 97-98.

[48] *The Philadelphia Times*, March 23, 1885, p 1. The Grover Cleveland Association a sort of early campaign committee or PAC, formed to support Cleveland's election.

[49] Scranton, *supra*, p 222, citing Biographical Album of Prominent Pennsylvanians, Third Series, Philadelphia, 1890, p 221 and 1870 MCS, Philadelphia Co., p 566.

[50] *Inquirer*, March 23, p 8, and April 6, 1883, p 3.

[51] *Inquirer*, April 7, 1883, p 1.

[52] *Inquirer*, April 21, 1885, p 3.

[53] *Inquirer*, May 12, 1885, p 8, reported the walk out. *The Times* of May 31 and *The Inquirer* of June 1, p 2, reported the return to work.

[54] The strike lasted for several days. Progress (or lack of it) was reported in the papers every one of those days. (*Inquirer*, Sept 1, 1885, p 8, and Sept 2, 1885, p 8; the *Times* on September 2; both the *Times* and the *Inquirer* on September 3; the *Inquirer* on September 4; and both papers again on September 5, 1885.) Finally, on September 6, the *Times* reported that Murphy's 176 striking weavers would resume work the following morning, Murphy having agreed "to advance the price three cents per cut on heavy and light linneys and pay for narrow shawls by the shawl instead of by the cut… He also advanced the price on shawls seven, ten, twelve and fifteen cents per cut, according to grade." (*The Times*, Sept 6, 1885, p 1.)

[55] *The Times* and *Inquirer* of September 8 reported the strikers' return to work using words like "happy" and even "merry" to describe their mood. (*Inquirer*, Sept 8, 1885, p 2; *The Times*, Sept 8, 1885, p 2) The increases Murphy agreed to at that time may help explain why *The Times* later called him among the "more progressive" of the city's textile manufacturers. (*The Times*, Feb 5, 1890.)

[56] *Inquirer*, March 20, 1886. With labor peace, Murphy may have been picking up extra business that competitors with labor problems couldn't handle.

[57] *The Times*, April 1, 1886. Like other things Murphy did at the time, the discharge of strikers would later be made illegal under labor laws adopted many decades later.

[58] *The Times* of October 30, 1886. It's unclear whether the lockout came to pass, but the *Inquirer* of December 5th reported that "the troubles in the shawl and cloth mill of Joseph P. Murphy, at Fourth and Cumberland, will probably be settled by arbitration." In years to come, arbitration of individual employee grievances would become the centerpiece of labor contracts, but it's doubtful Murphy had any contractual obligation to arbitrate; more likely, he simply agreed to that method of dispute resolution *ad hoc*.

[59] *Inquirer*, Sept 27, 1886, p 2.

[60] A group of industrial leaders founded the Manufacturer's Club of Philadelphia on May 19, 1887. "The membership was made up largely of textile manufacturing executives from the area." (*History, Manufacturers' Golf & Country Club*, accessed at https://www.mg-cc.org/club-information/history.) That being the case, given Murphy's stature as one of the larger textile manufacturers in the city, and given his son's later membership, it is hard to imagine that he wasn't involved.

[61] *Proclamation of Oct 25, 1887.* The American Presidency Project, U.C. Santa Barbara, accessed at https://www.presidency.ucsb.edu/documents/proclamation-281-thanksgiving-day-1887#:~:text=A%20Proclamation& text=To%20the%20 end%20that%20we,the%20people%20of%20the%20land.

[62] *Inquirer* of December 5, 1887: "The following judgments were entered Saturday in the office of the Common Pleas Courts on judgment notes: ... vs. Joseph P. Murphy, $5,000, dated 25th ultimo, with Johnson and Higgins as garnishee..."

[63] Phila Death Certificate of Adele Murphy, Dec 14, 1887, FHL Film No. 2078968. Mrs. Murphy was pregnant at the time and would soon give birth to another baby girl: Mary Regina Murphy, born February 20, 1888.

[64] Calvin D. Linton, The Bicentennial Almanac, Thomas Nelson, 1976, p 230.

[65] See, generally, Frank William Taussig, Some Aspects of the Tariff Question, Harvard University Press, 1915, accessed at https://oll-resources.s3.us-east-2.amazonaws.com/oll3/store/titles/293/0072_Bk.pdf, especially Chapter XIX, on Wool. Taussig's discussion of wool production, and the manufacture of carpet wool, woolens and worsteds in his Chapter XX, reveals the complexities of the economic issues involved, but concludes that the tariffs on wool were indeed increasing the cost of wool to American buyers.

[66] *The Times*, Sept 11, 1888, p 1; see also the *Inquirer*, Sept 11th, 1888, p 2. *The Times* of Sept 28, 1888, contained a front-page article titled *For Tariff Reform*, which explained the Democratic position that "the movement for tariff reduction had nothing of free trade in it, but was designed to give workingmen steady employment by opening the closed manufactories."

[67] *The Times*, Sept 11, 1888, p 1.

[68] *The Times,* October 3, 1888, p 4, and October 14, 1888, p 1.

[69] *The Times* of Jan 11 (p 3), 13 (p 2) and 17 (p 1), and the *Inquirer* of Jan 12 (p 2) and January 17 (p 3), all in 1889.

[70] *The Times*, Oct 16, 1889, p 2. Murphy was there with his father's old political ally, Richard Vaux. The proceedings included speeches by governors and other notables from Texas, West Virginia, New Jersey, Maryland and elsewhere (*The Times*, Oct 15, 1889, p 1). Joe had also been elected that year to membership in the Hibernian Society (*The Times*, March 19, 1889, p 1; see also John H. Campbell, History of the Friendly Sons of St. Patrick and of the Hibernian Society for the Relief of Emigrants from Ireland, March 17, 1771 – March 17, 1892, Hibernian Society, Phila, 1892, p 467.)

[71] *The Times*, Oct 17, 1889, p 1.

[72] *The Inquirer,* Oct 17, 1889, p 2.

[73] *The Times*, Oct 17, 1889, p 1.

[74] Address given by Joseph P. Murphy at the Convention of Democratic Societies of Pennsylvania, Oct 22, 1889, as reported in A Biographical Album of Prominent Pennsylvanians, Vol III, 1890, p 221-222.

[75] *The Times*, Nov 3, 1889, p 1. The issue reported Murphy's anti-tariff activities in two separate articles, "Bring Out the Voters" and "Organized Tariff Reform: Business Men Supporting the Doctrines of Grover Cleveland." See also *The Times*, Nov 2, 1889, p 1.

[76] *Inquirer*, Feb 5, 1890, p 2.

[77] *The Times,* Feb 5, 1890, p 1.

[78] *Inquirer*, Feb 5, 1890, p 2; *The Times*, Feb 6, 1890, p 2.

[79] Mr. Hamill (Murphy's wool supplier) said that up until the day before, he'd had no reason to apprehend any trouble. "There have been a series of untoward circumstances entirely unforeseen and unlooked for. Two open winters have caused a general depression in the wool trade. The past year particularly has witnessed a repeated number of failures in the wool business. [The goods of two firms that had failed] were slaughtered at forced sales and the prices they brought in a large measure set the price for Mr. Murphy and made the competition ruinous to many firms... Mr. Murphy has been in business for twenty years, never failed before and stood high in the business community, and his failure was quite unlooked for. He often owed as much as $56,000 in one week. He used our goods extensively and was our heaviest buyer." (*The Times*, Feb 5, 1890, p 1.)

[80] *Ibid.* "Joseph P. Murphy, the Woolen Manufacturer, whose large mills are located at Fourth and Cumberland Streets, made a general assignment yesterday to Hugh J. Hamill and John J. McDonald. At the same time Bridget and Hugh Hamill, trading as B. Hamill & Co., made a general assignment to David Scannell. The latter firm is a woolen yarn manufacturer, both firms being closely identified in business and financial relations. Mr. Murphy employs about 800 hands, and his mill was in full operation yesterday. It is five stories in height and is owned by Mr. Murphy and has but a slight incumbrance. The assets and liabilities of the two concerns are not definitely known, but Mr. Murphy's indebtedness is placed at about $500,000. The cause of the failures, that of Mr. Murphy leading to the Hamill collapse, is attributed to the general stagnation of the woolen business occasioned by the high tariff upon the imported article."

[81] *Inquirer*, Feb 6, 1890, p 6.

[82] *The Times,* Feb 6, 1890, p 2.

[83] *The Times,* Aug 17, 1890, p 6.

[84] *Inquirer* of Aug 10, 1890, p 12. Leon Abbett had been Governor of New Jersey from 1884 to 1887 and again from 1890 to 1893. A week later, Murphy was still in Atlantic City. "Joseph D. Murphy, the Kensington Manufacturer, was one of the well-known men at Shauffler's Garden to-night" and his daughter Annie was "the prettiest girl at the Westminster" *(Inquirer* of Aug 17, 1890, p 12).

[85] *The Times,* Jan 16, 1891, p 1, and Jan 21, 1891, p 1; *The Inquirer,* Jan 21, 1891, p 1; *The Times,* Oct 18, 1891, p 1, Dec 3, 1891, p 4, and Feb 4, 1892, p 1; *The Inquirer* Feb 4, 1892, p 2; to name just some of the many that documented Murphy's political involvement. (*The Times* referred to him as "an extensive manufacturer of cotton and woolen goods." The *Inquirer* had previously called his mill a "mammoth," one of the biggest in the city (*Inquirer*, Feb 5, 1890, p 2). Robert E. Pattison was the Democratic Governor of Pennsylvania from 1883 to 1886 and again from 1891 to 1894. Grover Cleveland was renominated in June of 1882, and defeated Benjamin Harrison in the election that November.

[86] *The Times*, Nov 4, 1891, p 4.

[87] *Inquirer,* Nov 11, 1892, p 1.

[88] "Judgment Against a Philadelphian," *The Times*, Jan 1, 1893, p 1. (Judgment in favor of B. Hamill & Co.)

[89] *The Times,* Mar 3, 1893, p 3, March 5, 1893, p 3, and Mar 12, 1893, p 4.

[90] *The Times,* Sept 8, 1893, p 4; the *Inquirer*, Oct 8, 1893, p 5.

[91] "Joseph P. Murphy, Ltd" first appears in the 1894 City Directory, presumably prepared in late 1893. That directory lists him not as his company's President, but as its treasurer. (The 1895 and 1896 Boyd's Philadelphia Business Directories are to the same effect). The new president was a man named Irving F. Moore, the new secretary a man named Samuel D. Dalley. Previously, Irving E. [sic] Moore had appeared in the 1893 and 1894 City Directories as manager of an unidentified company at 1835 E. Huntingdon (at the corner of East Huntingdon and Kensington Avenue); Samuel Dalley had not been listed at all, in either 1893 or 1894. Exactly who these men were, and what their true interest and control were, are unknown. The extent to which Joe had been forced to give up control of his operation is unclear.

[92] *Inquirer*, Feb 6, 1894, p 5 (O.H. Sampson & Co., judgments aggregating $21,123); *The Times*, Oct 8, 1894, p 8; *Inquirer*, Oct 14, 1894, p 7.

[93] Wilson-Gorman Tariff Act of 1894, Ch. 349, §73, 28 Stat. 570, 1894. See "Wilson-Gorman Tariff Act," Wikipedia.org.

[94] *Inquirer*, Oct 15, 1894, p 7. Dress goods used a higher grade of wool than did carpeting, and the *Inquirer* article reflects the greater use of higher-grade wools in worsted fabrics that characterized the industry at the time. But the article also reflects the tenuous fortunes of businesses so dependent on ever-changing tariff regulation.

[95] *The Times,* Jan 27, 1895, p 9, and Feb 6, 1895, p 4.

[96] *Inquirer,* August 24, 1895, p 3. The *Inquirer* of August 28, p 2, contained an update: "The weavers of Joseph P. Murphy's mill are still out and no attempt has as yet been made for a settlement."

[97] Taussig, *supra,* p. 299. Joe also attended to various family matters in the 1890's, including the continued employment of his brother John. When Dennis F. Murphy's widow Annie died (Oct 30, 1896), it was from Joe's house at 2529 North 6th Street that her funeral procession began (*Inquirer,* Nov 1, 1896). And in July of 1899, the procession for the funeral of seventy-one-year-old Mary A. Hood also began from his house (*The Times,* July 5, 1899). Mary Hood had appeared as a domestic servant in the household of James Murphy in the 1870 Census, had seen his brother James and his children die, and later served as nurse for James's widow, Mary Ann, and sole surviving son Charles, age 7 (1880 Census, Phila Dist 689, Fam 108, at 822 Firth Street). In her probated will executed June 27, 1899, just a week before her death, she left $100 to St. Edward the Confessor for masses to be said for the repose of her soul, and the rest of her estate to Elizabeth H., Anna Marie, Loretto Madeline, Maria Agnes, Mary Regina, Edward, Raymond and Walter Murphy, the children of Joseph P. Murphy, "these bequests being in recognition of his and their many and uniform kindnesses to me" (Phila Will No 1203, 1899).

[98] *The Inquirer,* Sept 18, 1898, p 10; *The Times,* Sept 18, 1898, p 4, and Sept 20, 1898, p 2.

[99] "Mr. Murphy when seen said that depression in the wool business was the cause of the embarrassment. During the past six months there had been enormous losses in fancy cloakings and fancy dress goods. In one instance alone, between two and three weeks ago, this was made strikingly apparent. The Arlington Mills, of Massachusetts, had a sale at auction, with the result that there was an actual loss, on the value of their dress goods, of $350,000... His own firm had sustained a loss of $35,000 in a single day of the past week, as a sequel to this tremendous sacrifice of prices, and the general depreciation in values. Fully 65 percent of the cloak mills of the country were, he said, shut down, and it was impossible to withstand such losses. He could not state the amount of the liabilities, but there were sufficient assets, he said, to pay all the creditors in full and leave a good surplus. He thought that after things were straightened out the firm would be able to resume in a few months." *The Inquirer,* Sept 18, 1898, p 10.

[100] The 1900 U.S. Census, Phila Ward 19, Dist 398, Fam 20, included eleven Murphys, including five adults (Joseph P., cloth mfr, b Feb 1846; wife Adele, b Feb 1850; daughter Anna, b Dec 1873; son Edward, cloth mfr, b Feb 1878; and Frank, clerk, b Mar 1881); five children in school (Elizabeth, b July, 1883; Agnes, b Dec, 1885; Mary R., b Feb 1888; Loretto, b July, 1890 and Walter, b Aug 1892); and one not yet in school (Raymond, b Aug 1894). It also included a live-in servant, German-born Teressa Huth, b Feb 1860. (This Teressa Huth appears to be the same woman who would still be with Mrs. Murphy 20 years later, although that Census would identify her as Augusta Huth.).

[101] Joe's son, Edward Vincent Murphy (1878-1964) should not be confused with Joe's brother, Edward Vincent Murphy (1843-1919) the former Port Collector and Senate shorthand reporter who'd reported the Lincoln Conspirators trial. The elder Joe Murphy continued to appear in the city directories after 1900, but inconsistently – sometimes with the occupation "woolens," sometimes with no occupation, and sometimes not at all. Any indication of his involvement with the company called "Murphy & Bro." eludes us – yet surely, his money and contacts were the seeds of the new business. The very name, "Murphy & Bro.," begs the question as to which of his sons was the named Murphy and which merely the brother. For over a decade to come, the directories would list "Murphy & Bro." with two principals – Joseph P's sons, Joseph and Edward – while never denoting one as a president or superior in any other way to the other. Joseph P. appears to have created a company in which fairness to his sons was paramount, as each appears to have become a 50% partner.

[102] *The Times,* May 29 and Aug 6, 1902. *The Inquirer* of March 19, 1903, p 6; and that of May 28, 1903. After suing Furbush, the lender who'd foreclosed on the company a decade earlier, the Joseph P. Murphy Co. was discharged in bankruptcy by the U.S. District Court on May 27, 1903.

[103] The exact time of the move is uncertain because Joseph P. was not listed in the 1904 Directory; but in 1905, he was listed at 4601 Pulaski Avenue, Germantown.

[104] The only exception to Joe's absence from the news media is the 1906 Obituary of his wife's aunt, Mrs. Margaret Clothier Owens (Adele Miller Murphy's mother being Ann Elizabeth Clothier, and Margaret being Ann Elizabeth's sister.) That obituary stated that her funeral procession would begin at Joe's home on Pulaski Avenue (*Inquirer* of May 14, 1906).

[105] *The Inquirer*, Dec 7, 1910; PA Dept of Health Certificate of Death 29462, certifying death on 12-5-1910 and listing cause as "Faulty Degeneration of Heart," with nephritis as a secondary cause. Just a year prior to his death, Joseph and Adele had moved to 6807 Old York Road, Oak Lane, even further away from center city Philadelphia. (The new address appeared on the death certificate and in the 1910 Directory.) The reason for the move is unknown; since he was only 65, it seems he intended to live in the new house for some time, and that the heart attack came as a surprise. His obituary read, "Suddenly, on December 5, 1910, Joseph P, husband of Adele G. Murphy. Relatives and friends are invited to attend the funeral, on Friday, at 8:30 A.M. from his late residence, 6807 York Road. Oak Lane. Solemn requiem mass at the Church of the Holy Angels at 10 A.M. Interment at Holy Sepulchre Cemetery." See also *Washington Herald*, Dec 6, 1910, p 2; *Washington Post*, Dec 6, 1910, p 3; and *Evening Star*, Dec 6, 1910, pp 7 & 18.

[106] 1910 U.S. Census, Phila Ward 42, Dist 1068, Fam 290, listing the household as Joseph P., Adele G., Elizabeth H., Agnes M., Mary R., Loretto M., Walter L and Raymond J. The Census gives the address as 6811 Old York Road, but appears to be mistaken, as the 1910 City Directory and obituary both list it as 6807, which is also the address listed for Adele Murphy in later years. Altogether, Adele had had 11 children during 40 years of marriage, of whom 10 (all but James) were still living in 1910.

[107] The household his widow Adele still headed on Old York Road nine years after Joe's death included four of her daughters, a son-in-law, three grandchildren and a maid (1920 U.S. Census, Phila Ward 42, Dist 1578, Fam 369), including more specifically her daughter Anna Rowsey and granddaughters Adele and Anita Rowsey, her daughter Elizabeth Murphy, her daughter Agnes Murphy, her daughter Loretto Coleman and son-in-law Joseph Colman (a dentist), her grandson Joseph Colman, and a sixty-one year old maid, Augusta Huth (who appears to be the same person as, or a relative of, Teressa Huth, maid to Joseph P.'s family in the 1900 Census). Adele kept the family piano, and the family continued to depend on her. With four daughters, all in their middle years, there was only one man among them: Loretto's husband, Joe Colman. Anna Marie's husband, Charles Allan Rowsey, was a salesman in Columbus Ohio when he registered for the draft in 1918, listing his nearest relative as Anna Marie in Philly – but by 1920, they had separated; he married again and moved to Fla. It seems that neither Elizabeth nor Agnes had ever married, although the reference to "Aunt Agnes and Uncle Tom" in a letter written by Joseph Dominick Murphy in 1909 raises an unanswered question (see Chapter 13). By 1930, Adele and her daughter, Anna Rowsey, lived in a household of women only; the new home was valued at $30,000 and owned outright. While the household no longer included a live-in maid, they had their own radio set. The household consisted of Adele G. Murphy (now 81); daughter Anna M. Rowsey, in her fifties, separated from her husband (who had remarried); granddaughters Adele and Anita Rowsey, both in their twenties; and daughters Elizabeth and Agnes, both single and in their forties, neither having ever had an occupation (1930 U.S. Census, Phila District 1029, Fam 52, living at 6610 N. 12th Street). Charles Rowsey was now living in Florida with daughters Anita and Adelle, new wife, Jean, and two daughters of hers, in their twenties (1935 Fla State Census, Dade County, Prec. 4). One imagines the Murphy women, in Philadelphia, sitting in straight-backed chairs, sometimes playing piano duets and listening to the radio, regularly attending mass on Sundays, and otherwise living sedate, spinsters' lives for many years. Adele died of cerebral apoplexy at 3:45 in the morning on August 3, 1931. The informant, for purposes of her death certificate, was her son, Joseph D. Murphy, who lived two blocks away (Phila Death Certif, 1931, Bureau of Vital Statistics File No. 74740, Reg. No. 16911). After Adele's death in 1931, the surviving Murphy spinsters (Anna Rowsey, Elizabeth Murphy and Agnes Murphy) moved in with their sister Adele and her husband, Dr. George Shoup (1940 U.S. Census, Phila, 51-2164, Household 104 at 7007 N 12th St).

[108] According to news accounts, Joe pledged an unstated amount for erection of a monument to the lately assassinated President James Garfield (*Inquirer*, July 6, 1882, p 2). At the conclusion of a solemn high mass celebrated by Father P.F. Sullivan, pastor of St. Edward the Confessor Catholic Church, Murphy was the one to present him with a check for $3,700, although the money was from the congregation – the portion contributed by Murphy personally was not stated (*The Times*, Feb 29, 1888). Ten years later, he served as chairman of a committee organizing a concert for St. Edward's (*Inquirer*, Jan 5, 1898 and Jan 15, 1898, p 2). Those are the only instances in which the news media reported any charitable activity by Murphy. His employees donated $31 to the Irish Relief Fund (*The Times*, March 5, 1880, p 2; *Inquirer*, March 8, 1880, p 2). Joe also provided employment for his youngest brother, John Aloysius Murphy (Sept 19, 1849 - April 4, 1942); John was an intelligent man, having graduated from Central High School like all the Murphy boys except Joe. (General Catalogue of the Central High School, Philadelphia, from 1838 to 1890, Bd of Educ, 1890, p 94, accessed at archive.org/details/generalcatalogue00phil/rich (admitted Feb, 1864, left March, 1865)). But for reasons unknown, John spent his life working various clerk and production jobs in Joe's textile mills, including mill hand and finisher. He outlived all his siblings, but he did not marry until age 52, and at age 80, he was a boarder with only $35 in personal property. The informant on his death certificate was the man at whose house he last boarded. (1870 U.S. Census Phila Ward 16, Dist 50, Fam 1474; 1880 U.S. Census Phila Dist 310, Fam 9; 1920 U.S. Census Phila Ward 40 Dist 1498, Fam 250; 1930 U.S. Census, Phila Dist 0379, Fam 222; PA Death Certificates 1906-1968, No. 32249.)

8. Thomas J. Carvin

The fourth of ten children, Thomas John Carvin was a toddler during the riots of 1844. He may have briefly attended the Master Street School, but as an adult, he was unable to read or write.[1] There was nothing he liked about the rules of arithmetic or homework, nothing he liked about following instructions. His job at the steam-powered cotton mill, an escape from home when he reported there at the age of fourteen, quickly led to drudgery among robotic co-workers in service to machines. He hung around the Austin brass shop whenever he could. There, at least, he had freedom to be himself.[2]

There was much talk of freedom in 1850's Kensington. Dominick Murphy, the 17th Ward's new Irish Common Councilman, spoke of democracy, of a brotherhood of races and religions, of a country that promised liberty for all. The whole country, people said, was a brave experiment in government, and according to most people, it didn't deserve to be split apart. Such ideas appealed to Thomas as much as any ideals could, for nothing about them was a constraint, nothing about them demanded anything from him. Things could certainly be better than they were. Neither his parents nor his brother James (always commended for his maturity, his common sense, his responsibility) seemed to understand just how important freedom was. And when war broke out in 1861, talk of freedom was joined by talk of the glory that could be had in fighting for it.

Altogether, such ideas might lift a man out of life in a cotton mill. So on May 15, 1861, when Oregon Senator E.D. Baker showed up in Philadelphia recruiting a regiment, his talk of high ideals and glory rang true.[3] Volunteering for war could impress girls; it could demonstrate courage to parents and younger brothers; it could immediately mean a life of freedom, away from the mill. So Thomas volunteered. According to his Consolidated Military Service Record (CMSR), he had blue eyes, brown hair and was only five feet five inches tall – not a big young man, to be sure, but big enough for glory, big enough for better things, at least, than standing alongside children and girls, tending steam-powered looms that hissed and boomed and deadened his ears.[4]

Baker's appeals to patriotism and the righteousness of God were so powerful, Thomas signed up for three years. Three years away from street-cluttered Kensington. None of the boys who signed up that day hesitated much. And none wanted a defensive unit; they all wanted action.

On May 21, they were mustered into federal service with gray uniforms and brass buttons. Assigned to Company B of what would become the 71st Pennsylvania Infantry regiment, they elected James Lingenfelter their captain. After training at Fort Schuyler until July 1, they were back in Philadelphia, marching in front of their parents, sisters and girlfriends, proud as they could be.[5]

From there, they were sent to Fort Monroe, the "American Gibraltar," its 32-pound guns a key part of the North's naval blockade on the south. (There were some who naively believed the seceding states could be forced back into the Union without the letting of blood.) How grand it was, imagining the stories they'd soon be able to tell. When Bill Vance deserted at the end of the month, it was a startling surprise to most of the company. His memory provoked harsh words.[6]

Between May and November of 1861, Thomas enjoyed the brave camaraderie of the other young men.[7] Then, when Lingenfelter led the company out of Fort Monroe and the regiment began making its way into Virginia on August 5, 1861, the boys came face to face with something few had thought much about: long, tedious hours marching, building huts, getting rained on, trying to stay dry. "I now realize the trooth of a soldier's life," Private Richard Margerum wrote home.[8] The other side of war – the side that had no glory – blistered feet, made muscles ache, made stomachs growl with nausea. On September 11, 1861, on reconnaissance in front of the main body of troops, Thomas's Company B was attacked while on picket duty. The gray uniforms worn by both north and south made men indistinguishable from each other. Many were shot by friendly fire. A fatal hit to Captain Lingenfelter was the culmination of a ghastly day, the rude interruption of a dream. Desertions began in earnest, Jim Kennedy, Lewis Fenner, Henry Hooten and Bill Osborn of Company B among them.[9]

War was not the freeing experience Thomas had imagined.

On Sept 29, 1861, the regiment advanced toward Munson's Hill, just across the Potomac River from D.C. "The night was dark and the road a narrow track through dense forest." Due to a miscommunication, a collision with the enemy left four soldiers killed and fourteen more wounded, several mortally.[10] A night march, with sudden gunfire, spooked several boys into staying awake, wide-eyed, all night.

Early in October, the regiment, now commanded by Col. Wistar, became part of a division commanded by Nathaniel Banks, a former Governor with no military experience, a man said to be a political sop. They were withdrawn from the front to a position north of Washington, where they were joined into a brigade with the 69th, 72nd and 106th Pennsylvania volunteers and assigned to guard the fords of the Potomac."[11] Things were quiet for several weeks. But on October 21, Gen. Baker and Colonel Wistar, leading half the companies of the regiment, crossed the river in an effort to surprise the rebels in Virginia. Coming under heavy fire on the opposite bank, Baker himself and several other officers were killed. The soldiers started to run, but there were no boats to get back across the river. Men jumped into the water, trying (desperately) to re-cross to safety. But weighed down by full battle gear, many drowned. 312 of 520 were lost; Captains Markoe and Keffar, wounded, were captured by the enemy. Colonel Wistar, also wounded, was borne from the battlefield to safety in the rear.[12]

The boys of Company B were thankful they hadn't been among those who crossed the river. But they joined in their comrades' complaints about the lack of boats and the generals responsible for it. A few envied the badge of honor worn by those who'd survived the deadly fire, making much of their desire to see action in the fight for freedom.[13]

When the brigade went into winter quarters at Camp Observation, Maryland, Congress had still not passed pension legislation for those who survived the war. Together with cold winds and wet weather, talk of being left without pensions brought more desertions: James Brady, Mike Kelly and Jim McGheeghan deserted in October; on the second of November, they were followed by John Boyd, Staten Boyles, John Brannin, Tom Dallas, Sam Dilly, Hugh Dougherty, Tom Murphy, and Bob Smith.[14] Plainly, desertion was no longer the shameful choice of a despicable few. It now seemed the choice of a growing number of the boys, more sensible than it had seemed from the safety of Fort Monroe. Following orders that came from men one couldn't see seemed insane when one's own life was at stake. On the 7th of December, 1861, Thomas himself deserted.

For six months he hid out in barns, alehouses, and brothels, trying to get back to the Philadelphia he'd once fled, while others stuck to their posts. But his own freedom was short-lived. On July 10, 1862, he was arrested and returned to his regiment with the notation, "$6 cost of arrest and transportation will be deducted from his pay. He is losing all back pay and allowances."[15] The life to which he'd escaped from the mills was now itself a prison that wouldn't let him go.

At Harrison's landing in July, finding himself in camp alongside the 7th Reserves, he learned that after being badly wounded at Beaver Dam Creek two weeks earlier, his brother James had been taken to the field hospital at Savage Station. Knowing nothing more, he could only hope that James had survived and was alive in some rebel prison or hospital. James, always dutiful, always obedient, had promised their mother to look after him, the "reckless" one, but he could see where James's obedience had gotten him. When he heard that the generals had ordered the abandonment of Savage Station, leaving James and hundreds of other wounded men behind to await capture, he was convinced that following orders was folly; all he could feel was anger at the top brass.[16]

Thomas saw more action soon. On the 17th of September, 1862, he was at the center of the Union forces wading across Antietam Creek.[17] "In 20 confused and terrible minutes, half the 5,000 man division fell; the frightened remnants raced to the rear."[18] When General Sedgwick was wounded, his command devolved on General Howard.[19] Leading a charge by the 71st, Colonel Wistar fell, severely wounded again.[20] ("[F]or three hours the tide of battle ebbed and flowed over him before he could be removed.") The 71st lost a third of the number engaged that day, Company B in the thick of it. The next morning, only four officers were present for duty.[21] The Company's Second Lieutenant, William Wilson, its Sergeant, Jacob LeBold, and two of its privates, John Migent and Charles Miller, had been killed. William Quinn had been wounded. James Campbell had deserted. Thomas had been under direct fire for hours – pinned down, unable to run, feeling his own death at any moment. Some of the bloodiest fighting of the war was at Antietam. Bates's history of the regiment, intended as a paean to the glories of the Pennsylvania Volunteers, says "a part of the troops fell into some confusion" but the 71st held its position. One wonders whether Thomas was part of the holding, part of the confusion, or frozen in place, unable to contribute to either.[22]

In November, he was fined and docked pay for shirking picket duty. In December he was with his regiment, attempting to drive the rebels out of Fredericksburg.[23] In darkness, fog, and freezing rain that had begun before dawn on the morning of December 11th, engineers built a pontoon bridge across the Rappahannock River. Under heavy cannon fire, they crossed the bridge and fought their way uphill toward the center of town, then moved south down Sophia toward William Street. Confederate General Barksdale had set up headquarters on the ridge along Princess Anne Street. Well into the night, confederate fire came from the Presbyterian Church at the corner of Princess Anne and George Street.[24] When Barksdale finally moved his troops back to the foot of Marye's Heights, Company B bedded down for the night on Caroline and Sophia, sleeping in the rubble, intending to help clear the town in the morning.[25] The following morning, advancing to the right and rear of town under heavy artillery fire, they suffered considerable losses."[26] Thomas's CSMR gives that day – December 12th – as the date he was captured.

At five-foot-five, having long lost all trace of machismo and desperate to end the torment, it's possible that Thomas was fully engaged in the battle, trying to kill enemy soldiers until it was no longer possible to avoid capture. More likely, he was looking for a chance to surrender from the moment the battle began. It was not an uncommon practice. For many caught in the heat of battle, there seemed little reason to do anything else.[27]

Absent witnesses, there was no way to know if a missing soldier had been captured, killed, or deserted. Few involved in the street fighting were focused on gathering evidence or keeping records. When his commanding officer first noticed his disappearance, he remembered that Thomas had deserted before and that he'd recently shirked picket duty. It was natural to assume he'd deserted once again. The muster roll covering January and February, 1863, reads "Absent. Declared deserter."[28]

But despite what he'd heard, Thomas found that getting captured was not an easy ticket home. He was taken to Libby prison in Richmond, which had earned an infamous reputation for the conditions under which its prisoners were kept."[29] From Libby, he was sent to Belle Isle or Castle Thunder prison. At Belle Isle, sergeants Hyatt and Marks tied men up by their thumbs, bucked and gagged others, and made some prisoners carry heavy sacks of sand until unable to stand under the burden.[30] Castle Thunder was worse:

> By January 1863, the 1,400-capacity prison housed 3,000 men and women, and diseases such as dysentery and smallpox were prevalent. Struggling to maintain order among such a large and diverse population, prison officials—including its commandant, Captain George W. Alexander—often resorted to violence. In April 1863, the Confederate Congress authorized an investigation and heard accusations of unauthorized lashings and Alexander's use of his large dog Nero to intimidate prisoners.[31]

Thomas remained in rebel prisons for more than three months.[32] According to his 1865 muster-out roll, he was finally released from Libby and ordered to Camp Parole (in Annapolis, Maryland) on April 1, 1863.

> Prisoners were brought up the Chesapeake Bay to Annapolis by the steamer, New York, in groups as large as 6,000. The eight wooden barracks, each meant to house 150 men, soon proved to be woefully inadequate. Men lived in tents, huts they built for themselves with lumber stolen from public buildings, and a few hastily erected wooden barracks. The camp population varied from 2,000 to more than 15,000 at any one time.[33]

Long suppressed memories of the 1844 riots now rose and played themselves out in his nightmares; the faces of friends lost in the Saint Michael's train crash, hidden away since he was thirteen, now came back to him; and now, with death and disease all around, with more comrades lost, with his brother lost, countless unnamed strangers were falling before his eyes. He'd been plagued by nightmares even before his nights on cold prison floors. Now still a prisoner even in Northern hands at Camp Parole, awaiting his official exchange in the midst of disease-ridden tents, he could see no wisdom in the men who claimed the authority of "superiors."

While he was away from his former comrades, the 71st was decimated at the battle of Chancellorsville. It lost many more at Gettysburg, including his own new Captain, William Dull, killed there on the third of July.[34]

Such had been the highlights of Thomas's life when, on July 17, 1863, he was finally set free from Camp Parole. Under military law, he was supposed to return to his unit.[35] But that course of action made no sense. The armies were trying their best not to reveal their locations from one day to the next. How was he supposed to rejoin such a unit, on the move and trying to keep its plans secret? Instead of heading west or south through hostile Virginia in search of his regiment, it only made sense to head north, back to Philadelphia.

He'd given no advance notice of his homecoming. As he arrived at home on Mascher Street, a deserter once again, his sisters Mary and Elizabeth, now 19 and 16, and his brothers William and Joseph, now 15 and 13, were working in a nearby cotton mill.[36] It was summer. His parents' illnesses were serious enough, by the end of July, to keep one or both of them home from work, coughing and weak. His youngest brothers, now 11 and 9, were the first to welcome him home.

Innocent, ignorant, they wanted to know all about his heroic exploits and adventures. What could he say? He wanted to unburden himself, but he could say nothing without disappointing the boys and catching the ire of his sisters. His horrible memories could be of no help to his sick parents. The only person he could really talk to was his sister Mary, two years his junior. Before the war, they'd been weavers at the same cotton mill; they'd had an interest in each other's friends. He spilled out all the horrors he'd experienced to her, explaining with no guilt, and much defiance, that he'd not come home as some sort of hero or fool, but as a free man – a sane, sound, intelligent deserter, no dupe of the powers that be.

Mary assured him he had done the right thing.

She also introduced him to her friend, Anna Siner. Anna worked as a gaiter binder in the same mill Mary did.[37] The Siners weren't well off. And they were not Catholics. But there was mutual attraction: Anna felt compassion for the young soldier; Thomas liked the attention.[38] The pleasure of a soft hand, a gentle kiss, was blissfully warm and comforting.

But with his eyes on Anna Siner, Thomas paid little heed to what others might think of his absence from his regiment.

Earlier that year, the government had passed a compulsory draft law.[39] In late May and early June, a census of young men of draftable age had been taken in Philadelphia's Third Congressional District. Information about him – his name, age, address, place of birth etc – had been willingly supplied by his family and local authorities who knew him.[40] The list of draft-eligible men included the notation that he was already serving in the 71st Pennsylvania Volunteers.[41] For draft purposes, therefore, the census had no effect on Thomas's military status.

The draft results, however, were made public. On July 27th – within days after Thomas's arrival in Philadelphia – *The Inquirer* published Thomas's name among a thousand others drafted in the 19th Ward.

Preston Curry,
Nicholas Spang,
John Gutznuger,
Simon Reinhart,
Thomas Carvin,

Henry Harver,
John Mahoney,
John Streckline.
Joseph Lukens,
Matthew Kline,

The neighborhood was still split between pro- and anti-war sentiments, and publication of his name led to discussion of his status. Patriotic eyes made sure that drafted men were fulfilling their obligations. Thomas's physical presence in town invited attention. Perhaps that attention added to his earthly desires in deciding to ask Anna Siner to marry him.[42]

Once Anna agreed, the question was where, and by whom, would they be married. His sister's marriage to George Austin had shown how the Catholic Church would react to marriage at a non-Catholic Church, in a ceremony performed by one not an ordained Catholic priest. A decision to marry in a Protestant church, as Anne had done, was a slap in the face to his ailing mother. But deferring to the desires of others had proven itself a disaster, and he was tired of such nonsense. On September 6, 1863, Thomas and Anna Siner were married by Anna's uncle, George Wilson, at the First Independent Church of Kensington.[43] The newlyweds took up residence next to the Siner home on Chenango Street.[44] If the decision didn't sit well with his parents, that was their problem, not his.

His mother's condition worsened, leading to her death on November 29th. But Thomas refused to accept blame. It was his mother's religion, and her church, that had driven them apart in the last weeks of her life. Meanwhile, from time to time, he looked over his shoulder for the agents of the Provost Marshal.[45]

Thomas's oldest sister, Ann, had a family of her own to care for. And his younger brothers were still interested in foolish, innocent things, playing games, making slingshots and skipping stones. His father's health was failing, his death fast approaching. Even his new wife was not a supportive listener. It was his dear sister Mary to whom Thomas turned with his horrific tales of war. She too had lost a brother at Beaver Dam Creek, thanks to the idiocy of uncaring generals. She, too, kept an eye peeled for the Provost's men.

But despite her vigilance, thirteen days after the death of their mother – on December 11, 1863 – Thomas was arrested again. Desperate to avoid being returned to the front, Thomas turned to Mary, wondering aloud if his sister could stop it from happening. Could she go to the Provost to beg? Seek help from influential men like Dominick Murphy? Write an appeal to Abraham Lincoln on his behalf?

No record of a court martial has survived, and Thomas's CMSR gives no clues about details. Yet his arrest did *not* lead to a simple handcuffed journey back to his regiment. Rather, Mary had heard his appeals. All other efforts exhausted, she enlisted the help of a friend, James McIlvaine, with whom she did the only thing she could to keep Thomas from returning to war. While history yields no contemporaneous account of the matter, four months later, the *Inquirer* carried a notice that revealed the lengths to which Mary had been willing to go:

> POLICE CASES. – JAMES MCILVAINE and MARY CARVIN have each been held in $800 bail, by Alderman FIELDS, to answer the charge of having rescued a deserter from the army after he had been taken into custody.[46]

In Thomas's eyes, Mary's arrest proved that the government had gone haywire. Her willingness to help him had made her a traitor to her country. Unless we forget Mary Surratt, we know that in such passionate times, patriotism could demand full punishment for traitorous acts. The *Inquirer* itself cost only two cents a copy. Hardly able to afford the $800 bail, Mary surely served time, paying a steep price for empathy with her brother. And as if to prove her gratitude to her partner in crime, she wasted no time marrying James McIlvaine and becoming pregnant with his child.[47]

But Thomas had problems of his own. Spending December 1863 until March 1864 behind bars, he was in prison when his father died in January of 1864. Then, on February 29th, General Webb issued an order allowing deserters to be returned to service, subject to forfeiture of pay. Thomas was returned to active military duty. His CMSR muster roll card for the period of January and February 1864 has a note which reads: "$30 to be deducted from pay for apprehension as deserter. Returned to duty March '64 by order of General Webb."[48] The next card, for March and April 1864, says he would forfeit all pay and allowances due up to 29 March, 1864, would pay $60 reward for his arrest, and – cruelest and most unimaginable punishment of all – he would make good the time he lost by desertion. That final sting meant he'd serve an additional 15 months and 14 days beyond the date his original three-year term of service expired.

As the third anniversary of their enlistment approached, most surviving members of the 71st Pennsylvania Infantry looked forward to imminent discharge from duty, wondering whether they'd be sent into battle one last time before being sent home. But now facing another fifteen months in the service of his country, Thomas was not one of them. One can only imagine how he felt about soldiers like Private Margerum, who'd applauded the ill treatment of deserters, and what soldiers like Margerum felt about him. Enduring their scorn likely toughened his disdain for them and all they stood for.

But events have a way of marching on. On May 3rd, Hancock's whole II Corps (including the 71st Pennsylvania) began moving south. On the night of the 5th, they slept on their arms. On the 6th, Colonel Kochersperger was severely wounded in fighting at the Wilderness. The Corps pushed forward, with severe fighting on the 7th, reaching Spotsylvania Courthouse on the 8th.[49] With Colonels Smith and Kochersperger out of action, the 71st was now under the command of a mere Captain, William Smith; and on the 9th or 10th, when Smith was severely wounded, command fell to yet another Captain, Mitchell Smith. On May 10, William G. Thompson of Company B was wounded and hospitalized. After heavy rains that began on the 11th, on the morning of the 12th, the regiment thin, its leaders green, movement began at daybreak under dense fog. That morning it seemed the war wouldn't end until every last soldier had been killed.

Skirmishes turned into hand-to-hand combat. When Captain Smith and Lieutenant Clark were killed, regimental command fell on a third Captain, Captain Grear.[50] The Army of the Potomac's historian called the fighting that lasted from 10 a.m. on May 12th through 4 a.m. on May 13th "the fiercest and most deadly struggle of the war," the area "transformed into a frightful rain-soaked and blood-drenched *abattoir*," the woods "one hideous Golgotha."[51] The rain and the fighting continued for several days. During this, the loudest, bloodiest, most horrific fighting that Thomas had ever experienced, he himself was finally wounded.

That said, the nature of Thomas's wound is worthy of particular consideration: namely, he'd taken a musket ball at the tip of his right middle finger. War does many things to men; among them, it sometimes causes soldiers to sacrifice limbs to avoid losing their lives. By the end of the war, fingertips had become a popular destination for that sort of bullet.[52] For Thomas, the tip of his right middle finger may have seemed a particularly apt place to shoot himself. Taken to Emory General Hospital in Washington, the fingertip was amputated and the stump dressed. The 71st Pennsylvania moved southward to join in the brutal, deadly assault at Cold Harbor. After that calamity, there was so little left of the 71st that the few who remained, including Thomas, were transferred to the 69th.

It may have made little difference to Thomas by that time. From September through December, 1864, he was detailed at the Division Hospital, near Petersburg. The casualties from Cold Harbor had little effect, his heart now cold as brass. Birds' songs sounded like bugle calls; pinecones hitting the ground like mortar fire. Even his superiors could see there was no fight left in him. And so, his service with the 69th lasted only six more months. With the war's end a foregone conclusion, he was mustered out near Petersburg on January 13, 1865, "by reason of expiration of term of service" – as if the Army, averse to spending more money for useless soldiers, was anxious for a face-saving compromise.[53]

And so, just as the last vestiges of the conflict settled into history, Thomas finally returned home, legally free of government service for the first time in years. Seeking respite in soft flesh, he wasted no time impregnating Anna. (Perhaps fatherhood seemed capable of restoring peace and normalcy.) But the senseless world he'd discovered at war refused to end. One of the bitterest, most *ridiculous* indications of that senselessness was an advertisement placed in the papers in February, 1865, by John Budd, former assistant tax assessor, now acting for the 2nd Precinct of the 17th Ward:

17th Ward: Avoid the Draft – At a meeting held on Thursday
evening, 16th inst., it was resolved that all persons liable to
the Draft be requested to pay to the Precinct Committee $25,
for the purpose of filling the quota of the Ward.[54]

The draft? *Bastards!* Did they think him stupid? The War was winding down, and he was free at last! If he didn't keep a watchful eye, hacks like John Budd would take his money, if they couldn't take his life. Things were different now. He was done with giving of himself. It was time to take back. He'd have to be vigilant, to safeguard the freedom he'd won.

How much attention he paid to Mary's baby – a boy born March 20 – isn't known, but within days of Lee's surrender to Grant came the assassination of President Lincoln.[55] And if that didn't prove the world had gone to hell, on July 5, 1865, the day Andrew Johnson signed Mary Surratt's death warrant, Mary's infant son died.[56] Thomas could do nothing to help with her grief or her legal troubles. War's aftermath was eating away at him. James, both his parents, and now his nephew were dead. Nightmares and flashbacks wouldn't let go. The rubble of 1844 kept piling up in the streets. If there was anything good in the world, a man had to take of it what he could. Perhaps he could get a pension – twelve dollars per month if he'd been disabled from a wound or disease caused by the war. Would his amputated finger be enough? He held it up before his eyes, wondering. The Pension office in Washington was dealing with a backlog of applications. Congress was already considering bills to change the standards for granting them.[57] Pension agents were everywhere, offering to assist applicants for a fee.[58] If he took a job, would it defeat his claim for disability? Anna, meanwhile, was pregnant; there'd soon be an infant underfoot. Work at the cotton mills was out of the question. What was a vet to do?

It didn't help that their new home in the rear of the Siner house on Chenango Street was in a low-lying neighborhood, near the miasmic Cohocksink Creek and the Canal by which city engineers had attempted to rid the area of disease. As a result of the sewage and mosquitoes, home values were low. From his new home, Thomas tried to work at odd jobs, but found it hard to focus. The trauma of war was splintering him. With animal passion, he turned to Anna for satisfaction. But with a child due in October, Anna now told others he was unreliable, his whereabouts often unknown. Indeed, as far as the records reveal, Thomas disappeared, gone underground, out of sight, as if afraid the Provost Marshal would find him and haul him back to the war. He worked, no doubt, to get money for whiskey. He avoided work, no doubt, hoping to prove his disability.[59] In 1868, still without a pension, still needing money to live, he worked as a driver on the south side of town, far away from anyone he'd ever known.[60]

That year an Irishman, Joseph Maguire, wrote after visiting America, "Drink, accursed drink is the cause why so many Irish in America fail."[61]

Thomas, one imagines, was a prime example. Between 1863 and his death in 1906, the city directories listed him as a soldier, an upholsterer, a peddler, a shoemaker, a salesman, an oyster dealer, a salesman, a huckster, a bartender, a superintendent, a watchman, and a brass finisher – rarely holding the same job two years in a row. His residence changed as often as his jobs, the pattern consistent with heavy drinking and with what we now call PTSD. [62]

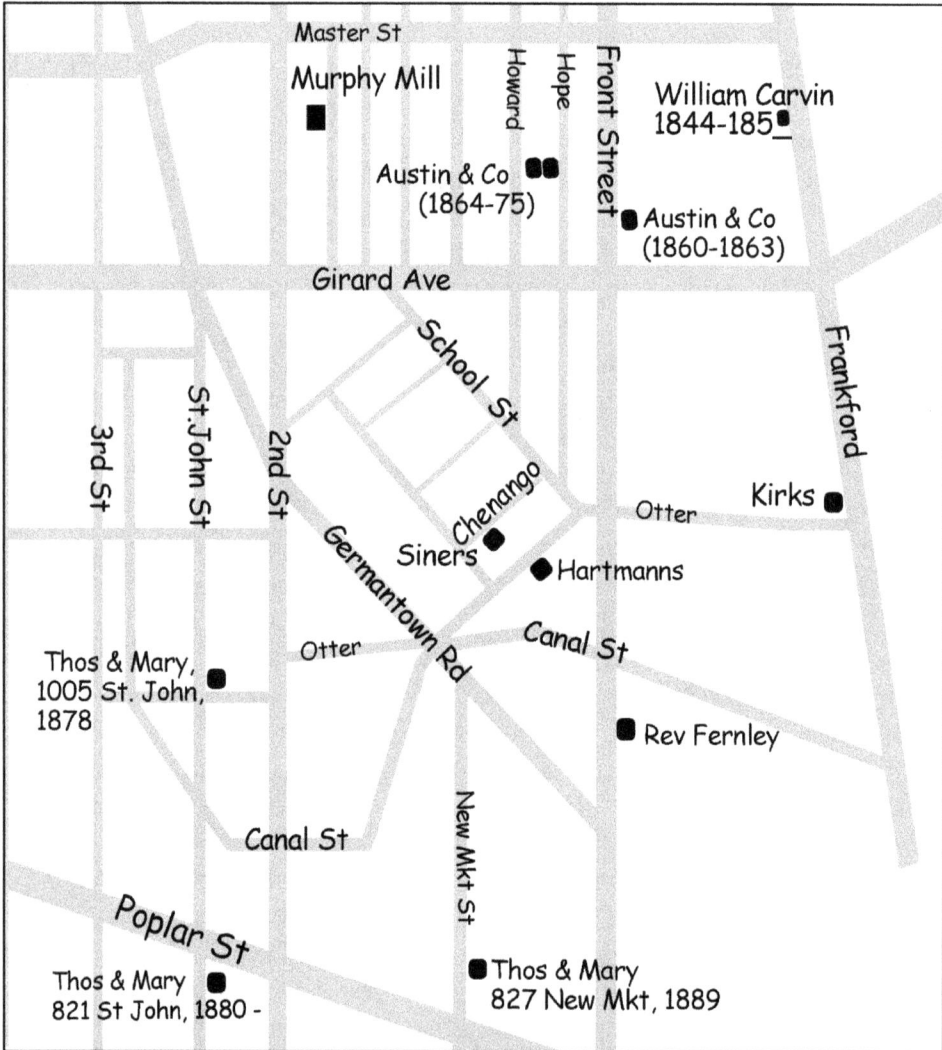

Solid black squares ■ indicate locations of various residences at different times. The Austin house where George and Ann Austin took in Ann's four younger brothers in 1864 was at 1347 Howard, near the Austin brass shops. Emily Hartmann lived at 117 Otter Street, Reverend T. A. Fernley at 1013 N Front, and Mary Kirk at 1104 Frankford. Water (full of sewage) flowed along the approximate path of Canal Street from higher ground in the northwest toward the Delaware River in the southeast.

Thomas's family life was even more problematic. Anna gave birth to a son, Andrew, on the 2nd of October, 1865.[63] In November, 1866, she became pregnant again. But neither pregnancy brought peace to their household. From their shelter in the rear of 105 Chenango Street, it was just a few more steps to Otter Street.

Obsessed with freedom and determined to have what he wanted, Thomas set his eyes on an eighteen-year-old girl who lived practically behind them, at 117 Otter Street. He soon got her pregnant too. The girl – one Emily Hartmann – must have insisted on marriage. But not a public church wedding: such a show might have drawn attention to her condition. Rather, on Christmas day, five or six months into Emily's pregnancy, they sought out the Reverend T. A. Fernley, who also lived in the neighborhood. Swearing that that there was "no impediment whatever in the way of their becoming man and wife" (despite the fact that Thomas's wife Anna was only a month or two into her own second pregnancy), the couple were married by Fernley.[64]

A separate record of the marriage at parson Fernley's house contains a notation in a very different handwriting, seemingly added shortly after the ceremony: "No fee!" it proclaims. "A deceiver. A Bad man having another wife living – ."[65]

Thomas's deceit in seducing Emily under Anna's nose was quickly discovered. When Emily gave birth to Elizabeth Carvin at the end of April, 1867, it seems she wanted nothing to do with Thomas or their child.[66] August must have been especially uncomfortable, as Anna then gave birth to Elizabeth's half-sister, Clara.[67] One wonders whether it was the disease rampant in the low-lying neighborhood that led to the early death of little Elizabeth, or the fact that no one really wanted her. Her burial in the Old Cathedral Cemetery that October raises questions about the circumstances of her short life.[68] Neither Anna nor Emily were Catholics, and Thomas had married them both in their churches, not his. While we can't be certain, it may be that one or more of Thomas's sisters, having taken care of Elizabeth during her short life, arranged for the Catholic burial that October.[69]

In any case, four years after the sordid affair, Anna and her two children were still living among the larger Siner family on Chenango Street. Thomas seems to have been only a sometime resident in the house, as he was included in one of that year's Census enumerations, but not in the other.[70] He may have been a complete brute who came home drunk and forced himself on his wife against her will; or he may have been charming enough, at times, for Anna to forgive him. In either case, in 1870 or early 1871, Anna became pregnant for the third time.[71] But wherever Thomas went when not at home, he got into trouble. On March 26, 1871, he was arrested on charges of disorderly conduct and sentenced to 30 days of hard labor in Allegheny County. The prison record asserts something Anna could surely verify: that Thomas's habits were "intemperate."[72]

Anna's third child, a son they named Thomas, was born later that year.[73]

If Thomas could be charming, he used it to his advantage with women. About this time, a young neighbor who lived on Frankford Avenue, at the end of Otter Street, also caught his eye. Mary Kirk, a barber's daughter, was twenty-two. About the same time Thomas impregnated Anna for the third time, he also impregnated young Mary. There's no record of a marriage, but Mary had a daughter by Thomas in 1872, and a son in 1873.[74]

About the time the second of these children was born, Thomas's namesake – his two-year-old son by Anna – passed away.[75] The low-lying neighborhood may have been a factor. The infant's death may have been enough to end all hope for the marriage with Anna, who had no apparent connections to Thomas thereafter. Thomas and Mary, on the other hand, lived as man and wife for several years.[76]

Post-war Philadelphia was becoming an industrial giant. Steam powered factories hissed and belched like rifle shot and cannon fire. But Thomas had learned to run from rifle shot and cannon fire, and he couldn't seem to stop running. When he next appeared in the 1876 city directory, his occupation was upholsterer; the next year, peddler; the next, shoemaker; the next, he was not listed again. Mary, like Anna before her, tried in vain to get Thomas to exercise responsibility.

At any rate, he wasn't about to let anyone's rules stand in the way. In the 1880 Census, Anna was still living with her birth family and her two children by Thomas in the rear of 105 Chenango Street.[77] Thomas himself, a peddler again, was living with Mary, their two children and two boarders (also peddlers) on St. John Street.[78] But Thomas didn't stay there for long; it seems he soon left Mary; by 1881, he was living with his younger brother Charles on North 3rd Street; the next few years found him working as a peddler, an upholsterer, a salesman, and an oyster huckster.[79] One wonders if he ever invited his son Andrew to a ball game,[80] if he got invited to his daughter Clara's wedding,[81] or if he was allowed to see Clara's daughter, his grandchild, when she was born.[82] One suspects he wasn't welcome on any of these occasions.

Catholic insistence on reading from their annotated Bible had once led to deadly rioting in the streets. Since then, Catholics had been intolerant of his sister's marriage. They'd disapproved of his marriage to Anna Siner in her uncle's Protestant church. They'd condemned his relationship with Emily Hartmann. When his marriage to Anna Siner failed, they wouldn't sanction a divorce, preventing his marriage to Mary Kirk. And now Mary Kirk, Catholic that she was, had rejected him too. Catholics, it seemed, were a judgmental lot; they threatened the very freedom he'd risked his life for.

With such thoughts moving him, Thomas joined a secret society, the Junior Order of United American Mechanics. The Order's stated mission was patriotic – to further the aims on which the country had been founded – and it was popular with veterans like Thomas, who'd risked their lives to preserve the Union. But the war had worked a strange alchemy in some veterans' hearts, in which the incompetence of top brass had proven the need for resistance to Generals, Provost Marshals, jailers, and ultimately, to authority in any form. Embracing devotion to their country, they were nonetheless bitter, not only toward those who'd sent them into battle, but toward all authorities that impinged on their personal freedom. Tracing its founding to the nativist movement in Kensington and Germantown in the 1840's, the J. O. U. A. M. was unabashedly anti-Catholic.[83] Its official history celebrated the anti-immigrant, anti-Catholic principles adopted by those early nativist groups, while blaming the Kensington riots entirely on the Catholics.[84]

Thomas's real problem with Catholicism may have been that like patriotism and marriage, Catholicism depended on faith in some sense, and Thomas had lost all faith in anything but his own freedom as an American. President Cleveland's veto of the generous Pension Act of 1887 gave Thomas and his fellow veterans more reason to resent their government.[85]

Meanwhile, having picked up his scent, trouble refused to leave him alone. On May 8, 1887, his son Andrew died, just 22 years old. The cause of his death was not given in the newspapers.[86] Neither Andrew's death nor the birth of a new grandchild brought Thomas back to either Anna or Mary. (By 1888, Anna was listing herself in the directory as his widow.[87]) But even if Thomas couldn't see it, there was always room for hope. The big-spending Republican Congress soon passed a new law, the Disability and Dependent Pension Act of 1890, providing pensions for all veterans who'd served at least ninety days and had been honorably discharged. Even better, a veteran was now eligible if he was unable to perform manual labor, regardless of his financial situation and regardless of when the disability began.[88] Claims for disability soared. When a Republican appointee, James R. Tanner, took over the Pension Bureau, Thomas was finally issued his pension certificate.[89]

Had Thomas been a complete scoundrel, his siblings would have given up on him, but they did not. His living arrangements with Charles proved a first step in bringing him closer to his birth family. In 1887, he moved north, living near several of his siblings who'd moved away from Old Kensington. He took a job as a bartender at a tavern opened by his younger brother Joe. His older sister, Ann, began to keep house for him on Mascher Street.[90] Ann's influence may have helped him hold down a job as a watchman for several years. In March, 1897, when Mary died, Thomas did the decent thing: the funeral procession left from his residence at 122 East Cumberland Street.[91]

But Thomas was still the old Thomas. Less than three months after Mary's death, Thomas proposed again, this time to twenty-six-year-old Amelia Buehn.[92] He was thirty years older than Amelia – a difference he could surely not hide – but honesty had never been Thomas's strong suit. In marrying Amelia, he claimed to be six years younger than he really was.

He'd never been able to sustain a long-term relationship, but the injustice of the world was to blame for that, not him. Among their war stories, he and other vets at the J. O. U. A. M. shared their resentments toward people who'd come to enjoy the benefits of being an American without having paid the price they had. By 1890, membership in the J. O. U. A. M. had grown to over eighty thousand people.[93] In 1891, the Order had adopted a new resolution, declaring that "there are great and powerful enemies within our midst" and that "the constant landing upon our shores of the hordes of ignorant, vicious and lawless criminals of the Old World should be viewed with alarm." The resolution approved a guarantee "to every man the liberty of worshipping God according to the dictates of his own conscience," and therefore resolved, "that no dogma or creed should be taught" in the schools, while the Bible – "the recognized standard of all moral and civil law" – should be required reading in those schools, "not to teach sectarianism, but to inculcate its teachings."[94] By 1896, the secret society had over 166,000 members across the country, including 85,000 members in Pennsylvania alone.[95] The swelling of their ranks heightened their anti-immigrant patriotism. Thomas was among like minds in the Order, and Amelia, perhaps, was impressed by his passion.

Meanwhile, despite his years living with Mary, Thomas had never divorced Anna. Despite her claim of being a widow, Anna and Thomas were both still very much alive, and very much still married.[96] There'd also been that short-lived marriage to Emily Hartman in Thomas's distant past.[97] Yet when Thomas applied to marry Amelia, he swore on the marriage application that he'd never been married before.[98]

Could Amelia have been so naïve as to believe him? Consider the address Thomas gave on his application to marry her. He'd been living at 112 East Cumberland when Mary died three months earlier. Now, on the marriage license, he gave his address as 2133 Mascher Street.[99] Such an address, if it existed, would have put him in the middle of Norris Square, which had become a city park at least twenty years earlier.[100] The houses fronting Norris Square were privileged places to live.[101] Claiming to live at an address that would have been in the middle of the park was a brazen lie, yet Thomas gave that as his address to the clerk at city hall, and to his young bride, while giving 2136 Mascher as his address to the church. It was rakish humor. Pretending to live in the lap of luxury likely struck Thomas as a harmless lie, the same sort of humor by which he'd given up the tip of his right middle finger.

And there was yet another departure from the truth: since his enlistment in the Army in 1861, Thomas had never worked as a brass finisher, yet he gave that as his profession now, on both the marriage application and in the church record, as he wed young Amelia Buehn.[102]

Buttons, candlesticks, broaches could impress some girls. There might be respectability in being a brass finisher. Who could blame him if he preferred to live in the past, when the Austin brass molding shop promised a bright future?

Whatever other lies he told to Amelia, they worked; Amelia agreed to marry him.[103] *The Inquirer* of June 17, 1897, p 10:

CARVIN—BUEHN.—On Thursday. June 10, at the parsonage of the Church of the Good Shepherd. by the Rev. John A. Goodfellow, Amelia Buehn to Thomas J. Carvin. both of Philadelphia.

The Nativist movement, having earlier joined forces with the Sunday School movement, now found common ground with the Temperance movement. In June of 1897, the National Council of the J.O.U.A.M. adopted a by-law providing that any member "engaging or continuing in the liquor business" after August 1, 1897, would be expelled.[104] The bylaw was consistent with the Order's anti-immigrant, anti-Catholic, anti-Irish philosophy. But when news of it reached the local Order in Philadelphia, it caused a stir. Thomas could despise a degenerate class of immigrants, but he could not despise his own Irishness, and certainly not his alcohol. Some pointed out that the new by-law didn't prohibit members from drinking, only from engaging in the liquor business. But Thomas was not one to make such fine distinctions, any more than he was one to do as he was told. For the next three years, Thomas again tended bar at his brother Joe's saloon.[105]

An earlier pattern now repeated yet again: by June of 1900, Thomas had left Amelia (or she had left him) and he was living a good distance further north, on East York Street, two doors down from his youngest brother, Charles. Both brothers were now tending bar for their brother Joe. The family was still sticking together. And Thomas was now living with yet another woman, also named Mary, apparently more tolerant of his drinking than Amelia had been.[106]

Thomas tended bar at Joe's saloon during most of the next six years.[107] In the meantime, there'd been a rift over control of the J. O. U. A. M.'s money; by 1902, the dispute had found its way into the courts.[108] In June of 1904, an insurgent group split off, forming a new organization that called itself, simply, the Order of Independent Americans.[109] While endorsing all the other principles of its parent organization, the O. I. A. did betray one of them: "At the afternoon session, a lengthy discussion ensued on the proposition to admit liquor dealers to membership in the order, the friends of the liquor men carrying the day."[110] Since the men of the new order would be able to drink to their hearts' content, Thomas didn't hesitate to join their ranks. They adopted an emblem and insignia that featured a Bible and an American flag.[111] Their mission became one of donating flags to the public schools, of fighting to keep other religions (Catholicism chief among them) out of the schools, and of defending the mandatory reading of the Bible in them. (And, of course, one of fighting to limit immigration and the rights of new immigrants.)

To further these aims, on November 21, 1904, the members of the O. I. A. marched *en masse* from City Hall to Park Theater to listen to a sermon by a Baptist preacher who was an officer of the society. His sermon was titled "Unrestricted Immigration."

> We have no room for the hyphenated American or for any people who do not act and vote simply as Americans... If the foreigners will not assimilate with us as American citizens, if they do not admire our American Sabbath and Christian Institutions bequeathed to us by our fathers; if they want social incendiarism and a continental Sabbath, they are welcome to enjoy them – by recrossing the Atlantic – the sooner the better, and that, too, with our warmest benedictions.
>
> But if they stay here, we demand the enforcement of that central truth of statecraft, the liberty of the individual subject to the sovereignty of the state, the subordination of individual rights and privileges to the general good...[112]

The Order was not alone in its anti-immigrant rhetoric. The sermon delivered at Northminster Presbyterian Church that Sunday was titled "Signs of the Times":

> In the past eight years, immigration has been so great that we are becoming blood-poisoned. Something must be done... The quality has changed. Ninety-one percent of the immigrants here have come from the most undesirable countries. They are the scum that are full of anarchy, infidelity and socialism, and instill their obnoxious beliefs in the hearts of our people.[113]

The sermon stirred the hearts of many Christians that day. In September, 1905, the men of the Order, protected by a line of mounted police, marched down Broad Street to present a large American flag while five hundred public school children shouted, screamed and waved smaller flags to the "rattle of musketry." A Methodist preacher gave an invocation before the children were schooled on the Order's cherished principles.[114] In May, 1906, after presentation of a flag to a Colwyn school, courtesy of the Order, addresses were given by Reverend Jones, pastor of the Colwyn Baptist Church, and Reverend Garber, pastor of the Mount Zion Methodist Episcopal Church.[115]

And so Thomas spent his final years fighting for liberty, marching for the separation of church and state, presenting flags and preaching against the threat of immigration. In November, 1906, the Orphans' Court of Pittsburg ruled in favor of the O. I. A. as to the fund over which they'd left their parent organization. For many, it was vindication of their righteousness, a time for celebration, a time to thank God for justice.[116] But Thomas wouldn't enjoy the celebration long. On Christmas eve, estranged from all his surviving wives and children, he died of heart and kidney disease at the age of sixty-four.[117]

He had worked as a peddler, an upholsterer, a salesman, a shoe-maker, an oyster dealer, a watchman and a bar tender, and yet, the person who informed the coroner of his death gave his occupation as brass finisher. Only one person believed that story: his recent bride, Amelia. Though estranged, Amelia also saw to it that Thomas had a proper obituary, and that his friends at the O. I. A. were invited to attend his funeral.[118]

> mantown avenue. Interment private.
> CARVIN.—On December 24. 1906. THOMAS J CARVIN. husband of Amelia Carvin. Relatives and friends and Lieutenant Cushing Council. No 829. O of I A. are invited to attend the funeral. on Tuesday. at 9.30 A M. from his late residence. 1811 E York st. Interment at Glenwood Cemetery.
> CLARK.—On December 25. 1906. BRIDGET

While Amelia may have believed many of Thomas's tall tales, she was not so naïve as to let his service to his country go unrewarded. The 1890 Dependent Pension Act not only expanded coverage to veterans, it also allowed widows to receive pensions if their husbands were disabled at the time of their death. Amelia finally succeeded. On December 18, 1916, she received her first pension check – $36 for the quarter.[119] The amount was later increased: at a time when the news stand price of *The Inquirer* had dropped to only one cent per copy, Amelia started receiving as much as $30 per month (about $3,900 in 2020 dollars) as a result of her late husband's service to his country.[120] Thomas's lifelong quest to be rewarded for his service was finally satisfied, and at least as far as Amelia Buehn was concerned, there was some justice in that.

Notes on Chapter 8, Thomas J. Carvin

[1] By all accounts, Thomas was the last in his family to be born in New York. His date of birth is here taken as April 4, 1842, the day and month based on his 1897 marriage license, since a man has no reason to leave a new wife ignorant of his birthday. But depending on choice of record authority, Thomas may have been born in 1842 (1860 Census, 1861 & 1864 CMSR entries); in 1843 (1850, 1870 and 1880 Censuses and 1906 funeral record); in 1845 (1900 Census and 1863 & 1865 CMSR entries); or in 1848 (1897 Marriage License). I discount 1848 because the family was already in Kensington by then and a man may subtract a few years when he marries a younger wife. I credit 1842 over 1843 or 1845 because the Army referred to him as 19 at the time of his enlistment in 1861. In the 1850 Census, Thomas was listed as a 7-year-old who'd attended school within the year. Since St. Michael's parochial school had not yet opened, Thomas must have attended the nearby Master Street School, but his education stopped early; in the 1880 Census, he was listed as unable to read or write.

[2] In the 1860 Census, he was listed as an eighteen-year-old weaver; he'd likely been working for several years by then. But when he enlisted in 1861, he gave his occupation as brass moulder.

[3] Because of a few early enlistments, Baker's regiment had been nicknamed the "California Regiment," despite its mostly Philadelphia ranks.

[4] Throughout this account of Thomas's military career, facts and dates for which sources are not otherwise stated are based on his CMSR – a collection of notations on pieces of card stock, indexed by the name of Private Thomas Carvin, Company B, 71st (and 69th) Pennsylvania Infantry Regiments, reviewed in 2009 at the National Archives in Washington, D.C.

[5] Samuel Bates, History of the Pennsylvania Volunteers, 1861-1865, Vol 2, Harrisburg, 1869, p 788.

[6] Bates, *supra*, pp 805-806.

[7] For these months, the rolls of Lingenfelter's company at Fort Monroe show that Thomas was present and getting paid.

[8] Margerum, Corp. Richard, *Letters, 1861-1864,* in Society autograph collection, Collection 22A, Company 'H,' 71st Pennsylvania Infantry Regiment, Historical Society of Pennsylvania, 1300 Locust Street, Phila, PA

[9] Bates p 788 – but see pg 805 where the date is Sept 21. Fenner, Kennedy and Hooten's desertions at p 806.

[10] Bates p 789

[11] *Ibid.* The Brigade was a part of Stone's Division, itself a part of Nathaniel P. Banks' Army. Banks was generally known as a "political sop" (see Curt Johnson and Mark McLaughlin in Civil War Battles, Crown Publishers, 1977, p. 63, and other sources) It seems likely the rank and file talked about him the same way.

[12] As described by Bates 789-790 and elsewhere, known as "Ball's Bluff".

[13] Few actions in the war have been more severely criticized, at the time and since. In November, 1861, upon the death of E.D. Baker, the regiment was "adopted" by the State of Pennsylvania and its name changed to the 71st Pennsylvania.

[14] These desertions are all as listed by Bates, supra, pp 805-807. One might ask why Thomas Carvin's name, and his own desertion, are not included in Bates' list with the others. Thomas's CMSR at the National Archives makes clear that he, too, was a deserter from Company B of the 71st Regiment, but as it happens, he was later transferred to Company B of the 69th Regiment, and Bates only picked up his later service in that Regiment. (See Bates p 713.)

[15] Thomas Carvin CMSR.

[16] Stephen Sears, To the Gates of Richmond: The Peninsula Campaign, Houghton Mifflin, 1992, p 264.

[17] Johnson and McLaughlin, *supra*, p 67. The 71st Pennsylvania was now a part of Sumner's Second Corps, at the center of the Union advance. The muster rolls mark Thomas as present during that time.

[18] Curt Johnson and Mark McLaughlin, Civil War Battles, Fairfax Press, 1977, p 67. In most histories, only the names of fallen officers are noted. How terrible, yet how convenient for historians of war, that 2,500 men can die in the space of nineteen words!

[19] Johnson and McLaughlin, *supra*, p 82.

[20] As noted earlier, Wistar had been previously wounded at Ball's Bluff.

[21] Bates, *supra*, p 794.

[22] Some six weeks later, Private Margerum, taken prisoner and waiting to be exchanged from Camp Parole in Annapolis, reported wide dissatisfaction among the troops and urged the need to make peace. (Corp. Richard Margerum to his brother, Oct 31, 1862, *Letters, 1861-1864,* in Society autograph collection, Collection 22A, Company 'H,' 71st Pennsylvania Infantry Regiment, Historical Society of Pennsylvania, 1300 Locust Street, Phila, PA.)

[23] At the end of December, a notation was made on the muster roll by Thomas's name: "Missing in action – one month's pay stopped for shirking picket duty per regimental order." Largely thanks to Francis O'Reilly's detailed account of the action at Fredericksburg, it is possible to track the movements of regiments, companies, and even smaller detachments during the battle, and so to identify where Thomas' company was during the action on December 11th. (Francis A O'Reilly, The Fredericksburg Campaign: Winter War on the Rappahannock, L.S.U. Press, 2003.)

[24] O'Reilly, pp 90-91, 93, 96-97, and map at p 88. See also the detailed maps provided in O'Reilly's separate article, "Slaughter at Fredericksburg," that appeared in Blue & Gray Magazine, Volume XXV, Issue No. 4, 2008. Of particular interest to some may be the fact that one of the rebel units Thomas faced at the corner of Princess Anne and George Street that night was the 17th Mississippi regiment, including one Private Alemeth Byers, whose perspective on this battle (together with a fictional encounter with Thomas Carvin) is recounted in the author's mostly historical novel, *Alemeth*. It appears that Carvin and Byers were in intense fighting, within eyesight of each other, albeit through clouds of gun smoke drifting between the buildings through doorways and shattered windows. Little did they know that while the conflict that had them shooting at each other, their families would join in marriage some hundred years later.

[25] Sometime after 11 p.m., they hooked up with men from the 9th Corps, who'd gotten across a second bridge their engineers had managed to complete that evening (O'Reilly, *supra*, pp 98, 100).

[26] Bates, *supra*, p 794.

[27] Early in the war, captured prisoners had been paroled and sent home to await notice of their exchange. But so many soldiers had allowed themselves to be captured just to get home, the federal army had set up the Parole Camps in order to discourage the practice. (Lonnie Speer, *Portals to Hell*, Stackpole Books, 1997, p 104.)

[28] The notation didn't read, "Proven deserter" or even just "deserter." Rather, "Absent – declared deserter," suggests that Thomas's absence was all that was known, and that after an initial designation as "missing in action," desertion was presumed to be the reason for it. He was of course not paid, regardless, as no one wearing his name badge stepped forward to ask for pay.

[29] Speer, *supra, seriatim,* incl. 121-125. Although Libby prison was used exclusively for the indefinite imprisonment of federal officers, Speer asserts that Libby was headquarters for the Confederate States Military Prisons beginning January 1, 1863, so it became the depot prison to which all POW's in the area were brought before being transported to their respective facilities. (Speer, *supra*, p 122, 302.) "Libby Prison," at Wikipedia.org, accessed November 3, 2020, recounts several graphic examples of harsh treatment there. *War of the Rebellion*, Official Records, Series 2 (on prisoners and exchanges) provides numerous reports/complaints about the conditions there (pp 513, 530, 544, 552, 569, 573, etc...)

[30] Speer, *supra*, p 118. On January 17, 1863, Belle Isle was "reactivated for a short time, emptied out and closed down, and then reopened again in May."

[31] Castle Thunder "was an infamous Confederate military prison during the American Civil War (1861–1865). In service from August 1862 until April 1865, the facility was established for political prisoners, Unionists, and deserters, but its use quickly expanded to include women, spies, and

African Americans. Castle Thunder's keepers—particularly Commandant George W. Alexander, who presided over the prison from October 1862 until February 1864—earned a reputation for brutality and were subject to investigation in 1863 by the Confederate House of Representatives." *Castle Thunder Prison*, Encyclopedia of Virginia, accessed at https://www.encyclopediavirginia.org/Castle_ Thunder_Prison. See also Speer, *supra*, p 302.

[32] As of July of 1862, the opposing governments had entered into a formal agreement by which "a parole, to be put into effect within ten days after capture, permits a prisoner to return to his own lines, provided that he does not take up arms until he is officially exchanged." The agreement required delivery of prisoners to specific sites, and there were frequent delays. For example, on December 28, 1862 – shortly after Thomas's capture – Stanton stopped exchanging commissioned officers; both sides were accusing each other of not complying with the agreement (Speer, p 104). There was also the problem of "excess numbers" of prisoners to process and handle. Some or all of this apparently resulted in Thomas being held in Richmond for the first three months of 1863 – *without* being paroled or exchanged.

[33] Camp Parole page at: https://www.pa-roots.com/pacw/Index/campparole.html, accessed November 3, 2020. At Camp Parole, "The prisoners stayed...... until they were officially exchanged on paper for a prisoner of equal rank or based on the higher-rank calculations of the cartel." Speer, *supra*, p 104.

[34] Bates, *supra*, pp 798, 805. There'd also been a scandal within Thomas's Brigade while Thomas was at Camp Parole: Captain Bernard McMahon of Thomas's 71st Regiment had shot and killed Captain McManus of the 69th. McMahon had been court martialed and convicted of murder but was later pardoned due to his gallant conduct at Gettysburg – such being the twisted justice of men committed to war.

[35] The significance of the release date in Thomas's discharge papers is a little ambiguous, but it sounds as if July 17, 1863, was the date he was exchanged and therefore released from Camp Parole. The essence of parole is the prisoner's promise not to engage in further combat, and earlier in the war, release on parole meant going home, but as we've seen, so many soldiers had abused the system that parolees were now to return to their units.

[36] Other mills in the area had fallen prey to the ravages of war, but Irwin and Stenson's Mill, just 6 minutes way, was still operating, and other mills had opened as well (whether despite the war or because of it).

[37] 1860 Census, Phila, Ward 16 East Division, Fam No 1365. Anna Siner seems to have descended from a family of brass founders that had lived in Northern Liberties and Kensington for decades. One Siner, still operating the brass foundry, was a very wealthy man, his estate worth over $100,000. Numerous Siner families lived near the foundry, just west of the Austin brass shop, and several still worked as brass founders. (See 1860 Phila Census: David S. Siner, age 50 brassfounder, and David S. Siner Jr., brassfounder, at Ward 16 West, Fam No 2068; William Siner, age 58 brassfounder, at Phila Ward 17, Fam No 175. See also the Philadelphia city directories tracing numerous Siner brass founders back as far as Northern Liberties in 1829, when five Siners were listed as brass founders; the peak had been in 1841, when seven different Siners were listed as brass founders: Jacob Siner Sr., Jacob Siner Jr., David Siner, two John Siners and two William Siners. Given the proximity to the Austin brass shop, George Austin's brothers may have worked at the Siner foundry before opening their own. If not through Mary, Thomas may have met Anna's family through the Austins.

[38] Whether the John Siner listed as a trader in the 1850 Census (1850 Census, Phila, Penn, Fam 1235) was Rebecca's father, father-in-law or much older husband is unclear, but he was not living with the rest of the family in 1860. Anna's mother, Rebecca, worked as a washerwoman (1870 Census, Phila Ward 16, Dist 49, Fam 1333).

[39] "An Act for enrolling and calling out the national Forces, and for other Purposes," *Congressional Globe*, 37th Cong. 3d. Sess. Ch. 74, 75, March 3, 1863, quoted in full at https://glc.yale.edu/act-enrolling-and-calling-out-national-forces. (Yale's website cites the Congressional Record, but in fact, the Congressional Record, as we saw in Chapter 3, did not yet exist for another ten years; the proper cite for an 1863 act of Congress is to the Congressional Globe.)

[40] Thomas's family would not have hesitated to share information about him, because they knew he was already serving, voluntarily. Being drafted would change nothing.

[41] Civil War Draft Registration Records, Pennsylvania, 3rd Congressional District, Microfilm Image 238. Another category of information captured in the census was marital status. Oddly, the Provost Marshal had recorded Thomas's status as *married*. In fact it was not until September 6, 1863, a few weeks after he got back to Philadelphia on parole – three months after the draft census was prepared – that Thomas and Anna were formally married in a church. The list of draft-age men had been enumerated in May and June, three months earlier. Which member of the family had told the Provost Marshal that Thomas was married, and why? One plausible explanation is that even before his enlistment, or during a prior trip home after his desertion in 1862, William and Mary had been led to believe that their son was married, when in fact he was not. Perhaps the September, 1863 wedding was intended to formalize a *fait accompli*, in part to please his parents. But William and Mary, both soon to be buried in the Catholic cemetery, would have wanted the marriage to be performed by a Catholic priest and blessed by the Catholic Church. Perhaps, the couple had claimed to be married, but religious differences had resulted in a stalemate over where the ceremony would be performed.

[42] If marriage, or even imminent fatherhood, could be considered a helpful factor in resisting a return to the front, better that it be formalized in an actual church wedding. The Conscription Act included various exemptions from service for family circumstances. Might a draft board, or even the Provost Marshal, consider marriage relevant in determining who ought to be sent to the front? Meanwhile, the new law also provided that "no person who has been convicted of any felony shall be enrolled or permitted to serve in said forces." Thomas may have wondered, was desertion a felony?

[43] Phila City Archives, 1863 Marriage Registrations, p 48, groom Thomas Carvin, occ. brass finisher, born NY, res. Phila, age 22, married Sept 6, 1863, to Anna Siner, born Phila, res. Phila, age 20. Marriage ceremony performed by Rev. J. G. Wilson of 1410 Columbia Ave, Kensington. Marriage registered Oct 1, 1863. Reverend Wilson was Anna's maternal uncle. (Anna's sister, Catherine, married William Brewer, and Catherine Brewer's death certificate shows her parents as John Siner and Rebecca *Wilson* (PA Death Certificates, 1912, Cert No. 100001, Oct 21, 1912).) City Directories in the 1860's list the First Independent Church of Kensington at Marlborough and West Street, and the Rev. John G. Wilson at 242 Columbia av. The church was there only two minutes from the Siner house at 105 Chenango Street and the Austin shop address at 1227 North Front Street. Perhaps the couple met through Anna's older brother Andrew, a wagon driver who may have called on the foundries or the mills where Thomas and his sister Mary worked. (The 1860 Census shows 18-year-old Anna with Rebecca Siner (56) as head of the household, Anna's siblings Andrew (25), Louisa (20) and Margaret (15) Siner, Louisa's husband William Ferris (24), their 3-month-old son John, and a John Siner (49), day laborer, who is not shown as the head of the household. (1860 Census Phila Ward 16 East, Fam No 1365). Since Andrew appears in the 1860 Directory living in the rear of 105 Chenango Street, and he and Rebecca both appear in the 1861 Directory living on Conrow Court (a small alley behind 105 Chenango), the entire household described in the 1860 Census – including Anna – were all living in the rear of 105 Chenango.) Or maybe it was through one of Anna's cousins, like David Siner, who had enlisted with Thomas in the 71st Pennsylvania Infantry. Anna actually had two cousins named David Siner, one a butcher (1860 Census, Phila Ward 17, Fam No 75) and the other a brass founder (1860 Census, Phila Ward 16 West, Fam No 2068) who were both in their twenties. It was apparently the butcher who served in the 71st with Thomas; the brass founder served in the 3rd Artillery.

[44] The later records in Thomas's CMSR reflect his marriage to Anna and their address as 107 Shenango [sic] Street in Philadelphia.

[45] After listing many of the usual difficulties encountered in collecting names, the January 1864 preface to that year's City Directory announced that the draft seemed to be "the terror of all classes," and "in no year have there been so many refusals to give names." The following year's preface declared, "[T]he 'terror' of the 'Draft' is, more extensively than ever, on the people. Every person carrying a City Directory in his hand is suspected of being an enrolling officer, either military or civil, and the very *sight* of this otherwise useful medium of information creates suspicion of ulterior designs."

[46] *Inquirer*, April 9, 1864.

[47] The date of their marriage is unknown, but Mary and James McIlvaine conceived their child in late May or early June of 1864, shortly after their arrest. The child was born on or about the 20th of March of 1865. *Inquirer,* July 8, 1865, p 5.

[48] Apparently, the General Order read that such deserters, as a condition of their return to duty, would forfeit all pay due up through the date of the order.

[49] Bates, *supra,* p 800, and Johnson and McLaughlin, *supra,* p 108.

[50] Bates, *supra,* p 800.

[51] Johnson and McLaughlin, *supra,* p 114.

[52] As but one example, "One member of the 154th New York shot off two fingers from his right hand in 1862 in an attempt to get a disability discharge. [The doctor], however, realized the wound for what it was and made him stay in the service." (Ronald D. Kirkwood, Too Much for Human Endurance: The George Spangler Farm Hospitals and the Battle of Gettysburg, Savas Beatie, 2019, pp 253-254.)

[53] Thomas's last military records reflect his residence address as 107 Chenango Street, next door to the Siner home at 105 Chenango. The CMSR record of Thomas Carvin's 1864 hospitalization asserts that he was married at age 22 in Philadelphia, address 107 Shenango [sic] Street, wife's name Anna Carvin. (Chenango is shown on both an 1862 map and an 1893 map as below Girard: see http://www.philageohistory.org/rdic-images/view-image.cfm/JES1893.Phila.016.Ward16.)

[54] *Inquirer*, Feb 20, 1865.

[55] That April, Abraham Lincoln's corpse was brought to Philadelphia by train, escorted to Independence Hall by a military procession amid much weeping and talk of revenge against the south. (Richard A. Sauers, "Philadelphia: Economy of War," at *History Net*. https://www.historynet. com/philadelphia-economy-of-war.htm, p 84.) "Half a million of sorrow-stricken people were upon the streets to do honor to all that was left of the man whom they respected, revered and loved with an affection never before bestowed upon any other, save the Father of his Country… The wet cheeks of the strong man, the tearful eyes of the maiden and the matron, the hush which pervaded the atmosphere and made it oppressive, the steady measured tread of the military and the civic procession, the mournful dirges of the bands, the dismal tolling of the bells and the boom of the minute guns, told more than it is possible for language to express… [N]ot a house along the line of procession, indeed, not a house in all this vast city, but exhibited the signs of grief, the weeds of woe." (*Inquirer,* April 24, 1865.)

[56] *The Inquirer* of July 8, 1865, p 5, reported the baby's name, John, the name of his parents (James and Mary McIlvaine), their address at Richmond and York Street, and the date of the infant's death on July 5th. According to that report, the infant was 3 months, 15 days old.) The fact that the report refers to the baby as John McIlvaine Jr. throws into question whether his father's name was actually James or John, complicating the challenge of tracking his identity among the James and John McIlvains, McIlvaines, McIlwains and McIlwaines of post-bellum Philadelphia. One possibility is that Mary's James was the James McIlvaine who resided at a hotel at the corner of Richmond and York during the war (1861 through 1866) and may have moved on, after his capers with Mary.

[57] Congress would debate possible changes in the veterans' pension laws for years to come. See, for example, *Inquirer*, Jan 18, 1864, p 1; Jan 4, 1866, p 2; Jan 6, 1866, p 4; Jan 10, 1866, p 4; May 19, 1866, p 2; Jan 2, 1867, p 8; Jan 21, 1868, p 8; *Evening Telegraph*, Jan 21, 1869, p 2; Jan 11, 1870, p 8; Jan 15, 1870, p 4; *National Tribune*, April 13, 1893, p 6; and many, many more – as well as Chapter 9, below.

[58] *Inquirer*, Jan 8, 1866, p 3.

[59] Living within a few blocks of Chenango, the 1866 Directory lists John Austin & Co. and George Austin; it lists the Siner Brass Foundry, Anna's brother George and sister Louisa, her uncle David, and her cousins David Jr., John, Jacob, Jackson, and two Williams; it even lists Dominick and Edward Murphy; but it does not list Thomas Carvin, there or anywhere else in the city. The 1867 Directory didn't either.

[60] Perhaps he'd taken a cue from Anna's brother, Andrew Siner, listed in various directories as a drayman and a teamster.

[61] Dennis Clark, The Irish in Philadelphia, Temple University Press (1973), p. 49, citing *Catholic World*, Vol. 6, No 36 (March, 1868).

[62] The following list reflects Thomas's occupations and addresses, year by year. (Years left blank are years in which no Thomas Carvin appears in the city directory and no other indication of occupation or address has been found.)

Year	Occupation	Address(es)	Source/Comment
1861	Brass finisher		CMSR
1863	Soldier	Mascher, west side	Census for the Draft; wed to Ann Siner
1864	Soldier	107 Chenango	CMSR. Arrested and returned.
1865			Children by Anna Siner
1866			Wed to Emily Hartmann
1867			
1868	Car man	712 Medina	Directory
1869			
1870		105 Chenango	U.S. Census, intermittently.
1871			Hard labor for disorderly conduct
1872			A child by Mary Kirk
1873			Another child by Mary Kirk
1874		1839 N 10th	Directory
1875			
1876	Upholsterer	206 N. 9th	Directory
1877	Peddler	1119 Olive	Directory
1878	Shoemaker	1005 St. John	Directory
1879			
1880	Pedlar	821 St. John	Directory
1880	Peddler	821 St. John	Census – living with Mary
1881	Peddler	529 N 3rd	Directory – living with brother Charles
1882	Upholsterer	529 N 3rd	Directory
1883	Salesman	529 N 3rd	Directory
1884	Oysters	533 N 3rd	Directory
1885	Oysters	533 N 3rd	Directory
1886	Oysters	533 N 3rd	Directory
1887	Oysters, bartender	807 Callowhill, 1942 E Lehigh	Directory
1888	Huckster	807 Callowhill,	Directory
1889	Oysters	827 New Market	Directory
1890		2130 Hope St	U.S. Census (Vet)
1891	Bartender	2425 Mutter	Directory
1892	Supt.	2425 Mutter	Directory – living w sister, Ann Austin
1893	Watchman	2427 Mutter	Directory
1894	Watchman	2429 Mutter	Directory
1895	Watchman	2427 Mutter	Directory
1896	Supt.	2427 Mutter	Directory
1897		112 E Cumberland	Obituary upon death of Mary
	Brass finisher	2136 Mascher St.	City Archives – wed to Amelia Buehn
1898	Bartender	2502 N Howard	Directory
1899	Bartender	2502 N Howard	Directory
1900	Bartender	2502 N Howard	Directory
1900	Bartender	1811 E York	U.S. Census – living with a second Mary
1901	Bartender	1811 E York	Directory
1902			
1903			
1904			
1905	Bartender	1811 E York	Directory
1906	Bartender	1811 E York	Directory
1906	Brass Finisher	1811 E York	Death Cert

[63] Andrew Carvin was born October 2 or 3, 1865 and named after his mother's brother. He was baptized on July 14, 1878. (Baptismal Records of the Emmanuel Episcopal Church, Phila, at the Historical Society of PA, Historic Pennsylvania Church & Town Records, Reel 907, microfilm image 103 of 335, accessed via Ancestry.com, Pennsylvania and New Jersey Church & Town Records, record his birth as having been on the 3rd.)

[64] Records of the Nazareth Methodist Episcopal Church, accessed in a data base online through Ancestry.com, microfilm image 781, originals at the Historical Society of Pennsylvania (Historic Pennsylvania Church and Town Records, Reel 367) and/or in the records of the Methodist Episcopal Church at Valley Forge.

[65] Ibid., microfilm image 298. The address given by Thomas in the Church record was not 105 Chenango, where Thomas lived with his wife Anna, but 1547 Howard Street. Much farther north. No matches have been found between this address and any other – it appears that Thomas may have simply made the address up to satisfy Emily and the Church.

[66] The birth of Elizabeth Carvin is evidenced by a burial record of the Old Cathedral Catholic Cemetery Record dated Oct 29, 1867, giving her age as six months, that is, reflecting a birth about April 29, 1867. (Historical Society of Pennsylvania, Cemetery Records of Old Cathedral Catholic Cemetery, Historic Church and Town Records, microfilm image 4605 of 6844.) The parentage of little Elizabeth Carvin could certainly be clearer, and the conclusion that Thomas and Emily were her parents is somewhat speculative. However, census, directory and other records make clear that all the Catholic Carvins in Philadelphia at this time were the offspring of William and Mary Carvin, who had passed away in late 1864 and early 1865, so the baby Elizabeth must have been their granddaughter. Since her last name was Carvin rather than Austin, McIlvaine or some other married name of a Carvin daughter, she must have been the daughter of a male Carvin. William and Mary's son James had died in 1862, and the next oldest male in the family (William) was only sixteen, so Elizabeth was almost certainly the daughter of Thomas. As for the baby's mother, she couldn't have been Thomas's wife, Anna, as Anna gave birth to her daughter Clara only four months later. So we conclude that Emily was the mother. The baby Elizabeth was conceived in late summer, 1866. Her mother would likely have realized her condition that autumn. If Thomas was faced by a demand that he marry her, one can see him accepting the risk of a bigamy charge, and further, that after Emily discovered Thomas was a cad, she might have wanted to forget the baby almost as much as Thomas himself. This creates the situation in which we can wonder who cared for the baby for six months, and then, upon her death, who arranged for her to be buried in a cemetery of her father's birth religion (on which he'd now turned his back), rather than Emily or Anna's.

[67] Baptismal Records of the Emmanuel Episcopal Church, Phila, Reel 907, microfilm image 101 of 335 at the Historical Society of Pennsylvania, record the baptism of Clara Carvin, daughter of Thomas and Annie Carvin, on December 9, 1877, and her birth date as August 20, 1867. (Other records refer to Clara as Carrie.)

[68] Old Cathedral Catholic Cemetery Record dated Oct 29, 1867, supra.

[69] Because virtually nothing is known of Thomas's sisters Catherine and Elizabeth after the 1860 Census, one can't rule out the possibility that either of them had cared for the infant Elizabeth and arranged for her burial in the Catholic cemetery. Thomas's sister Mary, having sprung Thomas from jail, might have done so, but how that might have impacted her relationship with James McIlvaine (who seems to have left Philadelphia by 1875) is uncertain. Perhaps Thomas's wife, Anna, took care of the little girl, and had her buried in the Catholic Cemetery because she was so clearly Thomas's child, not her own. Another interesting possibility is that the infant Elizabeth was cared for by Thomas's sister Ann Austin, whom we've already seen was devoted to the care of her larger family. Though Ann had herself married outside the Catholic Church, she apparently raised the four orphaned younger brothers she took in as Catholics; two of them remained Catholics as adults. Ann Austin could well have been the one responsible for her unfortunate niece's burial at Old Cathedral.

[70]   Due to dissatisfaction with the accuracy of the first 1870 Census in four cities, including Philadelphia, President Grant ordered a second enumeration of the Census in those cities. The first census taker enumerated Chenango Street on July 25th, the second on November 17th. On July 25th, the census taker found Anna, Anna's mother, Rebecca Siner, three of her siblings, her children Clara and Andrew, her sister Catherine, Catherine's husband, William Brewer, and two Brewer children, living in a small dwelling at the rear of 105 Chenango (1870 Phila Census, Ward 16, Dist 49, Fam Nos 1533 and 1534, accessed at Ancestry.com). A spelling error by which all Carvins were recorded as "Garvins" [sic] in the first enumeration was corrected in the second. The marriage of Catherine Siner to William Brewer is attested by the 1912 death certificate of Catherine Brewer, which shows her as the daughter of John Siner and Rebecca Wilson (Pa Bureau of Vital Statistics Death Cert #100001, accessed at Ancestry.com, microfilm image 396 of 3627). To avoid double-counting or missing anyone, standard census instructions are that a person whose time is divided between two addresses should be included at the address where he spends a majority of his time. Whoever was interviewed on Chenango Street on July 25 did not consider Thomas to be living there a majority of the time, as he is not included in that enumeration, but when Chenango Street was visited again in November, whoever answered questions *did* include Thomas living with the Siner household a majority of the time (1870 Phila Census, Ward 16, District 49, 2d enum of Nov 17, 1870, p 32, microfilm image 77 of 214).

[71]   August 3, 1873 entry for Thomas Carvin, Records of the Old Cathedral Catholic Cemetery, Historic PA Church & Town Records, Historical Society of PA.

[72]   Allegheny County Workhouse, Register of Prisoners Tried and Sentenced to Hard Labor, 1829-1971, p 46 of 6346, Prisoner No. 1357, in Ancestry.com database of Pennsylvania Prison, Reformatory and Workhouse Records 1829-1971. The Thomas Carvin incarcerated in Allegheny County was described as having sandy hair and blue eyes like the Thomas who'd enlisted in the 71st Infantry ten years earlier. He was listed as only 5'6" tall (cf Thomas's CSMR listing as 5' 5"). Prison records indicate that the occupation of their inmate was brass molder.

[73]   Old Cathedral Records, *supra*. The Church record shows the child two years old at the time of his burial in the summer of 1873. In the 1900 Census, Anna is listed as having had three children, of whom only one had survived (1900 Phila Census Ward 31, Dist 789, Fam 25). Anna's daughter Clara had survived; the two non-surviving children were her sons Andrew (1865-1887) and Thomas (1871-1873).

[74]   Mary Kirk, born in Pennsylvania in December 1859, was the daughter of William, a barber, and Elizabeth Kirk (1850 U.S. Census, Phila. North Ward, Fam 800; 1860 U.S. Census, Phila.Ward 16 East Div., Fam 566; 1870 U.S. Census, Phila. Ward 16, Dist 49, Fam 1146.) The Kirks were living at 1104 Frankford Av in 1870 (see Directory). The 1872 and 1873 births of Thomas and Mary's two children, named Mary and John, are reflected in the 1880 U.S. Census Phila, Enum Dist 196, 821 St. John Street, p 23, Fam No 258, which shows Thomas Carvin, pedlar, as head of the household and Mary as his wife. A Catholic mass said for Mary when she died suggests she may have been Catholic; if so, she might have understood Thomas's inability to divorce Anna, and agreed to be his common law wife even so.

[75]   Old Cathedral Records, 1873, *supra*.

[76]   1880 U.S. Census Phila, Enum Dist 196, 821 St. John Street, p 23, Fam No 258.

[77]   While Thomas and Mary were counted with their two children on St. John Street, Anna's family, including Thomas's two children by her, were counted at 1880 U.S. Census, Phila, Enum Dist 293, Fam No. 151, p 14, listing William and Catherine Brewer and their two children; Annie Siner, her mother Rebecca, her brother Andrew, and her two children, Andrew and Carrie Carvin. Anna told the census taker she was married, but she didn't claim Thomas as a member of her household.

[78]   1880 U.S. Census Phila, Enum Dist 196, 821 St. John Street, p 23, Fam No 258.

[79]   In the 1881 Directory, both Thomas and Charles are listed as living in the rear of 529 N 3rd Street, several blocks southwest of the neighborhood Thomas and Mary had been living in. It is possible that Mary moved with Thomas on this occasion, but the relocation, simultaneous with Charles and Thomas living together, suggests that Thomas and Mary separated at this time. Thomas remained at 529 N 3rd until 1884, when he moved next door to 533 N 3rd St, where he continued living until 1887.

[80] In 1882, when his son Andrew was about 17, the Athletics started playing baseball in Philadelphia; the following year, they were joined by the Phillies. (Weigley, *supra*, p 519.)

[81] Clara (Carrie) was married in 1884 to Jacob M Achenbach (sometimes Ashenbach). (See the 11 Aug 1906 death certificate of Florence Achenbach McKinley, giving her father's name as Jacob Achenbach and her mother's maiden name as Clara Carvin.)

[82] His daughter, now Clara Achenbach, gave birth to a daughter Florence on October 16, 1885. (See death certificate of Florence Achenbach, Phila Death Certificates 1906-1967, Cert. No 82160, accessed at Ancestry.com.) Was Thomas permitted to see the child? Did he want to?

[83] Edward S. Deemer, Official History of the Junior Order United American Mechanics and American Landmarks, The Fraternity Publishing Co, Boston, 1897, pp 102-107, accessed at https://books. google.com/books?id=k1jQVa4I7KIC&printsec=frontcover&dq=inauthor:%22Junior+Order+United +American+Mechanics%22&hl=en&newbks=1&newbksredir=0&sa=X&ved=2ahUKEwiJidqi6KD2 AhX2knIEHbxNCtMQ6AF6BAgFEAI#v=onepage&q&f=false. (Note that the 1909 edition of the official history, while similarly tracing its origins to nativist/Catholic riots of 1844, otherwise differs substantially. (Rev. M. D. Lichliter, The Official History of the Junior Order of United American Mechanics, J. B. Lippincott, Philadelphia, 1909, accessed at the Internet Archive, https://ia 600704.us.archive.org/18/items/historyofjunioro00lich/historyofjunioro00lich.pdf.)

[84] For the four principles and the origins of the Order in the "Bible Wars" that led to the 1844 Riots, see Chapter One, *supra*, Deemer, pp 17-18, or Lichliter, pp 2-8. The 1909 Lichliter edition declared that the Order "teaches the highest morality and believes in sound Christian Principles" (p 47), while including among its first objects to "prevent the present system of immigration of foreign paupers to our land" (p 48). Lichliter's History described how it was "foreigners" who interrupted a peaceful Nativist meeting in Kensington in 1844, claimed that all those wounded in the rioting were "Americans," and acknowledged the intense "hatred" of the nativists toward the Catholic "devotees of Rome" (pp 4-6). "While the fact is absolutely true that, aside from the Aborigines, there is no distinctively American race, yet, the claim, often made, "that this country owes all its wonderful progress to immigration," is open to positive contradiction ... The early settlers ... were a class of sturdy, able, and determined men, among the brightest and most intelligent of their native lands, from which they fled to escape from the oppression of conscience ... From the close of the Revolution to 1850 ... about two million, five hundred thousand immigrants landed upon our shores ... became conversant with our system of government, adopted our customs and our language, and must be classed as valuable acquisitions to our country ... These sturdy and liberty-loving foreigners had each braved the long and tedious journey across the ocean ... With the determination of progressive and aggressive pioneers, they... began to till the soil and sow the seed of civilization ... The hardships they endured, the battles for existence they fought, and their final reward in the possession of farms and homes, earned by years of honest toil, made better citizens and truer patriots ... Their descendants are among the noblest of our people ...

[F]rom 1850 to 1870 ... a marked change appears ... [M]any landed who were not animated by the noble spirit of those who had preceded them, and clannishness began to develop rapidly ... [T] steamship lines ... entered into a new traffic of living freight, in the shape of "steerage passage at low rates." [T]he arrival upon our shores of a promiscuous and undesirable class began in the latter part of this period, and continued into the next ..." (Deemer, *supra*, 1897 edition, "The Republic's Peril," pp 102-107.) Reverend Lichliter's 1909 History recounted how, in 1881, an additional object of the organization was approved to prevent "sectarian interference" with the public schools (p 52), and how in 1885 the Order's objectives were clarified to include "uphold[ing] the reading of the Holy Bible therein" (p 54). Lichliter described how, after discovering a nun teaching in the Pennsylvania public schools, the Order championed legislation in 1895 to prohibit anyone from teaching in the public schools "in religious garb" (p 265 *et seq*). He recounted how an 1898 bill to allow churches to build at the U.S. Military Academy at West Point seemed innocent enough, being open to any church, until "the nigger in the woodpile" [sic] was discovered in the form of news that the Roman Catholic Church had actually begun work to do so (pp 242-243). That members of the Order were required to be white almost went without saying. An 1873 resolution to strike that requirement was rejected. When "resolutions were offered setting forth that a foreign political church was sending emissaries to this country for the purpose of converting the colored people," it was proposed to "give the colored people the advantages of a patriotic Order, similar to our own." However, that suggestion, too, was rejected. (Deemer, *supra*, p 34, 36.)

[85] It had awarded a pension of twelve dollars per month to all disabled veterans, regardless of the origin of the disability. It also required veterans to prove that they were dependent on income from another source, a requirement President Cleveland felt would prove too difficult to enforce. The Democrat therefore vetoed the bill as being too costly and too difficult to administer.

[86] *Inquirer*, May 12, 1887, p 5; *The Times*, May 12, 1887, p 3. Thomas had seen so many people die, it's hard to imagine his reaction, especially not knowing how the boy had died. In prior years, the leading cause of death in Philadelphia had been consumption (2,822), followed by inflammation of the lungs (1,742) and marasmus (undernourishment) (862). A spike in diphtheria cases caused 857 deaths in 1886. The coroner had ruled 252 deaths accidental and 100 as suicides (*Inquirer*, Jan 1, 1887).

[87] The city directories of 1888, 1889, 1890, 1895 and 1900 all list her as Thomas's widow, first living at 1021 St. John Street, then 956 Marlborough and finally at 2442 East Cumberland. It may well have seemed to Anna as if Thomas really had died. Andrew's 1887 obituary had said the funeral would begin at "his mother's residence." The 1890 Veteran's Schedule (1890 U.S. Census, Special Schedule of Surviving Soldiers, Sailors, and Marines, & Widows, Etc., enum June 1890, Phila Enum Dist 371, p 1, Vet No 6) shows Thomas Carvin living at 2130 Hope Street, further away from Anna and the Siners, while the 1890 City Directory lists Anna Carvin at 1021 St. John Street.

[88] *National Tribune*, April 13, 1893, p 6. This was the Pension Act of June 27, 1890.

[89] Pension Certificates issued June 29, 1891, included one for Thos. Carvin (*Inquirer*, July 16, 1891, p 7).

[90] See Chapter 4, *supra*, and list of Thomas residences in note 62 above.

[91] *Inquirer,* March 9, 1867, p 9; *The Times*, March 10, 1897, p 8. A requiem mass was said for Mary at the Church of Our Lady of Visitation. This was surely not Thomas's doing. Thomas's separation from Mary may have been related to his separation from the Church.

[92] Phila City Archives, Death Certs 1803-1915, FHL Film No. 1869756, accessed via Ancestry.com, is the death certificate of Mary A. Carvin, married domestic worker, born in Phila abt 1853, died March 7, 1897, buried March 10, 1897, in Mechanics Cemetery. While the death certificate put her birth in 1853, she'd been 22 when the 1870 Census was taken. The death occurred on March 7, 1897, following d Thomas's move still further north, to 112 East Cumberland Street, to be close to the tavern his brother Joe had opened, and the funeral was from the residence of her husband at 112 East Cumberland Street. A Requiem Mass was said at the Church of Our Lady of Visitation, no doubting reflecting Mary's preferences, not Thomas's. (*Inquirer*, March 8, 1897, p 9; *Times*, March 8, 1897, p 8.)

[93] Deemer, p 50.

[94] Deemer, pp 49-50.

[95] Deemer, pp 59, 93.

[96] Anna died on Dec 2, 1904. See her obituary in the *Inquirer*, Dec 3, 1904, p 7, identifying her as Annie Carvin, the daughter of the late John and Rebecca Siner and wife of Thomas Carvin, but indicating that her funeral would be from the home of her son-in-law, Jacob Ashenbach [sic].

[97] Efforts to ascertain the later fate of Emily Hartman have not been successful, but she was quite young. When Thomas married Amelia Buehn, she was likely still alive, re-married and with her husband's name lost or among the many Emily Hartmans appearing in later records. Anna Siner Carvin's death certificate and obituary show that she did not die until December 2, 1904. (See FHL Film #1004061, orig Death Cert at Phila City Archives, and *The Inquirer*, Dec 3, 1904, identifying decedent Annie Carvin as the wife of Thomas Carvin and the daughter of the late John and Rebecca Siner.)

[98] Philadelphia City Archives, 1896 Marriage Licenses, License #93793, in which the groom, one Thomas J. Carvin, brass finisher, born in New York on April 4th, 1848, and residing at 2133 Mascher Street, swears to his bride Amelia Buehn, born Phila. May 6, 1871, residing at 2495 Howard St, employed at a mill, that he has never been married before. The application was sworn to on June 3,

---

1897, and the happy couple were married on June 10, 1897, by John A Goodfellow, Pastor of the Church of the Good Shepherd.

[99] The records of the Church of the Good Shepherd, where they married, gave his address as 2136 Mascher Street. This slight difference between 2133 and 2136 might not matter – it might be no more than an inadvertent scrivener's error – except that there were actually no residences at *either* such address.

[100] Maps between 1874 and 1895 show the park taking up all the land between Diamond and Susquehanna, precisely where it is today. The houses once occupying the 2100 block of Mascher Street had been leveled; the land was now covered with grass, paths, landscaping and squirrels. The Park had been created in the 1850's; in the 1880s', new water features, pathways, plantings and other improvements had been made. See https://tclf.org/landscapes/norris-square-park. Among the numerous maps showing Norris Square Park eliminating the 2100 block of Mascher Street are 1895's G.W. Bromley & Co., *Atlas of the City of Philadelphia, 1895*, Plate 15, accessed at http://www.philageohistory.org/rdic-images/view-image.cfm/bromley1895-plate15. Plate 15 shows that street addresses on Mascher below the park went no higher than 2033; the same map, plate 16, shows that addresses on Mascher above the park began at 2203. To the same effect are J.E. Scheidt, *Atlas of the City of Philadelphia by Wards, 1893, Ward 19*, and G.H. Jones & Co.'s *Atlas of Philadelphia, Vol II, 19th Ward, 1874*, at the same website.

[101] Kenneth W. Milano, Remembering Kensington & Fishtown, History Press, 2008, pp 89, 110. Milano found that "the big homes that lined the streets of Norris Square were highly represented" in Boyd's Philadelphia Blue Book.

[102] Telling the Army he was a brass finisher might have made sense thirty years earlier, when Thomas's experience in the Austin shop was fresh and he'd had no other career. Telling Anna Siner, back in his youth, that he was a brass finisher might have bolstered his credentials when he was courting her. Telling Emily Hartmann he was a brass finisher may have helped him with that seduction. But telling Amelia Buehn he was a brass finisher, thirty years later, was an outright lie or delusion.

[103] The marriage is attested at Pennsylvania & New Jersey Church and Town Records, 1669-2013, Phila, Episcopal, Church of the Good Shepherd, June 10, 1897, Thomas J. Carvin & Amelia Buehn, accessed at Ancestry.com.

[104] Deemer, *supra*, p 61.

[105] Thomas and Amelia lived across the street from where Amelia had been living when they were first married, (Phila City directories of 1898, 1899 and 1900.) The address Amelia gave in applying for the license was catty-corner across Cumberland Street, at 2495 North Howard.

[106] 1900 U.S. Census for Philadelphia Ward 31, District 0783, Family No 162. This woman, also named Mary, had never borne a child, and was seven years younger than the Irish Mary, mother to two of Thomas's children, who had died in 1897. Meanwhile, Anna Siner Carvin told the census taker that year that she was married, and had been for thirty-six years (1900 Census, Phila Ward 31, Dist 0789, p 3, Fam 25), but this admission did not prevent her from repeating the assertion in the 1901 and 1902 City Directories that she was Thomas's widow.

[107] It's likely that for some or all of this bartending work, Thomas was in the employ of his younger brother Joe. During that time (in 1904) Thomas's first wife, Anna Siner, died at the age of 61. (Death Certificate of Anna Carvin, housekeeper, died Dec 2, 1904, accessed from Ancestry.com database, Pennsylvania Death Certificates, 1803-1915, 1904, PA Historical and Museum Commission, FHL Film No.1004061; *Inquirer,* Dec 3, 1904, p 7 (funeral at home of her son-in-law, Jacob M. Ashenbach [sic]; burial at Hanover Cemetery.)

[108] "As a development of the long-standing strife existing in the Junior Order of United American Mechanics, the insurgent members have begun a fight in the courts for possession of the beneficiary degree fund, now held by the loyalists." (*The Times*, July 18, 1902, p 9.)

[109] *Inquirer*, June 26, 1904, p 3, and Sept 20, 1904, p 3; Sept 22, 1904, p 3. The "Order of Independent Americans" first appears in the 1906 Philadelphia Directory at 1345 Arch Street, p 1980. See also Arthur Preuss, *A Dictionary of Secret and other Societies*. St. Louis: B. Herder Book Co. 1924, republished Detroit: Gale Reference Company 1966; p 208.

[110] *Inquirer*, Sept 22, 1904, p 3.

[111] As its emblem, the new order adopted "an open Bible on a flag inside a compass and a square, the whole being circled by a shield." It adopted as regalia "a collar of red, white and blue, with the emblem suspended on a flag." (*Inquirer*, Sept 23, 1904, p 3.)

[112] *Inquirer*, Nov 21, 1904, p 7. The preacher was the Reverend Madison C. Peters.

[113] *Inquirer*, Nov 21, 1904, p 7. One imagines that Thomas was especially concerned about immigrant groups known for their anarchy and infidelity.

[114] *Inquirer,* Oct 1, 1905, p 6. The Methodist preacher was a Reverend Vivien.

[115] *Inquirer*, May 31, 1906, p 6.

[116] *Inquirer,* Nov 25, 1906, p 2 and Dec 9, 1906, 4th Sec., p 6. The members of McMorris Council No. 902 of the I. of O. A. celebrated by putting on a minstrel show (blackface) performance (*Inquirer*, Nov 30, 1906, p 2).

[117] Death Certificate 121715, 31259, accessed from Ancestry.com database, Pennsylvania Death Certificates, 1803-1915, 1906, PA Historical and Museum Commission, microfilm pg 2760 of 5310.

[118] *Inquirer*, December 27, 1906.

[119] Veterans Administration Records of Pension Payments, Certificate No 816752, dated Nov 15, 1916, for Thomas Carvin, 71 PA Inf, Private, Co B, commenced Sept 20, 1916, for Army Widow Amelia B. Carvin. Amelia's $36 per quarter was increased to $75 per quarter on Jan 1, 1918, and to $90 per quarter in the third quarter, 1920.

[120] After marrying Thomas in 1897, Amelia appears as Thomas's widow at 2316 N Howard Street in the City Directories of 1908 and 1909; at 3353 Malta in the 1910 Census (a widow living alone at age 38) and again as Thomas's widow in the 1911 City Directory. According to civil war pension records reviewed by the author, Amelia successfully applied for the pension of Pvt Thomas Carvin of Company B of the 71st Pennsylvania Infantry. The pension was initially set on December 18, 1916, at $36 per quarter; increased to $75 on January 1, 1918, and then to $90 for the third quarter of 1920, before being reduced to $30 in the first quarter of 1923. Certificate #816752, commenced 9/20/1916, dated 11/15/1916. The pension seems to have helped. Amelia last appears in the 1920 Census, at age 60, having taken in three boarders. (Phila Ward 23, District 0642, at 5103 Torresdale Avenue.)

9. Dominic I. Murphy

Dominic Ignatius Murphy (1847-1930) grew up in a house of great accomplishments. [1] His father was a well-known businessman and member of Common Council. Three of his older brothers reported proceedings in the U.S. Senate, while two had key roles in the federal taxation system. [2] Yet another was one of the most successful textile men in Philadelphia. In March of 1871, at the age of twenty-three, he took a job as a white-collar clerk in the federal government's Pension Office in Washington. The position might not seem much of a plum today, but at the time, it was "eagerly sought, and secured only upon the highest testimonials." [3] (In Dominic's case, the testimonials were no doubt from his brothers and the members of Congress they knew.)

But Dominic was a man of stalwart principle, not the type to take undue personal advantage of his situation. For five years, he processed the claims of disabled war veterans, examining their service records, witness statements, and medical reports, investigating possible fraud, deciding eligibility, and gaining insight into the lives of people who had fought for their country, people who'd lost limbs to enemy fire, people now unable to work because of that service. In 1873, he was involved in the founding of Washington's Carroll Institute, an organization that sought to involve poor Catholic youth in meaningful activities, including culture, arts, and theatrical productions. [4] After starting at $1200 per year, by July 1, 1876, Dominick's pay had reached $1800. [5]

Why Dominic applied for a passport on May 1, 1874, is unknown, but it may suggest something of the international direction Dominic's career later took. In any case, in August of 1875, at age 28, he married Kate Kearon, a clerk in the nearby Patent Office. He moved into her parents' house with her, a two-story, 13' x 23' brick "back building" her father had recently built. [6] There, Kate gave birth to two sons, Joseph (in 1877) and Dominick (in 1879). Sadly, however, three days after the birth of their second son, Kate was dead. [7]

For the sake of the boys, Dominic chose to remain in D.C., and he continued living at the Kearon house (where the boys' grandmother could look after them) for the next twelve years. Dominic busied himself by editing an eight-page Catholic daily, "The Fair Journal," to raise money for St. Patrick's

Church.[8] But mostly, he applied himself to his work, continuing to process claims, immersing himself in the lives of disabled veterans and their families.

To decide a pension claim, one had to understand not just facts, but attitudes and circumstances, especially when deciding whether the claims of the many soldiers who had deserted were defeated by the exclusion of "any person who in any manner aided or abetted the rebellion." Agents were sent to the hometowns of applicants all across the country to interview doctors, fellow soldiers, and neighbors about every aspect of a claimant's life.[9] In 1880, Dominic was promoted to Principal Examiner at a salary of $2,000 per year.[10]

The political spoils system that would play a role in Dominic's life was in its heyday in the early 1880's. After campaigning for James Garfield, one delusional office-seeker, indignant that he was not named consul in Paris (never mind that he spoke no French), shot and killed the ungrateful president, elevating the notoriously insensitive Chester Arthur to a term as president that was notable for its injustices.[11] When the Democrat Grover Cleveland won election in 1884, he did so as a vocal critic of Arthur's political patronage, announcing that he would not fire any Republican who was doing his job.[12] When Cleveland, as president, made good on that promise, he alienated supporters who expected their just rewards, but as Republican officials left the government, Cleveland replaced them almost exclusively with Democrats. Within two months of Cleveland's inauguration, Dominic Murphy, whose older brother had just been elected President of the Grover Cleveland Association in Philadelphia, became Acting Chief Examiner at the Pension Office. Within a few more months, he was appointed Chief of the Board of Review. And on December 1, 1885, he was promoted to Chief Clerk, at a salary of $2,250 per year. It was his third promotion in just the first year of the Cleveland administration.[13] Political patronage may have been widely criticized, but it was still alive and well.

Like most Democrats, Cleveland favored a small federal government and limited government spending. On one occasion, he went so far as to say the government had no business spending public money to relieve individual suffering.[14] But during Cleveland's first term, Congress passed hundreds of private laws granting pensions to potential political supporters, despite the fact that existing legal criteria (as enacted by Congress) made them ineligible, and despite the fact that the Pension Office had denied their claims for that reason. Every time Congress over-ruled the Pension Office with such a private bill, it struck Dominic as an obvious play for political favor. At one point in 1886, President Cleveland complained that 240 bills granting such private pensions had been presented to him on a single day.[15] Cleveland vetoed them all, proving to Murphy that he was a man of principle – while reaffirming, of course, that Murphy's Pension Office itself held the power to approve or disapprove a pension, no matter what an applicant did to curry favor with his Congressman.

After four years, Dominic's brother Joe, back in Philadelphia, was leading the President's 1888 re-election campaign there as President of the Grover Cleveland Association. With Cleveland facing a stiff challenge from his Republican opponent (Benjamin Harrison), Pennsylvania's 30 electoral votes were second only to New York's. In February of 1888, Dominic took a step down in responsibility, resigning his position as Chief Clerk of the Pension Office in D. C., publicly giving "ill health" as the reason. But the lower-level assignment he took instead was as supervising examiner of the federal pension district that included Pennsylvania.[16] Whatever the alleged health issue, it had no permanent consequences. On the other hand, direct responsibility for approval of pension claims in Pennsylvania was more than convenient for a family committed to Cleveland's reelection there.

Unfortunately for the Murphys, Benjamin Harrison took 52% of Pennsylvania's popular vote and won the national election. Dominic returned to his duties in Washington. But as soon as Harrison was inaugurated, he appointed James R. Tanner as Pension Commissioner. Tanner was a civil war veteran and amputee who had campaigned for Harrison.[17] The spoils system had worked as intended; without a government job, Dominic had to decide what else he might do.

He'd already accumulated enough savings to begin investing in outside interests.[18] Now, on the advice of his father-in-law, Robert Kearon, he went to work with his nephew, John D. Kinney, in the "general claim" business. "He was remarkably successful in this, and soon built up an extensive business."[19] A good number of the claims Dominic filed were for pensions, where his knowledge of the criteria and procedures benefited claimants able to pay him for breaking through the red tape. But he filed other sorts of claims as well, and perhaps it helped Murphy's business that his father-in-law was an auditor of just such claims at the Treasury Department.[20]

In 1890, while engaged in this business, Dominic was a presenter at the national convention of the Catholic Young Men's National Union, where another presenter – a black delegate from New York – said that most blacks had simply adopted the Protestant faiths of their slave masters, while the Catholic Church had been a genuine friend.[*] Among the several speakers on race relations, a Mr. Wood, a black delegate from Baltimore, spoke of the Church's duty to create manual training schools for colored youth. (In 1880, a third of the residents in the District of Columbia were African Americans.) A man of principle, Dominic also had an intellectual, artistic side to his nature; he liked music and the arts; he sometimes even wrote poetry. When he spoke, he was in alignment with both of the speakers before him:

---

[*] In fact, Wood was reported to have said, "for years the colored race was treated like dogs, and… now they [are] not much better off. But the fact that their condition [is] as much improved as it is now is due solely to the Catholic Church."

> [O]ne of the most interesting features of the morning session…
> was the paper read by Dominic I. Murphy, the president of the
> Carroll Institute of this city. His subject was the formation of
> societies for catholic young men and the advantages and
> blessings that must arise from such organizations… Reading
> rooms, gymnasiums and all such sorts of amusements should
> be held out to young men, giving them the advantages of social
> intercourse and intellectual training.[21]

Though part of a wealthy, powerful family himself, Dominic was
sympathetic to those less fortunate than himself, including both African-
Americans and veterans who'd risked their lives for the cause of national
unity. Knowledge of the pension process and influential contacts may not
have been the only reasons Murphy's private claims business was successful.
Perhaps he genuinely cared for those who lacked such advantages. Perhaps
he was guided, in part, by a sense of right and wrong.

Meanwhile, Miss Nellie Kearon, his late wife's younger sister by seven
years, who also lived in the house with Dominic and his sons, was an aspiring
young soprano,[22] and her teacher was Miss Mollie Byrne, one of those rare
women who'd made careers for themselves and were recognized in the
newspapers for their talents. It was later said about Mollie, "Never was there a
sweeter voice or sweeter woman."[23] In great demand, Mollie was singing at
events all over the city, including a role in "The Pirates of Penzance" at Lincoln
Hall.[24] No doubt Dominic wasn't the only man who took an interest in the
sweet-voiced star, even as some were heard to whisper slanderous things about
a single woman who dared to have her own career. How many suitors Miss
Mollie had is unknown, but by 1884, she was performing at Murphy's Carroll
Institute. For over a decade, Dominic listened to her lilting melodies, and at
some point a romantic relationship developed. As their common interest
included the arts, by 1889, they were performing together at the Unity Club[25]
in a program billed as "An Evening with Tom Moore."[26] Shedding light on
his own priorities, Dominic's role was to give a sketch of Moore's life, which
had been devoted to the arts, to tolerance and to harmony. Mollie's role for the
evening was to sing a solo of Moore's popular song, "The Last Rose of
Summer," a sad piece that highlighted the pain of loss, separation, and
loneliness.[27]

Having a common interest in harmony and unity, the couple's romantic
attraction grew. For reasons unknown – but perhaps in anticipation of a
honeymoon trip – Dominic applied for a passport again in April;[28] and then
on November 4, 1891, several years after their first acquaintance, the couple
were married. The *Sunday Herald* called it "the felicitous termination of a
love story that has won the interest and sympathy of a host of friends…"

> From the long list of names of ladies closely identified
> with local music, it would be difficult to select that of one

more cordially liked and respected than Miss Mollie Byrne, whose marriage last Wednesday to Mr. Dominic I. Murphy... was the occasion for hundreds of congratulations from the host of friends of both parties. And hundreds more, who could not claim a personal acquaintance with the fair soprano, but who know her through her voice, unite in wishing Mrs. Murphy all the happiness obtainable in this world.[29]

The home of Dominic's first wife and her family was obviously not the best place for the newlyweds to live, even absent concern about the character of a career woman, even absent concern about a man in the business of pressing claims on the government living in the same house as a man in charge of auditing them. The new Mr. and Mrs. Murphy, each of them celebrated for their own accomplishments, moved into a new home just a couple of blocks from the Kearon house.[30]

The Republican presidency lasted only four years. With support from several Murphys, Grover Cleveland won re-election in the autumn of 1892, and in January, 1893, when the Democrats' Inaugural Committee met to prepare for the inauguration, it appointed Dominic Murphy as one of its committee chairmen.[31] After Cleveland was re-inaugurated in March, Murphy waited for his due reward, and in April, he got it: President Cleveland appointed him First Deputy Commissioner of Pensions at a salary of $3,600 per year.[32] Reporting on the three top appointments at the Pension Bureau, the *National Tribune* wrote:

Dominic I. Murphy, the First Deputy Commissioner, was too young to enter the army during the war, but he has literally grown up in the Pension Bureau, having entered it when a boy in a very subordinate capacity, and risen through all the grades to Chief Clerk. No one in the country is better acquainted with all the manifold ramifications and workings of the great institution than he, and he has the disposition as well as the knowledge to make radical reforms in its administration...

The men who have been put at the head of the Bureau are thus seen to be all right. Now the important question is whether they will be given the authority and means to conduct the Bureau as they undoubtedly feel that it should be. The duty before them... is to... dispose of its vast accumulation of cases... If given the power and the means, they will settle every one of the hundreds of thousands of cases now on file in the Pension Bureau by the last day of December, 1894... It will be a grievous mistake, in every way, to allow these cases to drag along, year after year, in the way in which they have been dragging since the close of the war. The prematurely old and broken down men who are applicants for the Nation's justice should no longer be denied that which they have earned with their best blood.[33]

Life was looking good, and Murphy prepared once again to enjoy the status of a senior federal official. He later said that when Cleveland appointed him, the President's instructions were to bring greater liberality to the granting of pensions.[34] But the summer of 1893 brought disappointment, both for the Pension Bureau and for the family.

First, the happiness of marriage to the sweet-voiced soprano was short-lived. The new Mrs. Murphy died at the end of June, 1893, less than two years after the wedding.[35] One obituary said that she'd died after a brief illness, and that "Mr. Murphy, who has been seriously ill, is recovering."[36] Whether his illness was physical or emotional, Murphy once again felt personal loss. Twice he'd been married; twice his wife had died within a few years of the wedding. How fate would treat such a union of independent spirits would remain a mystery for later couples to discover.

Second, as the summer grew hot, it became apparent that the Pension Bureau was not eliminating its backlog of claims. Instead, under the leadership of the fiscally conservative Grover Cleveland, the Bureau announced a slew of reductions in pay and grade that autumn, reducing the rank and salary of much of its existing (largely Republican) staff amid accusations of disguised partisanship:

> The list of reduction which took place yesterday in the pension office is still in hiding. The officials will throw no light on the matter. They maintain that as a reduction in rank is a reflection upon the efficiency of those reduced, the suppression of this news is only merciful to the victims. Others interested in the matter declare that this reason for suppression is a sham. They say that it is merely to cover up partisan methods.

The *Evening Star* went on to report the details of two Republicans who'd been reduced, and to make public the question its reporter had asked Murphy: why the list of those reduced could not be divulged. According to the *Star*, Murphy had replied that he could see no good reason why it *shouldn't* be, except that "a contrary rule of the Department stood in the way."[37]

Dominic moved his personal residence again, this time setting up house with his nephew John Kinney.[38] (John had continued in the claims business, and Dominic may have kept a financial interest in that business even after becoming First Deputy Commissioner.) He was also among the notables at a November 1894 dinner given by the Union Veterans Legion, at which "the menu was of an elaborate and sumptuous kind. Rare viands, hearty substantials and choice wines and cigars were dispensed with lavish hand."[39] In late July, 1895, he joined a yachting party on Long Island Sound as the guest of Captain Merritt (of the Merritt Wrecking Company) on board Merritt's yacht "Carrie," said to be "one of the finest afloat."[40] While he was out of town, his friends put his name forward as a candidate for the District of Columbia Registrar of Wills, but upon his return, claiming surprise, he insisted he had no interest in that position.[41] In February, 1896, he attended a charity ball for the Ladies Southern Relief Society, also attended by Vice President Adlai Stevenson and several members of Cleveland's cabinet.[42] He was elected to the Interstate Democratic Association. Remaining connected in such powerful circles paid off. When Pension Commissioner William Lochner was appointed to a federal judgeship, President Cleveland nominated Dominic to be the next Commissioner of Pensions, the top position at the Pension Bureau.[43]

Needless to say, by that time, the pension office had become highly political. To grant a pension (especially one not granted by a prior administration) could be as effective as buying a vote outright. Both Republicans and Democrats portrayed themselves as friendly to those who'd served while portraying their opponents as indifferent. The Commissioner's job was clearly a political "plum." Yet, according to the *Evening Star*, "Mr. Murphy was selected purely on merit and his knowledge of the workings of the office."[44] And due to his family's longstanding connection to the Senate, that body had no problem confirming his appointment.

The Commissioner's job was no minor office. By the 1890's, civil war pensions were being paid to over a million pensioners, and they accounted for over forty per cent of the entire federal budget.[45] Nor was it only the number (and backlog) of pension claims that had risen since the war. Total employment at the pension office had been only 72 people in 1859; it had grown to 354 people when Dominic started in 1871, and by July 1, 1897, it numbered 2,272,[46] including Dominic's niece, Mary C. Kinney at a salary of $1400 per year,[47] and his sister-in-law, the young soprano, Nellie Kearon, at $1200 per year.[48] Principled as he was, Dominic not only knew the power of awarding pensions, but the value of having family members in good jobs.

Meanwhile, over 350 of the 1300 salaried clerks in the Pension Office were women. It was convenient for bachelors and widowers in search of companionship that the Registry labeled each of them as Mrs. or Miss. One of them, Bessie T. Atkinson, was clearly labeled as *Mrs.* Bessie Atkinson, and her husband, William Atkinson, also worked in the office. But Bessie soon came to Murphy's attention. Whether William, Bessie or Dominic fell short of proper decorum is unknown, but as future events would prove, at least some spark of attraction developed between the Pension Commissioner and his married clerk.

That attraction notwithstanding, Dominic had enjoyed the perks of being Commissioner for less than a year when William McKinley beat Grover Cleveland in the election of 1896. Dominic might have cleaned out his office even before McKinley was sworn in, but in a twist of irony for the long time Democrat, it was announced that the offices of the Pension Bureau would host the upcoming Inaugural Ball for the new Republican president. The walls of the place, "if endowed with speech, could unravel mysteries and tell tales of sadness connected with the soldier's life," but those walls would witness a different atmosphere for the festive inaugural ball.[49] Oddly enough, the *Washington Times* story about the inaugural ball ended up mostly about Murphy himself:

> After all, the glory of the Pension Bureau is more in the everyday life lived within its unadorned walls… Under its care falls the widow and the children of the soldier. Reward and not charity best describes its mission.
>
> During a recent visit through the East I heard murmurings of dissatisfaction because of the refusal of pensions; but while it is a granted fact that some deserving ones are passed by, they are certainly the exception and not the rule…
>
> This brings me to say that the present Commissioner of Pensions is a man possessing keen insight and rare discretion. He is most assuredly a true friend of the soldier. No commissioner has ever been more impartial in the work before him than the Hon. Dominic I. Murphy… [The article's recitation of Murphy's history with the Bureau is here omitted.] Mr. Murphy is a broad-minded man, and in no wise has he changed since being promoted above his fellow-clerks... [Recitation of the types of cases that came before Murphy are omitted.] The orphaned child, with no knowledge of the requirements of the law, must be dealt with as well as the shrewd fraud. No man has ever done more to secure justice to claimants… [Various procedural orders issued by Murphy are omitted.] No other commissioner has brought upon himself more favorable comment, and that Mr. Murphy's popularity is unlimited by party or creed is attested by an immense circle of friends, not only in Washington but in other cities as well, and by the fact that his nomination was promptly confirmed without opposition.[50]

The piece read like a testimonial designed to convince the new Republican president to keep his Democratic Commissioner of Pensions in office. The next month, a similar demonstration of support for Murphy came when

214

representatives of two army veterans' posts showed up and made a presentation to him. One showered praise on Murphy in a statement to the *Times*:

> For the first time in the history of this great department are all the old soldiers satisfied. I have been a soldier myself and I can speak for them... Every one of the 289 members of this post is opposed to you politically, always have been and always will be. Yet they come of their own accord with this proof of their respect. Not only that, but here is another post with 220 members, also all black Republicans, who have come to express their satisfaction with your administration.[51]

Murphy thanked the presenter, saying his purpose was to serve loyal soldiers and their families, "whether I remain here three days or three weeks or three years." Clearly, Dominic was anticipating the usual request for resignation, and his family using its pull in the reporting world to send a message to the incoming president: *keep Dominic in office.* In fact, the campaign was so great that *The Times* repeated the identical story the following day, with only the headline changed (to make the name 'Murphy' stand out even more).[52]

THE FRIEND OF SOLDIERS

Pension Commissioner Murphy Thanked by Two Posts.

A TRIBUTE TO MR. MURPHY

The Pension Commissioner Thanked by Two G. A. R. Posts.

McKinley was inaugurated on March 4, 1897. When the new President, his wife and other dignitaries arrived in Murphy's Pension Building for the inaugural ball, Murphy did his best to ingratiate himself to the new President. But as he soon learned, the campaign to keep his job had fallen short. Five days after the inauguration, Murphy was quoted in the *Evening Star* "emphatically express[ing] the hope that the Pension Building will never again be used for inaugural ball purposes." McKinley's ball, Murphy said, had cost the government $70,000 and had "caused a very injurious interruption to the business of the office."[53] Clearly, the campaign to curry favor with McKinley had ended, and Murphy now sought to drive a wedge between loyal veterans and their new president. A month after McKinley's inauguration, Murphy's resignation was accepted, and he was out of public service again. He would never have a say in deciding pension applications again.

On the other hand, we can be sure that as Murphy prepared to depart from the Pension Office, he took time to say a fond goodbye to Mrs. Atkinson.[54] And when her husband, William Atkinson, died in October of 1897 at the age of 40, Murphy surely gave the widow his condolences.[55]

Though out of office once again, he remained in the public eye. His listing in the D.C. Directory identified his new, private occupation as *insurance and loans*. He bought the *New Century*, a weekly news magazine "devoted to the interests of the Catholic Church" and installed his twenty-five year old son, Joseph, as its managing editor.[56] He was a speaker at an event attended by cabinet members.[57] He was elected chairman at a meeting of the city's United Irish Societies.[58] He served as toastmaster at the annual banquet of the National Union, Washington Council No. 205.[59] He served as one of three judges in a Gonzaga college debate over the annexation of Hawaii.[60] He delivered an address to the Catholic Benevolent Legion.[61] And while a Murphy may never have been Lord Mayor of Dublin, in November of 1899, when the actual Lord Mayor of Dublin arrived in Washington, two Irishmen called upon him at his hotel: Terence Powderly (Commissioner of Immigration) and Dominic Murphy. The following day – Thanksgiving Day – Powderly and Murphy accompanied the Lord Mayor and his secretary to the White House, where the four of them conferred in a private meeting with President McKinley.[62] Given the relationship between McKinley and Murphy, the meeting must have been awkward; yet Dominic, ever the harmonizer, sought to emphasize common interests with the President.

A few days later, along with the Civil Service Commissioner and Solicitor of the Treasury, Murphy was one of three judges for a debate at the Georgetown University School of Law on the proposition, "That the Boers are Justified in Their Present Stand Against Great Britain."[63] The following March, he served as toastmaster at a banquet urging Irish unity for Saint Patrick's Day, pleading with his fellow Irishmen, "Let us remember that in the struggle for Irish liberty, Protestants and Catholics fought side by side, and that their blood blended in one common stream to sanctify the Irish soil."[64] In June of 1900, he was mentioned as the likely appointee to the "Catholic seat" on the District of Columbia Board of Charities.[65]

In addition to his other pursuits, he joined two other lawyers in forming the patent law firm of Hopkins, Murphy & Hopkins.[66] In a surprising turn of events that reflects his efforts at unity, he served on the reception committee for the March 1901 Inaugural Ball (McKinley's second term). Less surprisingly, the planning for that year's Saint Patrick's day celebration again took place in his office.[67] As one of the trustees of the Saint Vincent's Orphan Asylum, he signed the deed selling the Asylum's property.[68] He was on the Board of the Catholic Summer School at Harper's Ferry.[69] He was a guest at the first meeting of the Iroquois Club (successor to the Washington Press Club), and later a master of ceremonies at one of its events.[70] He was elected president of the Friendly Sons of Saint Patrick; he opened the speechmaking on Saint Patrick's Day by declaring that the Friendly Sons had been organized "to always extend the hand of fellowship."[71] He was made secretary at a mass meeting at the

Columbia Theater organized in protest of Russian atrocities in the treatment of Jews.[72] And in March, 1904, he gave a speech (titled "The Press") at a Saint Patrick's Day meeting of the Shamrock Club.[73]

It would be wrong to think that all of Dominic's activities were charitable, Catholic, or apolitical. In his years of work at the Pension Bureau, Dominic had dealt with hundreds of veterans, their families, and the groups that represented them, most significantly the "Grand Army of the Republic" (G.A.R.), an organization of veterans who'd fought for the Union during the Civil War. The G. A. R. was among the first advocacy groups in American politics. Over the years, the political power of veterans and their families made it a group to be reckoned with, wooed for its support by politicians of all political parties.

In September of 1898, the G.A.R. voted to censure H. Clay Evans (Dominic's replacement as chief of the Pension Bureau), lambasting Evans's record of indifference while characterizing Murphy's record as one of solidarity with veterans and concern about their plight. The spokesperson for the G.A.R. said that Evans "could have no sympathy with a man who had marched, bivouacked, and fought, for the reason that he [Evans] had never marched, bivouacked, or fought."[74] Neither the G.A.R. nor the newspapers who reported its criticism of Evans pointed out that Murphy, too, had no military service of any kind.

Murphy was clearly courting the G.A.R. In February of 1900, he was a guest at a banquet paying tribute to the G.A.R.'s commander-in-chief, Albert Shaw.[75] In September, he gave an address at a rally held by the Virginia Democratic Association.[76] In November, he was named to the National Capital Centennial Committee charged with responsibility for ceremonies and parades.[77] And as the election of 1900 drew near, he went public with an allegation designed to drive another wedge between McKinley and veterans' groups, repeatedly telling the press what the President had said to representatives of the G.A.R. – something which, Murphy insinuated, revealed the president's real feelings:

> Mr. Murphy was a member of the Committee which called upon the President to urge a change in his pension policy. Mr. McKinley, as alleged, said: "There is no denying the fact, gentlemen, that the money power of the country is against any further expansion of the pension roll."[78]

Just three days before the election of 1900, Murphy was again denouncing McKinley's position on veterans.[79] The story was repeated verbatim in the next days' *Washington Times*.[80] Murphy's attempt to torpedo McKinley right before the election could hardly have been clearer, but it didn't work, as two days later, McKinley won re-election.

Murphy's efforts to curry support with the veterans did not cease, however. On the night of February 15, 1898, when the U.S.S. Maine was sunk in Havana Harbor, it took on a significance no one had anticipated. The sinking enflamed patriotic sentiment against Spain. "Remember the Maine" became the battle cry of those wanting war. Veterans – too old to fight but steeped in pride at what they once had done – anxious to preserve the honor of the country they'd fought for – were prominent among those calling for war. Four months after the sinking, Dominic was on the stage at a meeting of Union Veteran Legion No 69 – whose motto was "We Remembered the Maine" – when the commander of that ship, Captain Charles D. Sigsbee, was the honored speaker.[81] In the months to come, Dominic was elected an honorary member of the U.S. Naval Volunteers of the Spanish American War[82] and he participated in a "Tribute to the Flag" at the Carroll Institute.[83] In October of 1903, he gave a speech at a meeting of the G. A. R.[84] For a man no longer in government service, with no military background and no present official connection to veterans affairs, Murphy went to great lengths to endear himself to veterans, to the G.A.R., and to every politician wanting their support.

Thirty years after the end of the Civil War, American prosperity and population growth were fast transforming it into a world power. Sensing that their interests extended beyond her own shores, Americans were looking to the sea, imagining the creation of a cross-continental canal which would connect the Atlantic and Pacific oceans and constitute a huge boon to commerce and trade. Such a canal was key to American power throughout the hemisphere. Americans were also looking to the islands of the Caribbean and the Pacific that could provide harbors and ports for its growing navy, and to the natural resources those islands might also provide to help satisfy America's growing needs. All that was lacking were qualified men to accomplish the vision by actually building the canal, by actually controlling the islands – as outposts to defend any sea traffic that might someday use the canal.

And so, as Cubans fought for their independence from Spain, the McKinley government had anchored the *U.S.S. Maine* in Havana. And when it exploded, the McKinley government blamed Spain, demanding Spain withdraw from Cuba (which, once Spain withdrew, would clear the way for American control). And when Spain didn't withdraw, the McKinley government declared war on the imperial power.[85]

As West Virginia Senator Stephen Elkins noted:

> When Cuba shall become a part of the American Union and the isthmian canal shall be completed, which is now assured, Puerto Rico, Cuba, Hawaii and the Philippines will be outposts of the great Republic, standing guard over American interests in the track of the world's commerce in its triumphant march around the globe. Our people will soon see and feel that these island possessions belonging to the United States are natural and logical, and in the great part we are to play in the affairs of the world we would not only give them

up but wonder how the working of our natural destiny we could get on without them.[86]

It was a classic example of imperialist logic, buoyed by the spirit of *noblesse oblige*. In the ten weeks that the war on Spain lasted, America kept a keen eye on the islands and their vast supply of cane sugar. At its first opportunity, it secured not only Cuba, but Puerto Rico for itself. To protect its west coast, it looked across the Pacific to Manila Bay, and finding Spanish ships defending that bay, its navy's warships destroyed them.

During negotiations to end the brief war, McKinley instructed his negotiators that their statesmanship should not be indifferent to implications for "the commercial opportunity" that existed, saying, "It is just to use every legitimate means for the enlargement of American trade." Such comments certainly pleased American businessmen. But lest anyone think American interests primarily commercial, Senator Knute Nelson of Minnesota explained that "Providence has given the United States the duty of extending Christian civilization. We come as ministering angels, not despots."[87] In other words, as far as the world was concerned, it was noble Christianity, not rank commercial profit, that lay behind America's benevolence. McKinley earned high praise for his foreign policy from most Americans, not least from military, veterans and patriotic groups like the G. A. R.

The resulting Treaty of Paris made American interests clear: its government demanded that Spain cede Puerto Rico to it, which Spain did. (The island has been a non-voting U.S. possession ever since.) It demanded that Spain grant Cuba its freedom, which Spain did. (America did, however, reserve the right to appoint Cuba's governors, determine its laws, maintain its military occupation, and intervene unilaterally in Cuba's affairs.[88]) It demanded that Spain cede the colonies of Guam and the Philippines to it, which Spain did after initial resistance. (The impasse was broken when America added twenty million dollars to its promise of a better future for the islands.)

In 1902, Congress created a bicameral legislature for the Philippine islands, somewhat like America's own bicameral legislature except that the upper house of the Philippine version – the equivalent of the American Senate – consisted of the members of the U.S. "Philippine Commission," a slate of McKinley appointees headed by his Secretary of War, William Howard Taft. Skeptics accused America of acting like an imperial power, but McKinley called the policy one of "benevolent assimilation" and U.S. Senator Albert Beveridge defended the taking of the islands "to protect the Filipinos from European predators." If the distinction between European and American predators escaped some Filipinos, Beveridge was ready with another benevolent rationale – "and to tutor them in American-style democracy."[89]

To understand Murphy's views on American foreign policy, we must consider his own career at the turn of the century. A belief in unity and harmony had led him to see his country as a place where Catholics and

Protestants could co-exist, where inner city youth could be pulled out of poverty by exposure to culture. His work at the Pension Bureau had made him feel deeply for the tens of thousands of soldiers who'd fought to preserve diversity, equality, freedom and mutual respect. Their sacrifice was to preserve an awe-inspiring ideal; if others had to make sacrifices to spread that ideal beyond our shores, were they any less deserving of support?

In August, 1898, just days after the Spanish surrendered the Philippines, Dominic was elected vice president of a group organized to welcome our brave boys home.[90] The next day, he was on stage supporting those who'd waged war:

> That the people of Washington appreciate valor and honor the
> brave soldier boys who left their homes to uphold the cause of
> their country… was shown last night… [T]he galleries, boxes
> and stage being hung with great American flags…The Marine
> Band… stationed in the rear of the stage, its renditions of
> patriotic music keeping the audience in a constant ferment of
> patriotic demonstration…[91]

The Postmaster General called the Americans who'd freed Cuba from the Spaniards "the embodiment and personification of the nation's unquenchable spirit of patriotism." Their service had advanced the cause of humanity and freedom, he said. They'd fought not for conquest or plunder, but as the volunteer *defenders* of the republic, "impelled" by the mandates of justice to redress "wrongs which cried to heaven." And as for the aftermath of hostilities, new duties and responsibilities had been given to Americans, he said, "by the over-ruling hand of an all-wise Providence." Henceforth, America mustn't relinquish "the vantage ground of our moral rectitude." Rather, we must "accept the full mission of peaceful and commercial development."[92]

Another speaker, Reverend Stafford, proclaimed that

> men may fall, but when Providence works there must be
> order, symmetry and harmony; therefore, the great idea of
> liberty… did not appear among the poor population of some
> arid and melancholy waste, but here upon this great continent,
> a world of its own, with every material resource and every
> natural advantage, every form of beauty, and every
> possibility of growth…[93]

James Tanner, the double amputee who'd served as Pension Commissioner prior to Murphy, expressed his fear that upon returning home, the veterans of the war would have to "rap at Uncle Sam's pension door and cry for a pittance," because "there may be an economic pension commissioner who will think that the way to public favor and approval is in paring down pensions to the lowest degree."[94]

The message was clear: because God favored the growth of American

220

civilization, we had a *duty* to extend it to other countries, even declaring war on them, even sending warships their way, in order to do so. In the logic of the day, we were therefore not aggressors, but engaged in the "defense" of our country. Finally, the severest injustice lay not in waging war, not in causing young men to die, but in failing to pay survivors pensions, afterward, for having risked their lives.

Dominic embraced the goal of expanding American principles to others around the globe, so with Republicans and Democrats alike courting the veteran vote, Dominic supported the military, even if meant supporting McKinley. (So it is that having common enemies brings men together.)

Then, in September of 1901, a criminal act in Buffalo, New York, changed Dominic's future. A young steelworker, outraged over the plight of the working man, shot McKinley in the stomach with a pistol. When the President died eight days later, Murphy served as an Assistant Marshal at his funeral pageant and on the Music Committee charged with planning his memorial service.[95] Thus honoring the fallen President, Murphy welcomed the new one, for Theodore Roosevelt had strong views about Americans' duties abroad, and Dominic saw a chance to have a better relationship with the new President than he'd had with the old. Roosevelt was a champion of American involvement in both the Pacific and the Caribbean. He'd urged war with Spain even before the explosion of the *Maine*. He'd personally led American soldiers up San Juan Hill. And his interest in building a canal across the Americas was even stronger than McKinley's. In 1903, he was so intent on getting the right to build in Panama that he fomented a revolution there in order to do so.[96] Roosevelt's expansionist plans would soon play into Murphy's own future.

The Murphy family had never campaigned against Roosevelt, as they had McKinley. Roosevelt held no grudge against them. Dominic's brother Edward now had friends among Senate Republicans. * His Catholic publishing credentials were sufficient reason to consider him for a role in a Catholic country like the Philippines. A recommendation by Cardinal James Gibbons of Baltimore was enough to get Roosevelt to nominate him to a position on the Philippine Commission.[97] Dominic's name had been put forward repeatedly as a candidate for mayor of D.C., but he relished the idea of governing that Pacific archipelago instead.[98] When his longtime friend from the Pension office, Mrs. Bessie Atkinson, moved in with him in 1903 or

---

* Dennis, the dean of Senate reporters, had died in 1896, but brother Edward, who'd succeeded him, was now in his thirty-sixth year of reporting for the Senate, a major stockholder in several large corporations and hobnobbing with Senators and the Washington elite, while Dominic's nephew, James Wilmot Murphy, was well on his way to a sixty-four-year career as the Senate's next official chief reporter. Meanwhile, Dominic's brother Joe had become one of Philadelphia's major employers, now enjoying a comfortable retirement, having left a thriving business to his sons.

early 1904, she likely intended that she and her two children would go to the Philippines with him.[99]

But with his appointment still pending, politics intervened once again.

One of the Senators from Roosevelt's home state of New York, Thomas C. Platt, prided himself on being Roosevelt's "political godfather," instrumental in Roosevelt's nomination as vice president.[100] When Roosevelt became President, Platt was anxious to call the shots, and once Roosevelt obtained rights to build the transcontinental canal connecting Atlantic to Pacific, Platt and Benjamin Odell (Roosevelt's successor as Governor of New York), lobbied the new president for the appointment of a fellow New Yorker to the position of Secretary to the Canal Commission.[101] Their man, Edward C. O'Brien, was qualified for the job, having been Commissioner of Navigation in Washington and President of the New York Dock Board.[102] Overly anxious to claim credit for O'Brien's appointment, Platt wrote to O'Brien's brother (the N.Y. Secretary of State), as if he had inside information from the Oval Office, "It gives me pleasure to inform you that your brother has been appointed the Secretary to the Isthmian Canal Commission."[103] A few days later, on March 4, 1904, a New York paper announced the appointment as a *fait accompli*:

> Northern New York friends of General Edward C. O'Brien will be gratified to learn that he is to be made secretary of the Panama Canal Commission... General O'Brien is... an able, genial citizen whose success is well deserved.[104]

The unauthorized leak was a great embarrassment to the President. Roosevelt had been saying that no decision would be made for some time. His anger over the leak turned out to have a significant effect on Murphy's future. Less than a month after the French handed over control of the canal project, Roosevelt officially appointed Murphy (not O'Brien) as Secretary to the U.S. Isthmian Canal Commission.[105]

Dominic was no engineer; he spoke no Spanish; he had no ties to central American governments; he had no experience with docks, canals, navigation, or anything relevant to the building of a canal. But being well connected in Washington political circles, his qualifications for the position were clear:

> Mr. Murphy expresses himself as proud of the fact that among his indorsers for the position were Former President Grover Cleveland, Former Pension Commissioners Black, Dudley and Tanner, Former Secretary of the Interior Hoke Smith, and Mr. Francis, the latter now president of the St. Louis exposition; John M. Reynolds, former assistant secretary of the interior; Senators Blackburn, Gallinger, Mitchell and Aldrich and many members of the House of Representatives.[106]

After a headline calling Murphy's new position a "plum," the *Washington Times* went on to describe the context:

> The position of secretary is one of the most important the commission has to bestow. It is understood that ex-President Cleveland in his letter indorsing Mr. Murphy stated that if it had been in his power to select the Panama Canal Commission he would have undoubtedly given Mr. Murphy a place on the Board.
>
> Some surprise has been expressed at the announcement of the appointment as it was recently stated that the office would not be filled for at least six months. There were a number of prominent candidates for the position, and it was generally reported that Colonel O'Brien, of New York, would get the office. It is understood that the publication of Colonel O'Brien's picture in a magazine and newspaper with the statement that he had obtained the appointment greatly hurt his chances.[107]

DOMINIC L. MURPHY

SECRETARY OF PANAMA CANAL COMMISSION

Washingtonian Was Strongly Indorsed for the Position to Some of the Country's Most Prominent Citizens. His Appointment Is Regarded on All Sides as a Good One.

And so, as a result of other men's missteps, Dominic Murphy was called to serve his country once again – not in doling out pension benefits, not in governing the Philippines, but in oversight of the building of the Panama Canal.[108]

There were major decisions yet to be made. An exact route had not yet been determined; nor had a decision been made whether to build the canal at sea level or operate it with locks. The project was known to be deadly: over 30,000 people had already died during France's failed efforts to build the canal.[109] Now that the Commission had a green light to proceed with actual construction, it was time for the Commission to make decisions, time to demonstrate American ingenuity to the world.[110]

The day following his appointment, President Roosevelt called Murphy to the White House for a lengthy private meeting at which "many points of the canal building and zone government were gone over, and the President made the secretary acquainted with his ideas."[111]

Among the subjects likely discussed was the awarding of lucrative construction contracts under the direction of the Secretary of War. Murphy assumed his new office on Monday, June 13.[112] When the Commissioners sailed for Panama six weeks later (to "enact legislation for the government of the strip..."[113]) Murphy stayed behind in Washington. And once again, on the Tuesday following the Commissioners' departure, he met with Roosevelt. The two men discussed isthmian canal matters in "some detail," the President asking him about complaints from Panamanian officials regarding the work there. The Evening Star gave its report the subheading, "Secretary Murphy Explains Matters to the President."[114]

It is curious that the Canal Secretary didn't join the Commissioners on their trip. One might think it was appropriate for him to join them. But they were part-time policy makers, whereas Murphy, as Secretary, was a full time executive, in charge of daily operations. His "hands on" duties may well have made him closer to the actual construction than the part-time commissioners were. While the details of the two meetings between the President and his Democratic appointee aren't known, the two men apparently established a good relationship; ultimately, Murphy was instructed to keep the President apprised through his personal secretary, confidante and advisor, William Loeb. Before the summer was through, with Roosevelt facing Democrat Alton B. Parker in the November election, Murphy was corresponding with Loeb:

Aug 31, 1904

My dear Mr. Loeb:

I write to give you an extract from a letter written by my cousin, Rev. Wm. F. Marshall, who has been living in France for a number of years. From Aix-les-Bains, he writes, among other things: "I am not a politician, but I take an interest in all that appertains to dear America and I therefore would like to see Mr. Roosevelt elected. The European press favors Judge Parker and the reduction or abolition of the tariff, which is the best proof that we need Roosevelt and protection."

My cousin is sending me the two volumes recently published by M. Roux on "The World's Great Canals" and he tells me that if the President would like to have a copy, he will be glad to send it to him. I have already written him to send the work as I am sure the President will think it of value.

It might be interesting for the President to know that since the Associated Press dispatch went out, August 10th, to the Pacific Coast, there has not been received a single protest relative to the existence of the contract between the Panama Railroad Company and the Pacific Mail Steamship Company, either by wire or letter. The dissatisfaction on the Coast I believe, has been allayed.

With warmest regards and best wishes to the President and yourself, I am

Very truly yours,
D. I. Murphy,
Secretary.

Hon. W. Loeb, Jr.,
Secretary to the President[115]

Murphy had spent three decades dealing with important men in the Capital, and his letter could serve as a "how to" for how a high-ranking government official should deal with the White House. Notwithstanding his family's years of support for Democratic politicians and his brother's notorious opposition to high Republican tariffs, Murphy's first paragraph cited his cousin Marshall's support, both for the President's re-election and for his party's tariffs – implying, without so saying, that he himself joined in such support. Murphy's second paragraph promised the President a gift. His third assured the President that a political problem had been defused. The rest of the letter was in the same vein.[116] One imagines that in the face-to-face with Roosevelt in June, Dominic had similarly ingratiated himself to the President – even at the expense of the absent Canal Commissioners.

With so much money at stake, the building of the canal was naturally beset by controversy. One concern involved the difficulty of finding labor for the project, and the widely held assumption that black men were more suitable for work there.[117] Another problem was Panama's complaint that the U.S.-supported government of the Canal Zone was trying to turn it into an American colony. An example of American respect for the young country's independence came when Rear Admiral Walker (head of the Canal Commission) declared upon his arrival in Panama that the United States planned to keep its ports in the Canal Zone open "in spite of any protests which might be made by the Panama government."[118]

After a month in Panama, the Commissioners returned to the United States, "having enacted laws for the government of the zone and deciding questions of urgent importance."[119] But reports of disease, political unrest and dissatisfaction continued, prompting a number of Congressmen to visit the country in order to see conditions there for themselves.[120] Upon their return, according to the *Washington Post*, "practically every man [was] in favor of changes more or less sweeping, which may result in the reorganization of the Canal Commission." Several Congressmen wanted to reduce the Commission's size from nine to three and require that they reside and work in Panama.[121]

But of all the Commission's practices, none provoked more complaints than its method of awarding contracts for the work to be done. The number and size of such contracts was staggering. In just six weeks, the *Post* mentioned contracts for 43,000 tons of cast iron pipe, 2.6 million feet of lumber, a "very large quantity" of cement, a thousand steel "dump cars," two hundred flat cars, hydrants, valves, vitrified sewer pipe, a laundry plant, steam shovels, photographic equipment for surveying, four hundred sets of bedroom furniture, and "a large

WORKING ON ISTHMUS

Canal Commission Makes Report to the President.

BIG CONTRACTS TO BE LET

Bids Soon Will Be Opened for Vast Amount of Material to Be Used in Construction of the Canal—Cost of Excavating Already Reduced Below that of the French Company.

quantity of paper of various kinds and a lot of type, for use in connection with the Panama Canal printing office" [122] – and that was only the beginning. When the Commissioners returned from their visit in the summer of 1904 and reported on their mission, news coverage emphasized that "big contracts" for a "vast amount of material" would be awarded.[123] There was no system in place for competitive bidding, nothing to keep the Commission from awarding contracts to any business it saw fit. Once again, government officials were in a position to reward friendly financial interests. Meanwhile, for a nine-member Commission to deliberate or make any decision at all, they had to gather, to actually hold a meeting, a cumbersome matter that required coordinating the schedules of nine well-connected gentlemen. Not surprisingly, such meetings were few and far between. Unlike the Commissioners, Murphy's work for the Commission was full time. He was in fact the highest-ranking full-time official in the whole enterprise, at the day-to-day center of all contracts awarded by the Commission. Whether his involvement facilitated the award of contracts to political toadies or was a constraint on them, he was surely a factor in one direction or the other.

Meanwhile, running day-to-day functions like hiring of staff, he hired his twenty-one-year-old nephew Edward (his brother Edward's son) as a typist and stenographer in the Washington office. Normal protocol in the young man's appointment was not followed, as his position was designated "classified" on the order of the President himself. (It is not clear whether Edward's duties involved more than typing, taking dictation or recording discussions.) Hired on October 8, 1904, Edward resigned on November 30, 1904, less than two months later.[124] Whether his brief stint at the Commission represented a short-lived example of nepotism in a gravy job, or a classified role that ended when its purpose had been accomplished, is also unclear.

Complaints and controversy continued. As always, those in charge gave assurances that things were going well. [125] In response to continuing complaints of American excess, Roosevelt sent Secretary of War Howard Taft to assure the Panamanian Republic that "We have not the slightest intention of establishing an independent colony in the middle of the State of Panama." Taft took a large party of officials with him, so as to "do all honor to the little Panama state, showing its people that the United States government has as high a regard for their sovereign rights as for those of any other people."[126]

In the midst of all the controversy, Mrs. Bessie T. Atkinson and her two children moved into Murphy's apartment. In what was surely no coincidence, only two days after Bessie and Dominic were married, the couple left for Boston, where Murphy's son Joseph got married as well.[127]

Despite such respites for family matters, complaints about the Canal Commission only mounted over the winter, including calls for the nine gentlemen of the Commission to become more hands-on with respect to Canal construction. Finally, on April 1, 1905, the President issued an executive order that the make-up of the Commission would have to be changed. After new members were appointed, the Commission would have to delegate authority to an Executive Committee to facilitate quicker decision-making. The Commission would be required to maintain "a complete system of accounts." Its contracting practices would have to be revised. "Contracts… shall only be made after due public advertisement… and shall be awarded to the lowest responsible bidder…" And perhaps hardest for some to bear, the Commission would be required to hold regular meetings *in Panama*.[128] Letters of resignation were quickly accepted, new Commissioners appointed. One can imagine how Mrs. Atkinson felt about the prospect of moving to the tropics. Yellow fever and malaria had killed thousands. Many doubted whether the government's war on mosquitoes would work. Yet Murphy arranged to sail for Panama on May 23rd.[129]

Then, just a day prior to his scheduled departure, Murphy learned of the death of Albion Tourgee, U.S. Consul in Bordeaux, France.[130] According to the New York *Sun*, Murphy applied for Tourgee's post on May 22, the day before his scheduled sailing for Panama, "just after he had heard of Judge Tourgee's death." Remembering Murphy as a well-connected man with a cousin in Aix-les-Bains who'd expressed political support, Roosevelt appointed Murphy the same day, the Sun calling Murphy "a personal friend of President Roosevelt, who has great regard for his ability… He is now regarded as a Republican, although politics had nothing to do with his selection as secretary of the canal commission or his appointment to the consular service."[131]

Suddenly, instead of the Philippines or the mosquito-filled jungles of Panama, Dominic and his family were headed to Bordeaux, a city of art, history, magnificent architecture, golden facades, monumental squares, beautiful courtyards and temperate weather, all to be enjoyed while sipping French wine and enjoying its world-famous cuisine.[132] The wife and children were delighted. Dominic's success now clearly rivaled that of his brothers. For yet another Murphy, America had lived up to its promise.

It was an easy, idyllic time. Dominic and Bessie found Bordeaux so pleasant that in the summer of 1907, they received repeated visitors from home.[133] In June of 1907, the *Washington Post* republished an article from the *San Francisco Monitor* that, while lampooning Roosevelt's appointments, alluded to Murphy's efforts at writing poetry.[134]

The tasks required of the new consul were often ceremonial.[135] But the official responsibilities of a consul are not only to protect a country's citizens abroad; they are also to facilitate trade. That role involved sending home intelligence reports about a host country's people, resources, commerce and industry. It required Murphy to become familiar with everything Bordeaux had to offer, from its world-famous wines to less romantic products like hand saws and screw drivers.[136]

After two years in Bordeaux, Roosevelt appointed Dominic consul at St. Gall, Switzerland, on the country's border with Germany. From his new post, he reported on production facilities, machinery, power sources, equipment, technologies, methods, the labor force, export values and Switzerland's importation of coal and steel from Germany and Austria.[137] Since the canton was Switzerland's biggest producer of textiles, Dominic made sure to pass on his intelligence to his brother and nephew in Philadelphia, who still made their livings in textiles. Dominic's consular counterparts in Zurich and Basel updated him on the production of a new product: artificial silk. Courtaulds, the giant British textiles firm, was planning to produce it in Marcus Hook, Pennsylvania – only a half hour's drive from the Murphy Mill. And most interesting of all, it was said, the artificial stuff could be made at far less cost than genuine silk. Dominic passed his information on to his brothers in Philadelphia; one never knew when the family might put such intelligence to good use. [138]

Dominic may have had more to say about artificial silk when he returned home in 1913.[139] (His brother and nephew were surely eager to hear about it.) Then, in February of 1914, President Wilson nominated Dominic to be Consul General in Amsterdam, the Netherlands.[140] Dominic and his family moved to the city of canals, the home of Rembrandt, Van Gogh, and the Dutch East and West India Companies, sometimes called the "Venice of the North," its culture and long history at the center of world commerce. On June 17, 1914, while in Amsterdam, Dominic and Bessie announced the engagement of her daughter, Bessie, to a Swede, Johan Alfred Gösta Nordström.[141] It was a happy time for the sixty-seven-year-old Murphy; he had no reason to retire from a government service that was providing him such a sinecure.

Then, eleven days later, the assassination of Archduke Franz Ferdinand (heir to the Dual Monarchy of Austria and Hungary) began a chain of events that plunged the world into war.[142] Little more than a week after the Archduke's assassination, Germany pledged its support to the Dual Monarchy; three weeks later, the Dual Monarchy declared war on Serbia, prompting Russia to mobilize its troops and Germany to demand that they demobilize. When Russia did not, Germany sought land concessions from France (to demonstrate its neutrality in the event of war between Germany and Russia). France replied by mobilizing its troops, to which Germany responded by invading Belgium while declaring war on France and Russia as well. Due to its own alliance with France, Britain responded by declaring the existence of war with Germany. Even Japan got into the act, demanding that Germany withdraw its fleet from the Far East and surrender territory Germany had taken on the Shantung Peninsula of China; when Germany failed to respond, Japan, too, declared war on Germany.

In short, within a matter of weeks, the entire Eastern hemisphere had erupted into war. Germany had swept through Belgium and advanced into northern France. In the eyes of much of the world, Kaiser Wilhelm, the German leader of the Central Powers, was the villainous aggressor. And there were Americans at risk, both in Germany and in neighboring countries.

President Woodrow Wilson vowed to keep Americans out of the conflict.[143] But a hundred and twenty-five thousand American tourists, students and other citizens were suddenly unable to get home from Europe, their liberty at risk. Passenger ships were being refitted for war. Voyages were being cancelled. Travelers' checks were being turned down. Congress passed a joint resolution for "the relief, protection, and transportation of American citizens" in which it appropriated $2.5 million dollars to secure their return from Europe. Private bankers quickly came up with three million more.[144] Assistant Secretary of War Henry Breckenridge sped to Europe to buy what America wanted for its citizens abroad. Determining that "Holland was the normal point of egress for all Americans coming from Germany," Breckenridge called upon the Imperial German Government in Berlin to seek the safe extraction of Americans from the war zone. Thanks to Germany's "extreme courtesy" (and $150,000 in gold he'd brought for the purpose) Breckenridge was promised a special train to Holland every day until the Americans could be gotten out of that country.[145] Dominic Murphy's duties in Amsterdam were suddenly anything but ceremonial. Responsible for the protection of American citizens, he was sent $5,000 in gold to help with the evacuation of Americans from the Netherlands.[146]

America's political neutrality didn't restrain her business and commercial interests, however. With Britain at war, its need for arms and munitions skyrocketed. American businesses were free to supply their natural ally with arms. As this commercial cooperation became increasingly clear, America's officially neutral stance was questioned, both by the Central Powers (who resented the support America was giving) and by Britain and its allies (who considered the support not enough). Murphy's Netherlands maintained its neutrality, like the United States. But both sides in the conflict wooed America and other uncommitted countries to join the war as their allies. "The diplomacy of the first months of the war was to be devoted to efforts by both sides to win the support of Italy as well as smaller uncommitted countries such as Romania… Greece and Bulgaria."[147]

This was the state of affairs in March of 1915, when Woodrow Wilson reassigned Murphy from Amsterdam to Sofia, the capital of uncommitted, unaligned Bulgaria.[148] Bulgaria was a poor country, lacking Holland's rich history of international trade and finance. After five centuries of Ottoman rule and just a few decades of independence, Bulgaria was ruled by King Ferdinand I, a Catholic aristocrat whose close relatives included royal families in Portugal, Great Britain, Belgium and Mexico. Ferdinand's chief concern was regaining territory his country had lost in the Second Balkan War. It was a good bet that Bulgaria would not remain neutral but would ultimately ally itself with whichever side would support its own territorial claims. After much lobbying by both sides, Germany guaranteed Bulgaria that it would do so, and on October 11, 1915, Bulgaria entered the war on the side of the Central Powers.[149] The ramifications for Murphy were substantial. He was now a diplomat in a country that was at war with Britain and France, countries America was commercially supporting. To some extent, at least, Murphy's newest assignment left him representing American interests from within the borders of a hostile power.

An example of Murphy's duties as Consul in this awkward situation arose at the end of February, 1916, when his services were needed to assist in protecting an American citizen in Bulgaria, Frank E. Couche of Ohio. Having arrived in Sofia on his way to Saloniki, Couche – who had formerly served as attaché to the American Legation at Bucharest – was arrested by the Bulgarian Secret Police and charged by the State Prosecutor with espionage. Murphy succeeded in getting the Bulgarian Government to try Couche in a civil court, rather than before a military tribunal. (It was a difference Dominic's seventy-three-year-old brother Edward, remembering the trial of Mary Surratt, urged as an important one.) At his trial, Couche said he was going to Salonica not as a spy, but as a shoe salesman. He was acquitted, but the State Prosecutor appealed. Murphy then used his good offices to secure his release. According to the *New York Times*, Couche was expected to be permitted to leave Bulgaria rather than face a new trial there.[150]

Dominic also issued over a dozen emergency passports to American citizens living in the Balkans who were seeking to return to the U.S.[151] Meanwhile, due to the turbulent conditions of war, other diplomats had left Sofia. British bombing raids repeatedly forced Dominic to seek refuge in Sofia's bomb shelters.[152] As the sole remaining American diplomat in Bulgaria, he became the *de facto* Ambassador, taking on the role of intermediary between the American and Bulgarian governments in political as well as commercial matters. The assignment was a difficult one. In 1916, the Bulgarians, as allies of the Germans, regained control over much of Romania, which had allied with the French and Russians. Murphy's job was to reason with a country that was an American enemy in everything but name – and if possible, to look for – and exploit – cracks in its alliance with Germany.

With this in mind, what happened in the autumn of 1916 is not surprising. The Murphys had decided to visit Bessie's daughter, now living in Stockholm with her husband, Gösta Nordström.[153] Like the U.S., Sweden was still a neutral country, but travel from Sofia to Stockholm was problematic, even if the journey avoided war-torn Europe by sailing west through the Mediterranean and up the Atlantic coast. By October, Mr. and Mrs. Murphy had reached the Hague, in neutral Holland, where they obtained passports and a diplomatic pass from the German legation.[154] Their route passed through Germany to Warnemunde, a German port city on the Baltic Sea, from which they would sail up the Baltic to Stockholm. Despite his German pass, Murphy was treated with incivility by the German authorities at Warnemunde, both on the way to Stockholm and upon the return trip in November.[155] If the Germans suspected that the U.S. and its General Consul in Bulgaria were up to something, they may have been right. Back in Sofia on December 30th, Dominic handed a note to Bulgarian Premier Vasil Radoslavov from President Woodrow Wilson, containing Wilson's proposal for peace with Bulgaria.[156]

Peace, however, was still a long way off. In March, 1917, news of the Zimmerman telegram brought anti-German sentiment in the U.S. to the boiling point.[157] On April 6, just weeks after the telegram became public, the U.S. decided its liberty was threatened and so declared war on Germany. Churchill had finally gotten his wish that America become embroiled in the war. But while Bulgaria and the U.S. were now on opposite sides of the military conflict, neither country had declared war on each other. And despite the obvious dangers, Murphy remained in Sofia, continuing to operate as U.S. Consul General there, even though his consular duties included sending intelligence reports back to the State Department. The thin line between such "commercial" reporting and espionage could not have escaped his notice. It hadn't been long since he'd rescued Frank Couche from the Bulgarian Secret Police, and Couche had simply been selling shoes. Murphy was sending dispatches back to the U.S. State Department on such topics as Bulgarian grain production and its policies on "commerce with the enemy."[158] As it happens, while Murphy was never arrested for espionage, his position as *de facto* ambassador was about to put him in the middle of the biggest stink of his life. And the question is whether or not, at this late stage of his life, Murphy had become a brilliant statesman or had gotten in over his head, an expendable pawn in the brutal realities of covert operations and disinformation that characterize international relations during war time.

The intrigue began a few days before Christmas, 1917, when a Bulgarian newspaper, the *Kambana*, printed what it said was an interview with Murphy. The *Kambana*'s report was quickly picked up in a German newspaper, the *Vossische Zeitung*, and by Christmas day, it had made the *Washington Post*:

STATE DEPARTMENT SILENT ON MURPHY

U. S. Consul at Sofia Says German Paper Is Antiwar.

Headline in *Washington Post*, Dec 25, 1917, p 2.

Sensational charges were made recently in a Berlin newspaper, the Vossische Zeitung, to the effect that Consul General Dominic Murphy, of Sofia, for many years a resident of Washington, had declared in favor of Bulgarian land concessions and had opposed the declaration of war upon Austria.

The newspaper article also stated that Murphy deprecated as ugly the agitation which former Ambassador Gerard is carrying on with his lectures. He is quoted as saying that Gerard was always a friend of the entente and contributed a great deal toward America's rupture with Germany and President Wilson had not dared to contradict him because he was one of the prime movers in his election.

Officials of the State Department last night declined to comment on the reports.[159]

The State Department was receiving reports from various sources; but such reports, though confidential, were printed by the *Post* the following February. Some statements the *Kambana* attributed to Murphy sounded like things a loose-lipped or inexperienced diplomat – such as a long-time consul with no ambassadorial experience – might have said. For one thing, it quoted Murphy as implying that the U.S. Senate would not allow Italy to extend its territory into Dalmatia.[160] The Bulgarians had no doubt become aware of Murphy's family connections to the Senate – maybe even from Murphy himself. Dominic's aging brother Edward – known for his love of the podium more than his skill at keeping secrets – still held the contract for Senate reporting. What Edward may have said to Dominic about the Senate's attitude toward the war is anyone's guess – and whether Dominic repeated it to the Bulgarian press may never be resolved. Either way, if Dominic, in reliance on his brother, suggested that the President might not have the last word, one can imagine the President and State Department being more than upset.

The *Kambana* report further quoted Murphy as saying that "the commercial interests of the United States demand that the war should cease as soon as possible in order that American ships may be free to sail for Europe with raw materials and merchandise destined for the exhausted peoples of Europe."[161] Did Murphy really undermine Wilson's negotiating position by implying that such commercial interests left him no choice but to secure peace? The President and State Department could not have been happy.

Perhaps most importantly, the Bulgarian newspaper quoted Murphy as saying he'd convinced his government of the "legitimate nature" of Bulgaria's territorial claims. Such a boast amounted to guaranteeing that the U.S. was prepared to give Bulgaria all it could hope for. On top of that, in spite of President Wilson's threats to break off relations with Bulgaria if Bulgaria remained a belligerent German ally, Murphy reportedly assured the Bulgarian paper that the U.S. would never do so. (So, at least, claimed the *Kambana*.)

Finally, the paper said Murphy went on to assert that Wilson wouldn't dare oppose former Ambassador to Berlin, James Gerard, due to his financial support of the President. Though not mentioned in the report to the state department, Murphy also reportedly called the Bulgars "a wild and savage people" who "ought to be tamed."[162]

The State Department ordered Murphy to admit or deny the Kambana's report. Murphy insisted that the interview had been completely faked in order to discredit him, precisely because of his growing influence with Bulgaria at German expense.[163] According to the next day's editorial in the *Washington Post,* Murphy's efforts proved the folly of trying to maintain a relationship with an ally of Germany. The editorial called for cessation of relations with both Turkey and Bulgaria on the ground that "He that is not with me is against me."[164]

But Murphy was not sacked; relations with Bulgaria were not discontinued. In March, 1918, the *Post* accused the U.S. of being played for a fool by a treacherous, double-crossing Ferdinand.[165] The *Post* was not alone in its anxiety. But as the war took its toll on Bulgaria, Bulgarian confidence in the Central Powers, and therefore in the Radoslavov government, waned. In June of 1918, a new prime minister, Aleksandar Malinov, made clear he wanted to explore peace with the allies – assuming, of course, that Bulgaria could keep its territorial gains. But with the Bolsheviks in power in Russia, many in the U.S. were as concerned about Russian influence as they were about Germany's. On September 25, U.S. Secretary of State Robert Lansing telegrammed the Ambassador to Switzerland about a State Department circular on Russian atrocities, directing him to pass the circular on to Murphy, for delivery to the Bulgarian government.[166]

At the end of September, 1918, Murphy's friendships in Bulgaria finally paid off. According to him, King Ferdinand and his government had made a demand on Germany and Austria for immediate assistance, and when it was not promised, King Ferdinand had decided to come over to the allied side.

> What impelled the King most, the consul general's account indicates, was the fear of revolution. Anarchy was making serious progress in Sofia. Workmen and soldiers had held meetings and passed laws. Bolshevism in its most excessive form became the regular order and manifestations were held before the royal palace.
>
> King Ferdinand, it is added, haunted by recollections of the former Emperor Nicholas, was unable to sleep. He considered it essential for his country and for his own safety that a strong foreign military force should intervene and thus, it is added, as Germany could not give him that force, he turned to the entente.[167]

On September 28, Murphy accompanied a Bulgarian delegation to Saloniki to meet with French General Franchet d'Esperey, proposing the armistice. [168] The lead story in the *Washington Times* was headlined "Bulgaria Quits Germany: Accepts Allies' Terms."[169] The State Department said that Murphy had received no instructions from the Secretary of State, and had probably accompanied the Bulgarians strictly as an "observer," but a German telegram stated that Murphy had played "a very important part in recent events."[170]

Philadelphia's *Evening Public Ledger* said Murphy was "recognized as being very prudent and a deep student of international affairs." It further reported that Washington diplomats were "awaiting with interest" any word from him. [171] But most interesting was the analysis provided by the *Cincinnati Enquirer*:

Diplomatic Rules Are Made to Be Broken

There is at Sofia a diplomatist bearing the telltale name of Dominic Murphy, a name that recalls the Blarney stone and the soft "soothering" of the coaxing sons of Erin. He is accredited by the United States with the title of Consul General to Bulgaria. Germany's Foreign Office, the precise Wilhelmstrasse, complains that it was this man who detached the Bulgarian officials from their responsibility to the Central Powers alliance. The further point is made that he actually conducted the preliminary negotiations, and even went so far as to accompany the armistice delegation to Saloniki.

With more or less of a twinkle in his eye, though with a stern voice and air, Secretary of State Lansing admits that he coincides with the exasperated Berlin statesmen to the extent of agreeing that the diplomatic Dominic was functioning entirely without instructions and in an unofficial capacity. Orders have been issued peremptorily commanding him to return to his post of duty. The armistice having been accepted, it is quite possible that the bold fellow, also with a twinkle in his eye, will ride back to Sofia and compose some sort of a high-sounding instrument for filing in the archives of the State Department at Washington. No doubt it will read well, and the fluent and fox-like Murphy will humbly apologize for winning a high stake by going outside the prescribed rules.

The result should be rather shocking to the numerous as well as clamorous critics of the National Administration who insisted that Congress should forthwith declare war on Bulgaria. It may turn out that they are as far away from the inside of affairs in Turkey, against which President Wilson has also refused to issue the declaration of belligerency. Perhaps there is in Constantinople another Dominic Murphy acting without orders and in an entirely unofficial manner, against whom the German Foreign Office may soon have a cause of complaint.[172]

The very day of that article, October 3, 1918, the King who'd chosen to side with Germany abdicated his throne, leaving the Bulgarian Monarchy to his son, Boris – who (according to Murphy) was more "democratic" at heart.

Ferdinand's abdication and Bulgaria's defection had huge ramifications. According to the *Evening Star,*

> Germany is panic-stricken by events in Bulgaria, and justly so. Germany sees the consequent disaffection of Turkey, the complete reclamation of Serbia, Montenegro, Albania and Romania and the invasion of Austria, with the latter country's overrunning and consequent withdrawal from the struggle, leaving Germany alone to face the civilized world. Germany sees her own defeat writ large on the face of current events.[173]

Indeed, Bulgaria's defection marked the beginning of the end for Germany. Little more than a month later, the general Armistice was signed and the war was over. Arguably, Dominic Murphy's maverick adventures in diplomacy had played a major role in ending the First World War.

Murphy's diplomatic duties were not over, however. In Sofia on December 28, 1918, he applied for a passport for use in visiting Turkey, France, England, Switzerland, Italy and Holland, giving as the purpose of his travels "official duty." The usual duties of a Consul call for a relatively permanent and stable presence in a country, to develop relationships and learn its commercial business. A post-war tour of six countries suggests a mission of a different nature – perhaps helping to survey needs for the Red Cross or other American aid. Murphy was now 71 years old, however, and perhaps his work in Bulgaria had worn him down. Referred to as the *former* Consul General at Sofia, Murphy was reported in Saloniki soon thereafter, recovering from an attack of pneumonia.[174]

Still, Murphy's success in Bulgaria would prove to be his crowning achievement. The Municipal Council of Sofia named a street "Murphy Street" after him.[175] He appeared as a speaker at the American Club in Paris alongside Herbert Hoover and General Pershing.[176] In May, he arrived back in the states on a leave of absence, emphasizing in a press interview that Bulgaria was an excellent market for U.S. goods of any kind.[177] In June, he described the successful conversion of Bulgaria at a meeting of the Central High School Alumni.[178]

According to the *Washington Post*, it was on Murphy's advice that Bulgaria threw herself on the mercy of the allies after the defeat of her army."[179] Another who gave Murphy credit was General Erich Ludendorff, Germany's *de facto* co-dictator (along with Paul von Hindenburg). After the war, Ludendorff wrote of his frustration with events in Bulgaria, including Murphy in particular.

> "The American declaration of war included all the states of the quadruple alliance [Germany and her allies] with the exception of Bulgaria, where the American representative continued to hold his post at Sofia. The German government failed to secure his recall through the Bulgarian government, although I requested them several times to do so. This failure brought heavy retribution upon us later on."[180]

According to Ludendorff, Murphy "took advantage of [the situation] very cleverly, and held out prospects of large profits in good Swiss francs. Many failed to resist this temptation."[181]

But differences between people coalesce into different truths. In a world of international intrigue, there is never escape from controversy. While Murphy was widely congratulated for Bulgaria's defection from the German alliance, there were many who felt what he had done was short-sighted. During the war, anti-German sentiment in the U.S. had been whipped up by a massive public relations campaign in the U.S., designed to raise money for the military's needs. Anti-German sentiment persisted after the war ended, and extended to Germany's erstwhile ally, Bulgaria. One of the institutions that voiced such animosity repeatedly was the *Washington Post*. In February, 1919, the *Post* ran an article critical of Murphy titled "Bulgarian Lies."

> We are… informed that Bulgaria's virtues have even hypnotized the allied armies of occupation. They were so convinced of Bulgaria's good will that they let her keep and run her own railways… As the Bulgarian railways are being run with rolling stock stolen from Serbia and the cigarette tobacco is plunder from the Greek tobacco fields round Kavala, the generosity of the allies is calculated to excite our astonishment rather than our admiration.
>
> Consul General Dominic I. Murphy also, it would appear, made his little contribution to this policy of kiss and be friends by giving a dinner at which the guests were officers of the allied armies of occupation and members of the Bulgarian government… The idea of asking the relatives of the victims of Bulgarian cruelty to sit down at the same table with the men

who had the blood of thousands of helpless women and children on their hands could only appeal to a Bulgarian.[182]

At the end of March, the *Post* questioned Murphy's activities yet again:

> The fact that the United States and Bulgaria were not at war was said in official circles to have been the basis of the attitude of the missionaries, who were very friendly to the old Bulgarian government, although the country was at war with nations with which the United States was associated in fighting Germany.
>
> In this connection, officials recalled that Dominic I. Murphy, diplomatic representative of the United States in Bulgaria, went to Saloniki with the Bulgarian authorities to negotiate the armistice after Bulgaria surrendered. The State Department ordered Mr. Murphy back to Sofia and later instructed him to come to Washington. On his arrival his actions will be closely questioned.[183]

Like his older brothers before him, Dominic had grown to understand that in Washington, accusations fly freely; no one is given the benefit of a doubt. In his Pension Bureau days, he'd never cared for private bills in Congress which effectively overturned Bureau decisions. But in 1927, when Murphy was eighty-years old, he supported such a private bill involving himself and his own career. Despite the legal prohibitions against accepting gifts from foreign governments, the U.S. House of Representatives passed a bill authorizing Dominic to accept the gift of a silver fruit bowl from the British government in recognition of relief he'd given British prisoners in Bulgaria.[184]

In July, Murphy was reassigned as Consul General to Stockholm.[185] He continued to send reports back to the State Department, but despite having achieved greater fame than his father or any of his siblings, his career was clearly winding down.[186] He and Bessie lived out their lives with her daughter in Stockholm, even after his retirement from the Consular Service in 1924.[187] Murphy died in that city on April 13, 1930, having experienced all the controversy that government service could produce, and having done what he could to extend his country's influence to the rest of the world. His efforts were recognized by an Associated Press report of his death, carried in various newspapers.[188]

Notes on Chapter 9, Dominic I. Murphy

[1] 1850 U.S. Census, Phila, Kensington Ward 6, Fam 1128, and 1860 U.S. Census, Phila, Ward 17, Fam 454. Dominic was born May 31, 1847 (*National Tribune*, April 27, 1893, p 7). Early in life, Dominick's name was most often spelled with a k, like his father, but later, it was almost exclusively spelled without the k, probably to express his preference and to distinguish himself from his father. For clarity's sake, we have opted to use the shorter spelling throughout, even editing direct quotations of printed works to conform to the shorter spelling. Dominic was admitted to Central High School in July 1861 and attended until November 1864 (General Catalogue of the Central High School, Philadelphia, from 1838 to 1890, Bd of Educ, 1890, p 84, accessed at archive.org/details/generalcatalogue00phil/rich; and U.S. High School Student Lists 1821-1923, PA, Central High School, 1861, American Antiquarian Society, accessed through Ancestry.com). By this time, the Christian Brothers Academy had opened at St. Michael's, so Dominic's attendance at the public high school was a choice in favor of a secular education.

[2] After attending Central, Dominic worked for several years as a clerk in his father's textile mill. At age 23, he was a "manufacturer" (1870 U.S. Census Phila Ward 16, Dist 50, Fam 1474); in the 1872 City Directory, he was listed as a clerk, still living at his parents' house). See also *National Tribune*, April 27, 1893, p 7; *Phila Record*, April 15, 1930; 1900 U.S. Census, Wash D.C., Dist 0055, Fam 163.

[3] *National Tribune*, April 27, 1893, p 7; Claire Prechtel-Kluskens, "A Reasonable Degree of Promptitude," *Prologue Magazine*, Spring, 2010, Vol 42, No 1, National Archives, accessed at https://www.archives.gov/publications/prologue/2010/spring/civilwarpension.html.

[4] *Constitution and By-Laws of the Carroll Institute of Washington, D.C., Organized Sept 8, 1873, Constitution Revised, May 20, 1880,* American Catholic Pamphlets and Parish Histories Database, The Catholic University of America, accessed at https://www.lib.cua.edu/rarebook/node/3056.

[5] *Evening Star*, June 16, 1904, p 14. Government clerks at the time were paid an annual salary of either $1200, $1400, $1600 or $1800. By 1873, his salary of $1600 per year put him among 50 clerks in the Pension Office making that amount, compared to only 26 clerks making $1800 and quite a few more making less – either $1400 (83 clerks) or $1200 (85 clerks). (Register of Officers and Agents in the Service of the U.S. as of Sept 30, 1873, GPO 1873, p 322.) Whether Murphy's relatively high pay had more to do with merit, seniority, or family connections is unknown.

[6] The license for the marriage of Dominick and Mary Catherine Kearon was issued August 17, 1875 (*National Republican*, Aug 18, 1875, p 4). The house details are from the building permit for the south side of M Street NW, between 6th and 7th (*Evening Star*, May 24, 1875, p 4; *National Republican*, May 25, 1875, p 4). Catherine's father, Robert Kearon, a former employee of the Library of Congress, likely knew Murphy's older brothers. Kearon had been working as an auditing clerk in the Treasury Department since at least 1863 (Register of Officers and Agents in the Service of the U.S., Sept 30, 1863, GPO 1863, p 26). By 1875, he was one of only two clerks in the office of the Treasury's 4th Auditor making a salary of $1800 per year (Register of Officers (etc), Sept 30, 1875, GPO 1875, p 45). See also the 1870 Census (Wash, D.C. Ward 3, Fam 1393) valuing Kearon's personal and real estate at $5,500; and the 1880 Census (Wash., D.C., Dist 041, Fam 420).

[7] "The death of the lovely wife of Mr. D. I. Murphy, of the Pension office, is lamented by a large circle of friends." (*Evening Star*, Jan 28, 1879, p 5 and Jan 29, 1879, p 3.)

[8] *National Republican*, Nov 5, 1881, p 5; *Evening Star*, Nov 5, 1881, p 5.

[9] Prechtel-Kluskens, *supra*. As a result of the 1879 Pension Arrears Act, the workload and backlog increased significantly. Previously, pensions began to accrue from the time they were applied for; under the new law, pensions accrued from the date of the applicant's discharge from military service. Suddenly, tens of thousands of veterans found themselves facing the possible collection of fifteen years' worth of monthly payments all at once. Claims skyrocketed.

[10] *Evening Star*, June 16, 1904, p 14; Register of Officers (etc), as of July 1, 1883, GPO 1883, p 532. Murphy had joined the pension office during the administration of Republican Ulysses Grant and had continued working in that office during the administrations of Republicans Hayes, Garfield and Arthur.

[11] President Garfield's assassin was Charles Guiteau.

[12] As New York's Port Collector during the Tammany Hall era, Arthur had been identified with the most corrupt forces in politics. Taking a percentage of taxes collected, he had bettered his $6,500 salary as Collector several fold, earning more than $50,000 before being fired by Rutherford B. Hayes. Arthur's accomplishments as President included signing the Chinese Exclusion Act, which limited immigration by unsavory Chinese, and issuing an order that let tens of thousands of white settlers take possession of land a federal treaty had granted to native American tribes. Upon taking office, Cleveland quickly ordered the white settlers out of the tribes' territory, fortifying his reputation as a principled man.

[13] *National Tribune*, April 27, 1893, p 7. See also Register of Officers (etc) as of July 1, 1885, GPO 1885, Vol 1, p 487, and Register of Officers (etc) as of July 1, 1887, GPO 1887, Vol 1, p 513.

[14] "Cleveland's Veto of the Texas Seed Bill," in *The Writings and Speeches of Grover Cleveland*, Cassell Publishing, NY, 1892, p 450. Drought had ruined crops in several Texas counties, and Congress had voted to help Texas farmers by appropriating funds to buy seeds for them; but Cleveland vetoed the expenditure, saying, "I can find no warrant for such an appropriation in the Constitution, and I do not believe that the power and duty of the general government ought to be extended to the relief of individual suffering which is in no manner properly related to the public service or benefit. Though the people support the Government, the Government should not support the people. The friendliness and charity of our countrymen can always be relied upon to relieve their fellow-citizens in misfortune... Federal aid in such cases encourages the expectation of paternal care on the part of the government and weakens the sturdiness of our national character." Democrat Cleveland vetoed the Texas Seed bill on February 16, 1887.

[15] Calvin D. Linton, ed., The Bicentennial Almanac, Thomas Nelson, 1976, p 228.

[16] *Evening Star*, March 1, 1888, p 1.

[17] Tanner served as Pension Commissioner for only five months, giving jobs to disabled veterans and liberally approving pensions. Hayes requested his resignation in September, 1888, and Tanner opened a law practice devoted to securing pensions for disabled vets.

[18] In December of 1885, Dominick sold an investment lot in the District, adjacent to one being sold by his brother Edward, for $2,160, or close to a year's salary. (*Evening Star,* Dec 26, 1885, p 5.) The transaction suggests that the two brothers may have been making investments together but leaves unclear how or when Dominick acquired the property in the first place. When his father, Dominick Murphy, died in 1878, his brother Joe had enough money for a major expansion of his textile mills; perhaps Dominick had found a way to pass wealth to all of his sons.

[19] *National Tribune*, April 27, 1893, p 7. The Washington City Directories of 1888 and 1889 list him as Chief Clerk and Clerk in the Pension office; but the 1890 Directory lists both him and his nephew, John D. Kinney, as "claims," sharing the same office address, 930 F Street, NW. The following year, their claims business moved a tick to 941 F Street, but Murphy himself was still living with his sons at the Kearon house, 614 M Street NW, until he moved out, probably in November of 1891, to his own apartment at 403 M Street, NW. By 1893, Murphy had moved to 911 T Street, NW, where his nephew and now business partner John Kinney soon joined him – the two men separated by twenty-two years but having bachelorhood in common.

[20] Register of Officers and Agents (etc), 1889, Vol 1, p 76; Wash D.C. Directory, 1888-1890, Robt Kearon ("chf claims div 4th aud.") In the Register as of July 30, 1881, p 70, and thereafter, Kearon was listed as a Division Chief. The responsibility of the 4th Auditor's office primarily related to receipts and expenditures by the Navy, but it included naval pension claims and miscellaneous other (non-naval) claims. (See Robert Mayo, The Treasury Department and Its Various Fiscal Bureaus, Wm. Q. Force, 1847, Chpt IX, Office of the Fourth Auditor.) The nature of the responsibility for general claims is reflected in the listing for Kearon in the 1879 City Directory, "in chge gen claims div 4th aud o."

[21] *Evening Star*, Oct 8, 1890, p 6.

[22] 1870 U.S. Census, Washington Ward 3, Fam 1393; 1880 U.S. Census, Washington City Dist 41, Fam 420. When the Washington Choral Society began extending membership invitations, it included both Nellie and her Irish Catholic music teacher, Miss Mollie Byrne, the daughter of Mr. and Mrs. Patrick A. Byrne (*Evening Star*, July 1, 1893.) Patrick A. Byrne was in real estate (1885 Wash. D.C. City Directory) and his daughter Mary ("Mollie") was a music teacher (1888 Wash. D.C. City Directory.) Presumably, the younger Nellie Kearon was one of her students.

[23] *Evening Star*, June 29, 1895, p 18.

[24] Miss Byrne sang both as a soloist and in choral performances at churches, paid classical concerts, and other events. *Evening Star*, Jan 2, 1880, p 4; Jan 17, 1880, p 8; Jan 19, 1880, p 4; Dec 21, 1881, p 2; April 27, 1882, p 8; March 24, 1883, p 3; May 23, 1883, p 8; May 2, 1885, p 2; March 11, 1886, p 3; May 25, 1889, pp 3 and 12; April 17, 1890, p 8; April 19, 1890, p 11; Dec 24, 1890, p 3; and the *National Republican*, April 16, 1881, p 4. By 1890, Miss Byrne was being referred to as a "well known and distinguished concert singer." (*Evening Star*, Nov 8, 1890, p 9.) She was also associated with the Franz Abt Club when it organized a series of concerts in Atlantic City (*Evening Star*, June 22, 1889, p 5.)

[25] *Evening Star*, May 26, 1884, p 1; May 27, 1884, p 1; March 30, 1889, p 2; Jan 31, 1890, p 6. The "Unity Club" was one of several clubs interested in art, literature and metaphysics where "free exchanges of views could be given." (*National Republican*, April 15, 1876, p 1.)

[26] Moore was the Irish Catholic writer of prose, poetry and song who had married a Presbyterian and spent his life trying to promote harmony between faiths in Ireland. He had traveled to America, had opposed American slavery, and had been admitted to the American Philosophical Society in Philadelphia.

[27] Thomas Moore's "The Last Rose of Summer" was one of the most popular tunes known to the Irish in America – sad, but full of meaning for people who'd lost loved ones. It was set to a traditional Irish tune called "Aislean an Oigfear," or "The Young Man's Dream." Its lyrics: 'Tis the last rose of summer,/ Left blooming alone;/ All her lovely companions/ Are faded and gone;/ No flower of her kindred,/ No rose-bud is nigh,/ To reflect back her blushes/ Or give sigh for sigh!// I'll not leave thee, thou lone one,/ To pine on the stem;/ Since the lovely are sleeping,/ Go, sleep thou with them;/ Thus kindly I scatter/ Thy leaves o'er the bed,/ Where thy mates of the garden/ Lie scentless and dead.// So soon may *I* follow,/ When friendships decay,/ And from love's shining circle/ The gems drop away!/ When true hearts lie withered,/ And fond ones are flown,/ Oh! who would inhabit/ This bleak world alone?

[28] NARA Passport Applications, 1795-1905, 1890-1892, Roll 368, 23 Apr 1891 – 30 Apr 1891.

[29] *Sunday Herald*, Nov 1, 1891, p 5 and Nov 8, 1891, p 16.

[30] The Washington City Directory of 1891 still listed Dominick's residence as 614 M Street nw (the Kearon home); the 1892 Director lists his new residence as 403 M Street nw.

[31] *National Tribune*, Jan 12, 1893, p 7 and *Evening Star*, Jan 24, 1893, p 9.

[32] *Evening Star*, June 16, 1904, p 14; 1894 Washington City Directory; *Register of Officers (etc) as of July 1, 1895*, GPO 1895, Vol 1, p 683.

[33] *National Tribune*, April 13, 1893, p 6. The claim that Murphy was too young to have fought in the war is questionable. Murphy turned eighteen before the war ended, and many volunteered at a younger age, such as the fourteen-year-old Dominic Murphy who enlisted in Philadelphia as a bugler in the 13th Pennsylvania Cavalry on Nov 9, 1861, and after three years' service, was chief bugler of the regiment. (Bates, *supra*, Vol 3, pp 1267, 1275 and 1282.)

[34] *National Tribune*, March 22, 1900, p 4. The claim should probably be assessed against a background of both parties claiming to be the champions of those who had loyally served in the War; Grover Cleveland was otherwise known for his fiscal conservatism.

[35] *Evening Star*, July 1, 1893, p 16, June 29, 1895, p 18, and March 16, 1907, Part 3, p 8; *Washington Herald*, Jan 26, 1908, p 15. Date of death was June 30, 1893. She was buried at St. Aloysius, the couple's parish church where she had regularly sung in the choir.

[36] *Baltimore Sun*, July 3, 1893, p 2.

240

[37] *Evening Star,* Oct 31, 1893, p 1. Seven years later, the details of one such reduction in pay was in evidence at a murder trial: Murphy had reduced Benjamin Snell's salary from $1800 to $1200 per year; Snell was on trial for the 1899 murder of a thirteen-year-old girl; first called as a juror, Murphy was excused because of his knowledge of Snell; he was then called as a witness about the reduction in pay, but he was not allowed to testify. *Washington Times,* Jan 21, 1900 p 3 and Jan 31, 1900 p 8; *Evening Times,* Jan 19, 1900, p 2 and Jan 30, 1900, p 2.

[38] The 1893 City Directory listed the Murphy residence as 403 M Street nw. The 1894 directory, both alphabetically and in the Government listings at p 1073, listed it as 911 T Street nw, the same address as for John D. Kinney. See also John D. Kinney in the 1897 D.C. Directory, and both John and his mother, Hannah Kinney, in the 1901 Directory.

[39] *Evening Star,* Nov 22, 1894, p 2.

[40] *Washington Times,* July 21, 1895, p 5.

[41] *Evening Star,* Aug 7, 1895, p 1 and Aug 8, 1895, p 1. The D.C. Registrar of Wills was another position appointed by the President.

[42] *Evening Star,* Feb 5, 1896, p 7.

[43] *Evening Star,* June 18, 1894, p 8; *Washington Times,* Nov 25, 1909, p 16.

[44] The appointment was May 28, 1886. (*Washington Times,* March 10, 1897, p 2; *Evening Star,* June 16, 1904, p 14.) See also *Washington Times,* May 20, 1896, p 4; 1897 D.C. City Directory; and the brief biography of Murphy under *Key Figures, Statesmen,* in Kenneth Steuer, Pursuit of an Unparalleled Opportunity, Gutenburg Books, Columbia Univ. Press, accessed at http://www.gutenberg-e.org/ steuer/archive/AppendixB/steuer.appendixB.html. The appointment required Senate approval, but the Senate Committee on Pensions approved the nomination easily: to a man, they knew Dominic's brothers, Dennis, James and Edward. After his appointment as Commissioner, Dominick continued his involvement with the Carroll Institute; among other things, he helped organize a dinner in honor of the retiring Archbishop Keene of the District of Columbia, attended by such notables as the Presidents of the Columbian College, Georgetown and Howard Universities, and E.M. Gallaudet of the Deaf and Dumb Institute. (*Evening Star,* Oct 9, 1896, p 5) and at a similar banquet honoring the Archbishop a year later, also attended by Dominic's brother, E.V. Murphy (*Evening Star,* Oct 14, 1897, p 10).

[45] *Evening Star,* Jan 5, 1898, p 4; Susan Sterett, "Husbands & Wives, Dangerousness & Dependence: Public Pensions in the 1860s-1920s," *Denver Law Review,* Jan 2021, citing Megan J. McClintock, "Civil War Pensions and the Reconstruction of Union Families," 83 *J. Am. Hist.* 456, 458 (1996); Kathleen L. Gorman, "Civil War Pensions," Virginia Center for Civil War Studies at Virginia Tech, accessed at https://www.essentialcivilwarcurriculum.com/ civil-war-pensions.html.

[46] Register of Officers (etc) as of Sept 30, 1871, GPO 1871, Vol 1, pp 157-161; Register of Officers (etc) as of July 1, 1897, GPO 1897, Vol 1, pp 706-733.

[47] See 1893 and 1897 D.C. Directories; 1897 Register of Offices, p 712.

[48] See 1897 D.C. Directory; 1897 Register of Offices, p 716; Prechtel-Kluskens, *supra.* The Directory lists Nellie Kearon and Nannie Kearon (music teacher) still living at their father's address, "614 M Street nw."

[49] *Washington Times,* Jan 3, 1897, p 6.

[50] *Ibid.* Having brothers well connected in the Senate, with friends on both sides of the aisle, surely didn't hurt either.

[51] *Evening Times,* Feb 12, 1897, p 1.

[52] *Evening Times,* Feb 13, 1897, p 7.

[53] *Evening Star,* March 9, 1897, p 11.

[54] His resignation as effective April 3 (*Washington Times,* June 8, 1904, p 4; *National Tribune,* June 16, 1904, p 5).

[55] District of Columbia Deaths and Burials, 1840-1964, Salt Lake City, Utah, FamilySearch, 2013, FHL Film No 2115025, accessed at Ancestry.com.

[56] *Evening Star,* June 6, 1903, p 8; *Washington Times,* June 8, 1904, p 4; *National Tribune,* Nov 18, 1897, p 6; 1903 D.C. City Directory entry for Joseph James Murphy. The weekly magazine, bought

from Henry M. Beadle, was the successor to the 'Catholic,' which Beadle had started in 1870. It was said to have "the support of Cardinal Gibbons and other leaders of the Catholic Church" (*Washington Times*, May 21, 1904). Where Murphy got money to lend or with which to buy a magazine isn't clear. His salary as Commissioner had been a very healthy $5,000 a year, but that hardly left him enough to become a serious lender. Perhaps it came from the profits made filing government claims during his last term out of office. Murphy was reportedly editor and publisher of *The New Century* between 1903 and 1905 (*Catholic Advance*, Wichita, Kansas, May 3, 1930, p 3) but he is mentioned as manager of the weekly before that ("Carroll Institute Banquet" in the *Washington Times*, Feb 5, 1902, p 8). His son Joseph James Murphy left the weekly when he was appointed editor of the *Boston Republic* in 1903 and Dominic then took over the editor's duties until he sold the paper in 1904 (*Evening Star*, Sept 18, 1903, p 3; *Washington Times*, May 21, 1904, p 12).

[57] *Evening Star*, Oct 14, 1897, pp 10 and 15. The event was a tribute to Archbishop John J. Keane.

[58] *Evening Star*, Nov 25, 1897, p 12. The executive committee then met in Murphy's office (*Evening Star*, Nov 30, 1897, p 16). At the event, the guest speaker from Ireland, a Miss Gonne, Murphy and others spoke against the arbitration treaty between Great Britain and the U.S. (*Evening Star*, Dec 13, 1897, p 9; *Evening Times*, Dec 13, 1897, p 2.)

[59] *Evening Star*, Jan 7, 1898, p 16.

[60] *Washington Times*, March 16, 1898, p 5; *Evening Star*, March 16, 1898, p 10; *Evening Times*, March 16, 1898, p 6. His fellow judges at the Gonzaga debate included a Justice of the U.S. Supreme Court.

[61] *Evening Star*, Nov 25, 1899, p 10.

[62] *Washington Times*, Nov 30, 1899, p 4.

[63] *Evening Times*, Dec 2, 1899, p 1. (The judges found for the affirmative. *Washington Times*, Dec 3, 1899, p 3.)

[64] *Washington Times*, March 18, 1900, p 7; *Evening Star*, March 17, 1900, p 11 and March 19, 1900, p 10.

[65] *Evening Star*, June 23, p 2. In an early attempt at diversity, it was widely understood, and so reported, that the five-member Commission would include one Protestant, one Jew, one Catholic, one woman, and one "colored" man. The Catholic seat would likely go to Murphy; the "colored" seat to Professor George W. Cook of Howard University.

[66] *Washington Times,* June 8, 1904, p 4. Murphy is listed in the D.C. City Directories, 1902 through 1904, along with Thomas and Sherburne Hopkins, as part of the firm of "claims and patents" lawyers with offices in the Washington Loan and Trust Building. The 1902 listing reflects that Murphy joined the law firm between about December of 1900 and November of 1901. See also his obituary in *The Catholic Advance*, Wichita, Kansas, May 3, 1930, p 3. What he knew about patents and patent law is less than clear.

[67] Murphy also served as toastmaster at the St. Patrick's Day banquet. (*Evening Star*, March 4, 1901, pp 17-18, March 7, 1901, p 2 and March 19, 1901, p 10; *Washington Times*, March 5, 1901, p 5 and March 19, 1901, p 3.)

[68] The Asylum at the corner of 10th and G Street was sold to private parties for $450,000. (*Evening Times*, May 16, 1901, pp 2 & 3.)

[69] *Washington Times,* July 8, 1901, p 2.

[70] *Evening Star*, Jan 9, 1902, p 3 and May 5, 1902, p 13. At the latter event, one guest, the Chinese minister Mr. Wu Ting Fang, was asked to give a speech, and when he was finished, a club member "told an amusing anecdote at the expense of the Chinese minister." The modern reader may question contemporaneous reports that the minister thought the anecdote funny.

[71] *Washington Times,* Feb 16, 1902, p 26, and March 18, 1902, p 3.

[72] *Evening Star*, June 6, 1903, p 8; *Washington Times*, June 6, 1903, p 2.

[73] *Evening Star*, March 16, 1904, p 6.

[74] *Washington Times*, Sept 12, 1898, p 3.

[75] *Evening Star*, Feb 6, 1900, p 11.

[76] *Evening Times*, Sept 20, 1900, p 2.

[77] *Washington Times*, Nov 3, 1900, p 3.

---

[78] *Washington Times*, Sept 20, 1900, p 4.

[79] *Evening Times,* Nov 2, 1900, p 4. Murphy was quoted as saying, "Within the past month there have been two denials of my statement, both, I presume, coming from the Republican National Committee…If General Palmer, or any other member of the pension committee want the names of other gentlemen who know the facts in this matter, I shall be glad to furnish them. In this last denial, the three gentlemen who sign it have a great deal to say about the President's liberal attitude toward the pensioners of the civil war. This may do very well for a stump speech on the eve of election, but these same members of the G.A.R. committee, on several visits to Washington after the interview above referred to, told a very different story. Some of the gentlemen on the committee were loud in denouncing the attitude of this Administration toward the civil war veterans."

[80] *Washington Times*, Nov 3, 1900, p 2; see also *Evening Star*, Nov 3, 1900, p 16.

[81] *Washington Times*, June 16, 1901, p 2.

[82] *Evening Star*, Sept 21, 1901, p 16.

[83] *Evening Star*, Feb 7, 1902, p 10.

[84] *Washington Times*, Oct 10, 1903, p 7.

[85] A later investigation would conclude that the cause of the explosion had been internal – that burning coal next to a compartment containing ammunition had ignited and caused the explosion. But at the time, a Naval Commission decided (somewhat self-servingly) that the cause had been *external,* that a mine of some sort must have damaged the ship from the outside. (There'd been a "natural tendency to look for reasons for the loss that did not reflect upon the Navy." H. G. Rickover, *How the Battleship Maine Was Destroyed* (Annapolis, MD.: Naval Inst. Press, 1995 ed.), p 95; Louis Fisher, *Destruction of the Maine*, Law Library of Congress, August 4, 2009, accessed at https://www.loc.gov/law/help/usconlaw/pdf/Maine.1898.pdf.)

[86] Louis A. Pérez, *War of 1898: The United States and Cuba in History and Historiography*, "Intervention and Intent," (1998) p 49.

[87] Joshua Polster, <u>Stages of Engagement: U.S. Theatre and Performance, 1898-1949</u>, Routledge, 2015, p 25.

[88] It was a right later exercised when American Secretary of War William Howard Taft declared himself provisional governor of the Island.

[89] "Spanish-American War," "Treaty of Paris," and "Philippine-American War," on Wikipedia.org. Not surprisingly, there were those who opposed the treaty, sensing, like Massachusetts Senator George Hoar, that "This Treaty will make us a vulgar, commonplace empire, controlling subject races and vassal states, in which one class must forever rule and other classes must forever obey."

[90] *Evening Star*, August 24, 1898, p 10.

[91] *Evening Star*, Aug 25, 1898, p 3.

[92] *Ibid.* The Postmaster General said the soldiers had "eagerly" gone forth "to uphold the honor of the flag we all venerate and love, …which constrained us to unsheathe the sword… They went not… as the banded force of a self-aggrandizing power, but… *impelled* by the mandates of civilization, humanity and justice… They return with the highest badge which the citizens of the republic can wear, that of offering all for the *defense* of the country… The flags which come from their bloody conflicts will ever be kept among the treasured emblems of the nation's glory… He would not be a true American who does not recognize that our country is, and is to be, one of the great, peaceful and civilizing influences of the world… [emphasis added].

[93] *Ibid.*

[94] *Ibid.*

[95] *Evening Star*, Sept 16, 1901, p 6, Sept 20, 1901, p 3 and Sept 23, 1901, p 15; *Washington Times*, Sept 20, 1901, p 2, and Sept 21, 1901, p 3.

[96] The French Panama Canal Company had a contract with the government of Gran Columbia to build a canal across Panama (then a part of Columbia), but French efforts had stalled; the French investors were desperate, because their right to build in Panama expired in 1904. In 1901, the U.S. signed a treaty with

Nicaragua giving the U.S. rights to build a canal in that country. Desperate, the French Company began efforts to persuade the U.S. not to build in Nicaragua, but to buy out its rights in Panama instead. 1903, Roosevelt's Secretary of State John Hay negotiated a treaty with Tomas Herran (a graduate of Georgetown law school) giving the U.S. a renewable, hundred-year lease to the canal site in Panama, but in August, 1903, the Columbian Senate refused to ratify the treaty, insisting on terms more favorable to Columbia. An angry Roosevelt did not revert to the Nicaraguan plan. Instead, he struck a deal with the French Canal Company pursuant to which, that November, with the support of American marines and an American gunboat, Panamanian separatists declared a new, independent Republic of Panama; the U.S. guaranteed the independence of the new government; and for fifty million dollars (forty paid to the Canal Company and ten to the Panamanian separatists) the U.S. acquired permanent rights to the Zone. (*Hay-Bunau-Varilla Treaty, Separation of Panama from Columbia,* and *Panama Canal Zone,* all at Wikipedia.org.) The US gunboat Nashville was in Panama after putting down Filipino rebels in Manila who were trying to obtain Philippine independence from the U.S.

[97] Theodore Roosevelt to James Gibbons, June 25, 1903, and April 26, 1904, Theodore Roosevelt Center at Dickinson State University. Cardinal Gibbons, who'd been pushing to give the Filipinos their independence, had asked Roosevelt in 1903 to appoint Murphy to a position with the Commission; in 1904, he had written Roosevelt asking if he could recommend a Mr. Waring to the Commission; Roosevelt replied to Gibbons that he would not recommend Waring "until I find out if they act favorably on my recommendation of Dominic I. Murphy."

[98] In the summer of 1902, Murphy's name was repeatedly mentioned in the Washington Press as a candidate to succeed Commissioner John Wesley Ross as President of the District of Columbia Board of Commissioners, a position essentially equivalent to the capital's mayor. *Evening Star*, July 30, 1902, p 2, Aug 1, 1902, p 1, and Aug 13, 1902, p 2; *Washington Times*, July 31, 1902, p 2, Aug 1, 1902, p 2, Aug 9, 1902, p 2, and Sept 30, 1902, p 3; and *Evening Times*, July 30, 1902, p 2 and Sept 29, 1902, p 3.

[99] The 1905 City Directory – prepared toward the end of 1904 – shows Bessie Atkinson and Dominic I. Murphy with different last names but with the same home address, 1305 Kenyon av nw. Since the last names are different, the listing was probably prepared before their wedding. The couple may have been living together as early as the final months of 1903, when the prior year's Directory was prepared; if so, Bessie's two children by William Atkinson presumably lived with them as well.

[100] "Thomas C. Platt" at Wikipedia.org, citing Platt's own 1910 autobiography.

[101] The official name of the Commission was the Isthmian Canal Commission, but once it was decided to build the canal in Panama, it was often referred to as the Panama Canal Commission.

[102] Perhaps even more importantly, O'Brien's brother was New York's Republican Secretary of State, a political ally of Platt, Odell, and Roosevelt. In his February 24th letter recommending O'Brien to Roosevelt, Governor Odell wrote, "You may recall that I had written you some time ago in behalf of the appointment of General E. C. O'Brien as a member of the Panama Canal Commission. I understand that you cannot see your way clear to make that appointment. I think it would be good politics as well as a gratification to General O'Brien's friends if he could receive the appointment of Secretary to the Commission." Benjamin B. Odell to Theodore Roosevelt, Feb 24, 1904, Theodore Roosevelt Papers at Library of Congress, MS Division, Theodore Roosevelt Digital Library, Dickinson State Univ., www.theodorerooseveltcenter.org.

[103] Thomas Collier Platt to John F. O'Brien, Feb 25, 1904, Theodore Roosevelt Papers, *supra.*

[104] "A Capable Man," March 4, 1904 newspaper article, Theodore Roosevelt Papers, *supra.*

[105] *Washington Evening Star*, June 7, 1904, p 2, June 11, 1904, p 3, *National Tribune*, June 16, 1904, p 5, and *Washington Times*, July 15, 1904, p 2. Murphy must have gotten a heads-up as to what was coming, since on May 4, 1904, as if to clear his schedule, he sold his interest in his weekly news magazine to a Milwaukee man. *Washington Times*, May 21, 1904, p 12; *Washington Evening Star*, May 21, 1904, p 16.

[106] *Evening Star*, June 16, 1904, p 14.

---

[107] *Washington Times,* June 8, 1904, p 4, article under the headline, "Washington Man Wins Canal Commission Plum."

[108] *New York Times,* June 8, 1904; *Washington Times,* June 8, 1904, p 4; *Evening Star,* June 16, 1904, p 14; *National Tribune,* June 16, 1904, p 5.

[109] Yellow fever and malaria had so devastated the workforce as to bring construction to a halt. The theory that mosquitoes were responsible – and that they could be controlled by draining ponds and covering them with oil to prevent insects from breeding – was still the subject of much ridicule. Thinking the Canal would never be built unless disease could be controlled, the Commission engaged the services of Colonel William Gorgas, an army physician, in March 1904, to bring disease under control. "Health Measures during Construction of the Panama Canal," Wikipedia.org.

[110] The nine-member Commission had existed for many years as a largely advisory body without actually having to build anything.

[111] *Washington Times,* June 8, 1904, p 2. Murphy remained at the White House with Roosevelt for "some time" (*Evening Star,* June 8, 1904, p 1).

[112] *Washington Times,* June 8, 1904, p 4.

[113] *Washington Post,* July 19th, 1904 p 5; July 24, 1904, p 12; July 31, p 5. The Commissioners sailed for Panama on July 26th.

[114] *Evening Star,* Aug 2, 1904, p 1; *Washington Post,* Aug 3, 1904, p 7.

[115] Dominic I. Murphy to William Loeb, Aug. 31, 1904, *Theodore Roosevelt Papers,* Library of Congress Manuscript Division, https://theodorerooseveltcenter.org/Research/Digital-Library/Record?libID=o46614, Theodore Roosevelt Digital Library, Dickinson State University.

[116] *Ibid.* The letter implies two other points as well. First, Reverend Marshall was no backwoods country preacher, so being his cousin helped bolster Murphy's own credentials. (Marshall was a former President of Seton Hall, just a few miles outside New York City. As such, he had succeeded Roosevelt's own distant cousin, Reverend James Roosevelt Bayley, as president of that college. Marshall had also started the college's military department, creating the Seton Hall Battalion, commissioning dozens of officers who had served in the Spanish-American War alongside Roosevelt. (Seton Hall Univ. website, ROTC Program, History, at https://www.shu.edu/rotc/history.cfm.) Roosevelt therefore knew of Marshall, and his being Murphy's cousin showed that Murphy was well-connected. Second, the letter suggested that Murphy's connections in Europe were reporting to him on how European papers viewed American tariffs and political affairs. In a world where nothing is more important than being well-connected, Murphy was more worldly than one might expect for a mere pension office clerk, and additional connections in a country like France could never hurt a President looking beyond American shores.

[117] It was generally conceded that due to the brutal climate, disease and working conditions, work on the Canal would have to be performed by men of color. Just weeks after Murphy's appointment, a prediction that laborers would have to be "taken from the United States, preferably from the negro laborers of the Southern States," caused this reaction from the *Washington Post*: "We can see where the canal commission will have difficulty in securing workmen from the South. Every Southern State is already short of toilers, black and white, for the cotton fields and plantations. There are plenty of idle negroes in the Southern cities and States, but they do not take kindly to work at home, and could not be induced to go away from the United States under any promise of profitable reward for their work." *Washington Post,* July 4, 1904, p 6.

[118] *Washington Post,* Sept 15, 1904, p 2.

[119] *Washington Post,* Sept 7, p 4; Sept 16, p 3.

[120] *Washington Post,* Oct 20, 1904, p 9.

[121] *Washington Post,* December 7, 1904, p 4. One Congressman said, "I was unable to find that the Panama Canal Commission has accomplished very much up to date."

[122] *Washington Post*, Sept 16, p 3; Sept 29, p 6; Oct 7, p 4; Oct 9, p 6; Oct 14, p 6; Oct 20, p 6; Oct 25, p 1; Oct 26, p 11; Oct 29, p 9. Of course, work on the Canal hadn't even started yet; once it did, it would go on for ten years.

[123] *Washington Post*, Oct 13, 1904, p 11.

[124] *U.S., Panama Canal Zone, Employment Records and Sailing Lists, 1884-1937*, NARA Record Group 185, Box 27, 1904-1920, accessed via Ancestry.com. On Edward's Service Record Card, in a box intended to record whether the appointment was "Competitive, Excepted, [or] Unclassified," the words "Excepted, Unclassified" have been struck through, replaced with the handwritten note, "Classified. Executive Order 11-15-04." Young Edward went on to life employment in government as a reporter and clerk for the Interior Department.

[125] U.S. officials in Panama admitted that the isthmus was hot, but they downplayed or denied reports of serious sickness. In a September Report on conditions in Panama, the American Minister asserted, "The disagreeable and unhealthy features of the Panama climate have been ridiculously overstated by those who have studied the situation superficially... As a matter of fact there has not been... a single uncomfortable night for sleeping, while the average days have not been hotter than those of New York and Washington. There has been hardly a single instance of serious illness here... When the present able sanitary corps... have carried out their plans... there is no reason why this isthmus should not be one of the healthiest places in the world." (*Washington Post*, Sept 4, 1904, p 2.) Upon his return in December, Congressman Stevens asserted, "There is little sickness that we could discover." (*Washington Post*, Dec 7, 1904, p 4.) While Congressman Stevens' inability to find sickness in Panama may have been because Dr. Gorgas's work was beginning to pay off, many believed there was truth in the other possibility: that the Congressman and other dignitaries had seen no sickness because they hadn't been laboring in the jungles. After all, December also brought complaints that "the canal officials enjoy such luxuries as roof gardens and liveried coachmen at government expense" while clerks and laborers were "forced to live like pigs." (*Washington Post*, Dec 30, 1904, p 4.)

[126] *Washington Post*, Oct 20, 1904, p 9.

[127] Dominic, Bessie, her two children, and Dominic's younger son, Dominic F. Murphy, lived together at 1305 Kenyon Street, NW. Bessie and Dominic were married on October 24, 1904 (*Baltimore Sun*, Oct 25, 1904, p 2, and *Washington Post*, Oct 25, 1904, p 7. Bessie's children were Elizabeth E. "Bessie" Atkinson (b. May, 1889) and Randall W. Atkinson (b. Oct 6, 1894) (see 1900 U.S. Census, Washington D.C., Dist 0052, Fam 316, 1438 V Street).

[128] Minutes of Meetings of the Isthmian Canal Commission, April 23, 1905, pp 11-12, accessed at https://ufdc.ufl.edu/AA 00006399/00011/5x.

[129] *New York Tribune*, May 23, 1905, p 16.

[130] "Gets Tourgee's Consulate,*" New York Times*, May 23, 1905, p 1. Albion Tourgee, a lawyer, a novelist, and a civil rights icon, had advocated for former slaves, battled the KKK, and written novels dramatizing the plight of freedmen in America. In the landmark 1896 case of *Plessey v. Ferguson*, he had argued the unconstitutionality of the Louisiana law mandating segregation of the races. He had founded Bennett College as a normal school for freedmen. In 1897, President McKinley had appointed him U.S. Consul in Bordeaux, France. After eight years' service there, Tourgee had died of uremia on May 21, thought to be caused by a Civil War wound.

[131] *New York Sun*, May 23, 1905, p 3. Also, "Gets Tourgee's Consulate," *supra*, and Official Register, Persons in the Civil, Military & Naval Service of the U.S., G.P.O., Wash. D.C., 1905, 1907.) The news reports of the assignment stated that Murphy would not be replaced as Secretary to the Commission, as its recent reorganization had made the position unnecessary. But the elimination was only temporary. When the Senate failed to confirm Roosevelt's appointment of his friend Joseph Bishop to membership on the Commission itself, the President appointed Bishop to be the Commission's "Press Agent and Historian" instead, at a salary of $10,000 per year. When newspapers scoffed at the idea that the Canal Commission needed such an office, Roosevelt recreated the job of Secretary to the Commission and gave

it to Bishop at the same salary – $10,000 – namely twice what Murphy had been paid (*Washington Herald*, Nov 21, 1906, p 6.)

[132] In the 18th century, as the world's second largest port, Bordeaux had been the most important point of departure for the shipment of Africans to work the sugar cane fields of Haiti.

[133] First was Bessie's mother, Mrs. Catherine B. Throckmorton; later that summer, Dominic's nieces, Edward's twenty-seven-year-old daughter Josephine and Joe's twenty-four-year-old daughter Elizabeth; and lastly, Dominic's forty-year-old niece, Anna Kinney. (*Washington Times*, June 16, 1907, "Personal News and Gossip of the Government Departments" section, p 6; *Washington Herald*, Sept 18, 1907, p 5; *Washington Herald*, Sept 21, 1907, p 5; *Washington Times*, Sept 22, 1907, Society News & Chat, p 4.)

[134] "BANISHING THE POETS: President Sending All the Irish-American Bards Abroad. From the San Francisco Monitor. Editor O'Malley, of the Catholic Sun, brings a serious charge against President Roosevelt. He accuses him of being a bitter enemy of American poets, 'particularly Irish-American poets.' 'It may be that some will undertake to deny this statement,' writes Mr. O'Malley. But he cites some very damaging proof: for instance, 'Once upon a time, Dominic Murphy, at Washington, wrote a poem – something about bats flying in the twilight and red sunshine smoldering in the West. Roosevelt came to power and fixed him so he'd never do it again. He made him consul general at Bordeaux, and hustled him out of the country.'"

Whether Murphy really wrote such a poem is unclear, and whether O'Malley's reference to bats and a red sunset was meant to be taken literally is unknown. But the description of Murphy and his poem was followed by the assertion that Roosevelt had granted consulships to three other Irish Catholics, none of whom spoke the language of the country to which he was assigned. The article concluded, "[W]e see no hope for Mr. O'Malley... He'll go to Timbuctoo, if he doesn't look out." (Unnumbered page from the Sunday *Washington Post*, June 30, 1907 – possibly a page 5 – accessed at Newspapers.com. Next to that article appeared another, titled "Why Women Talk Most," describing how Dr. Marade, the inventor of voice telegraphy, had been experimenting in Paris with the physics of the energy involved in speech. Marade concluded, "Every second when an orator speaks in a hall he works as much as a porter who shoulders luggage weighing 400 pounds." Marade further determined that because of their narrower larynxes, women expend less energy, so that "a woman can talk four times as long as a man with the same expenditure of energy."

[135] In July, 1907, for example – the centennial anniversary of Robert Fulton's famous steamship – Dominic's duties included serving as an honorary U.S. commissioner at the International Maritime Exposition. As such, he had to give a speech showcasing America's role in the development of maritime technology and commerce. The American pavilion featured various American naval vessels and a scale model of the Panama Canal, about which Murphy could speak from experience. (*Washington Post*, April 12, 1907, p 4; *Washington Times*, July 21, 1907, Second Section, p 4; *Evening Star*, Aug 16, 1907, p 10 and Aug 26, 1907, p 10.)

[136] "American handsaws are not known here," he wrote, "the old fashioned 'buck' variety being exclusively used. It seems as though American manufacturers might successfully introduce their saws in this region. Other American tools, the quick-acting screw-driver, for instance, might also find a ready market. At the American pavilion at the Maritime Exposition... at Bordeaux... an American handsaw and a quick-acting screwdriver... were looked upon with admiration and wonder by the French workmen." Monthly Consular and Trade Reports, No 333, Govt Printing Office, June, 1908, accessed at https://www.google.com/books/edition/Monthly_Consular_and_Trade_Reports/FYNJAA AAMAAJ?hl=en&gbpv=1&bsq=Murphy

[137] *Evening Star*, Feb 10, 1909, p 2; *Washington Times*, Feb 10, 1909, p 6; *Philadelphia Inquirer*, Feb 11, 1909, p 5. One of Murphy's reports pointed out that St. Gall accounted for over nine million dollars in annual exports, compared to less than three million each from Basel, Zurich, Geneva and Berne. (Daily Consular and Trade Reports, Bureau of Manufactures, Dept of Commerce and Labor, October 4, 1910, No. 78, p 43, accessed at https://www.google.com/books/edition/Daily_Consular_and_

Trade_Reports/ZUUlAQAAIAAJ?hl=en&gbpv=1&dq=dominick+murphy+consul+switzerland+repo
rts&pg=PA43&printsec=frontcover)

[138] Silk was not a workingman's material, like cotton or wool; it was the fiber of emperors. Since it
required patience for Mulberry trees to grow and for little worms to do the work of spinning it, it carried
a price tag to match. But in 1891, Hilaire de Chardonnet had started to produce artificial silk, made
directly from tree cellulose. The idea of making things out of trees was catching the imagination of
chemists everywhere. By 1910, Henri and Camille Dreyfus were using wood pulp to make cellulose
acetate for motion picture film and toilet articles. In November, 1910, a British consular report noted
that "a considerable portion" of the increase in trade from Birmingham to the United States was "due
to the growth of shipments of one product – wood-pulp yarn, or artificial silk." (*Daily Consular and
Trade Reports, Issued by the Bureau of Manufactures, Dept of Commerce & Labor, Washington*, No
106, November 5, 1910.) In the year that followed, American Viscose opened its first rayon factory at
Marcus Hook (Russell Weigley *et al*, Philadelphia, a Three Hundred Year History, W.W. Norton &
Co. (1982), *supra*, p 533). Meanwhile, Henri and Camille Dreyfus produced the first acetate continuous
filament yarn in 1913. Most of their trees' cellulose went into film for motion pictures and into lacquers
to protect the fabric wraps of German Zeppelins and airplanes.

[139] When Murphy returned home briefly in March of that year, the *Washington Post* quoted his remarks
about the changes to Washington's skyline during his six years abroad. "I always liked Washington," he
said, "but after several years spent abroad, where I had opportunity to see the great capitals of Europe, I
am more than ever in love with it." (*Washington Post*, March 10, 1913, p 6.) While in D.C., he attended
the annual St. Patrick's banquet (*Evening Star,* March 16, 1913, p 2). The Murphys returned to St. Gall
in May. (Bessie's passport application dated April 14, 1917, asserts that she last left the U.S. on May
7, 1913; Dominic's Emergency Passport Application of December 28, 1918, asserts that he last left the
U.S. about May 10, 1913.)

[140] *Washington Post*, Feb 3, 1914, p 5; *Washington Herald*, Feb 3, 1914, p 2. "[B]y February 1914…
there seems to have been a general belief in government circles that war was inevitable." (James Joll,
The Origins of the First World War, Pearson Education, 1992, p 126.)

[141] *Washington Times*, June 17, 1914, p 7.

[142] The assassination occurred on June 28, 1914. Franz Ferdinand had favored the establishment of a
third crown, a Slavic kingdom which would have freed Serbia from Austrian-Hungarian control. The
aim of his Serbian assassins was to prevent him from doing so, believing such a plan would steal thunder
from Serbian ambitions to reclaim the region for itself. (See "Assassination of Archduke Franz
Ferdinand," Wikipedia.org, citing Luigi Albertini, Origins of the War of 1914, Oxford Univ Press,
1953, pp 87-88.) (Spencer C. Tucker, *The Great War, 1814-1918,* Indiana Univ. Press, 1998, pp 6-10.)

[143] Calling his progressive agenda *New Freedom*, Wilson the Democrat had lowered tariffs, introduced
taxes on incomes and estates, and used the Clayton Antitrust Act to break up big businesses. But Wilson
was also a Presbyterian minister from Georgia, a former Confederate who "infamously segregated the
nation's civil service after decades of racial integration." On June 26, 2020, Princeton University removed
Wilson's name from its public policy school due to his "racist thinking and policies." (Jason Slotkin,
Princeton to Remove Woodrow Wilson's Name from Public Policy School, NPR.org, June 27, 2020,
accessed at https://www.npr.org/sections/live-updates-protests-for-racial-justice/2020/06/27/884310403/
princeton-to-remove-woodrow-wilsons-name-from-public-policy-school.) Wilson intervened repeatedly
in Latin American countries – sending troops to the Dominican Republic, Haiti, Cuba, Panama, Honduras,
and Mexico, saying in 1913, "I am going to teach the South American republics to elect good men." But
when war broke out in Europe, Wilson insisted that America remain neutral, "impartial in thought as well
as in action." ("Woodrow Wilson," Wikipedia.org, and various sources cited therein.)

[144] H. J. Res. 314. Two days after the initiation of war between Great Britain and Germany, the *U. S.
S. Tennessee* sailed from New York with its crew, 24 officers of the Army; various officers of the Navy
and Marine Corps; 8 War Department clerks; a diplomatic advisor from the State Department; the
national director of the American Red Cross and his secretary; 5 representatives of the Treasury

---

Department; $1,500,000 gold coin from the Congressional appropriation; 5 private bankers; $3,000,000 of private bankers' gold; and a messenger. (Henry S. Breckenridge, *Report on Operation of the United States Relief Commission in Europe*, Washington, 1914, accessed at https://books.google.com/books?id=Uh7dxQEACAAJ&pg=PP7&focus=viewport&output=html_text.)

[145] Breckenridge, *supra*.

[146] *Ibid.*, Appendix D, paragraph 12.

[147] Joll, *supra*, p 35. Bulgaria, like the U.S., the Netherlands, and Romania, had quickly declared its neutrality in 1914. (I have opted to modify Joll's spelling of "Rumania" to conform to the country's current official English spelling.)

[148] *Evening Star*, March 7, 1915, p 12. Still in Amsterdam on April 17, Murphy applied for a passport there.

[149] Russia had been instrumental in freeing Bulgaria from Ottoman rule, a fact which might have encouraged Bulgaria to side with Russia, France and Britain in the war. But King Ferdinand had significant personal ties to Austria, which was allied with Germany. (He'd been baptized in Vienna, his godfather was Austria's Archduke Maximilian, and he was serving as an officer in the Austro-Hungarian army when he was elected prince of Bulgaria in 1887.) Besides, King Ferdinand had been impressed by the anti-Russian rhetoric of his new prime minister, Vasil Radoslavov. He had declared Bulgaria a kingdom, with himself as tsar, or king in 1908. The 1878 Treaty of San Stefano, between Russia and the Ottoman Empire, had recognized Bulgaria as consisting of Moesia, Macedonia and Thrace, but the other Great Powers had rejected giving Bulgaria so much, and Bulgaria was left a mere fraction of its former size, with many Bulgars left outside the newly recognized state. Bulgaria had fought two wars in 1912-1913, one successful against the Ottomans, the other unsuccessful when Bulgaria attacked its former allies in an effort to regain Macedonia. (Jacob Gould Schurman, The Balkan Wars, 1912-1913, 1916, accessed courtesy of Project Gutenberg, at https://www.gutenberg.org/files/11676/11676.txt.) In 1912 through June of 1914, there was much talk of the French making a sizable loan to Bulgaria, but due to poor coordination between the French government and its private bankers, the French loan never materialized, while German and Austria-Hungry came through with a large loan of their own. (Joll, *supra*, pp 125, 152; "Bulgaria During World War I," Wikipedia.org.) Then, Russia backed Serbia (a Bulgarian rival in the Balkan land dispute), further alienating Bulgaria from Russia. Finally, in October of 1915, Germany promised Bulgaria what it most wanted: restoration of its lost territories. (Joll, *supra*, pp 93, 125; "Bulgaria During World War I," *supra*.)

[150] *New York Times*, March 28, 1916, p 3; *Evening Star*, March 29, 1916, p 22.

[151] His signature appears as the approving authority on emergency passport applications issued in Sofia between May of 1916 and June of 1918, for the benefit of American missionaries, businessmen, and their wives seeking passage out of the Balkans, back to the U.S. (General Emergency Passport Applications, 1907-1923, 1915-1925, for Bulgaria.)

[152] *Evening Star*, May 17, 1919, Part Two, p 10.

[153] Emergency Passport Applications, Argentina thru Venezuela, 1906-1925, 1914-1919, Vol 1, Holland, No 475 for Dominic Murphy, dated Oct 26 and Oct 28, 1916, purpose: "visiting my daughter at Stockholm, and afterwards returning to my post at Sofia, Bulgaria."

[154] *Ibid*; and Passport No 473, obtained October 26, 1916, referenced in the Diplomatic Passport Application of Bessie T. Murphy dated April 14, 1917, Special Diplomatic Passport Applications, 1916-1925, 1916-1917, Vol 1.

[155] *Evening Star*, Nov 22, 1916, p 10; *Washington Post*, Nov 22, 1916, p 1.

[156] *Evening Star*, Dec 31, 1916, p 2.

[157] Germany's Foreign Minister had made a proposal for Mexico to consider in the event the United States should join the war against Germany. Mexico, Zimmerman proposed, might ally itself with Germany and make war on the U.S. Its reward, if successful, would be that Mexico could recover Texas, Arizona and New Mexico for itself.

[158] Murphy's consular reports included, on January 25, "Bulgarian Cereal Acreage Reported by Consul General." On January 29, "Turkey's Foreign Commerce for the Last Half of 1916." And on January 30, "Bulgaria's Regulations on Commerce with the Enemy." *Washington Post*, March 15, 1918, p 5.

[159] *Washington Post*, Dec 25, 1917, p 2. Background information about Murphy, at article's end, is here omitted.

[160] To Italy's great chagrin, at war's end, it was in fact prevented from doing so. Italy had entered the war on the Allied side only because the Treaty of London promised to honor its territorial claims in Dalmatia. Then, during the war, Italy was allowed to occupy essentially all the territory it had been promised. But by advocating self-determination, Wilson's 14 Points effectively negated Italy's gains; most of Dalmatia ended up taken back from Italy in the final post-war negotiations, becoming Albania and Yugoslavia.

[161] The "confidential" report received by the State Department raised disturbing questions about the Murphy interview:

The *Kambana*, the Germanophile newspaper of Sofia, has published an interview with Mr. Murphy, consul general of the United States at Sofia, of which the following is the text:

"According to the latest information, the government and Senate at Washington have intimated to those whom it concerns that the military aims of Italy will not be allowed to extend to Dalmatia. This will accelerate the conclusion of peace.

"The Americans understand the motives which urge the bolsheviki of Petrograd to hasten to conclude the peace. London and Paris have been informed that the commercial interests of the United States demand that the war should cease as soon as possible in order that American ships may be free to sail for Europe with raw materials and merchandise destined for the exhausted peoples of Europe.

"Consul general Murphy who is of Irish origin and who has the reputation of being a partisan of the liberty of the oppressed peoples has convinced his government by the reports sent by him during the past two years of the legitimate nature of the Bulgarian claims to unite Macedonia, the Dobrudja and the valley of the Morova to Bulgaria.

"He affirms that America will never pronounce against this Bulgarian unity. In spite of the threats of Wilson, the relations between the United States and Bulgaria will not be broken off, for it is the Senate that decided this.

"Murphy recalls with regret the malicious declarations and acts of the American Ambassador to Berlin, Gerard, who as an enthusiastic friend of the *entente* contributed to the rupture of relations between Germany and the United States. Wilson did not dare oppose Gerard, as the latter was one of the most influential propagandists for his election."

– *Washington Post*, Feb 23, 1918, pp 1-2. (Also *Evening Star*, Feb 23, 1918, p 3.)

[162] *Evening Star*, May 17, 1919, Part Two, p 10.

[163] *Washington Post*, Feb 23, 1918, p 1. The full article:

DENIES SOFIA 'VIEWS'

Consul General Murphy Did Not
Denounce Gerard, as Quoted.

VICTIM OF TEUTON INTRIGUE

Germans Apparently Hope to Drive
District Man from Bulgaria

Fear His Influence at the Foreign Office – Harsh
Criticism of Wilson Published in Semi-Official Organ

and Credited to Murphy Denied by Him in Cablegram
– Had Stirred the Allied Diplomats – Some Skeptical

By ALBERT W. FOX.

The attention of the State Department has been directed, through confidential reports from Allied Sources, to a remarkable situation involving Dominic I. Murphy, the American representative and consul general at Sofia, Bulgaria. The semiofficial Bulgarian newspaper *Kambana* has printed what purports to be the quoted language of an interview with Mr. Murphy wherein the latter pledges the United States to remain friendly to Bulgarian aspirations and predicts early peace forced by President Wilson to benefit America at the expense of the exhausted allies.

Mr. Murphy is also quoted as having denounced Mr. Gerard, former American Ambassador to Berlin, and having claimed that President Wilson would have rebuked him had it not been for the fact that Gerard was a "heavy contributor to the election of Wilson."

Comes From Three Sources.

After receiving word from three different allied sources as to the existence of the alleged interview, the State Department took immediate action and cabled to Mr. Murphy for confirmation or denial.

Mr. Murphy's excellent record in the service made officials here loath to believe that he could have even informally expressed the views attributed to him.

Reply from Mr. Murphy has now been received by cable, and it has put the whole matter in an entirely new light. He states that he never gave such an interview as printed in the *Kambana* and adds further that the whole affair appears to be a deliberate effort on the part of German and Bulgarian officials to discredit him for reasons which can be readily understood.

Might Damage Teutons.

The State Department has other information indicating that German agents are seeking deliberately to get Mr. Murphy out of Sofia on the ground that he has too much influence with the Bulgarian foreign office, and is in a position to obtain information concerning German underground methods which might be damaging to the Teuton cause.

Mr. Murphy, who is a native of the District of Columbia and very well known in Washington, is described by officials as a man of strong personality and the most lofty ideals of patriotism, and opinion here is crystalizing into the conviction that he has been made the victim of a German-Bulgarian plot.

The United States government has not severed relations with Bulgaria, and it is an open secret that this government hopes to avoid the necessity of doing so.

May Strain Situation

But if the Bulgarian government is found guilty of having had a hand in this intrigue against the American representative, the situation may easily become strained to the breaking point.

An embarrassing feature of the situation is that while officials who know Mr. Murphy are convinced that he never formally or informally expressed the views attributed to him, some of the allied diplomats are still skeptical. They say that Mr. Murphy had apparently made no effort to repudiate the interview until his attention was called to it by the State Department.

The interview was printed in Sofia on December 19, they point out, and there would have been plenty of time for repudiation, even by mail.

Further Details Expected.

The State Department expects to probe deeper into the matter in the hope of ascertaining the reasons which prompted the German-Bulgarian propagandists to conspire against the American consul-general. Further word from Mr. Murphy is also expected.

The *Post* concluded by quoting the "confidential" report received by the State Department, above. See also *Evening Star*, Feb 23, 1918, p 3 and *Evening Public Ledger*, Feb 23, 1918, p 3.

[164] *Washington Post*, Feb 24, 1918, p 4. (Digitally, pp 23 and 90 of 131 at Newspapers.com.)

[165] *Washington Post*, March 15, 1918, p 1, 5.

[166] Robert Lansing to Pleasant Stovall, Sept 25, 1918 (*Papers Relating to the Foreign Relations of the United States, 1918, Russia, Vol I*, Doc 641, accessed at https://history.state.gov/historical documents/frus1918Russiav01/d641).

[167] *Philadelphia Inquirer*, Oct 2, 1918, p 2.

[168] *Evening Star*, Sept 30, 1918, p 1 and May 17, 1919, Part Two, p 10.

[169] *Washington Times*, Sept 30, 1918, pp 1-2. "Murphy is sole agent of U.S. in Bulgaria, other diplomats having left, so any peace initiatives would go through him."

[170] *Evening Star*, Sept 30, 1918, p 1.

[171] *Evening Public Ledger*, Sept 30, 1918, p 8.

[172] *Cincinnati Enquirer*, Oct 3, 1918, p 6.

[173] *Evening Star*, Sept 30, 1918, p 6. (I have modified the original spelling of "Rumania" to conform to modern usage.)

[174] *Evening Star*, January 27, 1919, p 1.

[175] *Evening Public Ledger*, Jan 27, 1919, p 3; *Washington Times,* January 29, 1919, p 8.

[176] *Evening Star*, Feb 23, 1919, p 19. The occasion was a luncheon at the Palais D'Orsay in Paris, celebrating the birthday of George Washington; those attending also included French President Poincare, the American labor leader Samuel Gompers, Ambassador William Sharp and Admiral William Benson.

[177] Arriving Passenger and Crew Lists, New York, 1820-1957, May 2, 1919, on the ship Nieuw Amsterdam, accessed at Ancestry.com. (Dominic and Bessie had left Plymouth, England, on April 21st.) *Evening Star*, May 17, 1919, Part Two, p 10.

[178] *Evening Public Ledger*, June 25, 1919, p 8 and June 26, p 11. Also on the podium with Mr. Murphy was Major Bill Hollenbeck, a former football star at the University of Pennsylvania who had served overseas in a general staff capacity; Hollenbeck criticized the absence of the American flag in the public schools, "declaring that reverence to the flag was essential if this country is to successfully combat the evils of bolshevism now threatening to envelop it."

[179] *Washington Post*, Sept 10, 1919, p 2.

[180] *Washington Post*, Sept 7, 1919, p 1.

[181] *Washington Post*, Sept 10, 1919, pp 1-2, and Sept 28, 1919, p 1.

[182] *Washington Post*, Feb 21, 1919, p 6.

[183] *Washington Post*, Mar 30, 1919, p 15; *Evening Star*, March 30, 1919, p 20. The assertion that Murphy would be "closely questioned" might mean he would be closely questioned by the news media or others concerned about pro-German sympathies; the *Post* article had begun by pointing out that the State Department had said it would probably not pursue the matter.

[184] *Evening Star,* Feb 17, 1927, p 17.

[185] *Evening Star,* Sept 20, 1919, p 2. The article suggests he was appointed in September, but the assignment had been reported in the July 1919 issue of the *Foreign Service Journal* (Vol I, No 5, p 6) accessed at htes/defattps://afsa.org/siult/files/fsj-1919-07-july_0.pdf, and Murphy's passport application dated July 10, 1919, gives his destinations as England, Holland and Sweden, and states his purpose as, "to take charge of consulate at Stockholm." (Special Diplomatic Passport Applications, 1916-1925, 1919, NARA Vol 6, p 889 & 890.)

[186] In August, 1920, there was a report about the dissolution of the national flour monopoly in Bulgaria, as a result of which Murphy said it was a great time for American manufacturers to do business there (*Washington Post*, Oct 3, 1920, p 13.) He later reported that the outlook for Swedish iron output was gloomy (*Washington Post*, Oct 17, 1920, p 4).

[187] *Evening Star*, July 17, 1924, p 9.

[188] See, for example, *Chicago Tribune*, April 14, 1930, p 20; *The Catholic Advance* (Wichita, Kansas), May 3, 1930, p 3; *Philadelphia Record*, April 15, 1930.

10. Joseph J. "Jimmy" Carvin

In 1862, when he was eight, war took his brother James. When he was ten, steam-powered, dust-filled cotton mills took his parents, and that same year, the government returned his brother Thomas to the hell that was war. battle lines. His family had neither Murphy renown nor Murphy advantages. He and his brothers might have been divvied up among the city's orphanages were it not for Ann, dear Ann, who took them in and (briefly) two of their sisters (Mary and Elizabeth) too, though Ann and her husband already had four children of their own.

The Austin household at 1347 Howard Street barely rose above the water that flowed through the culverts and down to the river, especially on rainy days. Joe and his brothers (William thirteen, George eight and Charles five) lived on the edge of despair, but Ann and George gave them hope. [1] And fragile as hope could be, it at least let them totter between failure and success, between today's bad luck and the possibility of good luck tomorrow. Absent luck, life would bring nothing but pain, so it had to be real. Luck became his lodestar, his mentor, his guide.

And so, comparing his healthy limbs to the sawed-off stumps of amputees, he understood how lucky he'd been to be too young for the war, to be spared the bloodshed and horror: luckier than James, who'd ended up dead, luckier than Thomas, whose nightmares persisted. About two million men had fought to preserve the Union, and half a million had been killed or wounded. The way he saw it, the odds had been three to one that James and Thomas would survive unscathed; luck had clearly not been with them. And though he'd returned alive, Thomas had been swallowed up by helplessness, succumbing to bad luck even after it ended. Everyone suffers *some* bad luck. If a person understands the fickle lady, calculates chances, takes good risks but not bad ones, bounces back from the bad, uses opportunities to advantage, he may well find a path through life. Though small for his age, Joe figured he could do well at some sports, if not others, and he could follow them all, even if only as a spectator – foot racing, bicycle racing, horse racing, fishing, wrestling, boxing, and any game of chance that called for strategy or skill.

The fifteen years between their ages meant he'd never been close to his brother James. But Ann, Catherine and Mary had all shared memories of their oldest brother. Clearly they'd all admired the dutiful man. They'd even begun to call him by his middle name – Jimmy – as if they saw something of their beloved older brother in him. He was officially Joe, but to family and friends, he would always be Jimmy, like his unlucky brother. As easy as a coin flip, he could have been either one of his older brothers; as it was, he really had been born lucky.[2]

Though no longer welcome in the Catholic church herself, Ann had honored their parents' wishes that they be buried in St. Michaels cemetery. She'd encouraged "Jimmy" and his brothers to attend St Michael's.[3] And Mary, dear sister Mary, had even gone to jail for Thomas. Joe could see the value his sisters placed on caring for their family. And so he tried to be as good to them as they were to him; he tried to get the most he could from school; he helped Ann with his nephews as much as he could.

He was ten when brother Thomas married Anna Siner, twelve when Thomas seduced Emily Hartman. Always fearless, always daring, always out to have fun, always quick to take a risk, Jimmy admired Thomas in a way, but one thing kept him from wanting to be exactly like his living older brother: Thomas was reckless. Thomas was selfish. He made bad choices, not just once or twice, but all the time. And he didn't care a whit about long term consequences.

Jimmy felt sure he could do better.

In 1867, perhaps as a result of the Emily Hartmann scandal, George, Ann, their children and her four younger siblings all moved out of the old neighborhood, away from their home on Howard Street, away from the Murphy mill, the Austin brass foundry and Chenango Street. Then they moved a second time, even farther north, so that by 1870, they were living off Diamond Street, west of Norris Square, nearly an hour's walk from their childhood haunts.[4] For reasons unknown, George Austin had gone out on his own, getting work as a common laborer.[5]

They were not alone in their move northward. The city itself now extended about seven miles up the Delaware river. Farmland had been built over with more row houses and industry. The city had earned itself a new nickname, 'the workshop of the world.' Radiators and factory whistles hissed. In Kensington, people worked behind the brick-walled, iron-barred windows of W. W. Altemus & Son, Richard C. Borchers & Co., the John H. Dearnley Co., and the Philadelphia Textile Machinery Company. They made bobbin winders, warpers, spoolers, beamers, dryers, pneumatic conveyors, condensers, nappers, carders – always more machines with which to make carpets and clothes, weaves and knits, broadcloths, twills satins and more at Mills like those of Dominick and Joseph Murphy. Industry intertwined with home life, workshops with bedrooms and kitchens.

By age sixteen, Jimmy was working in one of the new steam-powered cotton factories, he and his co-workers not unlike shuttles themselves, carrying the bare threads of their lives through iron, wood, and brick as they walked from home to work and back again, day after day. They were all parts of the same enormous machine, it sometimes seemed, liable to wear out someday, just as their parents had. With every shift, Jimmy dreamed of fishing, playing ball, racing bicycles. Surely, if he played his cards right, if he kept his eye out for opportunity and made good bets, he could someday get the life he wanted.

The youngest four boys in the family – William, Joe ("Jimmy"), George and Charles – had become a team of sorts – a family within a family – even before Ann took them in. By the summer of 1870, their older sisters having left, the Austin household included John Austin (apprentice plumber at age 18), George Austin (14), Emma Austin (11), Thomas Austin (6), Ida Austin (1), William Carvin (wheelwright at age 21), Joseph Carvin (working in a cotton factory at age 16), George Carvin (driving a horse and wagon at age 15), and Charles (13).[6] For twelve years, Jimmy worked in the heat and dust, dreaming of the day he might leave the cotton factory. Then, in the summer of 1876, the Centennial Exposition came to town.

Jimmy had no interest in the massive Corliss engine, none in the Sholes typewriters or Bell telephones, and certainly none in the new shuttle looms; the exhibit that attracted him was the forty-two-foot copper arm that rose above the crowds like the fist of a triumphant warrior, holding a torch that symbolized the light of liberty, defying brick walls and steel-barred windows. [7] Out-of-town visitors stared up in awe. For Jimmy, it was a sign. His plans were not without risk, but since life was a gamble anyway, he'd feel like a fool to let opportunity pass.

You could bet on any sport if you were smart about it, and prize fighting, popular among Irish saloon-owners and their patrons, was especially attractive to a certain sort of betting man.[8] Bare-knuckle fighters like Jimmy Elliot, Jem Mace, and Mike McCoole were rough and violent men, often personally at odds with the law.[9] There were legal issues about their sport; many courts, district attorneys and politicians claimed that prize fighting amounted to assault and battery.[10] But with the purse at $100 a side and tickets selling for $5 each, there was money to be made. At the age of twenty-two, Jimmy was already known as a "sporting man." That year, as the Centennial Exposition brought tourists into town, he backed a prize fighter, John Hoover of Kensington, at a bare-knuckle fight on Pettys Island.[11]

Pennsylvania authorities had no jurisdiction on Pettys Island, while any New Jersey authorities who might arrive by boat could easily be spotted. Besides, taking a chance on what policemen and district attorneys might do was no riskier than a bet on the fight itself; with a little luck, a man could make a lot of money. And so Jimmy decided to take a chance on John Hoover.

He likely didn't coach Hoover to do what he did, but in the thirty-fourth round of the fight, Hoover "took McGarver by the legs and threw him." The wrestling move didn't pay off. Deciding it had been a foul, the referee gave the battle to McGarver.[12] Jimmy had learned a lesson about playing by the rules. But having seen McGarver's fist raised in victory while his handler raked in cash, he knew that the Hoover-McGarver fight would not be his last.[13]

Public and legal outrage from another fight in September – in which spectators shot at, the losing fighter killed and the victorious fighter charged with murder – resulted in the establishment of the so-called Philadelphia Rules for boxing. Matches were henceforth required to take place within the city limits and contests could last no longer than four rounds, a restriction that was later changed to six rounds for scoring purposes.[14] Problem was, four rounds was simply too short for money to be made. Fight fans wanted fights that went thirty, fifty, sometimes eighty rounds before a fighter gave up. Though such slugfests were illegal, inconsistent law enforcement ensured that they continued. The rowdy, hard-drinking crowds that watched these brawls made a perfect crowd of mates for a gregarious man like Jimmy. In 1877, he made his move, leaving the mill and the Austin house to take a job as a bartender among the sporting crowd.[15] Alcohol loosened lips. Customers opened up, divulging secrets, telling jokes that Jimmy could repeat to others. Their bold claims led to foolish bets. And Jimmy made good on them, making friends, paying off when he had to, but for the most part, accumulating a growing sum of money.

Luck was good to him. In 1878, he used his prize-fighting cash to open his own bar on Emerald Street. His brother William had meanwhile learned a skill of great importance to the saloon business: the fitting of iron to wood.[16] Not coincidentally, just as Jimmy opened his own saloon, William and George became barrel-makers.[17] Still in their twenties, the team of brothers now embarked on a common business enterprise, brewing, barreling and selling beer. And unlike many in the prize fight world, Jimmy did not end up murdered. In fact, he had the friendly, outgoing personality essential to being a tavern keeper.[18]

Jimmy's friendly spirit extended to the fairer sex as well. Soon after his start in the liquor business, he married Catherine Hagen, a young Irish girl whose parents and older sister also worked in the mill. The girl was smitten by the sporting young man who always seemed to have plenty of cash.[19] Although Jimmy went to church only occasionally – mostly to be forgiven his sins and to pray for his gambles to pay off – Catherine and her family were good Roman Catholics. So when Jimmy asked the priest at St. Edward's to perform the marriage, the Church saw no problem blessing their union with the sacrament, provided Jimmy promised to improve his church attendance. The wedding went forward and on June 24, 1879, Catherine gave birth to a baby boy, whom they named William after Jimmy's father and older brother.[20]

While Jimmy's bar on Emerald Street was only a few blocks east of Norris Square, it was tucked away behind other buildings on the east side of Front Street, where neither the traffic around the Square nor anyone else was likely to pass. Business was not what Jimmy had hoped, and the experience taught him the importance of location. Expecting a second child, Catherine could use a place with more room for a family. Determined to learn from his mistake, Jimmy's eyes quickly came to rest on one of the main intersections in Kensington, a five-way junction of Front Street (a major thoroughfare running north-south from Kensington to downtown Philadelphia), York Street (a major street coming in from the west and heading southeast toward the river, at the terminal point of the Reading Railroad and Pettys Island), and Kensington Avenue (a major street starting at the intersection and heading to the northeast, up river). The building on the southeast corner of the intersection – 2401 Kensington Avenue – not only seemed a good location for a saloon, but the flat upstairs could accommodate a family. At mass on Sundays, Jimmy prayed that the pricier spot would pay off.

By June of 1880, Catherine and their child had moved in to the flat above the saloon. His older brother William also lived with them, tending bar downstairs, while younger brother George (still a cooper, but probably starting to tend bar part time) moved to a place just a minute's walk west.[21]

Jimmy's Tavern soon became a magnet, drawing in customers while also drawing family close; the pub at the intersection would prove to be the hub at which relatives would work for years to come. Two of his brothers would name sons after Jimmy, suggesting their high regard for him.[22]

There are always setbacks, of course. Jimmy and Catherine's infant son William died that September, just short of fifteen months old.[23] (After all, life itself was clearly a gamble.) But over the next several years, Jimmy and Catherine had seven more children, of whom three – a son, Joseph James Jr. (1881 – 1919) and two daughters, Sadie (1884 – 1963) and Florence (1888 – 1958), survived infancy.[24] As the children grew taller, horse-drawn wagons, carriages, and bicycles jostled for position on the streets. Across the river in Camden, Walt Whitman was expanding on *Leaves of Grass*, while in West Philadelphia, Louisa Knapp Curtis was preparing early issues of the *Ladies Home Journal*. In 1884, Jimmy opened a second location, half a mile south at 1746 North Front Street. He invested in yet another property on Amber Street.[25] With two taverns to run, he hired other members of the family to share in bar tending duties, sometimes renting them rooms above the bars; in various combinations, he employed at least four brothers and a nephew at different times.[26]

Jimmy continued to follow prizefighting, often backing fighters he believed in. He also started playing cricket for the Girard Club.[27] Two days before Christmas, 1885, he was one of the "well known sporting men of this city" attending a prize fight between two Englishmen staged in a barn in Bucks County, "one of the hardest fought prize fights that has been seen in Pennsylvania in a long time." The stakes were $250 per side plus ticket sale at $5 per ticket. There was lively betting throughout the fight, and a surge by the underdog in the thirteenth round caused the betting to shift:

As soon as the men stepped to the center, Beatty drove his left straight on Magic's nose and mouth, making the blood fly in every direction. Beatty at this time was the strongest and made a great rally, chasing his opponent all over the ring. The spectators now became very boisterous and odds of 6 to 4 were freely bet that Beatty would win, with very few takers… The fourteenth and last round put the spectators in an uproar…

The fighters went down and got back up again. But when both declined to return to the ring at the end of the fourteenth round, the fight was declared a draw. For reasons unknown, the newspapers made no mention of any effort by law enforcement to stop the event or make arrests in connection with it. [28]

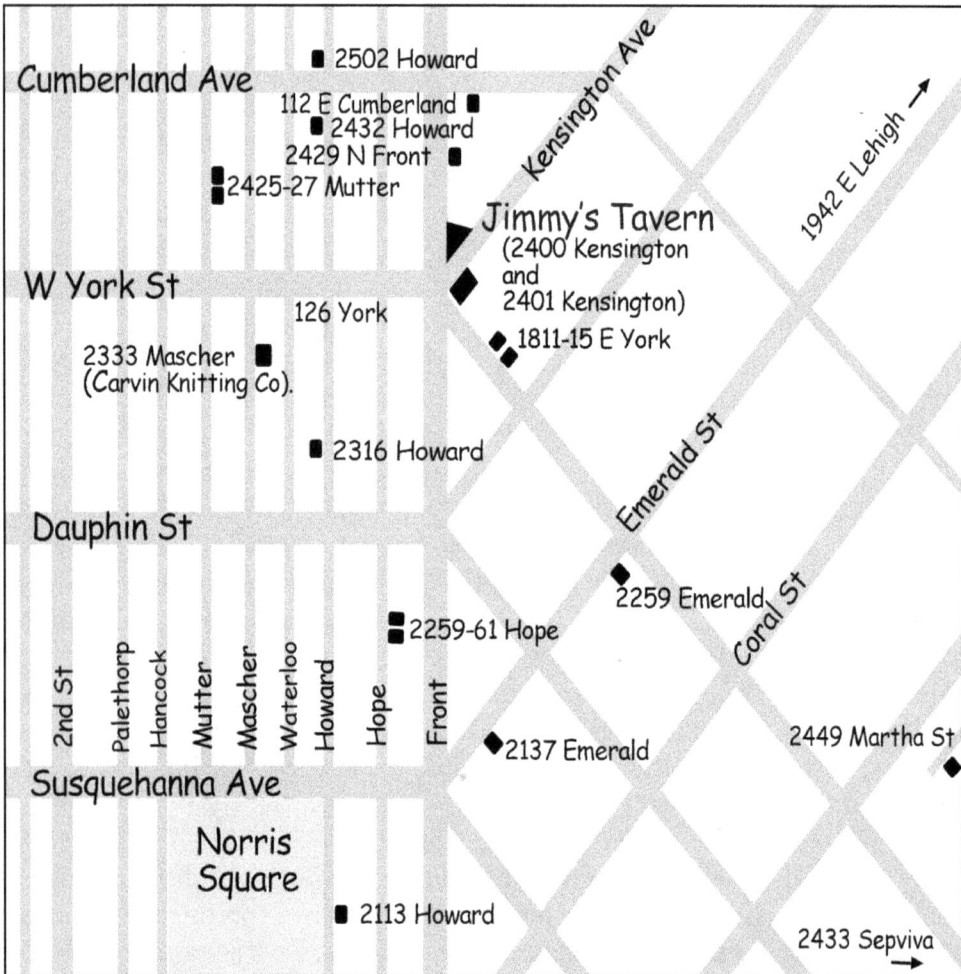

Solid black squares ■ indicate locations of various residences at different times

Neighborhood around Jimmy's Tavern, 1878-1920

1878-1879: Joseph J. (Jimmy) Carvin, Liquors, at **2139 Emerald** in 1878 (w brother Wm), then **2137 Emerald** in 1879.

1880-1920: Joseph J. Carvin, Liquors (occasionally Tavern Keeper, Saloon Proprietor, or Lager, and "Kensington-Av mkt" in 1909) listed as **2401 Kensington** in 1880-1883; as **h 2401 Kensington** in 1884-1886; as **2401 N Front** in 1887 (both with and without the "h"); as **2400 Kensington** 1889-1920, including **N Front c Ken av** in 1910; and as **2400 Kensington** in the 1920 Census.

Joseph J. Carvin, Liquors, was also listed at **1746 N Front Street** (with nephew John Austin) in 1884-1888; and living at **2316 Howard** in 1890; at **2113 Howard** in 1891; at **2432 Howard** in 1892-1894; at 636 York in 1895-1896; at 2418 N 6th in 1898; at 1317 Lehigh in 1900-1904; at 1229 Lehigh in 1905-1907; and at 1935 Somerset in 1908-1919.

Living with, or working for, Joseph J. (Jimmy) Carvin or his tavern:

William Carvin (Jimmy's brother), Wheelwright 1872-1873; Bedsteadmaker / Cabinet-maker 1875-1877; Cooper 1878; then Bartender for Jimmy at **2401 Kensington** in 1880-1881 and at **1746 N Front** (second tavern) in 1884-1885; then boilermaker at 2433 Sepviva in 1886.

George W. Carvin (Jimmy's brother), Cooper at 2259 Hope in 1880-1881, Sawyer at 2259 Hope in 1883, Cooper at 2261 Hope in 1884-1885; Bartender for Jimmy living at **2261 Hope** in 1886-1890; Liquors at **2401 N Front** in 1888.

John Austin (Jimmy's nephew), Bartender for Jimmy at **2401 N Front** in 1882, at **2401 Kensington** in 1883-1884 and at **2400 Kensington** in 1885; living at **2400 Kensington** in 1886; Clerk with home at 1746 N Front (Jimmy's address) in 1887; Bartender at 2624 Howard in 1890 and 1892, at 2918 Howard in 1893-1894, at 2429 N Front in 1896-1897, and at **2449 Martha** in 1898.

Thomas Carvin (Jimmy's brother), Bartender for Jimmy living at **1942 E Lehigh** in 1887; at **2425 Mutter** with Ann Austin in 1891-1892; at **2427 Mutter** in 1893; at **112 E. Cumberland** in 1897; at **2502 N Howard** in 1898-1900; at **1811 E York** in 1900 (Census), 1901 and 1905-1906 (including death certificate).

Charles (J?) Carvin (Jimmy's brother), Bartender for Jimmy, living at 2163 Gordon in 1890, at **2311 Mutter** in 1891-1892, at 1907 Firth in 1893-1894, at **126 York** in 1896-1897 and 1899; at **1815 E York** in 1901-1902; and at **1813 E York** in 1905-1911 and 1916, at 1912 Hart Lane in 1916.

Amelia Carvin, widow of Thomas, at **2316 N Howard** (where Jimmy lived in 1890) in 1908-1909.

Carvin Knitting Company at **2333 N Mascher (c. York)** in 1903-1906; Jasper and E Orleans in 1907.

Jimmy's brother William had worked as a bartender at the Kensington saloon since it opened, but after getting married in 1886, he left bartending to become a boilermaker.[29] (It was similar to cooper's work, but now, instead of wooden barrels, he made copper or steel casks or vats, the sort of thing good for making beer.) On March 11, 1886, Jimmy paid $550 to buy a property where William and his new wife now made their home. Whether Jimmy also invested in William's new trade, bought his products or charged the newlyweds rent, is unknown.[30]

Although Jimmy surely had contacts in law enforcement, they were not completely reliable. Less than a week after buying the property, Jimmy was arrested at a Saint Patrick's eve prizefight at a saloon right around the corner from his own.[31]

A PRIZE-FIGHT RAIDED.

SEVEN ROUNDS FOUGHT WHEN THE POLICE ARRIVED.

A Kid-Glove Battle Between John Coburn and Martin Brannon, Professional Feather-Weights—Forty-Eight Men, Including the Principals, Arrested.

Lieutenant Ferguson, of the Eighteenth District, was informed yesterday afternoon that a prize-fight was in progress at the sporting resort of Thomas Clark, 2406 North Front Street. Hastily gathering twenty-six officers, he placed details in charge of Special Officer Geyer and Sergeants Snyder and Henry. About five o'clock the saloon was surrounded and at a given signal the different squads swarmed down upon the place...

When the officers entered they found the bar room and a small room in the rear crowded with excited men. John Coburn, one of the principals, was in his fighting costume and was bleeding copiously from the ears. He was badly battered up about the face. The other principal, Martin Brannon, was attired in his street clothing. His face showed that he had been badly pounded. The floor of the room, which was in great confusion, was spattered with blood.

FORTY-EIGHT MEN ARRESTED

The prisoners, forty-eight in number, were marched to the Eighteenth district station house, where they gave the following names:

Joseph Carvin, 2401 North Front... Samuel Kershaw, 2221 North Front... John Long, 2406 North Front; Henry Conway, 2414 North Front... (etc) [*other names omitted*]

The proprietor of the saloon where the fight occurred was held in $800 bail, while the other prisoners were released upon furnishing $400 bail each. Most of them gave fictitious names.[32]

While unknown men could give fictitious names, Jimmy was known by the arresting officers as the saloon-owner right around the corner. He had no choice but to give his real name. As for the $400 bail, losses were necessary from time to time; heck, if every gamble proved to be a winner, it wouldn't be gambling. Besides, always willing to take a risk, Jimmy may have found a way to beat the charges against him; the papers made no reports of a conviction.

Despite his brushes with the law, Jimmy continued to look after his relatives. His nephew, John Austin, was about his own age. With the Austin family brass business having finally disappeared from the directories, Jimmy employed John Austin for some thirteen years, between 1885 and 1898.[33] After William's departure from the tavern in 1886 left him short of help, Jimmy hired his brother George. George continued to live just a block from the tavern for the rest of his short life, tending bar there from 1886 through his death in 1890.[34] Jimmy even hired the black sheep of the family, the wayward, anti-Catholic Thomas, going so far as to purchase a property ten minutes from the tavern as a place for Thomas to live. But never dependable, Thomas worked at the bar less than a year before he quit; the following year, he moved out of the place Jimmy had bought as well.[35]

Their youngest brother, Charles, had been spending time with Thomas – perhaps too much time – and by February, 1887, Thomas's ways had worn off on him. Charles was arrested for selling cakes of soap on a downtown street corner, telling passersby that some of them contained five-dollar bills. (The arrest came after a young boy complained to police that he'd lost two dollars trying for the prize.)[36] But good-hearted Jimmy was always looking out for his family. Different as they were from each other, they were family, and family should stick by family. Despite the arrest, in 1890, Jimmy employed Charles to tend bar for him too.[37]

Despite being plagued by scandals and corruption, the number of the city's saloons had been increasing steadily for decades until, in the late 1880's, the politics of temperance caused many to close. Owners scrambled for ways to stay in business. Jimmy had been operating two saloons, one at 2401 North Kensington and a second at 1746 North Front. Anticipating a legal crackdown, Jimmy gambled again in 1888: his brother George applied for the license on Front Street, while Joe applied for a license in his own name, not at 2401 Kensington (where he'd been operating for years) but across the street, at 2400

Kensington, a doctor's office that sat on the wedge-shaped property fronting both Front Street and Kensington Avenue.[38]

In those days, a four-judge License Court heard testimony about applications for license renewal. There was testimony about a knife fight in front of one applicant's establishment, and testimony from doctors about the quality of another's liquor. One doctor called an establishment a "low groggery," testifying that "nobody went there but the poorest of the poor." Several owners denied selling five cent whiskey. One was questioned about having a pool table on the premises. Another testified he sold on Sundays to churchgoers who wanted to slake their thirst after church (to which one of the judges wryly commented, "it must have been a dry sermon.") Joseph Acton's application for a license at 2406 North Front Street – the "sporting resort" where Jimmy had been arrested two and a half years earlier – was denied. Altogether, when the License Court issued its decisions that May, there was a drastic reduction in the number of liquor licenses in the city: only 193 of 625 applications in the 19th ward were granted.[39] Yet somehow, despite his own arrest at Acton's, Jimmy's application for 2400 Kensington Avenue was approved.[40]

The building was a "four and three-story" brick structure, including both a store front and a dwelling above it.[41] It was, if anything, an even better location than the one across the street. But Jimmy's former competitors did not rest; with their licenses revoked, they now schemed to return to the game. Some made an issue of the merry-go-round next to Jimmy's new tavern. Merry-go-rounds at Oktoberfest parties in German neighborhoods attracted families, young people in love, and anyone out to have a good time. They were also good for business, as they helped the free flow of beer. But riders on merry-go-rounds were often minors, and that fact led to problems. In November of 1888, a neighborhood man called the police to report that his twelve-year-old daughter – whom he described as "tall and well-developed for her age" – had been missing for three days, and that the merry-go-round next to Jimmy's tavern had "much to do with her incorrigibility." The girl's father explained to the *Inquirer* that the cause of her running away "was the punishment he had administered in order to break her of the habit of disobedience." In fact, he had whipped her Sunday morning. By dinner time, he'd noticed her missing. When she was found three days later hiding in the family cellar (she'd been coming up at night to get food from the kitchen), he accepted no personal responsibility: he blamed the merry-go-round.[42] The following spring, when the Liquor License Court heard testimony for license renewals,

> Joseph Carvin, a licensed dealer at No. 2400 Kensington avenue, was asked questions concerning his moral character and denied the insinuations. He declared that his place was not frequented by the patrons of the merry-go-round, which is located in the rear of it.[43]

One wonders how many other wrongs (real or not) were blamed on the merry-go-round. Even more, one wonders how Jimmy got his license renewed in the face of such charges, especially given his prior gambling arrest. Strict morality was abundant in those days, not just in the pressure to stop drinking; not just in the commandment to attend mass every Sunday. Pressure was increasing for Catholic parents to register their children in parochial school.[44] In such a rigid environment, sporadic church attendance and occasional prayer were hardly enough to secure a liquor license for a man with a merry-go-round behind his tavern and a history of sponsoring prize fights. However – maybe it was blind luck – Jimmy managed to get his license renewed, year after year, as if he'd found some other way to influence the authorities.[45]

Meanwhile, Jimmy looked for other opportunities. In 1888, he was among several merchants on North Front Street who founded the Merchants Electric Light Company to furnish light in the northeast section of the city. In fact, he was one of nine members of Merchant Electric's Board of Directors. The company built a generating plant on Hope Street and ran its transmission lines underground, charging forty cents per lamp per night – compared to the sixty cents being charged by its competitor, the Northern Company. Things went smoothly until March of 1892, when the City Council – one of whose members, Harry Clay, happened to be the President of Northern – gave Northern permission to run its overhead wires in the Merchants' operating area.[46] To defend itself, Merchants' got Mayor Sydney Stuart to veto Northern's ordinance. Northern retaliated by reducing its Front Street rates to twenty cents; Merchants responded by reducing its own to twenty-five. Frustrated, Clay then announced his intention to buy Merchants' stock. Merchants' Board members (who were also its major stockholders) deposited their shares in a trust to prevent Clay from doing so. But eventually, the competition proved too fierce; that autumn, Jimmy and Merchants' other directors reversed course, selling their shares to Clay and giving him a controlling interest for a tidy sum.

In October of 1892, Merchants' minority shareholders sued Jimmy and the other members of the Board, alleging that the business was doing well, that it was earning a healthy profit even at the reduced rate it was now charging, that Northern's Clay planned to shut down the Merchants' generator and make its shares worthless, and that the Board had violated its duty to the minority shareholders, colluding with Clay at their expense and for their own profit. A temporary restraining order was issued. In February, Clay called a meeting of Merchants' stockholders (of whom Clay was now the majority stockholder) at which (as predicted) Clay voted his shares to ask the City Council to dissolve the corporation on the ground that its business did not warrant its continuance.[47] In a day when business advantage could be bought and sold as easily as pints of beer, it seems Jimmy was not only spending time at the intersection of Front Street, Kensington and York, but at the intersection between business and local ward politics.

Meanwhile, with competition reduced by the cutback on liquor licenses, and with Front Street well-lit by gas lamps, business at the intersection with York and Kensington Avenue was good. Jimmy's bet on the prime location was paying off. On March 20, 1890, he purchased the doctor's-office-turned-tavern on the northeast corner – the wedge between Kensington and Front – for thirty-thousand dollars.[48] The same year, Jimmy's own family – he and wife Catherine, together with Joe Jr., Sadie, and now another daughter, Florence – moved to Howard Street, cutting the walk to the family tavern to less than two minutes. And in 1891, kind-hearted Jimmy gave another chance to his brother Thomas, taking him in again to tend bar.[49]

Jimmy was using his success for the betterment of those he loved.

One doubts that Catherine was able to get Jimmy to church except on Easter Sunday, if then. But if Jimmy was not a church goer, he was a solid family man. The arrangement of family residences over the years (see Map p 258) makes clear just how central his tavern became to his siblings' lives, the focal point for family jobs and relationships. Considering 2401 and 2400 Kensington as one, Jimmy ran his business there for forty years, providing work for relatives the whole time.

His friendliness and willingness to take a risk extended even to strangers, and it sometimes got him into trouble. Consistent with Godkin's observation that the Irish tavernkeeper often served as the community's lender, when Arthur Bromley (an Englishman new to the city) asked Jimmy to cash his $75 check, Jimmy obliged; and when the check bounced, the man (tracked down by police in Atlantic City) he admitted the swindle.[50] The police had not been so helpful to Irishmen in Mayor Conrad's day. The Irish had gained a great deal of influence in the city by then, Jimmy had found connections in politics, and those connections were serving him well.

By 1893, Catherine was pregnant for the eighth time when Jimmy brought her and daughter Sadie to the Colonnade Hotel in Sea Isle City for a summer vacation.[51] But as that pregnancy came to an end, fate was unkind yet again. On October 29, barely thirty years old, both Catherine and the baby daughter she'd been carrying died in childbirth.[52] With five children dead in infancy and now his young wife as well, thirty-nine-year-old Jimmy could be forgiven if had a few drinks at the bar.

Jimmy moved again, this time a mile west, to a house on York Street, a full fifteen-minute walk to work.[53] The new neighborhood was less congested than the major intersection where his tavern was, and not far from those 6th Street addresses Milano called prestigious – a much nicer location in which to raise a family. The change of address brought Jimmy and his children to a new parish, that of St. Edward the Confessor, where (five years earlier) Joseph P. Murphy had presented the parish a check on behalf of the congregation. It had been forty years since his father had worked for Dominick Murphy, but the Carvins and Murphys were neighbors again.

With others tending bar for him, Joe could afford to be further away from work: financially, if not emotionally, he was doing well. But his three surviving children were still young – Joseph, Jr. was twelve, Sadie nine, and Florence, five. The older two were in school that winter, but going to work now meant leaving five-year-old Florence at home alone. Jimmy had to find childcare.

The neighborhood also included the German Baptist widow, Margaret Kiker and her children.[54] Her daughter Mary had married a man named Charles Sherick, also German, [55] and the Shericks lived at 604 York Street. [56] Numbered 636 and 604, the Carvin and Sherick houses were less than a hundred feet apart, and just a block and a half south of the Kikers and Murphys. The Carvin and Sherick families seemed an ideal match. Jimmy was in his forties, as were Charles and Mary Sherick. Each house included a single teenage boy (one fifteen and the other thirteen). More importantly, while Jimmy's motherless home included two pre-teen girls in need of childcare, the Sherick household included two older daughters, aged nineteen and twenty, capable of giving it. That made three women of the Sherick house available to help care for Jimmy's daughters while their father tended to his saloon.

Jimmy would do anything for his daughters. By the autumn of 1894, he had enrolled them in Professor Samuel F. Givens' Dance Academy. [57] Meanwhile, to escape the summer heat, he rented a cottage for the summer in Sea Isle City. He and three other men "took a trip to sea and returned home with over three hundred pounds of fine weak-fish, flounders and croakers." The following summer, he was back at the shore again, staying at the Ocean View Cottage and labeled "quite an expert angler" in the paper.[58]

At this point in our story, we must consider oral tradition. For now came events that, according to that tradition, scandalized the family.

As the Sherick women helped look after his daughters, it wasn't long before Jimmy, now in his mid-forties, found himself looking at one of them: twenty-year old Katie Sherick. Katie made him feel young again; and after a couple of years, he asked her to marry him.

A man who was renowned for telling stories – a grandfather to some of us – was tight-lipped about what transpired next. When asked about his parents, he had little to say about them. And when some of us asked our own father what he knew, he too claimed to know little. But after much begging, he finally told us that our grandfather was the product of a scandalous marriage. He knew few of the details, and saw little point in guessing, but those were different times, he stressed; expectations were different than they are today; people were less tolerant, more insistent on abiding by society's unwritten rules.[59]

He seemed to know more than he let on. We pressed for more.

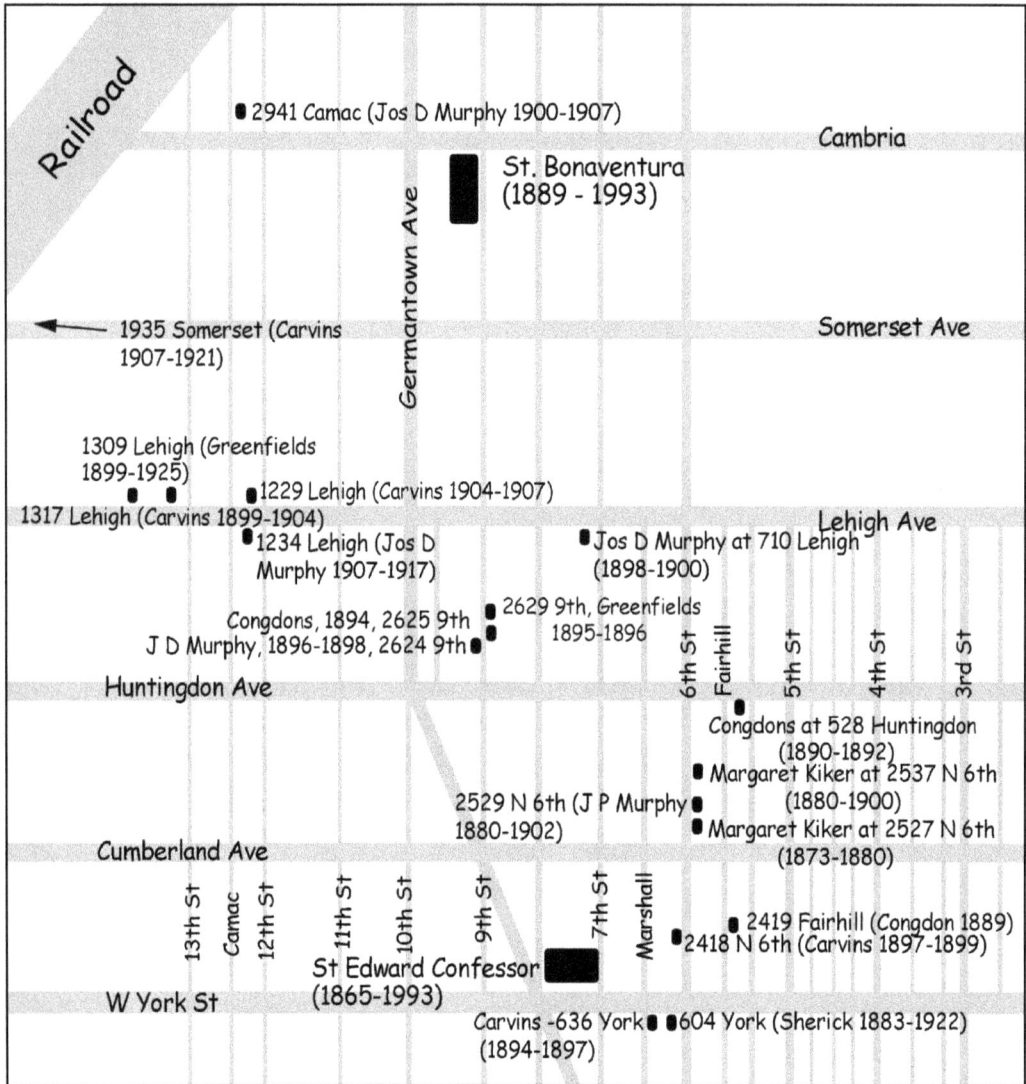

Railroad

2941 Camac (Jos D Murphy 1900-1907)

Cambria

St. Bonaventura
(1889 - 1993)

Germantown Ave

1935 Somerset (Carvins 1907-1921)

Somerset Ave

1309 Lehigh (Greenfields 1899-1925)

1229 Lehigh (Carvins 1904-1907)

1317 Lehigh (Carvins 1899-1904)

Lehigh Ave

1234 Lehigh (Jos D Murphy 1907-1917)

Jos D Murphy at 710 Lehigh (1898-1900)

2629 9th, Greenfields 1895-1896

Congdons, 1894, 2625 9th
J D Murphy, 1896-1898, 2624 9th

6th St

Fairhill

5th St

4th St

3rd St

Huntingdon Ave

Congdons at 528 Huntingdon (1890-1892)

Margaret Kiker at 2537 N 6th (1880-1900)

2529 N 6th (J P Murphy 1880-1902)

Margaret Kiker at 2527 N 6th (1873-1880)

Cumberland Ave

13th St

Camac

12th St

11th St

10th St

9th St

7th St

Marshall

2419 Fairhill (Congdon 1889)

2418 N 6th (Carvins 1897-1899)

St Edward Confessor
(1865-1993)

W York St

Carvins -636 York (1894-1897)

604 York (Sherick 1883-1922)

Solid black squares ■ *indicate locations of various residences. As of 1880, six families were scattered in five separate Enumeration Districts: plumber William H. Greenfield at 2268 Memphis St; saloon keeper Richard Congdon at 323 Girard Ave; oyster dealer Charles Sherick at 532 W York St; manufacturer Jos. P. Murphy at 123 Susquehanna; widow Margaret Kiker at 2527 N 6th St; and saloon keeper Jimmy Carvin at 2401 Kensington Ave. (1880 U.S. Census, E.D. 679, Fam 243; E.D. 315 Fam 174; E.D. 374 Fam 211; E.D. 370, Fam 83; E.D. 376, Fam 190; E.D. 674, Fam 166.) By 1890, Greenfield was at 2413 Marshall, working as a carpenter; Congdon was at 528 Huntingdon, working as a clerk; Sherick, still an oyster dealer, had moved to 604 West York; and Murphy had built a home at 2529 N 6th. Kiker had moved to 2537 N 6th when Murphy moved in. And Carvin, still running his saloon at 2401 Kensington, had moved to 2316 Howard. In 1894, Carvin, recently widowed, moved to 636 York, near the Shericks.*

In 1895, the Congdon sisters started marrying: Stella Cecelia to Jos D. Murphy and Marie Irene to William H. Greenfield Jr. The newlyweds all lived next to the sisters' parents on North 9th Street. In February, 1896, Katie Sherick married Jimmy Carvin; she soon became pregnant, and when visiting her grandmother (Margaret Kiker) while Jimmy was at work, she'd have walked past the elder Murphy house on N 6th St.

For one thing, he finally said, Katie Sherick had been much younger than Jimmy – and the age difference alone was scandalous. Still, we pressed.

Alright, there was more to it than that. Jimmy had remarried too soon after the death of his first wife; in those days, respectable people wore black for years after loved ones died. Besides, Katie Sherick was German, and Jimmy Carvin was Irish. People believed that an Irishman should only take an Irish wife. And while he wasn't sure, he thought it might have had something to do with Katie's occupation.

"Her *occupation*? Was she a – dancer?"

"I don't know. Why are you so curious about this?"

"We want to know."

"Well, maybe she was… something like a masseuse. A German masseuse."

He could be wrong about that, he admitted. But again, he stressed, he was sure the standards in the 1890's were less tolerant than "today." (Keep in mind when this conversation occurred – by 'today" he meant the 1950's). He stressed that the Murphys were a very proper, well-to-do family, and had never approved of the marriage to Katie Sherick. And he was certain his father had never wanted to talk about it. In fact, neither did he; it was too painful.

And that was that. Conversation ended.

In the decades since, we've learned a few things. For example, while there was in fact a very large difference in their ages, nearly three years passed between Catherine's death and Jimmy's marriage to Katie Sherick. The Shericks were a prosperous, successful and stable family. Katie had no occupation at all, much less a scandalous one. But perhaps because it touched his own life too closely, another element of the "scandal" was never mentioned: the wealthy matriarch Margaret Kiker had raised her family, including Katie Sherick, as strict Baptists.[60] Religion had been divisive in the old country; it had been divisive in 1844; it had divided Jimmy's sister Ann from her parents; it had thwarted Thomas at every turn; and several generations later, it would remain divisive in our own lives. In 1896, it posed a major obstacle for Jimmy and Katie Sherick as well. Teetotaling Baptists were the antithesis of hard drinking Irish Catholics. Margaret Kiker had moved away when the Murphys moved in; Jimmy's saloon must have represented Sodom and Gomorrah to her.

But let's not get ahead of ourselves. Suffice it to say, there were those on both sides who objected to marriages across the religious divide. The position of the Catholic Church, certainly, was clear: unless a couple was married by a Catholic priest, empowered by the sacrament of ordination to administer the holy sacrament of matrimony, no marriage would be recognized in the eyes of God: any children born of such a union would not be legitimate. Unless Katie Sherick agreed to convert to Catholicism, and to raise any children she might bear in the Catholic faith, the couple would be barred from communion with the Holy Mother Church. And the position of the Baptists was equally clear: it wasn't Katie's occupation that was a problem, it was Jimmy's – being a saloon keeper was sinful, decadent, and a threat to their innocent daughter Katie. Strict Baptists and strict Catholics alike saw the marriage as a sin in the eyes of the one true God in which they believed.

It was in the midst of such conflict that Katie agreed to marry Jimmy, whether her family liked it or not. On February 3, 1896, Jimmy and Katie were married at St. Edward the Confessor by that Church's rector, P.F. Sullivan. And it's important to note that Sullivan couldn't have performed the rite absent Katie's agreement to the Church's conditions.[61]

On June 6, 1896, Jimmy applied for a passport, stating his intention to go abroad temporarily, accompanied by his wife.[62] (One imagines they spent their honeymoon somewhere where Jimmy might teach Katie how to fish.) By the time they returned, young Katie was pregnant. They moved to a nice home up the street, at 2418 N 6th Street, even closer to Katie's grandmother, the aging Margaret Kiker. (The move did not likely please those Catholics who were counting on a Catholic child.)[63] Pregnant Katie no doubt visited her grandmother's house often. And – see Map – since the Kikers lived just a few doors past Joe Murphy,[64] the residents of the Murphy house – including twenty-four-year-old Anna Murphy and her teenage sisters Elizabeth, Agnes and Mary – no doubt watched the pregnant girl walking past their house many times. They surely frowned on the fact that Jimmy was practically their father's age, while his pregnant wife was closer to their own. At a minimum, still faithful to the church their grandfather had helped to build, they saw Katie's promises to convert to Catholicism and to raise her child as a Catholic as essential to their acceptance of the young Baptist bride. But the expectation that she would make good on her promise was in jeopardy: every time Katie passed by their window on the way to visit her strong-willed Baptist grandmother, they could only imagine what the old widow had to say about her granddaughter converting to Catholicism.[65]

Friendly and carefree by nature, Jimmy simply wanted happiness for himself and those around him: the partisans on both sides of the divide were unreasonable. On the 5th of March, 1897, when Katie gave birth to a healthy baby boy, Jimmy was a happy man. They named the baby Charles, after Katie's father and Jimmy's youngest brother.[66] Four months later, Jimmy won a judgment for $650 on a loan he'd made.[67] Just days after the judgment, the family checked in to the Atglen Hotel in Ocean City to celebrate, to get away from the midsummer city heat, to enjoy the ocean breezes and a bit of fishing. The group included Jimmy, his wife Katie, his children by Catherine (Sadie, Florence and Joe) and even a "Miss Rittenhouse" (19-year-old Clara Rittenhouse, Katie Sherick's German-American sister-in-law).[68] Life must have seemed promising; Jimmy picked up the tab for the whole group.[69] But the group did not include the four-month old infant; the baby had been left at home, cared for by his Baptist grandmother, even as the Murphy women looked on.

Still loyal to his old family, Jimmy continued to give jobs to his brothers. Even wayward Thomas – having married Amelia Buehn in 1897 and straightaway taken up with his second Mary – now tended bar for Jimmy, this time for what would turn out to be several years straight. But as good as business was, Jimmy's homelife was destined to be unkind. Katie and the baby continued to spend time with her family – passing by the Murphy house every time – while Jimmy took care of business at the tavern. But a month after the baby's first birthday, Katie fell sick. She had a bellyache for much of the week. Her Protestant mother and grandmother looked in on her. On April 21, 1898, a Thursday, one of the women – maybe even thirteen-year-old Sadie – went to the bar to tell Jimmy he'd better come home, that things had taken a turn for the worse. Katie'd had a bloody stool, and now she was vomiting, a sorry sight when Jimmy saw her, grimacing, holding her belly, pulling her knees to her chest. As Florence and Sadie prayed the *Hail Mary,* the natural question was whether a priest should be called to administer last rites. For the Catholics, the question was steeped in doctrinal niceties. Some members of the church questioned whether Katie was even eligible for the sacrament, and Jimmy found himself caught between grief, contemplation of the Almighty, and the legalisms of Catholic ritual.[70] But there wasn't time to sort out the legalisms. The same Dr. Wood who'd certified little Charley's birth the year before now faced a much less pleasant task: certifying the cause of Katie's death. When he did so, he described it as invagination (a twisting) of the bowels.[71]

Katie had died even younger than Jimmy's first wife. His natural inclination was to bury her where Catherine had been buried, at New Cathedral Cemetery, but Katie's Baptist family objected. The obituary prepared that Thursday, the very day Katie died, appeared in Friday's editions of *The Times* and *The Inquirer,* announcing that the funeral would be at two o'clock Sunday afternoon with interment at Green Mount Cemetery, a site that would please the Baptist matriarch, Margaret Kiker, and the rest of her family, because Green Mount was not connected with the Roman Catholic Church.

But much like the discussion of last rites, the discussions about Katie's remains had been hurried. While there were some condolences from Katie's friends that Friday, there was also strenuous objection by Catholics. They'd been shocked to read in that morning's papers that Katie would not be buried in a Catholic cemetery.[72] The same announcement was repeated in the Saturday editions: the funeral would be at two o'clock Sunday afternoon; interment would be at Green Mount cemetery. *The Times* of Saturday, April 23, 1898 (page 10) carried it:

CARVIN.—On the 21st instant. KATIE. wife of
Joseph J. Carvin and daughter of Charles and
Mary Sherick. In her 25th year.
The relatives and friends of the family are
respectfully invited to attend the funeral, on
Sunday afternoon at 2 o'clock, from the resi-
dence of her husband, 2418 North Sixth street.
Interment at Greenmount Cemetery.

As opinions and Catholic complaints poured in, doubts began to weigh
on Jimmy. Wasn't Green Mount a Protestant cemetery? Hadn't Katie agreed
to convert to Catholicism? Didn't Jimmy want a Catholic Priest to say the
funeral mass? Florence and Sadie's Catholic teachers were telling them their
father had a moral obligation to bury his wife in the Catholic faith to which
she'd agreed to convert. Others, including Margaret Kiker, asked why Katie
should be buried as if she'd converted, rather than in the Baptist faith to which
she had always belonged. Wasn't it a slap in the face to her Protestant family,
and to her own memory?

After much debate about the eternal well-being of Katie's soul, Jimmy
made three decisions that Saturday. For one thing, he bought a substantial
family plot, large enough for a dozen burials, at the Catholic Holy Sepulchre
Cemetery. [73] Second, he arranged for a solemn requiem mass at St. Edward's
for the repose of Katie's soul. At the last minute, he broke the arrangements
for the Protestant funeral and substituted a Catholic one. (St. Edward's was
delighted.) And finally, he arranged for revised obituaries. The
announcement of the new arrangements appeared in the Sunday morning
papers – the day for which the funeral had originally been announced. Of
course, the obituaries were buried toward the backs of both papers. Many
failed to notice that the funeral would not take place at 2:00 that afternoon at
Greenmount, but at 8:30 Monday morning at Holy Sepulchre – or that a
solemn requiem mass was to be said for Katie at St. Edward's.[74]

CARVIN.—On April 21. 1898. Katie. wife of
Joseph J. Carvin, and daughter of Charles and
Mary Sherick, in her 25th year. The relatives
and friends of the family are respectfully invited to attend the funeral. on Monday morning, at 8.30 o'clock. from husband's residence.
2418 North Sixth street. Solemn mass of requiem at St. Edward's Church.

Mayhem was inevitable that Sunday afternoon. Those who showed up
planning to go to Green Mount to hear prayers by a Baptist preacher were
told that their condolences were appreciated, but that if they wished to return

they could pay their respects at St. Edward's or at Holy Sepulchre the following day. Awkward. Embarrassing. Enough to still be scandalous fifty years later, when the man who was grandfather to some of us – a man who loved telling stories more than anything – didn't want to talk about it.[75]

Jimmy tried to focus on business, tending bar, listening to others' stories of woe, trying to escape his own problems by delving into those of his customers. Perhaps to avoid the conflict between Baptists and Catholics on North 6th Street, he moved to a rented house at 1317 Lehigh Avenue, a mile away. That summer and fall, he renewed his liquor license.[76] The tavern at 2401 Kensington began appearing in newspaper ads for Schaeffer's draught beer.[77] Noting that Sadie and Florence were at the Cordova Hotel "for an extended stay" and that Sadie was an "accomplished musician," social items described Jimmy as "the well-known businessman of Kensington."[78] Even as brother Thomas marched with the anti-immigrant, anti-Catholic A. O. M., Jimmy himself became a charter member of a very different society, Philadelphia's Aerie No. 42 of the Fraternal Order of Eagles.

> Non-sectarian, non-political and non-racial, it invites all who
> believe in the brotherhood of man, believing that the observance
> of its motto, "Liberty, Justice, Truth and Equality," will add to
> the world's good fellowship. [79]

The tolerant, non-sectarian Eagles were just what Jimmy needed.

Meanwhile, the religious controversy had left the Shericks and Kikers dealing with tensions of their own. When a daughter was born to Katie's married sister, Laura, she honored her deceased sister by naming the infant Katie after her. Soon thereafter, the wealthy widow Margaret Kiker died – and just twelve days after that, there was a mass baptism: not just Laura's new infant, but four other Kiker family members were baptized with her, suggesting a shift in allegiance larger than the yearnings of a single soul.[80] The baptism was not at the deceased Margaret Kiker's Baptist church, but at the more tolerant and ecumenical Methodist Episcopal Church. It seems some of the Baptist Kikers had been waiting for their matriarch to die before asserting their own religious preferences. Clearly, some people adhere strictly to traditions of faith, while others are more willing to compromise.[81]

Jimmy and his children now lived in a rented apartment at 1317 Lehigh Avenue.[82] The liquor business had done well, and Jimmy had money to invest.[83] No longer neighbors, his family had little in common with the Shericks any more, apart from sharing the infant Charles. Jimmy spent his social time with his fellow Eagles instead. Their frequent allusions to brotherhood may have got him thinking about his tavern as a family enterprise – and remembering his sisters' kindnesses to him, Jimmy started taking more interest in his son and namesake, Joseph James Carvin Jr.

In the summer of 1901, either Jimmy or Joe Jr. vacationed with Florence and Sadie at the Jackson hotel in Atlantic City.[84] And then, his son presented him with yet another business opportunity: the young man had worked for a couple of years at a knitting company, and knew how easily a profit could be made in hosiery. As with any new business, there was risk involved, but the way Joe Jr. talked, significant profits were to be had. It sounded to Jimmy like a good bet. In 1903, with the help of tavern, real estate, and gambling profits, father and son opened the Carvin Knitting Company on Mascher and York, about four blocks west of the tavern, with Jimmy as company president and twenty-two-year-old Joe Jr. as General Manager.

The company placed an ad in the "Female Help Wanted" section of *The Inquirer* of May 22, 1903: [85]

HOSIERY—Bar toppers. Carvin Knitting Co., Mascher and York sts.

By November 29, the company was advertising for knitters as well. And on December 30, it advertised for an "experienced boy on boxing." In the weeks and months to come, ads were placed for a "boy with some experience on rib machines," "experienced knitters and toppers on Mayo machines," "experienced menders," "experienced operators on Roman machines and toppers on Mayo machines," "experienced Bonaz operator on glove stitch machine," "knitters and toppers on Keystone machines; operators or learners on glove stitch machine," "cylinder toppers; no stiches to double, and "experienced boy on sleecer." The company must have been busy, as it clearly had a constant need for help.[86]

Jimmy had not abandoned his tavern; it continued to thrive. In 1905, his nephew James (Charles's son) joined the ranks of other relatives who'd tended bar at his tavern. And even wayward brother Thomas showed signs of responsibility toward the end of his life, tending bar for Jimmy with as much consistency as he'd ever shown for anything.

Soon after Joe Jr. married a German American named Elsie Preuss, Elsie made Jimmy a grandfather.[87] Then, in late May of 1906, daughter Sadie delighted him by marrying a German-American railroad conductor, Harry Gekler.[88] But not everything was going Jimmy's way. Less than three weeks after daughter Florence turned eighteen, *The Inquirer* reported that Joe *Jr.* had been appointed her legal guardian.[89]

Why would Florence's brother be appointed her guardian? The girl had no apparently need of a guardian, and even if she did have a need, Jimmy was a successful, fully competent businessman; except for his occasional brushes with the law, he had neither a criminal record nor any known addictions or bad habits. Only one explanation makes sense: an eighteen-year-old girl could not marry without her father's permission, and Jimmy did not approve. Sadie's beloved was the butcher, Wendell Young, a Catholic and (as far as we know) upright and responsible. There was no apparent reason for disapproval. Meanwhile, it's hard to imagine that a guardianship petition could be granted without Jimmy's being notified of it, so it seems Jimmy must have acquiesced in his son being made his daughter's guardian. Perhaps Jimmy simply refused, as a matter of principle, to give his blessing to a marriage he didn't approve of. ("Fine, son. If you approve of your sister's choice, you be the one to give your permission.") Of course, this too is pure speculation. Why go to the extent of a guardianship proceeding for such a thing? We know only that Joe Jr. was, in fact, appointed guardian, and that Florence did in fact marry the butcher Wendell Young soon thereafter.[90]

As it turns out, Joe Jr's appointment as his sister's guardian would be the last record of his living in Philadelphia. At least as far as Jimmy could tell, the knitting business Joe Jr. managed had been doing well; the young man never had a problem he couldn't solve, and nothing seemed to phase him. But to Jimmy's surprise, the business soon closed, and rather suddenly, the investment in it exposed as a bad decision after all. But a gambler doesn't expect to win all of his bets, and thanks to the liquor business, Joe continued to prosper.

Shortly after the knitting business closed, Joe left for California. Jimmy remained behind to manage his tavern. By 1907, he'd moved to a new home even farther from work, where Sadie and Harry Gekler moved in with him. They continued to live with him even as they began to have children of their own.[91]

Public transportion now made for an easier commute, but the move away from the tavern only made sense because Jimmy, now in his mid-fifties, planned to put in fewer hours there. He left much responsibility for the business to his brother Charles, who continued living within a couple minutes of the place.[92] One suspects that Joe spent more time fishing, more time at the race track or at prize fights. He may even have spent more time with his youngest son, Charley – at least until 1917, when Charley enlisted for the duration of the First World War. Meanwhile, Sadie, her husband and her children continued to live with Jimmy throughout the war years and the pandemic of 1918.[93]

The following year, unexpected events changed Jimmy's life in a number of important ways. For one thing, Joe Jr. fell victim to a capital crime. For another, the Geklers moved out of the house and relocated to Los Angeles.[94] For another, his son Charley returned to Philadelphia after his service in the war. And finally – perhaps most importantly – in October of 1919, Congress approved the Volstead Act.

The 18th Amendment, outlawing "intoxicating liquors," had been ratified in January of 1918; ever since, there'd been heated debate about the level at which alcohol content would make a drink "intoxicating." Opinions had varied: Was it just hard liquor that was illegal, or also beer and wine? It was up to Congress to pass legislation detailing the effect of the amendment. Bowing to the forces of Temperance, Congress declared in the Volstead Act that *all* alcoholic beverages were "intoxicating."[95] After forty years in

274

business, Jimmy's livelihood had been made a crime. The Wine & Liquors category of the City Directory disappeared.

Jimmy had been a generous man. He'd taken gambles, but he'd made good decisions. (He could hardly be blamed for his occasional misfortunes.) If anything, he'd been too generous, too trusting, too soft a touch, both to family and to others. Now in his mid-sixties, he faced a choice between operating an illegal speakeasy, retiring, or doing something else entirely. Sadie had moved to California. Florence already had five children of her own, and soon had a sixth on the way.[96] Even his youngest child, Charley, recently discharged from the Army, had moved in with his grandmother Sherick, and was soon starting a family of his own. In at least some ways, it all left Jimmy Carvin alone in the world.

The Census was enumerated in Kensington beginning on the 2nd of January, 1920, fifteen days before the effective date of the Volstead Act. As if making a statement of defiance, Jimmy gave his occupation to the Census taker as "Proprietor/Saloon." But now, with his children gone, he found himself living alone in the flat above the tavern. And though he'd owned it for thirty of the forty years he'd been running it, there was now a mortgage on the property.[97]

We can imagine Jimmy going downtown to see the new satirical comedy, "How Dry We Are; the Worst Is Yet to Come" at Dumont's Theatre.[98] Most saloon owners in Philadelphia continued to operate during Prohibition: in 1925, there were over ten thousand arrested in the city, and only about four percent of them met with a fine; typically the fine was so low that most proprietors considered it a routine business expense.[99] Jimmy had always been a sporting man; it's hard to imagine him giving up the business rather than absorbing such a cost of doing business. But if Jimmy operated an illegal speakeasy, the public records don't so reflect. The 1921 Directory gave no business address, only his home address at 1935 Somerset, followed thereafter by a new home address on Herbert Street. By 1924, in any case, he'd sold the saloon property.[100]

We know that he made more than one trip to California, to visit the Geklers there, but for the most part, Jimmy's activities in the 1920's elude us. Efforts to locate him in the 1930 Census have fallen short. But sometimes, one's sense of a man points in the right direction. As a former fight promoter, he surely attended the Jack Dempsey – Gene Tunney heavyweight title fight held in Philadelphia September 23, 1926. And we know that the sportsman liked the seashore where he'd often gone fishing. Once his business was gone, it's hard to imagine him staying away from the shore, which Nucky Thompson was turning into a haven for wine, women and gambling. There were card games, slot machines, numbers running, and illegal liquor running up and down the Boardwalk. The once quiet town on the seashore was now a place the *Inquirer* would call a "lively and wide-open gambling and merry-making town where practically nothing [was] barred."[101] Always willing to take a good risk, the gambler, sportsman and former fight promoter with nothing tying him to Philadelphia could hardly have stayed away.

Front: Sadie Carvin Gekler, Henry Carvin Gekler, Catherine Gekler, unknown, and Joseph J. ("Jimmy") Carvin. Rear: Harry Gekler. Circ 1921.

Though maintaining his own address in the city until the day he died, Jimmy dropped by Drexel Hill for visits from time to time, spending enough time with Charley and Charley's children that they later remembered him (though only vaguely) as "Uncle Jimmy."[102] But in 1930, he was likely at a hotel or speakeasy at the shore when the census taker came around. And on December 11, 1934, he died in Philadelphia of diabetes and chronic nephritis. The friendly, generous man was buried with both his wives in the family plot he'd bought at Holy Sepulchre Cemetery over thirty-five years before. The informant at his death was listed as his son, Charley. Funeral arrangements were made through family friends of his daughter-in-law.[103]

Jimmy had never attained the fame or financial success of the Murphys. But by keeping an eye out for opportunities, by taking the right risks and by betting only when the odds were favorable, Jimmy had done well by his siblings and his children. The iron bars in the factory windows of Kensington had not held him back. He'd not succumbed to bad breaks. His children had gotten an education. With a little bit of luck, they could attain whatever success they were willing to devote themselves to.

Jimmy may not have descended from the Lord Mayor of Dublin, but he'd done alright for himself.

And so it is that, on that note, our account of the second generation of Murphys and Carvins comes to an end.

Notes on Chapter 10, Joseph J. ("Jimmy") Carvin

[1] We find much contradiction in the censuses as to the ages of Joseph and his siblings William, George and Charles. (See especially the 1860 U.S. Census, Phila Ward 17, Families 658 and 660; 1870 U.S. Census, Phila Ward 19, Dist 058, Fam 243; and 1870 U.S. Census Ward 19, Dist 058 (2d Enum), Dwelling 2128 (Diamond Street).) The 1860 and 1870 Censuses bear all the hallmarks of error and approximation. (1) The 1850 Census shows William as three months old. His 1929 Death Certificate and Funeral Record both give his date of birth as February 20, 1850. (PA Historic and Museum Commission, PA Death Cert No 51478; Historical Society of PA, Historic PA Church and Town Records, Phila, John F. Fluehr & Sons Funeral Home, Permit No 12700.) (2) George's death certificate and the obituary based on it (in January 1891) assert that he was 35 years old when he died, and the 1880 Census gives his age as 24, both suggesting that George's birth year was 1855, not 1852 as suggested by the 1860 Census. (3) Charles's birthdate was apparently May 7, but the year of birth (1861) given in his death certificate is impossible because he appeared in the 1860 Census, enumerated Aug 16 of that year. The 1900 Census gives his birth month as May 1860, which seems possible, but earlier birth years are suggested by the ages shown for him in earlier censuses, and by the ages of his mother and siblings. All things considered, 1858 may be the likeliest year of his birth. (4) The 1860 Census listed Joseph himself (later "Jimmy") as 10. In 1896, he swore on an application for a marriage license to a younger woman that he was born August 12, 1855. His headstone gives his birth year as 1851, but it was commissioned by survivors who were not alive at the time of his birth and such a birth date would conflict with the known birthdate of his older brother William. The 1900 Census gives his birth as August of 1854, his 1896 passport application gives his birthdate as August 12, 1854, and the 1880 Census gives his age as 26, all of which point to 1854 as the year of his birth. We here adopt that date, sworn to on his passport application, as mostly likely correct.

[2] His grandson, Charles W. Carvin Jr., said that in the early 1930's, his grandfather was known to him as "Uncle Jimmy."

[3] The new St. Michael's parochial school had opened in 1853. Ann had married in the Presbyterian Church around the corner from St. Michael's, and she would go on to be buried in the Odd Fellows Cemetery, rather than at St. Michael's. (*Historic PA Church & Town Records, First Presb. Church of Kensington, Feb 1, 1853*, George Austin to Ann Cravan [sic], Historical Soc. of PA; PA Death Certificates 1906-1968, Cert. No 118653, PA Historic & Museum Commission, accessed via Ancestry.com.) But of the four boys she took in, William, Jimmy and Charles all grew up as Roman Catholics, like their parents. As adults, Joe and Charles would both buy plots for themselves and their families in the Roman Catholic Holy Sepulchre cemetery; William would bury his daughter Ellen in the Roman Catholic New Cathedral Cemetery in 1900. Of the four boys, only George would be buried in a non-Catholic Cemetery (Northwood). Ann seems to have supported the boys in maintaining their Catholic faith while in her house.

[4] In the 1868 Directory, George Austin is listed at 2043 North 7th Street. In the 1870 Census, Phila Ward 19, Dist 58 (1st Enum), Fam 243, he was identified as a laborer. In the second enumeration (1870 Census, Phila Ward 19, Dist 58 (2d Enum), p 19, he appears at 2123 Leithgow St. (just north of Diamond).

[5] City Directory of 1870. The Austin brass foundry continued on Hope Street, the directory listing John Austin as a brass worker there until at least 1875 – but George himself was never again associated with the family brass business. The directories make no further mention of laborer George Austin until 1875, when he is listed as a driver at 2122 N 5th St. He remained at that location and in that occupation for some time. The 1880 Census listed him as a teamster at 2111 N 5th (1880 U.S Census Phila Dist 365, Fam 4).

[6] The Austin household was counted in that year's census first on June 10 and again on November 17th with conflicting results. The discrepancies between the two counts, both as to the members of the

household and as to their ages, are more than can be explained by the five months that separated them; simply put, one or both were replete with error. For example, while George and Ann are both listed as 25 years old in the first enumeration, they are both listed as 45 only five months later. (Compare 1870 Census, Phila Ward 19, Dist 58, p 29, enumerated June 10, Fam 243, to 1870 Census, Phila Ward 19, Dist 58 (2d Enum), enumerated November 17th.) The representation of the household given here is based on the two enumerations as starting points but then corrected and/or heavily influenced by other records.

[7] The huge arm would later become the right arm of the Statue of Liberty in New York Harbor.

[8] The social, cultural and ethnic factors which combined to put prize fighting into saloons – especially Irish ones – are thoroughly described in Greggory M. Ross, "Boxing in the Union Blue: A Social History of American Boxing in the United States During the Late Antebellum and Civil War Years" (2014), *Electronic Thesis and Dissertation Repository, 2043,* pp 193-194, accessed at https://ir. lib.uwo.ca/cgi/viewcontent. cgi?article=3423&context=etd.

[9] The heavyweight champion of the world between 1865 and 1868 had been Jimmy Elliot, an Irishman who was arrested in 1870, charged with highway robbery and assault with intent to kill, for which he spent nearly 17 years in a Philadelphia prison. He died after being shot by an unhappy gambler. Jem Mace, the 1870 champ, was English, not Irish, but owned a saloon in which Philadelphia gangster Jimmy Haggarty had been mortally wounded in an 1871 barfight. McCoole, who was champion between 1870 and 1873, was an Irish saloon owner later arrested on charges of murdering another boxer after a quarrel in his saloon. ("Jimmy Elliot," "Jem Mace," "Jimmy Haggarty" and "Mike McCoole," all at Wikipedia.org.)

[10] In Pennsylvania, an 1866 law had made prize fights and boxing matches illegal, but only in five counties (including adjacent Montgomery County, Philadelphia's northern neighbor). (Act No. 184, Laws of Pennsylvania, 1866, p 210). The legality of prizefighting in Philadelphia in 1876 was still a matter of interpretation of common law principles of assault, battery, riot, and the like. Courts were divided about whether prize fights were legal under the common law. That very year, the Massachusetts Supreme Court had declared that "prize-fighting, boxing matches and encounters of that kind serve no useful purpose, tend to breaches of the peace, and are unlawful, even when entered into by agreement and without anger or ill will." (Commonwealth v. Collberg, 119 Mass. 350, Jan 4, 1876; the court found precedent in decisions in North Carolina, Indiana and Alabama, but it acknowledged contrary decisions in Ohio and South Carolina.) As late as 1889, Philadelphia papers were carrying blow-by-blow accounts of prize fights in that city, though a grand jury that included four clergymen had no problem indicting the participants (*The Times,* Jan 4, 1889, p 1; Jan 13, 1889, p 2; Jan 16, 1889, p 4.)

[11] Pettys Island is in the Delaware River, directly offshore from the end of York and Lehigh Avenues but within the jurisdiction of New Jersey. (See Map preceding Table of Contents.) "The island was a hotbed for gambling and dueling in the 18th and 19th centuries, and acquired a reputation for lawlessness and danger…" (Wikipedia.org, "Pettys Island.")

[12] *Inquirer,* August 23, 1876, p 2.

[13] Later that year, Johnny Clark, a Filbert Street saloon keeper, put up Jimmy Weeden against another Philadelphian named Walker. "Roughs" from surrounding areas attempted in vain to learn where the bout was to take place. Those willing to pay three dollars a head boarded a large barge on the river, holding a thousand passengers; with two tugboats carrying the fighters, they and the spectators were transported to Salem County, New Jersey, one of the first states to make prize fights unlawful (see https://www.encyclopedia.com/history/united-states-and-canada/us-history/prizefighting). New Jersey law provided that "Any person engaging in a prize fight in this state, and any person aiding, assisting or abetting therein, is liable to a fine of $1,000, or imprisonment at hard labor for two years, or both" (*Trenton State Gazette,* May 15, 1863). So the decision to stage it there seems curious – unless the promoters felt it safer to go "out of state" or onto inter-state waters, expecting that to give them jurisdictional advantage. The fight, refereed by Patsy O'Hara, lasted seventy-six rounds before Weeden was declared the victor. Ignored when he urged the fighters to desist, the Salem County sheriff tied the spectators' barge to the dock to keep the crowd under his jurisdiction pending arrest, but when the

fight was over, the crowd ignored him again, untying the barge and making off for a safe return to Philadelphia. The Sheriff's men fired pistol shots at the departing barge. One man fell wounded, but the barge was soon out of pistol range. The matter seemed over until the following day, when it was determined that the fighter identified as Walker, carried out of the ring in bad shape, had died immediately after the fight (*Inquirer*, Sept 1, 1876, p 8). New Jersey officials charged Clark and his victorious fighter with murder; they and others, including the tugboat captains and Patsy O'Hara, were arrested by Pennsylvania law enforcement officials and turned over to New Jersey (*The Times*, Sept 6, 1876, p 1 and Sept 7, 1876, p 1). The defendants were represented by none other than Lewis Cassidy, the lawyer who'd once been Dennis Murphy's classmate at Central High School and Dominic Murphy's political ally in Philadelphia politics. Weeden, the winner of the fight, was tried, convicted, sentenced to eighteen months, and died after a year in a Trenton prison.

[14] Matthew Ward, "Boxing and Boxers," Encyclopedia of Greater Philadelphia, accessed at https://philadelphiaencyclopedia.org/archive/boxing-and-boxers/. Clark went on to open a boxing school / gym in Philadelphia.

[15] The 1875 Directory showed brother William still living with the Austins at 2155 North 5th Street – Jimmy did not appear in the directory, but he, too, was likely living with the Austins that year. Jimmy's first appearance in the directories was in 1877, when he was listed twice – once in the Austin house on North Fifth Street, but also at 2149 N Front Street. In both entries, his occupation was listed as bartender.

[16] Phila City Directories of 1868 through 1875 show William employed as a sawyer, a wheelwright and a bedstead maker.

[17] "Many coopers worked for breweries. They made the large wooden vats in which beer was brewed. They also made the wooden kegs in which the beer was shipped to liquor retailers. Beer kegs had to be particularly strong in order to contain the pressure of the fermenting liquid, and the rough handling they received when transported, sometime over long distances, to pubs where they were rolled into tap-rooms or were lowered into cellars." (Wikipedia.org, "Cooper (Profession).") Jimmy's occupation, as given in the directories, changed from "bartender" to "liquors" in 1878; William was first listed as a cooper in 1878; George in 1879. Jimmy's 1878 address was given as 2139 Emerald Street, while George's was given as 2137 Emerald. The following year, Jimmy's was given as 2137 Emerald. Neither listing includes the "h" used to designate home addresses. Although not entirely clear, it seems likely that the two neighboring addresses were both a residence and a place of business. Perhaps William and George also contributed to the opening of Jimmy's first saloon: though Jimmy appeared to be the proprietor, William, George and others only later appeared as bartenders. Whatever the details, at this point, William, Joe, and George had clearly left the Austin household, and were now living and working with each other.

[18] The personality was that suited to being what E. L. Godkin called the "guide, philosopher [and] creditor" of the Irish community. (E. L. Godkin, *supra*. See Chapter One.) Jimmy fit Godkin's description to a tee.

[19] The exact date of Jimmy's marriage to Catherine Hagen is unknown, but assuming that Catherine's family was the one reflected in the 1870 Census, Phila Ward 19, Dist 60, Fam 1531, and Phila Ward 19, Dist 60 (2d Enum), Dwelling 318, Catherine had been born about 1860 to Bridget and James Hagen (a laborer), and so was several years younger than Jimmy. Their first child was born in June of 1879, suggesting conception in the autumn of 1878, when Catherine was eighteen.

[20] The 1880 Census, enumerated in June, indicates the child William was then 11 months old. The actual date of his birth is calculated based on the age that appears on his death certificate, indicating death on Sept 7, 1880, at 14 months and 14 days old. (PA Death Certificate of William Carvin, Phila Ward 31, FHL No 2047250.)

[21] Jimmy's family lived in the apartment above the tavern (1880 U.S. Census Phila Dist 674, p 20, 2401 Kensington Avenue). At Census time, living with them was John Roth, a German, occupation bar tender. The Census counted Jimmy's brother William as a cabinet maker, living with the Austins at 2111 N 5th Street (1880 U.S. Census Phila Dist 365, Fam 4). But both the 1880 and 1881 City Directories listed William as a bartender and gave his home address as 2401 Kensington. Perhaps he was working at two

jobs and living above the saloon on nights he tended bar. George, meanwhile, had moved to 2259 Hope Street, just a block to the south, and later to 2261 Hope Street, where he worked as a sawyer, a cooper and later as a bar tender.

[22] His brother George named a son Joseph James Carvin in 1876. (This young man died in 1897 at age 21. *Inquirer*, Nov 26, 1897, p 9.) Jimmy's brother Charles named a son James Joseph Carvin in 1881 or 1883 (1900 Census Phila Ward 31, Dist 0783, Fam 160, and PA Death Certificate 54413 for James Joseph Carvin, May 14, 1923.)

[23] William's death certificate gives his date of death as September 7, 1880. (Phila PA Death Cert Index, 1803-1915, FHL Film No 2047250.) His burial at the Roman Catholic New Cathedral Cemetery was the following day. (Historic PA Church & Town Records, Reel 838, New Cathedral Cemetery, Range 2, No 13, September 8, 1880, Historical Society of PA). Both accessed via Ancestry.com.

[24] Contemporaneous news accounts make no mention of any infant deaths in the family. The report of eight births is according to notes of the author's interview with their granddaughter, Mary McLaughlin, in the early 2000's. Within only fifteen years of marriage (1878-1893), eight births would suggest an active reproductive life. Sadie is called Sarah in at least one record, but according to oral tradition and other records, she went by the name Sadie. Joe eventually bought a family plot at the Catholic Holy Sepulchre Cemetery, and some of Florence's daughters became nuns, so whatever their number, Joe passed his parents' and Catherine's Catholicism on to his own offspring.

[25] In October of 1884, Jimmy bought property at Virginia and Amber Street; on May 25, 1886, he sold a property at 4th Street and Clearfield for $900; and on December 4, 1988, he paid $400 for a property at Fifth Street and Rising Sun (*Inquirer*, Oct 27, 1884, p 7; May 28, 1886, p 7; and Dec 17, 1888, p 6).

[26] Jimmy employed his brothers William, George, Charles, and Thomas, and George's son ("George W."), his nephew Charles, and Ann's son (John Austin). See Map and Legend pp 258-259. The placement of an "h" in the directories, indicating a home address, frequently attests to family members living at the bar addresses, probably upstairs. The 1884 and 1885 Directories listed both "Carvin Joseph J., liquors, 1746 N Front, h 2401 Ktn av," and "Carvin William H., bartender, h 1746 N Front," while the 1885 Directory listed his nephew, Ann's son John Austin, at 'h 2400 Ktn av." In 1887, Jimmy's listing was "liquors, 1746 & 2401 & h 2401 N Front," while nephew John was listed as a clerk with a home address of 1746 N Front.

[27] Though already surpassed by baseball in popularity, cricket was still a popular sport. Numerous reports in the papers refer to the cricketer simply as "Carvin" or as "J. Carvin" (e.g. *The Times* of Oct 12, 1880; May 15, 1881; June 19, 1881; July 17, 1881; May 31, 1882; March 25, 1883; May 25, 1884; *Inquirer*, Aug 7, 1892, p 7) but some refer to him as J.J. Carvin (*The Times*, July 2, 1882, p 2; July 23, 1882, p 2; Sept 14, 1883; June 22, 1884; and *The Inquirer*, June 12, 1898.) The name "J. J. Carvin" was unique; there is no mention in the Philadelphia media of anyone else with that name, other than Joseph James Carvin, the liquor dealer, and his son of the same name (who hadn't been born when the cricketer began playing).

[28] *The Times*, December 23, 1885, p 1.

[29] Phila Marriage Lic No. 5912, William Carvin to Mary O'Brien, 1886, Phila Marriage Lic Index 1885-1951, Clerk of Orphan's Court, Phila, Digital GSU # 4140411. Maybe Mary didn't like William working in saloons. After the marriage, the directories listed him as a boilermaker for a year, then as a fireman for thirty years, until he was listed as a bartender again in 1916. William died May 31, 1929.

[30] The 1886 Directory shows William, boilermaker, living at 2433 Sepviva Street. On March 11, 1886, Jimmy paid $550 for a property on Sepviva, near Jackson, which ran between Memphis and Martha in East Kensington (*Inquirer*, May 26, 1886, p 7). Jackson was at the location of modern Hagert Street (see 1886 Street Name Guide) – making 2433 Sepviva almost certainly the property he bought.

[31] *The Times*, March 17, 1886, p 1. The article calls Clark's place at 2406 N Front St both a "sporting resort" and a "saloon." The 1886 City Directory identifies Clark's occupation as "lager."

[32] *Ibid.* The report continued with a lengthy description of the fight: "SEVEN HARD ROUNDS. The fight was with kid gloves, for $150 a side. Coburn hails from Manchester, England, and Brannon belongs in Port Richmond. Seven hard rounds were fought and Brannon was terribly punished. The men are known, in the

language of the prize ring, as feather-weights. Coburn weighed one hundred and twelve pounds and Brannon was two pounds lighter. For a short fight it was one of the hardest battles between feather-weights that has ever taken place in this city ... Jack Fogarty, who recently fought twenty-seven rounds with Jack Dempsey, was referee and Jimmy Ryan was time-keeper ... In the first round ... [blow by blow description of the bloody fight omitted, including its enlargement to include the fighters' seconds] ... a general fight was likely to take place when Jack Fogarty, who feared police interference, declared the fight a draw. Coburn and his friends were not satisfied with the decision and Coburn immediately challenged Brannon to fight another battle. The decision had just been given when the police appeared."

[33] John Austin was the son of George and Ann Austin; he and Jimmy had lived together as children after the death of William and Mary. At 15 years old, he was an apprentice plumber (1870 Census Phila Ward 19 Dist 58, Fam 243) but ten years later, though still living at home, he was tending bar for Jimmy (1880 Census Phila Dist 365, Fam 4). He was still listed as a bartender in various 1890's directories as late as the 1898 edition, but efforts to determine his fate thereafter have failed.

[34] The 1880 Census, Phila Dist 369, makes clear that George Carvin had gotten married and moved in with the family of his wife Allabina (*nee* Snyder) at 2259 Hope Street. (When he and Allabina moved to 2261 Hope a few years later, they were renting the house next door to her parents.) Allabina Snyder Carvin gave birth to a daughter Carrie (1873-1903), a son they named Joseph James Carvin (1876-1897) after his uncle Joe, a daughter Annie (1884-?) and another son, George Washington Carvin (1887-1945). In February, 1884, the latter was made First Lieutenant in Company G, 2nd Regiment of the National Guard at Gettysburg (*The Times*, Feb 3, 1884, p 3), and on June 2, 1886, he was appointed assistant county tax assessor as a Republican (*Inquirer*, June 3, 1886, p 2). George Sr. appeared as a bartender in the city directories between 1886 and 1890, including one year (1888) that gave an address of 2401 N Front. George died January 20, 1891, a member of Washington Lodge No. 29, Knights of Pythias, and of Peskewha Tribe No 220 of the Improved Order of Red Men (*The Times*, Jan 22, 1891, p 5, and Phila PA Death Certificates, 1803-1915, Index, FHL Film No 1887795, accessed at Ancestry.com). The original death certificate in the Philadelphia City Archives has not been reviewed, so the reasons for George's death are unknown. Allabina married again the year after George's death and went on to live a long life as Mrs. Abraham Swartz Kaisinger. Sadly, George's son Joseph died less than seven years after George did, at the age of 21 (*The Times*, Nov 28, 1897, p 28; *Inquirer* Nov 28,1897, p 17).

[35] On October 1, 1886, Jimmy paid $2600 for a property on the southwest side of E. Lehigh Avenue, 65 feet from the Northwest Side of Emerald (*Inquirer*, Oct 19, 1886, p 7). As described in Chapter 8, Thomas had moved around a good bit, changing addresses more often than he changed jobs or wives, but the first year (1887) that he appears in the City Directory as a bar tender, his residence address is 1942 East Lehigh Avenue, which is precisely where Jimmy had bought on Emerald and Lehigh. Maybe the walk, or Jimmy's demands, proved too much for Thomas, as the following year (1888) the Directory listed him as a huckster living on Callowhill Street, downtown. (Thomas appears as a bartender again in the Directories of 1891, he and brother Charles both living on Mutter Street, only 4 minutes away from 2401 Kensington, when Jimmy apparently employed him again.)

[36] *The Times*, Feb 24, 1887, p 3. The address given, 529 N 3rd Street, is the address shown for Charles in the 1886 Directory, right next door to the address shown for Thomas, at 533. The storied soap may have come from their cousin, George Austin Jr., who had been listed as a soap-maker (living with his parents) in the 1877 City Directory.

[37] Charles had married in 1879. (In 1900 he and his wife (Catherine, *nee* Welch (1862-1930)) asserted they'd been married for 21 years (1900 U.S. Census Phila Ward 31, Dist 0783, Fam 150 at 1815 E York St). Their first child, John, was born in 1880 according to the 1900 Census, and their second, James, in 1881. From 1882 through 1885, Charles had been listed in the directories as an agent and salesman living some forty minutes south in the rear of 133 Dana Street. His move in the 1887 Directory was to the rear of 529 North 3rd Street, next door to Thomas. A year after Charles appeared as a bartender in the 1890 directory, he moved to Mutter Street, just four minutes from Joe's Tavern,

where he stayed for several years while tending bar. Even Charles's move to 1907 Firth Street, reflected in the 1893 Directory, only increased his walking time to 2401 Kensington from four minutes to six. Charles was married to the same woman for over 50 years and fathered six children by her. By all indications, he became a stable and successful family man. By 1900, he even had a live-in servant in his house. (See 1900 U.S. Census, Phila Ward 31, Dist 0783, Fam 160.)

[38] Phineas J. Horwitz was a physician who lived at 1919 Walnut Street (1888 City Directory, p 852). His ownership of the property at 2400 Kensington is shown by the report of Jimmy's March, 1890 purchase of it from Horwitz: "Front st., N.E. cor. Kensington ave. – P. J. Horwitz to J. J. Carvin; March 20, '90; 128 x 53.1-7/8 .$30,000" (*Inquirer*, April 2, 1890, p 7). Because Kensington Avenue forks off to the northeast from Front Street, the two streets form a Y at the 2400 block (See Map, p 258). The doctor's office sat in the triangular wedge of the Y, one wall facing west toward Front Street and another facing east toward Kensington Avenue. With odd numbers on the east side and even numbers on the west, 2400 Kensington was the same location as 2401 Front Street.

[39] City-wide, there'd been 4,206 licensed taverns in 1887; as of June 1, 1888, there would be only 924. The 19th Ward, where Jimmy's tavern was located, was hard hit. "In the Nineteenth ward, where 139 saloons were refused, there was consternation last night. After the first of June the ward won't look like the banner saloon ward of the city. It has lost its reputation."

[40] *The Times*, May 1, 1888, p 1, reported the granting of Jimmy's application for the license at 2400 N Kensington. Jimmy's brother George's application for a liquor license at 1746 North Front St was withdrawn before it was denied or approved (*Inquirer*, May 1, 1888, p 2). (That may have been simply a contingency plan, in case Jimmy's application was denied, or part of a "deal" struck by which one application would be withdrawn if the other was granted.) While competition was drastically reduced in 1888, it was not eliminated. The 19th Ward was still one of the three wards in the city with over sixty approved saloons. Those granted licenses in the 19th Ward also included Charles Martin, a block away at 2500 N Kensington; Robert Graham, at 2560 N Kensington, Peter Ward a block away at 2304 North Front; and Joe's former bartender (see 1880 Census) J.A. Roth, at 301 West York; but none of these were at the major intersection occupied by Jimmy.

[41] *Inquirer*, June 25, 1925, p 16 b.

[42] *Inquirer*, Nov 28, 1888, p 8.

[43] *Inquirer*, April 3, 1889, p 8.

[44] The Archbishop of Boston had just announced that parents of school-age children were required to send them to parochial school "under pain of sin" (*Inquirer*, Sept 11, 1888, p 1; *The Times*, Sept 11, 1888, p 1).

[45] For example, see *The Times*, May 15, 1889, p 3. The license was renewed by the License Court again in later years (*Inquirer*, April 15, 1890, p 2; May 23, 1891, p 23; *The Times*, April 8, 1892, p 6)

[46] Northern's President, Harry Clay, was a member of the Select Council.

[47] *The Times*, Oct 28, 1892, p 7 and April 5 & 6, 1893, p 1. Legislative and political haggling continued for the rest of the year and beyond. (*The Times*, April 12, 1893, p 4, April 29, 1893, p 1, April 30, 1893, p 1, and May 6, 1893, p 3; and *The Inquirer*, April 22, 1893, p 1, April 29, 1893, p 7.)

[48] *Inquirer*, April 2, 1890, p 7. Thereafter, the tavern's address appeared in the directories as 2400 N Kensington.

[49] The 1891 City Directory shows Thomas, bartender, living nearby at 2425 Mutter Street.

[50] *Inquirer*, June 28, 1891, p 2.

[51] *Inquirer*, July 23, 1893, p 10. "Fishermen are well pleased over the appearance of blue-fish, weak-fish and hake, and a successful raid on the denizens of the deep has been in order during the past week." That August, Joe was still at the shore, registered at the Hotel Germantown (*Inquirer*, Aug 20, 1893, p 10).

[52] Obits in *The Times,* 31 Oct 1893, p 5, and the *Inquirer*, Oct 31, 1893, p 7, list both deaths as occurring Oct 29. She was buried at New Cathedral Cemetery. See Burial Records of New Cathedral Cemetery, 2nd & Butler St, 31 Oct 1893, PA & NJ Church & Town Records, 1669-2013, accessed through Ancestry.com (microfilm p 742 of 3191), stating that Catherine was buried "with infant." If Mary

McLaughlin's assertion was correct that Catherine bore eight children altogether, she must have lost a second, third and fourth after William.

[53] The 1894 City Directory lists Jimmy at 2432 Howard Street; the 1895 Directory lists him at 636 York Street.

[54] 1870 Census for Phila Ward 20, Dist 68, Fam 145; 1880 Census for Phila Dist 376, Fam 190, and the 1893 City Directory listing for Margaret Kiker at 2537 N 6th Street; see Chapter 7 above. By 1894, Joseph P. Murphy was at 2529 N 6th and Margaret Kiker was at 2537 N 6th.

[55] The name Sherick derives from German Scherich, a variant of Scheurich. Charles Sherick was the son of the late Alexander Sherick (1831-1867) and his widow, Margaret (neé Donahue). Born in Germany, Alexander had met Margaret, born in Ireland, in about 1850, when they were 19 and 18, respectively, boarders at the same house in Philadelphia (1850 U.S. Census, Phila, Dwelling No 587). (Phila Death Certif Index, 1803-1915, originals at Phila City Archives, accessed via Ancestry.com, lists Alexander Sherick's birth as 1831, occupation moulder, married, address 6th and Meetler St, 20th Ward, death as March 20, 1867, and burial at Cohocksink Church Vault.) By June 1, 1880, Charles Sherick was a 28-year-old "Dealer in Oysters," with wife Mary Sherick, age 26, keeping house; Catherine Sherick, age 6; Laura V. Sherick, age 5; and Charles H. Sherick, age 1 (1880 U.S. Census, Phila, Dist 374, p 21, 538 West York Street).

[56] Charles Sherick owned the house (and oyster restaurant) at 604 York Street from no later than 1883 until his death in 1912; his son Charles operated it until at least 1922. By the 1900 Census, he would own it free and clear of any mortgage debt. Charles's occupation was "oyster dealer," but unlike Thomas Carvin, whose occasional employment as oyster dealer likely meant pushing a street cart, Charles Sherick operated a more substantial dine-in oyster house. The length of time the Shericks were at that address suggests stability, if not also prosperity.

[57] *Inquirer*, Oct 21, 1894, p 15. The newspaper simply lists Sadie Carvin and nine other children as "among the most advanced." It seems likely that Sadie's younger sister, Florence, was also enrolled.

[58] *The Inquirer* of July 8, 1894, p 11; Aug 12, 1894, p 10; June 9, 1895, p 9; July 7, 1895, p 16; and July 14, 1895, p 15; all originating in Sea Isle. A year later, Joe donated $10 to the Kensington Aid Association (*The Times*, Oct 21, 1896, p 3).

[59] This account of changing standards was given to us by our father in the mid 1950's.

[60] The Cohocksink Church, where Charles's father Alexander Sherick had been buried, was a Methodist Episcopal Church, so Charles may have been raised as a Methodist. But Margaret Kiker, the domineering matriarch of the family, had raised all the women in her family in the Baptist faith. Her funeral services were at the Fiftieth Baptist Church; she was buried with her husband Antony Kiker at Mount Vernon Cemetery (*The Inquirer,* May 21, 1900, p 14).

[61] Marriage Cert 83053, Reel 1331, Phila City Archives. In the application, the applicants swore that Joseph J. Carvin of 636 W York Street, occupation liquors, was born in Phila on August 12, 1855, and that he'd been married once before, dissolved by his first wife's death about October of 1893. The bride, Katie Sherick, of 604 W York Street, swore she'd been born in Phila in June of 1872, was 23 years old, and had never married before. The license, reported in *The Inquirer* of Feb 4, 1896, p 9, was sworn to and attested by one P.F. Sullivan on Feb 3, 1896. P. F. Sullivan is identified in the 1896 City Directory as the rector of St. Edward the Confessor.

[62] Passport Applications, National Archives & Records Admin (NARA), Washington, D.C., Roll No. 470, June 6, 1896, Application of "Joseph James Carvin, accompanied by his wife," employed as a saloonkeeper.

[63] Both of Margaret's sons who lived with her – Katie Sherick's uncles Harry & Philip – were butchers, like their father had been, an occupation which was surely related to the Kiker grocery business.

[64] In 1894, the Kikers still lived a few houses north of the Murphys, on the east side of North 6th Street (having left the house next door to the Murphys when the Murphys moved in). The Carvins' new house was at 2418 N 6th Street. The Joseph P. Murphy house was at 2529 N 6th St., and the Margaret Kiker house was 2537 N 6th St.

[65] The fact that the Murphys' disapproval of the marriage persisted for many years thereafter suggests that Katie never did convert.

[66] His youngest brother Charles was still tending bar for him at the time.

[67] *Inquirer*, July 9, 1897, p 3. The judgment was against one August Hoffman. The 1897 City Directory shows Hoffman – occupation "stoves" – with a work address of 2404 North Front Street, right across the street from Joe's tavern – he was probably a regular customer. If Carvin hadn't let Hoffman run up a bar tab, he'd simply loaned Hoffman the money. Friendly Joe Carvin, who'd given a job to his wayward brother Thomas, had been willing to bet on the high-risk loan.

[68] The judgment on the promissory note is reported in *The Inquirer* of July 9, 1897, p 3. The group checking in at the Atglen is described in *The Inquirer* of July 11, 1897, p 22. "Miss Rittenhouse" (Clara Rittenhouse (1873 - 1961) was the sister of Henry J. "Harry" Rittenhouse (1874 - 1945), who would soon (1898) marry Katie Sherick's sister Laura V. Sherick (1876 – 1933).

[69] One suspects that six-month old Charley was left at home with his grandmother, Mary Sherick, when the rest of the family vacationed in Ocean City that summer. After all, people with means and a sense of responsibility were expected to look after family members in need.

[70] The 1913 Catholic Encyclopedia stated, "Extreme Unction may be validly administered only to Christians who have had the use of reason and who are in danger of death from sickness. That the subject must be baptized is obvious, since all the sacraments, besides baptism itself, are subject to this condition." (https://en.wikisource.org/wiki/Catholic_Encyclopedia_(1913)/Extreme_Unction.) Whether Katie, as an arguable convert, had been baptized at all was, to the Catholic mind, itself a complicated matter: "[T]he particular case of each convert must be examined into when there is question of his reception into the Church. For not only are there religious denominations in which baptism is in all probability not validly administered, but there are those also which have a ritual sufficient indeed for validity, but in practice the likelihood of their members having received baptism validly is more than doubtful… [T]he Baptists use the rite only for adults, and the efficacy of their baptism has been called in question owing to the separation of the matter and the form, for the latter is pronounced before the immersion takes place…" (https://en.wikisource.org/wiki/Catholic_Encyclopedia_(1913)/Baptism.) Accordingly, there was room for interpretation whether Katie had been legitimately baptized, and therefore eligible for extreme unction.

[71] Philadelphia City Archives, 1898 Deaths, Cert No. 21084, Return of a Death, states that Mrs. Catherine Carvin, white female, married, age 24 years, address 2418 N 6th Street, died April 21, 1898, Cause of Death "Invagination of the bowels," determined by physician M.A. Wood, M.D. 155 Susquehanna Ave. Decedent's place of birth: Pennsylvania. Burial 4-25-98 at Holy Sepulchre Cemetery.

[72] After Katie's friend Clara Rittenhouse had come along on the Carvins' 1897 vacation in Ocean City, Clara's brother, Harry Rittenhouse, had married Katie's younger sister, Laura. Jimmy may have been the same age as Charles and Mary Sherick, but he was part of an extended social group dominated by his wife's generation. Since hardly anyone owned a telephone, notification of death was by word of mouth and by newspaper. For the slow expansion of telephones into private households, see Lucy Davis, *Telephones,* Encyclopedia of Greater Philadelphia, accessed at https://philadelphiaencyclopedia.org/archive/telephones/#:~:text=Philadelphia%20gained%20its%20first%20private,Pennsylvania%20Railroad%20president%20Thomas%20A.

[73] The diocese had opened Holy Sepulchre in 1894, after Joe's first wife died and was buried at New Cathedral.

[74] *Inquirer,* Sunday April 24, 1898, p 22.

[75] Our own father told us there was no love lost between the Murphys and the Shericks. Had the Murphys, with their influence at St. Edward's, spoken to Father Sullivan in Jimmy's behalf? Had promises been made? Was the purchase of a large family plot in the diocesan cemetery, and the sponsoring of a requiem mass, enough to persuade the Church to accept the body of a woman who had not converted as promised?

284

[76] The *Times*, Feb 15, 1900, p 9; the *Inquirer*, Feb 16, 1898, p 13; Feb 15, 1899, p 13; Feb 14, 1900, p 11; Jan 6, 1901, p 15; Feb 12, 1902, p 16.

[77] See, for example, the "Take the Same" and "What'll You Have?" ads for Arnholdt & Schaeffer Brewing's "Braun-Beer" in the *Inquirer* of Aug 12, 1898, p 5, Sept 2, 1898, p 4, and Feb 15, 1899, p 13, listing Joe's tavern, along with 20 other bars in the city, as a place to buy the beer.

[78] *Inquirer*, July 16, 1899, p 26, "Personal Pencilings." In the *Inquirer* of Aug 21, 1898, p 15, he was "the well-known businessman of Philadelphia," staying with his family at the Cordova in Atlantic City.

[79] The Eagles chapter was organized on Sunday, January 7 of the new century. The description of its nature was set forth in the subtitle of the article on it that appeared in *The Inquirer*, Jan 8, 1900, p 6.

[80] About the time of Katie's death in 1898, Harry Rittenhouse had married Katie's sister, Laura Sherick; Laura had become pregnant; and in February of 1900, she'd given birth to a baby girl, whom she named Catherine after her recently deceased sister. As of the 1900 Census, Harry and Laura were living with her father and mother, Charles and Mary Sherick; her 20-year-old brother, Charles Sherick; the infant Catherine; and Charles's 19-year-old niece, Emma Sherick (1900 Census, Phila Ward 19, Dist 0390, Fam 84, at 604 W York Street). Meanwhile, the wealthy widow and matriarch, Margaret Kiker, now entering her eighties, had been focused a great deal on her will, revising it repeatedly, adjusting bequests to her children to account for loans and debts among them, managing her estate as if trying to manage the lives of her heirs. (Since its execution in 1894, she had revised the will several times; the adjustment amounts suggest that the estate was substantial; heirs included her stepson, Reuben Kiker; her fifty-year-old daughter, Emily Breisch; her forty-six-year-old daughter, Mary Sherick; her forty-five-year-old daughter, Anna Murphy (no known relation to Joseph Patrick Murphy), and her sons Philip, John and Theodore Kiker.) (Applic for Prob. and Letters Test. No 1287, Phila Wills, accessed in Ancestry.com's PA Wills & Prob. Records, 1683-1993.) Then, on May 19, 1900, Margaret died. Her funeral, naturally enough, was at the Fiftieth Baptist church, where she'd long been a member (*Inquirer*, May 21, 1900, p 14.) But just ten days later, baptized together on the 31st of May were Emily Breisch, Mary Sherick, Anna Murphy; Mary Sherick's twenty-four-year-old daughter, Laura Rittenhouse; and Laura's three-month-old daughter, Catherine Rittenhouse. (Baptismal Records of St. John's Methodist Episcopal Church, Philadelphia, May 31, 1900, Historic PA Church & Town Records, PA Historical Society, accessed at Ancestry.com.)

[81] The hand of God was not yet ready to rest in their family. On December 31, 1900, the newly baptized infant, Catherine Rittenhouse, died. She was buried at Green Mount cemetery. (Phila City Death Certificates, 1803-1915, FHL Film No 1011829, accessed at Ancestry.com.)

[82] The household, as recorded by the 1900 Census, Phila Ward 37, Dist 957, Fam 192, looked like this:

Name	Birth & Age		Marital	Occupation
Jos. J. Carvin	Aug. 1854	- 45	Wd	Saloon Keeper
Jos. J. Carvin Jr.	Apr. 1881	- 19	S	Clerk – Hosiery
Sarah Carvin	Oct. 1884	- 15	S	At School
Florence Carvin	Oct. 1888	- 11	S	At School
Charles Carvin	Mar. 1897	- 3	S	

[83] In January 1900, he was issued a permit for a renovation at the saloon (described as the northeast corner of York Street and Kensington Avenue: *Inquirer*, Jan 16, 1900, p 12). In April of 1902, he invested $500 to purchase a rental property at Cambria Street and East Rosebill. On May 1, 1903, he sold another investment property for $1,050. (*Inquirer*, April 8, 1902, p 16, and May 6, 1903, p 6.) These were the only transactions that made it to the papers; perhaps he was buying and selling other properties as well.

[84] *Inquirer*, July 21, 1901, Sec 2 p 11. The reference to Joseph J. Carvin could have referred to either father or son.

[85] "Bar topper" was an occupation "suitable for girls, age sixteen and over," who transferred hosiery, during its manufacture, from a legging machine to a foot machine. (Occupation Studies: Bulletin Series; White Williams Foundation, January, 1923, accessed at Google Books, https://play.google.com/store/books/details?id=N004AAAAMAAJ&rdid=book-N004AAAAMAAJ&rdot=1.)

[86] In addition to the dates already listed, see *The Inquirer* Help Wanted section for Jan 18, Jan 19, Jan 24, Jan 25, Feb 29, Mar 21, Mar 31, Apr 1, Apr 20, Apr 22, Apr 23, Apr 25, May 25, Sept 3, Sept 11, Oct 18, Oct 23, Oct 24, Oct 25, Oct 26, Oct 27, Oct 30, Nov 20, Nov 28, 1904, with similar ads in 1905. Curiously, we find no similar series of help-wanted ads for any of the Murphy mills. Was the knitting business so different from the weaving business? Maybe the Murphys placed their help-wanted ads anonymously, inviting interested applicants to apply to the newspaper. Or did they simply have a way to get better textile help than the Carvins did? (E.g., did they pay better wages?)

[87] Marriage Records, PA Marriages, Various County Register of Wills Offices, June 5, 1905, Film No 001276765, accessed at Ancestry.com; Birth Certificate No. 84121, certifying the birth of Joseph James Carvin III was born on April 9, 1906. Mother's name was spelled Preuss. Father's occupation listed as "manufacturer." Address 1229 W Lehigh Avenue.

[88] Sadie had turned 18 on October 10, 1906. She had known Henry ("Harry") F. Gekler for years. (An article in *The Inquirer* of Aug 27, 1899 (Sec 3, p 7) had included her as one of the guests at a birthday party his parents held for him.) They were married in 1906 (Marriage License 199331, Phila Marriage Index accessed via Ancestry.com. The marriage was reported in *The Inquirer* on May 24, suggesting a marriage date of May 23.) Their daughter Catherine was born July 23, 1909, and their son, Henry Carvin Gekler, on October 4, 1917. Later events make clear that Joe remained close to the Geklers for many years.

[89] *The Inquirer* of October 29, 1906, p 6, under the headline "Guardians Appointed."

[90] Florence and Wendell were married May 22 of 1907 (Marriage Lic 213615, Phila Marriage Index accessed via Ancestry.com). Their daughter Virginia was born March 11, 1908 (PA Birth Cert 048501); their son, Wendell Jr., on March 6, 1909 (PA Birth Cert 048675); their daughter Florence Marie (1910); Martha Jane (1920), and Mary E. (1925). Virginia became the head of a religious order, Sister Mary David, Superior General of the Order of the Blessed Sacrament; Florence Marie and Martha Jane became nuns in the same order; Mary E. Young married John V. McLaughlin. (See 1910 Census Phila Ward 37 Dist 924 Fam 77; 1920 Census Phila Ward 17 Dist 1303 Fam 27; 1930 Census Phil Dist 1219 Fam 266; and obituary of Wendell Young, *The Inquirer*, Jan 3, 1973, p 30.)

[91] The new address, a forty-five minute walk from work at the tavern, was 1935 Somerset St (1908 Phila City Directory listings under both Gekler and Carvin). Catherine Gekler was born July 23, 1909; Henry Carvin Gekler was born Oct 4, 1917.

[92] The Directories show Charles, bartender, at 1813 E York between 1905 and 1916. Even his move to Hart Lane (first noted in the 1918 Directory) put Charles only fifteen minutes from the tavern, compared to Joe's forty-five (though public transportation – and now, even automobiles – were making walk times far less relevant).

[93] The Geklers were still living with Jimmy at 1935 Somerset in the 1910 U.S. Census (Phila Ward 38, District 0956, with Jimmy listed as head of household). Harry appeared there again in the 1912 Directory (as a "foreman"), in the 1916 and 1918 Directories (as "investigator"), and in the 1919 Directory as "inspr" (inspector).

[94] The Geklers appear (listed as Harry F. Gekler, adjuster, Am Indemnity Exchange) at 4535 Prospect Avenue, LA, in that City's 1920 Directory. So he appears to have moved to L.A. during 1919. Exactly when he did so, and why, is unclear, but Sadie's brother Joe was his only connection in L.A., as far as we're aware. The Geklers didn't likely move due to any major falling out with Jimmy, since Jimmy visited them in California more than once, according to a social tidbit that appeared in the *Los Angeles Evening Citizen News* of September 17, 1920: "Is Visiting Daughter and Family – Mr. James Carvin of Philadelphia arrived in Hollywood last Saturday to visit his daughter, Mrs. Harry Gekler, and family, of De Longpre avenue for some time. This is not Mr. Carvin's first visit to the Pacific coast; consequently, he has noted the improvements hereabouts."

---

[95] The government did this by defining "intoxicating liquor" to include any beverage containing more than *half a percent* of alcohol.

[96] Florence Cathryn Carvin (Oct 10, 1888 – May 4, 1958) married the butcher, Wendell Young, in 1907. Their children included Virginia E. Young (1908 -) who became an accomplished nun, Wendell Young, Jr. (1909-1984), Florence Marie Young (1919-2007), also a nun, Martha Jane (1920 -), and Mary E. Young (1925 - 2009), who married John McLaughlin and spoke to the author about her grandfather shortly before her death.

[97] 1920 U.S. Census Phila Ward 19, Dist 047, Fam 1.

[98] *The Inquirer* of March 14, 1920, p 39. The show was advertised as "the Funniest Burlesque of the Season" and according to the *Inquirer*, "as may be imagined, [it's] a satire on the arid conditions now prevailing, and is wildly amusing" (*Inquirer*, March 16, 1920, p 6).

[99] "Arrests were made, but bringing the arrested to trial and persuading the courts to convict them remained another matter." (Russell Weigley *et al*, Philadelphia, a Three Hundred Year History, W.W. Norton & Co. (1982) *supra*, p 578, citing a 1925 Report by Mayor Kendrick.)

[100] The building was reported sold in June of 1925 by one Robert McNeil for $77,500 (*Inquirer*, June 25, 1925, p 16 b). Since none of the Robert McNeils in the 1925 City Directory are listed as realtors, it seems Jimmy had sold the property to McNeil between 1920 and 1925. Jimmy's granddaughter Mary McLaughlin, who was born about 1925, recalled in a conversation with the author that he opened a bar or restaurant at the Reading Terminal when she was very young, but she acknowledged that her recollection almost ninety years later was uncertain, and in any case, the directories don't list Jimmy at that address.

[101] *Inquirer*, May 14, 1939, p 8.

[102] As for "Jimmy," it's natural his grandchildren called him the name by which he'd always been known. But why they called him "uncle" is not clear.

[103] Philadelphia Death Certificate No 24425 for Joseph J. Carvin, 936 Herbert Street, dated Dec 13, 1934. Oddly, we've been unable to locate Jimmy in the 1930 Census. He may have been living with one of his children (or more than one, in succession) so never counted in any of their households. His death certificate contained some anomalies. The listing of his spouse as Katherine Sherick comported with the fact that the informant was his son Charles Carvin. But the handwriting in which the name Charles Carvin was entered is not that of his son Charles, and the middle initial given (A rather than W) was wrong – suggesting that someone other than Charles may have actually provided the information or at least completed the form. The maiden name given for decedent's mother (Morrow) was right, but the decedent's father's name, "James" rather than William, was incorrect (though not surprising given Charles' own apparent lack of understanding about his father's past, and the fact that his father was known as "Jimmy.") Listing the decedent's occupation as "retired manufacturer" was perhaps plausible, but certainly surprising, given his very brief stint in the knitting business compared to his many years operating multiple saloons. The embalmer was Frank A. Hookey, Lancaster Ave – the father of Stella Marie Murphy's friends, Jane and Mary Hookey. (See 1920 U.S. Census Phil Ward 47, Dis 1196, Fam 150 and 1920 Census Phila Ward 47 Dist 1790 Fam 178 listing Frank Hookey as an undertaker.)

11. Joseph D. Murphy

The immigrants who'd faced prejudice at the hands of the native-born had struggled, survived, and left the country to their children. Being native-born Americans themselves, some of those children had looked down upon the Chinese, Poles, and other immigrants who threatened their country's shores. But now it was time for a third generation to show what they could do. [1]

Joseph Dominick Murphy, the first son of Joseph Patrick Murphy and Adele Miller, didn't arrive until June 17, 1873, so he never faced bloody riots as a child, didn't live through the horror of the civil war. The distinction of being his parents' first child belonged to Joe's older sister Adele. But Joe was their first son, and that made all the difference. Taking his first name from his father and his middle name from his grandfather, Joe's own name (like so many others) constantly reminded him of patrilineal descent. There was no space on the Division of Vital Statistics' new birth-registry form for the occupation of his mother – there'd have been little need for yet another "housewife" or "waif" – but there was a space for "Occupation of Father" because that seemed to matter (though no one could explain how). In the case of Joseph D. Murphy, that occupation was "Manufacturer." He was one of the biggest in the city dominated by men.[2]

Joe's grandparents, the immigrants, were still alive; some Murphy family fortunes had been preserved and others were still on the rise. Joe's famous uncles, Dennis, James and Edward, were the pre-eminent reporters of the U.S. Senate, and his Uncle Dominic was rising through the ranks of the Pension Bureau. In 1881, when Joe was eight, his father built a prestigious home on North 6th, a pretty, tree-lined street, just a couple of blocks from St. Edward the Confessor Church. The ten members of the Murphy household included two parents (a manufacturer and his wife), two grandparents (a clerk with the Treasury Department and his wife), an uncle (a clerk in the Government Printing Office), an older and a younger sister, a little brother, and a live-in-servant. Joe and his three siblings were cared for by the servant, twenty-two-year-old German-born Louisa Pfaefer.[3]

Children didn't speak unless spoken to. Talk at the dinner table centered around politics, finance, and business. After dinner, while the men smoked cigars and the women retired to sew or discuss the latest parish news, there was little for a boy like Joe to do, sandwiched between his older and younger sisters.

Should he play with the girls? None of Joe's male cousins lived in Philadelphia.[4] His little brother, Edward, was five years younger than him – and for a child, five years is a very long time. For all intents and purposes, Joe was the only male child in a world full of women.

For the first twelve years of his life, the newspapers were full of news about their father's accomplishments – strikes by employees, the building of a major new woolen mill, speeches on tariffs, chairmanship at meetings, leadership in parades. The record of Joe's own life, and that of his little brother Edward, is silent. What school did they attend? How did they spend their time? The unknowns force us to grasp at straws in search of clues.

A photograph taken many years later shows Joe to be a hefty, robust man of substantial weight. His 1918 draft registration card confirms the robust picture: the examiner described Joe's height medium, but faced with the choice of describing his build as slender, medium or "stout," the examiner opted for "stout."

> "Stout"… Of persons: Thick in the body, not lean or slender; usually in unfavourable sense, inclined to corpulence; often *euphemistically* = corpulent, fat.[5]

Joe, it seems, had never suffered for lack of food.

One family living just a block from the Murphy's new house – the Congdons – were close friends who would come to play a significant role in Joe's life.[6] If we take the Murphy and Congdon families together, the oldest five were all girls, prone to dominate or ignore younger boys as fancy struck them.[7] To divine the atmosphere of the Murphy household at this point, we might consider the older men's domination of the house and their focus on prices, profits and public policy. We might consider the plight of the older women who lived in their shadows. And if we look ahead to what the younger girls' futures held in store, we find that Anna Marie Murphy's marriage would not end happily. That neither Elizabeth nor Maria Agnes Murphy would ever marry or have children of their own. That the three women would live out their lives with their mother (and then, after their mother's death, with each other, at the house of their younger sister), with not a man among them. At a minimum, the Murphy sisters were very close – certainly not the type to run loosely with men.[8]

At the same time, sandwiched between his older sister Adele and his younger sister Anna Marie, and having no brother close to his own age, Joe had a natural friend in Richard Congdon, who was just a year his junior. When boyish fancy struck, the pair played tricks on the older girls, and spied on them. But when Adele Murphy came down with typhoid fever and died a terrible death at age sixteen, Joe became the oldest of the Murphy children. The Congdon girls' compassion for his loss softened their adolescent rivalries. And barely two years later, Mrs. Congdon also died; each family now shared in the other's loss, Joe and Richard two boys in a neighborhood full of girls.[9]

Like the other Murphys, Joe continued in school.[10] Then, just a week after Mrs. Congdon was buried, the papers announced a shocking surprise: the Murphy mills had gone bankrupt. The children had not seen it coming. Their relationships with their father grew even more stressful as he dismissed their emotions as weakness in the face of his important business trials.

How exactly life among his sisters affected young Joe has been lost to history, but about the time he turned eighteen, his relationship to Richard's sisters was changing.[11] They were practically the only girls Joe knew who weren't his relatives. Problem was, they were older than he was. Worse still, he wasn't the only one interested in them. On the other side of the Congdons, on Marshall Street, the builder William Henry Greenfield had moved into the neighborhood. The Greenfield's son, William Jr., some three months younger than Joe, also had an eye on the Congdon girls.

Because Irene Congdon was only a few months the boys' senior, competition for her was inevitable. But who else did Joe have to choose from? In vying for Irene's affections, he should have had the edge, as he was older than William, but as it seemed to him, his hefty waistline was in the way. Sure enough, Irene expressed interest in his slenderer rival, William. On the verge of losing out, Joe's attentions turned to Irene's older sister, Stella. Something must have led them to decide they were suited to each other, for within a couple of years, Joe Murphy and Stella Cecelia Congdon were married.

Their license to marry was reported in *The Times* on May 1, 1895. William Greenfield's license to marry Irene Congdon was reported two months later. But unlike society's other engagements, the betrothals were not mentioned in the newspapers, nor were parties, bridal showers, dances, or even the weddings themselves. Content with their close circle of family and friends, the younger generation stayed out of the newspapers. Joe and Stella made their first home directly across the street from the Congdon house on North 9th Street. William and Irene moved to the same street. With the three homes so close together, the Congdon girls remained at the center of all their small gatherings.[12]

Just a month after the wedding, however, the senior Murphy was in the news (again). His weavers had gone out on strike (again). While Joseph P. was absorbed in his business problems, his son tried to figure out where he fit in to the world of powerful men. Maybe he'd had his fill of the publicity surrounding his father, his grandfather, and their businesses. When it came to labor strikes, lawsuits and finances, the news was nearly always unfavorable. The older Murphy's anger when the new president, William McKinley, promised to raise tariffs again made his son wonder if politics wasn't a waste of time anyway. He could never compete with the sort of fame the older generation had attained. Being stout had made him an introvert. If he engaged in any civic activities, they didn't land him in the news.[13] His absence from the historical record suggests a more private man than either his father or grandfather had been.[14]

Meanwhile, nine months and one week after their marriage, Stella Cecelia Murphy gave birth to a daughter they named Stella Marie.[15] Joe enjoyed staying home with his wife; watching his daughter learn to crawl, and walk, and talk. Soon, Stella was expecting again, and little Stella Marie was asking questions about her mother's changing shape. The parents gave answers intended to satisfy before the questions became too graphic. The Murphys decided that if their second child were a girl, they would name her Genevieve after Stella's older sister Genevieve Congdon, who lived just three blocks away and had become little Stella's favorite aunt. The thought of having a sister just like her Aunt Genevieve certainly pleased little Stella Marie. But the second pregnancy did not end happily. On Sept 17, 1897, when the infant Genevieve was born, she lived for only an hour.[16]

The house was full of memories, but all of them – their hopes for the child, Stella Marie's questions, the answers they'd given her, the labor itself – were suddenly painful. It was hard to think of politics or national news, especially when it involved the suffering of others. And the news often involved the suffering of others.

For example, two months later, when a group of white supremacists overthrew the newly elected (and largely black) government of Wilmington, North Carolina, it made the national news, but the Murphys, focused on their own problems, didn't give it much thought.[17] President McKinley maintained there was nothing he could do about such racism, as it was not a federal matter. African-Americans chastised McKinley for refusing even to publicly condemn the insurrection. But Joe and Stella Murphy, in need of comfort themselves, contented themselves by pointing out that the Murphys had never been fond of McKinley.[18]

Joe finally began to find his niche in the world by designing fabrics, shawls, and other products for his father's mills.[19] His focus was on the materials, the dyes, the patterns of weave, the threads per inch, the choice of sizings used, the hand and appearance of the yarn and the finished cloth. But with their child's death still on his mind, he could bring scant softness to the weaves, little brightness or color to the fabrics he designed. It was hard to design his manufactured goods with breathability.

With so much reminding them of their loss, the Murphys moved to a new home, several blocks away, at 710 Lehigh Avenue.[20] When Stella became pregnant for the third time in the spring of 1899, Joe insisted she get plenty of rest, that she do absolutely nothing strenuous at all. He knew, now, that both his Stellas were special; that all conceivable measures had to be taken to ensure their health and happiness. As he looked forward to another birth, he tried to infuse his fabrics with hope.

About that time, a new business entity promised good things to come. Its name – 'Murphy & Bro." – suggests the participation of two principals, Joe and his younger brother Edward.[21] Their father, now in his mid-fifties, struggling with creditors and cash flow, had figured out a way to pass some of his wealth to the younger generation. While the details of loans, gifts, or investments elude us, the new company now belonged to Joe and his brother. Joe was no longer a mere designer. Even if he was five years older than Edward, the two boys were equal partners. Each could think of himself as the named "Murphy," his brother the "& Bro." Father Murphy advised them; he used his contacts to support them; but he passed actual control to the younger generation.[22] Joe was now a businessman in his own right – an owner, a capitalist.

His image of himself began to improve. The looms were all powered by steam, of course, but Joe had no connection to the old world of hand-loom weaving, in which neighborhood craftsmen cooperated and worked with each other; he knew nothing of what his grandfather meant about men who powered their looms with their own two feet. The new Murphy & Bro. mill was no neighborhood operation, it was all the way on the south side of town, and transportation to and from it was an issue.[23] Helpful as it might have been for someone else's waistline, an hour-and-a-half walk to work was out of the question. Fortunately, by 1897, electric trolleys had replaced horse-drawn streetcars.[24] They were far more reliable, and they lacked the foul odors of the horse drawn trolleys that still ran on the side streets. Joe could walk to the street on which the trolleys ran. The wait for a connection was not as unpleasant as it might have been had he had to walk farther.

On November 27, 1899, Stella gave birth to another daughter, this one named Mary. This time, the infant lived. She was fed, loved, cradled, burped, and rocked to sleep. But small and frail, she lived for only two weeks.[25] It wasn't long, but two weeks of love had been enough to make her life palpable, her absence even more painful, even harder to bear than Genevieve's. Joe found it hard to focus on Murphy & Bro. At least for a time, brother Edward bore the greater part of the business load. And four-year-old Stella Marie became all the more precious, all the more coddled.

The house at 710 Lehigh now bore painful memories of its own. Late in 1900, the Murphys moved again, this time several blocks further north, even farther from the Murphy & Bro. mill.[26] Transportation became a bigger issue than ever. Fortunately, technology had begun to accelerate. The 1890's had ushered in the era of the automobile, and the new self-propelled machines were the talk of the town. In Philadelphia, the James Hill Company and the Keystone Motor Company had started making two-passenger runabouts.[27] Ads by the bicycle maker, Roach and Barnes, could be found throughout the pages of the 1900 City Directory:

A runabout could turn the difficult daily commute into a ten- or fifteen-minute adventure, and for Joe, it was surely tempting. But if he bought such a vehicle, he was one of a privileged few. Even by 1905, there were fewer than 500 automobiles registered in Philadelphia – about one car for every 400 families.[28] Perhaps Stella saw a runabout as an unnecessary expense. Perhaps Joe took the trolley to work a while longer, only dreaming of owning a car. But he knew he wouldn't be able to resist for long.

In the meantime, contraception being a sin, Stella Cecelia soon conceived again. The fourth pregnancy was more anxious than ever before, and though it was filled with painful memories and worries about complications, it further heightened the level of care and attention paid to the precious little Stella Marie. Then, on April 10, 1901, a healthy baby was born: Joseph Edward Murphy. And to everyone's delight, the boy lived.[29]

Joe's attentions turned once again to the bigger world. When it took the government only six weeks to electrocute McKinley's Polish assassin, Joe Murphy did not complain about the speed of the punishment. Such criminals deserved what they got. Besides, he was more concerned about demands for a 55-hour workweek and complaints about child labor in the textile mills. In the summer and autumn of 1902, such conflicts led to the biggest labor strike Philadelphia had ever seen, a strike that threatened to cripple the family's business.[30] Joe encouraged his father to follow Roosevelt's example: the President had dealing with the anthracite coal strike through negotiation and compromise. But the textile mills held firm and at least in the short run, the strike failed.[31] When the bankruptcy proceedings were finally over, the elder Murphys sold their prestigious home on North 6th Street and moved to Germantown, two-and-a-half miles north, taking Joe's sisters with them. Joe and Edward were now fully in charge of the business their father had left behind.

After tying the knot in August of 1906, Edward moved to West Philadelphia.[32] And now, with scores of employees and their families depending on them, Joe and Edward began to taste the fruits of success. They added a new, twenty-five by thirty-six-foot brick dye house to the mill at 16th and Fitzwater,[33] and they opened a second mill in the suburbs.[34] They placed frequent want ads, including one that read, "Boys wanted, about 14 years old."[35] They advertised their desire to buy a 100 horsepower return tubular boiler.[36] As equal partners at Murphy & Bro., neither Edward nor Joe could make a decision without the consent of the other, but the occasional conflict this caused was not fatal. Their households revealed their success with better radios. Bigger pianos. A New Victrola. A live-in servant of their own.[37]

While a runabout was all Joe needed for a trip to the mill, Stella and children begged him to consider a larger touring car so that they could ride too.[38] Unable to say no, Joe bought a machine large enough to take the whole family for rides in the country. On the first warm days of spring, he took them to the beach at Atlantic City, where trips up and down Atlantic Avenue kept them even cooler than walks on the Boardwalk and new attractions included the Steel Pier, the Million Dollar Pier, and the six-story wood and tin elephant known as "Lucy."[39] Speeding along the highway toward home, it seemed the ocean breeze would never abandon them. Their touring car made the larger world seem pleasant. Lacking the smell of horse manure, the new fuel – gasoline – seemed to vanish without so much as a trace.[40]

They were prosperous times, and his daughter deserved the very best he could give her, so Joe started sending Stella Marie to a prestigious private school.[41] The school's yearbook, "The Patrician," was said to be named after its founder (Mother Patricia Waldon), but the double meaning of the name could hardly be lost on parents. Joe became a member of the Whitemarsh Country Club.[42] His eight-year-old son begged to attend opening day at the new Shibe Park stadium, just a few blocks away.[43]

The Athletics won the World Series there in 1910, 1911 and 1913. But while the A's were winning baseball games, workers were finding it hard to make ends meet. Crop failures and lynching threats in the south had caused thousands of African-Americans to come to Philadelphia, Sarah Scott, the Murphys' nineteen-year old live-in servant, among them.[44] America had been good to the Murphys, and Joe assured Sarah that if she only applied herself, she could improve her lot, just as so many Germans and Irishmen had. But as we've seen, the Murphys had fathers, brothers, sisters, and uncles to help them; family that meant capital, education and contacts among successful people. Germans and Irish shared neighborhoods. When a black woman dared to move into a white neighborhood, a mob threw stones at her house; two days of rioting followed, leaving three people (two white and one black) dead.[45]

During a 1910 strike by carmen of the new Philadelphia Rapid Transit System, angry carmen attacked street cars along Lehigh Avenue, leaving dozens injured and almost 300 street cars heavily damaged. More than 3,000 deputized police arrested hundreds of strikers. When a demand for arbitration was denied by the PRT, the Central Labor Union called for a general strike.[46] 45,000 textile workers struck their employers.[47]

Joe had little stomach for such disputes. His heart was in design, where durability, comfort, even beauty were his focus. And now, as Uncle Dominic had predicted from his consulate in Switzerland, a silk factory was being built in Marcus Hook, a half hour's drive down the Delaware River. Chemistry moved design to a far more basic level, from visible things like fabrics, yarns and dyes down to invisible things like molecules and the elements of matter itself. But Joe was a man of vision, who could see chemistry's potential. If he could produce fabric made of such man-made yarns, he could undercut those who relied on silkworms, prove to his father that his love for design had not been wasted. He even thought of making the new synthetic himself, something greater than anything their father had ever done. Little did he know that when he spoke to his father about making yarn from wood pulp, it would be one of the last conversations they ever had. Joseph P. Murphy died on December 5, 1910. Two months later, Stella Cecelia's father followed.[48]

Much as he grieved over the loss of his parents, the cloud had a silver lining: Joe now had the freedom to do as he pleased, and the enjoyment of all that a successful life had to offer was high on his list. He took the family to see *The Man Between,* Rupert Hughes' serious play about "the eternal struggle of capital and labor, class against class." The subject was of no small interest to the Murphy family. According to *The Inquirer,*

> The scene showing a huge cantilever bridge in full course of construction was a splendid example of stagecraft, while the gathering of an angry mob and its outburst on the arrival of troops to quell them into submission was worked up in a way that caused a thrill of excitement to reach the audience... [T]he role of the bridge builder, John Stoddart, who stands between his capitalist employer and the men under him, assumed a real dignity that entitles it to serious consideration.[49]

We cannot know Joe's innermost thoughts: whether he felt empathy with the laboring classes; whether he was solidly aligned with the capitalists. But whatever his personal views, the Murphys did not give up their business. Their father's death put capital at their disposal. They acquired and began making alterations to another mill at 30th and Reed Street.[50] In 1912, they bought yet another mill at Cobb's Creek in West Philadelphia, where they started a new company, "West End Woolen Mills, Inc."[51] Classified ads showed activity at all the locations: in August, 1912, the brothers put their Chester mill up for sale; a year later they were hiring at the West End Mill.[52] Even if Joe had sympathy for the working class, that sympathy did not extend to labor unions. In keeping with the prevailing attitude of employers in 1913, they advertised for "non-union beamers" at the Fitzwater mill.[53] And on February 22, 1914, they advertised their desire to buy a 50-horsepower upright boiler and large tank to dye the fabrics they wove.[54]

The city, meanwhile, was filling up with skyscrapers. More than 100,000 cars would soon be registered there. One writer viewed Market Street as "dimmed by the summer haze that is part atmospheric and part gasoline vapor."[55] The only bad news, as far as the Murphys were concerned, was that artificial silk was proving difficult to manufacture. They'd not been able to produce more than a few samples when, on June 28, 1914, the assassination of Franz Ferdinand plunged Europe and much of Asia into war. By late summer, Germany had invaded France. Lines of battle had been drawn up along the Marne. And by the end of 1914, opposing trenches stretched from the English Channel to Switzerland.[56]

Like most Americans, Joe Murphy had little interest in getting involved overseas – he only wanted to be sure that his imports of wool from Ireland would not be interrupted. On October 5, 1914, the *Inquirer* reported (under the heading "Philadelphians on Boardwalk") that Mr. and Mrs. Joseph Murphy were "among the Philadelphians on the promenade" in Atlantic City. As they looked out at the Atlantic Ocean, Joe assured Stella there was nothing to worry about; everything would turn out well. Generations of Murphys had prospered in the textile business, even in the worst of times. While Uncle Dominic shepherded Americans out of Germany and Holland, Joe decided he would wait patiently for hostilities to end; after all, President Woodrow Wilson had promised to keep America out of the war, and America had declared itself officially neutral.

Still, the war had an impact on American business. Trade with Germany and the other central powers all but disappeared. European shortages amid increased demands pushed prices higher. With higher prices making the chance for profit irresistible, increased exports to England, France and their allies more than made up for the loss of trade with Germany: American exports to Europe nearly tripled from 1,293 million dollars in 1911 to 3,814 million in 1916. Mineral oil, flour, brass, horses, wheat, oats, corn, pork, mules, cotton and gunpowder led the way as America profited from Europe's war.[57]

The Murphy textile mills experienced similar upheavals. In the first year of the war, the building that housed the West End Woolen Mills was condemned and the mill closed its doors.[58] But by February of 1917, Joe was placing help-wanted ads to staff the mill at 30th and Reed.[59] And Joe did not lose sight of his Uncle Dominic's reports about the wonders of artificial silk. With Dominic's help, he tracked down a German chemist named Christian Greiner; together, they started experimenting with wood-pulp in an effort to make artificial silk.[60]

Meanwhile, exports of food, arms and munitions to England and France made clear which side of the war American business was supporting. Germany threatened to sink American ships caught supplying arms to its enemies, publicly targeting the Lusitania, an ocean liner it claimed was secretly carrying munitions to England. Despite the warnings, the Lusitania defiantly left New York for Britain, its civilian passengers trusting their governments' denials that there were munitions on board and that any attack by Germany would therefore violate the rules of war. When Germany carried through with its explicit threat and torpedoed the Lusitania, newspapers demonized the Kaiser's "Huns." Outraged over the sinking and unaware that the Lusitania had, in fact, been carrying munitions, Americans directed their hostility toward Germany and

German-American citizens, rather than at the governments that had used them as human shields.[61]

And so, Wilson sought and received a declaration of war against Germany. Ironically, once he did so, he became intolerant of the very opposition to involvement he himself had so recently expressed. To stir up support for the war, he established the first modern propaganda office, the Committee on Public Information, headed by newspaper man George Creel. Creel's Committee orchestrated a campaign of so-called "Four Minute Men" to give short speeches at public gatherings, to rally support for the war, and to pitch Americans on the purchase of Liberty Bonds to finance it. To suppress dissent, Wilson got Congress to pass the Espionage Act of 1917, which made it a crime "willfully to cause or attempt to cause ... disloyalty ... [or] refusal of duty." A year later, the Sedition Act went further, outlawing "disloyal ... or abusive language" about the government or the military. The Department of Justice began targeting antiwar groups and arresting many of their leaders.

The government also invited the Dreyfus brothers to make cellulose acetate dope for American warplanes in Maryland.[62] The Ford Motor Company started making steel helmets for American troops at a ten-story plant just a block and a half west of Murphy's home. American business was now making artillery shells, gun mounts, boots, leathers, mortars, knives – everything an army could need – for its own combatants. "Few Quaker City manufacturers went uninvolved in the production for war."[63] The War Revenue Acts of 1917 and 1918 raised the top income tax rate to seventy-seven percent and levied an excess profits tax on both businesses and individuals. Yet the papers reported that the Germans had invented a better way of making clothes out of "paper cloth," which Joe knew to be artificial silk.[64] When Creel's Committee on Public Information began fanning the flames of anti-German sentiment, Joe had his eyes on the German success while other Americans found only the enemy in the faces of their German neighbors, people like the Roderers, Reintanzes, Althouses, Demmers, Yoders, Kirchners and Klemms who lived on the same street as the Murphys.[65]

Creel called his later account of his Committee's work "How We Advertised America: The First Telling of the Amazing Story of the Committee on Public Information That Carried the Gospel of Americanism to Every Corner of the Globe." The war in Europe was characterized as one to defend "liberty." To sell "Liberty Bonds," Creel's Committee guided America into anti-German hysteria. Rumors abounded about German spies and enemy plots. Sauerkraut was renamed "Liberty cabbage"; "German measles" became "Liberty measles." "[G]roups campaigned for the suppression of the German press and language... [T]he Philadelphia School Board voted to end the teaching of the German language in the public schools."[66] Under the Espionage and Sedition Acts, it became a crime to write a "disloyal" letter or express anti-war sentiments to any audience which included men of draft age.

Altogether, over two thousand Americans were prosecuted under the two laws. Americans who declined to buy Liberty Bonds woke to find their homes streaked with yellow paint. Churches of pacifist sects were set ablaze. Men suspected of disloyalty were tarred and feathered. Most of the violence was carried out in the dark by vigilantes who marched their victims to a spot outside the city limits, where the local police had no jurisdiction.[67]

Irish and Germans had long lived side in their workplaces and apartments; the people of Kensington and Germantown had grown together like interwoven vines, Irish and Germans intermarrying (Sherick to Rittenhouse; Carvin to Gekler; Carvin to Preuss.) Stella Marie's friends included Germans like Lillian Hengen, Dora Klemm, Sara Yoder and Lillian Kirchner.[68] Yet the rhetoric stirred up by Creel made everyone with German blood suspect.

With Joe's interest in artificial silk outpacing Edward's, even the Murphy brothers soon found disagreement hard to manage. Murphy & Bro came to an end. When Edward and two of the younger Murphy brothers – Francis and Walter – combined to buy Joe out, a new entity appeared at 16th and Fitzwater called "Murphy Bros," with Edward as president and treasurer, Francis and Walter as vice-president and secretary, Joe having no role at all. (He simply kept the mill at 30th and Reed Street, where he kept his own office.)[69]

Now entirely on his own with only one mill to manage (the "Joseph D. Murphy Textile Co."), and comfortable with the money he'd received in the buyout, Joe didn't need to work as hard as before. He took an apartment on prestigious Rittenhouse Square, downtown. But ever a designer at heart, ever dreaming of making greater things than the other men ins his family, Joe and his German technician, Christian Greiner, kept trying to make artificial silk.[70]

The food crisis in Europe affected his family as well. Even before the United States entered the war, Charles Lathrop Pack had organized the National War Garden Commission to encourage Americans to grow their own fruits and vegetables so that more food could be exported to Europe. Citizens were urged to plant vegetables in school and company grounds, parks, backyards and vacant lots. Propaganda posters urged Americans to "sow the seeds of victory." The federal Bureau of Education initiated a U.S. School Garden Army (USSGA) to mobilize children to enlist as "soldiers of the soil." Caught up in the patriotism of the day, Joe's son (Joseph Edward Murphy) took an intensive three-week farming course at the State College. After a brief visit home, he spent the summer at a government farm camp.[71]

While young Joe was learning to grow food to support the war, father, mother and Stella Marie spent the summer at a new cottage on South LaClede Street in Chelsea, some twenty miles west of the city.[72] But technology and war and meant massive movements of people around the globe, and together, they had created a new problem: flu was killing thousands, all over the world, and especially among soldiers. Encouraged to ignore the disease's spread by a federal government that wanted only positive news in support of the war, Philadelphians ignored the advice of their own local health officials. When the Murphys returned to Philadelphia that autumn, they found the city hit hard by the pandemic. In early October, 139 Philadelphians died from the flu in a single day. By the time city officials took notice, it was too late. They ordered all Philadelphians to wear gauze masks in public. Even spitting became a criminal offense. But the *Inquirer* asked, "What are the authorities trying to do? Scare everyone to death? ... Live a clean life. Do not even discuss influenza. ... Talk of cheerful things."[73] And so the public remained skeptical.

Worldwide, a third of the world's population were infected. As many as a hundred million people died.[74] Twelve thousand Philadelphians died in just the month of October. With almost a third of its employees stricken, Bell Telephone implored people to limit telephone calls to emergencies. Victims seemed fine one minute but delirious with fever the next, their skin turning purple from a lack of oxygen, pneumonia filling their lungs with fluid, blood gushing from the nose, from the ears and even from women's vaginas. Theaters, schools, churches and saloons were closed. Hospitals were put under police protection, with patrol cars serving as ambulances. Highway crews used steam shovels to dig trenches for the dead. With some seventy-five percent of the hospitals' physicians and nurses serving in the war overseas, medical students were used to tend to the sick. Children who lost both parents to the flu lived for days in their homes without food.

And then, by month's end, it was mostly over. The city allowed public places to reopen on October 27.

All the while, to keep up morale (since a world war was on), President Wilson had ordered his administration to limit news to positive reports. He never made a single public statement about the pandemic, even when the war ended on November 11, 1918, even though sporadic outbreaks of the flu continued through the spring of 1919.[75]

Things quieted some after the war and pandemic were over. Joe Murphy and his German chemist, Christian Greiner, could be heard talking once again about ways to turn trees into silk. They learned what they could from the tight-lipped people at Marcus Hook, but there was natural reluctance to describe failures, just as there was natural secrecy about anything that worked.

A gang broke into the Murphy mill, robbing it of inventory. The headline read "Thieves Flee in Car; Patrolman Hits One in Revolver Battle." The subhead: "Blood on Abandoned Motorcar Shows One of Gang that Escaped Was Wounded."

> Revolver shots were exchanged early today between
> a patrolman of the Twentieth and Federal streets station
> and five alleged motor bandits who were said to have
> been forcing an entrance to the textile mill of Joseph D.
> Murphy, Thirtieth and Reed streets. The men escaped.

Blood spots found on the rear seat of an abandoned automobile that the police say was used by the thieves indicate one of the five was wounded. Hospital authorities here have been told to hold anyone applying for treatment of a bullet wound.

The abandoned machine was found at Twenty-second and Pine streets. It is said to be the property of Alfred Fikentscher, of 2306 North Myrtlewood street, whose car was stolen last night from Broad and Vine streets. When recovered, the machine had a bullet hole through the radiator. The shot had lodged in the engine.[76]

Why robbers would risk death in order to steal cloth is hard to say – unless some competitor thought Murphy had discovered the secret for making fabrics from trees. The bold taking made Murphy feel violated, but no one had ever said running a business would be easy. Labor strikes … Sabotage … Armed robbery … If only he didn't have be a manufacturer, he thought. If only he could design and patent an artificial silk product – yarn, fabric, anything – he could simply collect royalties, be forever free of market swings, equipment breakdowns and gangs who break and enter. To quit the world of manufacturing, he would need just one more success to ensure his family's well being. There *had* to be a way to turn trees into silk.

In the spring and summer of 1919, the Great War over, Uncle Dominic reported that the Germans had mastered the necessary chemistry. Dominic gave him names and places, contacts in Switzerland and Germany who might share the new science with him. On July 16th, both Joe and Christian Greiner applied for passports. Murphy's application attached a copy of his birth certificate; Greiner's attached an affidavit regarding his naturalization as a United States citizen. Both men stated the intention to leave from New York about August 1st. Given the changes later made to the applications, it's interesting to compare the versions.[77]

At first, the applications stated an intention to visit Holland and Belgium, the purpose of visiting those countries phrased cryptically as "en route," while the purpose of visiting a third country – Germany – was stated simply as "business." Attached to the applications, also dated July 16th, was a typewritten letter on Murphy's business letterhead, clearly stating his intention to visit the Vereinigte Glanzstoff Frabriken plant in Germany where artificial silk was being successfully made. Also attached was a typewritten statement dated July 16th to the effect that Christian Greiner had been in his employ for some years "as a foreman and demonstrator of Artificial Silk," and stating the desire that he (Greiner) go to Germany with Murphy, in order to "examine some of the factories that produce this Silk successfully."

Greiner's original application mirrored Murphy's in all relevant respects.

300

JOSEPH D. MURPHY

MANUFACTURER OF

TEXTILES

THIRTIETH AND REED STREETS

OFFICE

WOOLEN BUILDING

PHILADELPHIA. July 16th, 191 9.

To the Clerk of the United States Court,
Philadelphia, Pa.

Dear Sir:

I herewith submit my reasons for wanting Passport to Germany. For the last four or five years we have been experimenting in making Artificial Silk, have not been successful in making it in a large commercial way, have only been successful in making in small quantities. Have spent not only the time developing this product but many thousands of dollars and are anxious to examine the property of Vereinigte Glanzstoff Fabriken or any of the Artificial Silk plants of Germany where they make it on a large scale and very successfully.

Artificial Silk is only made successfully by one large concern in this Country and under another system from the one we use. Regret to state that in this Country many firms have failed trying to produce Artificial Silk but feel we can see some of our mistakes by examing these German plants.

Very respectfully yours,

Joseph D. Murphy

JDM/M

Sworn and subscribed to before me this 16th day of July A.D. 1919.

Frances P. Kelly

NOTARY PUBLIC,
My Commission Expires March 3rd, 1920

JOSEPH D. MURPHY

MANUFACTURER OF

TEXTILES

THIRTIETH AND REED STREETS

MX OFFICE
DOLEN BUILDING

PHILADELPHIA.   July 16th,   191 9.

To the Clerk of the United States Court,

Philadelphia, Pa.

Dear Sir;

This is to certify that C. A. Greiner
is in my employ and has been for some years as
foreman and demonstrator of Artificial Silk.
I am desirous that he should go to Germany to
examine some of the factories that produce
this silk successfully.

Respectfully yours,

Joseph D. Murphy

JDM/M

But then, there were identical revisions made to each. The purpose was now given simply as "commercial" And the intention to visit Germany was replaced with an intention to visit France, as if Murphy – or someone advising him – had decided it easier to get a passport to visit America's recent ally in the war than to visit its recent enemy. A change was also made on the back of the application. Originally, both Murphy and Greiner had requested that their passports be sent to Murphy's home address, 1830 Rittenhouse Square in Philadelphia. But new requests asked that both passports be sent to Dominic I. Murphy, American Consul General, Wardman Park, Washington, D.C.

Surely, Uncle Dominic had suggested the changes. Had he advised that visiting Germany would be impossible, unwise, or unnecessary? That making the changes he recommended would bypass Government obstacles, allowing them to get to Germany less "directly"?

The passports were issued on July 22nd. Then, on the 9th of September, having made it as far as the American consulate in Paris, Murphy and Greiner made further amendments to their applications, swearing that it had become necessary to visit Switzerland.[78] (It was easier to pass into Germany from a place where Dominic had contacts, like St. Gall, Switzerland, than it might have been from Belgium or France.[79])

With Uncle Dominic's help, the September 9th passport amendment was approved. In the month that elapsed before their return to the States,[80] they learned as much about the manufacture of artificial silk as the capitalists of a defeated Germany would allow. Upon their return to Philadelphia, business went on as before: the manufacture of cotton goods continued to weaken as it had before the war: between 1909 and 1919, Pennsylvania's production of cotton goods decreased 31%, with Philadelphia bearing the brunt of the loss. That loss was partially offset by a rise in production of ready-made clothing, much

Joseph D. Murphy
1919 Passport Photo

of it the product of Jewish hand-labor.[81] The classified ads Murphy now placed suggest a movement toward the finished and dyed piece goods that, as a designer, Joe had always preferred to simple undyed broadcloths. The piece goods market was growing.[82] But Joe Murphy produced no artificial silk.

Dominant as it was in his life, running the textile business wasn't Joe's only responsibility. While his father and uncles had been part of an extended family dominated by men, Joe was the only male his age in his family. His mother and sisters continued to live at 6807 York Road in Kensington, an enclave of women and children a few miles north of his stylish apartment on Rittenhouse Square. Headed by Joe's seventy-year-old mother Adele, it included four of Adele's daughters and three of her grandchildren. The only income-earning male in that house was Adele's son-in-law, the twenty-eight-year-old dentist, Joe Colman. Of course, even if there'd been a social security program in those days, the never-married, never employed Murphy women would not have been eligible for it. Since the household could not support itself financially, Joe Murphy remained responsible. And as the women didn't drive, Joe and his touring car were frequently put to good use.[83]

Although the women had no careers, the family was nevertheless wealthy enough to have cooks, maids, and other servants doing their household chores. It was what was expected of a well-off family, a sign of Joe's success (and that of his younger brothers) that he could provide such a life for them. We hear no more of his efforts to make artificial silk; it seems the Murphy women could still afford the real thing.

It was in this affluent lifestyle that Joe and Stella had raised their precious daughter, Stella Marie. She was raised in silk and lace, with books, and music, and theater, and the rigid morals of the Catholic church. Aspiring to assimilate into mainstream America, Joe and Stella Murphy sought to distance themselves from one habit of common Irish Catholicism: in their dignified circles, there was a stigma attached to drinking. The Murphys were proper, church-going Philadelphians and law-abiding citizens. Much of the city blatantly violated the new Prohibition laws, frequenting speakeasys and drinking openly while campaigning for repeal. In the 1921 election, much to Joe and Stella's dismay, the political machine run by "wet" William S. Vare regained the control it had enjoyed before Prohibition began; Republican J. Hampton Moore was elected mayor with a whopping 85% of the vote.[84] Joe and Stella Murphy counted themselves among the supporters of Prohibition.

But while he avoided public drinking, Joe played cards twice a month with a regular group of like-minded men.[85] Meanwhile, his only surviving daughter had reached marriageable age. Having once addressed her as "the best girl in the world," he now treated her as if she were. With years invested in her education, and now wanting her to marry into a good family, now wanting the best that success in America could provide, he showed her off wherever he could. In September of 1920, when three hundred and fifty businessmen pushed three hundred and fifty young girls down the Boardwalk in wicker chairs in what became the Miss America Pageant, Joe must have imagined his daughter among them. He showed her off at every Philadelphia society opportunity he could, even volunteering to oversee arrangements for the first annual dance of the Avon Country Club at McCrea's Dancing Academy.[86] In the absence of making a fortune in artificial silk, find the right husband for dis daughter had become his loftiest dream.

But his and Stella's efforts to find the right kind of family for Stella Marie came too late. She'd already taken a liking to a boy from the old neighborhood. His family background fell short of what they had in mind: he'd been raised with no mother; his father was a liquor salesman, a gambler, and a lecher who liked younger women, even non-Catholics. The young man who'd captured their daughter's interest was constantly cracking jokes and making light of things, never taking life seriously. He liked to dress in ridiculous costumes, to play ridiculous characters; he loved funny papers and minstrel shows; he risked his life going up in flying machines. In short, he was an immature lad, uninterested in serious business pursuits. He'd never be able to support their daughter in the way she deserved.

And on top of that, he was a drinker. His loose habits were frowned upon by the stricter nuns at the Academy of Mercy. (And Stella Marie enjoyed alcohol too much as it was.) For some reason, Stella Marie seemed more attracted to the young man than to anyone in the country club set. Ignoring her parents' advice, she insisted on having her own way, and in June of 1922, she married her fun-loving beau. When she left home to start a family of her own, her absence left a hole Joe and his wife hadn't felt since little Genevieve and Mary had died.

With his starlet gone, Joe had little to do but entertain himself. He helped form the new Penn Athletic Club.[87] He and the other members of the Manufacturers' Club purchased a farm and mansion in Upper Dublin for the purpose of constructing a golf course.[88] But no matter how he tried to enjoy the good life, problems kept after him. In April of 1924, his mill was looted again, clothing and cloth worth $3000 stolen from his inventory.[89] He felt violated yet again. And the month after that, Stella Cecilia passed away at the age of fifty-two.[90]

After the funeral, left to fend for himself, Joe moved into the Manufacturers' Club at Broad Street and Walnut, "an organization where ethnically and economically homogenous citizens gathered in large, well-appointed rooms to discuss matters of great importance."[91] He spent several weeks at the Princess Hotel in Atlantic City.[92] Secretly, he decided to sell the textile mill. It came as a total surprise to his children. As described by Stella Marie in a March, 1926 letter to her Aunt Genevieve:

Friday

Dear Aunt G,

The Murphys are surely going in the real estate business – today, Father sold the mill – it all happened so suddenly – we don't know what to think – I haven't been talking to Father yet – Joseph told me the news when he came home for dinner – the men came down to the mill this morning, came back this afternoon and said they would buy it – left $5,000 deposit – I sincerely hope it is for the best – Mother always wanted it – thought the place was entirely too big – too much worry...

Will write more details later –
With much love –
Stella Marie –

Six weeks later, Murphy ran his last classified ad for the mill at 30th & Reed. It advertised various pieces of equipment "For Sale Cheap."[93] His late wife had long wanted him to sell the business, and after hundreds of years in textiles, it seemed Joe was calling it quits at last.

But Joe had one more thing to accomplish before he retired. By the end of July, he was placing classified ads for a stenographer, a clerk, a designer, a boss weaver, a loom fixer, a percher, and a mender on piece goods at yet another address: Bellfield and Wister Street. His thinking can only be guessed at, but the new location was the very spot at which LaSalle University, that same year, was opening its new campus, between Germantown and Oak Lane.[94] The new mill location got Joe closer to the golf links at White Marsh Country Club, as well as to the soon-to-be-built Manufacturers' Golf Course.[95] More importantly, Joe had convinced his son, Joseph Edward, now in his early twenties, to give up the idea of becoming a farmer: in the tradition of many generations of Murphys, the boy was now learning the textile business. Buying the Wister Street mill was a way to pass on a business to his son, while Joe himself played golf.[96]

For six years after his wife died, Joe remained a single widower, playing cards, playing the links, teaching his son the woolens business, and adhering to the proper life of a widower. Then – about three years after his son married, Joe Murphy saw an opportunity for a new life in the person of one Isabell Hoeflich, *nee* Reybould. Joe and Isabell had taken up with each other despite the fact that Isabell's German husband was still alive. They lived together in Philadelphia as man and wife (and with Isabell's daughter, Marion) for some time before going to New York City to marry. [97]

In obedience to the Catholic Church, Isabell had never gotten divorced. Once again, the Murphy family condemned the marriage: Joe's daughter, Stella Marie, refused to have anything to do with her father's new wife.[98] Perhaps the illicit marriage was the last straw for Joe's mother as well. A year and a day after the wedding, Adele Murphy died. Joe arranged for a solemn requiem mass for her at the Church of the Holy Angels and had her interred in the Murphy family plot at Holy Sepulchre.[99]

At age 58, he'd never attained the fame of his grandfather, father, or uncles. A "stout" man, he wasn't one to march in parades, give speeches or hobnob with powerful men, unless it was to engage in a private game of cards or round of golf. He was a sensitive, simple designer at heart. His financial success, such as it was, was in the use of capital and know-how to provide for his family, which he did in a quiet but dignified and law-abiding way. His one dream – to master the alchemy of turning trees into silk – was never realized: by the time he married Isabella Hoeflich, he'd clearly given up on it. Other, younger men were making it happen, and that, it seems, was quite alright with him.

In the summer of 1932, he and Isabella vacationed in Ireland, a country Joe had never seen; in 1935, they visited Chile. But by his early sixties, overweight and suffering heart problems, Joe was looking for a place to rest and recuperate. Hot Springs, Arkansas, was said to be the perfect place for such recuperation, and he and his wife left for the celebrated, life-restoring place on Saturday, March 21st.

The next day, he was dead.

The obituary that appeared in the *Inquirer* may have been composed by Isabella, by Joe Jr., or even by Stella Marie. Whoever authored it, it reflected an opinion about what Joe had thought most important: it recited that he'd been president of Joseph D. Murphy, Inc, and that "His family had been engaged in the textile business in this country and Ireland for more than two hundred years."[100]

Notes on Chapter 11, Joseph D. Murphy

[1] Joseph D. Murphy may be of particular interest to us because, as a product of all that had gone before him, he (like us) was an example of what many Americans were becoming, which is to say more modern, and ever more proud of our heritage. Curiously, though, while sharing a common interest in everything about ourselves, some of us are proud of our early blue-blooded ancestry in America, while others are proud to have risen up from poverty and oppression as mere immigrants. Some of us even seem to think that we and our ancestors go back further than other people and their ancestors do.

[2] The place of birth given on birth certificate #14689 – "York near Amber," rather than the numerical 427 East York recorded elsewhere – also shows that even in 1873, seventeen years after the City adopted its uniform numbering system for street addresses, that system still had not yet entirely caught on.

[3] 1880 U.S. Census Phila Dist 370, Fam 83 at 123 Susquehanna Ave. The residents were Joseph P. Murphy and his wife Adele; their children Adele, Joseph, Anna and Edward; John J. Miller and his wife Annie; their son Joseph R. Miller; and the servant, Louisa Pfaefer. Louisa's older countrymen, like the Protestant Irish, had come to Philadelphia in search of a better life in a land of opportunity and upward mobility, but so far, they had not done as well as the Murphys.

[4] Several of Joe's male cousins died in childhood, but those who'd survived were all successful. His older cousins included John Miller Carson (1864-1956), a man's man who'd graduated from West Point and was on his way to becoming a Brigadier General; Richard S. Murphy (1861-1907), personal secretary to Senators who was listed in the 1900 Census with the occupation "capitalist;" and John D. Kinney (1869-1939), a pension attorney in D.C. who worked with their Uncle Dominic Murphy, Commissioner of Pensions. Joe's younger male cousins in D.C. included James Wilmot Murphy (1878-1960), who would follow in his father's footsteps to become the dean of Senate Reporters for fifty years (see postscript to Chpt 5).

[5] Excerpt from the Oxford English Dictionary entry on "Stout." The O.E.D. gives an example from an 1856 Tailor's Guide asserting that a man is considered stout "when the waist is large in comparison with the breast." It's always possible Joe put on his weight later in life. (He was forty-five years old by the time the draft registrar described him as "stout.") But it seems likely his waistline began its expansion when he was a young boy.

[6] Richard Congdon, son of John and Mary Congdon, had served in the 192nd Pennsylvania Infantry, Co E or G, during the civil war. (See 1890 U.S. Census Veterans Schedule, Phila, Dist 392, p 2.) After the war, he had married Boston-born Mary Elizabeth Connelly, a daughter of James and Mary Connelly, and ran a hotel and saloon in Old Kensington (1860 Census Phila Ward 17, Fam 119; 1870 Census Phila Ward 17, Dist 52, Fam 69; 1880 Census, Phila Dist 316, Fam 174; and City Directories 1870 – 1884). He appears as a watchman in the 1885 City Directory at 2513 Marshall St – one street west of the Murphy home at 2529 North 6th. In 1889, the Congdons moved to 2419 Fairhill St – one street east of the Murphy home (see the 1890 Directory and Map, p 266).

[7] Names and birth years in the two families were Anna May Congdon (1868), Genevieve Congdon (1869), Adele Murphy (1871), Stella Congdon (Feb 1872), Irene Congdon (Dec 1872), Joe Murphy (1873) Richard Congdon (1874), Anna Marie Murphy (1875), Walter Congdon (1877), Edward Murphy (1878), Francis Murphy (1881), Elizabeth Murphy (1883), and Maria Agnes Murphy (1885).

[8] Did Adele's death affect them in some lasting way? Were they "stout" like their brother? Did their relationship with their father affect their attitudes toward men? Or did they simply prefer the company of women?

[9] Death Certificate, FHL Film No 2080370, accessed via Ancestry.com; *The Inquirer,* Jan 28, 1890, p 5.

[10] Joe Murphy is not listed among the graduates in Central High School's publications. He may have attended the old Catholic high school that began at St. Michaels and was now the preparatory division of LaSalle College (https://www.lschs.org/about-la-salle/history). We have found no obituary or other

3

record clearly indicating college attendance. A 1931 newspaper article refers to one Joseph Murphy being elected a vice president of the Alumni Association of St. Joseph's College, but the article includes no middle initial and does not indicate what year this Murphy graduated (*Inquirer*, June 8, 1931, p 2). A yearbook of the University of North Carolina lists a "J. D. Murphy" as a member of the Class of 1899, but that seems too late for a young man Joe's age. In light of Joe's late-life move to the campus of LaSalle College, it may well be that he attended both LaSalle's preparatory division – which had grown from the old St. Michael's Church where the 1844 riots occurred – and its College (https://www.lschs.org/about-la-salle/history).

[11] A few months after the Murphy bankruptcy, the Congdons moved to a new home around the corner, about the same distance as previously. In June of 1890, Richard Congdon (father of the Congdon family) appears in the U.S. Census Veterans' Schedule at 528 Huntingdon Ave, and at the same address in the 1891 City Directory.

[12] The Greenfield-Congdon license was reported in *The Times*, July 3, 1895. The 1896 Directory shows William Greenfield at 2629 North 9th, next door to the Congdons. The first address for Joe Murphy after the marriages was not until the Directory of 1898, but that address was 2624 N 9th Street, right across the street. Keeping in mind that the directories reflected addresses late the prior year, the most plausible conclusion is that both of the new husbands had taken hómes next to the Congdon house immediately upon marrying, so that both their Congdon wives could remain close to their families during their first years of marriage, when first pregnancies were hoped for. Meanwhile, although literally adjacent to the Congdon home, the houses were all still just three blocks away from the senior Murphy's home at 2529 N 6th Street.

[13] The name Joseph D. Murphy was common in the papers, but most of the stories were about another Joseph D. Murphy, a journalist, member of the School Board, and Cashier of the U.S. Mint. (See his obituary, *The Inquirer,* Nov 20, 1912, p. 7.) The Joseph D. Murphy elected treasurer of "The Asparagus Club" and the man on the planning committee for the Philopatrian Ball were surely the same very public man too. The only stories that may refer to the more private son of Joseph P. Murphy are a couple datelined Atlantic City, reporting on summer visitors from Philadelphia, such as the report that "Joseph D. Murphy, a prominent businessman, is resting here. He is stopping at the Champlaine." (*The Times*, July 11, 1897) and the report, six weeks later, that he was still at the beach. (On Aug 22, 1897, "Ryan's Cottage" included simply "Joseph D. Murphy, Philadelphia.") The following summer, another report (Aug 14, 1898) from Atlantic City might also refer to Joseph D., the son of Joseph P. Murphy.

[14] Neither the 1896 nor the 1897 City Directory gave any clue of his existence. Conceivably, Joe was the "Jos. D. Murphy" listed as a "dyer" down by the waterfront, at 2318 Moyer Street, but that location seems unlikely, given its distance from the neighborhood of his parents, his sisters, and the Congdons and Greenfields. As common as the Murphy name was, it seems unlikely that entry referred to him.

[15] Stella Marie Murphy was born on February 6, 1896.

[16] Phila Death Certs Index, 1803-1915, FHL Film No 1011826, for Genevieve Stella Murphy, address 2624 N 9th Street, accessed via Ancestry.com. Burial Sept 20, 1897, New Cathedral Cemetery.

[17] The coup was the work of white men outraged that freed slaves had gained too much political power.

[18] "Wilmington Insurrection of 1898," *Wikipedia.org.*

[19] The 1898 City Directory gave Joe's occupation as "designer."

[20] See Map p 266. The move may also have been prompted by the departure of their friends, the Greenfields, who had moved to Lawndale the year before, some five or six miles to the north. Both the 1898 and 1899 Directories show the Greenfields having moved to Lawndale; both the 1899 and 1900 Directories show the Murphys at 710 Lehigh.

[21] The first evidence of the new company and mill location is in the 1900 City Directory, which lists "Murphy & Bro. (Jos D. and Edwd V.), cotton gds, 746 S 16th." The 1900 U.S. Census at 710 Lehigh Avenue listed Joseph D. not as a "designer" but as a "manufacturer." While the Directories list only the two older brothers as principals, we can't rule out the possibility that their younger brothers, Francis, Walter and even Raymond, may have also been employed at the mill and/or owned a share of the

company. But the Directory listings make it clear that Joseph and Edward were in charge. When the family nurse, Mary Hood, died in July, 1899 without a husband or children of her own, leaving her savings to St. Edward the Confessor church and to each of Joe's younger siblings, she left nothing to Joe (presumably because he was independent and didn't need it).

[22] Between 1900 and 1910, listings for Joseph P. Murphy in the city directories include five years in which the word "woolens" or "woolengds" follows his name, two in which "cotton" or "cottongds" does, and three in which he is not listed at all. In no case is he listed as an officer or principal of any company, and no evidence of his involvement in Murphy & Bro. appears elsewhere -- all facts consistent with a strategy to shield the business from Joe P's creditors by putting everything in his sons' names.

[23] Murphy & Bro., Cotton Goods, was listed in the 1900 City Directory at 746 South 16th Street.

[24] John Hepp, "Public Transportation," Encyclopedia of Greater Philadelphia, accessed at https://Phil adelphiaencyclopedia.org/archive/public-transportation/

[25] Philadelphia Death Certificate Index, FHL Film No 1011828, Mary L Murphy, death Dec 12, 1899, 16 days old, burial at Holy Sepulcher Cemetery Dec 13, 1899.

[26] The 1901 Directory shows them at 2943 Camac Street. Although they soon moved to 2941 Camac, and then to 2932 Camac, they remained on the 2900 block of Camac Street (north of Cambria) continuously until 1907. Meanwhile, in 1890, a new church had opened in a building at 9th and Richfield Street, and with it, a new parish: St. Bonaventura's. (A new church on Hutchinson Street, near 9th, dedicated with a solemn high mass held in the basement on May 17, 1896, would not be completed until 1906 (The Times, May 18, 1896, p 8; The Inquirer, May 18, 1896, p 7).) Recently torn down, the new church was beautiful: its beauty can still be appreciated through the photographs at https://www.abandonedamerica.us/st-bonaventure. The Murphys' move to Camac Street put them far from St. Edward and very near St. Bonaventura. Lehigh Avenue, about midway between St. Edward Confessor and St. Bonaventura was likely the parish dividing line, but St. Bonaventura was a German church; its rector, Father Hubert Hammeke, was a German; at least some of its masses were conducted in German, and non-Germans may have continued to attend St. Edward. Whether the Carvins or Murphys began attending the new church is hard to say.

[27] https://www.earlyamericanautomobiles.com/1900.htm

[28] Russell Weigley et al, Philadelphia, a Three Hundred Year History, W.W. Norton & Co. (1982) supra, p 524.

[29] Like his father, the younger Joe Murphy would grow up to be stout.

[30] When the United Mine Workers struck the anthracite coal operators of Pennsylvania in 1902, the age-old conflicts between management and labor entered a new phase. President Roosevelt sought no injunctions against the strikers; he called in no federal troops; rather, he invited management and labor to the White House, where he urged both sides to compromise. In the end, the miners and operators agreed to binding arbitration by which their differences were eventually resolved. The textile strike that began in Philadelphia on June 1 of 1903, idling some 100,000 workers, was chiefly to support the demand for a 55-hour workweek and to protest the use of child labor. On June 2, The Inquirer's frontpage headlined "Textile Strike Is Largest Known," and the lead article called it "one of the greatest conflicts between employer and employee that Philadelphia has ever seen." The celebrated Mother Jones came to town, as did the famous socialist, Eugene Debs, giving speeches in support of the striking workers.

[31] The strike in Philadelphia spared 47 firms that had already agreed to the 55-hour week, which seems to have included Murphy's: when The Inquirer listed all the mills whose employees attended a union meeting, Murphy's was not among them. In any case, by August there was talk of the strike failing; by October, The Inquirer was reporting that the strike had been unsuccessful, the (local) Central Textile union all but dissolved, and a new plan afoot to affiliate with the national Textile Workers Union and A. F. of L. (Weigley, supra, p 495; The Inquirer of May 15, June 1, June 2, June 6, June 24, June 26, Aug 12, Aug 29, and Oct 22, 1903.)

---

[32] *The Inquirer*, August 24, 1906, p. 6. Edward and his sweetheart – a woman twelve years his senior, with a sixteen-year-old son – got married in New York City, with no prior notice and none of the bride's family in attendance. Her former husband was still alive, and since the Church did not recognize divorce, it would not recognize Edward's marriage. The newspaper account of the wedding asserts that "Mr. Murphy's brother attended him," but doesn't reveal which brother. The 1907-1909 Directories showed Edward living at 3413 Chestnut; the 1910 Census and 1910-1913 Directories showed him living with Marian, her teenage son Richard Levis, and an African-American servant, Sarah Jones, further west at 4516 Locust Street (1910 U.S. Census, Phila Ward 46, Dist 1163, Fam 177) and Edward's move to West Philadelphia coincided with the opening, on March 4, 1907, of regular subway-elevated service between the Fifteenth Street and Sixty-Ninth Street PRT stations, extended to Second Street station on August 3, 1908. This route provided a direct link between Edward's new residence and the Murphy & Bro. plant at 16th and Fitzwater. Meanwhile, younger brother Frank Murphy also married in 1903. Some in the family thought him too young to get married, as he was only 22; but he and his wife had a healthy daughter in 1904 (who they named Adele Gertrude Murphy, after his mother), and a healthy baby boy in 1906 (whom they named Joseph P. Murphy, after his father).

[33] "Permits Issue Yesterday," *The Inquirer*, Sept 26, 1905, p 7.

[34] Help wanted ads from *The Inquirer*, March 12, 1905, p 17, and July 23, 1905, p 17. "Designer and manager on woolen goods for Chester Mill." "Superintendent for woolen mill. Address Murphy & Bro, Chester, stating where employed, wages wanted." While no Murphys or Murphy & Bro. mill appear in the 1904 or 1906 Chester Directory, the latter directory contains a listing for "The Marion Mills Co." at 15th and Highland Terrace – the address given when the mill was put up for sale in 1912, identified as a 32,000-foot mill with a large yard (*Inquirer*, August 18, 1912, p 32, and January 12, 1913, p 36).

[35] *The Inquirer*, Feb 22, 1906, p 12.

[36] *The Inquirer*, January 5, 1908, p 31.

[37] The 1910 U.S. Census, Phila Ward 37, Dist 928, Fam 145, shows the Murphys at 1234 Lehigh Ave, living with servant Sarah Scott; their neighbors included two physicians and others whose occupations were listed as "real estate properties" and "own income."

[38] The early craze for horseless carriages soon caused automobile plants to "spring up like mushroom growths all over the country" (Fred H. Colvin, *Sixty Years with Men and Machines*, McGraw-Hill, 1947, p 124, quoted in *Brass Era Car*, Wikipedia.org). In January, 1904, Frank Leslie's *Popular Monthly* magazine listed sixty-one companies making cars in the United States, including such notables as the Eisenhuth Horseless Vehicle Company, the Locomobile Company of America, and the Singer Sewing Machine Company.

[39] The sixty-five-foot-tall wooden and tin elephant was the brainchild of another Irish Catholic from Philadelphia, James V. Lafferty, Jr (1856-1898), who had it built in 1881 to attract visitors to the area then known as South Atlantic City. The elephant's tusks suggest it was a bull, and the origins of the name "Lucy" are unclear. ("Lucy the Elephant" at www.lucytheelephant.org).

[40] We know that Joe Murphy had a touring car by 1909 or earlier from Stella Marie's letter of July 20, 1909, Chapter 13, below.

[41] The Academy of the Sisters of Mercy was older than most of the city's public and parochial schools. Founded by the Sisters of Mercy in 1861, it was located at Broad and Columbia Street, about .6 miles (a 15 minute walk) south of the Murphy home. Whether Stella Marie walked, took a public carriage, or was driven to school, likely depended on the weather and mood of the day. See Phila city directories 1904-1916 (under A for Academy) and the websites of the modern schools, Gwynedd Mercy Academy's High School and Elementary School, at https://www.gmahs.org/mercy-mission/history and https://www.gmaelem.org/about-us/history.

[42] Organized in April of 1908.

[43] The stadium opened on April 12, 1909.

[44] Sarah Scott had been born in Virginia (1910 U.S. Census, Phila Ward 37, Dist 928, Fam 145). The African-American population of Philadelphia more than doubled between 1900 and 1920. Weigley, *supra*, p 531.

[45] Weigley, *supra*, p 532.

[46] Weigley, *supra*, pp 548-549.

[47] *Inquirer*, March 8, 1910, p 2. The firms themselves said the unions' numbers were inflated.

[48] On December 5, 1910, the elder Murphy, Joseph P., died of a heart attack at the age of sixty-five. (See Death Certificate, and his obit in *The Inquirer* of Dec 7, 1910.) His funeral services were held at the Church of the Holy Angels. Stella's father followed in early February, 1911. (See obituary of Richard Congdon in *The Inquirer* of Feb 9, 1911.) The Congdon funeral took place from Joe Murphy's home, and a solemn requiem mass was said at the Church of Our Lady of Mercy.

[49] *The Inquirer*, February 21, 1911. A later write-up in *The Inquirer* called the play "unique and compelling, inasmuch as it does not commit itself unreservedly to the standpoint of either capital or labor, but takes that of the average citizen who is 'The Man Between.'" (*The Inquirer*, October 15, 1911.)

[50] Real Estate Transfers, *The Inquirer*, May 26, 1911, p 5. The existing mill, first designated as 744 and 746 S. 16th Street, was now being identified as occupying the southwest corner of 16th and Fitzwater Street – the same location by a new name. The new mill was also on the south side, but further west: 30th Street was fourteen blocks west of 16th, and Reed seven blocks south of Fitzwater. Alterations to the Murphy & Bro. mill, S.W. corner 30th and Reed, by one William H. Gavell, cost $750 (*Inquirer*, June 11, 1912, p 11).

[51] The new address of the building was given in one newspaper piece as 64th and South. The real property had been the site of a cotton mill since ante-bellum days, but the Murphy building itself may have been newer. As a resident of West Philadelphia, Edward was deeply involved in the new mill's daily operation. But unlike Murphy & Bro., the new company was no 50/50 proposition. Joseph was its President, Edward only its Treasurer. (In the *Inquirer* of April 27, 1913, Sec 2, p 16, one Joe Murphy (not necessarily the same man) advertised boathouses for rent near Darby Creek.)

[52] *The Inquirer*, Aug 18, 1912, p 32, and Jan 12, 1913, p 36, reflect efforts to sell the Chester Mill. Meanwhile, the Murphys offered eleven dollars a week for a fireman willing to watch over their West End boilers at night (*Inquirer,* Sept 25, 1913, p 12).

[53] "BEAMERS. Non-union beamers on cotton warps. Murphy & Bro., 16th and Fitzwater." (*Inquirer*, Oct 16, 1913.) Such ads would be illegal little more than two decades later.

[54] *Inquirer*, Feb 22, 1914, Sec 2, p 6.

[55] Weigley, *supra*, pp 524-526, quoting Christopher Morley, Travels in Philadelphia (David McKay, 1920). Textiles, meanwhile, remained "by far the largest and most productive" industrial enterprise in the city.

[56] Dietrich Orlow, A History of Modern Germany: 1871 to Present, 4th Ed, Prentice Hall, 1999, p 77.

[57] Mark Jefferson, "Our Trade in the Great War," *Geographical Review*, Vol 3, No 6, June 1917, pp 474-480, accessed at https://www.jstor.org/stable/207691. The Dreyfus brothers, who'd been using their tree-pulp lacquer to make film for moving pictures, were now using it to protect Zeppelins and the wings of airplanes.

[58] Douglas Ewbank, "The Boothroyd and Goodyear Families of Mill Workers and the West End Mill," West Philadelphia Collaborative History, accessed at https://collaborativehistory.gse.upenn.edu/stories/boothroyd-and-goodyear-families-mill-workers-and-west-end-mill. The history of the building dated back before the civil war. The West End Woolen Mills, Inc, advertised for a night fireman to attend its boilers in 1913 for a wage of $11 per week. (*Inquirer*, Sept 26, 1913, p 12). The company was listed in the 1915 City Directory, but not in the 1916, suggesting that corporate entity may have shut down in the latter part of 1915. At about the same time, Irvin and Harper Wilson won a court judgement against Murphy for $150 (*Inquirer,* Oct 8, 1915, p 8).

[59] *The Inquirer* of Feb 25, 1917, p 51, ran a help wanted ad for a "Boss Carder, 7 sets 60" cards on Merino yarn" placed by Joseph D. Murphy, 30th and Reed.

[60] The German chemist, Christian Adolf Greiner, had been born in Thuringen, Germany, in 1866 and immigrated from Rotterdam in 1893, becoming a naturalized American citizen on September 26, 1910. (U.S. Passport Applications, NARA Roll 0843, Certificate 99308 (Christian Adolph Greiner), July 19, 1919.) In 1910, he lived in Norristown, N.J., and worked as a chemist in the manufacturing industry (1910 U.S. Census, Montgomery County, Norristown Ward 10, Dist 0125, Fam 120). He first appeared with a Philadelphia address in the 1919 City Directory, at 5412 Angora Street, in West Philadelphia, closer to the old West End Mill than to 30th and Reed. By 1920, he had moved just past Cobbs Creek, at 5019 Baltimore Ave (US Census 1920, Phila Ward 46, Dist 1739, Fam 274).

[61] *Evening Ledger*, May 8, 1915, p 1. American and British outrage against Germany was fanned by their governments. American papers falsely reported that German school children were given a holiday to celebrate the sinking of the Lusitania and loss of civilian life. A good argument can be made that American outrage should have been directed at the governments of Britain and the U.S. They were complicit in efforts to disguise the Lusitania – in many respects, a war ship, carrying munitions to Britain – as a passenger ship, sailing with women and children aboard. Successive British governments denied that the Lusitania had been carrying munitions until 1982, when finally, out of concern for the safety of salvage teams, it admitted the presence of highly explosive munitions on board. In effect, the passengers aboard the Lusitania had been used as civilian shields. Many years would pass before the revelation that, a week before the sinking, Winston Churchill had written to Walter Runciman, the President of the Board of Trade, that it is "most important to attract neutral shipping to our shores, in the hope especially of embroiling the United States with Germany."

[62] http://gpktt.weebly.com/a-short-history-of-manufactured-fibers.html

[63] Weigley, *supra*, pp 558-559. Ford's plant at the corner of Broad Street (14th) and Lehigh was a block and a half west of Murphy home at 1234 Lehigh.

[64] "Perfecting Paper Cloth: Germans Seek Soft Substitutes for Cotton and Wool Fabrics" *(Inquirer,* Feb 12, 1918, p 4) reported that workmen's clothes were already being made of the new fabric, and that "by next spring, men, women and children of all classes will probably be wearing complete outfits made of the new material."

[65] Some of the people living near the Murphys in the 1910 U.S. Census, Phila Ward 37, Dist 928. Roderer was an undertaker, Hengen a liquor dealer.

[66] Weigley, *supra*, p 560; *Evening Public Ledger*, May 15, 1918, p 10.

[67] Patricia O'Toole, "How the U.S. Government Used Propaganda to Sell Americans on World War I," Jan 26, 2022, accessed at https://www.history.com/news/world-war-1-propaganda-woodrow-wilson-fake-news.

[68] Lillian Hengen, 18, lived next door at 1232 Lehigh, Lillian Kirchner, 10, at 1228, Lora and Elizabeth Klemm, 17 and 11, at 1204. Sara Yoder, 14, lived a block south at 1223 Tucker Street.

[69] Francis Dominic Murphy (1881-1959) had been listed in the 1910 Census as a textile manufacturer (U.S. Census PA, Delaware, Sharon Hill, Dist 0158, Fam 102) but Walter Leo Murphy (1892-1959) had only appeared in the 1916 Directory with the occupation "clerk," still living at his parents' house. He got married on February 4, 1918, to Anna McHugh, and was still living with her parents in 1920. (*Evening Public Ledger,* Feb 5, 1918, p 11; U.S. Census Phila, Ward 40, Dist 1506, Fam 103.)

[70] By this time, Camille and Henri Dreyfus were using cellulose acetate dope to coat the fabric skins of British war planes. *The Inquirer*, June 16, 1918, p 46; Aug 2, 1918, p 18, and Aug 4, 1918. Obit of Edward F Marley, *Evening Public Ledger*, Aug 20, 1918.

[71] Joe's farming course was in May, 1918 (*Evening Public Ledger*, June 14, 1918, p 13; *Inquirer*, May 5, 1918, p 10.) "At least 80% of male college students will spend their vacations this summer working on farms, according to the Department of Labor. The youths will be lodged for the most part in farm labor camps." (*Evening Public Ledger*, May 11, 1918, p 11).

[72] The new Murphy address in town was 1830 Rittenhouse Square, lying between 18th and 19th Streets between Walnut and Spruce – about two miles from Murphy's office at 30th and Reed. The same June 21 Public Ledger that reported the Murphys' summer stay in Chelsea reported that "Mrs. William H.

Greenfield and Miss Marie Greenfield, of 1309 West Lehigh avenue, are spending the week in New York as the guests of Mrs. Greenfield's brother and sister-in-law, Mr. and Mrs. Walter H. Congdon. Mrs. Congdon will be remembered as Miss Agnes Loughran, of this city." (*The Evening Public Ledger,* June 14, 1918, p 13, and June 21, 1918, p 11.) Bridgit Agnes Loughran had married Walter Congdon in 1917.

[73] "Philadelphia 1918: The Flu Pandemic Hits Home," Jefferson University, accessed at https://www.jefferson.edu/alumni/connect/alumni-bulletin/summer-2020/the-flu-pandemic-hits-home.html.

[74] In comparison, the "Black Death" in the 14th century killed fewer than thirty million.

[75] "Philadelphia 1918: The Flu Pandemic Hits Home," *supra.*

[76] *Evening Public Ledger*, May 19, 1919, p 2. See the similar article in the *Inquirer*, May 20, 1919, p 5, which concluded, "It is believed the men were a gang of organized cloth robbers who had been operating here and in New York."

[77] U.S. Passport Applications, NARA Roll 0843, Certificate 99307 (Murphy) and 99308 (Greiner), July 19, 1919.

[78] The applications stated that the visit to Switzerland was for the reasons set forth in an attached telegram, but no telegram has been found.

[79] The fact that Stella Cecelia Murphy accompanied her husband on the trip is interesting – surprising if it was indeed a business trip.

[80] The Murphy party left Southampton, England, on October 8, 1919, and it arrived in New York on October 17th.

[81] Weigley, *supra*, pp 529 and 533.

[82] Classified ads were placed for an experienced bookkeeper, $25 per week to start (*Inquirer*, Feb 15, 1920, p 44); weavers on narrow Bridesburg looms, and loom fixers on Crompton & Knowles looms (Inquirer, Oct 22, 1922, pp 65 and 68, and subsequent days); a dyer on woolens, gloves and cotton yarn (*Inquirer*, Feb 11, 1923, p 61 and subsequent days); weavers on Crompton & Knowles looms (*Inquirer,* June 24th and 25th, 1923); a beamer for pattern work (*Inquirer*, Sept 10, 1924, p 26); a finisher familiar with wet and dry finishing of woolen piece goods (*Inquirer*, Oct 20 and 21, 1924, p 24). Significant employment at the 30th & Reed mill is also attested by the obituary of one of Joe's employees, John Duane, inviting all the employees of "Joseph D. Murphy Mills" at 30th and Reed to attend the funeral. (*Inquirer,* June 3, 1924).

[83] 1920 U.S. Census, Phila Ward 42, Dist 1578, Fam 369. Joe's support for his mother and her matronly household continued until her death in May of 1924 (*The Inquirer*, May 10, 1924, p 26).

[84] Joe's support of "dry" candidates is demonstrated by his 1926 attendance at a fundraiser for Joseph R. Grundy and George Wharton Pepper (see Appendix 5, Ltr 9).

[85] *Evening Public Ledger,* Feb 23, 1921, p 11.

[86] *Evening Public Ledger,* April 23, 1921.

[87] The Penn Athletic Club was organized about 1922 by Jack Kelly and his friends on Rittenhouse Square, just around the corner from the Murphy's apartment. Joe was among its founding members, but a new pandemic in 2020 foreclosed the possibility of details being investigated for this book. Some future historian may find more information at the Philadelphia Historical Society, 1300 Locust St, Phila, which maintains a collection of early papers of the Penn Athletic Club. See http://www2.hsp.org/collections/manuscripts/p/PennAC1820D0078.html.

[88] Manufacturers' officially opened on May 15, 1925 with a match that pitted Walter Hagen and Joe Kirkwood against Huntingdon Valley's "Ducky" Corkran and Merion's Max Marston. (Manufacturers'(etc), *supra*, accessed at https://www.mg-cc.org/club-information/history.)

[89] *Inquirer*, April 19, 1924, p 9. Weigley *et al*, at p 568, refer to "the ever-increasing challenge of automobile traffic, including a new kind of criminal, the motorized bandit," stating that "the tasks of upholding the Prohibition law and of controlling crime by automobile threatened to overwhelm the police department."

---

[90] A solemn requiem mass was said at St. Patrick's church. The funeral would leave from Stella Cecelia's late residence at 1830 Rittenhouse Square. The obituary (*Inquirer*, May 9, 1924, p 29) gave the date of death as May 8th.

[91] Website of OCF Realty, accessed at http://www.ocfrealty.com/naked-philly/rittenhouse/delorean-time-machine-banana-republic-on-broad-street. Murphy's obituary confirms his membership in the Club; the first evidence of his residence there is his listing in the 1925 City Directory.

[92] *Inquirer*, May 10, 1925, p 29, and May 17, 1925, p 30.

[93] *The Inquirer*, May 9, 1926, p 95. Namely 1 Warner & Pfiderer, 2-barrel mixer, 1 Permultit water filter, 4 large jacket botiers, 2 jacketed mixers, 2 filter presses, and a large lot of leather belts, pulleys and hangers.

[94] The move to the new location, at the same time LaSalle was moving its campus there, may suggest that Murphy had attended LaSalle prep, or College, or both – and indeed, may also suggested that his father, Joseph P. Murphy, had also attended LaSalle. There may be a multi-generational connection to LaSalle that has not been found by our research. If so, Joe's move there continued a Murphy family connection to the old St. Michael's Church which was now closing in on a hundred years. (See https://www.lschs.org/about-la-salle/history.)

[95] *Inquirer*, July 30th, 1926, p 29; July 17, 1927; Sept 25, 1927; Sept 16, 1928; Sept 20, 1929; and Oct 3, 1929, p 31.

[96] Joseph Edward Murphy (1901-1983) was married to May Young in 1928. He placed ads for help at the Wister Street mill in 1941 (e.g. *Inquirer*, July 9, 1941, p 28), and operated it until he liquidated it at auction on October 9, 1951. His auction notice asserted that it was in complete liquidation of the Woolen mill at Belfield and Wister. To be put up for bid were: 6 sets of 60x48 woolen cards; Davis & Farber late-type tape condensers; 2 120-spindle spinning frames; 6 500-spindle mules; 36 Crompton & Knowles looms; novelty twisters; 2 Shears; 2 Gessner cloth presses; 1 Whitin Schweiter winder; a picker; a shredder; a Garnet machine; washers, dye kettles, nappers, dryers, mixing pickers, bobbins, shuttles, shafting, belting, office furniture, and other items (*Inquirer*, Sept 29, 1951, p 27).

[97] Isabell's father David T Raybould was an Englishman who'd immigrated in 1871, her mother Harriet a native Pennsylvanian (1900 Census Phila Ward 28, Fam 399). Isabell was still living with her first husband, a bookkeeper, George Hoeflich, with an infant daughter Marion, at 2535 Lehigh in 1910 (1910 Census Phila Ward 38, Dist 0963, Fam 162), but by 1920, she and her daughter Marion were living with her father (1920 Census Ward 28, Fam 89) at 3311 Harold St. George Hoeflich did not die until 1951. The 1930 Census, enumerated on April 11 of that year, shows Joe and Isabell Murphy living together as husband and wife, with daughter Marion Hoeflich (1930 Census Phila Dist 1028, Fam 240) at 6655 Lawton Avenue. But their marriage in New York did not take place until August 2, 1930. (NY Marriage License Indexes, Manhattan, 1930, Joseph D. Murphy & Isabell Hoeflich, Vol 8, No 18430, Aug 2, 1930, Certificate 20434.) Whether Joe and Isabell met at church, Whitemarsh, or elsewhere is unknown.

[98] This according to oral family tradition. Stella Marie's staunch Catholicism would be reflected in her position regarding the marriages of her oldest son as well.

[99] The death of Adele G. Murphy, wife of the late Joseph P. Murphy, was on August 3, 1931 (*Inquirer*, Aug 4, 1931, p 27). According to the obituary, she was still living at 6610 N 12th.

[100] *Inquirer*, March 23, 1936, p 2. *The Inquirer* of April 5, 1936, Classifieds (p 8 W a), has an article on the estate that asserts its total value was $57,000, divided between his second wife, Isabella, his two children, and his siblings. The article mistakenly refers to his daughter, Stella Marie, as his stepdaughter – perhaps an inadvertent slip, perhaps a parting slight by a rejected stepmother.

12. Joseph J. Carvin Jr.

Joe Carvin Jr. was born April 24, 1881, the year President Garfield was assassinated. It was only the second time in U.S. history there were three presidents in a single year,[1] and Joe grew up in an unstable house. Athough kind and generous, his father was a saloon owner, a gambler, a cricket player, and a fight promoter, arrested in a police raid when Joe Jr. was four, accused of corrupting a young girl at his merry-go-round when Joe Jr. was seven, tangling with city politicians most of his life. Four of his uncles and two of his cousins tended bar at his father's saloon.[2] His Uncle Charles was arrested for swindling customers with claims of five dollar bills in bars of soap, and his Uncle Thomas was an intemperate philanderer with children in multiple households. His mother died when he was twelve, and when he was fourteen, his father married his sisters' babysitter, Katie Sherick, just nine years older than he was. In his father's saloon, the men who drank ale had little good to say about the brandy-drinking country club set., but his own father had gambled his way into a profitable business of his own. Joe Jr. wanted to be a successful American businessman too.

Of medium height and slender build, with blue eyes and dark brown hair, Joe was enrolled in high school in the late 1890's, either at the Roman Catholic High School or at LaSalle Prep.[3] When he was eighteen, he was listed as a student in the city directory at a time when students were rarely given listings of their own.[4] In the 1900 Census, he was listed as a clerk in a hosiery mill; in the 1902 city directory, as a bookkeeper, probably at the same hosiery mill.[5] But Joe Jr. was a sportsman like his father, willing to take risks. Crunching numbers in the mill's office one day, looking at healthy profits for his brandy-drinking owners, he decided he couldn't live keeping books for others. Clearly, running his own business was within his reach. His father knew nothing of the margins involved in knitting hosiery, but based on the numbers in his employer's books, making a good profit looked easy. There was no reason such numbers couldn't be matched by anyone, and he was able to impress his father with his grasp of them. They could start small, he said. His father had questions, but he could answer them all, and ultimately, he persuaded Jimmy to back him, though Jimmy insisted it was a calculated risk. In May, 1903, father and son entered the hosiery business together. The "Carvin Knitting Company" placed a help-wanted ad for "bar-toppers" for their mill.[6]

The 1904 City Directory lists the Carvin Knitting Company in the hosiery business, Joe Sr. as President and twenty-three year old Joe Jr. as its treasurer and general manager. As general manager, Joe Jr. ran the operation, doing the hiring, the filling of orders, and the supervision of production, while his father continued running his successful saloon. As treasurer, Joe Jr. also paid bills, collected receipts, and otherwise handled the cash.

The city directory also listed two other officers of the new company: George Caruthers, Vice-President, and Robert P. Steele, Secretary.[7] Who these two men were, and how they entered the picture, is anything but clear. A person didn't need a large factory to be in the hosiery business – he could start knitting socks with no more than a few knitting machines in a vacant apartment.[8] It's fair to ask, then – why did such an operation need a Vice President and a Secretary?[9] Rather strangely, the 1904 Philadelphia Directory lists both their residence addresses simply as "New York" – no rental house, boarding house, or even hotel address in Philadelphia. The listing suggests a very temporary presence, if not a desire to be hard to find. The need for corporate officers who didn't even have Philadelphia addresses is even harder to explain.

The want ads that began in May, 1903, continued until Dec 4, 1905. The company was clearly making a go of it. But as the ads continued and the needs they expressed changed, the emphasis on wanting "experienced" help grew. Eventually, the ads started including rates of pay, suggesting the company may have found it harder than anticipated to find people with the right skills. (Certainly, neither father nor son had the ability to train them on the knitting machinery.) If finding experienced help was a problem, defects in the quality of their product may have been a problem as well.[10]

In June of 1905, young Joe married a German girl, Elsie Preuss.[11] In the latter months of that year, Elsie discovered she was pregnant, and on April 9, 1906, their baby was born – a son, Joseph James Carvin III.[12] At that point, all signs pointed toward Joe becoming a successful manufacturing man, with a stable domestic life in Philadelphia. But 1906 did not turn out as expected. For one thing, the ad placed for the Carvin Knitting Company on December 4, 1905, was the last one ever placed. After months in which they'd placed ads nearly every week, there were none placed during 1906. It seems that after a run of about three years, the Carvin Knitting Company had ceased operations.[13]

Furthermore, it was in October, 1906, that Joe Jr. was appointed his sister Florence's legal guardian. Whether that odd appointment had anything to do with Florence's attraction to her husband-to-be, Wendell Young, it was the last record of Joe Jr. living in Philadelphia. The later Philadelphia directories make no mention of him, nor is he ever mentioned in any of the city's later newspapers.

Something significant had clearly happened in 1906.

A story, told to us as children in the 1950's and 60's, suggests at least part of the answer.[14] Having gotten into serious trouble with money he owed to some unsavory characters, Joe Jr. was suddenly compelled to flee Philadelphia in fear for his life. The problem, we were told, was a gambling debt owed to loan sharks, numbers runners, or some other criminal types, a purely personal problem young Joe had faced on account of a weakness for gambling or other bad habits.[15] He'd gone all the way to Los Angeles, taking Elsie and their infant son with him. In L.A. he took up work driving a milk wagon, and he didn't dare return to Philadelphia for as long as he lived.

In the story we heard, no mention was made of anything like the Carvin Knitting Company. When we discovered the existence of that company some sixty years later, an obvious question was the nature of the connection, if any, between the failure of the Knitting Company and the sudden flight of its treasurer, Joe Jr. Perhaps, after a couple of years in the office of someone else's hosiery company, a confident young man had decided he could make a lot of money for himself in that business. Perhaps he'd convinced his father to back him in the enterprise. Perhaps they found other men (from New York) who had money to lend, and perhaps, as both general manager and treasurer of the operation, Joe Jr. had found the business more difficult than he'd anticipated. Perhaps he'd faced problems repaying the loan to the New Yorkers.

The last ad was placed by the Knitting Company on December 4, 1905; at that point, trying to fill a vacancy, Joe's expectation was clearly to continue in business. It's reasonable to assume, therefore, that operations continued until some point in early 1906. Joe had then left for L.A. as early as October of 1906 (after appointment as his sister's guardian) and in any case no later than June 25, 1907, when his and Elsie's second son, Edward, was born in Los Angeles.[16] For some reason, Joe Jr. had left town soon after the business disappeared from the records. What happened? And did it have anything to do with Caruthers and Steele?

The effort to identify these two New Yorkers has proven inconclusive. A search of Philadelphia newspapers between 1900 and 1910 reveals not a single mention of them – suggesting that they lacked any connection to Philadelphia or its textile manufacturing.[17] It doesn't take much to imagine that a fight promoter like Jimmy, who found ways to get his liquor license renewed despite having an arrest record, had some tough connections. It doesn't take much to imagine that as the knitting business struggled, the gambling which got young Joe into trouble (whether from poker, craps, running numbers, prize fights or betting on horses) affected his handling of cash for the business itself. That a big-time gambler – or any lender from New York – might be serious about seeking retribution for a loss seems more than plausible. The Carvin Knitting Company would never appear in the records again, and Joe Jr.'s flight to L.A.

followed within the year. Because Jimmy, president of the company, remained in Philadelphia, we would not be surprised to learn that at some point he paid off the loans out of his own pocket – perhaps explaining why, in 1920, there was a mortgage on his saloon.

In any case, by 1908, having "escaped with their lives," Joe, Elsie and their two little boys were living at 154 W Slauson Avenue in Los Angeles, then a small, almost rustic town compared to Philadelphia. Joe's occupation was described in that year's directory as "produce" – presumably, a wagon or stand at a farmer's market.[18] But that job didn't last long. The 1909-1911 L. A. city directories gave his occupation as "dairy," and by May of 1908, he and other dairy wagon drivers were petitioning the city for a lower license tax for "butter and egg men."[19]

According to oral family tradition, Joe's little half-brother, Charley, came to live with Elsie and him; their father sent Joe money to put Charley through school, but Joe pocketed the money and put his little brother to work as a helper on his milk wagon. (That money, too, may have gone to gambling. If it did, it was no worse than what might be expected from a young son of a gambler, raised as Joe had been.) But maybe their father had every right to be angry. After all, Joe Jr. had let him down yet again.

By March of 1910, Elsie had given birth to her third child, a daughter.[20] Joe soon stopped driving his milk wagon and entered the gas and electric business in L.A. He worked for utilities there for five or six years, sometimes in sales, sometimes collecting bills.[21] In 1917, the family moved to a new apartment in Van Nuys, and the following year, after buying a car, he went into the jitney business with it, becoming a sort of primitive Uber driver.[22]

> The recession-plagued year 1914 saw the explosive rise of the "jitney," an unlicensed taxi that took passengers for just a nickel. The private streetcar companies refused to improve their service in a time of recession and as a result drove more and more people to alternatives like the jitney and buying their own vehicle.[23]

In his efforts to get steady fares, he hired himself out from a taxi stand on Pershing Square. At 2 a.m. on the morning of April 18, 1919, two well dressed young men asked him for a ride to an address on Merengo Street in Pasadena, about a half hour's drive northwest. Then, just outside the city limits, his passengers asked that he take them by way of Oak Knoll. He obliged. At Los Robles and Oak Knoll, they ordered him to stop the vehicle. And at 8 a.m. that morning, he was found by a passerby, shot and seriously wounded by a gunshot wound to his head, jaw and neck.

Taken to the hospital, he regained consciousness long enough to make a statement to the police. The front page of that day's *Long Beach Press* contained the following article:[24]

Taxicab Driver Is Shot by Murderous Passenger

PASADENA, Calif, April 18.

— Joseph Carvin, taxi driver, 817 East Washington Street, Los Angeles, was found shot and seriously wounded in his own taxi at South Los Robles Avenue and Oak Lane this morning at 8 o'clock by passersby.

He was taken to the local emergency hospital and regaining consciousness said he had been shot without warning by one of two young men who engaged his car in Los Angeles to bring them to Pasadena. He said the passengers were strangers to him. At the spot where Carvin and his taxi were found, Carvin said he stopped the machine and it was then, he said, that one of the passengers shot him. The bullet entered his left cheek and passed through his spine, causing paralysis of his entire body. He was taken to the Los Angeles County hospital.

Carvin said he started with his fares from Los Angeles at 2 a.m.

Local and Los Angeles police are working on the case. This morning the local police received a mysterious telephone message from Los Angeles saying that a man there knew the motive for the shooting. The Los Angeles police are looking for the man.

The following day, the front page of the Los Angeles *Times* carried a much longer story under the headline "Fresh Clew to Strange Crime."[25] The text of *The Times* article:

Encouraged by a gasping statement that a third man saw the shooting, made by Joseph J. Carvin at the County Hospital, Captain of Detectives George Home, Chief of Police McIntyre of Pasadena and a score of detectives combed Pasadena last night for this witness to the shooting by two bandits of Carvin, shot down as he stood beside his automobile at Oak Knoll and Los Robles avenue early yesterday morning.

That someone in Pasadena is implicated in the shooting the police stated as a fact late yesterday afternoon. The person is alleged to live somewhere on South Marengo Avenue. The two bandits, according to the wounded taxi man's statement, mentioned Marengo Avenue several times during the drive from this city to Pasadena. Both of the wanted men are thought by the local police to reside in Pasadena or Oak Knoll.

MYSTERIOUS CASE.

According to Capt. Home, the shooting is one of the strangest cases ever placed before the local police. No motive for the crime can be found by the police. Nothing to point to robbery or revenge could be uncovered.

"After a careful personal investigation of the shooting," said Capt. Home, "the facts in this case are these: two well-dressed young men hired Joseph J. Carvin, 37 years of age, who lives with his wife and two small children at 817 East Washington Street, and conducts a taxi business from Pershing Square, to drive them to Pasadena. The two "fares" arrived at the taxi stand at 2 a.m. yesterday.

"Just after leaving the Los Angeles City limits, one of the men, both of whom were riding in the rear seat of the automobile, instructed the driver to go to Pasadena by way of Oak Knoll. The two men then spoke of an address on Marengo Avenue, in Pasadena, but Carvin was unable to hear the number. The drive took about half an hour.

"Ordering Carvin to stop the machine at Oak Knoll and Los Robles avenue, the two passengers asked him to open the side curtains, which were buttoned about the car. As he stepped to the automobile door one of the passengers drew a revolver and shot him through the head. As Carvin fell he thought he saw a third person run in the direction the bandits had taken. He lost consciousness and was found in the ditch beside the road at about 8 a.m. yesterday morning. He was removed to the Pasadena Receiving Hospital and then to the County Hospital.

"The bandits' bullet, according to reports received by me from the hospital, struck the taxi driver in the right side of the face, below the temple. It lodged near the spine at the base of the neck. He has, according to the surgeons, about an even chance of recovery."

THE DESCRIPTIONS

The description given the police by Carvin is:

No. 1: About 25 years, five feet six inches, 135 pounds. He wore a brown suit, looks like khaki, a cap to match. Had medium complexion, was smooth shaven, and looked like an American.

No. 2: About 25 years old, five feet five inches, 145 pounds. Wore a black coat and a dark soft hat. Looked like an American."

One account of the crime asserted that the motive was not robbery, as no valuables were taken.[26] The police were perplexed by the complete absence of any apparent motive for the crime.

The Times article included a photograph of the victim:

Joseph J. Carvin.

The doctors put his chance of recovery at 50/50. As it happens, it wasn't Joe's lucky day. Soon after giving his statement to the police, he died. His brief obituary:

> CARVIN, April 19, Joseph Carvin, beloved husband of Elsie Carvin, aged 37 years. Remains at chapel of Cunningham & O'Connor.[27]

Two weeks later, on May 2nd, an article in the *Van Nuys News* reported that there'd been no further progress in the case.[28] With a witness having called in to say someone knew the motive for the crime, one might think the news stories would have continued. But they did not. Media coverage ended for two years. Then, after all that time, in a general report about unsolved cases, the papers said there'd still been no arrests.[29]

The case was never solved.

Why had the two passengers directed the driver to go to their destination "by way of" Oak Knoll, then ordered him to stop the vehicle there? Who was the person who called the police with the statement that someone knew the motive for the killing? And who was the third man who'd run in the same direction as the perpetrators – someone who'd apparently known about the planned killing?

The victim's wife, Elsie, and his father, Jimmy Carvin (still living in Philadelphia) were surely shocked by news of the murder. But one has to wonder what Jimmy thought of the detectives' assertion that they'd found no motive in robbery or revenge. Might Jimmy not have had at least a *suspicion* of such a motive? He knew that his son had left Philadelphia in fear for his life twelve years earlier. He knew that Joe Jr. had owed money to *somebody*, whether it was Caruthers and Steele or not. And given their business relationship, it's hard to imagine that Jimmy didn't have ideas about who his son's creditors were. Did he communicate what he knew to the Los Angeles police? Did they really have *no clue* as to a motive?

Meanwhile, Henry ("Harry") Gekler, Sadie's husband, now identified as an insurance adjuster, had moved with Sadie to the L.A. area at the very time of the murder – possibly weeks before or after it.[30] His only connection to L.A. at the time was Sadie's brother Joe. Was there a connection between his move to L.A. and Joe's murder there?

Two possibilities present themselves: First, if Gekler's move preceded the murder, there's the possibility that the loan sharks from whom Joe had fled were able to track him down in L.A. by following the Geklers there, confident that there'd be contact between them. Surely, the L. A. Police would have wanted to look into that.

Alternatively, if the Gekler move followed the murder, it seems more than plausible than an insurance adjuster – trained in detective work – might have moved to L. A. at least in part to see if he could solve a puzzle that the L. A. Police could not.

And then we have the fact that at precisely this time, Jimmy visited the Geklers in L. A., more than once.[31] Did Harry and Jimmy hound the L. A. Police to make progress in their investigation? Were they conducting one of their own? Regardless of exactly when or why the Geklers moved to LA, it is hard to imagine otherwise.

Over a hundred years have now passed. It's a cold case file now, all the participants long dead and buried. But the story remains, unsolved and, in the minds of some, still very much alive.[32]

COUNTY OF LOS ANGELES • REGISTRAR-RECORDER

California State Board of Health
BUREAU OF VITAL STATISTICS
STANDARD CERTIFICATE OF DEATH

PLACE OF DEATH. DIST. No.
County of
City or Town of
or Rural Registration District .... (No. County Hospital St.; .... Ward)

State Index No.
Local Registered No. 3246

FULL NAME Joseph Carvin

PERSONAL AND STATISTICAL PARTICULARS

SEX: male
COLOR OR RACE: White
Single Married Widowed or Divorced: married

HUSBAND OF / WIFE OF: Elsie Carvin

DATE OF BIRTH: April 24 ——

AGE: 37 years 11 months ... days

OCCUPATION: (a) Trade, profession, or particular kind of work: Taxi D
(b) General nature of industry, business, or establishment in which employed (or employer)

BIRTHPLACE (State or country)

NAME OF FATHER
BIRTHPLACE OF FATHER (State or country)
MAIDEN NAME OF MOTHER
BIRTHPLACE OF MOTHER (State or country)

LENGTH OF RESIDENCE
At Place of Death (Primary registered in state):
In California: 12 ...... days

THE ABOVE IS TRUE TO THE BEST (Informant): Elsie Carvin
(Address): 817 E Washington

Filed .... 191 L. H. Powers M. D. Registrar
Apr 23 191 9 H. Litz Deputy

CORONER'S CERTIFICATE OF DEATH

DATE OF DEATH: April 19 191 9 (Month) (Day) (Year)

I HEREBY CERTIFY, as to the person above named and herein described. That on ... 23 191 9 I held an inquest and ... a verdict on the death. Or, That I have ... officially on account of

The CAUSE OF DEATH was as follows:

Gunshot wound of the neck the neck

Homicidal

Wagner Calvin Hartwell Coroner's Surgeon
23 9 L A Coroner

*State the DISEASE CAUSING DEATH, or, in deaths from VIOLENT CAUSES, state (1) MEANS OF INJURY, and (2) whether (probably) ACCIDENTAL, SUICIDAL, or HOMICIDAL.

SPECIAL INFORMATION for Hospitals, Institutions, Transients or Recent Residents. Where was disease contracted, if not at place of death?
Former or usual residence: 817 E Washington St

PLACE OF BURIAL OR REMOVAL: Calvary
DATE OF BURIAL: April 191

UNDERTAKER: Cunningham & O'Connor
ADDRESS: 1031 S Grand ave

EMBALMER'S LICENSE No.: 676

This is to certify that this document is a true copy of the official record filed with the Registrar-Recorder.

Charles Weissburd
CHARLES WEISSBURD
Registrar-Recorder

FEB 1 3 1991

19-754946

This copy not valid unless prepared on engraved border displaying the County of Los Angeles Seal and Signature of Registrar-Recorder.

Notes on Chapter 12, Joseph J. Carvin Jr.

[1] When the year began, Rutherford B. Hayes was president, but Hayes had not run for a second term and James Garfield succeeded him on March 4th, 1881 – only to be assassinated and succeeded by Chester Arthur on September 19th.

[2] Joe's uncles William, Charles, George and Thomas, and his cousins, John Austin and Uncle Charles's son James Joseph Carvin, all tended bar for Jimmy at one time or another.

[3] The physical description is from Joe Jr.'s Sept 12, 1918 draft card, Los Angeles County, California. By the turn of the century, the growth of the Carvin family meant there were more Carvins in Philadelphia than there had been in the 1830's and 40's. For example, Joe Jr. had a cousin Joseph James Carvin (the son of George and Allabina Carvin), who attended the Sabbath School of the Norris Square Church before dying in 1897 at the age of 21 (*Inquirer*, Nov 26, 1897, p 9). Another, slightly younger Joseph Carvin, of the third preparatory class for LaSalle College, received a gold medal for excellence in 1896 (*The Times*, June 20, 1896, p 6). And another was his cousin, James Joseph Carvin (the son of Charles and Catherine Carvin) also born in 1881, who married Florence Stinger in 1901 (*Inquirer*, Aug 22, 1901, p 12). Born in 1881, Jimmy's son, Joe Jr., would likely have been in the class of 1898, and it wouldn't be surprising if he shared his father's interest in sports. A boy identified only as a Carvin, of the Roman Catholic High School class of '98, was in a track meet at Franklin Field in 1896 (*The Times*, May 9, 1896, p 5). It seems one of these was probably the Joe Jr. who is the subject of this chapter, so the conclusion that the Joe Jr. of this chapter attended either the Roman Catholic High School or LaSalle Prep seems sound.

[4] Occupations were generally listed for commercial reasons. One imagines Joe Sr. approved his son having his own listing as a reward of some kind.

[5] The 1900 U.S. Census (Phila Ward 37, Dist 0957, Fam 192) described Joe Jr. as a clerk in a hosiery mill, and the 1902 City Directory as a bookkeeper – one might guess at the same hosiery mill.

[6] *Inquirer*, May 22, 1903, p 12.

[7] 1904 Philadelphia City Directory, Carvin Knitting Co. at 2333 North Mascher Street

[8] The listings in the hosiery category of the business directories suggest that hosiery was frequently made in small residential shops. Whatever the size of the Carvin Knitting Company operation, it was small enough to move to a new address in October of 1905. On October 17, 1905, a help wanted ad – the first since August – shows a new address: "Jasper and Orleans sts, top floor."

[9] How and why had these two New Yorkers, Steele and Caruthers, gotten involved in a small, Philadelphia based start-up? Had they owned the knitting machines, and made them their contribution to capital? Had they been Joe Jr's employer, then sold him and his father a majority share of their ongoing business? Had they loaned the new enterprise money? If so, were they the type to lean heavily if not timely paid back? The answer to such questions may be relevant to what happened next.

[10] The machines referred to in the knitting company's ads included Mavl machines, Bonnaz or Bonnax machines, glove-stitch embroidering machines, Champion machines, National machines, heelers, and footers. Jobs the company was trying to fill included end pullers on embroidered work, pairers, folders on full fashioned work, an experienced girl to box goods, bar toppers on transfer work, an experienced boy on legger, an experienced operator to welt and shape, a boy who has run rib machines, an experienced boy on full fashion leggers, "an experienced boy to fill in paper press and help about wareroom," experienced cutters of ribbed loops, experienced helpers on heelers, experienced welters girls to ravel, girls to lace, girls to end-pull embroidery work, a girl to loose course, and even just "small girls wanted." On December 4, 1905, for the first time, one ad included the phrase "highest wages paid" and another an actual wage: "9 c. a dozen" for experienced bar toppers. Joe may have been learning that to get experienced help, he had to offer more money.

[11] The marriage occurred on June 5th. (Marriage License No. 186417, Phila City Archives, accessed via Ancestry.com; *Inquirer,* June 6, 1905, p 7 (spelling the bride's name as "Price").) Note that "Preuss" in German would be pronounced something like "Proice," and Elsie's name appears with the spelling "Price" in many records.

[12] Birth Certificate No. 84121, certifying the birth on April 9, 1906. Mother's name was spelled Preuss. Father's occupation listed as "manufacturer." Address 1229 W Lehigh Avenue, a block away from his father's house at the time.

[13] After the company's appearance in the 1906 Directory at "Jasper bel Orleans," there is no mention of it, in the newspapers or in the directories, in 1907 or any later years.

[14] The story was told to us, as children, by our father and grandfather.

[15] The story of Joe Jr.'s flight from Philadelphia and the reasons for it seem entirely plausible in view of the various wayward influences that had filled the young man's youth.

[16] Los Angeles County Birth records accessed via Ancestry.com. See also the 1908 Los Angeles City Directory, p 275.

[17] The search included alternate spellings. Various Caruthers, Carothers, Carruthers and Carrothers appear in the newspapers of New York State, including a George Caruthers said to be in the real estate business in Brooklyn (*Brooklyn Citizen,* Dec 30, 1905, p 5). None suggest any connection to the hosiery business, or textiles of any kind, and there are no similar references in the Philadelphia papers. (The Philadelphia papers do include a few references to a Robert P. Steele but do not identify him as a Philadelphia resident or give any other information about him (*The Times,* April 20, 1895, p 11; *Inquirer,* April 22, 1895, p 9; *Inquirer,* Feb 25, 1907, p 14). The papers' sports sections frequently report on a Robert Steele (without the middle initial P) who was the owner of Cedar Park Stock Farm, where he bred, trained and sold race horses (*Inquirer,* Jan 10, 1895, p 11, Feb 23, 1895, p 6, Sept 5, 1895, p 5, May 8, 1896, p 5, July 26, 1896, p 22, May 15, 1898, p 13, June 19, 1899, p 4, Feb 4, 1900, Jan 31, March 11, May 4, May 26, and June 9, 1902. *The Times,* Jan 10, 1895, p 8, Oct 29, 1900 and Feb 4, 1901). Mrs. Robert Steele, meanwhile, helped put on a New Year's Eve dance at the Belmont Cricket Club. *(The Times,* December 15, 1895, p 25 and Jan 1, 1896, p 4.) So if the Secretary of the Carvin Knitting Company were actually a Philadelphian, it was very likely this "sporting man." But the Secretary of the Knitting Company went by Robert "P." Steele, and is clearly identified as a resident of New York. Only a single mention is made of a Robert Steele, hosiery man, in the Philadelphia papers: the *Inquirer* of Nov 11, 1905, mentions Robert Steele as one of thirty-five men on an arrangements committee for a convention of the national hosiery manufacturers' association, to be held at the Manufacturers' Club in Philadelphia. The article contains no suggestion that this Steele was a Philadelphian; the single mention suggests that the hosiery business may not have been his full-time career, but some casual connection – as if he were some other "sporting man" Joe had met at the racetrack or cricket club, who had then made an investment in a small hosiery business on Mascher Street.

[18] The actual listing is "Carvin Jos pro h 154 W Slauson av." A list of abbreviations at page 52 of the directory indicates that "pro" means "produce."

[19] *Los Angeles Herald,* May 29, 1908, p 9. The 1910 U.S. Census, L.A., Assembly District 70, Dist 244, Fam 94, shows Joe's family at 154 Slauson Avenue in L.A. as of April 15, 1910, including Joseph J. Carvin, wife Elsie, and three children – Joe (age 4), Edward (age 2), and daughter Elsie (one month old).

[20] Elsie Carvin (March 9, 1910 – June 14, 2000), married Gordon B. Keller, and had a son, George Bernard Keller (1946 – 1996). Her brother Joseph James III (April 9, 1906 – Aug 18, 1991) attended Loyola University and married Zoe Porter on Sept 5, 1970. Her brother Edward Charles Carvin (June 25 1907 – Dec 22, 2002) married Marie Klose and they had two children, Charles (1932 -) and George (1935 -).

[21] In the 1912 LA Directory, Joe was listed as "clk to mgr new business LA Gas and Elec Corp." with a new home address, 5922 Howard. In 1913, it was "solr" (solicitor) and in 1914 and 1915, "collr" (collector) for the LA Gas and Elec Corp, new home address 5922 Mettler. In 1916, it was the same occupation but the new address of 453 S Hope. In 1917, "bkpr" (bookkeeper) for a new company (S E C Co) in Van Nuys.

[22] The 1918 L.A. City Directory still listed Joe as a collector, living in the rear of 132 C[alvert] Street, Van Nuys. Joe's September 1918 Draft Registration Card lists Elsie as his wife at 132 Calvert Street, Van Nuys. By 1916, you could buy one of Henry Ford's Model T's for $360, and cars were popping up everywhere.

[23] Matt Novak, "Nobody Walks in L.A.," *The Smithsonian Magazine*, April 26, 2013, accessed at https://www.smithsonianmag.com/history/nobody-walks-in-la-the-rise-of-cars-and-the-monorails-that-never-were-43267593/

[24] *The Long Beach Press*, April 18, 1919, page 1. The same article appeared in the *Daily Telegram* that afternoon under the headline, "WITHOUT WARNING: Taxi Driver is Shot and Seriously Wounded by One of Two Passengers." According to another paper's account, Carvin told police that engine trouble had developed and that he "alighted to investigate" and was shot "while bending over the machine." (*The Monrovia Daily News,* April 18, 1919, under the Headline, "Last Minute News.")

[25] *Los Angeles Times*, Saturday morning, April 19, 1919. A one sentence summary also appeared under the headline "The Day's News Summed Up."

[26] *Los Angeles Evening Post Record*, May 17, 1923.

[27] *Los Angeles Times* of April 21, 1919.

[28] The full text of that article read: "MURDERED MAN WAS FORMER RESIDENT OF VAN NUYS. J.J. Carvin, the passenger motor car operator whose mysterious death was chronicled in the Los Angeles papers last week, was formerly a resident of Van Nuys and at the time of his death owned a house and four lots on East Calvert street, near the home of J. M. Orrell. Carvin operated a passenger car for hire in Los Angeles, and was hired to carry some unknown parties to Pasadena on the night of the 17th. The next morning Carvin was found murdered on the outskirts of Pasadena. No motive has been found for the deed and no trace of the person who shot him. His family lived here for about a year and a half and only recently moved to East Washington street in Los Angeles."

[29] Los Angeles Evening Post Record, May 17, 1923. Listed as one of 30 reasons police should stop arguing and get down to solving crimes: "Joseph Carvin, taxi-driver. Hired to drive two men to Pasadena. Slain. His valuables were not disturbed. No arrests." The report echoed one that had appeared in the LA Evening Express on February 17, which had concluded, "the motive was other than robbery."

[30] Henry Gekler, "inspr," appears in the 1919 Philadelphia City Directory living at 1935 Somerset, with Joseph J. Sr. He then appears (listed as Harry F. Gekler, adjuster, Am Indemnity Exchange) at 4535 Prospect Avenue, LA, in 1920. When he and why he moved his family to Los Angeles is unclear, but his wife's brother Joe was his only connection in L.A., as far as I am aware.

[31] This social tidbit appeared in the Los Angeles Evening Citizen News of September 17, 1920.

[32] Elsie Carvin worked as a postal clerk in L.A. for years to come. In the 1920 and 1930 Censuses, she listed herself as a widow, but in the 1940 Census, as divorced. (Perhaps she remarried and got divorced between 1930 and 1940?) See 1920 U.S. Census, L.A. Assembly Dist 64, Dist 0226, Fam 289 at 1511 Bellevue; 1930 Census, L.A. Dist 0721, Fam 96 at 609 LaVeta Terrace; and 1940 U.S. Census, L.A. Enum Dist 60-1115, Fam 348 at 609 LaVeta Terrace. Elsie died March 7, 1974. (This date per the California Death Index. The Social Security record of her death, SSN 556-70-9208, gives the date of death as March 15, 1974.) Elsie was survived by her children Elsie Marie Carvin Keller (1910-2000) and Edward Charles Carvin (1907-2002).

13. Stella Marie Murphy

Few families were better known in Kensington than the Murphys. In politics, business, and church affairs, Stella Marie's family had been prominent for three generations. Her great grandfather had served on City Council. Her grandfather and father had been among the largest employers in Kensington. Her great uncles were famous in the nation's capital, hobnobbing with presidents, senators, and supreme court justices. Still, we must consider what we know of her personal perspective.

She was born in Philadelphia to Joseph D. and Stella Cecelia Murphy on February 6, 1896.[1] She likely cradled her baby sister, Mary, before that infant died; she certainly felt her parents' sadness, shared their sense of loss. Told that Mary had not been the first, that a sister named Genevieve had also died when she was too young to remember it, Stella Marie lived her most formative years with ghosts whose souls, she was taught, were still very much alive in limbo. Their real presence made them like imaginary friends she would soon see again. And as the only one of the three able to cling to life, she would always wonder why she'd been privileged to live while her sisters had not.

Meanwhile, she had no fewer than eight attentive aunts, ages 9 to 32, living within a stone's throw of her home, each practicing for eventual duty as mothers and ladies. Even compared to other young girls of the wealthier class, Stella Marie was doted on as children seldom are. Anna May Congdon, Elizabeth Murphy, and Marie Agnes Murphy would never marry, so for them, having a little girl nearby was the next best thing to having one of their own. Her favorite aunt of all – Genevieve Congdon, "Aunt G" – had not yet married, and even when she did, she would remain childless. Anna Marie, Mary Regina, and Loretto Murphy were not yet married either, and their children would not be born for years to come; they, too, treated Stella like a doll, teaching her how to curtsy, to cover her head before stepping into church, to genuflect and make the sign of the cross before turning away from the alter rail.[2] Irene Greenfield was the only one of Stella Marie's aunts to be a mother herself, and her first two children were not princesses, but boys.[3]

Although talk of tariffs, assassinations and wars was boring, conversation at the dinner table often turned to family, and from such talk, Stella Marie learned how important the men in her family were. Manufacturing, always.

The U.S. Senate. Leadership of the Pension Bureau. The Congressional Record. The Panama Canal. Most people – most common people, that is – had no understanding of the great events in which her family was involved. Stella Marie was privileged to be a member of the upper crust. Even her younger brother Joe, was five years her junior: by the time he could compete for the attention, she was already the apple of their father's eye.

When her beloved Aunt Genevieve got married, the wedding dress, the train, the flowers in the church, the priest's sonorous Latin, all made the world seem as divine as holy communion itself.[4] After the wedding, "Aunt G" didn't move far away, at first, and continued to dote as if Stella Marie were her own.[5] But when Stella Marie was seven and Joe two, the world began to change. Aunt G's husband, Joe Dulanty, took a new job; he and Aunt G moved to faraway Buffalo, New York.[6] It was the first step in the dismantling of the princess's court that had formed her sense of who she was. Her cousins, the Greenfields, lived less than a block west on Lehigh Avenue, and her favorite cousin, Marie Greenfield, three years her junior, had always looked up to her. In the absence of Aunt G, Stella mothered her younger cousin. The two became fast friends.[7]

In the summer of 1909, her eight-year-old brother was sent to rural upstate Pennsylvania to experience life on a farm. Already thirteen, Stella Marie made clear that milking cows was not for her. When Uncle Joe and Aunt G came back to Philadelphia for a business meeting that summer, Aunt G was like a fairy godmother come to take her to the royal ball. The Dulantys took Stella Marie with them, in their new car, back to Buffalo, where (since Uncle Joe was on the road so much) they lived at the Castle Inn.

It wasn't a castle in the medieval sense, but it was as close to a real castle as a hotel could get. U.S. President Millard Fillmore had bought the gothic structure in 1858 and made it his home until his death in 1874; his sons had then converted it into the Fillmore Hotel. (It had just been renamed "Castle Inn" when the Dulantys arrived.)[8] The childless couple treated their niece to luxurious hotel living, to food prepared by great chefs and served by fancy waiters. Stella wrote penny postals home about how fabulous it felt to be living in a President's house.[9] From the hotel, she looked out the window onto Niagara Square and the new McKinley monument there. She went with Aunt G to see Niagara Falls, and even to Toronto.

Her father's reply to the postcards she sent from Buffalo was addressed to "the best girl in the world." (He squeezed a question mark into the margin, as if asking her to reflect on whether she deserved that distinction.)

> Philadelphia. July 20, 1909
>
> To the best girl in the world, Stella Marie — ?
>
> We received your many postals and were delighted to hear that you were having such a fine time, traveling so much and had been out of the United States. When you come home I am

going to take a month off from office so as you can tell me all about the things you have seen.

Last Tuesday, we took Aunt Agnes and Uncle Tom up to Scott's in the automobile to see Joseph. He had grown so tall and gotten so stout that at first we did not recognize him. He is having such a fine time, working on the farm, milking the cows and driving the horses that he says he is going to stay until school starts and then he might stay all winter and go to school with Yerbie and Bud.[10]

Mother is going up with Uncle Will to spend a few weeks with Aunt Irene. Walter and Willie are now at Tumbling Run with their mother; send them some postals.[11]

Do Aunt G and Uncle Joe intend to go to Atlantic City this summer?

Give Aunt G and Uncle Joe our dearest love and a great big kiss and a hug for yourself.

If you were now at school, would you get an X or V. P. for conduct? Hope you would get 50 extras and the medal.

Affectionately,
Your Papa.

Sarah J. Scott, the nineteen-year-old Virginian, did the cooking and other chores in the Murphy house; neither Stella Marie nor her mother performed such common tasks.[12] Stella Marie was being groomed to be an educated, cultured lady, a goal for which generations had striven. Success was not something to be dismissed or begrudged; it was a cause for pride. So Stella Marie began taking lessons on the family piano. Her parents enrolled her at the Academy of Mercy, where she read the Catholic Bible and was guided by nuns through the study of French, philosophy, and literature. She even learned to play the concert harp her father had bought her.

When (years later) her grandchildren saw the gargantuan instrument in her living room, they were told she'd become rather accomplished on it. But when they asked her to play it for them, she laughed, saying the time had passed since that was a possibility; over a period of years, its strings had loosened until a few were detached at one end and hanging out of the frame; and by that time, Stella herself had also aged. (Time spares no one.) But a modern description speaks to the instrument's original grandeur:

> Created by Lyon & Healy in 1890, this intricate harp is symbolic of the Victorian era during which it was made. The Style 23 has become the most recognized harp in the world and showcases the woodworking artistry of the Lyon & Healy craftspeople. Its sound is unmistakable: even, responsive and resonant. The highly embellished floral carving at the crown, top of the column, base and feet, is coupled with a *fleur de lis*

pattern at the bottom of the column - both notable features of the time. The carving of the Style 23 Gold is accented with 23+ karat hand-gilding. A complimentary sweeping floral decoration accents the extended Sitka Spruce soundboard which also features a double Rosewood inlay along the edges. The Style 23 Gold features solid brass action plates with richly stylized lettering and ornamentation."[13]

The Lyon & Healy Model 23 Gold now sells for over fifty thousand dollars. When Stella Marie's father bought it the early twentieth century, it cost him less, but so did Sarah Scott's labor.

Coming down from Buffalo to celebrate Stella Marie's fifteenth birthday with her, Aunt G bought her tickets to a play at the Grand Opera House, Vaughan Glaser starring in Rupert Hughes's "The Man Between." She may have given Stella opera glasses too. The Murphys all went to the play together. The newspapers advertised reserved seats at the matinee for twenty-five cents, but the Murphys didn't sit with the general public. They went in the evening, in their theater attire, and sat in a proper box. In the

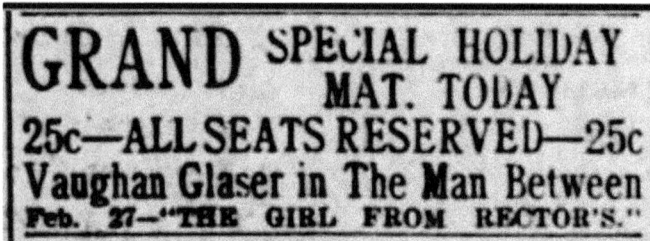

GRAND SPECIAL HOLIDAY MAT. TODAY
25c—ALL SEATS RESERVED—25c
Vaughan Glaser in The Man Between
Feb. 27—"THE GIRL FROM RECTOR'S."

thank-you letter Stella Marie wrote to Aunt Genevieve, Stella passed on love from her friend, Lillian Hengen, one of the neighborhood's numerous German girls, and she told her Aunt G of reading a story by Anne Katharine Green.[14]

"Do you remember how we used to sit on the porch and criticize her?" she asked.

Anna Katharine Green was called "the mother of the detective novel," predating even Sir Arthur Conan Doyle. She'd invented a nosy society spinster who assisted a male detective; her stories featured a young debutante, Violet Strange, solving mysteries on her own. It's easy to see the young Stella Marie and her Aunt G sitting on the porch, parroting man's skepticism about a woman's ability to write a detective novel – only to see Stella Marie, as she grew older, begin to change her mind.[15] Stella Marie had been bitten by the story-telling bug. A box at the theater offered a very different view of the world; Stella Marie now immersed herself in the world of drama and literature. Philadelphia's magazine, *The Ladies Home Journal*, carried articles by muckrakers, social protestors, exposers of corruption and scandalous social conditions.[16] For the first time in history, there was plenty of material a young woman could read, much of it written by women. Edith Wharton's 1905 *The House of Mirth* mounted a cutting attack on an irresponsible, morally corrupt upper class. In Sylvia Chatfield Bates' *The*

Vintage (1916), a young man had asked why he should raise a flag at a patriotic ceremony.

"Why should I raise it? It's a very pretty flag, of course. But look at what it has come to stand for, what it countenances, shelters! Look at the suffering, and sin, and dirt, and inequality! Think of the tricks and grabbing and piling up of vulgar dollars! And the hypocrisy! Lord! And the grinding down of those who are borne to the earth already with loads! Land of the free, is it?"[17]

A well-read young woman like Stella could hardly avoid such themes.[18] "The eternal struggle of capital and labor, class against class," was a goad that aroused hers interest in story-telling. As she aspired to comment on the great questions of the day, there were many who held old fashioned views.[19] Spectators physically blocked marchers at the first national woman's suffrage parade in Washington; more than two hundred people were injured as police stood by.[20] As the men debated events around Joe Murphy's dinner table, Stella wrestled with the questions herself: Did capitalists contribute to the economic good of all, or were they leeches on the backs of labor? Were women capable of more than making babies? She dreamed of putting her own views into stories.

She had the chance to do so in a short story she wrote for Mercy Academy's yearbook and literary magazine, *The Patrician,* in 1916.* In Stella's story, "Weighed in the Balance," the roguish Jean Ruffin had approached a Paris house under cover of night with burglary on his mind, but at the last second, he'd knocked on a door instead, intending only to beg. As fate would have it, he'd knocked on the door of an abbey. The kind monk who answered the door ended up scolding him.

"You bewail the fate that made you the son of poor parents," chided the monk. "You blame circumstances for your crimes, but 'honor and shame from no condition rise.' It depends entirely upon yourself." The monk warned Ruffin that if he didn't make the best of what he'd been given, God's judgment would be "swift and severe." And in Stella's story, it was: the story ended with gold, stolen from the abbey, filling the rogue's pockets, while Ruffin's dead body lay crushed by a sudden snowslide that had fallen from the abbey roof.

If the story reflected the teachings of the Sisters of Mercy, it was also Stella's response to socialist sentiment elsewhere. She knew that her father, grandfather and great uncles were among those who stood accused of what *The Man Between* had called "quelling their workers into submission." In response, she denied that poverty is to blame for crime: if the poor would only accept faith in God, they could overcome the circumstances of their birth. Blame lay not on the upper classes, but on a lack of faith, on a lack of will to change, among the "rogues" of the world themselves.

---

* Reproduced in full in Appendix 3, below.

But Stella was herself clearly a creature of the upper class. The newspapers were full of her; her photograph appeared again and again, especially in connection with Catholic charities, even when others were in charge and Stella's own role was minor or not even mentioned.[21]

POPULAR YOUNG CHARITY WORKERS OF THIS CITY

MISS ELEANOR O'LOUGHLIN (in circle)
MISS STELLA MARIE MURPHY   MISS ELIZABETH SMART

Photo by J. Mitchell Elliot.
MISS STELLA MURPHY
Miss Murphy will take part in the large lawn fete given on the attractive grounds of the Mercy Convent at Merion today and tomorrow in aid of the new Mater Misericordiae Hospital, which is being rushed to completion for the country's needs

Photo by J. Mitchell Elliot.
MISS STELLA MARIE MURPHY
Miss Murphy, who is one of the earnest workers in behalf of the musical comedy to be given at the Bellevue-Stratford this week for St. Francis Country House, will be one of the chorus girls in the "Millionaire" number that will be one of the features of the show.

Such attention had not been paid to earlier generations of young women. Mary Ann Carvin and Adele Miller had lived before the days of newspaper photographs. But even the later women – Catherine Hagan, Katie Sherick, Stella Congdon, and the sweet-voiced Molly Byrne, star of theatrical productions – had not been so put on display. The attention paid to Stella Marie could not have been on account of her beauty – an overbite ruled that out – but women were claiming rights to a higher status in the world. The men who published newspapers were looking for ways to acknowledge the "fairer sex." And since 1848, the men in Stella's family had figured large in the world of news reporting; many had connections to newspapers. When Stella Marie's parents sought to recognize their daughter's importance by marketing her to the young men of Philadelphia, their newspaper connections were happy to oblige. The flattering portraits her parents arranged avoided a straight-on view of her overbite.

Photo by J. Mitchell Elliot.
MISS STELLA MURPHY
She will be an aide at the fete Cham...

It wasn't only women who posed a threat to the dominance of American men. Due to the situation in Europe, the *Evening Public Ledger* began the new year by predicting that 1917 would prove a turning point in world history, "either a new birth of liberty and peace or the abomination of desolation itself" in which "the yellow race [would] clamor for ascendancy over Christendom." Fifteen centuries, declared the paper, had not "dimmed the glories" of the year 451, "when civilization stopped the Huns at Chalons." The piece ended with the warning that "The white race holds its fate in its hands."

It was a base trick of logic that, with the yellow race the natural enemy of the white one, placed German "Huns" in the camp of the enemy. The U.S. entered the war three months later, and over the next two years, the Philadelphia press would describe Germans as "Huns" nearly six thousand times.[22]

While Dominic Murphy was in Bulgaria convincing that country to join the allies, Congress passed the Sedition Act of 1918, making it a federal offense to use "disloyal" language about the government or the flag. Socialists who opposed the war suffered most for their opposition. Eugene Debs was convicted and imprisoned for three years. When Kate Richards O'Hare called the women of the United States no more than "brood sows, to raise children to get into the army and be made into fertilizer," it took a North Dakota jury only thirty minutes to convict her of violating the Espionage Act on account of the insult.[23] When Rose Pastor Stokes wrote a letter to the *Kansas City Star* asserting that "no government which is for the profiteers can also be for the people, and I am for the people while the government is for the profiteers," she was indicted under the espionage act, convicted, and sentenced to ten years in a federal penitentiary.[24] When armed men rounded up 1,186 strikers at the Phelps Dodge copper mine in Arizona and placed them on railroad cattle cars without food or water, the *Los Angeles Times* editorialized that the people responsible had "written a lesson that the whole of America would do well to copy."[25] And so they did. The Schools organized contests in which students composed their own four-minute speeches; winners received government certificates certifying them as Junior Four Minute Men.[26] The *Evening Public Ledger* published a four-minute speech on "The Meaning of America."

> Forged in the flames of freedom, fanned by the winds of tyranny, welded into shape by the hearts and brains of early patriots … our Government is a machine with a soul ... For America is not only a country – it is an ideal … a system of government which promises freedom to all men …"[27]

When the Fourth Liberty Loan Drive was kicked off in Philadelphia, organizers published a schedule of how many bonds a man should buy, depending on his salary and number of dependents. More and more "charity" work went to support the military machine, raising money for uniforms, hospitals, food, and – above all – the sale of Liberty Bonds to pay for weapons and supplies. Like many young women of the day, Stella Marie Murphy played her own part in the war effort: in January, 1918, she sang and danced at the Bellevue-Stratford in a benefit for the St. Francis Home for Convalescents.[28] Just as in prior wars, the government led the media (and the media, in turn, led the people) in patriotic zeal. All things German were depicted as evil. The Committee on Public Information declared that winning the war would save the world for God,[29] and following its lead, America's hawks – including those who claimed to represent the Prince of Peace – emphasized God's support:

PEACE SERMONS ARE TRAITOROUS, MINISTERS TOLD

Bishop Warns Those Who Refuse to Urge Righteous War

Methodist ministers who do not preach from the text "The Cause of the Allies is the Cause of Righteousness" will be prosecuted for treason, according to Bishop Theodores Henderron, of Detroit, presiding at the 131st session of the Philadelphia annual conference in Simpson Memorial Church...

"Any preacher who wabbles from this text is just as guilty as an out-and-out traitor," he declared, launching a plan for the organization among laymen of aides to the Department of Justice...

"There will be patriotic demonstrations in all of our churches lasting until May to stiffen the morale of the country and give religious interpretation of the war," he said. "The slogan will be "The Cause of the Allies is the Cause of Righteousness." If any preacher cannot preach this text he is a traitor. If he can't be regenerated, he will be eliminated...

He asked each minister to appoint one layman to co-operate with the Department of Justice in keeping "tabs" on ministers' sermons, and asked that the laymen's names be given to the district superintendents. "I am a pacifist," said the Bishop, "with the accent on the -fist...."[30]

The Committee appealed to Jews, Italians, Poles and Native Americans by enlisting speakers of their "own race" in their own languages.[31] In her theater outings, Stella Marie could choose to see the Committee's own production, "The Beast of Berlin" (i.e., the German Kaiser Wilhelm), or "Good Bye Bill" (about the Kaiser's capture and ultimate dispatch). There were pitches to buy Liberty Bonds at both.[32] If Stella preferred a performance that didn't villainize Germany, she could go to the People's Theater in Kensington which, in April of 1918, was featuring "The Golden Crook" burlesque act. But if she'd gone there on Tuesday night, April 9, 1918, she'd have witnessed an increasingly common way of supporting American ideals. That night, when Frank Kellman failed to stand up during the playing of the Star-Spangled Banner, he was grabbed by a soldier and a sailor, forced to the stage, forced to kiss the American flag and made to apologize to the audience. Despite his apology, he was "severely pummeled by the enraged men and women in the audience" before being turned over to the Department of Justice for investigation.[33]

As summer approached, newspaper advertisements proclaimed it every citizen's duty to see such anti-German films as *My Four Years in Germany* and D.W. Griffith's *Hearts of the World*.[34] At the Forrest Theatre, one could opt instead to see *Pershing's Crusaders*. (Released by the Committee on Public Education, it was advertised as "The Truth About the War.") If Stella hoped to avoid such propaganda, she could see *All for Democracy* instead, "the most picturesque patriotic production ever presented."[35]

In addition to dominating the movie theaters, Creel's Committee on Public Education demanded that cartoonists produce only "anti-Hun" cartoons.[36] The socialist journal, *The Masses* was prosecuted because of cartoons that opposed the war, including this one by H.J. Glintenkamp:

The four-minute men proclaimed the existence of German spies in our midst; they accused Germans of the murder of American women and children.[37] One four-minute speech in Pennsylvania declared that the people of the town were "determined to wipe out seditious talk among pro-Germans here even if it requires tar and feathers and a stout rope in the hands of a necktie party."[38]

On September 28, more than 200,000 people crowded Broad Street to witness a Liberty Loan Parade featuring horse-drawn howitzers, biplanes, and marching bands led by John Philip Sousa. Stella may have seen God's hand in what happened next: within 24 hours of the parade, reports of the "Spanish Flu" were skyrocketing; within a week, 4,500 Philadelphians had died of the disease that was soon declared a pandemic – over three times the number of Philadelphians killed in Europe during the war.[39]

As the end of the Fourth Liberty Loan Drive approached in October 1918, the *Inquirer's* headline warned of possible disgrace if the city did not achieve its fund-raising goal. "That this district, and particularly this city, the cradle of liberty, shall not be disgraced ... prayers were offered in thousands of homes yesterday ..." A new plan was laid out by which "every citizen is expected to display the Fourth Liberty Loan emblem in his home or store window ..." 2500 city policemen, 2500 Boy Scout "color bearers" and 2100 "solicitors" would scour the city, the solicitor's duty being to visit every one of the 450,000 homes in the city to ensure that every one of them displayed an appropriate pro-war decoration and that every citizen had bought bonds.[40]

Maybe love for her German grandmother, Adele Gertrude Murphy, or her childhood friendship with Lillian Hengen had cooled Stella Marie to the anti-German rhetoric of the day, preventing her from demonizing all Germans. Maybe she'd been offended by the abuse directed toward people like Frank Kellman. For whatever reason, she refused to vilify Germans. Even as her parents promoted her to Philadelphia's bachelors, even as the constitutional amendment giving women the right to vote fell short in the U. S. Senate by three votes, she questioned America's decision to go to war.[41]

But the heart is a peculiar thing. Stella had long ago taken an interest in a young man who lacked her family's wealth, education, and privileged class, a young man born of a scandalous marriage, a man she'd first met as a young girl when he (briefly) lived across the street. Whatever his shortcomings, he shared her interest in stories; he even had a knack for telling them himself, mimicking the voices of his characters. Nothing her parents could say squelched her interest in him, even when he enlisted in the army with plans to become an aviator and fight against the Germans. In the autumn of 1917, she spent two romantic weeks with him at ground school in Princeton, New Jersey.

Mocking her pacifist anti-war views, the young aviator called the aspiring writer "Dutchie," a common nickname for a German soldier.[42] Stella Marie's distaste for socialism may have prompted her to side more with industrial Germany in the war, but calling someone "Dutchie" was an insult, not a term of endearment. It must have been a tease, since the young cadet clearly thought himself more than a casual acquaintance:

> *Barracks 35*
> *Dearest,*
>> *It seems I've waited ages for word from you. Time is lengthened no doubt by the fact that I think of you continually – Life here is far different from that at Princeton and I have plenty of time to think and wonder why I've received no word...*
>> *Oh I miss you during the day, Dutchie, but it is the nights I can hardly stand – wonderful starry moonlight nights – wasted – our best days spent apart...*[43]

Valentine's Day of 1918 brought new ways of expressing love. That Sunday's *Inquirer* headlined, "American Artillery Trained to Deal Death to Treacherous Hun." Tuesday's carried an article headlined "Wife-Beater a Rabid Pro-German." Another, titled "Hang a Few of These Traitors," reported that fifty-five members of the I.W.W. labor union had been indicted for anti-war activities. "Such men are traitors and, upon conviction, should be treated as such. High time to resort to the hangman's noose." The front page on Valentine's day itself featured a Valentine four columns wide, with hearts around U.S. servicemen and the word, "Victory!"[44]

338

So much for the world of men. For young ladies of Philadelphia society, life was full of invitations. After one society dance, Stella Marie's letter to her man in Texas expressed doubts about loving him. But her doubts did not deter him. His reply was addressed to "Dutchie Dear."

> *Please never again tell me of your doubt as you did a week or so ago. Nothing makes me more miserable, because dreaming and loving you as I do, I can't understand how you can doubt – it is like throwing cold water on my dreams.*[45]

The following April, she boarded a train for Texas with three close girlfriends, ostensibly to visit an army Lieutenant stationed there (the brother of two of her friends).[46] For Stella, the friend's brother was not the attraction; her young storyteller had also reported for duty in San Antonio. But by early 1918, just before her train left, her beau was reassigned to Dallas; he was soon flying all over Texas, teaching other cadets how to fly and stirring up support for the war by selling Liberty Bonds. There's no evidence she was ever able to connect with him in Texas that summer.

After her return to Philadelphia, her social calendar occupied most of her attention. Dances, parties, charity events filled her days. On June 1st, there was another *Fete Champetre* to benefit the Mercy Convent in Merion.[47]

The pandemic that spread across the world that summer did not originate in Spain. It may even have originated in the U.S. Americans called it the "Spanish" flu for the simple reason that the Committee on Public Information had called for nothing but positive news in support of the war, so American media had largely ignored the flu, whereas neutral Spain had chosen to be open about its existence there.[48] But Philadelphia was among the first American cities to feel the full force of the virus, and it was among the hardest hit by it. Stella stayed in Chelsea with her parents, writing occasional stories and frequent letters to her Texas aviator.[49] Her parents hoped that the beach and fresh air would help her avoid the deadly disease that summer, and perhaps even meet a man more to their liking. But Stella's doubts faded; in fact, her interest in her aviator only deepened, especially when he wrote from a hospital bed in July that his legs had been broken when his plane crashed. Waiting for the war to end, pining for her beau to come home, was neither easy nor quick. Though the Armistice was signed in November 1918, he didn't return to Philadelphia until the following

April. The delight she took in his return was matched only by the fact that finally, on June 4, 1919, Congress passed the amendment which, if ratified, would give women the right to vote.

Stella Marie introduced her beloved to all her friends; they went from affair to affair with the Greenfields, Strouds, Congdons, Hookeys, Loughrans and Scannells.[50] She was a small woman, but she impressed him with performances on her enormous golden concert harp.[51] She and Marie Greenfield performed at the Bellevue Stratford hotel in the comedy, "In Fancy's Garden."[52] The books she read strengthened her aspirations to write stories of her own.[53] When Tennessee's ratification made the 19th Amendment official in August of 1920, it seemed nothing could stand in her way. The story-telling and romance continued until September of 1921 when, after reports of "a mass of scantily-clad feminine loveliness" in Atlantic City's first Miss America Pageant, Stella's own engagement was announced in the *Inquirer* under the heading, "Returning from Seashore." Stella had been in Chelsea, not on the shore. The headline seemed meant to suggest that Stella herself had been one of the pageant contestants.[54]

THE PHILADELPHIA INQUIRER, MONDAY MORNING, SEPTEMBER 19, 1921
RETURNING FROM SEASHORE
MISS STELLA MURPHY
Of 1830 Rittenhouse Square, who will return home this week from Chelsea. The engagement of Miss Murphy and Charles Carven was recently

A month before the wedding, Alice Loughran gave a dance in her honor at the Whitemarsh Country Club.[55] The Monday prior to the wedding, her father gave her a party at the Manufacturer's Club.[56] And on Saturday, June

340

3, 1922, at Saint Patrick's Roman Catholic Church, with Alice Loughran and Marie Greenfield her bridesmaids, the princess around whom the world revolved was finally married to the man of her dreams.[57]

Although now a new bride, Stella had never learned how to drive a car, never learned how to cook. And so, as a wedding present, her parents gave her something to help her in her new life: the services of a cook and chambermaid.[58]

She would certainly have time on her hands in which to do what she'd always wanted to do. She'd be able to write to her heart's content. If all went well, she might become an accomplished author, another Anna Katherine Green, with mysteries and detective stories of her own to tell. Stella Marie Murphy was on the verge of having everything she'd ever wanted.

But time and marriage would eventually change her life. Her patrician family was about to merge with her husband's plebian one. Despite all its advantages, all its wealth and history and power, her own life was about to be overtaken by his.

Notes on Chapter 13, Stella Marie Murphy

[1] 1900 U.S. Census Phila Ward 19, Dist 400, Fam 710, at 710 Lehigh Avenue; https://www.findagrave.com/memorial/147704555/stella-marie-carvin.

[2] Anna Marie Murphy married Charles Allan Rowsey April 26, 1904; their daughters Adele and Anita Marie Rowsey were not born until September 5, 1905, and January 31, 1908. Mary Regina Murphy did not marry William Edwards Pascoe until 30 Nov 1916; they went on to have six children. Loretto Madelaide Murphy did not marry Joseph A. Colman until June 19, 1917, and the first of their eight children was not born until 1918.

[3] Walter H. Greenfield was born Jun 7, 1896, four months after Stella; William Congdon Greenfield was born August 15, 1897. Stella Murphy's closest female cousin was Marie Irene Greenfield, born Nov 13, 1899.

[4] Elizabeth Genevieve Congdon married Joseph F. Dulanty on 15 August, 1901. Phila Marriage License No. 139018.

[5] Aunt G and her new husband, Joe Dulanty, lived on Arizona Street for three years.

[6] Joseph F. Dulanty's family had owned a home in St. Edward's parish – at 1024 Arizona Street – since 1880, when he was a child; his brothers had become roofers, while Joe became a salesman. His employer in 1904 was the Philadelphia firm of John B. Ellison & Sons. Since they were wholesalers of woolen goods, it seems likely that they were one of Joe Murphy's customers. Perhaps it was at Murphy's suggestion that Ellison & Sons made Dulanty their new agent in Buffalo. (The 1905 City Directory for Buffalo shows Dulanty's connection with Ellison & Sons as its agent there, and the Directory for Philadelphia shows the firm's home office there.)

[7] Stella Marie's cousin, Marie Irene Greenfield (1899-1989), was the daughter of her aunt, Marie Irene Congdon (1872 – 1956), who had married William H. Greenfield, Jr. (1873 - 1944). After their 1895 marriage, William and Irene Greenfield had moved briefly from North 9th Street to Lawndale, but by 1900, they had returned, moving in to 1309 West Lehigh Avenue, less than a block west of the Murphys at 1231 West Lehigh (1900 U.S. Census, Phila Ward 37, Dist 0957, Fam 196; and 1910 U.S. Census, Phila Ward 37, Dist 0924, Fam 4). Future events would make their close friendship clear.

[8] Todd Hariaczyi, "Torn Down Tuesday: The Millard Fillmore Mansion," *Buffalo News*, April 25, 2017, accessed at https://buffalonews.com/news/local/history/torn-down-tuesday-the-millard-fillmore-mansion/article_8d0d99b0-175f-5e75-9506-54936e81a765.html; Steve Cichon, "Millard Fillmore's Downtown Buffalo Addresses," http://blog.buffalostories.com/tag/castle-inn/.

[9] Stella was likely unaware of the former President's connections to the nativist Know-Nothing Party, or the fact that when he lost the New York gubernatorial race in 1844, he had blamed his defeat on "foreign Catholics." (Paul Finkelman, *Millard Fillmore*, p 24, quoted in *Millard Fillmore*, Wikipedia.)

[10] "Aunt Agnes" could have been Joe Murphy's sister, Maria Agnes Murphy, or Bridget Agnes Loughran, who went by the name Agnes and had married Stella Marie's Uncle, Walter Hilman Congdon. But all available records reflect that Joe's sister was never married, and the identity of "Uncle Tom" is a mystery. Possibly, given that the Murphy's new live-in servant was a young black woman named Sarah Scott, little Joe had gone to live for the summer on a farm associated with her family – "Uncle Tom" might even have been what the children called Sarah Scott's husband or father. But "Yerbie and Bud" have also escaped identification.

[11] "Uncle Will" was Aunt Irene's husband, William Greenfield; Walter and Willie Greenfield were Stella's cousins, the older brothers of her favorite, Marie Greenfield. Tumbling Run was a popular resort in Schuylkill County, "one of the most beautiful in the state," that "consisted of a large and elegantly decorated Victorian hotel, a theater, dance pavilion, amusement hall, roller coaster, skating rink, bowling alley and a carousel. On the hill behind the hotel, a baseball park hosted teams from the Atlantic League. Boathouses lined the northern and eastern shores of the upper dam and a steamboat

offered nickel rides around the lake. Trolley cars transported visitors to and from the area on a schedule of 10-minute intervals. By 1908, more than 750,000 people visited the park during the three-month summer season..." (Colleen Hoptak, *Turning the Pages of Time*, 2020, accessed at reading eagle.com/news/south-schuylkill-news/turning-the-pages-of-time-a-century-ago-tumbling-run-was-a-top-notch-resort/article_0b333ec2-3612-11ea-b96b-47d4dd5f0402.html.)

[12] 1910 U.S. Census, Phila Ward 37, Dist 0928, Fam 146 at 1234 Lehigh Avenue.

[13] Promotional language taken from https://www.lyonhealy.com/harps-collections/premium-harps/ in 2021.

[14] Daniel Hengen, Liquors, was in the 1911 City Directory at 1232 Lehigh Ave – that is, right next door to the Murphys. Lillian was his daughter – one of Stella Marie's German friends from a neighborhood where Irish and Germans were thoroughly mixed from house to house. The thank-you letter to Aunt Gert was addressed to the Castle Inn, postmarked Tuesday, Feb. 28, 1911, and bore a two-cent stamp.

[15] The Pennsylvania State Senate had debated whether such a well-plotted book as Green had written could really have been written by a woman. ("Anna Katharine Green," *Wikipedia*. com.)

[16] Its editor, Anna Robeson Burr, "railed wittily and angrily against self-important men and the silly women who encourage them" (Eleanor Robson, *The Discovery of Professor Von Saalbrandt: A Philadelphia Story*, in Strings and Threads: A Celebration of the Work of Anne Draffkorn Kilmer, Eisenbrauns, Inc., 2011, p 226). In her 1897 short story, *A Feline Fate*, Burr had written about a young man who'd "chosen to fall in love with a very superior person – with a girl of wit as well as beauty; with a young lady who had seen and traveled much, who barely tolerated the average young man, and who, as she counted among her friends many prominent people, could afford to pick and choose" (Tales from McClure's: Romance, Doubleday and McClure's, 1899). The story must have reminded Stella Marie of her own relationship with the young man she'd first known as the boy who swept up a factory floor. In Sir Mark, a Tale of the First Capital (D. Appleton & Co, 1896) Burr had written a story about the foundations of America in the city of brotherly love. Stella Marie likely read it; her own story, *Weighed in the Balance* (Appendix 3), seems patterned after its highly dramatic, moralistic style.

[17] Sylvia Chatfield Bates, The Vintage, Duffield & Co, N. Y. (1916), pp 5-6.

[18] Mary Wilkins Freeman's 1908 work, *The Shoulders of Atlas,* involved money, family conflict, and suspicions of crime and murder. Jane Addams, who wrote 1910's *Twenty Years at Hull House* – was a radical reformer, lesbian, and suffragist.

[19] Texas Senator Joseph Bailey resigned from the Senate in January, 1913, with a four hour speech describing his befuddlement: "I cannot understand," he said, "how any woman wants to step down from the high pedestal on which man has placed her to mingle in the broils and debaucheries of politics. No. The Southern States believe in the rule of the men people. And not only in that, but in the white men people." (*Inquirer*, Jan 3, 1913, pp 1 and 5.)

[20] *Evening Star,* March 4, 1913, pp 1 and 21; *Washington Times*, March 6, 1913, p 5.

[21] "Miss Murphy" and Mrs. Frank Rowsey (surely related to Charles Rowsey, Stella Marie's uncle by marriage) were mentioned simply due to their attendance at a young people's *fete* at a Catholic church near Bryn Mawr (*Evening Public Ledger*, June 11, 1915, p 11). An *Evening Ledger* story about a musical comedy at the Bellevue Stratford to benefit the St. Francis Country House (in which production Stella Marie was but one of many chorus girls, and only in a single number) was accompanied by a large photograph of her (*Evening Public Ledger*, Jan 29, 1917, p 9). At an event to raise money for the construction of Mater Misericordiae Hospital, Stella's picture was included (rather than those of the organizers and committee heads) because she was "taking part" (*Evening Public Ledger*, May 25, 1917, p 15). When completed, the hospital was to be given to the army for the treatment of wounded veterans (*Evening Public Ledger*, March 18, 1918, pp 1 and 6). On January 30, 1918, the *Ledger* described a group raising money to send garments to soldiers in Europe; another organizing an "endless chain of small bridge parties" for the Red Cross; another raising money for a school in Tennessee, and so on. The articles described the individual efforts of numerous organizers, sponsors and volunteers whose

photographs were not included, and not one mentioned any contribution by Stella Marie, yet her picture was prominently displayed under the caption, "Popular Young Charity Workers of This City" (*Evening Public Ledger*, Jan 30, 1918, p 9). An article on the Junior Auxiliary's Memorial Day fundraiser for the Convent of Mercy at Merion (Misericordia Hospital) named scores of young women whose roles were identified, Stella Marie's efforts not among them. Yet her picture appeared prominently, next to the article (*Evening Public Ledger*, May 13, 1918, p 13).

[22] This estimate is based on a search for the word "Hun" in 1917-1918 Philadelphia newspapers at Newspapers.com, which returned 5,965 instances of the word.

[23] *Bismarck North Dakota Tribune*, Dec 8, 1917, p 1; *Dickinson North Dakota Press*, Dec 15, 1917, p 3; *Kansas City Star*, Dec 30, 1917, p 8; *New York Tribune*, Feb 10, 1918, p 2. (As O'Hare wrote later in Appeal to Reason (1920) "… War and profits was the one subject the Democratic administration dared not permit me to discuss.")

[24] *Inquirer,* June 2, 1918, p 1. (Her conviction was overturned on appeal.)

[25] "The Espionage and Sedition Acts," Digital History 3479, accessed at https://www.digital history.uh.edu/disp_textbook.cfm?smtID=2&psid=3479#:~:text=In%20June%201917%2C%20Cong ress%20passed%20the%20Espionage%20Act.&text=Congress%20passed%20the%20Sedition%20A ct,2%2C100%20people%20under%20these%20acts.

[26] *Inquirer,* March 19, 1918, p 10.

[27] *Evening Public Ledger*, July 9, 1918, p 18.

[28] *Evening Public Ledger*, Jan 4, 1918, p 13 and Jan 25, 1918, p 9; *Inquirer,* Jan 20, 1918, p 20. The production of the musical comedy "Dr. Optimist" was directed by Charles S. Morgan of Mask & Wig fame.

[29] "I am everywhere helping to win this greatest of wars and to save the world for God and man. *I am the Four Minute Man."* (Four Minute Men News, Edition C, reprinted in Alfred Cornbise, *War As Advertised: The Four Minute Men and America's Crusade, 1917–1918* (Philadelphia: American Philosophical Society, 1984).

[30] *Evening Public Ledger,* March 18, 1918, pp 1, 7. The First Presbyterian Church of Kensington hosted a patriotic rally featuring speeches by four-minute men and music by a Marine Corps Band (*Evening Public Ledger*, May, 1918, p 11).

[31] "Full-Blooded Sioux Acts as Four Minute Man. Dupree, S. Dak., has a full-blooded Sioux Indian, Thomas J. Rouillaurd, acting as a Four Minute Man, largely among people of his own race." "We expect soon to have every Jewish audience in a motion-picture house or a Jewish playhouse addressed by a Jewish speaker…." Also, "…There was an address in Italian by Michelo Riccio, Italian consul; in Polish by Rev. Stanislau Musiel; in Lithuanian by Rev. John J. Ambot; in Magyar-Hungarian by Rev. Peter Dolin; in Russian by Rev. Constantin Bukstoff; in Ukrainian by Rev. Theodore Helanda and Rev. Romen Zalitsch; in Armenian by Prof. Armidos Ananakian and Mr. Partovan; and in Bohemian-Slovak by William Shultz." (Committee on Public Information, *Four Minute Men Bulletin* 1, May 22, 1917, Cornbise, *supra.*)

[32] *Inquirer,* April 7, 1918, pp 43-45.

[33] The same night, the Chester County School Board voted to discontinue teaching the German language, a month before the City of Philadelphia's School Board did so (*Evening Public Ledger,* April 10, 1918, p 3).

[34] The star of Griffith's *Hearts*, actress Lillian Gish, later said the film's depiction of German brutality "bordered on the absurd." (Tim Lussier, "What Others Said About Hearts of the World," Silents Are Golden webpage, accessed at http://www. silentsaregolden.com/heartsofworldfeature.html.)

[35] *Inquirer*, June 2, 1918, p 11.

[36] Philadelphians were proud to have the youngest anti-Hun cartoonist of them all: eleven-year-old T. Hilton Haines (*Evening Public Ledger*, April 10, 1918, p 13).

[37] "Speech by a Four Minute Man: Ladies and Gentlemen: I have just received the information that there is a German spy among us – a German spy watching *us.* He is around, here somewhere, reporting upon you and me—sending reports about us to Berlin … Money means everything now; it means

quicker victory and therefore less bloodshed. We are *in* the war, and now Americans can have but *one* opinion, only *one* wish in the Liberty Loan … For treachery here, attempted treachery in Mexico, treachery everywhere—*one billion.* For murder of American women and children—*one billion more.* For broken faith and promise to murder more Americans—*billions and billions more.* (Committee on Public Information, *Four Minute Man Bulletin,* No. 17, Oct 8, 1917, Cornbise, *supra.*)

[38] *Scranton Tribune*, July 27, 1918, p 4; Carbondale Daily News, July 27, 1918, p 2. The Committee denied that the speaker had been authorized by it (Committee on Public Information, *Four Minute Men Bulletin* 1, May 22, 1917; Cornbise, *supra*).

[39] Russell Weigley *et al*, Philadelphia, a Three Hundred Year History, W.W. Norton & Co. (1982) *supra*, p 561; "Philadelphia Liberty Loans Parade," Wikipedia.org, accessed Jan 15, 2022. The *Evening Public Ledger* of May 10, 1919 (p 6) reported on the fund-raising efforts of the Industrial Committee of the Victory Liberty Loan campaign in Philadelphia. Group 2, including Cotton, Wool and Carpets, was chaired by Charles J. Webb, whose company had subscribed to the tune of 1.6 million dollars, second only to the 4-million-dollar subscription of George H. McFadden & Bro. Joseph Bromley subscribed for $100,000, while William F. Taubel subscribed for $70,000. Joseph D. Murphy's subscription for $11,150 was small by comparison, but joined by many others of about the same amount. Was it a sign of a smaller company? Lesser support for the war?

[40] *Inquirer*, Oct 7, 1918, pp 1 and 3, and October 19, 1918, p 5. The plan was that of George Wharton Pepper, the Republican lawyer and "dry" candidate whose fund raiser Joe Murphy attended in 1926 (see Appendix 5, Ltr 9).

[41] The Senate vote on the Constitutional Amendment on October 1, 1918 was 53-31, three votes shy of the 56 (two thirds of those present and voting) needed to pass. The Senate voted again on February 10, 1919, after Republican gains in the mid-term elections: this time, the vote fell one vote short, 55-29. Stella Marie's views on the war are presumed based on all the circumstances, including her privileged status, her religion, her friendships and kinship with Germans, and the nickname "Dutchie."

[42] The name "Dutchie" was used, sometimes insultingly, to refer to a German, due to the Germans' own word for themselves and their country as "Deutsch" and Deutschland. (See, for example, *Buffalo Times Illustrated Sunday Magazine*, March 3, 1918, p 9; "Yankees Here and Over There," St. John Weekly News, Oct 17, 1918, p 5; and "Tag, Dutchie, You're It" in *Everybody's Magazine*, quoted in the *Santa Fe New Mexican*, Aug 26, 1918, p 4 and the *Charlotte News*, Oct 5, 1918, p 8.) The name could even be used by an American soldier to refer to the German enemy ("St. Louis Boys Tell Thrilling Stories From Battlefront," letter of Corp. Ben Dietz, in *St. Louis Post-Dispatch*, Dec 4, 1918, p 4; "A Letter to the Soldiers," *Angola* (Indiana) *Herald,* Sept 20, 1918, p 1; "Dare Devils of War," *The Citizen*, Aug 22, 1918, p 2.) Even if not used to designate a German, the nickname could have been used to designate someone *too* neutral in the war, the Dutch having refused to sell war materials to the Allies, generating tension with "neutral" America, which sold such material even before entering the war (*Inquirer*, March 24, 1918, p 10).

[43] Charley Carvin to Stella Marie Murphy, Jan 19, 1918. See, Appendix 5, Ltr 2.

[44] *Inquirer*, Feb 10, 1918, p 1; Feb 12, 1918, p 7; Feb 14, 1918, p 1. On the 12th, Strawbridge and Clothier advertised "thrift stamps" as alternatives to cards, saying "anyone would be pleased to get one from you as a love-token – an expression of love for country as well as of the person to whom you send it." In the same issue, a half page advertisement by Columbia Records (one of Great-Uncle Edward Murphy's companies) touted its collection of military marches set to dance tunes.

[45] Charley Carvin to Stella Marie Murphy, Feb 5, 1918. See Appendix 5, Ltr 3.

[46] *Evening Public Ledger*, April 27, 1918, p 11. According to the Ledger, the travelers left on Wednesday, April 24, to spend a month visiting Lieutenant Edward P. Loughran and his new wife, the former Miss Jane Hookey, both of Philadelphia and part of Stella's social circle. The four young ladies who made the trip together were Stella Marie, Miss Mary Hookey, and two Loughran sisters, Catherine and Elizabeth. The newspaper report may have contained an error, as none of the censuses, none of the newspaper searches performed, and none of the other documents found on Ancestry.com make

mention of a Loughran sister named Elizabeth; we wonder if the fourth traveler was actually Miss Ella (or Ellen) Loughran, named after their mother; or whether it was actually Bridget Agnes Loughran, who later married Stella's cousin, Walter Congdon; or, perhaps most likely of all, the youngest Loughran sister, Alice J. Loughran, who was so close to Stella as to serve as a bridesmaid at her wedding, and who married another family friend, Frank J. Scannell; the Scanells remained close to Stella and her husband for years to come.

47 *Inquirer*, June 2, 1918, p 3.

48 "Pandemic 1918," *America's Hidden Stories*, Smithsonian Channel, aired March 18, 2019; John Barry, "How the Horrific 1918 Flu Spread Across America," *Smithsonian Magazine*, Nov 2017, https://www.smithsonianmag.com/history/journal-plague-year-180965222/; John Barry, The Great Influenza, Viking Penguin, 2004; Nancy Bristow, American Pandemic, Oxford Univ. Press, 2012.

49 They opened the cottage that June. (*Evening Public Ledger*, June 21, 1918, p 11.) This was the cottage on South LaClede Street in Chelsea.

50 Mrs. Frank Hookey and Mrs. John Loughran had been involved in the fundraising for Mater Misericordiae Hospital (*Evening Public Ledger*, May 25, 1917, p 15). Mrs. Hookey was the mother of Jane and Mary Hookey, Mrs. Loughran the mother of Alice and Agnes Loughran, with whom Stella Marie had travelled to Texas during the war. Jane Hookey married Edward Loughran; Agnes Loughran married Walter Congdon; Mrs. Loughran hosted Stella Marie's own engagement party. In February, 1918, Stella and her Aunt G spent the weekend in Atlantic City as guests of Stella's favorite cousin and fellow cast member, Marie Greenfield (*Evening Public Ledger*, Feb 27, 1918, p 11). When Stella's cousin Walter Greenfield and Virginia Stroud were married on April 27, 1921 at St. Stephen's Church, reception at the Bellevue Stratford, both Stella and her aviator were in the wedding party (*Inquirer*, April 21, 1921, p 10; April 24, 1921, p 37; April 25, 1921, p 10; and April 28, 1921, p 10). Marie Greenfield, Katherine Scannell and Frank Scannell (1897-1958), Katherine's brother, had participated with Stella in the production of Dr. Optimist (*Evening Public Ledger*, Jan 4, 1918, p 13 and Jan 25, 1918, p 9; *Inquirer*, Jan 20, 1918, p 20). Stella's work for St. Francis continued in the months leading up to her marriage (*Evening Public Ledger*, Jan 24, 1920, p 9, and *Inquirer*, Jan 16, 1921, p 36).

51 Three years after her graduation, and just weeks after the aviator's return from military service, Stella Marie played harp at the graduation ceremony for the Mercy Academy class of 1919 (*Evening Public Ledger*, June 10, 1919, p 4).

52 *Evening Public Ledger*, Jan 24, 1920, p 9. The benefit was to aid the St. Francis Country House in Darby.

53 Her reading may have included the new book by Virginia Woolf, *The Voyage Out.* Woolf's feelings about the horrors of the war, and about the status of women, likely mirrored Stella's own.

54 *Inquirer*, September 19, 1921, p 4. Occupying two full column widths, the enormous photograph was accompanied only by that headline and the caption, "Miss Stella Murphy, of 1830 Rittenhouse Square, who will return home this week from Chelsea. The engagement of Miss Murphy to Charles Carven [sic] was recently announced." Since Chelsea was on the Delaware River just south of Philly, it is curious that, just after the beauty pageant, the engagement announcement was headlined "Returning From Shore." No other explanation appeared for the prominent announcement, which appeared right next to an article asserting that Prohibition had caused more and more young people to turn to drink.

55 The dance at the Whitemarsh was on Friday, May 5, 1922 (*Inquirer*, April 28, 1922, p 12).

56 Mr. Murphy entertained the bridal party at their home on Rittenhouse Square the night before the wedding. See *Evening Public Ledger*, June 2, 1922, p 13, which misidentifies the groom as "Joseph" Carvin, a resident of Northwood, PA, while reporting that the groom had entertained his best man (Stella's brother, Joe Murphy III) and ushers at the Manufacturer's Club – Mr. Murphy's domain – the prior Monday.

57 *Inquirer*, April 30, 1922, p 38.

[58] The chambermaid and cook was Ida Johnson. According to Ida's great great granddaughter, Nicole Lee, Ida's original 1977 death certificate shows her date of birth as 2 October 1888, in Alabama, and her parents as Eugene Milligan and Mary Pierce. Ida Milligan had married one Juno Taylor when she was nineteen; her daughter Louise was born in Spring Hill, Alabama, on April 20, 1912. She'd been working as a servant in a private home in Birmingham when Juno left her (1910 U.S. Census, Jefferson County, Alabama, Birmingham Ward 4, Dist 53, Fam 85). She was married a second time, to a Mr. James Johnson, and by 1920, Ida had moved to Philadelphia, where James worked as a laborer in a brass factory (1920 U.S. Census Phila Ward 37, Dist 1312, Fam 12). Soon thereafter, Mr. Murphy hired her to work for his daughter. Ida's daughter Louise married James Townes and lived until 5 February 1989. Louise and James Townes had several children, including Leonard (1930-2009) and Mary Louise (1932-2005) Townes, whose granddaughter, Nicole Lee, suppled the background information about Ida for this book. The assertion that Mr. Murphy paid for Ida's services is speculation, based on his wealth and general treatment of his daughter, as well as the fact that Stella's aviator husband, working in the basement of a hosiery mill and going to textile school at night, would not have been able to afford such a luxury in 1922.

14. Charles Walter Carvin

Charles Walter Carvin claimed to know little about his mother or his birth – only that he'd been raised by his sisters, Sadie and Florence, when they were still just little girls themselves. His grandchildren heard rumors that scandal had been involved; that Charley's father, Jimmy, had been far older than his mother; that too little time had elapsed since Jimmy's first wife died; that there was objection to Katie Sherick's background – her German descent, perhaps, or her occupation – she'd been a professional dancer, perhaps, or a masseuse, or involved in some other "common" occupation. The implication was strong that the Murphys had disapproved of the marriage, but it was all for nothing, because the young bride died soon after Charley was born. Charley's own eldest son (Charley Jr., called "Sonny") would reluctantly share these ideas with his own children, but of course he hadn't been alive when his father was born, and everything he'd heard was from his mother's side, which is to say, from the Murphys. It wasn't until all these generations were gone that some truths about Charley's birth finally came to light.

Philadelphia's birth registry lists the baby born to Katie Sherick on March 5, 1897 only as a "white male," the only infant for whom the delivering doctor (Dr. Wood) did not record a name.[1] Since his mother died when he was one, he remembered nothing of the woman who lay beneath the sod at Holy Sepulchre, nothing of the indecision, the tension, the confusion about where she would be buried. The sisters who'd raised him were twelve and nine when he was born. He'd have relied on what they told him about his earliest years, and they of course remembered all the time they'd spent with him, all the care they'd shown him, sacrificing parts of their own young lives for his sake; but as children themselves, they could hardly appreciate the role played by others. When the two girls spent the summer at the shore a year after their stepmother's death, their baby half-brother wasn't with them, the beach being no place for a motherless infant. As adolescents themselves, with lives of their own, they'd have been pleased when Jimmy left the toddler at home in the care of his grandmother, Mary Sherick. Mary, no doubt, had more to do with raising the boy than his Catholic sisters were aware.[2]

But she, it seems, did not impress on the boy how much she'd had to do with his upbringing. Mary was one of the five who took part in the mass exodus from the Baptist Church when Charley was three.[3] When marriages cross a cultural divide, as his parents' had – when the old guard sees a young couple's union as naïve, irreligious, or both – the division may strengthen in some, but in others it breaks down. While some cling to their childhood faiths, the dogmatic faiths of others soften, or sometimes even disappear.

We now know that Katie Sherick had no scandalous occupation. There was no rush to remarry after Jimmy's first wife's death. Apart from the age difference, it was religion that had caused the Murphys to consider the marriage between Charley's parents scandalous. Realizing the folly of it, Mary Sherick had abandoned the faith of her childhood to raise the infant in the spirit of religious tolerance.

Jimmy, meanwhile, had moved with his children away from his saloon to a new home on Lehigh Avenue (See Map p 266). Florence and Sadie ensured their little half-brother's regular Catholic church attendance, but while the girls were in school, Mary looked after the little boy.

Still, without a mother's love, Charley's first few years were not entirely happy ones, and he created better worlds from sheer imagination. His best friends – neighbors just a couple doors down the street – were two boys, William and Walter Greenfield, whose ages straddled his own by just a few months each.[4] The three friends were enamored of comic strips and animated cartoons. They talked of the latest reels to be watched at the Olympia Nickelodeon Theatre on Eighth Street, and on special occasions, they may have even dropped some hard-earned coins there. When his half-brother's new Knitting Company venture opened its doors, Charley was put to work sweeping the cotton-strewn floor. In 1906, when he was nine, he and the Greenfield boys toyed with the idea of answering the Nickelodeon's ad for a "neat-appearing American boy to act as usher, also two small boys to operate graphophone."[5]

But operating the theater's graphophone was not to be a part of Charley's future: his whole life changed that year. His sister Sadie married. The knitting business closed. Brother Joe disappeared, fleeing unnamed creditors, destination unknown. (His father said Charley was better off not knowing where his brother had gone). And in this unsettled state, Charley met the Greenfield's boys' cousin, the privileged princess, Stella Marie Murphy.[6]

She was slightly-built – smaller than Charley – but a year his senior. She had little time for a boy who swept factory floors; if she noticed him at all, she pretended not to. Then, in 1907, her family moved to 1234 Lehigh Avenue, right across the street from his (See Map p 266). Ever so briefly, the two became close. For the third time in a hundred years, the families of this story, different as two families could be, were in direct contact with each other, every day.

Stella Marie knew about things Charley didn't, like books, music, and theater. She had things he didn't have, like a mother, a little brother, an upright piano, even a copy of *The Autobiography of Buster Brown*. He envied everything she had. But their association as close neighbors was not the beginning of a great adventure. Her parents didn't think well of his family. And when the Murphys moved to Lehigh Avenue, practically next door, Charley's family moved to a new home further west, on Somerset.[7]

When his sister Florence got married that May, the ten-year-old boy was left alone in the house with his saloon-keeper father. He knew no one in the Somerset neighborhood. Busy running his saloon, Jimmy could hardly do a good job of raising the youngster alone. So Charley was put on a train to Los Angeles to live with Elsie and Joe. Jimmy sent along money for them to feed him and put him in school.

L. A. was nothing like Philadelphia in those days. For one thing, it was far smaller. For another, the adventurous people who lived there were more interested in entertainment than the staid people of Kensington. The annual Tournament of Roses featured two miles of floats, flowers, marching bands and wild animals. At Tally's Electric Theater, you could buy a ticket to watch a moving picture for just ten cents. The newspapers carried comic strips like *Buster Brown, Happy Hooligan* and two unlikely fellows named *Mutt and Jeff* – a far cry from staid Pennsylvania, which had enacted anti-cartooning legislation after its Governor was portrayed in a cartoon as a parrot.[8] There was a new motion picture studio, and a downtown funicular called *Angel's Flight*. People were even talking about annexing nearby Hollywood.

Altogether, Los Angeles was a heavenly place for a boy of ten to find himself. And to make it even better for Charley, Joe was soon pocketing the money their father sent for his schooling. Instead of sending him to school, Joe put him to work making milk deliveries. The work wasn't all heaven, but it sure beat going to school.

Decades later, Charley would say that the years he spent in L. A. had a profound effect on him. Inspired by the comics in the L. A. papers, he began to draw cartoons of his own. And while working on the milk wagon, he dealt with shop owners from Chinatown, little Italy, the town's Negro quarter, and its German, Japanese, Polish and Jewish neighborhoods.

In 1908, people routinely identified themselves and others by ethnicity: Happy Hooligan and the Yellow Kid were proud to be Irish; the Katzenjammer Kids were proud to be German. The classified portion of the L. A. city directory devoted a separate section to the Chinese laundries of Charley Wong, Duck Sing, Hop Chung, Soon Woo, and others. It provided addresses for the Laundrymen's Club, the French Benevolent Society, the German-American Alliance, the Hebrew Benevolent Society, the Italian Mutual Benefit Association, the Japanese Association, the Polish Young Men's Association, the Spanish Mutual Benefit Society, the Italian-American Club, the Colored Men's YMCA and the Orphan Asylum for Italian and Mexican Children. The world was a mix of cultures and identities, each one more fascinating than anything the youngster had seen in Philadelphia. Ears open, he began to repeat the rhythms and accents of the stories he heard. Decades later, his dialect stories would be condemned as cruel stereotyping, but in Charley's eyes, there was nothing cruel about them. His soties made people laugh, and the talent served him well.

At the same time, the age of flight was beginning. In 1910, Los Angeles hosted the country's first international air show. Airplanes, hot air balloons, midway rides, circus animals, and spectators all passed within a stone's throw of Charley's window on Slauson Street as they made their way to the show. Joining tens of thousands of others, Charley looked up at the aviators with envy. The famous Glenn Curtiss, who'd won the Gordon Bennett Cup in Rheims, set a new air speed record of 55 m.p.h. Amateurs – even the newspaperman, William Randolph Hearst – took to the air. And as Charley watched, it seemed possible he might someday fly himself.

But Charley's heavenly time in L. A. did not last. After two or three years, Jimmy somehow learned about Joe's dishonesty; outraged that Charley wasn't in school, he demanded that the boy be sent home right away. Within days, Charley was on the train, heading back to Philadelphia.[9] He found himself in the old-fashioned city of his birth once again, a city built on steel, on steam, on industry. Given his interests, he likely managed the cost of admission to the People's Theater, just two blocks north of his father's saloon, where the acts included a woman ventriloquist, a team of comedy bicyclists, and other vaudevillian fare, but he yearned for more.[10]

He wouldn't have missed the international air show in Atlantic City that summer. The boardwalk stretched for seven miles in those days; the town's saltwater taffy and ocean breezes rivaled what he'd seen out west. Then, that October, *The Curtiss Aviation Book* came out. Having seen its author fly in Los Angeles and again in Atlantic City, Charley couldn't have missed the book's prediction of a bold future for aviation:

> The time has come when the world is going to need a new type of man – almost a new race. These are the Flying Men. The great dream of centuries has come true, and man now has the key to the sky.

Curtiss's book described the motors he'd attached to bicycles as a boy; his first experimental flights; the very air show in Los Angeles Charley himself had just attended.[11] How could Charley *not* dream of flying his own plane someday?

Meanwhile, young Catholics attended parish schools and social events together; on Sundays, they attended mass together. Being a friend of the Greenfield brothers, it wasn't long before Charley found himself in the company of their sister, Marie, and their cousin, Stella Marie Murphy, again. As she was reading and writing stories, Charley was entertaining friends by telling his own. He began to take a greater interest in the girl whose interests so aligned with his own. After three years of avoiding school and dreaming of life as an aviator and cartoonist, Charley was tempted to live for fun the way his brother had, the way his Uncle Thomas had. But he had also inherited his father's industry and ambition. To make some money, he got a job as a cashier with Adams Express.[12]

There was much in Stella Marie's upbringing to suggest she have nothing to do with such a boy. But the words she wrote in the 1916 *Patrician* were heartfelt, and they could have applied to young Charley as much as to the rogue who'd appeared at the abbey door: "You bewail the fate that made you the son of poor parents; you blame circumstances for your crimes, but 'honor and shame from no condition rise.' It depends entirely upon yourself…[God] has offered you an opportunity better than any circumstances of birth could have done, and if you do not make the best of it, I warn you, his judgment will be swift and severe."[13] Such words could not have escaped young Charley. But as he saw it, Stella Marie herself was the reward he'd reap if he proved himself worthy. We can imagine him promising her that he'd go to mass, that he'd go to confession, that he'd be a good Catholic.[14]

He was still grappling with how to win Stella when, on April 6, 1917, Congress declared war on Germany. With America now going overseas, it was time to make a decision, and the decision he made was to serve his country in the fight against the Huns. He first enlisted as a reservist in the Quartermaster Corps: a month after the declaration of war, he began his service at Fort Niagara, New York.[15] But at Fort Niagara, Charley heard that the army was looking for fliers. Air shows were glamorous affairs. Aviators were romantic heroes. Charley applied and was accepted to the flight training program. From September to December, he attended a ground school at Princeton University. On November 21, former President Theodore Roosevelt gave a lecture on "National Strength and International Duty" before reviewing Charley and the other cadets on the Princeton parade field. But impressive as the former President could be, the young man would later make no mention of the President's visit: he better remembered his time with Stella Marie during her visits there, and the fanciful stories they'd shared, and all he'd done to impress her.[16]

On January 5, 1918, he was assigned to Kelly Field in San Antonio, Texas, far from his new love.[17] Once there, having picked up derisive military lingo for enemy soldiers, he teasingly addressed Stella as "Dutchie." His letters referred to their time together at Princeton, to "happy [moments] of long ago," and to the irresistible love he felt for her:

> … *With boys around discussing how the "air is full of pockets" – how "my ole plane bucked today"— one can hardly… describe one's deep feelings.*
>
> *Oh I miss you during the day, Dutchie, but it is the nights I can hardly stand – wonderful starry moonlight nights – wasted – our best days spent apart…*

At five we tumble out and at six thirty start flying – just as the dawn's breaking – a wonderful sight, Dutchie, but wasted because you are not here to enjoy it with me ... [T]his war came along when I was very much in love and took from me the thing that is dearer to me than anything in life ...

I'd like to feel, but hate to think, that you have missed me as I have you.

Later –

This remarkable composition was just interrupted by a summons to the "Dual Control" station and I have just finished an hour flight. The air was wonderful today Dutchie; warmer than on the ground and our camp looks like the tiny soldier camps you see on the cards at Christmas. The towns look like doll villages and the earth grows prettier and more picture-like the higher you go. Only up eleven hundred this morning. The air acts as a great stimulant and I no longer am quite as lonesome as I was this morning, at least on the surface I'm not, but that longing is there and I will be until I have my little darling again ...

... Needless to ask as to how you got home Saturday night. Have you been good since? I have – even if it must be attributed to lack of opportunity to be otherwise. We had a great experience after we missed the train at Pittsburgh and were entertained on the train we took by a real honest-to-goodness detective. I'll be able to tell you some real stories now. Remember our stories?*

He complained of receiving no mail, depicting himself as a neglected "Kidet" with biplane in hand. He told her he'd go to confession, as he'd promised he would.

"They are shipping thousands of troops away from here each day," he wrote, "and each day hundreds of recruits from all over the country are coming in – all green men, so we have lots of trouble with the crews on our ships. It is quite romantic (although that doesn't quite fit) to see them go –

---

* The letters are set out in full in Appendix No 5, this one being excerpts from Letter 2.

the band plays 'Should Auld Acquaintance Be Forgot' and it is 'So long Mack – g'bye 'arry, see ya over there' etc."[18]

The Committee on Public Information included a "Bureau of Cartoons" whose mission was to arouse support for the war by getting cartoonists to vilify the enemy.[19] The Bureau called upon cartoonists to think of their cartoons as four-minute-man speeches, selling liberty bonds. Most newspapers got wholly on board; cartoonists Boardman Robinson and Robert Minor were both fired from newspapers for refusing to draw pro-war cartoons.[20] Charley did what his country asked of him: he penned not just pin-up girls, but pro-American, anti-German cartoons everywhere he could, including envelopes he shared with other airmen, and in at least one case, on the envelope of a letter he sent to Stella Marie.[21] When Stella complained, he apologized, making excuses. When she complained about his having joined the air corps so far away, he wrote of taking leave to go home in March.[22] But on March 21, he accepted his Lieutenant's commission.[23] Now authorized to train others to fly, he could not return home. When he wrote to Stella on April 17 from the Officer's Mess at Camp Dick in Dallas, his letter was postmarked with the stamp, "BUY NOW U.S. GOVERNMENT BONDS 3RD LIBERTY LOAN."[24]

The government knew well that Americans cherished their liberty, that the key to getting young men to take up arms was to convince them that the enemy threatened that liberty, and that war was necessary to preserve it.

Dallas's Camp Dick had been established at the state fairgrounds to serve as an army training camp.[25] Stella had already made plans to visit him in San Antonio; her train left Philadelphia on April 24th, but news of his reassignment to Dallas reached her too late for her to back out of the trip. It seems Charley and Stella never saw each other in Texas.[26] After all, the war had to be financed; "Liberty" bonds had to be sold.[27] In Dallas on July 4, 1918, there were events in the morning at Love Field and more in the afternoon at Camp Dick, the public enticed to drop by with offers of free lunches and tours which allowed them "the chance of going through the barracks and seeing exactly how the boys live. A demonstration of assembling airplanes, a machine gun race, a showing of anti-aircraft work, stunt flying, a blindfold drill and a baseball game make up the remainder of the program."[28] On Saturdays from August through October, baseball teams from the various military bases competed against each other, providing more entertainment for the citizenry. Clearly, the Army wasn't only training soldiers to fight. To generate public support for the war, airplanes from the camps dumped literature from the sky, advertising the ball games and other events at the camps.[29]

While much attention has been paid to the four-minute speeches made by celebrities to sell bonds, celebrities most often appeared in cities, where they could get the most bang for the buck.[30] In the less populated rural areas of Texas, it was the early aviators and the novelty of their planes by which the government sold Liberty Bonds:

> [I]n 1917 the Aviation Section of the U.S. Army Signal Corps established an elite group of Army pilots assigned to the Liberty Bond campaign. The plan for selling bonds was for the pilots to crisscross the country in their Curtiss JN-4 "Jenny" training aircraft in flights of 3 to 5 aircraft. When they arrived over a town, they would perform aerobatic stunts and put on mock dog fights for the populace. After performing their air show, they would land on a road, a golf course, or a pasture nearby. By the time they shut down their engines, most of the townspeople, attracted by their performance, would have gathered. At that point, most people had never seen an airplane, nor ridden in one. Routinely each pilot stood in the rear cockpit of his craft and told the assemblage that every person who purchased a Liberty Bond would be taken for a ride in one of the airplanes.[31]

Standing up in his JN-4, Charley told stories and made people laugh at the German characters he portrayed. The Committee on Public Education instructed the four-minute men to try slogans like... "A cause that is worth living for is worth dying for, and a cause that is worth dying for is worth fighting for."[32] Invoking Gettysburg, San Juan Hill, and the will of God, the Committee published poetry accusing "slackers" of disgracing their forefathers. ("I'd rather you had died at birth or not been born at all, than know that I had raised a son who cannot hear the call... To save the world from sin, my boy, God gave his only son. He's asking for My boy, to-day, and may His will be done."[33])

Many years later, Charley's grandchildren would discover a leather photograph album he'd brought home at the end of the Great War. Flyers in their leathers stood beside their cockpits. Planes were hardly more than tiny specks in the clouds overhead. One photograph of Charley and two other men was captioned *The Three Aces*. When his grandchildren pestered him about what it meant to be an "ace," he admitted he'd never shot down a real German. But when they asked if he'd ever killed a man, he hesitated.

They were particularly interested in a photograph depicting the wreckage of a JN-4 in the top of a tree.

"Is that your plane?" they asked.

Yes, it was.

After much effort, they were able to draw out what had happened.

The Wright Brothers' planes, called "pushers," had engines mounted behind the pilot. When pushers crashed, inertia sent the engines forward and the result was predictable. Glen Curtiss built "tractors" – planes with front-mounted engines that *pulled* the cockpit. Crashes in a tractor gave the flyers much better odds of survival. By 1916, Glen Curtiss's "JN" model biplanes had become the Army's favorites. Pulled by a 90 horsepower, liquid-cooled V-8 engine nicknamed a "Liberty" engine, a JN-4 flew up to 75 miles per hour and as high as 11,000 feet. With two cockpits, one behind the other, it was ideal for training new pilots to fly. The trainee sat in the front; the more experienced pilot behind him.

One night, on a Liberty Loan Drive over Trinity, Texas, Charley had been in the rear (instructor's seat) of the "Night Hawk," another man up front. Guided only by vague shadows cast by the light of the moon, there were troublesome pockets of wind. The plane started throwing oil. An unexpected fog blinded them. There were suddenly branches of trees, and then nothing.

The shot of the crashed plane was captioned "The Night Hawk's Roost – Trinity, Texas, July 1918 – Liberty Loan Drive – Lt Bellzor killed; Lt Carvin injured."[34] Another photo pictured Charley on crutches. If he was overcome with guilt or a feeling of responsibility with respect to the other man's death, evidence of such feelings have not survived.[35]

The Armistice ending the war was signed on November 11, but Charley remained in the service for some months longer. Many years later, he claimed to have been promoted to Captain and put "in charge of night flying" at Ellington Field; he said that he wasn't released from service until "late in 1919 because his job at Ellington Field in charge of night flying was considered too important to permit an earlier discharge."[36] But his letter written a month after the war ended tells a different story:

Monday, Dec 8th, 1918

Dearest Dutchie –

I suppose you are beginning to think I am quite a wanderer and I really suppose I am sorta one especially with things as fascinating for me as they are in Dallas. I am really afraid I am being spoiled with this flying about and luxurious life, with splendid machines, beautiful homes and exclusive clubs.

This club is really beautiful and so hard to get a card to – that I am always wishing I could have Stella here to enjoy it with me – but we can't have everything and I am extremely fortunate having all I have...

The writer of that letter had gone to two movies in Ft. Worth one day, spent the next morning looking for his friend Bill in town, and after being told by Bill's girlfriend that Bill was on a picnic, spent the next afternoon flying around Fort Worth, looking for Bill's picnic.[37] Indeed, Charley's job was important: the government was still in need of money to pay off its war debt, and Charley was involved in the *Fifth* Liberty Loan Drive – called the "Victory" drive – conducted after the war had ended.[38]

His December letter refers to his liberty loan trips. Since the publicity for them was the plane itself, circling overhead, such trips needn't be advertised in advance; they could be entirely spontaneous. After spending the afternoon flying over Forth Worth looking for Bill's picnic, Charley described "incidentally landing at S.M.U. where the entire student body turned out to see me (the plane)."

Charley's discharge from the service was not late in 1919, as he would later claim. In fact, he was discharged on April 10, 1919 – eight days prior to the murder of his half-brother Joe in California. While his father traveled west to assist in a police investigation, Charley headed to Philadelphia to pursue his romance with Stella. He also maintained his interest in flying. In July, he became a founding member (and secretary) of the Aviator's Club of Pennsylvania. Atlantic City opened the first commercial airport in the nation that year, and one of the new club's goals was to establish a municipal aerodrome for Philadelphia.[39]

At the same time, given the widespread opposition to Prohibition – and the expectation of great profits to be made from bootlegging – the flyers found their skills in strong demand for smuggling high-end liquor into Atlantic City from boats offshore. A small plane couldn't carry barrels of the cheap stuff, but profits from a few cases of fine Scotch or Cognac could make a night of flying from ship to shore profitable.

Local historian Donald Nyce, 79, of Egg Harbor Township... said his father had taken part in a few deliveries, transporting the liquor by boat to establishments around the back bays. Because authorities had virtually no ability to stop the planes as they entered U.S. waters, seaplanes were used to offload cargo from "Rum Row," a flotilla of schooners that sat off the East Coast full of liquor from the Caribbean and Europe.[40]

For some reason, when asked years later to describe his return to Philadelphia after the war, Charley said nothing about being secretary of the Aviator's Club, nothing about the temptations of bootlegging. Rather, he described himself as "jobless and without training," wondering about a career.[41] The "dry" Murphys wouldn't abide their daughter marrying a cartoonist, much less having a rum-runner in the family.[42] Prohibition made Charley choose between joining his father as a bootlegger and settling down to an honest living with his true love. As it happened, he didn't continue night flying with the Aviator's Club for long.

Joe Murphy had plenty of contacts in the textile business, and if he was to win Stella Marie's hand, it was Joe Murphy Charley needed most to please. Joe insisted that Charley settled down and put his mind to it, there was much money to be made in textiles, especially in the new artificial silk they were making in Europe. With Prohibition set to put his father's saloon out of business forever, Jimmy's advice was to go into food or the clothing business; "the government," he said, "will never make it illegal to eat or wear clothes."[43] So Charley took his father's advice: he got a job throwing crates of yarn in the basement of the Taubel textile mill. Spending his days at the mill, he also started attending night classes at the Philadelphia Textile

School.[44] He quickly found that the school was his kind of place: its Bradley Algeo told the *Evening Public Ledger*, "we plan to make men more than mere machinery."[45] Telling stories and making people laugh with his cartoons, he was definitely more than an inanimate adjunct to battens and gears. Charley was soon promoted into front line management at Taubel.[46]

> During this period, he earned some money with a facile pen – by cartooning. Nor did he lose his sense of humor. One time, when asked on a test to list a thousand ways of adjusting a knitting machine, he instead drew a cartoon of an angry man kicking the bejabers out of one of the machines. Called up to the PTI dean's office for the expected reprimand, he instead found his hand shaken, with the dean remarking: "I'm a weaver. That's what I think too."[47]

Still in school and selected "most likely to succeed," he was offered a sales job; the base salary was only half of what he'd been making at Taubel, but it also paid commissions.[48] Being a four-minute man had honed Charley's skills at making a sales pitch: the gamble he took by accepting the job paid off. He graduated from PTI in 1923, and by 1924, he had tripled his income.[49] After Charles Webb was quoted in the papers saying that to be successful you have to love your work, Charley was soon selling for him and (apparently) he did love the work. "Charley's position was as head of the one-man cotton fabric department: he was the one man. But shortly after that Webb began to work with rayon and Charley, sensing the opportunities inherent in what was then considered 'artificial silk,' moved into that department."[50]

One can't help but wonder about the importance of family, and in this case, about the trail that led from Dominic Murphy's reports from Switzerland, to Joe Murphy's postwar visits to Germany, to Charley's interest in the synthetic fabric that men had learned to make from trees.

As a child and adolescent, Charley had been mostly independent. After his marriage to Stella Marie on June 3, 1922, he was expected to be a family man, but as his father had proven, having a family didn't mean he couldn't also have a sporting life. So Charley started frequenting race tracks, gambling joints and speakeasies, entertaining customers there and often bringing Stella along. The mood was positive in the Carvin house, as it was in the rest of the nation.[51] The newlyweds could see Vaudeville acts like those of Philadelphia's own comedians Mae West or W. C. Fields.[52] While they delighted in such fare, Stella Marie – postponing the stories she intended to write – wrote to her Aunt G that she and her mother were making lace curtains for the windows at the couple's new house on Pratt Street.[53]

As it turned out, while enjoying stories told by others, Stella Marie found little time to write her own, especially when (in 1923 and again in 1926) she found herself enduring months of pregnancy and giving birth to sons.[54] For his part, Charley left Stella and Ida to handle the babies in the house.

There is much to be said for the ingenuity of man. Thanks to the war, Joe Murphy's dream had become a reality: harvesting trees in huge numbers, companies were now treating wood pulp with seaweed, caustic soda, carbon disulfide, and sulfuric acid, then spinning the material into long, silky fibers to make "paper fabric." "Artificial silk" was strong and light enough for airplane wings. It had a silky hand, and it was cheaper than the real stuff from Asia. Westerners, it seemed plain, could do anything better than Asians could – or Nature itself, for that matter. Americans saw their man-made substitute as a boon for the masses. No longer would it be only the rich who dressed in silk. The European invention had become the American dream: thanks to the ingenuity of man, everyone could dress like a king or a queen.[55]

So Charley joined Clifton Yarn Mills, introduced rayon to that company. "Like the Fuller Brush man I used to go from mill to mill with my samples and hawk the new yarn," he said. (It was a natural transition for a four-minute man.) "The kids used to ask who the man was who slept in the house on Sunday." Before long, he was in charge of Clifton's sales. Endearing himself to prospects with jokes and dialect stories, he sold enough wool, cotton, and cheap rayon yarn to earn a shareholder's interest in Clifton.[56]

Meanwhile, with two children and a third on the way, Stella found no time to write. She waited days for Charley to come home from his out-of-town sales trips. But even in Charley's absence, the family would soon be too big for their little house. Stella heard that the Society of the Holy Child of Jesus had founded a private Catholic school in Drexel Hill, just west of the city, and she prevailed on Charley to buy a house near the school. The family moved from Frankford out to the suburbs in Drexel Hill.[57]

For the first time since Consolidation, Carvins lived outside city limits.

Charley was fond of saying, "The key to success in business is treating your friends like customers, and your customers like friends." He did exactly that in 1928 by drawing his own Christmas card – a caricature of himself and his family – and having enough copies printed to mail one to each of his friends and customers. It was a great idea, making his love for drawing cartoons part of his sales strategy. The card pictured him peeking from around a corner at a scene in his own living room: Stella Marie, talking on the phone.

> "This is Stella Marie. We received your card! Great!! I feel so mortified... Well you know Charley... One of those 'so clever' men – can't see Bailey's for cards – Wants something original – This is the twenty first and he can't find a pencil – same last year – we didn't send a card – I'm desperate. I think I'll send penny postals marked 'Careless but sincere – Merry Christmas' – The Carvins."

He also drew his sons, the younger one playing with the dog, saying "Mama love Papa," while the older, looking miffed, said "He promised to fix my bike too."

Charley would send such home-focused cards every Christmas for the rest of his life.[58] Buyers who couldn't distinguish one salesman's product from another fell in love with the self-deprecating humor of the man's stories and cartoons. Meanwhile, it being the age of flappers, suffrage and liberated women, nothing sold better than women's hosiery – a phenomenon that would soon be known as the "Synthetic Revolution." Rayon meant every woman in America could experience the feel of wearing genuine silk. Charley's 1929 card pictured himself in the midst of his family, dancing for joy over the birth of a daughter.[59] His 1930 card – drawn after the stock market crash – pictured him in his living room, puffing on a cigar, expressing the hope that his friends hadn't gotten "caught in the market."

If the twenties had been good for America, they'd been especially good for Charley. By the time of the Great Depression, he was already doing rather well, able to support his wife and three children in a manner that fulfilled all of Stella's expectations.

All, that is, except for her desire to write.

Stella found herself bored at home, thinking of Charley, watching Ida cook, do chores and take care of the kids. Her life was not the stuff of which detective novels were made. As she searched for inspiration, for something in her experience she could write about, she found herself waiting, wondering, and making herself a drink while she waited.

Charley convinced Clifton Mills to open a sales office in New York. And nothing but the best and newest would do. A building under construction at Fifth Avenue and 34th Street promised to be the tallest building in the world. Upon signing his lease, Charley became among the first tenants of the Empire State Building. His business announcement informed customers he'd be moving in on April 1st, 1931 – a month prior to the official opening of the building – and featured the sort of homespun humor that was becoming his brand.[60] On the outside of the announcement, he portrayed himself as a country bumpkin facing the New York gentry; the details on the inside were rendered in one of Charley's many voices.[61]

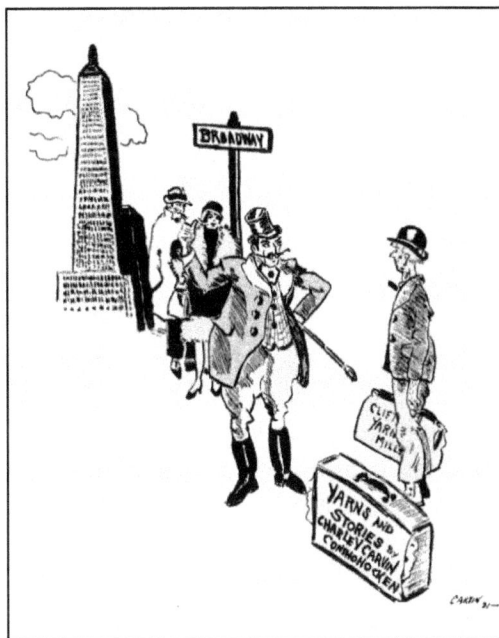

As the rest of the country (and Stella, at home) sank ever deeper into depression, Charley's 78-year-old grandmother – the woman who'd helped to raise him, as an infant – joined the Carvin household. Stella Marie was not overly fond of her new houseguest. A sort of super-mother-in-law, Mary Sherick was not only the Baptist-turned-Methodist whose family had been at odds with the Murphys for years, she also disapproved of Stella's drinking, and regularly greeted Charley, on his return from business trips, with reports about her intemperance. Stella resented having such a person in her house, and the friction between the women was strong enough to be remembered by the children many years later.[62]

Charley, on the other hand, continued to prosper. His sales techniques expanded from telling dialect stories and drawing cartoons to delivering roasts from podiums, giving zany, full-costume stage performances and doing impromptu impersonations. After the 1934 appearance of Mae West in *Belle of the Nineties*, Charley talked Stella Marie into spoofing West's role at a costume party; he himself played Belle's boyfriend (a mustachioed prize fighter in horizontal striped pants), mimicking the gestures, the gait, the voice, and the lines. After the successful performance, he mailed photographs of the event to customers as post cards. Finally, he reprised the gala evening in that year's Christmas card, poking fun at Stella for insisting he draw them clothed in something more appropriate to the season.[63]

While others stood in bread lines, Charley sold rayon for bed sheets, for curtains, for lingerie, for hosiery. To sell more yarn, he extended credit to a new company, Burlington Industries.[64] By the end of the 1930s, American clothing contained six times as much rayon as silk, and even the Industrial Rayon Corporation – a Cleveland, Ohio company that manufactured the new synthetic for industrial uses – wanted in on the growing consumer market. Charley and Industrial agreed he was the right man to make that happen, and Charley left Clifton for Industrial.[65]

As sales manager for his new company, Charley pushed its new product line, "Spun-lo." A typical Spun-lo ad bore the headline "Millions of Women Switch to New Stabilized Rayon." The text of the ad made bold (if unsupported) claims:

"'It's amazingly run-resisting,' say women everywhere. 'Brings utterly new beauty to rayon undergarments,' say famous designers... Every inch of this *Spun-lo* rayon is pre-tested and inspected by rigid scientific processes of the Industrial Rayon Corporation."[66]

While venturing into consumer goods, Industrial didn't entirely turn its back on heavy industry. By 1940, the top eight U.S. automakers were selling nearly three million cars a year. Since rayon made good tire cord, Charley's goal was to reinforce every tire in America with his product.[67]

Conveniently for Industrial, if not for Charley, the tire industry was centered in Akron, near Industrial's Cleveland headquarters. For Charley, it meant frequent trips to Ohio.

Leaving the Empire State Building to Clifton (and others), he opened a sales office in the sixty-story skyscraper at New York's 500 Fifth Avenue. In Philadelphia, Ohio, and New York, he told stories and made people laugh. With success came promotion: in early 1941, he was elected a Vice President of Industrial.[68] Almost immediately, there was good luck: in July, 1941, when the government cut off imports of Japanese silk, Industrial's stock jumped nearly ten per cent to a new high.[69] And finally, when Japan attacked Pearl Harbor and the U.S. mobilized for war in Europe and the Pacific, the Army found itself in need of tires for Jeeps and personnel carriers, as well as fabric for tents, tarps, uniforms, and parachutes. Once again, the fight to preserve liberty meant sending soldiers overseas freedom for American businesses to profit. Charley added Washington to his itinerary, touting Industrial's rayon as suitable for all the country's wartime needs. [70]

Still, as well as things were going in business, all was not right at home. Charley's grandmother had only been a constraint on Stella's drinking for a couple of years before she died – without her influence, Stella could drink as much as she pleased.[71] As one member of his family explained, Stella Marie had been raised as a princess, the apple of her father's eye, the center of attention in everything. With Charley on the road all the time, Stella unable to drive and Ida taking care of the children, loneliness and depression only got worse. Much as she missed him when he was gone, Charley's stays at home only magnified the problem: his wit, his charm, his voices, his knack for story-telling, made him the center of attention wherever they went. Unable to thrive in his shadow, Stella continued to find comfort in drink.[72]

The best treatment for an alcoholic being fresh air, sunlight and salt water, the family rented a house for a week or two every summer in Atlantic City, Philadelphians' preferred destination for escapes from summer heat and enjoyments suited to sporting men like Charley. (Their trips to the shore also gave Ida a chance for time off.) Vacationing at the beach in the summer of 1935, their breakfasts were prepared, their beds made, their laundry and linens washed, by an old woman of color named Nancy. An old man of color named Sam emptied their trash, hosed down the paths around the cottage, trimmed the hedges and cut the grass. Charley and Stella assumed the couple's work was an amenity included in the rent they paid. But when it came time to leave – after Sam had packed the car with the family's luggage and they were ready to go – Charley and Stella found the couple standing by the car, their own small bags in hand.

"What are you doing?" asked Charley.

"Sam and I are going home with you, if that's okay. We want to work for you."

"But I already have help at home. I can't afford to pay any more help."

"That's alright. It's been weeks since Mr. Straus paid us. If you'll give us a place to stay and food to eat, we'd rather work for you."

"But what can you do?"

"I can cook, clean, take care of babies; I can do anything you need."

"And Sam?"

"Sam can do anything."

"Well, since Mrs. Carvin doesn't drive, she might like someone to drive for her. Can Sam drive?"

"No, sir. But he could learn."

Finding the couple's plight irresistible, Charley agreed. Once he took them back to Drexel Hill, the family had three servants, two of them live-ins. Charley taught Sam to drive a car. But having never learned to read, Sam couldn't pass Pennsylvania's written driving test. So Sam simply did odd chores around the house, took care of landscaping, and waited on the table at dinner time.

Between frequent trips to Ohio, Charley commuted from Philadelphia to New York, spending weeknights in the city, coming home only on weekends. It eventually proved too much. In 1937, to be closer to his New York office, Charley rented a house in affluent Scarsdale, in Westchester County, where Stella Marie (who loved drinking sidecars while watching thoroughbreds race) had easy access to Yonkers Raceway.[73] He also joined the exclusive Westchester Country Club, where he could play golf at one of its three golf courses and where Stella could sun herself at its beach location on Long Island Sound while their teenage sons did cannonballs off its 25-foot high diving platform. Ida, Nancy and Sam all went to Scarsdale too; the following year, Charley bought a house big enough for the whole family, including all three servants.[74]

The family had finally and officially moved out of Philadelphia. But they still had many friends and relatives there, especially the Murphys and other friends of Stella Marie's. Between memories and frequent visits, they'd certainly not forgotten the city of brotherly love.

Yet the next few years were full of laughter and pain. For a long time, Charley believed the best treatment for Stella's alcohol problem was practice – that if she drank often enough, forcing herself to stop after two or three drinks, she'd learn self-control. He encouraged her to drink often, in managed amounts. But the "treatment" didn't seem to work. They were repeatedly frustrated at the consequences.[75]

Charley was always playing roles. When Clarence Day's book "Life with Father" was turned into a Broadway play, the men of the Westchester Country Club decided to put on a zanier version of the show, casting Charley as a scandalous neighbor named Lulu; dressed in drag and flaunting his assets, he stole the show.[76]

Without Sam to drive them anywhere, Nancy and Ida had little to do on their days off; Charley agreed to take them for Sunday drives himself. He even bought a black chauffeur's cap for the job. It wasn't long before the neighbors were gossiping: the family must be the richest people in Scarsdale – even their servants had servants!

But in the midst of outward mirth, family was posing even more challenges. Daughter Stella was a typical pre-teen, and doing well in school. (Like her mother, she loved to read.) But the boys were more of a problem. Charley's 1939 card called Joe a "mirthquake" and "a gyp off the old block." As an April Fool's Day prank, he left a sack of dog manure on the principal's desk. When the irate principal called Charley to inform him of Joe's suspension from school, the fact

that it was April Fool's Day led Charley to smell a joke in the air; feeling sure the call was a prank arranged by Joe and determined not to be bested, he told the voice on the line he didn't think suspension was adequate – he thought Joe should be expelled. The voice accepted Charley's suggestion. After the actual dismissal, it took some back-pedaling to keep Joe in school. Charley bristled, at first, being the target of a prank for once. But such pranks were near and dear to his heart, and in light of Joe's other accomplishments, they were easily weathered.[77]

Stella Marie's drinking, however, only got worse in New York. The Great Depression brought news of people's hardship and plight on a daily basis. Treated in a hospital for alcoholics, Stella Marie was one of the first to be involved with the seminal group that became Alcoholics Anonymous. Writing from home while Stella was away in rehabilitation, Charley wrote to her, "Keep your chin up, Mom – not much further to go."[78]

Charley Junior – whom they called "Sonny" – was also a challenge. Back in 1925, when Sonny was two, Stella Marie had written to her Aunt G that the toddler was "so used to hearing that he is a Bad Boy that he calls *himself* 'Bad Boy.' Say he is good, and he says 'No, Bad Boy' – even whips himself."[79]

A healthy child doesn't call himself bad, and he most certainly doesn't whip himself – unless mimicking what someone else does to him. It seems Charley and Stella Marie had told the little boy he was bad repeatedly. When the nuns of the Holy Child assigned him to make his mother a scrapbook for Mother's Day, he cut and pasted items from pamphlets and magazines into it, including whatever he thought would most please his habitually sick mother: Prayers and hymns to the Blessed Virgin; a list of the Holy Days of Obligation, another list of feast days, a third of days for fasting. He included an article on the importance of Catholic boys wearing scapulars ("If you are among Catholics, you should be ashamed to be seen without them") and an article on the Act of Contrition ("Every time you go to Confession, remember that on the sincerity of one of your ordinary Acts of Contrition, your eternal salvation may depend.") He included images of Jesus himself and clippings of verse.

> Lord, I'm just a little boy,
> Hidden in the night;
> Let Your angels spy me out
> Long before it's light. [80]

He did it all to please his mother. And while the scrapbook may have pleased her, Sonny's report card did not: it revealed poor schoolwork and a clear pattern of absences.[81]

Most of Sonny's behaviors might be expected from a boy who'd whipped himself, whose mother was often drunk, whose father was always absent. As an adolescent, Sonny had servants in the house, nice cars to drive, and girls who wanted to ride in them. Thanks to his mother, he also had a well-stocked bar in the basement.[82] But when Charley got him a summer job at Industrial's plant in Cleveland, the boy quit after a couple of weeks due to machinery grease and too much heat. When a pregnant classmate named him the father of her child, Sonny had empathy for the girl – but it was Charley who had to pay for the adoption.[83] Within a few weeks of starting college, the boy got drunk and smashed his car into a telephone pole, then dropped out of school. College, he concluded, was not for him. Success would be his without it.[84]

Then, of course, came Pearl Harbor. Still only fifteen years old, Joe could hardly wait until he got his chance: he enrolled at Valley Forge Military Academy.[85] Sonny, on the other hand, put off military service as long as he could, eventually enlisted in the Quartermaster Corps to avoid the draft.[86]

The new war did nothing to hurt Charley's business. As we've seen, the conflict with Japan had sent Industrial's stock to an all-time high. In the spring of 1942, Charley and Stella took their daughter Stel (then thirteen) to Hollywood Beach, Florida in hopes that sun and ocean air would help Stella

Marie stay sober.[87] The same year, he bought a second house in Scarsdale.[88] He gave more speeches, including one at a New York dinner honoring Ernest Katz of Macy's.[89] By 1943, he'd been promoted at Industrial again and was including *Spun-lo* cartoons in his Christmas cards.[90] But Charley was not insensitive to those who served. He began to appear at U.S.O. shows, on military bases and before Veterans' groups, entertaining with his trademark dialect stories.

He later described one appearance this way:

I was working with the chaplains in the Chaplains Corps Fund and they asked me if I wouldn't go out to Camp Upton and give a little show for the boys. Well, they wanted me out there at 11 a.m. and the idea of being funny that early in the morning didn't appeal to me. But orders are orders, so I went.

When I got to the hospital I saw signs all over the place announcing that Carvin was coming in to tell some stories. I didn't expect that many people would show up at that hour, but when I went into the auditorium, there they all were, jamming the place to the doors – with their nurses in attendance.

So up I got and started to tell a few stories. No response. I was laying the biggest egg in history. After about the third story I figured something had to be done so I walked to the edge of the stage and asked the nurses if they wouldn't please step out of the room so that I could relax with the boys.

Obligingly they left, and then I let go. The crowd roared and clapped for more – and I gave it to them. While I was telling my stories – each a little bluer than the one before – I noticed that the corporal on one side who was taking care of the public address system was being besieged by calls. He'd pick up the phone, listen for a second, then roar into it, 'What of it?' and slam it back into the cradle.

After I'd finished my story-telling, I went over to him and asked him about it. "Aw," he answered, "just some cranks complainin' because I was sendin' you through the loudspeaker system all over the hospital."[91]

In April of 1945, Charley was back in Florida, entertaining a group of wounded vets there. In May, he organized a dinner at the Lambs Club on West 44th Street to benefit the Army and Navy Chaplains' Fund.[92]

The Lambs was an exclusive club of Broadway's best; its members included such greats as Fred Astaire, Irving Berlin, Charlie Chaplin, James Cagney, W.C. Fields, George Gershwin. Charley's jokes must have gone over well, as the next year, though lacking the credentials of a professional entertainer, he was elected to membership in the exclusive club.[93]

Charley was also national fund-raising chairman for his old school, now the Philadelphia Textile Institute. Joining him in the fund-raising was fellow

PTI alumnus Fred C. Scholler, who had become a textile chemical (soap) supplier.[94] As it turned out, Scholler and Carvin shared not only their history at PTI and numerous industry connections, but also a love for golf and thoroughbred horse racing.

Charley hadn't summered in Atlantic City much since his move to New York, but he'd maintained an active interest in the resort town's legendary gambling establishments. He'd carefully followed the legal troubles of the city's legendary boss, Nucky Johnson, and Johnson's 1941 imprisonment, but those troubles had neither ended the city's gambling nor kept Charley from introducing Sonny to it.[95] Because Fred Scholler maintained a home in Ventnor (also on the Boardwalk, just south of Atlantic City) Charley got plenty of local gossip as well. Before his demise, Johnson had been seeking the legalization of betting on thoroughbred horse racing in the state, with Atlantic City the ideal site for it.[96] Johnson's fall from power left others willing to take up the cause. Fred Scholler and several other Philadelphia businessmen who were golfing buddies began to talk about getting into thoroughbred racing.[97] In 1944, one of them became President of the Atlantic City Horse Racing Association; Scholler became Chairman of the Board. By that time, on the Board of Directors of Industrial Rayon and one of the highest paid men in Ohio, Charley was an obvious choice to join the effort to open a track.[98] Charley invested. The group's efforts proved successful. When the 3.5 million dollar Atlantic City Race Track finally opened in 1946, Charley found himself an owner along with comedy legend Bob Hope and several other celebrities.[99] By 1949, he'd bought his own enormous house in Ventnor, just a block from the Boardwalk, and was celebrating his track ownership with a self-portrait in his annual Christmas card.[100]

In addition to his membership in the Westchester Country Club, Charley became a member of Seaview and of the Atlantic City Country Club. He also began entertaining with Bob Hope.[101]

Charley's humor played out in his daily life as much as it did from the stage. With great relish he told how Nancy had bought herself a Cadillac (despite the fact that neither she nor Sam could drive). The car had sat in the garage all year round; the only time it came out was on Sundays, when Charley drove Nancy and Ida around the neighborhood. But in late 1945, as the family prepared to winter in Florida, Nancy decided she wanted to bring the car to Florida with her. Stella Marie went ahead by plane while Charley stayed behind, working. But when Sam still didn't pass the driver's test, Charley ended up driving Nancy and Ida to Florida in Nancy's Cadillac.

He wore his chauffeur's cap, of course. With Nancy and Ida in the back seat, he headed south. Somewhere in Georgia, after dark, he saw a flashing light in the rear-view mirror. Pulled over by state troopers, he watched with amusement at the trooper's reaction as they noticed his chauffeur's cap, and alternated glances at it and at the two elderly ladies in the rear seat.

"Who's the owner of the car?" they wanted to know.

Charley motioned to the back seat.

"I own the car," Nancy announced.

"*She* owns the car?" the trooper asked Charley.

"Yes, officer. *She* owns the car."

"Registration, please."

When the registration confirmed that Nancy owned the Cadillac, the troopers' reaction was what one might expect in those Jim Crow days: the trio were obviously troublemakers up to no good. But lacking hard evidence of wrongdoing, they simply told Charley to get out of town with his ladies as fast as he could. The troopers accompanied the Cadillac as far as the next county. But it was already late, and Charley had no compelling concern about the troopers, so that night, defying the *Whites Only* sign, Charley announced that they'd all stay in the same motel. Nancy and Ida insisted they'd feel safer elsewhere, but Charley would hear none of it. He snuck them into the room next to his without incident, and they all enjoyed a quiet night's sleep. But the next morning, as Charley was checking out, a customer spotted the ladies coming out of their room; first one person cried out, then another. An irate customer burst into the motel office demanding that the police be called. Not waiting for change, Charley slammed a few bills onto the countertop and hustled Nancy and Ida back into the back seat, scrambling to make a getaway before the police arrived.[102]

It was the sort of adventure that often arose from the mischievous roles Charley liked to play. But in the meantime, family problems had continued to plague him. Sonny had been in the army only a few months when, still stateside, he'd taken an army jeep on a date, leading to a drunken crash that left the date and Sonny himself in a ditch, unconscious. After months in an army hospital and his discharge from the service in December, 1943, Sonny spurned the idea of going into industry like his father; instead, he and a friend had gone into business selling remnants and converting fabrics for the linings of clothes.[103] Then, at the age of twenty-two, he announced an unlikely engagement: he would be marrying Julia Logan, a flight attendant for American Airlines, a southerner more than a year his senior who was descended from a long line of Presbyterian preachers and church elders.[104] Charley took a liking to the young woman, but her Presbyterian beliefs were a problem for Stella Marie, especially when the young woman refused to convert to Catholicism.

It was Ann Carvin and George Austin again. It was Thomas Carvin and Anna Siner. It was Jimmy Carvin and Katie Sherick. Each of these Carvins had disobeyed their Catholic church by marrying Protestants. The Murphys were still followers of the great Irish unifier, Thomas Moore, to be sure, but to their way of thinking, living in harmony with Protestants didn't mean marrying them. Stella Marie could not condone her son being the first in her line to disobey generations of proper Catholic behavior.

But Julie wouldn't convert. And when Sonny didn't abandon the requirements of his faith, she broke off the engagement. Raised in part by his Methodist grandmother, Charley invited Julie to take a ride with him in his car. Religion didn't matter, he told her, Sonny loved her, that was all that mattered. With Charley's help, the engagement was resumed. But to Stella Marie Murphy, religion *did* matter. At her urging, Sonny told Julie that if she wouldn't convert, she'd at least have to sign a document agreeing to raise her children as Catholics. That much, at least, was required by his Church.

But for Julie, this proved an even worse affront; she broke off the engagement again. And this time, to escape the pressure, she joined friends in California for the summer. Relentless, Sonny flew after her. When he dropped his demand for any sort of papers to be signed, she agreed to be married – but not back east, where Sonny's family was; only there in Santa Monica, and only by a Presbyterian minister. Sonny agreed. With just a few days' notice, Charley himself, and his son Joe, were in California for the wedding. Julie's family also managed to get there. But after some tense conversation, Stella Marie and the other Murphys refused to attend. Charley told the bride that his wife, being ill, was unable to travel.[105]

Some things never change.

After the wedding, Charley returned to work, where he resumed making sales with good-natured humor. Now that the war was over, rayon was getting into everything. On November 9, 1946, Industrial's competitor, American Viscose, took out a full-page ad in the *New Yorker* headlined *What! Build Furniture with Rayon?* The ad boasted that American's rayon was being used in gears, propellers, coffee tables and baby carriages. On December 7, another ad pictured a housewife holding a cup of tea, the copy asking, "What's this tea bag made of?" The answer, of course, was rayon.[106]

(The stuff made from trees.)

Charley renewed his efforts to coach Sam to pass the driver's exam. On January 27, 1947, he wrote to Stella that he'd taken Sam for the test that morning, but he still didn't know the results.[107] (In fact, Sam had failed the test again.) Charley had written some songs for a rehearsal – "doin' a 'What Comes Naturally'" he wrote – but Stella was depressed without him. They had spoken by phone. "Enjoyed talking to you but you get disappointed so easily – Buck up – I understand." Stella Marie wanted him to join the rest of the family in Florida, where she hadn't abandoned her hopes of converting her new daughter-in-law to Catholicism. Julie did not convert, but at least the two women got along civilly, despite their religious differences. Still, Charley was busy and couldn't join them. "I too would love to wonder around Florida with you and our family – but we must eat and I am getting ready to retire."[108]

When spring brought the news that Julie was pregnant, Charley could not have been more excited.[109] Soon to be a grandfather, there was much to think about that summer. Sonny told him that if the baby was a boy, it would be named after them: *Charles Walter Carvin III*. (They would call him Chick, to distinguish him from Charley and Sonny.) With the coming of a new generation in mind, there was talk of joining forces – of starting a family business in the Carvin name, a business that could provide for Sonny's family, for Joe's (when he had one) and someday, farther down the road, to be passed on to the generation about to begin. Though vague about the specifics, Sonny acknowledged that his current business could profit from an infusion of cash. (Without it, he and his partner were limited in what they could accomplish; in fact, without it, their future itself was uncertain.) Now that he had a baby on the way, he wondered: might Charley be willing to help out, by investing in their business?[110]

Considering the possibility, Charley remembered the trouble his father had gotten into when he invested in the knitting business run entirely by his older son. Was Sonny's business a risk worth taking? Would he have to be closer to its daily operation than his father had been to the knitting company? Would he have to quit his own job, to pay attention to such an investment in his son?

When he heard the news that the baby had arrived, a boy to be named Charles W. Carvin III, he shot off a telegram: "Congratulations to the proud parents!" At the office, he uncorked the champagne and passed out cigars. He sent bolts of rayon fabric (otherwise impossible-to-find) to Julie by way of congratulations. Having purchased a small rental home in Scarsdale for an investment, he gave it to Sonny, who would only have to take over the mortgage payments. Courtesy of Charley, the young couple and their new baby moved into their new house.[111]

All thoughts were on the future of the first grandchild, in line to become the family patriarch of a future generation. To marry and have children of his own. To fight for liberty, if need be. To be an aviator, or a cartoonist, or to tell funny stories from the stage.

But that November, all plans were put on hold with news that the infant would never do any of those things.

From the moment Charley heard Sonny's voice, he could tell there was a problem. "What's wrong?"

The baby was precious, but his eyes were slanted; his head small and round; his fingers stubby. There were creases in the soles of his feet. The doctor was calling him a *mongoloid.* [112]

"Sonny, you've got to get a second opinion...."

But other doctors confirmed that the child would be retarded – a moron, perhaps, or an idiot. He'd be infertile. His vision and speech would be impaired. He'd have heart problems; and as a result of them, he'd have a short life.

Sonny related the experts' advice: *Send him away to a home. Forget he exists. Have another baby, just as soon as you can.*

A tough decision would have to be made. How would Sonny, only thwenty-three, handle such a child? Charley asked around. St. Rita's home, in upstate New York, was devoted to such children. (St. Rita was the patron saint of lost causes.) The home had a waiting list, but maybe Charley could pull some strings.

Julie, however, could not make up her mind. With constant reassurance that a second child should be normal, she agreed to try for one. Charley suggested they go to Florida to start their family anew and consider their options for their first-born. With its tropical palms and white beaches, its planter's punches and Latin-American rhythms, Florida was just the place to conceive another child. And while the parents considered what to do, the newborn could stay in Scarsdale with Stella Marie and the servants.

Hotel **SHELDON**
ON THE BEACH

Hollywood, Florida
November 23, 1947

Dear Mother C,

Your letter was wonderful and I really think that was so thoughtful of you to write me just what you knew I wanted to hear – all about Chickie. I miss him so much I don't know how I'm going to stand it. Charley has been wonderful in trying to help me get my mind on something else but even though I say I'm going to, my darling baby is ever in the back of my mind. I know you are all helping to take good care of him and I do appreciate it so much. Wouldn't I love to see him eating his vegetables now. Does he love them like he does his pablum?

Hope Dad can come down next weekend because Charley and I are having a terrible time making any decisions. Wish we could get a place soon because living in a hotel doesn't offer much for me to do except think and that's always bad. If I had something to do to keep me busy it wouldn't be so hard.

Thanks again for keeping me posted on the behavior of my little one. Here's much love to you from Charley and me –

Julie

Flying to Florida, Charley spent two days helping Sonny and Julie think through all the difficulties that a decision to keep the baby would bring. But no matter what he said, the young parents could not make up their minds. When he flew home from Florida – when he sat down once again to consider the year's Christmas card – the fate of the baby was still up in the air.

*   *   *

As winter sets in, Charley has a peculiar problem. His dilemma is simple. If Sonny and Julie decide to keep the child, then of course, he should be in the card. The birth should be announced as one more step in the growth of the family. (He has promised family, friends and customers to give them an "intimate glimpse" into his family's life every year. He'll have to say *something*; if he says nothing, people will never stop asking what's wrong with him, leaving out his first grandson, his namesake.)

But if Sonny and Julie decide to put the infant in a home, to move on with their lives, to forget the child forever – if they give the baby up to St. Rita's as doctors and close friends are urging – then to celebrate the birth in the Christmas card will mean that no one *can* forget him. After twenty years documenting the family's progress, the cards are telling a story. *I've depicted us surviving Prohibition, the Great Depression, the Second World War. I've drawn Popeye and Mickey Mouse, FDR and Winston Churchill. If I draw my grandson in them, I'll be subjecting Sonny and Julie to the lasting scrutiny and judgment of others, should they decide to abandon him.*

*   *   *

The bitter irony was that the drawing of the Christmas card would have to wait until the young people made up their minds.

Once drawn, the card would have to be sent to the printers. The printed cards would have to be stamped, addressed and mailed. Stella Marie was little help. *We can't wait to send the card after Christmas, Charley; you've got to draw it now. Think of something!* But he couldn't. The young couple's indecision was maddening.

By mid-December, the baby was four months old. As Christmas approached, Julie wanted to spend the holiday in Scarsdale with the rest of the family. But after much discussion, she agreed she and Sonny would spend the holiday in Scarsdale while Nancy would take the baby to Florida with her. Perhaps, with the child gone, it would be easier to decide his fate.

The week before Christmas there was no snow – just harsh, drizzling cold. On Christmas Eve, snow began to fall in New England. By Christmas day, the foul weather was making its way toward New York with no sign of weakening. Still, Charley had drawn no card. The decision not made hung

374

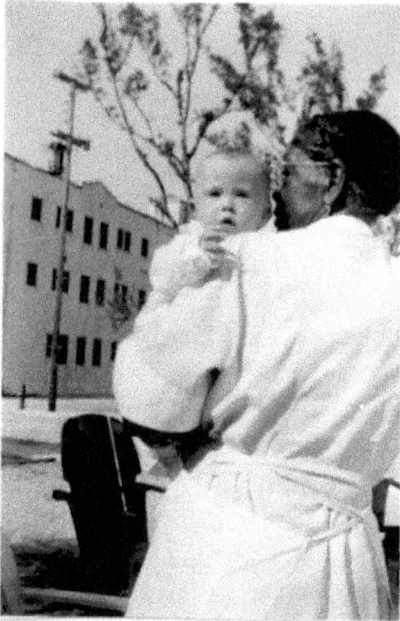

heavy over the holiday. And during these somber days, the oil heater blew up. (The system, apparently, was under too much pressure.) When the heat went out, the house grew even colder. Then, about midnight on the 25th, the snow reached Westchester County. By the early hours of Friday, the 26th, it graced all the lawns in Scarsdale. By the following Saturday, a hundred *million* tons of snow had fallen in the city – the biggest snowfall since 1888. Charley was stranded there, cars and trains not moving, all sound muffled, light reflected in millions of directions at once. The New Year's Eve crowd in Times Square was thin. By the time Charley got home, Scarsdale was as white as it had ever been.

It wasn't until January 11 that Sonny and Julie finally made their decision. They would send the baby away, as the experts advised. They would forget he'd ever been born; pretend he'd never existed. Charley pulled his strings, making it happen, separating the family from the infant forever. Sonny and Julie drove to Saint Rita's, trying not to think about what they were about to do, while Nancy comforted the baby in the back seat.[113]

And when Charley finally sat down to draw his Christmas card, he made no mention of the baby. He did, however, include the headline, "Advice to the Man Who Draws His Christmas Card: Don't."

The birth of the child was a stark reminder about the importance of a healthy, loving family. The torment spared no one. With Sonny and Julie bearing the weight of the world on their shoulders, it was clear that the family needed him more than ever. And so, within just a few weeks, Charley announced his own retirement. "Carvin Quits Industrial Rayon," read the headline in the *New York Times*.[114] Determined to make things right between himself and his eldest son once and for all, Charley took out his check book. With a stroke of the pen, he entered the converting business with Sonny.

Charley had been reluctant to take the plunge, but family was more important than all the money in the world. Even the company's new name spoke to good intentions: father and son, senior and junior, could both lay claim to being the principal figure behind the "Charles W. Carvin Company."

To some extent, a company bearing such a name – not only theirs, but the name of the abandoned child – might help fill the void they all were feeling.

Charley told himself it was the least he could do.

Sonny's business was nothing like Industrial's. Charley had simply been selling the undyed, untreated rayon yarns produced by Industrial, a big chemical manufacturer with few competitors. In contrast, there were hundreds of small firms in the converting business, all small-time entrepreneurs brokering deals, contracting with knitters and weavers to buy their fabrics, contracting with dyers, printers and finishers to treat those fabrics and selling the "converted" fabrics to manufacturers for turning into clothes, curtains, bedspreads, tablecloths, upholstery, and all the other things that dyed and printed fabrics could be used for. The cutthroat, competitive business wasn't just competitive; it was also subject to the whims of changing fashion and design. But Sonny had fallen in love with the excitement of it – being close to designers, to fashion models, to all the glamor of women's wear. And now Charley was in it too.

With the infusion of his cash, reputation and irrepressible sense of humor, the company did well; after a year, it bought a controlling interest in a Rhode Island converter named Pondel Fabrics.[115] At an industry convention, attendees found what appeared to be a copy of that morning's textile newspaper, the *Daily News Record*. But it wasn't that paper at all: the four-page forgery, carefully printed on newsprint, looked every bit like its real counterpart, complete with masthead, advertisements, and even a grainy photograph. But the bogus articles in the *Daily News Racket* lampooned the big suppliers like Textron, J.P. Stevens, and Burlington Mills. The lead article – titled "New Selling Vehicle to Serve Customers" – described how a thinly disguised version of Charley himself – "Carlos W. Starvin'" – had acquired "Ponderous Fabrics." In a nod to the French influence on fashion, the company's new sales vehicle was dubbed the "Pousse-Carte" and the story's continuation, on page two, included a photograph of Charley standing on a New York street corner in front of the actual "Ponderous Pousse Carte," along with the push-carts of other street vendors reminiscent of Charley's days on the milk wagon in L. A.[116]

The business prospered.[117] Its printed fabrics were displayed at New York's Fashion Institute of Technology and featured in a new fashion line by designer Dorothy O'Hara.[118] Charley was honored with an Annual Achievement award from the Textile Veterans Association, selected to an industry committee to formulate a marketing strategy for synthetics, and elected to the Board of the Textile Distributors Institute.[119] He made podium appearances for the Silk and Rayon Printers Association and for the National Council of Salesmen's Organizations.[120] And when another (this time healthy) grandchild was born in September, 1948, the birth was announced as Sonny and Julie's first child. Charley's Christmas card celebrated it with much fanfare. The birth of a third grandson in 1950 was announced as the birth of a second grandchild. His Christmas card said Sonny and Julie now had *two* children to keep them busy.[121] In this and every respect, the very existence of the first grandchild, Charley's human namesake, was denied.

But Charley's problems weren't over. The seeds of impending disaster began with the introduction of *Milium*.[122] As futurists who saw no limit to the wonders of chemistry, Charley and Sonny believed in the new synthetic fibers, the natural result of a belief that man could do anything. Patented by the Deering Milliken company, *Milium* was said to give fabric extra warmth without extra weight, due to application of a lightweight aluminum coating to the fabric. On May 5, 1950, Deering Milliken announced that *Milium* was ready for introduction to the marketplace, and the five companies authorized to distribute it included the Charles W. Carvin Company.[123]

Rayon pricing was favorable; production exploded to nearly two and a half *billion* yards a year. High prices for cotton and wool had fueled demand for synthetics. The rayon industry was overbooked.[124] Meanwhile, new technologies were spawning even newer synthetic fibers. The future could hardly look brighter.[125]

Then, on June 25, 1950, North Korean forces under Kim Il-sung crossed the 38th parallel, and the world was at war once again. Congress gave President Truman the power to impose rationing and price controls while business geared up to meet the demand.[126] Businessmen like Charley faced a dilemma: supplying the government's war-time needs was bound to be profitable, but also temporary. Abandoning civilian customers for short-term gains risked losing those customers in the long run. But raw materials were hard to come by, and experience showed that those who won government contracts would be given priority for them. Like most businesses, Charley made the decision to bid on government contracts.[127] He won at least one: a contract for a million and a half yards of rayon twill at 42 cents a yard, a contract worth over seven million dollars in 2022 currency.[128] Charley favored selling such a large volume of a basic product, even if it lacked the fashion glamor his son found so attractive.

A month later, Charley was part of an industry committee working with government agencies on national defense. While vacationing in Florida for Christmas, he got a surprise invitation from Spencer Love, founder of Burlington Industries, to join him for dinner at his home in Palm Beach. Charley learned the real reason for the invitation when he arrived to find none other than President Harry Truman there. Love had been on the government payroll during the Second World War, working with industry to meet the military's need for textiles; he had now recommended Charley as the right man

for the new war, running the textile department of the Office of Price Stabilization. Charley found it impossible to say no.[129]

On 26 January 1951, the OPS announced a price freeze. Charley found himself speaking to the textile industry on behalf of government, defending the unpopular measure.[130] Ultimately, the problem facing the OPS was the need to balance the requirements of three constituencies: the military, private industry, and the American customer. For the consumer, it had to keep prices as low as possible while ensuring an adequate supply of basic goods. For the military, it had to meet a demand for huge quantities of manufactured products that was bound to put upward pressure on prices. And for businesses, it had to ensure sufficient prices and profits to make production for both constituencies worthwhile. As with any such balancing act, those responsible know they've struck the right balance when no constituency gets everything it wants – which is to say, when everyone's unhappy, to some degree. The job of public spokesperson becomes one of deflecting criticism from all sides, while assuring each sector the administration is keeping its interests in mind.

Charley got a taste of the public figure's life when he addressed a group of wool manufacturers the following month. The muckraking columnist Drew Pearson, personally in attendance, devoted one of his columns to the meeting. Though he himself had been there, he described the occasion as a "closed-door meeting" between Charley and representatives of the woolen industry.

"The group consisted entirely of wool manufacturers," Pearson wrote in his column, "with the exception of Charles Carvin, the government's man. Carvin, however, is not exactly a friend of the consumer…" Pearson ignored the balancing act which the OPS faced, asserting the partial truth that "Carvin is supposed to protect the consumer, prevent inflation. That is the job for which OPS was created." He described the meeting as an example of the "public-be-hanged" behavior of government officials who "seem more interested in upping prices than in preventing inflation."

The basis for Pearson's attack? Charley had dared to say there was nothing he could do about the wool manufacturers' complaints about controls on their prices; he had suggested they take their complaints to his higher ups.[131] But Pearson (called a "chronic liar" by FDR and much criticized for his methods) had given Charley a taste of the public life, smearing his reputation coast-to-coast in a forum where Charley had no means to reply.[132]

Charley addressed the Wool Manufacturers again two weeks later.[133] He addressed a meeting of B'Nai Brith at the Astor Hotel.[134] His duties for the OPS kept him busy through the summer of 1951, on leave from his own business, which left Sonny full rein theres. As a teenager, Sonny had thrown parties in the basement when Charley was away. Charley had drawn him in the 1944 Christmas card saying, "Pop, as a veteran of World War II and a businessman, I think you are not modern." Now seven years later, Charley worried that Sonny hadn't changed, and that, in his absence, Sonny might "modernize" the company, playing up the more glamorous side of the textile business.[135]

In the late summer or fall of 1951, finishing his stint at the OPS and focusing again on his own company, Charley discovered that Sonny had done just that. The younger man had always wanted the company to develop its own line of prints. Problem was, he'd been unable to make a profit with them; every original design was quickly knocked off by competitors. [136] Now, he'd bought a great deal of lightweight fabric, mostly crepe, made of DuPont's newest synthetic, an acrylic fiber called Orlon. [137] In demonstrations arranged by DuPont, the ability of the new fiber to hold color and a crease had been highly touted. Sonny had walked away from the presentations with visions of pleated fabrics that never needed pressing. Confident and thinking big, Sonny had bought ad space and filled it with the slogan, "If it's new, it's created by Carvin." The ads pictured women in pleated dresses claiming that their "Carvinet" fabric could be "tied in knots – then discard its wrinkles and emerge 'free' and fresh."

our orlon*
can be tied in knots

if it's
new
it's
created by
Carvin

Sonny had also bought a vast quantity of the Deering-Milliken product, *Milium*, with its lightweight aluminum coating. His big purchases gave Charley pause, but the younger man had a quick and ready answer: he'd also put together a deal with one of the country's largest dressmakers, the Puritan Dress Company, to capitalize on the come-back success of the famous fashion icon and sex symbol, Gloria Swanson. Her celebrity, Sonny insisted, was bound to help sell the new synthetics.[138]

Swanson had played in silent movies opposite such men as Rudolph Valentino and Laurence Olivier. She was well known for her off-screen affairs with men like Joe Kennedy. Now, she'd made a stunning comeback in 1950's *Sunset Boulevard*. Just as Charley was starting work with the OPS in Washington, she'd been nominated for the best actress Oscar; she was playing on Broadway again; her name and all the celebrity fashion she stood for were on people's minds. Betting on her iconic reputation for stylish (and sometimes extravagant) dress, Puritan had hired her as the new designer for its "Forever Young" fashion line, and Sonny had Puritan to feature his Orlon fabrics in her new collection. [139]

Charley had good cause to be nervous, but the very point of joining Sonny's converting business was to show support for the boy. They'd even brought Sonny's younger brother Joe on board to help with sales. At this point, there was no undoing what Sonny had done anyway; the only option was to stand solidly behind him.

Puritan announced the hiring of Swanson and the new *Forever Young* line at events in Boston and Philadelphia.[140] Then, rolling out her new collection to the fashion world at New York's Waldorf-Astoria, Swanson touted the new synthetics. After the show, there was a demonstration for the press in which a dress made of a nylon-Orlon blend was doused in water, hung up to dry, "and about 18 minutes later, was dry and practically ready to wear again, without the benefit of pressing." [141]

Without pressing. DuPont had used the point to convince Sonny of the near-miraculous benefits of Orlon. Sonny had used it in his pitches to Swanson and Puritan. He'd relied on it in buying huge amounts of the fabric for Swanson's line. Orlon was the fiber of the future; there was much money to be made in it; he knew what he was doing; he told his father to just trust him.

But Charley was back from Washington now, and when Swanson announced she was about to embark on a tour of the country to promote her new line, he pulled rank. He, not Sonny, should accompany the famous actress on the tour; after all, he was the senior partner. Besides, he, not Sonny, was Swanson's age. Whatever hard feelings it may have caused, Charley got his way. Seven days after the roll-out at the Waldorf-Astoria, Charley and Swanson stepped off the train together in Greenville, South Carolina.[142]

Swanson was taken with Charley, and Charley taken with the famous star. They toured the country together by train. It's said that Swanson wanted Charley to go into show business, that she even offered to act as his agent.[143]

Textile Officials Greet Gloria Swanson

MR. YERKES   MR. SIBLEY

MRS. SIBLEY   MR. CARVIN   MISS SWANSON

A smiling Gloria Swanson alighted from the Southern Railroad's Peach Queen here this morning for a whirlwind tour of textile plants. The screen and stage star's features displayed her glamorous radiance in contrast to the black shawl she wore in keeping with the fact that she is a grandmother. Shown with the star are Vice-President Alan B. Sibley of Judson Mills, Mrs. Sibley, Charles W. Carvin, a New York textile converter, and Leonard A. Yerkes, Jr., of the DuPont Company. Miss Swanson is vice-president of and designed for a New York dress manufacturing firm. (Piedmont photo by Bennie J. Granger).

Stella Marie did not approve, and Charley chose to remain in business.

An ad by Abraham & Straus reported that Miss Diana Carroll of Charles Carvin Fabrics would be on hand at its stores to "describe and illustrate the wonders of these new fiber blends."[144] Charley was named a member of the advisory board to Manufacturer's Trust in New York.[145] In May, a *New York Times* article titled "Metallic Linings Boon to Apparel" quoted Charley saying that *Milium* fabrics provided "warmth without weight," that some 10,000 retailers had become acquainted with it, that stores would "push metallic-lined coats to the limit of available production," and that more than ten million yards of *Milium* would go into garments in the fall. At a price of $1.17 to $1.30 per yard, that would mean sales of over ten million dollars (the equivalent of over a hundred million dollars today).[146]

It was the success story that defined America: and Charley, the motherless son of tavern-keeper, was on the verge of attaining it.

He continued his charitable work, serving as toastmaster at a banquet of the Textile Veterans Association.[147] At the Textile Distributors Institute's annual musical revue, he played the role of Doctor Fraud, a psychiatrist diagnosing "the complex ills of the textile industry." At one industry dinner, he upstaged the famous comedian Morey Amsterdam:

> When Charley reached his first punch-line the crowd roared and behind the stage there was sudden agitation. The response to the second story was even greater, and so was the agitation. Morey Amsterdam, looking through the curtain, was white with fury.
> "What is this, a gag?" he roared. "Who rung in this pro on me?" It took a half-hour of persuasion and the presentation of irrefutable proofs that Charley was really a bona-fide member of the trade and no entertainer before Morey would consent to go through his act."[148]

In his 1951 Christmas card, Charley drew Santa with a huge sack over his shoulder labeled "Orlon." He drew Joe "on the road selling Milium." By the end of 1952, expecting to make millions, Charley drew Stella in mink, Sonny touting Milium, and Joe screaming into a telephone, "But you *must* see our line – it's Orlon blended with Milium and Dacron!"

In its December 1952 issue, *Modern Textiles* noted Charley's "tremendous sense of humor which has made him famous as the almost official raconteur of the whole textile industry… [H]is ability at story-telling is such that he is favorably compared with the great raconteurs." The article pointed out that he was "gambling on his faith in the new fibers," but quoted him in a moment of candor, explaining why he'd left Industrial Rayon: "the opportunity for a hard-working man with a will to gamble to build something permanent for himself and his family. Being a high-salaried man is swell while you're around, but it doesn't give you much of a chance to leave anything behind…"[149]

If his first grandson was to be forgotten, he could at least create a fortune to leave to the rest of his family. And so he pressed on.

As it happens, however, customers began complaining that the company's crepes and pleated Orlon fabrics did not hold creases the way Sonny had promised. (The "pucker cloths" were "puckering out.") And Orlon wasn't always holding color the way it should. In March 1953, when Deering Milliken sued two other companies for infringing on its *Milium* patent, the other companies countersued, alleging unfair competition between Milliken and Carvin in violation of the anti-trust laws.[150]

For most of the year, despite the pleats losing their creases, the crepes puckering and the Orlon not holding its color, the *Milium* business, at least, remained good. Charley continued to back the metallic fabric, singing the praises of its "warmth without weight." Their customers – the clothing manufacturers – kept promoting the same line to the consumer. But as the year went on, consumers started complaining to retailers that *Milium,* too, was not living up to the claims being made for it.

By autumn, customers were returning the company's fabrics in droves. Charley was not used to having dissatisfied customers: each time a complaint was made or a shipment returned, he accepted responsibility, returning the purchase price, eating the loss. As the depth of the problem became apparent, Sonny wanted to hold Deering Milliken and DuPont responsible: if he and his father were going to stand by the products, why shouldn't their suppliers do likewise? Sonny wanted to the suppliers, but Charley refused: their relationships in the industry mattered most in the long-term, he said.

To downsize rather than sue, Charley abandoned his uptown offices, moving to smaller, more affordable quarters. At his suggestion, son Joe left the family business to work for Tennessee Eastman. But this left Sonny feeling responsible and unsatisfied, as if the blame was his. Charley didn't try to correct the feeling. Sonny was also drinking too much. Whether said or not, "I told you so" was all over Charley's face. So Sonny walked out, demanding that since his work over the past five years had earned him an equity share, he should be "bought" out. He deserved to be paid for his share.

His demands did not sit well with Charley, who saw his gamble with fashion as the cause of their common catastrophe. Like a dog-bitten man who's been asked to compensate the dog for injuries, he did what he could to stifle sarcastic wisecracks.

It should have been the happiest of times: the Korean war had ended; Charley's daughter Stel had married a young but towering Irish Catholic man named Frank Carmody.[151] Outwardly, Charley went on with business as usual, doing his best to maintain his good humor.[152] At a dinner party given by Stel's new mother-in-law, Charley's impersonation of a visiting bishop from Eastern Europe – intended as a joke, and understood as such by those who knew him – prompted one guest to ask if he would hear her confession. Unwilling to spoil his gag, Charley agreed – and by evening's end, he'd heard confessions from several others too. (When Mrs. Carmody learned what he'd done, she refused to let him back in her house ever again.) On another occasion, he entertained industry peers at the Waldorf with a routine in which he played the part of a Russian general who wiped his hands on Vice President Richard Nixon's coat.[153]

But while there was laughter on the outside, on the inside, Charley was stressed and depressed. In his 1953 Christmas card, he depicted himself

382

begging on the streets of New York, destitute from the expensive wedding reception his daughter had just enjoyed.[154] On January 5, 1954, the new bride tried to cheer him up:

Daddy

I have thought about you a lot lately, and how you must get at times. I know that the move downtown was a hard one on you, and want to say that at no moment in this life should you get depressed! I know it was a move down for you, you may have many more in business... The main thought in my mind is that when my children have reached the age that yours have, I only hope that I can give them some of your strength, your character, your kindness, and all the hundreds of qualities that made you the most perfect parent in the world...

Right now, Charley [i.e., Sonny] is having difficulty, maybe these will never straighten out, maybe all of his life he will be a "problem."[155]

But 1954 would prove to be a difficult year. That January, Charley had a heart attack.[156] His doctor instructed him to relax, to get out of the city, to spend time in Florida. He had accomplished much; there was no need to do more. But Charley spent the year attempting to rebuild his business, his schedule including the usual speaking engagements, another big wedding (his son Joe), and new challenges as a Florida real estate developer.[157] In September, the Textile Veterans Association announced the Charles W. Carvin Sr. Scholarship Award at PTI, where Charley had now become a member of the board.[158] The combination of business, speeches, philanthropy, weddings and real estate deals, marred by the soured relationship with his eldest son, were not what the doctor ordered.

By this time, his grandchildren were frequent visitors to his house on the Jersey shore. A block from the Boardwalk and the Atlantic Ocean, weathered by salty beach winds, the elegant structure he'd bought in 1949 was filled with chandeliered ceilings, high-backed chairs, mahogany tables, grandfather clocks, paintings of red-coated Englishmen and dogs hunting foxes and pheasants, all of which testified to his success. In the living room, ashtrays inscribed with bawdy jokes and figurines of beer-guzzling drunks suggested his discomfort with aristocracy. Charley told bawdy stories to a never-ending succession of guests. But the grand Lyon & Healey concert harp lay by a side wall, silent. And Stella had never written any more stories.

On the second floor, five bedrooms surrounded an open landing decorated with porcelain statues and portraits of Chinese elders whose faces bore the countenance of death. On the topmost floor, Charley told visiting grandchildren stories before tucking them in at night: old-fashioned stories about a noble hero to whom he gave the name *Bobolink*. Known the world over for his goodness and cunning, Bobolink had a crew who would follow him anywhere. With these newest stories, Charley put another audience under his spell. And every chance he got, he took them boating on Absecon Bay, where they watched the world's fastest boats, equipped with old Liberty engines that had been taken from Curtiss JN-4's.[159]

In May of 1955, Charley was on the dais in the Grand Ballroom of the Waldorf-Astoria Hotel. In the midst of crystal, linen and roses, under dazzling chandeliers, cuff-linked men and white-gloved women turned their chairs toward him after dinner. Leaning toward the microphone, the man beside him cleared his throat: amidst the tinkling of glasses and muffled coughs, he introduced the novelist Fannie Hurst, who gave thanks to the National Conference of Christians and Jews (which had sponsored the evening's program) for its opposition to hate groups. And she commended the work done on the organization's behalf by the man everyone had been waiting to hear, the evening's guest of honor, Charley. After thanks for the flattering introduction, he began telling stories of Chinamen and Jews, of Catholic priests, black porters, stuffy Brits and Irish bartenders, stories that had the audience of over seven hundred and fifty people howling with laughter.

At Table 24, seated in two empty chairs, two of his grandchildren listened to the stories, seeing for themselves what greatness existed in their family. As his stories ended, tears came to Charley's eyes. His voice cracked, ruffled by emotion, as he reflected on the honor being paid.[160]

Charley's Christmas cards soon announced the births of other grandchildren.[161] He was given an honorary LLD degree by St. Joseph's University and he became a member of its Board.[162] To enjoy his grandchildren and hard0-earned freedom, he stepped down as president of his company.[163] Soon thereafter, Dwight Eisenhower stepped down as President of the United States, warning of the dangers of the "military industrial complex."[164]

With the Cuban missile Crisis and yet another assassination gaining the nation's attention, John Kennedy appeared in his Christmas cards, as did a little orphaned boy saluting his fallen father. He drew new enemies in the cards, Nikita Khrushchev and Fidel Castro among them. The space race, Sputnik and Yuri Gagarin prompted him to draw Santa guiding his sleigh through rocket fire.

Spending summers in Ventnor and winters in Florida, he became the outdoor sportsman his father had been. In 1962, he served as toastmaster at a "Stag Football Dinner" of high-profile sports figures raising money for the upcoming Liberty Bowl.[165] He beamed with pride when Sonny was profiled in the *Daily News Record* and on the cover of *Modern Textiles,* touting his commitment to man-made fibers. He was especially pleased to read that his son was "not just anybody in textiles." but "a special somebody by the accident of his birth as the son of the famous Charley Carvin, the textile industry's greatest wit, story-teller, jokesmith and toastmaster."[166]

The following year, Congress passed the Gulf of Tonkin Resolution, giving the President unfettered authority to take "all necessary measures" to defeat enemy forces in Vietnam. By this time, some 400 Americans had been killed in the new war. And more had died across the U.S. in lynchings, murders and bombings on account of their race. But for Charley and his family, the good life went on. When jockey Bill Hartack rode Northern Dancer to victory in the 1964 Kentucky Derby, the *Evening Bulletin* devoted five paragraphs of its story to "one of the most magnificent sports spectacles of this or any other century," and four to the twenty-two members of "the Philadelphia Society for the Propagation of the Kentucky Derby," a group of prominent Philadelphia men who rode to Louisville on the rear end of a Pennsylvania Railroad Special. According to the article, the expedition had been going on for 20 years. "The purpose is social," said the *Bulletin*, "and it has to be heard and seen to be appreciated, especially when Charley Carvin, a retired textile tycoon, takes over with his dialect stories. His yarn about the unfortunate man who made the pockets in the pants is a classic that Myron Cohen couldn't match."[167]

Charley told his stories on the golf course, during fishing trips on Absecon Bay, between races at Hialeah or the Atlantic City Raceway, or at the dinner table with his family and friends.[168] His Christmas cards and the leather-bound photo album of his days flying biplanes stoked his grandchildren's interest in history, prompting questions about Will Rogers, Adolf Hitler, and whether Charley had really had dinner with Truman. When Frank Carmody's family fell on hard times, Stel and her children moved into the house in Ventnor for three years. Frank (who drank more than Charley approved) stayed in the house only on weekends, often arriving in the wee hours and climbing to his wife's second floor bedroom more than a little tipsy. One Saturday morning, Charley was pulling down the garage door when he cut off the tip of his finger. When Stel rushed him to the hospital, doctors announced that the finger could be reattached if quickly retrieved, so Stel immediately called Frank, assigning him the task of going to the garage to get the finger. Only half awake and still very hung over, Frank grasped the situation and did as duty demanded, wrapping Charley's severed finger in a handkerchief and racing to the hospital with it. Asked if he'd found the finger, he proudly announced that he had – but upon opening the handkerchief, discovered he'd lost the finger somewhere along the way. It was never found. Frank had missed his chance to become a hero. Charley had to live his remaining years with flesh from his buttocks doing a job for which his fingertip was better suited. But incident served Frank's children – who'd watched with eyes agog – for decades as they practiced the story-telling art they'd learned by listening to their grandfather.[169]

Even as Charley captured his grandchildren's hearts, not only with his story-telling but with boating, water-skiing, fishing and riding the ocean surf, Stella Marie spent most of her days "resting" upstairs in her perfumed, silver-laden bedroom suite. When she descended the stairs, she sometimes took the grandchildren by the hand and walked them to the beach for an hour in the sun, but she usually stayed indoors, teaching them (on good days) to play solitaire – a game she admitted having played for many, many hours. She insisted that they dress properly for dinner, that they not let their chairs scrape the tile floor when they sat down, and that – once properly seated – they sit with their backs straight, chew with their mouths closed, and speak only when spoken to.

She'd never had a paying job. She'd never learned to drive a car. She never entered her own kitchen. When she rang the little bell she kept at the head of her table, Henry – the house man hired after Sam Lowry passed away – brought dinner in, one course at a time, while Stella schooled her grandchildren on the proper way to take helpings from the serving dish he held over their little shoulders.

In June of 1966, Charley sold out his interest in the Carvin Corporation to Abe and Burt Bordow.[170] Life for Charley and Stella was becoming more about memories of the past, more about dreams for the future of children and grandchildren.[171] They had no problem getting underage grandchildren into the racetrack, and after teaching them how to rate the horses, taught them how to mix their favorite cocktails.[172]

In the summer of 1971, Sonny asked Charley for money again. This time he wanted to buy a business in Miami that wove heavy, industrial grade nylon into seat belts for the auto industry. Sonny had always been a borrower. (Charley had drawn him with empty pockets, asking for loans, in his Christmas cards thirty years earlier.) Charley obliged, as did Chase Manhattan bank. Sonny was able to buy the business, which ran around the clock in three shifts, seven days a week. Nylon came not from trees, but from petroleum. As far back as World War II, crude oil had become the material of choice for man-made synthetics. Detroit was now producing over ten million gas-guzzling cars a year. As Charley toured his son's factory, watching rows of women tend looms in the stifling heat, steam pouring from the dye room while battens and picker sticks made the weave room louder than a locomotive, tears of pride came to his eyes that his son had become a success.[173]

Sonny hired four of his own sons at that mill, marking the sixth generation of the family to work in the textile business in America.[174] And Sonny wasn't the only success. Charley's son Joe was approaching his third decade selling man-made fibers for Tennessee-Eastman. Charley was a happy man.

But a year later, when an OPEC embargo sent oil prices (and the price of nylon) soaring, automobile production dropped by more than half. Sonny's sales shriveled up and, with it, his ability to pay off his loans. He laid off his employees. He started bouncing paychecks. He fought a daily battle to avoid bankruptcy. The worst came when the EPA found out that to dye its seat belts, the company – the largest user of water in Hialeah – was pumping wastewater full of dyestuffs and toxic chemicals into the city's sewers. Sonny pled with Charley to borrow more money, to keep him afloat – but this time, Charley finally said no.[175]

Ida Johnson and Nancy Lowrie could always be found in the kitchen or in the basement laundry room at Charley's house in Ventnor, throughout these years. Awake before anyone else in the mornings, it was only after washing the dinner dishes that they climbed the narrow stairs back to their rooms among the attics. The three Carmody grandchildren visited them there, playing games with them and their grandchildren. The women remained as loyal to Charley and Stella Marie as the sailors on Bobolink's crew. They were still employed in 1972, when Charley and Stella Marie celebrated not only fifty years of marriage, but fifty years of Ida's labor with the family.[176]

In January of 1972, when the first of his grandchildren was married, the ceremony took place in a Unitarian church in Philadelphia, and Unitarians did not believe in the Holy Trinity. The ceremony would not be performed by a Catholic priest. Charley, Nancy and Ida all attended the wedding, but just as with Sonny's wedding 25 years earlier, Stella Marie did not. And Sonny himself, father of the groom, threatened to boycott the service, only showing up at the last minute when it became apparent he wouldn't get his way.

For his last Christmas card, Charley drew himself in a hospital bed, "cramming for his finals." On the bed beside him were a copy of the Bible and the daily racing sheet. When asked where he wished to be buried, his response was all Charley: "Surprise me," he said.

He died on March 19, 1974.[177] His funeral mass was said in Philadelphia, at the Cathedral of Saints Peter & Paul, the very Cathedral built by Bishop Kendrick after the riots of 1844. A long line of Philadelphians accompanied the hearse to his burial place, which was next to his father and mother in the family plot Jimmy had bought at Holy Sepulchre in 1898.

When she followed him on December 7, 1976, Stella Marie was buried beside him, having never written another story. Her passing was barely noticed in the papers, her funeral conducted with far less fanfare.

Notes on Chapter 14, Charles W. Carvin

[1] City of Philadelphia Archives, Microfiche Reel No. 289, 1897 Births, p 467.

[2] Charley was two in the summer of 1899. "Miss Florence Carvin and Miss Sadie Carvin, daughters of Joseph Carvin, the well-known businessman of Kensington, are at the Cordova for an extended period. Miss Sadie is an accomplished musician." (*Inquirer*, July 16, 1999, 3rd Sec, p 2, "Personal Pencilings.") After Katie Sherick's death, Charley remained close to his grandmother Mary Sherick; according to the 1920 sentence, he lived with the Shericks upon his return from service in Texas; according to his Christmas cards and Dad's memories, Mary Sherick lived with them in the 1930's.

[3] See Chapter 10, *supra*.

[4] The Greenfields had moved to 1309 Lehigh Avenue in 1899; the Carvins moved to 1317 Lehigh in 1900, then to 1229 Lehigh in 1904. (See 1905 City Directory.) The Greenfield boys likely didn't pay much attention to their cousin, Stella Marie Murphy, who spent more time with their sister, Marie.

[5] *Inquirer,* Jan 19, 1900, p 9. A 1906 paper reported the incorporation of the Amusement Company of America to manufacture nickelodeons, touring cars, "and other pleasure devices." (*Inquirer*, May 13, 1906, p 10).

[6] The Carvins' neighbors on Lehigh included not only William H Greenfield, the coal dealer, and his family, but also the thirty-something Congdon sisters, Anna and Genevieve (1900 U.S. Census, Phila Ward 37, Dist 0957, Fams 187 to 194) whom Stella Marie also visited. Charley's 1958 Christmas card included a line of verse stating that when he met Stella Marie, he was nine, while she was ten, going on eleven. That would put their meeting in late 1906 or early 1907. While this could mean they only met when the Murphys moved across the street, to 1234 Lehigh, it seems far more likely they met when she visited her cousins, the Greenfields, or her two Congdon aunts. One can only guess what the elder Murphys thought when their privileged princess took an interest in the barkeep's son, raised by his Methodist grandmother, whose father was a sporting man and saloon keeper who'd married a younger Baptist girl, and whose brother had just left town in flight from creditors.

[7] The Carvins were listed at 1229 Lehigh in the 1907 Directory, and at 1935 Somerset in the 1908 Directory.

[8]   Law No 265, Laws of the Commonwealth of Pennsylvania, 1903, accessed at https://babel.hathi trust.org/cgi/pt?id=uc1.a0001822881&view=1up&seq=355&skin=2021; Philadelphia North American, Jan 21, 1903; Chris Lamb, "Drawn and Quartered: The Government and Cartoonists During World War I," Ph.D. Thesis, Central Michigan University, 1996.

[9] Charley's stay in Los Angeles was likely from 1907 to 1910. He was probably sent there when his older sisters, who'd been taking care of him, married and left the house. (Florence married Wendell Young on May 22, 1907, and he likely went west soon thereafter.) Since his time there was working milk deliveries with his brother Joe, his stay could not have extended past 1911, as that is the last directory which gives "dairy" as Joe's occupation. Being only a youngster, it's no surprise that Charley doesn't appear in the city directories or newspaper accounts. But he also doesn't appear in the 1910 U.S. Census, not in the Philadelphia household his father was sharing with the Geklers, the household of Florence and Wendell Young, the household headed by his uncle, Charles Sherick, and not in the L. A. census. (The 1910 U.S. Census (L. A., Assembly District 70, Dist 244, Fam 94) shows his brother Joe's family in L. A. as of April 15 including only Joseph J. Carvin, wife Elsie, and his three children Joe (age 4), Edward (age 2), and daughter Elsie (one month old) at 154 Slauson Avenue.) Since Charley is not included in any of these censuses, the mystery of the thirteen-year-old's whereabouts in 1910 persists to this day. It may be that Charley was *en route* back to Philadelphia in April of 1910, and so failed to be caught by any of the Census-takers that year.

[10] *Inquirer*, June 7, 1910, p 11 and July 3, 1910, 2d Section, p 1. The People's Theater, at 2465 Kensington Avenue, was a humbler establishment than the theaters downtown.

388

[11] In addition to Curtiss' seminal 1910 book, <u>The Aeroplane</u> (1914) by Claude Grahame-White and <u>Flying Machines: Construction and Operation (1918),</u> by Octave Chanute, were two of the more popular books of the era.

[12] Charley's maternal grandfather, Charles Sherick, died on Dec 31, 1912 (PA 1912 Death Cert No. 120219), leaving his estate to Charley's grandmother, Mary Kiker Sherick (PA Wills and Probate Records, Phila, 1913, Petition No 65, Will Book 338, p 534). What school Charley attended is uncertain. Bill Colman reports a family recollection that young Charley attended St. Joe's Prep; the report seems plausible, as Charley was later a supporter and trustee of St. Joseph's college; but no documentary support has been found for the recollection. The job with Adams Express was noted on Charley's WWI draft card, NARA Roll M1509, Phila Draft Board 37, 1917-1918, alphabetical under C, on which Charley gave his address as his father's house, at 1935 West Somerset in Philadelphia.

[13] Stella Marie Murphy, "Weighed in the Balance," *The Patrician* (yearbook of the Academy of Mercy), 1916. The story is set out in full in Appendix 3.

[14] In one of his letters, he did tell her he'd keep his promise and go to confession (Appendix 5, Ltr 2).

[15] 1935 Veteran's Compensation Application of Charles Walter Carvin, Serial #1,162,987; Application No 1844 – 332782, WW I Veterans Service and Compensation Files, 1934–1948. RG 19, Series 19.91, Pennsylvania Historical and Museum Commission, Harrisburg PA. Charley's service at Niagara was also noted on his draft card, *supra*. Fort Niagara had been an army fort since colonial days; because Canada was already in the war and had been training flyers at The University of Toronto School of Military Aeronautics, Niagara was a natural place for early flight training. But Charley's penchant for telling stories was also beginning to manifest itself, even on official government forms. The 1917 draft card gave his date of birth as March 5, 1896 [sic] (making him a year older than he actually was) and also made the questionable claim that he had already served three years as a private in the cavalry, in California. His service began at Fort Niagara on May 12, 1917 (per his 1935 Application for Veterans Benefits).

[16] Princeton was one of eight U.S. Universities where the U.S. had opened ground training schools. Having lost half of its normal enrollment due to enlistments in the army, Princeton was struggling financially. ("United States Army, World War I Flight Training," accessed at https://en. wikipedia.org/wiki/United_States_Army_World_War_I_Flight_Training, *and* Alden Hunt, Brett Tomlinson, and Nina Sheridan, "Timeline: Princeton in the Great War," Princeton Alumni Weekly, May 30, Oct 3, and Nov 21, 1917, accessed at https://paw.princeton.edu/article/timeline-princeton-great-war.) "Princeton in the fall of 1918 was almost unrecognizable as an institution of higher education, as almost all the old college routines had changed. The eating clubs had closed for the duration of the war, *The Daily Princetonian* had suspended publication, and the football team played only an informal schedule. [Princeton President John] Hibben, who had been an early advocate of military preparedness, 'lost no time in placing the University's resources at the disposal of the government' (in the words of Alexander Leitch '24, author of *A Princeton Companion*) once the United States declared war on Germany in April 1917 and the faculty unanimously endorsed compulsory military service. Those students who did not enlist immediately joined ROTC, drilled, and studied tactics." "In August 1918, Congress created the Student Army Training Corps (SATC), paying some colleges and universities to host military training camps. By the time classes started at Princeton the next month, 711 students had enrolled in its SATC program under the command of Col. John A. Pearson, a West Point graduate who had been appointed the previous year to teach military science ... Six hundred more young men studied in a School of Military Aeronautics. The campus that fall had only 95 regular students, known derisively as the 'Diplomatic Corps,' most of whom were either too young to enlist or had some physical impairment." (Mark F. Bernstein, "Why Princeton Was Spared," *Princeton Alumni Weekly*, Dec 17, 2008, accessed at https://paw.princeton.edu/article/why-princeton-was-spared.) Stella Marie Murphy's visits at Princeton are mentioned in Charley's letter to her of January 19, 1918 (Appendix 5, Ltr 2).

[17] Veteran's Compensation Application, *supra*. Back in Philadelphia, Stella Marie might have gone to the People's Theater to see "Reilly and the Seminary Girl" or "Liberty Girls" (*Inquirer*, Jan 15, 1918).

[18] Charley Carvin to Stella Marie Murphy, Feb 5, 1918, Appendix 5, Ltr 3.

[19] Robert A. Wells, "Propaganda at Home," 1914-1918-online. International Encyclopedia of the First World War, ed. by Ute Daniel, Peter Gatrell, Oliver Janz, Heather Jones, Jennifer Keene, Alan Kramer, and Bill Nasson, issued by Freie Universität Berlin, Berlin 2014-10-08; "Cartooning for Victory," WWI Instructions to Artists, Committee on Public Information, Bureau of Cartoons, Bulletin No. 16, Sept 28, 1919, accessed at http://historymatters.gmu.edu/d/5052/. It was headed by George J. Hecht.

[20] Lamb, *supra*, citing Richard Fitzgerald, Art and Politics (Westport, CT: Greenwood Press, 1973), 82 and Rebecca Zurier, Art for the Masses, 1911-1917: A Radical Magazine and Its Graphics (New Haven: Yale University Press), 40.

[21] Charley Carvin to Stella Marie Murphy, Feb 5, 1918, Appendix 5, Ltr 3. From Charley's comment, "You must pardon the drawing on the envelope, I know you don't like them, I drew a few last week and this is the only envelope I have left," we can assume that the drawings were either pin-up girls or, more likely, anti-German cartoons of the type the Bureau of Cartoons was promoting.

[22] Charley Carvin to Stella Marie Murphy, Feb 28, 1918, Appendix 5, Ltr 4. Stella's complaint about him joining the air corps is suggested by his asking her if she'd have been satisfied had he remained in the Quartermaster Corps or joined the infantry.

[23] World War I Veterans Service and Compensation File, 1934–1948. RG 19, Series 19.91, Pennsylvania Historical and Museum Commission, Harrisburg, PA, Army, alphabetical under Carvin.

[24] Charley Carvin to Stella Marie Murphy, postmarked April 17, 1918, Appendix 5, Ltr 5.

[25] Camp Dick "was originally established January 31, 1918, in Dallas, Texas on the State Fair Grounds, as an aviation concentration camp to which graduates of ground schools were sent to await admittance to primary flying schools and for graduate reserve military aviators awaiting admittance to advanced schools. On February 5, 1918, the post was named Camp Dick in honor of Flying Cadet James F. Dick, Jr., who was killed January 6, 1918, at Dallas. Camp Dick was closed in January 1919." (Organization Authority Record, War Department, National Archives Catalog, accessed at https://catalog.archives.gov/id/10454301.)

[26] Dallas is some 275 miles from San Antonio, and to make such a trip, Stella Marie would need a chaperone; there was also the flu outbreak at Camp Dick that summer; and Charley's letter of April 17th gives no hint of plans for a meeting.

[27] Camp Dick was overcome by the flu pandemic of 1918, beginning in the summer and peaking in October. The Army imposed a quarantine for newly arriving soldiers, but large crowds fueled the spread of the virus. By September of 1918, the City of Dallas was holding yet another Liberty Loan parade, its fourth since 1917. Immediately after the widely-attended parade, reports of infections increased twentyfold and the Mayor banned further public gatherings. By the following spring, the pandemic had taken fifty million lives worldwide. (Jennifer Anderson, "Flashback to October 12, 1918," in *Dallas During WWI & II,* October 18, 2018, City of Dallas Office of Historic Preservation, accessed at https://cityofdallaspreservation.wordpress.com/2018/10/12/on-this-day-in-dallas-oct-12-1918-mayor-lawther-bans-all-public-gatherings-in-effort-to-slow-spread-of-spanish-flu/.)

[28] *Dallas Morning News*, May 29, 1918, p 1.

[29] "The day before the game, airplanes will circle both cities and literally make life miserable for the street cleaners with the thousands of handbills the six athletic departments have had printed." (*Dallas Morning News*, Aug 11, 1918, p 1.)

[30] After the first Liberty Loan Drive fared poorly, the government used George Creel's propaganda machine, the "Committee on Public Information," to make the later drives successful. Movie stars included Charlie Chaplin, Al Jolson, Ethel Barrymore, Lillian Gish, Fatty Arbuckle, Douglas Fairbanks, and Mary Pickford. ("Liberty Bond," Wikipedia.org; "First World War on Film," accessed at https://shootingthegreatwar.blogspot.com/2018/08/movie-stars-on-liberty-loan-drive-usa.html.)

[31] "Liberty Bond," Wikipedia.org, accessed January 15, 2022.

[32] Committee on Public Information, *Four Minute Men Bulletin* 1, May 22, 1917. Cornbise, *supra.*

[33] *Four Minute Men News, Edition D,* Cornbise, *supra.*) For the complete poem, see Appendix 4 below.

[34] Private collection of the author.

[35] Two photographs in the leather album depict a group of fliers sitting in a flatboat, with rifles, on a duck hunt. One of the men is identified as "Hecht." Efforts to determine whether the man might have been George Hecht, head of the Committee on Public Information's Bureau of Cartoons, were inconclusive, but George Hecht's

[36] Gene Boyo, "No Innocent on 7th Avenue," Modern Textiles, Dec 1952. But Charley's 1935 application for Veteran's benefits says nothing of a promotion to Captain, describing his rank simply as Lieutenant and giving his date of discharge as April, 1919, exactly two years after his enlistment. (Veteran's Compensation Application, *supra*.)

[37] Charley Carvin to Stella Marie Murphy Dec 8, 1918, Appendix 5, Ltr 6.

[38] The 4th Liberty Loan Drive raised seven billion dollars from the American public, its terms including the guarantee that "The principal and interest hereof are payable in United States gold coin of the present standard of value." The bonds were to mature in October of 1938. However, in 1934, FDR's Treasury Department called the bond, refused to redeem it in gold, and declined to account for the extreme devaluation of the paper currency by that time – all of which the Supreme Court, in Perry vs. United States, 294 U.S. 330 (1935), found unconstitutional. The default cost the buying public the equivalent of 250 billion dollars in 2021 currency ("Liberty Bond," Wikipedia.org, accessed Jan 15, 2022).

[39] Aviation magazines of the day referred to Charley as a "night flying instructor" (whether in reference to his past duties in the war or to more current employment being unclear). "Philadelphia aviators who served during the war met at the Hotel Walton on July 24 and formed the Aviator's Club of Pennsylvania. About ninety fliers were present … No time was lost in getting to the election of officers with the following results:… C. W. Carvin, secretary…" (*Flying*, Vol. VIII, No. 8, September, 1919, p 706; "Aero Club of Pennsylvania Merge with Aviators Club of Pennsylvania," *Aerial Age Weekly* (Vol 9, Part 2, 18 Aug 1819, p 1046) accessed at https://books.google.com/books?id=sVBR AQAAMAAJ&pg=PA1046&dq=Aviator%27s+Club+of+Pennsylvania&hl=en&sa=X&ved=0ahUK EwiAh4bayoHUAhVKziYKHZLjD78Q6AEIPDAF#v=onepage&q=Aviator's%20Club%20of%20Pe nnsylvania&f=false.) Atlantic City's municipal airfield was the first "airport" in the nation, a name given to it by its founder, Henry Woodhouse, an aviation enthusiast and promoter of the Atlantic City Aero Club (the same group that sponsored the 1910 AeroMeet.) (Wallace McKelvey, "Atlantic City Played Prominent Role in Birth of Commercial Aviation," *The Press of Atlantic City*, Aug 14, 2012, accessed at https://pressofatlanticcity.com/news/top_three/atlantic-city-played-prominent-role-in-birth -of-commercial-aviation/article_2ec0961a-e66e-11e1-852d-001a4bcf887a.html).

The September 1919 issue of *Flying* also reported that the Curtiss Aeroplane Corp had just purchased the Atlantic City Airport, the official field of the Atlantic City Aero Club. As an officer of the new Aviator's Club, Charley was among those charged with discussing a possible merger with the older Aero Club of Pennsylvania, but sources conflict about whether the merger went forward. Compare the report in *Aerial Age Weekly* to that in *Aircraft Journal*, No. 5, Sept 20, 1919, pg 10, which reported that the Aviator's Club had decided NOT to merge with the Aero club, saying that the Aviators' Club, consisting of former Army, Navy and Marine Corps fliers, who flew propeller aircraft in the war, didn't want to combine with the older association of balloonists.

[40] McKelvey, *supra.*

[41] Boyo, *supra.* There are signs that Charley's relationship with his father may have been tenuous. On January 2, the 1920 Census counted Joseph J. Carvin living alone above his saloon at 2400 Kensington, while on January 6, it enumerated the Sherick household at 604 York Street, six blocks west, as consisting of Mary Sherick, her son Charles Sherick (occ "oyster dealer, own business"), and Charley Carvin (occ "manager, hosiery mill." (1920 Census, Phila, Ward 19, Dist 0417, Fam 1, and Dist 0434, Fam 83.) The flat above the saloon had been home to multiple occupants before, so it's not clear why Charley would have lived with the Shericks, rather than with his father. Perhaps, dealing with the loss of his business to Prohibition and making frequent trips to California to investigate the murder of his son, Jimmy was simply pre-occupied. But religion, too, may have been a factor: the adult Charles

Sherick had recently been baptized in the Methodist Church on October 6, 1918 (Historical Soc of PA, Historic PA Church and Town Records, Reel 367, Baptisms at the Cumberland Street Methodist Episcopal Church); raised in part by his Methodist grandmother, Charley may have felt more comfortable with her and her son Charles.

[42] Charley would later teach his grandchildren how to draw cartoons with dark bold lines; going through the Sunday comics, he would tell them about his early favorites (among the oldest of them) and how much he had always wanted to draw. He had drawn one on the envelope of his February, 1918 letter to Stella, apologizing because he knew she didn't like them, but he was out of envelopes because he'd been drawing such things on them. (One suspects his drawings on envelopes in 1918 may have been of scantily clad pinup girls he was selling to other cadets, or anti-Hun sketches he was using to practice for Liberty Bond sales). In any case, Stella Marie kept Charley's letter, but the envelope with the unwanted drawing on it did not survive.

[43] This advice to go into food or textiles was shared with his grandchildren, some fifty years later, Charley giving them the same advice his father had once given him.

[44] The Philadelphia Textile School had been founded by private textile manufacturers in 1884 as a trade school, to train workers for work in their mills. By 1916, it had become a division of the Pennsylvania Museum and School of Industrial Art. (See 1916 City Directory under "School of Industrial Art," "Penna Museum and School of Industrial Art," and "Philadelphia Textile School.") It later became known as the Philadelphia Textile Institute, later still as Philadelphia University and, after a 2017 merger, Jefferson University. (See website of Jefferson University, https://www.jefferson.edu/content/dam/academic/history/Combined-TJU-PhilaU-History-02152018.pdf.) Charley graduated from the Philadelphia Textile Institute in 1923 (*New York Times*, March 22, 1974, p 42). Since the regular course of study was three years, Charley likely began in 1920; PTI opened for the fall on September 20 of that year (*Public Ledger*, Sept 6, 1920, p 13). Charley's throwing of crates of yarn in the basement at Taubel was reportedly in 1922. (Boyo, *supra*; Modern Textiles, May 1963.) See also various help wanted ads in 1922 for Taubel Bros Hosiery Mill at Cedar and Huntingdon Streets (such as *Inquirer* April 12, 1922, p 24).

[45] Algeo foresaw "grave losses to the spirit of co-operation among weavers, dyers, knitters and spinners if something is not done to lift them above the level of being mere adjuncts to the machines they tend… [T]he making of textiles is bound up in its history with the growth of this community. But the spirit of craftsmanship, upon which so much depends, is failing. Many mills can no longer boast a personnel built up for generations. In some, grandfather, father and son work together. Theirs is the old-time heritage of patient skill, of delight in the beauty of a humble but a very necessary calling. Recent changes have tended to drive this spirit out of the laboring man's consciousness… Here at the textile school we plan to make men more than mere machinery" (*Evening Public Ledger*, May 25, 1921, p 10).

[46] As early as the January 1920 Census, Charley had listed his occupation as a "manager" at the hosiery mill.

[47] Boyo, *supra*.

[48] The selection as most likely to succeed, and the job offer, were from a representative of Franklin D'Olier *(Ibid.)*. D'Olier is known for being, among other things, a Philadelphia cotton merchant, the first National Commander of the American Legion, and later Chairman of Prudential Insurance and grandfather of the actor, Christopher Reeve.

[49] Boyo, *supra*. Meanwhile, in January 1921, Stella Murphy and Katherine Scannell had been among those selling flowers, candy, cigarettes and programs at the St. Francis Junior Aids' production of Willard Spenser's "Miss Bob White" at the Bellevue Stratford; Loretta Scannell had an acting role (*The Inquirer*, Jan 16, 1921, p 36).

[50] *Inquirer*, Aug 11, 1923, p 15; Boyo, *supra*.

[51] President Warren Harding had released political prisoners arrested for their opposition to the World War, but he died of a heart attack half way through his term. His vice-president, Calvin Coolidge, was a fiscal conservative. Becoming President, he signed into law the Indian Citizenship Act of 1924,

which granted US citizenship to indigenous peoples. His presidency was characterized by a period of economic growth and great optimism.

[52] Weigley, *supra*, p 534; *Evening Public Ledger*, Oct 30, 1920, p 14, April 9, 1921, p 11 and Feb 18, 1922, p. 15; *Inquirer,* April 10, 1921 (Entertainment Section) p 3, March 13, 1921 (Entertainment Section) p 2; May 9, 1922, p 3 and Dec 24, 1922, p 13.

[53] Appendix 5, Ltr 7. The 1922 City Directory shows Charley for the first time living at 958 Pratt Street in Frankford, a neighborhood within the city limits of Philadelphia.

[54] Charles Walter Carvin, Jr., born Oct 12, 1923, was named after his father. Both grandfathers, Joseph "Jimmy" Carvin and Joseph D. Murphy, were named Joseph; but Joseph Edward Carvin, born May 20, 1926, was primarily named after Stella's brother, Joseph Edward Murphy.

[55] The first commercial textile uses for acetate in fiber form were developed by the Celanese Company in 1924.

[56] "It was at this time…that he introduced [rayon] into Clifton Yarn Mills and obtained an interest in the firm." (Boyo, *supra*). Clifton was headquartered in the Philadelphia suburb of Conshohocken.

[57] In 1921 and 1922, while Charley was single and attending PTI, he lived with his father at 936 Herbert Street in Frankford, a couple of miles to the northeast of Jimmy's saloon. Immediately after the wedding, the newlyweds continued to live there (see 1921 – 1923 City Directories). But by February 6, 1923, when Stella wrote to Aunt G about the furnishing of their new house, they had moved to 958 Pratt Street in Frankford (Directories of 1924 and 1925). The move to Drexel Hill was probably in 1928.

[58] The complete collection of Charley's cards is available in <u>Oh Mother, That Man's Here Again!!</u> <u>The Christmas Cards of Charles W. Carvin,</u> 2018, ISBN 978-0-9768183-5-9, edited and annotated by jwcarvin.

[59] Stella Marie Carvin, born Nov 20, 1929, was named after her mother.

[60] Charley was proud of this quirk of historical irrelevance; for many years, he displayed his humorous business announcement, announcing the move, on his living room mantelpiece and claiming that he had been the first tenant to move in. Assuming he did move in on April 1, 1931, that claim would be correct – it was a month prior to the building's "official" opening ceremonies scheduled for May 1st . On the occasion of the building's seventy-fifth anniversary in 2005, its owners gave a great deal of publicity to their longest continuous tenant, a Mr. Jack Broad, a jeweler whose Empire Diamond Company they referred to in press reports as an "original" tenant and sometimes as the building's "first" tenant. Unwilling to let Charley's status go unrecognized, the author contacted the building's Public Relations Department, asserting the contrary claim, attested to by the fact that Charley's 1931 business announcement notified his customers that he'd be moving in on April 1st. The building's public relations department asserted in reply that they'd reviewed the early building leases; that Empire Jewelry had moved in on September 1, 1931; that yes, Charley Carvin and Clifton Mills had been "among" the first tenants, but that the building's widely reported press releases had been correct in saying that Empire Jewelry was "the first." On the contrary, it has been well documented that the building was already occupied by several tenants prior to the official opening on May 1st. (See, for example, John Tauranac, <u>The Empire State Building</u>, St. Martin's Press (1995), especially pp 161, 183, and 275, which specifically mentions Clifton Mills among them.) Jack Broad's Empire Jewelry may have been the longest continuous tenant, but the claim that Empire's arrival on September 1st somehow predated the tenants who moved in prior to the May 1st opening is patently absurd. See *New York Times*, March 22, 1931, p 26 (scaffolding removed, construction complete; "has been renting for some time …"); *New York Times*, March 24, 1931, Real Estate p 49 (DuPont signs lease for three floors); and *New York Times*, May 3, 1931, p 2 ("Several tenants have already moved in …)

[61] There was some truth on the inside of the announcement: Clifton's offices were on the 31st Floor; they were moving in on April 1; they were offering yarn for sale as described; and they could be contacted (after the 1st) at Longacre 2536. But the truth was wrapped up in preposterous claims, made in the voice of the country bumpkin Charley had drawn on the announcement's cover: "It seems I can't get out of movin' to New York. Texas Guinan and Belle Livingstone have been coaxin' me and when John Raskob

and Al Smith bilt me a bildin I just couldn't refuse. I'm taking the thirty-first floor and the rest of the Buildin' will be rest rooms, restaurants, etc., for our convenience… They put a Zeppelin mooring mast on our Buildin' (104th floor) so you can come any way at all and we can take care of you."

[62] Mary Kiker Sherick had been living with her daughter and son-in-law, Laura and Harry Rittenhouse. (1930 U.S. Census Phila Dist 1076, Fam 400.) Laura's death on March 14, 1933, was likely the reason the elderly woman moved in with Charley and Stella in Drexel Hill. The children of the house knew Mary as "Gram Sherick," though she was not their biological grandmother, but Charley's. The uncomfortable nature of the relationship between Mary and Stella Marie is as recalled later by Charley Jr., who was just a child at the time, and it helps in the interpretation of a line in Charley's 1933 Christmas card. Composed just after the repeal of Prohibition had been announced on December 5, 1933, the card included a drawing of a Speakeasy with a "Closed" sign on its door, next to which two lines of forced verse are, "And granny who has seen so many years/ Smiles at Repeal through her tears." The mixed image of smiles and tears might be thought to indicate that Gram Sherick was a drinker herself, but her Baptist background and Charley's Jr's recollection that she disapproved of his mother's drinking suggest otherwise.

[63] Earlier that year, a popular song by Al Sherman, Al Lewis and Abner Silver had featured a man seeking to bully his way into the heart of an innocent lady; the song's refrain contained the lady's response: "No, no, a thousand times no! I'd rather die than say yes!"

[64] Eventually becoming the biggest textile manufacturer in the world, Burlington credited its own success to the fact that, in its early days, it was extended credit. (Annette Cox, "Marketing at Burlington Industries," Business and Economic History, 2d Series, Vol 18, 1989.) Charley, meanwhile, remembered extending credit to Spencer Love, founder of Burlington, and worried for days whether Love's credit was good (Boyo, *supra*).

[65] For the rapid growth in rayon sales, see Tegan Kehoe and Camille Meyers Breeze, "Rayon Through the Years," *Museum Textile Services* (2013), accessed at January 16, 2022 at http://www.Museum textiles.com/blog/rayon-through-the-years-part-i. According to Gene Boyo's article in *Modern Textiles, supra,* Charley applied for the job at Industrial Rayon when Percy Howe left – but efforts to determine when Percy Howe left have failed. According to Boyo, Charley said that Industrial had sued Clifton for $30,000 just the prior year. Industrial had won a judgment against Clifton Yarn Mills for $29,425 in 1931; Clifton appealed, and the judgment was affirmed January 16, 1933, in Industrial Rayon v Clifton Yarn Mills, S. Ct. PA, 165 A. 385 (1933). If Industrial sued Clifton in 1931, and Howe left in 1932, then Charley started with Industrial Rayon about 1932 or 1933 – not long after his move to the Empire State Building in 1931.

[66] *New York Daily News*, April 5, 1936, Sunday News, p 7.

[67] U.S. Automobile Production Figures," Wikipedia.org, accessed Jan 16, 2022, at https://en. wikipedia.org/wiki/U.S._Automobile_Production_Figures

[68] *Cincinnati Enquirer*, March 15, 1941, pp 18, 20.

[69] "Rayon Stocks Up on Jap Freezing," *New York Daily News*, July 27, 1941, p 42.

[70] Parachutes had previously been made of silk, and rayon was an obvious substitute. By this time, however, a new synthetic yarn – nylon – had become a strong competitor of rayon. Rayon was sometimes called only a partial synthetic since it was made from natural trees. Nylon was considered a pure synthetic – made from petrochemicals (chiefly benzene) derived from crude oil. Nylon eventually took most of the market for tire cord, and it won Army contracts for the parachutes intended for human use – but rayon became the yarn of choice for the parachutes used for dropping non-human provisions, supplies, and propaganda. [The original authority for this assertion has been lost, but it was asserted by Charley himself; see also confirmation in Major Raymond C. Altermatt, "Aerial Delivery of Supplies," *The Quarter-Master Review,* Sept-Oct 1945, Army Quartermaster Museum, Ft. Lee, VA, accessed March, 2022, at https://qmmuseum.lee.army.mil/wwii/aerialsupplies.htm.]

[71] Mary Kiker Sherick died of a heart attack in Haverford, PA, on Nov 16, 1935 (PA Death Certificate File No 97589).

72 The description of Stella Marie's reaction to being in her husband's "shadow" was often given by their daughter-in-law, Julia Logan Carvin (the author's mother).

73 Then called the Empire City Racetrack.

74 Mr. and Mrs. Carvin of White Plains attended the 21st birthday party of Miss Frances Baldwin (Mamaroneck, NY *Daily Times*, Feb 7, 1938, p 5.) When Charley purchased 7 Chesterfield Road in Scarsdale later that year, he was still sales manager for Industrial Rayon (*New York Times,* Dec 24, 1938, p 29).

75 This early "controlled drinking" strategy was described to the author by Charley himself.

76 "Life with Father" premiered on Broadway on November 8th, 1939 and the "Westchester Follies" quickly followed. In that year's Christmas card, Charley drew his younger son Joe remarking, "Yeh – that's my Pop – the pride of the Westchester Follies. He stops the show 'Life with Father.' Wait until I write my memoirs…"

77 After attending Scarsdale High School, Joe (briefly) attended Valley Forge Military Academy. He enlisted in the Navy and served in the Pacific during WWII. Inheriting his father's love for drawing, he helped draw some of the family's Christmas cards and studied art at the University of Miami (Florida) and the University of Zurich (Switzerland). Upon his return, he joined his father and brother in the textile converting business. (In the 1950 Christmas card, Charley wrote that Joe was "now dickering with his draft board to be in every other war;" and drew him wearing lederhosen, carrying a briefcase labeled "Carvin Retail Sales." The drawing was captioned, "Since his Switzerland trip, he also yodels.")

78 Charley's asking Stella Marie to keep her chin up was advice given in the undated, handwritten letter (Appendix 15, Ltr 11) probably written in 1939 or 1940. Charley later told the author that Stella Marie was one of Bill Wilson's first associates and one of the first to participate in seminal A. A. meetings. This squares with the fact that Dr. Bob Smith was a surgeon in Akron, Ohio who founded what became A. A. with Wilson, a New York stockbroker, in 1935. Exactly where and how Stella Marie became involved is unknown, but the first A. A. group met in Akron in 1935, where Charley called on the tire industry; the second group met in New York in the autumn of 1935, where Charley lived and had his sales office (the founders began the Alcoholic Foundation there in 1938); the third A. A. group began meeting in Cleveland (Industrial Rayon's headquarters town) in 1939. ("The Start and Growth of A. A.," Alcoholics Anonymous, accessed at https://www.aa.org/the-start-and-growth-of-aa, and "The History of Alcoholics Anonymous" at Wikipedia.org.) Stella was likely an inpatient at either the Towns Hospital in Manhattan (Stella lived near the city, was precisely the sort of wealthy alcoholic to which Towns catered, and A. A.'s founder, Bill W., had often been a patient there) or the St. Thomas Hospital in Akron (Stella had strong Catholic beliefs; A. A. founder Dr. Smith and Sister Ignatia admitted alcoholics beginning in 1939.) Prior to 1935, because alcoholism was considered a moral failing rather than a disease, religious institutions treated it only as such; when Dr. Smith and Sister Ignatia admitted their first alcoholic patient in 1935 with a diagnosis of acute gastritis, they reportedly became the first hospital in the world to treat alcoholism as a medical condition. ("Summa St. Thomas Hospital," Wikipedia.org.)

79 Stella Marie Carvin to Mrs. Joseph Dulanty, undated, Appendix 5, Ltr 8.

80 Private possession of the author. The title page bears the writer's name and the date: May, 1934.

81 Many years later, the boy explained the absences by telling his children he'd stayed home to keep his mother from drinking at times, to help her cope with hangovers at others. That he and Ida had worked together, trying to keep her sober, but since she had her phone, her checkbook, and her deliverymen, they failed. He said he'd lied, at school, about being sick, in order to protect his mother. But the many absences had caused the nuns to insist on written notes from home to verify that he'd been sick. Since his mother didn't remember him ever being sick, he'd had to write the notes to Holy Child himself.

82 In his 1939 Christmas card, Charley depicted Sonny saying, "According to Dad, I'm training for shirking my way through college," and in the 1941 card, he drew him reaching into an empty pocket

above the caption, "Always broke." Sonny later told how, after being expelled from the basketball team due to misbehavior in the cafeteria, he formed an unofficial team with others who'd been expelled; they called themselves "the Nicotines." His high school yearbook is full of classmates' comments about that episode, about his taking girlfriends for drives in his fancy new car, about the parties he hosted in his basement when Charley was out of town, and about his reputation for drinking. Frequent absences and poor grades delayed his advancement. When incomplete coursework kept him from graduating, Charley had to pull strings to get him a late diploma. Although the rest of his class graduated in June, Sonny's diploma was not dated or granted until August 22, 1941. Both the yearbook and the diploma are in the author's possession.

[83] The unsuccessful summer job was related by several relatives (in different versions); the family account contrasts with the public one: as *Modern Textiles* later published Sonny's own account, he worked "in the hot and steamy spinning room of Industrial's big rayon plant at Painesville, Ohio" for two summers (1938 and 1939), and after that "sulphur-scented" experience "as an ordinary plant worker," the following summer (1940) he took his father's car to New England, where he called on hosiery companies, selling processing oils (*Modern Textiles*, May 1963). The name of the impregnated classmate need not be mentioned.

[84] Charley Jr. had enrolled at North Carolina State College in Greensboro, which had a strong textile program (*Modern Textiles*, May 1963). According to the story later told by his brother Joe, when he hit the telephone pole, it knocked out power to half the city – no doubt an exaggeration by a rival sibling genetically prone to that style of expression.

[85] Joe (1926-2011) eventually enlisted in the Navy. He boarded the ship U.S.S. Tarawa (CV-40) on Feb 5, 1946 (Navy Muster Rolls, 1938-1949, accessed via Ancestry.com) and was home in time to attend his brother Sonny's wedding in August 1946. He attended the University of Miami in 1949-1950 and worked for Charles W. Carvin & Co before starting a long career selling fibers for Tennessee Eastman. Joe died on March 10, 2011 (*South Florida Sun-Sentinel*, March 16, 2011, p 8B).

[86] According to his 1943 WWII draft card. Charley was 5'9" and 183 lbs. (Draft Registration Cards for Fourth Registration for NY State, 04/27/1942, NAI Number 2555973, Records of the Selective Service System, Group No 14, Nat'l Archives at St. Louis, MO.) Though relatively fit, at 45, he was too old to enlist. Sonny registered for the draft on June 30, 1942, and didn't enlist until Jan 29, 1943 (U.S., World War II Draft Cards Young Men, 1940-1947 [database on-line]. Lehi, UT, USA: Ancestry.com Operations, Inc., 2011, Carver – Case; Dept of Veterans Affairs BIRLS Death file, 1850-2010, SSN 288-14-8360.)

[87] *New York Times*, March 25, 1942, p 28.

[88] *New York Times*, April 3, 1942, p 36. The seven-room house in a nice neighborhood at 173 Madison Rd was presumably an investment property.

[89] A speech to a South Carolina Rotary Club was reported in the *Spartanburg Herald*, May 5, 1942; the speech honoring Katz was reported in the *New York Times*, April 29, 1943, p 18. Charley's 1942 Draft Card showed him as 5'9," 183 lbs employed by Industrial Rayon, 500 Fifth Ave NYC. (WWII Draft Cards (Fourth Registration) for NY State, Record Group 147, Roll No 94.)

[90] In September of 1943, he was named to replace his boss at Industrial, Vice President George F. Brooks. *New York Times,* Sept 18, 1943, p 24.

[91] Quoted in Boyo, *supra.*

[92] *Miami Daily News,* April 10, 1945, p 10-B ("following a brief speech, he entertained those present with a number of jokes in various dialects"); *New York Times*, May 16, 1945, p 21. According to the *Times*, the proceeds of the event at the Lambs would be "derived from the $200 contributions from the executives of the rayon industry invited by Charles Carvin, president of the Denier Club." The invitation to speak at the event likely came from Burlington Industries executive Frank H. Leslie, who had often appeared clowning with Charley at Industry events, and who had himself been a member of the Lambs since 1936.

[93] Such greats as Gene Autry, Eddie Albert, Lionel Barrymore, Bernard Baruch, Ed Begley, Ralph Bellamy, Edgar Bergen, Milton Berle, Ray Bolger, Matthew Broderick, Joe E. Brown, Sid Caesar, Eddie Cantor, Art Carney, George M. Cohan, Hume Cronyn, Cecil B. DeMille, Douglas Fairbanks, Bob Fosse, Oscar Hammerstein II, Hal Holbrook, George Jessel, Al Jolson, Boris Karloff, Danny Kaye, Jerome Kern, Bert Lahr, Ring Lardner, Alan Jay Lerner, Frederick Loewe, Joseph E. Levine, Harold Lloyd, Ted Mack, Gordon MacRae, Raymond Massey, Louis B. Mayer, Edward R. Murrow, Eugene O'Neill, Tyrone Power, Hal Prince, George Reeves, John Ringling, Cliff Robertson, Edward G. Robinson, Will Rogers, John Philip Sousa, Loretta Swit, Booth Tarkington, Spencer Tracy, Rudy Vallee, Abe Vigoda, John Wayne, Orson Welles, Jonathan Winters and Ed Wynn were Lambs members. The complete list can be found on the Lambs' website; the page devoted to Charley Carvin is at https://the-lambs.org/club_member/carvin-charles-w/.

[94] *New York Times*, Aug 15, 1945, p 35, May 25, 1948, p 55, and Jul 1, 1948, p 31; *Inquirer*, Aug 20, 1945, p 11 and Oct 6, 1957, p 49; *Rayon Textile Monthly*, Vol 29, Issues 1-12, pp 100 and 114 (1948).

[95] Nucky Johnson's demise had been followed in the *Inquirer* of May 13, 1939, p 3 (shut-down of the resort's gambling operations); of May 17, 1939, p 2 (Johnson's backing of a race track bill); of Dec 28, 1940, p 2 (Johnson's reappointment as City Treasurer); of Jun 12, 1941, p 3 (Johnson's indictment); of July 13, 1941, p 7 (the arrest of Johnson ally Louis Kessel for alleged jury tampering, one day before the start of the Johnson trial); and of Jul 26, 1941, p 1 (Johnson's conviction). Johnson was paroled in August 1945 (*Inquirer*, Aug 11, 1945, p 5), too late to be further involved in efforts to build a track. But Sonny told of strolling down the Boardwalk and enjoying the resort town's amenities with his friend Bill Rogers early in the war (he claimed the army had lost his paperwork) and he would later impress his fiancée by introducing her to the city's gambling dens. He told his children of these exploits, and proudly showed them a watch he said he'd been given by the New York crime boss Lucky Luciano. The author doubted all such stories until one night in 1971 when he witnessed a phone conversation in which Luciano associate Mike McLaney asked Sonny to act as front man for a gambling operation in the Bahamas, with the approval of Premier Lynden Pindling.

[96] After the citizens voted to approve the amendment in 1939, the legislature had to agree on a plan to authorize and regulate the tracks, which took it many months. Once the legislation was enacted, before racing could begin, tracks had to be licensed and built, and before tracks could be licensed, a Racing Commission had to be appointed. After months of delay, the Governor did not appoint the first Racing Commission until March 1940 (*Inquirer*, Sep 12, 1939, p 21; March 19, 1940, p 12; and March 26, 1940, p 11).

[97] Before PTI, Scholler had graduated from Central High School in 1905. The three others included James "Sonny" Fraser, Scholler's frequent golf partner and president of the Atlantic City Country Club (*Inquirer*, Oct 24, 1944, p 21); Glendon Robertson, a Philadelphia hosiery manufacturer (*New York Times*, July 22, 1946, p 26); and Jack Kelly, Philadelphia's largest construction contractor (whose daughter, Grace, was a movie star). It was Kelly who became President of the Horse Racing Association. Fraser and Scholler had played together at a charity fundraiser at the Manufacturer's Club in 1943 and later against teams including Robertson at the Riverton Country Club (*Inquirer*, Aug 27, 1943, p 29; Sept 2, 1943 p 26; Sept 30, 1943, p 28; Nov 8, 1943, p 25).

[98] *New York Times*, Feb 6, 1946, p 39; *Times Recorder* (Zanesville, Ohio), July 6, 1948, p 6. As a Director of Industrial, Charley made speeches about the role of rayon in the tire industry and defended Industrial against charges that quality had declined after the war (*New York Times*, Jan 23, 1947, pp 33, 39, and Aug 17, 1947, p 81, "Fiber Producers Respond to Critics.") Three months after joining the Board, Charley and an anonymous co-seller sold a property in Manhattan for an undisclosed amount (*New York Times*, May 23, 1946, p 37). Ohio's department of revenue reported that in 1946, Charley was paid $90,630 by Industrial Rayon. The 1940 Census had reported the annual earnings of Nancy Lowrie and Ida Johnson as $740, the earnings of Sam Lowrie as $600 (1940 Census, New York, Westchester, Scarsdale, Dist 60-338, Fam 88). The minimum wage of 25 cents an hour was increased

to 40 cents an hour in 1948, but in light of room-and-board benefits they sometimes received, domestic workers weren't covered by minimum wage laws until 1974. Of course, Charley's earnings were not the highest in Ohio. Industrial's President, Hiram S. Ravitz, was paid $180,890 in 1946, and the Kroger Company's Harry W. Bracy was paid $380,733. As far back as 1937, a similar list of the nation's highest paid executives was topped by Louis B. Mayer at $1,296,503, more than two thousand times Sam Lowrie's pay *(New York Times,* Apr 8, 1939, p 7).

[99] *New York Times,* Feb 28, 1944, p 21, and *Inquirer,* Feb 28, 1944, p 16. See also *Inquirer,* Aug 17, 1945, p 24. As work proceeded on construction of their new race track in Atlantic City, former Senator George Smathers charged at a meeting of the Racing Commission that Fraser, Robertson and Scholler were unfit to run a track because they'd allowed illegal slot machine gambling at the Atlantic City Country Club, but Fraser shot back that slot machines were in country clubs all across the state (*Inquirer,* Oct 4, 1945, p 11 and Oct 6, 1945, p 22). The flap did not prevent plans going forward. By opening day on July 22, 1946, the $3.5 million dollar track had 85 investors, including Frank Sinatra, Bob Hope, Harry James, Sammy Kaye, Xavier Cougat and Charley, who got to know both Hope (whom he described as a wonderful, friendly man) and Sinatra (whom he described as a self-absorbed, condescending jerk.)

[100] 5901 Atlantic Avenue, Ventnor, N.J.

[101] We've been unable to find a contemporaneous record attesting to any such appearance. But Charley's daughter in law, Barbara Hickey Carvin, normally the guardian of truth in the face of efforts at exaggeration, tells of an evening in the 1960's when she and her husband, Joe, hailed a cab after leaving Sardi's restaurant. A cab pulled up to let a passenger out; it was Bob Hope, about to enter Sardi's just as she and her husband left. Barbara says that Joe said to Hope, "You don't know me, but my name's Joe Carvin, and I believe you knew my father." "Your Charley Carvin's son?" asked Hope, and when Joe confirmed that he was, Hope said, "Charley Carvin was the funniest act I ever had to follow."

[102] Charley made the story of the drive to Florida in Nancy's Cadillac a very funny one, and told it often. When he interviewed Nancy on tape in 1962, she confirmed the story (see Appendix 6).

[103] After his release from a military hospital in 1944, Sonny (Charley Jr.) had gone into business with a friend, Hank Jacoby, selling rayon and nylon stockings in Chicago. Sonny had then gone into business with Burt Bordow and his father, Abraham Bordow, forming "Borvin" Company, "selling remnants" in Chicago and "doing a little fabric converting as well." They soon moved into the New York market, "specializing in converting linings fabrics" (*Modern Textiles,* May 1963).

[104] The engagement of Charley Carvin Jr. to Julia Logan was announced on May 12, 1946 (*New York Times,* May 12, 1946, p 41). Julie would later recall being swept off her feet, not only by Sonny's attentions, but by his savoir-faire: at a time when rayon and nylon were rationed and all but impossible to find, Sonny was able to get all the hosiery a woman could desire.

[105] Sonny and Julia Logan were married in Santa Monica on August 4th 1946 by a Presbyterian minister, Joseph Vance. In attendance were Charley's sister Florence; his sister Sadie Gekler (and her husband Harry); their son Carvin Gekler (and his wife Val), and their daughter Kaye Gekler Bergdahl (and her husband Lenny); Charley's sister-in-law, Elsie Preuss, and her son, Joseph James Carvin III (and his wife Margaret) and Elsie's daughter, Elsie Carvin Keller, and Sonny's cousin Florence Littlefield (and her husband Bob). Also attending were relatives of the bride and various friends, including the actor, Roscoe Karnes, and Sonny's recent business partner in Chicago, Hank Jacoby. No Murphys were in attendance. But eight years later, when a misunderstanding led to the baptism of Julie's children in the Catholic Church, Julie was surprised to receive a flurry of wedding presents, belated sent by various Murphys in recognition of her marriage. (Bride's bridebook, private collection of the author, and recollections of the bride as orally conveyed to the author.)

[106] *The New Yorker* Magazine, Nov 9, 1946, p 93, and Dec 7, 1946, p 77.

[107] The letter was addressed to Stella Marie in Hollywood, Fla (Appendix 5, Ltr 12).

[108] *Ibid.* Also in Florida with Stella Marie at the time were Charley's sister Florence Young and Stella Marie's cousin Marie Irene (Greenfield) McShane.

[109] Julie later remembered sitting on the beach, telling the other ladies how she was feeling, when Florence asked her if she didn't yet realize that she was pregnant. Julie doubted it, but Marie agreed with Florence; they insisted that Julie visit Marie's husband James, a doctor practicing in Miami. Dr. McShane confirmed the pregnancy.

[110] Their business was the Borvin Corporation.

[111] 32 Claremont Road, Scarsdale, NY.

[112] Down Syndrome and Trisomy 21 are the modern terms for the condition first described medically in 1866 by Dr. John Down. In his paper, "Observations on an Ethnic Classification of Idiots," Down named it Mongolian Idiocy in the belief that it represented the reappearance of ancient Mongolian factors in the bloodline.

[113] Julie's account of the trip to St. Rita's, as told to the author.

[114] *New York Times*, March 3, 1948, p 39.

[115] The new company was Sonny's firm, the old Borvin Co., renamed as Charles W. Carvin & Co. Pondel Fabrics, Inc., of Pawtucket, Rhode Island, a converter of rayon fabrics, had offices at 450 Seventh Avenue in New York. For a while, at least, the merged company continued working out of that office and their existing office at 649 Avenue of the Americas (*New York Times*, April 17, 1948, p 30). The new firm did a "roaring business in linings, dress goods, underwear fabrics and ribbons" (*Modern Textiles*, May 1963).

[116] *Daily News Racket*, June 9, 1948, private collection of the author.

[117] The company was joined by Edwin Lord, William Schwab and print designer Harvey Seltzer (*New York Times*, June 30, 1948, p 42; July 5, 1949, p 36; and Oct 23, 1949, p 83). *Modern Textiles*' May 1963 issue reported that it was soon the largest company in the converting business.

[118] *New York Times*, May 17, 1950, p 38 and Nov 2, 1950, p 36.

[119] *New York Times*, May 4, 1950, p 54, June 22, 1950, p 41, and Sept 27, 1950, p 63.

[120] *New York Times*, June 21, 1950, p 45 and Nov 7, 1950, p 55. (At the latter event, Charley was joined on the podium by FDR Jr. and Harry Reimer, editor of the *Daily News Record*.)

[121] Sonny and Julie's own 1949 Christmas card was sent "From Charley, Julie and David." The birth of grandson Joseph William in July 1950, was announced in a local newspaper as the birth of Sonny and Julie's second child. (Original news clipping in collection of the author; paper and date unknown.)

[122] Deering Milliken placed an ad for Milium in *Life Magazine*, Aug 21, 1950.

[123] *New York Times*, May 5, 1950, p 36; <u>Deering, Milliken & Co. v. Temp-Resisto Corporation</u>, 160 F. Supp. 463 (S.D.N.Y., 1958).

[124] With increased volume and productivity, the wholesale price of rayon yarn had dropped from six dollars a pound in 1920 to about 53 cents by 1940; then, by 1950, inflationary pressure from the war had started to push prices back up again; it had risen to 78 cents by 1950 (Spencer Love, "Planning Textiles Production for War," Feb 27, 1951, Publication No. L51-113, Industrial College of the Armed Forces, Washington, D.C., pp 1706-1707; National Bureau of Economic Research, Wholesale Price of Rayon Yarn for New York, NY [M04130US35620M292NNBR], retrieved from FRED, Federal Reserve Bank of St. Louis; https://fred.stlouisfed.org/series/M04130US35620M292NNBR, January 25, 2022). Meanwhile, the company's prints were not limited to synthetics. An article on print fashions in the *New York Times* would soon opine that "One house, Carvin, has developed modern-artist designs to a refined degree in soft, lightweight cottons which are refreshingly different" (*New York Times*, March 3, 1951, p 16).

[125] Optimism for the man-made synthetics was evident everywhere. In his speech to the war college, Spencer Love had said, "The picture of the future is more and more man-made yarns. It is the answer to the ravages of the weather, to the uncertainties of agriculture. Don't worry about agriculture. There will be plenty of other things the farmers can do ... I believe a suitable fiber will eventually be developed that will even take the place of cotton" (Love, *supra*, p 1714). Charley and Stella Marie's

younger children were in college, Stel doing secretarial work for Charley during the summer, typing his letters to her mother and sending racetrack tickets to her, while he played golf at Westchester and Winged Foot. (See Appendix 5, Ltr 9, dated Aug 8, 1949.)

[126] The Defense Production Act of 1950. "On 9 September 1950, Executive Order 10161 created the Economic Stabilization Agency (ESA) and Wage Stabilization Board (WSB). The order also allowed for a director of price stabilization under the aegis of the ESA. General Order Number 2 of the ESA formally established the Office of Price Stabilization on 24 January 1951, with Michael DiSalle, mayor of Toledo, as its administrator." ("Office of Price Stabilization" at Encyclopedia.com; Executive Order 10161, Section 401(a), accessed at https://www.trumanlibrary.gov/library/executive-orders/10161/executive-order-10161). ESA General Order 2 (16 Fed. Reg. 738) established the Office of Price Stability.

[127] Love, *supra*, p 1711.

[128] *New York Times*, Nov 10, 1950, p 56. The contract's 1950 value of $630,000 would be equivalent to 7.3 million 2022 dollars. The author's unverified sixty-year-old recollection is that the rayon twill was to go into the linings of army uniforms.

[129] For Charley's appointment to the industry committee, see *New York Times*, Dec 14, 1950, p 58. His dinner with the President at Love's was not publicly reported but was orally described to the author by Charley's daughter-in-law, whose own 1948 visit to the Loves in Palm Beach was also mentioned in a letter to her parents (Julia Carvin to Will and Corinne Logan, June 10, 1960, private collection of the author). Charley's visit to Love and his meeting with Truman were also mentioned, with the usual humorous twist, in Charley's 1950 Christmas card: Charley was a member of the Republican Union League in New York. In the 1950 card, he drew his son Joe saying, "Since the Ole Boy had dinner with Truman at Love's, he won't go in the Union League." (See Carvin, Oh Mother, That Man's Here Again!!, *supra*.) Spencer Love had served as director of the Textile, Clothing and Leather Bureau with the agency that had been called the War Production Board in World War II.

[130] "This stopgap measure proved unpopular and unwieldy, and, in many cases, OPS was forced to increase prices. It was not until April 1951 that OPS issued a long-range price control strategy. However, that plan also failed to gather popular support. OPS operations were hampered throughout its existence by the continuous debate over the appropriate level of mobilization and governmental economic control required for an undeclared war." ("Office of Price Stabilization," at Encyclopedia.com.) In late February 1951, Charley spoke for the OPS at a meeting in Portland, Maine and addressed the International Association of Garment Manufacturers in New York *(Portland Press Herald*, Feb 21, 1951, p 18; *New York Times,* Feb 27, 1951, p 45). Even as he did so, Love himself was in the capital addressing the Industrial College of the Armed Forces, sharing his insights from the prior war. Love's comments to the Industrial College could have described Charley's current job as well: "I should say that 80% of our time at WPB was spent struggling with the office of Civilian Requirements and the OPA, and about 20 percent was spent in servicing the armed services ... The trouble was in finding adequate ways to get people to produce for the civilian economy what we wanted them to make and not cut across other programs." When Love's February address to the Industrial College was printed in April 1951, it was stamped "Restricted." (Love, *supra*.)

[131] Truman's Executive Order 10161, creating the Economic Stabilization Agency, was all about meeting the needs of the military; it said nothing of controlling prices. Pearson's column, *The Merry-Go-Round,* was the most widely syndicated column in America. His piece on Charley's speech was called "Why Prices Remain High" and appeared nationally in such papers as the *Alabama Journal* (Montgomery, Ala) April 2, 1951, p 4, and (of the same date), the Detroit *Free Press* (p 6); the Troy, NY *Record* (p 6); the Santa Rosa, CA *Press Democrat* (p 4); the Winona, MN *Daily News* (p 6); the York, PA *Gazette* (p 16); the Marshall, TX *News Messenger* (p 4); the Tampa, Fl *Tribune* (p 6); the Honolulu *Star Bulletin* (p 8) and hundreds of other papers across the country.

[132] See "Drew Pearson (journalist)" at Wikipedia.org, and sources cited therein.

[133] *New York Times*, April 12, 1951, p 61.

[134] *New York Times,* April 10, 1951, p 24.

[135] Charley had drawn Sonny "always broke" in his 1941 Christmas card. Later in life, Sonny would get asked for his resignation from two big corporate jobs for exceeding his budget; he would be in debt his whole life; he would later tell his own children that his strength was his "big ideas," that "to make money, you have to spend money," and that you should never spend your own money when you can spend someone else's instead." He was always proud of the nickname he eventually earned as a big spender: "Champagne Charley."

[136] Boyo, *supra.*

[137] Charley's 1951 Christmas card pictures Santa carrying a white sack over his shoulder labeled "Orlon," calls Charley Jr. the "Orlon King," and pictures young Joe "on the road" selling Milium. (Carvin, Oh Mother, *supra.*) Orlon was a DuPont trademark for an acrylic fiber that was produced between 1950 and 1990 (Tony Kornheiser, *The Washington Post*, June 13, 1990).

[138] Puritan was the largest maker of women's "half-size" dresses in the country (*Richmond News Leader*, Sept 7, 1951, p 35).

[139] In 1950 and early 1951, Puritan's "Forever Young" fashions had featured wool, cotton and rayon fabrics marketed with an emphasis on French designs by Paris designers like Alwynn, Pierre Balmain, Jacques Fath, Robert Piguet, and Jean Desses. (See, for example, the *Akron Beacon Journal*, Dec 20, 1950, p 16; the *Atlanta Constitution*, Dec 20, 1950, p 20; the *Baltimore Sun*, Dec 21, 1950, p 2; the *Kansas City Times*, Dec 27, 1950, p 11; the *Miami News*, Dec 27, 1950, p 19; the *Wilkes-Barre Times Leader*, Sept 3, 1951, p 5.) DuPont, meanwhile, had started producing Orlon in 1950, and a smattering of ads for Orlon clothing were appearing by 1951 (*Springfield Reporter*, March 14, 1951, p 34; Longbranch, N.J. *Daily Record*, Oct 2, 1951, p 2). But beginning in September 1951, the relationship between Puritan, Swanson and Sonny's Orlon fabrics was becoming clear. Almost simultaneously, ads for Puritan's *Forever Young* line began emphasizing crepe fabrics (*Los Angeles Times*, Sept 4, 1951, p 26) and including endorsements by Swanson (*Sacramento Bee*, Sept 13, 1951, p 14).

[140] Swanson's hiring as a Puritan Vice President and designer for its *Forever Young* label was announced to the Boston Press Club in September (*Boston Globe*, Sept 30, 1951, p 15). She appeared in Philadelphia for the label in November (*Inquirer*, Nov 16, 1951, p 37).

[141] *Indianapolis News*, Jan 7, 1952, p 19.

[142] *Greenville Piedmont*, Jan 14, 1952, p 1.

[143] 2010 author interview with Charley's son Joe, a salesman with the company in 1952.

[144] *NY Daily News,* Feb 24, 1952, Brooklyn Section, p 21B. The announcement appeared under the heading *Orlon and Nylon News.*

[145] *New York Times*, March 21, 1952, p 33.

[146] *New York Times*, May 4, 1952, Business Section p F7. Spencer Love, founder of Burlington Mills, was less optimistic about Milium. After his February 27, 1951 address to the Armed Forces Industrial College, he replied that Burlington's chemists "haven't been very enthusiastic about it," their main objection being its lack of porosity, making it (in his opinion) unsuitable as a substitute for wool (Love, *supra*, p 1717).

[147] The banquet recognized four industry men, including Spencer Love of Burlington, for outstanding service in civic and philanthropic endeavors (*New York Times*, Sept 25, 1952, p 47).

[148] Boyo, *supra.*

[149] Boyo, *supra.*

[150] Deering, Milliken & Co. v. Temp-Resisto Corporation, 160 F. Supp. 463 (S.D.N.Y., 1958). The suit was brought on March 10, 1953. In fact, although a special master and the lower court found in favor of Milliken and the Carvin Corporation, the Second Circuit Court of appeals ultimately reversed that decision, finding that what success Milium had enjoyed was not due to new science or technology (and so patentable) but rather, due to "intensive advertising campaigns." The Appeals Court expressly declined to rule on the conflicting evidence about whether those advertising claims had merit. (Deering, Milliken & Co v. Temp-resisto etc, 274 F. 2d 626 (2d Cir. 1960).)

[151] Young Stella Marie (1929-1994) had attended Edgewood Park School in Briarcliff Manor and Marymount Academy in Tarrytown NY. She was betrothed to Francis Arthur Carmody, a graduate of Scarsdale High School, in November 1952 *(New York Times,* Nov 30, 1952, p 101) and that year's Christmas card portrayed the elder Stella Marie on the phone (as usual), telling someone, "Of course a big wedding – *everybody*. Only have one daughter. I'm giving Charley a brand-new checkbook for Christmas and he'll come around." Stella (a small woman) and big Frank – who was 6' 4" and weighed 270 pounds – were married on May 2, 1953 in a ceremony that included the saying of a Roman Catholic mass by Father Benno Brink at the Immaculate Heart of Mary; Charley paid for a gala reception at the Westchester Country Club (*New York Times*, May 3, 1953, p 113). The armistice ending the Korean War was signed shortly thereafter (on July 27, 1953).

[152] Charley was master of ceremonies at a meeting of the Textile Veterans Association at the Roosevelt Hotel; the guest of honor at the Plaza Hotel for a dinner hosted by the rayon division of the Federation of Jewish Philanthropies; appointed to a committee of the Textile Distributors Institute to oppose contractual disclaimers of responsibility by suppliers for their products; and toastmaster at the annual meeting of the PTI Alumni Association at the Warwick Hotel (*New York Times*, Oct 1, 1953, p 46; Nov 12, 1953, p 28; Nov 16, 1953, p 33; and Nov 29, 1953, p 114).

[153] As recalled by Charley's son, Joseph Edward, in a conversation with the author.

[154] The reception was at the exclusive Westchester Country Club. The unshaven man in the Christmas card was standing outside a church, passing a collection plate among departing parishioners. Though he drew his own cartoon, Charley's drawing was clearly based on one drawn by Claude Smith that had appeared in *The New Yorker* of April 12, 1952.

[155] Excerpted from a letter from Stella Marie Carmody to Charles Carvin, Jan 5, 1954, return address 320 Maine Ave, Syracuse, New York.

[156] "Caprolan's Tower on 42 Street," *Modern Textiles*, May 1963. That same year, Sonny started work selling Acrilan fiber for Chemstrand Corporation *(ibid.),* and Joe went to work for Tennessee Eastman.

[157] Charley's 1954 focus included (1) continuing to run Charles W. Carvin Corporation; (2) the marriage, on May 23, 1954, of their son Joe to Barbara Hickey at the Immaculate Heart of Mary, with another reception at the Westchester Country Club (*New York Times*, May 23, 1954, p 102); (3) the purchase of 200 feet of land stretching from the Atlantic Ocean to Florida's intracoastal waterway straddling Highway A-1A in Hillsboro Beach, Florida, where Charley began the development of the Palm Hill Ocean Club, including a club house, inland-waterway dock, swimming pool and twenty-six two- and three-bedroom single-story homes; a description of the property ran in the *Fort Lauderdale Daily News*, Feb 23, 1957, p 3-C, announcing that a few of the units were left and using the word "exclusive" three times; Charley himself bought one of the four ocean-front homes on the property; (4) service as a featured speaker at a meeting of the National Association of Shirt, Pajamas and Sportswear Manufacturers (*New York Times*, March 21, 1954, p 171); (5) the November sale of his home at 7 Chesterfield Road in Scarsdale (*Port Chester Daily Item*, Nov 5, 1955, p 13; *New York Times*, Sept 23, 1954, p 53); and (6) the heart attack.

[158] *New York Times*, Sept 23, 1954, p 53; Boyo, *supra*.

[159] Charley gave his first boat the name "Night Hawk," the same as the JN-4 he'd flown into the tree in Texas during WWI. In it, he used to take a group of priests up to Somers Point, where they watched the people at the Sunshine Park nudist colony while drinking flasks of whiskey. He called his second boat "The Two Stels," and after daughter Stella Marie named her own daughter Stella Marie, he named his third boat "The Three Stels." In the early 1950's, he took his grandchildren fishing in the Bay, and on occasion, drove them down to Ocean City, where a flotilla of old rum-runner boats from Prohibition days, built with V-12 Liberty aircraft engines because of their speed, were advertised as the fastest boats in the world.

[160] Based in part on personal recollections. The dinner in honor of Charley was tendered by the Man-Made Fibres and Fabrics Division of the National Conference of Christians and Jews on May 18, 1955. Over 750 attendees filled seventy-five tables plus a dais seating twenty-two more. The guests included

three Millikens from Deering, Milliken Co (including Roger Milliken on the dais); Frank Leslie of Burlington Mills, also on the dais; and Ely Callaway, later the noted golf equipment manufacturer, then also of Burlington. Half tables were taken by Fairchild Publications (publisher of *Women's Wear Daily* and the *Daily News Record*) and Duplan Silk (makers of rayon since 1911). Whole tables were reserved by Owens-Corning Fiber Glass and the Celanese Corporation of America. (A program and seating chart for the event are in the private collection of the author.)

[161] Charley's 1952 card announced the (May 26) birth of a granddaughter, Corinne Carvin, to Charley and Julie. Joe and Barbara's first son, Joseph Edward Carvin Jr. (born February 15, 1955) and Frank and Stel's first son, Patrick Carmody (born November 12, 1955) were introduced in the 1955 card.

[162] *Inquirer,* June 10, 1957, p 10.

[163] Charley stepped down as CEO of Charles W. Carvin Corporation in 1959, succeeded by Burt Bordow; Charley became the Company's Chairman. *Daily News Record*, March 21, 1974, p 5. On May 10, 1961, he made a final payment to his three children from his trust fund, which had paid out half a million dollars (Letter from Charley to "Stel, Charley and Joe" dated May 10, 1961, in possession of the author.)

[164] "We have been compelled to create a permanent armaments industry of vast proportions ... This conjunction of an immense military establishment and a large arms industry is new in the American experience ... Yet we must not fail to comprehend its grave implications ... In the councils of government, we must guard against the acquisition of unwarranted influence, whether sought or unsought, by the military-industrial complex. The potential for the disastrous rise of misplaced power exists and will persist." (Excerpted from televised comments of Dwight Eisenhower from the Oval Office, Jan 17, 1961, Box 38, Speech Series, Papers of Dwight D. Eisenhower as President, 1953-61, Eisenhower Library; National Archives and Records Administration.)

[165] According to the guest list for the November 2, 1962 dinner, the thirty-six guests included: from the Liberty Bowl itself, its Director, A. F. "Bud" Dudley; from the College Football Hall of Fame, Director (and former head coach at Penn and at Rutgers) Harvey Harman; from the Naval Academy, Superintendent of the Academy Rear Admiral Charles C. Kirkpatrick, Commandant of Midshipmen Charles S. Minter Jr, Board of Control member Walter Welham, and Director of Athletics William Busik; from the 4th Naval District, Rear-Admiral Robert W. Cavenagh and Chaplain R. W. Ricker; from the Naval Academy Alumni Association, President of its Philadelphia Chapter Capt. Frederick J. Ilsemann; from Notre Dame University, trustee Joseph M. Byrne, Jr. , Director of Athletics Edward W. Krause, Director of Public Relations J. Arthur Haley, Business Manager of Athletics Herbert E. Jones, and Director of Ticket Sales Robert Cahill; from the Philadelphia Notre Dame Club, President Barton B. Johnson; from the Notre Dame Foundation, Director Rev. John E. Walsh; from the University of Pennsylvania, Head of the Department of Physical Education George A. Munger, Vice President of Business Affairs Rev. Jerome J. Wilson, and former line coach Ray Crowther; from the Eastern College Athletic Conference, Dr. Ellwood A. Geiges; from the Middle Atlantic College Conference Commissioner Leo Weinroth; from the City of Philadelphia, Commissioner of Recreation Robert W. Crawford; from the President's Philadelphia Committee, Paul B. Henkels and John H. Neeson Jr; from the Philadelphia Inquirer, sports editor Fred Byrod; sportscaster and former Eagles star Bosh Pritchard; sportscaster Jack Whitaker; ex All American football players Ed McGinley and Ed Morrison; and ex-heavyweight prize-fighting champion Gene "Long Count" Tunney. (At the game itself, played December 15, Oregon State beat Villanova 6-0.)

[166] "Allied's Bold Move West: Caprolan's Tower on 42 Street," *Modern Textiles*, May 1963; *Daily News Record*, Oct 19, 1964, p 50 and Dec 22, 1965, p 4.

[167] *Evening Bulletin*, May 4, 1964, Sports Section, p 31. Other members of the Society mentioned in the article were Jack Kelly's brother-in-law, Don Levine, Dutch Schroedel, vice president of the Turner Construction Company, and federal Judge J. Cullen Ganey. Myron Cohen was a Jewish comedian who, like Charley, had started as a salesman – showing samples in the garment district, he may even

have sold some Carvinet. Though he spoke perfect English, he exceled, like Charley, at coloring his stories with ethnic accents ("Myron Cohen," Wikipedia.org).

[168] Charley had several commemorative plaques attesting to holes-in-one; when asked how many he'd had, he said he wasn't sure, but it's been said there were six. Though seldom out and about, our grandmother loved to visit the racetrack and often joined us for fishing trips on the boat "The Three Stels."

[169] Charley's grandson Pat Carmody's hilarious rendition of the story can be seen at https://www.youtube.com/watch? v=jwwyv_jj4lA.

[170] *Daily News Record*, March 21, 1974, p 5.

[171] Sonny married Julia Logan on August 4, 1946 (*LA Times*, Aug 2, 1946, p 20), and had six children: Charles Walter III ("Chickie") (1947-1996); David Anthony (1948-); Joseph William (1950-); Corinne (1952-2016); Christopher Charles (1956-2017); and James Dominick (1958-). Joe married Barbara Hickey on May 22, 1954 (*New York Times*, May 23, 1954, p 102), and had three children, Joseph Edward (1955-), Michael Anthony (1956-) and Lisa Ann (1958-). Stella Marie (1929-1994) married Francis Carmody on May 3, 1953 (*New York Times*, May 3, 1953, p 113) and had Patrick Charles (1955-), Stella Marie (1956-) and Michael Francis (1959-).

[172] Approaching the front gate of the Atlantic City Racetrack with his grandfather at age 15, the author was very concerned about all the signage warning patrons that one had to be 21 to enter. But at the last minute, Charley pulled off to a side-entrance, where a guard greeted Charley and the author from a distance. "Good afternoon, Mr. Carvin – I see you've brought a fine young lad with you today. Your grandson?" Admittance was never in doubt. Charley and Stella brought flasks of cocktails ("sidecars") to the racetrack with them and taught the author the importance of shaking them with plenty of ice.

[173] Personal recollections of the author. Sonny had named his Hialeah, Florida seatbelt company "Charley Company" after himself.

[174] Sonny even put Frank Carmody on his payroll so that Stel and her children could have health insurance.

[175] All information personally known to the author.

[176] At least part of the reason for Nancy and Ida's loyalty was that Charley had helped them purchase homes in White Plains, to have something to leave to their own families. As the working relationship evolved, Charley began telling stories about how old Nancy was. Amidst speculation that she may once have been a slave, Nancy denied it, while claiming not to know exactly how old she was. When asked, she'd say, "Oh, now, I don't rightly know, but I must be about eighty, I reckon."

"Nancy, you know that can't be right," Charley would say. "You've been saying you were eighty for as long as I've known you, and that's been twenty-five years now."

"Well, Mr. Carvin, I really don't know. All I know is, I can still work. I can still cook. I never been too old to work, have I?"

[177] *New York Times*, March 22, 1974, p 41; *Women's Wear Daily*, March 21, 1974; *Daily News Record*, March 21, 1974, p 5.

15. Then and Now

We can't know what will happen when a butterfly flaps its wings, but one thing seems certain: generations must pass before the consequences of some decisions can be realized. To appreciate what happened when Glenn Curtiss's JN-4s took to the sky, it helps to know something about NASA and SpaceX. To understand the impact of artificial silk, it helps to know something of the miles of plastic waste that float across the world's oceans today. Decisions made by the Philadelphians continue to play out in the world.

In 1955, when Charley was honored by the Conference of Christians and Jews, two of his grandchildren listened to him delight an audience for the first time. After he'd finished, strangers in black ties and silk dresses came up to my older brother David and me.

"So you're Charley's grandsons. Quite some man, your grandfather. We bet you're proud of him."

We'd seen the way he'd made everyone laugh, the praise heaped on him, the tears in his eyes at the ovation. We were very proud.

But we thought, at the time, that we were his first two grandchildren. We didn't know, then, that our older brother had been sent away, or that our family had been trying to forget him since before we were born.

A few months after the event at the Waldorf, Mom called us together for a serious announcement.

"I've got something to tell you boys. So come here and listen; it's very important."

We exchanged curious glances.

"I'm not sure how to say it, so I'll just tell you. You boys will be getting a new brother this Christmas."

"Are you going to have a baby?"

"No, I'm not having a baby. Your brother is – well, let's just say he's –"

"Adopted?"

"No. He's not adopted. He's …"

When Mom finally found the right words, she told us we had a brother, Chickie, and that he was already eight years old – older, that is, than we were.

Had we failed to notice him in the kitchen? Sleeping in our room, taking baths with us?

He'd been away at school, Mom explained. And now, he was coming home. There'd be time enough to explain the details later, but we should know that things would play out the way God had always known they would.

"Just get ready to welcome him," Mom said. "To make him feel at home."

Make an older brother feel at home? Chickie was an oddity before we'd ever laid eyes on him, different from the moment we first heard of him. Where would he sleep? What sort of games did he like to play? Would he be going to school with us? As the day of Chickie's arrival approached, the questions wouldn't leave us alone.

And then the day arrived. As he discovered a home he'd never seen, our own bewilderment turned to delight. Our new brother was better than any Christmas present. Being smaller than we were, he seemed younger than us. Despite being thirteen months older than David, he was completely cooperative, willing to play whatever we wanted to play, doing whatever we told him to do. The freedom that gave me, in all my dealings with him, was nothing like anything I'd ever experienced before.

But his face, meanwhile, looked a little older than ours. He stood like a tree with roots in the ground to keep the wind from knocking him over, his gait labored and slow: a foot returning to earth was like an anchor dropping on high seas. We imitated his lumbering walk, plodding around the house behind him as if following Godzilla. We showed him off to our neighborhood friends, designating him "it" in games of tag, tempting fate by how close we dared come to him. Adults might have thought our mimicry unkind, but as far as we could tell, he seemed to enjoy our attention, to enjoy showing off, and that was easy for him because he could do things we could not, like put an ankle behind his head with ease. He could extend a hand (behind his back) all the way up to his neck. When he sat "Indian style," his ankles easily went on top of his knees. When we tried and failed to do such things, he smiled all the more.

But as wonderful as Chickie was, there were obviously things wrong with him. The most obvious were his crossed eyes, which revealed nothing of how he felt about things. Aimed inward toward his nose, they formed a barrier, less "windows into his thoughts" than revolving doors that had jammed. With no idea what the world looked like from behind them, we began to cross our own eyes in an effort to see what he saw. But when we crossed our eyes in the mirror, to see what we'd look like if we were him, we couldn't see ourselves. As we shared our mimicry, laughing at each other, we got no similar feedback from him. Could he tell us apart? Could he tell that we were imitating him? Mom told us that if we kept on with it, our eyes might lock up and stay crossed forever like his, but that didn't stop us.

His lips were cracked and dry. When he opened his mouth, saliva clung to the corners. There was also something wrong with his speech – a dull, wet frog-like rasp, as if a cough drop had caught in his throat, making it flap at all the wrong times. His tongue moved sluggishly. His words came out muddied, his *k*'s guttural like *g*'s, his *t*'s thick and dull like *d*'s or *th*'s. We sometimes imitated the way he tried to talk.

406

Chickie's wrongness was different than ours. We could forget to clean our room, we could be mean to each other, we couldn't run as fast as some of our friends. But Chickie wasn't just slow. Adults called him severely retarded. A "mongoloid."

God's will? An accident of birth? Nothing in our world really explained why Chickie was the way he was.

He was sent back to "school" when the holidays were over, but he returned for another visit that Easter, and again the following summer. There would soon be six of us, and for many years, though he was affected more severely than many people with Trisomy 21, Chickie remained a beloved member of the family. This is not to say that the experience was all a blessing. When Chickie was a teenager, he protested, fighting back when it was time for him to return to the home for developmentally challenged boys run by the Little Brothers of the Good Shepherd. (It was not until after Chickie died that we read of the pervasive sexual abuse there.[1]) Chickie always smiled when he came home and greeted us, and he never fought against anything else but returning to Good Shepherd Manor.

The grandfather who told us stories of the strong, crafty, kind-hearted Bobolink was himself strong, crafty, and kind-hearted in our eyes, and I never imagined that he'd played a role in sending Chickie away. There was a great deal more we didn't know about the Philadelphians when we were children.[2] At the height of the McCarthy era (the year the words "under God" were added to the pledge of allegiance) my teacher at Mrs. David's nursery school explained the difference between Russian communism and American democracy.

"Russia," she said, "is run by dictators, so it is full of lies and propaganda. They show their schoolchildren movies of lynchings and sit-ins in America, claiming it represents who we really are. They say our whole country is divided by racism, with colored people having nothing and whites having everything. With no way to know any better, Russian children accept such lies. We should give thanks to God that we live in a country where our government only tells us what's true."

The simple truth – that America was a land of liberty, equality and truth, was easy for a child to understand.

While our parents left to play golf or go to the racetrack, we were left in the care of the elderly Ida Johnson and Nancy Lowrie. We watched them cook, do laundry, and change bedsheets. It had especially fallen to Nancy (the older of the two) to care for us. She changed our diapers, nursed us, patted our backs, rocked us on her knees, sang us to sleep with spirituals. As we grew older, she taught us to sing *He's Got the Whole World In His Hands* and tickled our necks with cold fingers. "Good meat! Mmnn, mmnn, mmnn, what good meat!" We'd squeal and try to get away, but she was relentless. "I'm going to eat you up! Let me in there! Let me get more of that good meat!"

We loved going to our grandparents' house on the Jersey Shore. Four stories tall. Twenty-five rooms. Two separate stairways. One was a grand piece of architecture visible from the front entrance, with wide stone steps, a fancy banister, and a porcelain Chinese foo dog on the landing. Huge paintings of Chinese ancestors stood guard, protecting the bedrooms at the top of the stairs. (According to Chinese tradition, the leonine foo dog, with his ivory teeth, guarded the house against enemies; he only let us ascend because we were family.)

The house was divided between public rooms, in which to entertain company, family living quarters (the bedrooms on the second floor) and a set of hidden stairways, passages and utility rooms through which servants could move, invisible to the public eye.[3] The servants' staircase, a narrow, wooden one hidden behind a plain white closet door led from the basement to the kitchen hallway, and from there, up to another closet door near the bedrooms upstairs, and finally, from behind a third closet door, up to the four plain bedrooms among the attics on the topmost floor. Its wooden steps were narrow and steep.

At its bottom, in the basement, underclothes dripped from a clothesline onto a beveled floor with a drain. In the big tub sink next to the drain, Nancy washed the sand out of our bathing suits after a morning at the beach.

Our plain wooden bedrooms on the fourth floor were right next to Ida's and hers. Neither of the two elderly ladies ever addressed a harsh word to us. As a child, I always felt their love for me. But as I grew older, I realized I knew nothing about them.

On Christmas Day, 1962, with a new tape recorder and microphone he'd received that morning, with all twelve of his grandchildren there to hear, our grandfather, Charley, interviewed Nancy about her past. She'd grown up on a cotton plantation in Georgia. Since her parents were the first slaves the planter ever owned, she'd grown up in the big house. She'd picked cotton on the plantation. ("I could pick two hundred pound of cotton... I picked two hundred, I made fifty cents.")[4]

Four years later, when I was sixteen, I asked Nancy about her past. She remembered jumping from the barn window into wagons full of cotton. She remembered standing barefoot on the dining table, using a palm frond to shoo flies away as the "white folks" ate their Sunday dinner. When I asked her how old she was, she said she didn't know, but her mother had told her she was born two years after the emancipation. When I asked her how many children she'd had, her answer was astounding:

"Do you mean my *white* children?"

Content to bask in Ida's and Nancy's love, I'd watched James Meredith on television. Medgar Evers. Rocks thrown. Billy clubs wielded. But my grandmother had drawn my picture in his Christmas cards. He had placed me among presidents, world leaders, and celebrities. I was proud to be an American.

Years later, hearing Nancy was ill, I wrote to her. Starting to feel something toward her, I wrote because I wanted to express it to her, though I wasn't sure what I was feeling. That being fifty years ago, I don't recall what I wrote. But I still have the letter she sent me in reply, in which she asked if I remembered that it was she who'd taught me how to spell my name.

Vaguely, I did. Even now I remember sitting next to her in the back seat of a car, waiting for Mom to come out of a store, Nancy taking me through the alphabet, and then the letters of my name, one by one.

The year after Nancy wrote me that letter, in 1973, she died. Many things happened after that, in all our lives. But after the millennium turned, I listened again to the tape-recorded Christmas interview. (I'd transferred the voices from the degrading magnetic tape to bits and bytes on a floppy disk by then.) And as I listened, I heard things I hadn't heard as a child.

Nancy had been born on the Maddux Plantation in Pineville, Georgia, taught in a school built there by Judge Bivens. Her first teacher, Mr. Huffman, and later two others, Mr. King and Mr. Smith, had taught her to read and write. She remembered that before she went to work for our grandparents, she'd worked "night and day" for a Mr. Straus. "Sometime I'd go home at one o'clock, two o'clock, and I was back at six o'clock in the morning there to get breakfast... And I'd have three fires to make, and a heater. And I'd make – I'd have those three fires made – the heater – and those three heaters – and his breakfast ready when he come sittin' at the table, and his table set..."[5]

Brother David and I made a trip to Pineville in search of Nancy's roots. A local history in the public library described a resolution adopted at the Buena Vista courthouse before the Civil War, according to which politicians, teachers and news media had aroused

...a feeling of hatred, which has caused insurrections in the south, where innocent citizens have been murdered in cold blood and their homes destroyed by the torch of the incendiary. A terrible conflict has been started between free and slave labor. A party has been formed in the north declaring that the negro is the social equal of the white man, that the fugitive slave law must be abolished, that they are determined to seize the government and alter its constitution. These black Republicans are planning to destroy the dearest rights and principles guaranteed by the Constitution.

The people of Marion County regard the election of Abraham Lincoln to the presidency as an overt act of hostility upon the part of the North and as a declaration of war upon the rights of the South, and recommend the citizens of Georgia, upon the election of Lincoln being known, to meet immediately in convention to determine the mode and manner of redress.[6]

As a result of the war that ensued, Marion County lost four-fifths of her wealth, including slaves valued at three million dollars. "It was hard for the white people to adjust themselves to the new conditions," said the local history, "for there were many lazy, worthless darkies who refused to work and tried to live by stealing."[7] The KKK arrived in March, 1868.[8] Such was the place in which Nancy had been raised.

In that same local history, I read that in 1873, the state of Georgia had given the county $2,738.60 to be used for public schools, including schools for freedmen's children; one of the teachers had been the J. H. Huffman Nancy remembered.[9] In an old graveyard, David and I found the freedmen's graves all grown over with weeds; none had headstones; few had legible markings. But among the graves in the separate white section, one of the largest, cordoned off from the others, was still legibly identified as the grave of Judge Bivens, with a loving inscription carved in it for posterity.[10]

After that trip to Pineville, another decade passed before another advance of technology – the Internet – made it possible to explore Nancy's life from the comfort of home.

David Neal Maddux, the plantation owner where Nancy was born, had been high sheriff of the county. His overseer, twenty-two-year-old John Benson, had been responsible for eighteen slaves.[11] Nancy had been born on May 13, 1866. Like the other freedmen of her time, her parents had taken the names of their white masters.[12] By 1880, at age 14, Nancy Maddux was listed as a farm laborer herself, unable to read or write.[13] At thirty-four years old, married to one Robert Brooks (a "banjo picker" four years her junior) she'd already given birth to fourteen of his children, of whom only six were still living at the time (1900). Those still alive included fourteen-year-old Ernest (a laborer in a brick yard) and ten-year-old Leon (a day laborer). Nancy and Ernest were able to read and write; Robert and Leon were not.[14]

She'd said in her 1962 interview with Charley Carvin that Robert had never given her a penny, and that she'd eventually asked him to leave the house with the promise she never would ask him for one.[15] The old censuses revealed that Robert didn't leave until Nancy had borne two more of his children. By 1910, she and her children were living with her brother Dennis in Jacksonville, Florida. Within three years, they'd moved out on their own, to a house on Jacksonville's Florida Alley.[16] As late as 1920, Nancy's ninety-three-year-old mother, Sarah – the first slave David N. Maddux had ever owned – was still living with her in Jacksonville.[17]

We loved and admired our grandfather. As a child plucking the strings of our grandmother's golden harp, trying my best to press pedals my feet couldn't reach, I believed the stories told about the great accomplishments of the Philadelphians, the country of freedom for all. But the pride I felt was growing inside me like some unseen cancer, blinding me to see the world as others saw it. In later years, I became obsessed with one question, above all others: had my grandfather urged the abandonment of my brother?

He'd learned tolerance from his grandmother, Mary Sherick. He'd been honored for his philanthropy by the Conference of Christians and Jews. He'd told us stories of kind-hearted Bobolink. Had he counseled the young couple to keep the innocent child? Or, as I grew to suspect, had he urged them to send his namesake away? And if so, did I dare to judge him for it?

In the 1860's, science accepted around the civilized world had divided humanity into three distinct races: the Caucasian, the Ethiopian and the Mongol. That division was accepted nowhere more than at London's Royal Earlswood Asylum for Idiots, overseen by a group known as the Commissioners in Lunacy. Since a number of the asylum's residents seemed to share a Mongolian appearance, its superintendent, Dr. Down, came to call their condition Mongolian Idiocy. And since he knew of no cases arising from injury or contagion, he concluded that the condition was hereditary. He reasoned that a Caucasian infant born with Mongolian features was therefore a throwback to an ancient bloodline. And ironically, Down saw this as evidence that all the peoples of the world were not created as separate species, as some thought, but were all related, all part of a single, unified humanity.[18]

By 1924, when Sonny was whipping himself and calling himself a "bad boy," the science of human biology had not much changed since the 1860's, and eugenics was all the rage. Most states were enacting mandatory sterilization laws to protect the population from "mental defectives." A doctor named Crookshank wrote an extremely popular book, *The Mongol in Our Midst: the Three Faces of Man*, which asserted that the Caucasian, Mongol and Negro races were descended from chimpanzees, orangutans and gorillas respectively. In accordance with that understanding, when a child was born with "Mongolian idiocy," it showed that one of the parents was descended from the yellow race – which is to say, from orangutans.

Even by 1947, when Chickie was born, the state of medical science had not much changed. The world was still ignorant of chromosomes, then. People didn't know what we do now.

But the long-term effects of human science and technology have yet to be fully understood. Steam-powered looms; the cotton gin; the income tax; the typewriter; the linotype machine; the automobile ... Today's wars are fought not with cannon pulled by horse-drawn wagons, but by cruise missiles and nuclear submarines, while our clothes, curtains, bedsheets, carpets, tablecloths, chairs, plates, coffee cups, spoons and toothbrushes are made of plastics, all synthesized by chemists in the laboratory, most of them from crude oil. Polyester, polyvinyl chloride, polypropylene, Mylar, Kevlar, Styrofoam and polystyrene pile high in landfills. They coat the ocean. There were three billion people on earth in 1960; there will soon be nine. The forests have all but disappeared. Yet Americans, we're told, use seven times as much energy from natural resources as the average citizen of India.

America was founded on the principle of liberty, and with the freedom we've been given, we now truly live in a world that we ourselves have made.[19] Looking back, it's easy to judge the mistakes of prior generations. But which of the things we hold dear will our great grandchildren expose as *our* colossal blunders? If the Philadelphians tell us anything, it is that we've all been trying, in one way or another, to make the world what we want it to be, and that, very often, we get it very wrong.

In 1955, Sonny and Julie acknowledged their mistake in sending Chickie away, and for more than four decades, those who knew him benefited from his presence. But let's rewind the clock to 1955, the year they first brought him home. Their reversal left Charley with a problem. For eight years, he'd celebrated the births of his other grandchildren, explicitly calling his second the first, his third the second, and so on, repeating and digging ever deeper into the lie begun by denying the existence of his actual first-born. Now that Chickie was coming home for Christmas, what would he do in his hand-drawn cards? Continue to maintain silence about his namesake? Fess up to the wrong? Acknowledge the eight-year lie he, and Sonny and Julie, had all been telling? Over the years, I'd labored hard to find evidence about where Charley stood, as if my judgment about him would come down to that one thing.

It was years before I looked closely enough to see how he'd handled the dilemma. 1955's card, drawn after the catastrophe with Hollywood star Gloria Swanson, was headlined, "The Stars of Our Tree," and it celebrated each of his grandchildren as a Hollywood star. Names and dates of birth were treated as productions; on the marquees with that year's "stars" were their mothers, credited as "Producers," and their fathers, credited as "Directors." He drew tiny caricatures of each of us, with appropriate captions, personally suited to each of us. And in the center, named only as a "Previous Production" but drawn as a winged cherub blowing a horn, were the critical words:

Producer: Julia Logan Carvin
Director: Charles W. Carvin, Jr.
First Production: 1947.
Most recent but not last: 1952.

After eight years of lying, it would be pointless to turn a Christmas card into a confession, pointless even to draw unnecessary attention to the matter by referring to his namesake by name. But by including the previous production, the date, and the drawing, Charley did make sure that Chickie was included after all, and I can only love him for that.[20]

PREVIOUS PRODUCTIONS
PRODUCER *Julie Logan Carvin*
DIRECTOR *Charles W. Carvin Jr*
FIRST PRODUCTION – 1942
MORE RECENT BUT NOT LAST – 1952

Notes on Chapter 15, Then and Now

[1] After a brief year or two at St. Rita's Home in upstate New York, Chickie was enrolled at St. Coletta's School in Hanover, Massachusetts. Between 1964 and 1968 (i.e., once he turned sixteen) Chickie was a resident at Good Shepherd Manor in Wakefield, Ohio, a home for disabled young men run by a small order of Catholic brothers known as the Little Brothers of the Good Shepherd. In 1985, an investigation of sexual abuse initiated by several state agencies and the local Sheriff's department resulted in the indictment of two of the brothers, one of whom was sentenced to a year in prison for sexual battery on a resident (Sylvia Brooks, "Suit Says Man Got AIDS Virus from Religious Group," *Columbus Dispatch*, May 22, 1993, accessed at https://www.bishop-accountability.org/news3/1993_05_22_Brooks_SuitSays_Robert_Hayden_ETC_1.htm.) In 1993, a lawsuit was brought by the family of a man who entered the home in 1967, alleging widespread sexual abuse of residents by the brothers. ("Faith, Death and Betrayal," *U.S. News and World Report*, March 11, 1996; "Family Sues Church in Son's AIDS Death; Religious Order Denies Sodomizing Retarded Man," Associated Press, accessed at http://www.spokesman.com/ stories/1996/mar/03/family-sues-church-in-sons-aids-death-religious/). In 1968, Sonny and Julie moved Chickie to Florida, where he became a resident at the Sunland Training Center in Miami. Sunland was soon beset with its own sex abuse scandal, beginning with the headline,

"Director of Sunland, Six Others, Suspended In Torture Scandal," and an article stating that "retarded young male inmates were subjected to physical torture and homosexual attacks as part of a training program." (*Miami Herald*, Jan 19, 1968, p 3, and April 1, 1972, p 1-2A; *Miami News*, April 4, 1972, p 5A.) The scandal included residents being compelled to wear women's underwear, to masturbate in front of others, and to eat bars of soap; after an initial investigation, two staffers were fired and the chief psychologist allowed to resign, but other allegations surfaced and investigations widened, leading to a grand jury proceeding. (*Miami Herald*, April 5, 1972, p 2 and 1B, April 26, 1972, p 1D, and May 9, 1973, p 2B; 11th Judicial Circuit, Dade County, Grand Jury Report, May 8, 1973, accessed at http://miamisao.com/wp-content/uploads/2021/02/gj1972f4.pdf.) Meanwhile, a Sunland housemother was arrested for beating a 14-year-old female resident with a broom handle (*Miami News,* July 22, 1972, p 3).

[2] As a child, I believed everything our grandfather told us, including his start throwing crates of cotton hosiery in the Taubel mill. Only later did I begin to wonder about the "Liberty" engines taken from old JN-4s, put into the speedboats – "the fastest boats in the world" – he'd taken us to see in Absecon Bay. (The boats, we learned, had run rum from offshore during Prohibition.) There were wisecracks about alcohol and Prohibition in his Christmas cards. He'd supported "wet" Al Smith, for President. He'd taught me to drink sidecars when I was fifteen. Only recently, digging into his past, did I discover his election as an officer of the Aviator's Club of Pennsylvania in 1919, when pilots were scarce, and learn how airplanes had smuggled booze into Atlantic City in the early days of Prohibition.

[3] As children, we never once saw our grandmother in the kitchen. When we grew up, Mom informed us that her mother-in-law intentionally avoided the place, thinking it undignified for the lady of the house to enter that particular room. According to her, Stella Marie had never learned how to boil water – in fact, didn't even know where the pots and pans were kept.

[4] A transcript of the full 1962 tape-recorded interview is set forth in Appendix 12.

[5] She also remembered the time Charley had driven her and Ida to Florida, when the Georgia state troopers couldn't believe that the Cadillac belonged to her. Appendix 12.

[6] Nettie Powell, History of Marion County, Historical Publishing Co, Columbus, Ga., 1931, pp 54-55.

[7] *Ibid.*, pp 65-66.

[8] *Ibid.*, p 68.

[9] *Ibid.*, pp 77-78.

[10] Martin Luther Bivens (1816-1878) had been a judge of the Inferior Court 1849-1852. He'd been elected to represent Marion County in the state legislature in 1859. (Rena S, Cobb, A History of Marion County, GA, Wolfe Publishing, 1997; Nettie Powell, *supra*, p 51.) The inscription on his headstone: "Thou once loved form, now with the dead,/ Each mournful thought employs;/ We weep, our earthly comforts fled,/ And withered all our joys."

[11] 1860 U.S. Census, Marion County, GA, Buena Vista, Fam 464; 1860 Federal Slave Schedule, GA, Marion County, Kinchafoona Dist, p 31.

[12] The white plantation owner who'd owned Nancy's parents in Pineville was David Neal Maddux, b. Feb 5, 1813, d. Oct 24, 1894, buried at Buena Vista Cemetery. The first U.S. Census to include former slaves by name was that of 1870, in which the African-American Madduxes were listed as Darrel (43), Sarah (43), Thomas (17), Addison (15), Dinnis (11), Nancy H (4), Coraline (22) and Mella (or Mellant, 6 mo's) – all born in Georgia except for Sarah (born in Virginia). All but Nancy and Mella were listed as "working on farm." No one was recorded as able to read or write. (1870 U.S. Census, Marion County, Georgia, Kinchafoonee, Fam 959.)

That census was enumerated in August, 1870, meaning that four-year old Nancy H Maddux had been born in 1866. What Nancy's mother had told her – that she'd been born two years after the emancipation – apparently referred not to Lincoln's legal proclamation, but to the *de facto* emancipation resulting from Sherman's sweep through that part of Georgia in 1864.

[13] 1880 U.S. Census, Marion County, Georgia, Kitchafoonee Dist 41, Fam 263.

[14] 1900 U.S. Census, Muscogee County, GA, Columbus War 06, Dist 0094, Fam 124 at 502 Fifth Street. Nancy's younger children at the time were her son Claud (8) and daughters Theodosia (8), Roberta (3) and Alma (2). I remember Theodosia and Alma living in a basement room at our grandfather's house, a room into which, as a young boy, I never ventured.

[15] Appendix 12.

[16] In the 1910 Census, Nancy was living with her older brother Dennis, a bartender in a saloon, along with her daughter Alma and two new children, Robert (7) and Fred (6). Her occupation was listed as "house girl" for a private family. (1910 U.S. Census, Duval County, Fla, Jacksonville Ward 2, Dist 0073, Fam 487.) By 1913, she'd moved out of Dennis's house and was listed in the Jacksonville City Directory living at 1342 Florida Alley. (The Directory, p 41, noted that in its list of state and local government officials, those who were colored were marked with an asterisk; colored schools were listed separate from white schools; and so on.)

[17] 1920 U.S. Census, Duval County, Fla, Jacksonville Ward 6, Dist 55, Fam 20 at 1416 Cleaveland Street. Nancy was listed in the Census as a maid in a boarding house. Her age was listed as 52; her mother's as 64.

[18] In 1947, the actual causes of the condition (a genetic mutation resulting in an extra copy of the 21st chromosome) had not yet been discovered, and the condition was still thought to indicate the reemergence of ancient Mongolian blood.

[19] In December, 1952, *Modern Textiles* described Charley as "gambling on his faith in the new fibers," believing "in the latest developments: the acrylics, high polymers, and the others." Eleven years later, the same magazine quoted Sonny saying that the synthetic fiber business is the "best business in the world." "Allied's Bold Move West: Caprolan's Tower on 42 Street," *Modern Textiles*, May, 1961, Vol 44, Iss 5, p 19. Brother David remains in textiles to this day. (His synthetic pine straw, he says, is far better than the natural stuff it replaces.)

[20] Meanwhile, by referring to the 1952 production (his first granddaughter, Corinne) as most recent, but "not the last," he was clearly referring to the fact that both Julie and Barbara were pregnant again.

Appendix 1: The City Directories

Prior to 1856, property owners decided what addresses to use for their properties – and the result was mayhem. Houses were numbered and streets were named based on a myriad of individual ideas for how best to do so. Much research for this book, and inferences drawn from that research, were based on information in city directories, which tried to make sense of the mayhem without complete success. Because these and various other difficulties affect the accuracy of the directories, the reader is invited to consider the following:

"The numbering of the Houses and Stores throughout the whole of the City and Districts is, in many instances, very irregular – and on some of the main streets, it frequently occurs that houses more than a square apart have the *same* number – besides, many of the houses are not numbered at all; to which add the fact, that the numerous titles of *squares*, *rows* and *places*, given to small sections of different streets – and the difficulties from this source will be apparent…. The same name is frequently given to streets in different sections of the City – for instance, not less than four are called Ann Street; two Carpenter; three or four Penn; etc etc…. [D]ue regard has been paid to the proper orthography of the names, although compelled frequently to receive information from persons ignorant, not only of the proper spelling, but of the name of the occupant of the house, as well as his business and its location." — *M'Elroy's Philadelphia Directory, 1837.*

"As Kensington grew, an ever-larger portion of the population lived in shacks and sheds behind the houses that fronted the streets… Census records listed many households as being "in the rear of" a stated address. These unpaved dirt lanes, courts and alleys could physically change in just a few years; many were never named, and those that were might change with every new purchaser. Not until 1856 did major streets mark off blocks of a hundred numbers each, with even numbers on the south and west sides of streets, odd numbers on the north and east, and even then, the plan was not universally welcomed: many businesses continued to use their old numbers alongside the new ones." – Russell F. Weigley *et al*, Philadelphia: A 300 – Year History, Norton & Co., 1982, *pp 374- 375.*

Even after the City of Philadelphia began to systematically regulate street naming and numbering in 1856, misnumbering persisted, as many residents and business proprietors wished to retain the naming and numbering by which they'd previously been known. In its 1858 edition, McElroy's Directory first introduced the new numbering system in a chart showing even numbers on the west side of N-S streets and the north side of E-W streets, odd numbers on the east and south sides. It explained:

"The Decimal System of Numbering Houses: One Hundred numbers are set apart for each square, which leaves a few spare numbers for each, so that one square can, in future, be renumbered without disarranging the entire street. The initial, or starting points are at the Delaware River and Market Street. Persons can, by merely looking at the numbers on the Houses, no how many squares they are from the Delaware or Market Street. By-streets are numbered as though they extended to the Delaware or Market Street. Numbers properly arranged, suggest distances to the mind; but improperly placed, they lead to confusion." – *McElroy's Philadelphia Directory, 1858.*

"The collection and proper arrangement of so large a number of names required an amount of energy, labor and skill, only to be appreciated by those actually engaged in the work. Nor is it alone with the large number of names printed, we have to do; probably more than double that amount are returned by the canvassers. This mass, from all parts of the consolidated city, must all be assorted, alphabetically arranged, read carefully, removing the duplicates and triplicates, having, at the same time, strict regard to the proper spelling of the most difficult of all spelling, – that of proper names.... To say that errors have not occurred would be to... repudiate the lessons of experience." – *McElroy's Philadelphia Directory, 1860.*

The Civil War years brought additional difficulties.

"One of the greatest difficulties experienced by canvassers is the reticence of "domestics." Some of these flatly refused to give the needed information until the whole system of directory-publishing, with its attendant benefits, is set forth to their satisfaction; others, fancying the canvasser a tax-collector in disguise, purposely gives incorrect information for the sake of a laugh in their sleeves at having so shrewdly outwitted him; with others the answer is "call again," or "leave your name and residence, and Mr. So-and-so will call when he is in the neighborhood... In fact, a hundred different pretexts for evading his proper and necessary questions are trumped up by silly housekeepers...

"After the canvassing is complete, the assorting of the material is proceeded with; next in order comes the compilation... and, finally, the writing of a preface. The work is then placed in the hands of a printer, and the sheets are ready for the binder in about twenty days thereafter..."

"The collection of the names alone occupies from thirty to forty men during the entire months of October and November. The mass of names thus collected, amounting to nearly 300,000, must then be compiled and collated, and the duplicates destroyed..... Mr. Smith tells the collector who calls on him that he does not wish his residence put down; Mr. Jones asks to be put down only as a gentleman, and Mr. Brown refuses to give his name entirely, stating that he thinks 'directories are only good for thieves and detectives.'

"The hardest part of the labor connected with the publication, however, is the reading of the proofs... [T]o go over a hundred thousand names, and afterwards remain uncertain whether fifty thousand of them are correctly spelled, is indeed discouraging." – *Unidentified newspaper articles pasted into Internet Archive copy of McElroy's Philadelphia Directory, 1863.*

"[T]o obtain the names of business people and housekeepers, together with young men residing at home and in boardinghouses, and to compile from over 200,000 names, written indiscriminately on slips... so as to avoid duplicates and other inaccuracies, – may be considered by the inexperienced quite an easy matter... [D]ifficulties meet the canvasser at almost every door. The man of business is engaged with his customer... and if perchance the canvasser may find someone having leisure enough to give information, he is doubtful as to whether the name is Joseph or James, John Smith or John Smyth, whether the number of the building is 920 Green Street or 920 Coates Street... And thus from door to door the same difficulties are to be encountered and overcome. Nor is this all. The utter carelessness in reference to the matter at all is not among the least... many persons are out of the city, and information has to be obtained as best the canvasser can. These, and other difficulties which might be named, superabound this year. The 'draft' seemed to be the terror of all classes, and in no year have there been so many refusals to give names..." – *McElroy's Philadelphia Directory, 1864*

"... a far more difficult city [than New York, Boston or Chicago], viewed either from its peculiar conformation, its countless courts and alleys changing their name with each purchaser, or the nomenclature of its streets, in many cases the same name applying to four, five and six streets... Hereafter the annual issue is to be released on April 1 of the year it represented, thereby containing changes occurring in January and February of the year in question." – *Gopsill's Philadelphia Directory, 1867*

Appendix 2: Reflections of Edward V. Murphy
on the Lincoln Conspirators' Trial*

The Military Court by which the 'Lincoln Conspirators' were tried opened on the tenth day of May, 1865. Sessions were held in the old Penitentiary building, which stood in the Arsenal grounds on the point of land marking the junction of the Potomac River and the Eastern Branch. Even while the trial was in progress the body of John Wilkes Booth whose mad deed had started the whirlwind of passion which was to consume four of the 'conspirators' lay buried in secret beneath the floor of the building.

The courtroom itself, in the northeast corner of the third story, was big and bare. The windows were guarded by iron gratings. A door communicated with the cells in which the prisoners were confined between sessions of the court. Members of the Military Commission occupied a table near the eastern side of the room, Major General David Hunter presiding. At the foot of this table stood another, used by the three prosecuting officers. The center of the room was given over to the witness stand, while to the left was the table at which sat the official reporters. The dock in which the prisoners were ranged was a narrow railed-off platform along the western wall.

Such was the setting of the inquiry, which was the most extraordinary hearing with which I have ever had anything to do. The work of reporting the trial itself was extremely arduous. There were no typewriters in those days and carbon paper was unknown; therefore the reporters worked from 9 o'clock in the morning, when the court met, until late in the evening taking testimony, and from late in the evening until five o'clock the next morning transcribing it. It was also necessary to make another copy besides the official transcript for the National Intelligencer, which printed the testimony verbatim. Some idea of the volume of this may be gained from the fact that this paper devoted three or four of its pages each day in the publication of the evidence. The reporters get their sleep from five o'clock in the morning until 8.

One of the deepest impressions left upon me by that ordeal is that, were I ever to be tried for any crime, I should most earnestly wish for a civil and not a military court before which to plead. Another point which I recall, and which shows, I believe, the prevailing attitude of the court, was that every objection made by counsel for the accused was summarily overruled, while all objections made by the Government prosecutors were sustained without question.   I am thoroughly convinced that, had the trial been conducted before a civil court rather than a military commission, the chances are largely in favor of, but two of the conspirators, Payne and Alzerodt, ever having been sentenced to death.

Mrs. Suratt was convicted on the testimony of two witnesses. One had received for years her motherly care, and was the companion of her son John, of Booth,

* "Lincoln Trial Court Reporter Tells His Story," *New York Times Magazine*, April 9, 1916. Included here is the complete text of Murphy's own comments about the trial; excluded are the introductory and transitional comments of the Times Magazine's reporter.

Payne, …[gap in copying]… was undoubtedly aware of the conspiracy to abduct the President and a participant in it, although at the same time a clerk in the War Department. The other was a tavernkeeper at Surrattsville, Md, a man so terrified by detectives that he made statements that would best serve their purpose.

Mrs. Surratt was a woman of most exemplary life and character, a mother devoted to the care and welfare of her children, and a devout Christian. Every action of her life cries out against her complicity in Lincoln's murder and against 'the deep damnation of her taking off' on the purchased and perjured testimony of two interested and discredited witnesses.

The late Father Walter of St. Patrick's Church, in Washington, who had been for years her confessor, and who administered to her the consolations of religion down to the moment of her execution, proclaimed her entire innocence of any knowledge of the crime. David Miller DeWitt, in his two books dealing with the trial, proves the execution of Mrs. Surratt to have been a 'judicial murder.' Reverdy Johnson, long an honored member of the Senate and one of the greatest leaders of the American bar, who was her counsel, was of the same opinion.

John Randolph Tucker, in his work 'The Constitution of the United States,' in speaking of the military commission which tried her, said: "The military power was left without restraint to work the death of its victims in defiance of the Constitution of the country."

General Benjamin F. Butler, on the floor of the House of Representatives, denounced John A. Bingham, a fellow member, and the man who played the most active role in the prosecution, as 'the murderer of an innocent woman."

Benn Pitman, who was the Recorder of the Military Commission, in the last days of his life proclaimed his belief in the innocence of Mrs. Surratt.

I was personally present during the entire trial, and I assert now, as I have from the beginning, my firm conviction of the absolute innocence of this unfortunate woman.

And furthermore, although it has frequently been denied, it is nevertheless a fact that for the first few days of the trial, Mrs. Surratt was brought into the courtroom with an iron ball and chain fastened to her ankles and with her hands manacled. The manacles were removed later because of comments made by the press. Some or all of the other prisoners were manacled throughout the trial.

Her demeanor during the dreadful ordeal was such as might be expected of any modest matron. Overwhelmed with the terrible nature of the charges against her, and with the base ingratitude of which she was the helpless victim, she shrank from the gaze of those around her, a sorrowful and broken-hearted woman. It was said by those who saw her led – or, rather, carried – to the place of execution that she was more dead than alive when the hangman's noose was placed around her neck.

The principal witness against Mrs. Surratt was Lewis J. Weichmann. He and I had been fellow pupils at the Philadelphia High School. I came to Washington upon leaving school, and about two years later met him. I recall vividly my conversation with him, so far as its salient features are concerned. He asked me to call, and thereupon launched into an account of the family with whom he was staying. He extolled in the highest terms the virtues and delightful character of the family, that of Mrs. Mary E. Surratt, and added that the latter was so kind and considerate to him that he venerated her as if she were his mother. At infrequent intervals thereafter I met him on the street, and upon all such occasions he would renew his invitation.

And this was invariably followed by praise of the family, and particularly of its head. The call, however, was never made.

After the close of the short session of Congress in 1865,[*] I accepted a position to serve during the recess as private secretary to Provost Marshal General Fry. Shortly after the assassination of the President, under the direction of General Baker, Chief of the Government's detective corps, many persons were brought to Washington who claimed to have knowledge of the conspiracy to assassinate Lincoln; as well as of what they described as movements on the part of prominent Confederates in Canada, not only to remove Lincoln… [gap in copying]… General Jeffries, and the preliminary testimony was reported and transcribed by me.

While engaged in this work in the War Department one Sunday morning, I had occasion to visit the room assigned to Colonel Burnett, who had been summoned to Washington to assist in the prosecution of the alleged conspirators. Seated in the room, I observed my old schoolmate, Weichmann, whom I at once cordially greeted. Upon leaving, I was followed into the corridor by Colonel Burnett, who proceeded to question me about Weichmann, my relation with and my knowledge of him. Amazed at the character of the examination, I inquired the reason. Colonel Burnett replied: "You will learn in good time." The following morning in front of the White House I saw Weichmann in manacles being escorted by an armed guard of soldiers to the War Department. The next day I learned that he was charged with being in the conspiracy to murder the President.

I saw nothing more of him until he was placed upon the stand as a witness for the Government during the trial. I observed closely his testimony and the manner in which it was given, and became convinced that he was perjuring himself to save his own neck. When the daily recess for luncheon took place, after Weichmann had been on the stand all morning, he approached me and asked what I thought of his testimony. I replied that I was satisfied that he was falsely swearing away the life of an innocent woman, whom he had repeatedly told me he loved as a mother, in order to save his own worthless carcass, and that I would hold no further communication with him.

Mrs. Surratt was executed and Lewis J. Weichmann was rewarded with an appointment as clerk in the Philadelphia Custom House.

Passing through one of the offices in the Custom House during the brief incumbency of ex-Governor Johnston of Philadelphia as Collector, I happened to see Weichmann there. On reaching the Collector's Office I expressed my surprise to him. Having been installed in office but a short time previous, he had had no opportunity to acquaint himself with the personnel of the staff. He was amazed to learn that Weichmann had found lodgment there, denounced him as a perjurer, and immediately sent a letter to Secretary of the Treasury McCullough removing Weichmann and nominating another in his stead.

Several days later the recommendation was returned disapproved. That very night the Governor went to Washington and appeared next morning at the Treasury

---

[*] After a brief session from March 4th to March 11th, 1865, the 39th Congress was in recess until December 4, 1865. Lincoln was shot on April 14th and died on April 15th. The Military Tribunal began its proceedings on May 10th. So Murphy apparently accepted the position with Fry between March 11 and April 14, and transcribed the preliminary testimony of witnesses between April 15 and May 10th.

Department. There he saw McCullough. 'Mr. Secretary,' he said, 'one of two things must happen; either Lewis J. Weichmann leaves the Philadelphia Custom House or I do. Which shall it be?'

The Secretary tried to appease the Governor, telling him, among other things, that Weichmann had been appointed on the personal request of a Cabinet colleague, who might regard his removal as a personal affront. Governor Johnston said he knew the Cabinet officer, who did not hesitate to stoop to subornation of perjury, and still vehemently insisted that he or Weichmann would have to leave. Weichmann was removed. Governor Johnston, however, failing of confirmation by the Senate, which at that time rejected all nominations of the President, vacated the office. The old Collector was reinstated and Weichmann was restored to his former position. Of his later history I know nothing, except that he died a few years ago somewhere in the West.

Another point tending to prove the innocence of Mrs. Surratt was in connection with Lewis Payne, a fellow prisoner.

Payne was a mystery throughout the entire trial. Little was known of him save that he had served for a time in the Confederate Army, and had deserted. At first he declined to ask for counsel to assist him, and for a long time refused to communicate with General Doster, who had been asked by the Judge Advocate to defend him.

His only request, so far as I know, was on the day before the execution, when he asked permission to make a statement, to be taken down by one of the official reporters of the court. He desired to exonerate Mrs. Surratt from any connection, near or remote, with either the conspiracy to abduct or kill the President. The statement, we were told, he would swear to, knowing that he was about to die.

On one occasion, it seems, Booth, Atzerodt, and other conspirators were the guests of John Surratt, and were discussing plans for the abduction. Mrs. Surratt entered the room just as some remark was made that might excite her suspicions. John Surratt, who was sitting by the door through which she entered, her back being toward him, sprang to his feet, and, with forefinger to his lips, motioned for silence. The moment Mrs. Surratt left the room he cautioned the party to be most careful, and under no circumstances even to hint at anything which was going on, for his mother, if aware of the plot, would give the whole thing away and ruin them all. Payne was denied the opportunity to make his statement.

He made no denial of his brutal attack on Secretary Seward and his son Frederick, who rushed to the aid of his father. He did, however, express regret for the injuries inflicted on the latter.

During the entire trial, with his hands manacled and wearing only an undershirt, trousers and shoes, Payne sat like a statue, apparently oblivious or totally indifferent to the scene. Knowing the evidence against him was conclusive and that his conviction was certain, he had nerved himself – if indeed her possessed nerves or sensibility at all – to face the fate that was in store for him. When it came, he met it unflinchingly.

Atzerodt and Herold, with Mrs. Surratt and Payne, were the two others who paid with their lives for Lincoln's death. Atzerodt, according to his own confession, knew nothing of the assassination plot until two hours before it was carried out, and then refused to have anything to do with it. And whether from fear or otherwise, it is at least certain that he made no attempt to carry out his allotted share in that plot – of killing Vice President Johnson.

That he had been in the plot to abduct the President there can be no question, and had he been tried on that charge would have been justly convicted. It is questionable, however, whether he should have paid the price he did for the charge on which he was tried.

Most interesting of all the prisoners, Atzerodt had a stupid, stolid look, indicating a low order of mental development, and a total absence of any spirit that would have led to the commission of any act requiring the slightest degree of courage or daring.

Herold seemed entirely unaware of the gravity of the situation in which he was placed, or of the probable fate that was before him. He had accompanied Booth after the murder, and was with him when he was shot. According to the testimony, he was a boy of light and trifling character.

To me it seems impossible that a man of Booth's attainments and shrewdness would have confided his plans and plots to a creature so irresponsible. Herold, however, was familiar with the roads, and had a large acquaintance among the people of that portion of Maryland through which Booth had planned to make his escape, so that his use of the immature youth merely as a pilot would seem the far more logical. Also, it would be but natural for Herold to have been highly flattered by being made the companion of a man so eminent in the dramatic world as Booth and to become his willing tool and slave. But he was not the stuff of which conspirators are made. Booth himself, just before he died, said, "I declare before my Maker that the man here is innocent of any crime whatever."

The four remaining prisoners were all convicted of being "conspirators." Three were sentenced to life imprisonment at Dry Tortugas, the other for six years at hard labor. These men were Doctor Samuel A. Mudd, Edward Spangler, Samuel Arnold, and Michael O'Laughlin.

When Booth fled into Maryland, his first thought was for a physician, in order that his leg, broken when he leaped from the box at Ford's Theater after shooting Lincoln, might be set. Upon reaching the locality in which Dr. Mudd lived, he sought his services, and the physician, not having heard of the assassination, treated and splinted the wounded limb. Booth when he left was unable to put his boot on the injured foot, and left it in the doctor's office. Upon hearing of the assassination of the President, Dr. Mudd, in common with all the people of that vicinity, was terrified. Cavalrymen and detectives were scouring the country in pursuit of Booth, and all those who knowingly or unknowingly harbored the fugitives were in dread of swift punishment. Upon discovering the initials "J.W.B." in the boot left in his office, Dr. Mudd's terror was increased to such a point that when questioned by the pursuers regarding any knowledge of the assassins, he declared he knew nothing. A search was made, however, and the boot being discovered, the doctor was arrested and hurried to Washington.

It was testified that Booth had made a trip through the section of country over which he subsequently attempted to escape, under pretext of desiring to buy a farm, and that he called upon Dr. Mudd to make inquiries as to the character of the land there. It was also claimed that he had previously met the doctor in Washington. If this was so, Dr. Mudd probably recognized Booth in the first instance, and told the lie to shield himself. But he does not appear to have had any connection whatever with the conspiracy.

The Dry Tortugas to which he and the others were sent are a group of islands off the Florida Keys. Upon Graden Key stood Fort Jefferson, a military prison during the civil war. This group of islands was made a federal bird… [gap in copying]…

During Dr. Mudd's imprisonment there an epidemic of yellow fever broke out and among its first victims was the resident physician. Dr. Mudd stepped into the breach and worked so untiringly and to such good purpose that he was soon pardoned. Spangler and Arnold were pardoned about a year subsequently, and O'Laughlin died of yellow fever.

Spangler was a ne'er-do-well, a scene shifter in Ford's Theater. On the night of the assassination, when Booth dismounted from his horse at the stage entrance, it was Ned Spangler whom he called to hold the animal. In a few minutes, however, Spangler was summoned to shift the scenes, and he, in his turn, called a boy named Burroughs, known as 'Peanut John,' to care for his charge.

When Booth rushed from the glare of the stage lights into the dark alley he saw a shadowy figure which in size and outline strikingly resembled Spangler. He struck at the man with the unsheathed knife he carried, and leaped upon his horse. Strange treatment for a co-conspirator!

Save for the fact that he held Booth's horse, the only other evidence against Spangler was that upon hearing of the crime Booth had committed, he exclaimed, raising his arm, 'Shut up! Booth didn't shoot him!"

But it must be taken into consideration that Booth, in his many visits to the theater, was in the habit of tossing a quarter to obscure Ned Spangler; add to this the high position held by Booth in the dramatic world, and it seems but natural that when his patron was accused of such a heinous crime he should have attempted to defend him.

I recall but little of the other two – Arnold and O'Laughlin – save that the testimony against them was of the flimsiest character imaginable. Certainly neither of them committed any act warranting life imprisonment, though they were probably for a time participants in the plot to abduct the President. The charge on which all the prisoners were charged, however, was assassination, and not abduction. On the latter charge four or five of them might properly have been convicted before a competent court having jurisdiction.

Appendix 3:

"Weighed in the Balance" by Stella Marie Murphy (1916)

The snow fell over Paris with vigorous, relentless persistence. Here and there a window was lighted up; and the noise of people making merry within came forth and was swallowed up and carried away by the wind.

A solitary figure staggered through the drifts, stopping now and again to look backward. The figure was that of Jean Ruffin, a rogue of Paris wanted for many crimes. He carried his eight and twenty years with feverish animation. Greed had made folds about his eyes; evil smiles had puckered his mouth. It was an eloquent, sharp, ugly countenance. Just now he stood piercing into the inky darkness, his body rigid and leaning slightly forward. Wherever he went, he must weave with his own plodding the rope that bound him to crime and would bind him to the gallows.

He snapped his fingers as if to pluck up his own spirits and, choosing a street at random, he stepped boldly forward through the snow. He kept quickening his pace as if he could escape from unpleasant thoughts by mere fleetness of foot. He could only see one way of getting a lodging and that was to take it. He passed a house which looked as if it might be easily broken into, so he retraced his steps, entertaining himself on the way with the idea of a room still hot, with the table still loaded with the remains of supper, where he might spend the black hours of the night and issue forth on the morrow with an armful of valuable plate.

The house in question looked dark at first sight, but as Ruffin made a preliminary inspection, in search of the handiest point of attack, a little twinkle of light caught his eye from behind a curtained window.

At this discovery he cried out in anger and disappointment; then, seeing where it was leading him, he said, "Every man to his business after all! If they are awake, I may come by a supper honestly for once and cheat the devil."

He went boldly to the door and knocked. Usually when seeking alms he knocked timidly, but now when he had just discarded the thought of a burglarous entry, knocking seemed a mighty simple and innocent proceeding. His knocks had scarcely died away before a measured tread drew near, a couple of bolts pushed aside, and the door was opened wide as though no fear of guile were known to those within. A tall monk, muscular and spare, but a little bent, confronted Ruffin.

"You knock late," said the monk in courteous tones.

Ruffin cringed and brought up many servile words of apology. In a crisis of this sort, the beggar was uppermost in him.

"You are cold and hungry? Well, step in." He preceded the beggar upstairs into a large apartment, warmed with a pan of charcoal and lit by a great lamp hanging from the roof. It was very bare of furniture; only some gold plate on the sideboard, some tapestry hung upon the walls, representing the Crucifixion of Our Lord, and another representing the Blessed Virgin Mary.

"Will you seat yourself," said the monk, "and forgive me if I leave you? I am alone in the house tonight and if you are to eat I must serve you."

No sooner had he gone than Ruffin leaped from the chair and began examining the room with the stealth of a cat. He weighed the gold ornaments in his hand, opened all the drawers, and examined the tapestries.

"Five pieces of gold," he said; "if there were only ten I would risk it. A fine house and a fine old saint for a master."

And just then, hearing the monk returning, he stole back to his chair and began humbly warming his wet hands before the charcoal pan.

The monk entered with a plate piled high in one hand, and a cup of steaming coffee in the other. "Drink to your better fortune," he said gravely.

"To our better acquaintance," said the guest boldly, as he devoted himself to the viands with a ravenous gusto, while the monk, leaning back, watched him with steady, curious eyes.

"You seem nervous. What brings you here at this hour?" he asked.

"I had but one franc, and then the cold gives a man fancies or the fancies give a man cold, I know not which."

"My brothers were administering to the poor and, owing to the storm, have presumably stayed the night out, but you, my friend, with your apparent learning, what brings you about?"

Ruffin rose. "I am called Jean Ruffin, a poor master of arts, of this University. I know some Latin and a great deal of vice. I was born in a garret and shall probably die in one, if not upon the gallows, and from tonight on, dear father, you may consider me your most humble servant."

"No servant of mine," said the monk; "my guest for this evening."

"Truly, I am a guest of whom you may be proud," said Jean humorously.

"You are one of God's children. I am honored to be able to serve Him, and although you confess your familiarity with vice, I am sure that this very minute you are sorry for your wrongs, because you committed them for gain and received but dishonor."

"Gain!" repeated Ruffin with a shrug. "Gain! The poor fellow wants his supper and takes it; so does the soldier in a campaign. Do they both receive honor? No! The poor fellow is jailed as a thief, the soldier hailed as a hero. I steal a couple of mutton chops without so much as disturbing people's sleep; the farmer grumbles, but eats none the less enjoyably of what remains. The soldier comes up blowing gloriously on a trumpet, takes away the whole sheep and beats the farmer into the bargain. I am only Tom, Dick or Harry; I am a rogue, a dog, and hanging's too good for me, but just ask the farmer which of us he prefers."

"My man, your argument verges on the ridiculous. Listen to me, I beg of you. I am old and honored. If I were to be turned from this house tomorrow, many would be glad to shelter me. I fear no man. I have seen you tremble and lose countenance at a word. I await God's summons, contentedly giving what joy I can to others. You look for the gallows, a death without honor. You bewail the fate that made you the son of poor parents; you blame circumstances for your crimes, but 'honor and shame from no condition rise.' It depends entirely upon yourself, how you act your part. You claim that you steal only from the want of food. Very well, I will give you your opportunity. Never again shall you go hungry; you shall live here with me a straight, honorable life of repentance. You shall never again want for any bodily comfort. On the morrow you shall be able to see if it is, as you say, so easy to be good and honest when one has all comfort. Now, my man, follow me. I will show you your chamber, and remember that it was the will of God that made you come to me tonight for lodging.

He has offered you an opportunity better than any circumstances of birth could have done, and if you do not make the best of it, I warn you His judgment shall be swift and severe. So come, and God bless you; we shall see what comes of this night's lodging." And the old man passed from the room, followed by his guest.

The next day the workmen, clearing the streets of snow, due to the snowslide from the roof of the monastery, found a body horribly crushed, clutching five pieces of gold and two rich tapestries.

And that day, as the Angelus rang out, the good monk gazed solidly heavenward and begged that God be merciful to all sinners, "for, Father, they know not what they do."

– STELLA MARIE MURPHY, '16.

Appendix 4: Four-Minute-Man Samples (1917)

"It's Duty Boy" (Poem Read by Four Minute Men)

> My boy must never bring disgrace to his immortal sires—
> At Valley Forge and Lexington they kindled freedom's fires,
> John's father died at Gettysburg, mine fell at Chancellorsville;
> While John himself was with the boys who charged up San Juan Hill.
> And John, if he was living now, would surely say with me,
> "No son of ours shall e'er disgrace our grand old family tree
> By turning out a slacker when his country needs his aid."
> It is not of such timber that America was made.
> I'd rather you had died at birth or not been born at all,
> Than know that I had raised a son who cannot hear the call
> That freedom has sent round the world, its previous rights to save—
> This call is meant for you, my boy, and I would have you brave;
> And though my heart is breaking, boy, I bid you do your part,
> And show the world no son of mine is cursed with craven heart;
> And if, perchance, you ne'er return, my later days to cheer,
> And I have only memories of my brave boy, so dear,
> I'd rather have it so, my boy, and know you bravely died
> Than have a living coward sit supinely by my side.
> To save the world from sin, my boy, God gave his only son—
> He's asking for My boy, to-day, and may His will be done.

Speech by a Four Minute Man

Ladies and Gentlemen: I have just received the information that there is a German spy among us – a German spy watching *us*.

He is around, here somewhere, reporting upon you and me – sending reports about us to Berlin and telling the Germans just what we are doing with the Liberty Loan. From every section of the country these spies have been getting reports over to Potsdam – not general reports but details – where the loan is going well and where its success seems weak, and what people are saying in each community.

For the German Government is worried about our great loan. Those Junkers fear its effect upon the German *morale*. They're raising a loan this month, too.

If the American people lend their billions now, one and all with a hip-hip-hurrah, it means that America is united and strong. While, if we lend our money half-heartedly, America seems weak and autocracy remains strong.

Money means everything now; it means quicker victory and therefore less bloodshed. We are *in* the war, and now Americans can have but *one* opinion, only *one* wish in the Liberty Loan.

Well, I hope these spies are getting their messages straight, letting Potsdam know that America is *hurling back* to the autocrats these answers:

For treachery here, attempted treachery in Mexico, treachery everywhere – *one billion*.

For murder of American women and children – *one billion more*.

For broken faith and promise to murder more Americans – *billions and billions more*.

And then we will add:

In the world fight for Liberty, our share – *billions and billions and billions and endless billions*.

Do not let the German spy hear and report that *you* are a slacker.

> – Committee on Public Information, *Four Minute Man Bulletin* No. 17
> (October 8, 1917).

Appendix 5: Selected Letters (1911-1952)

Letter No. 1: Stella Marie Murphy to Mrs. Joseph Dulanty, Castle Inn, Buffalo, N.Y., postmarked Feb 28, 1911, at Fairhill Station, bearing a two-cent stamp

1234 Lehigh Ave
Philadelphia Pa

Dear Aunt G,

Received your two loving letters and was delighted to hear that you had arrived safe and sound but was very sorry to learn that you were so homesick for dear old Philly. Of course we are complimented to know that you think so much of us but still we like to know that you are happy and having a glorious time. I am reading a story by Anna Katherine Greene and am enjoying it very much. Do you remember how we used to sit on the porch and criticize her? On Saturday we had the pleasure of going to the theater to see "The Man Between." If it had not been for your thoughtfulness we would not have had that pleasure. We had a box.

I just met Lillian Hengen a little while ago and told her I was going to write to you and she said to give you her love.* Just think, I had to go all the way over to McCordle's to buy this paper to write to you. Don't you think that is an honor?

I am sorry to inform you that Genevieve Maloney died a few days ago and was buried from Our Lady of Mercy this morning. It was very sad.†

Aunt Anna May is giving a party tomorrow evening and is going to entertain about twenty people.‡ I wonder where they will sit. Sorry you are not home to get into the trouble. It is her sewing circle.

With much love from everyone and to everyone, I am your loving

Niece Stella
February twenty-eighth

---

* Daniel Hengen, Liquors, was in the 1911 City Directory at 1232 Lehigh Ave – that is, right next door to the Murphys. Lillian was his daughter – one of Stella Marie's German friends from a neighborhood where Irish and Germans were thoroughly mixed from house to house.

† Miss Genevieve E. Maloney was the seventeen-year-old daughter of William Maloney and "a niece of Martin Maloney, the Philadelphia Capitalist and Philanthropist," address 2306 N Park Avenue, Phila (*The Scranton Truth*, Feb 23, 1911).

‡ The never-married Anna May Congdon.

Letter No. 2: Charles W. Carvin to Stella Marie Murphy, return address Cadet C. W. Carvin, Cadet Flying Squadron, Kelly Field No. 2, San Antonio, Texas, postmarked January 19, 1918, San Antonio Military Branch, addressed to Miss S. M. Murphy, 1830 So. Rittenhouse Square, Philadelphia.

Barracks 35
Dearest,

It seems I've waited ages for word from you. Time is lengthened no doubt by the fact that I think of you continually – always every thought is of my little Stella Marie – Are you happy – do you miss me – are you faithful – what are you doing and thousands of such things. I wonder and wonder and arrive nowhere. Life here is far different from that at Princeton and I have plenty of time to think and wonder why I've received no word.

I felt last night like writing and telling you how much you are to me. I arranged phrases that I thought exactly expressed my feelings for you. I had thought I use several little quotations from a book I've just read. I should have written last night. I would have been better able to do so – today I can not – in the light these things I had thought to say seem foolish – with boys around discussing how the "air is full of pockets" – how "my ole plane bucked today" one can hardly word choice love phrases and describe one's deep feelings.

Oh I miss you during the day, Dutchie, but it is the nights I can hardly stand – wonderful starry moonlight nights – wasted – our best days spent apart.

I still find the same difficulty in getting to sleep, dear, after I've gone to bed – and I use the time to go over every pleasant moment of our two weeks and sometimes of happy ones of long ago. We must be in bed at nine and it is sometimes one or two and I am still dreaming—wide awake – of my little girl. I've tried Peter Ibbetson's "dreaming tune" but in his forty years he must have worked it all out.

At five we tumble out and at six thirty start flying – just as the dawn's breaking – a wonderful sight, Dutchie, but wasted because you are not here to enjoy it with me.

Don't imagine dear that I am horribly homesick or lonely. There are many moments of fun – many of excitement and many of work. It is only that this war came along when I was very much in love and took from me the thing that is dearer to me than anything in life. I do not regret doing my duty dear – because doing my duty give me more liberty, more right to love you, but I do regret being away from you – regret every moment of it.

I suppose being in town now and in the St. Francis play your time is rather taken up. I'd like to feel, but hate to think, that you have missed me as I have you.

Later – *[in darker ink]*

This remarkable composition was just interrupted by a summons to the "Dual Control" station and I have just finished an hour flight. The air was wonderful today Dutchie; warmer than on the ground and our camp looks like the tiny soldier camps you see on the cards at Christmas. The towns look like doll villages and the earth grows prettier and more picture-like the higher you go. Only up eleven hundred this morning. The air acts as a great stimulant and I no longer am quite as lonesome as I was this morning at least on the surface I'm not but that longing is there and I will be until I have my little darling again.

I bought you the most wonderful leather coat. I was rather extravagant but it is a great one – better than we saw in Blatt's. The same style. I say I bought it for you meaning that I thought Stella will want this and I can wear it. I do not use it flying – they issue coats for that. The coat is convertible – O.D. on one side and leather on the other with a polo coat that buttons inside for very cold weather – very English.

Went to ten o'clock mass Sunday in San Antonio – the nearest church – 6 miles – Martin and I – I am going to confession next Saturday as I promised you.

Just finished writing to Charlie Quinlan – have not heard from him since Christmas.

To whom have you been writing? Do you see Bate often? I'd like to hear from you soon Dutch – a little news – I really feel forgotten.

Needless to ask as to how you got home Saturday night. Have you been good since? I have – even if it must be attributed to lack of opportunity to be otherwise.

I just returned from the mail room where I went in hopes that I'd hear from someone – but not a word – I haven't heard a thing from anyone since I left. I am hoping however. One can at least do that. I have told you, have I not, that I do not like the town of San Antonio.

We had a great experience after we missed the train at Pittsburgh and were entertained on the train we took by a real honest-to-goodness detective. I'll be able to tell you some real stories now. Remember our stories?

I just finished "The Dwelling Place of Light" by Winston Churchill but I do not want you to read it. Also read "Over the Top" – very ordinary. M. Butler liked it, did she not? Of course it gives one lots of dope and apparently made a hit but the writing was far from gripping.

Wrote to my Grandmother and Father last night – sisters and Aunt due now and I really hate to write Irish – what'll I do?

With lots of love I close as I just heard our dinner call, "Come get it"!! I've kisses and kisses that I am just longing to give you so I'll enclose a few.

> *Carvin xxx*

Tuesday 3 p.m.
January 15, 1918. *

* "Being in town now" refers to the Murphys' recent move from Kensington to Rittenhouse Square in downtown Philadelphia. Being in the St. Francis play refers to the performance of "Dr. Optimist" to benefit St. Francis Home for Convalescents, for which Stella had been practicing all month, the actual performance yet to occur on January 25th (*Evening Public Ledger*, Jan 25, 1918, p 20).

Letter No. 3: Charles W. Carvin to Stella Marie Murphy, without an envelope. Dated "Tuesday – 5th" [February, 1918]

CADET FLYING SQUADRON
KELLY FIELD No 2
SAN ANTONIO TEXAS

Tuesday- 5th
My dear Stella,

Another miserable day too foggy to fly – another day longer before I am back to you. No letter again today – making five straight I've missed – have I been that terrible? I am terribly repentant now and lonesome as well.

Nothing to tell you, dear, all my days about the same – uneventful, unexciting, I am very glad that you go to church for me. I've not been able to get there for two weeks now!

Received a letter from my sister. She told me she called you up while you were away. She evidently knew where to look for news of me. Too bad you were not home.

Martin's fiancé is at Wichita Falls visiting her brother so of course Martin calls up every day that he gets a chance – he still receives his daily letters and sneaks off and reads them in a corner. And smiles – they must be nice!

Give Tex my love
You have it!!
(And do not want it do you)?

You must pardon the drawing on the envelope, I know you don't like them, I drew a few last week and this is the only envelope I have left.

I suppose you have been busy lately. Are they having dances or anything new in town? I get the "Ledger" but have seen nothing of any of our friends in it. I cut several articles out of San Antonio papers to send to you but in spite of the fact that I brought my writing paper to the Hangar this morning I forgot the clips.

They are shipping thousands of troops away from here each day and each day hundreds of recruits from all over the country are coming in – all green men so we have lots of trouble with the crews on our ships. It is quite romantic (although that doesn't quite fit) to see them go – the band plays "Should Auld Acquaintance Be Forgot" and it is "So long Mack – g'bye 'arry, see ya over there" etc.

I enclose my dearest love Stella Marie and confess that I am greatly disappointed in myself and my affairs. Your own,
Carvin xxx

Letter No. 4: Charles W. Carvin to Miss Stella Marie Murphy, 1830 So. Rittenhouse Square, Philadelphia, Pennsylvania, on letterhead of Cadet Flying Squadron, Kelly Field No. 2, postmarked San Antonio, Feb 28, 1918, 4 p.m. (Encloses a letter from Charles Quinlan to "Dearest Carvin" dated Sunday 24th.)

Tuesday – Wednesday

Dutchie Dear –

I am certainly delighted to hear that you at last have a real appetite – keep it up 'cause I've worried often about the little sweetheart of mine and her small appetite and I am very proud of my little girl and want you to stay just as you are – sweet, lovable – but why go on? I love just everything about you and don't even want a single change.

Do I dream anymore dearest? Well indeed I do – all about you. I try to picture myself burying my lips in your soft hair and just hug the old pillow tighter and tighter and try to bring back some of those very blissful minutes that I've had you so close to me – so very close – and to think how far away you are now dear – how far bodily but even closer spiritually. Closer now dear because I really think you trust me at last – you didn't absolutely before, did you? And, Dutchie, we can't really be everything to one another unless we do. I realize that, don't you?

I suppose I will be home in several weeks, maybe for Easter,* most likely before – but I'll only have a few days there and I am certainly going to make the best of them – never going to sleep a'tall a'tall!!

Dutchie Dear, I've missed you so – it hurts – honestly you can't imagine – the nights awful, a wonderful moon, can't go to town – nothing to drive away my homesick thoughts – no life, just a vast stillness and a still more empty and vast loneliness and an unstilled longing with an unforgettable feeling of you in my arms and that contented, wistful look in the eyes I love. Sometimes I think never again will it be and I try hard to drive such thoughts away but they come back. What evil genius spoils my happy dreams – the only pleasure I have. Dutchie, it simply must come true – you are all I have – all I want, and I do want you so – can anything prevent my having you.

Please never again tell me of your doubt as you did a week or so ago. Nothing makes me more miserable because dreaming and loving you as I do I can't understand how you can doubt – it is like throwing cold water on my dreams.

I always intend writing to Bill and yet I never get to do it – he won't get flying for five months, I know, so calm Mrs. Greenfield's fears – to some extent, at least – and Stella's too.

Why never tell me anything of Gallagher? What is he doing in Washington? Is he in uniform? Look well? Feel well? And Tony and Fran? When I said not to tell me of them I meant of your engagements – your letters etc – however I like to hear how they are doing! And what?

I am sending you my last letter from Charley Quinlan! What do you think of him. Does it help to remove any foolish doubts? If I receive any more of them I'll be angry. So take heed! Beware!

Didn't I tell you Doyle left for Garden City? Then France. He leaves a heartbroken mother.

I too am sorry you did not get flowers on Valentines Day and I am glad to think you thought of me when you saw the flowers 'cause I think I inherit my mother's

---

* Easter fell on March 31, 1918.

love of them – I can't resist pretty ones! You are like a flower I think – aren't you! I won't anumberate [sic] the various likenesses now! Perhaps when I come home!

Dearest would you have been satisfied had I remained in the Q.M. or Infantry? Honest now? I believe this is the first time you ever told me you thought of my flowers – you thanked me of course, but anyone would have done that – had I known perhaps you would have received more.

I started this letter yesterday but did not hear from you and will send it special. I received four letters from Runnymeade today, Wednesday.

With all my love, little sweetheart, hoping you found time to write Sat. & Sunday – I am your very own

Charlé xxx

Letter No. 5: CWC to Miss Stella Marie Murphy, 1830 So. Rittenhouse Sq., Philadelphia, Penna, return address Officer's Mess, Camp Dick, Aviation Concentration Camp, Dallas, Texas, postmarked Dallas, Texas, April 17, 1918, "BUY NOW U.S. GOVERNMENT BONDS 3RD LIBERTY LOAN."

Wednesday

Dearest - Just read yours of Saturday – I understand your restlessness and you most certainly are forgiven darling – your letters have been wonderful and have really been the one big event of each day – the one thing I really look forward to.

It seems we have both reached that uneasy stage – due no doubt to our separation – at least I know mine is due to that. The necessity of it is hard to stand and impossible to understand. Every time I read the little book you gave me I look at the little note on the card – Dutchie, I think that is the sweetest thing you ever wrote, and surely the dearest I ever read. You cannot imagine how I long for you each time, it is so like you.

I got orders to leave Camp last Wednesday but have not done so as yet, owing to a mix-up in my pay voucher, found a notice in my mailbox to come see the Adjutant at once so I suppose I am in for it. War hath its terrors!!

The Parkers act about my departure, as one would, that of an only son. They certainly have made my stay as homelike as possible and revived my belief in southern hospitality.

Don't fail to send me the Inquirer and your picture – you hear? Now mind.

Sorry you did not get to see my sister Thursday – I am sure she looked for you. In her letter she asked me if I did not envy her the tete-a-tete – do I? Perhaps you can tell her about that!!

It seems there is an awful muddle about the pictures. I think I'll have some good one taken just for you. So be secretive.

Don't forget to send me the snaps from Atlantic no matter how poor they are – I haven't a snapshot of you with me!

I certainly am surprised to hear that Stef & Charley O'B__ are in the Navy. Stef is evidently trying them both out!! Does Charley still go with H. Conroy?

I believe I remember Michell but have not heard anything about him.

About Mr. Sheehan, Ed Loughran told me he was in a gambling and Booze house that was raided in Jacksonville and was under arrest – He is still a Second Lieut. Awful isn't it!!

Rosanna's domestic duties proved rather fatal. Advise her for me not to attempt to dust any valuable articles around the house. Still I suppose she and Raymond can live without can tomatoes. Perhaps you had better start practicing on cans etc – start easy things first such as removing the stopper from milk bottles etc. Be gentle with them dear!!

Love, hugs, kisses from your own
Charlé

<u>Letter No. 6</u>: Charles W. Carvin Miss Stella Marie Murphy, 1830 So. Rittenhouse Sq., Philadelphia, Penna, return address City Club, Dallas, postmarked Dallas, Texas, Dec 9, 1918.

Monday, Dec 8th, 1918

Dearest Dutchie –

I suppose you are beginning to think I am quite a wanderer and I really suppose I am sorta one especially with things as fascinating for me as they are in Dallas. I am really afraid I am being spoiled with this flying about and luxurious life, with splendid machines, beautiful homes and exclusive clubs.

This club is really beautiful and so hard to get a card to – that I am always wishing I could have Stella here to enjoy it with me – but we can't have everything and I am extremely fortunate having all I have.

About our trip, we left Saturday morning and had trouble all the way up with a leaking radiator and throwing oil. We flew in relays stopping at each town and oiling and watering up. Of course that consumed a great deal of time and we did not arrive in Waco until five thirty. We decided we simply could not stay in Waco Saturday night so we left there at dark and flew toward Dallas but somehow or other we got off to the West and flew over Fort Worth so I succeeded in landing at Barrew Field about 7:30. We washed, had dinner, and I looked for Bill but he was not there so we went to town and the Movies and saw Bryant Washburn in "the Gypsy Trail" – terrible – then "Stolen Orders" – that started very well and had many stars in it but it ended so melodramatically. However we slept thru it alright!

We returned to camp and stayed at the Colonel's house. In the morning I looked for Bill but he was in Dallas so we flew over here and I went to every hotel in town but he was not registered – finally I remembered a girl here who he knows and called there but Bill was out in the country on a picnic – so I spent the afternoon flying around the country looking for a picnic – incidentally landing at S.M.U. where the entire student body turned out to see me (the <u>plane</u>). So Bill got cheated out of his ride.

I have not seen the Parkers this week – possibly Bill called there for me.

The only drawback to these trips dearest is the fact that I never hear from you and I think of you always and love you more than that. I certainly hope that I have many nice letters when I return. I dread the thoughts of spending Christmas in Texas away from you. I suppose you will get your collection of wonderful presents, as always –

I am having the plane fired today – in fact just came in from Love Field. I'll leave early in the morning if the weather permits.

Be real good dearest and be true and wait and write to your very own

Carvin

who loves and misses you

Letter No. 7: Stella Marie Murphy to Mrs. Joseph G. Dulanty, the Stuyvesant, Buffalo, NY, postmarked Feb 6, 1923:

Monday,

Dear Aunt G,

Your wedding gift, needless to say, was wonderful and came at a very appropriate time – the gloves were very useful – you know Mom – she wore hers the first day.

Rosanna has another daughter – they are going to name her Marie Louise. She is a little beauty – fat as can be – looks like a two month old child – weighed 9 lbs when she was born.

Tomorrow Textile School closes for the day, so the boys can go to the Silk Show in N.Y. Joseph is going over. Charles, Mother and I may go on Wednesday.

The house is coming along great – the living room is not furnished yet and I think that will be the hardest room of all – have the blue loveseat – that is beautiful – the light taupe rug – the dining room is gorgeous – Mother and I are making the lace curtains – cream colored net – lace edging – very pretty – but there are so many windows – we have the dotted marquisette ruffled peek-a-boo in the blue room – saw some pretty net curtains ruffled for the front bedroom – in Wanamaker's – the next time we go in town we expect to buy them.

Mother just called in – be sure and tell Aunt G how pretty my gloves were, also thank you again for mine, and again and again for the wonderful wedding gift – with much love to you and Uncle Joe –

Stella Marie –

<u>Letter No. 8</u>: Stella Marie Carvin to Mrs. Joseph G. Dulanty, no envelope, dated only "Friday," but probably late 1925 or 1926.

Friday

Dear G –

 I suppose Aunt Irene writes you all the news of their family – Marie's engagement – her ring – the new arrivals expected – I suppose Stella will want a girl this time. I had a chair ride with Stella – Mary F. and Billy at the Shore – they all looked well – Billy certainly is the cutest youngster – adorable. Mary Frances has a new coat and hat. Stella made her coat out of the blue tweed Father gave Marie a couple years ago – it was a piece left over.

 Charley is fine. Looks very well. He wears little suits now – at least when he is all dressed up. Has added a number of words to his vocabulary – calls Aunt Anna May "May" – "monk" for monkey – Boy – he is so used to hearing that he is a Bad Boy that he calls himself "Bad Boy." Say he is good and he says "no, Bad Boy" – even whips himself. He fell out of his ~~crib~~ pen – I suppose the next thing he will walk off the porch – Charles's vocabulary – a few of the words he said before you left. Here's the list as far as I can remember:

 Mamma, Daddy, Papa (for father), Doe (for Joe), gee, May, Marie, Ida, book, down, dog, door, duck, boy, cuke, dear, cab, girl, monk, drink, man, off, chocolate bud, horse, doll, pocketbook, baby, tick tick, sock, clock, car, chair, hot, cold, good, bird, Pete, egg, bacon, bean, hat, spoon, porch, bye bye, howdy-do, hello, cracker.

 He says almost everything after you but he has not started on sentences yet – he loves chocolate Buds – always wants one. Soon as I go out on the porch – "Mamma – chocolate Bud." He was vaccinated on Monday. So far it hasn't bothered him. Hope it takes – the doctor thought he was great – wants his picture for his Baby book. Alice Loughran and Frank Scannell were out last evening – she looked very well – I suppose that is a go. I'm trying to write with Joe's fountain pen and having a terrible time – so will close with much love to Uncle Joe and you and hoping you are quite recovered by now.

Affectionately,
Stella Marie

Letter No. 9: Stella Marie Carvin to Mrs. J. F. Dulanty, The Stuyvesant, Buffalo, N.Y. postmarked March 29, 1926

Friday

Dear Aunt G,

The Murphys are surely going in the real estate business – today, Father sold the mill – it all happened so suddenly – we don't know what to think – I haven't been talking to Father yet – he went to the Grundy & Pepper dinner tonight* – Joseph told me the news when he came home for dinner – the men came down to the mill this morning, came back this afternoon and said they would buy it – left $5,000 deposit – I sincerely hope it is for the best – Mother always wanted it – thought the place was entirely too big – too much worry.

We start painting and papering our house Easter Monday – each day I try to do a little but you really can do very little until almost time to move – got the big rug out of the attic – aired that – we were so afraid there would be moths in it – but it looks alright. You would never know Sonny – he is developing so – talks all the time – can say anything – a regular chatterbox – he has never been in a trolley – except that time in Atlantic – if you took him now you would have to pay car fare – 35 inches is average for a 3 yr old and he is 36 in – he has a great time with "Anna May" (he calls her) – but when he wants to tease her, he says "Annie". I'm "Mother dear."

I don't care for this writing paper – but I won it – so must use it – will write more details later – with much love –

Stella Marie –

---

* The description of Joe Murphy attending a "Grundy-Pepper" dinner is an indication that Murphy supported the "dry" political reformers within the Republican party. Republican George Wharton Pepper was a University of Pennsylvania law professor and Christian activist who'd been appointed to a seat in the U.S. Senate and was up for re-election. (With Mayor Kendrick, he'd called on Calvin Coolidge in October of 1925 to ask that General Smedley Butler of the U.S. Marines be permitted to remain as chief Prohibition enforcement officer in Philadelphia, suggesting a "dry" position on Prohibition.) In 1926, as a candidate for re-election, he was opposed in the Republican primary by William S. Vare, the "machine" candidate who was "wet" (anti-Prohibition). Vare won the election, but the Senate refused to seat him based on allegations of election fraud. Republican Joseph R. Grundy, from Bristol, was a textile manufacturer and head of the Pennsylvania Manufacturer's Association who opposed limitations on child labor and favored enforcement of the Volstead Act. In 1926, he was involved in party politics but was not a candidate himself. (See, for example, *Inquirer*, March 21, 1926, p 18.) However, in December, 1929, when the Senate refused to seat Vare, Grundy was appointed to the Senate by Governor Fisher. It would seem that the 1926 "Grundy-Pepper dinner" was one to support "dry" Pepper's renomination to the Senate seat, in the face of the challenge by "wet" machine candidate Vare.

438

<u>Letter No. 10</u>: Charles W. Carvin to Stella Marie Carvin, no envelope, not dated.[*]

INDUSTRIAL RAYON CORPORATION
GENERAL OFFICES

PLANTS   CLEVELAND, OHIO   SALES
OFFICES
CLEVELAND, OHIO   500 FIFTH
AVENUE
PAINESVILLE, OHIO   NEW
YORK, N.Y.
COVINGTON, VIRGINIA
AND

PRINCIPAL TEXTILE

CENTERS

Mom Darling –

Made very good time going home. Arrived at 9:20 and right to bed. Joe was home with Jimmy Fallon & Cal – Sonny returned (had the car) at 1:15 – I left a note to have him awaken me. Good Lord, I just remembered I forgot to select the Bathroom paper today – well.

Certainly enjoyed being with you – showing we can be happy anyplace – It is now 5:45 and this is the first minute I have had today. Ritchie did not come so I'll catch the six fifteen and do the income tax tomorrow.

I feel much better but not well – still hungry tho –

I am so weary I cannot coordinate my thoughts – I think Virginia Beach will be very inviting–

Enclosing Jean Eichman's letter – return it, as I have not answered it yet –

Keep your chin up, Mom – not much further to go –

Stay beautiful and write to

           Daddy –

---

[*] This letter was clearly written after 1938, as Industrial's Painesville plant didn't open until 11-25-38. (See *Lancaster Eagle-Gazette*, Nov 26, 1938, p 4.) Since Charley Jr. and Joe were still living at home, neither were yet in the service, and since the letterhead does not yet read VP of Sales, this letter was probably written in 1939 or 1940.

Letter No. 11: Charles W. Carvin to Stella Marie Carvin, no envelope, dated only 6:30 PM Monday. Possibly written Monday, March 11, 1940.[*]

500 FIFTH AVENUE
NEW YORK, N.Y.

6:30 P.M. Monday

Darling –

The Income tax man just left – I phoned home – getting the 6:50 Scarsdale – 7:31 – Dinner 7:45 – Homework 8:30-9:30 – Success is mine – for God's sake come home – I thought I had finished homework in 1914 – then the war – then textile school – now HOMEWORK.

The trip home was bad but not dangerous. Your blouse things from Altman did not come. I phoned them – they are tracing – will get Music tomorrow and send Ida up while I am in Cleveland. Brooks says to leave Tuesday nite but I sorta hate to leave – HOMEWORK – maybe I like it – you know – big Boss – etc. etc.

Dearest, you really are doing fine and I hope I may make a date with you for Easter – if Selnek (?)[†] is not ahead of me – of course I am no musician – but I too used to sing and I dance in a nice fatherly way. Then too I am faithful – and – trustworthy – and – dull –

No news from McL. so I put this dame in her place – maybe I am really a cave man – Your birthday card was swell – just received it – how come? – maybe the storm affected the mails – (males) – did you get my letter.

For Gawd's sake – don't tell me you took a ride – I did not write – I have a Stenog – I can dictate that too and you know my spelling and writing – Oh – Boy.

Well, plenty of love – our future's ahead.

Your own Daddy –

---

[*] Since he was commuting to Scarsdale/White Plains, this letter was probably written in 1938 or later. Since he was still working for George F. Brooks, it was written prior to his 1943 promotion, and since "Sonny" (Charley Jr.) was still living at home, it was written prior to Sonny's enlistment in 1942. Since he just received a birthday card, late for his March 5 birthday, it was probably written in March, soon after the 5th. Finally, he says he is looking forward to Easter. The dates of Easter were April 17th in '38; April 9th in '39; March 24th in '40; and April 13th in '41. Since a possible date for Easter seems in the near future, mid-March of 1940 seems the likeliest date for this letter – perhaps Monday, March 11, 1940.

[†] May refer to David O. Selznick, whose "Gone with the Wind" was making millions after six weeks in theaters (article by Ed Sullivan, NY *Daily News*, Feb 7, 1940, p 50) or to his brother, Myron Selznick, a wealthy actor's agent (for such stars as Vivien Leigh and Carole Lombard) who was also the owner of well-known racehorses of the day and was, in 1940, being sued for divorce. (NY *Daily News*, Oct 27, 1940, p 39C; San Pedro Cal. *News-Pilot*, Oct 28, 1939, p 5). As for Charley's rendition of the name, "Selnek (?)," he was a notoriously bad speller.

Letter No. 12: Charles W. Carvin to Mrs. Charles W. Carvin, 315 Grant St., Hollywood, Fla., Airmail, return address Industrial Rayon Corporation, 500 Fifth Avenue, New York, N.Y., written c. 5:30 pm and postmarked New York, N.Y., Jan 31, 1947, 11:30 p.m.

INDUSTRIAL RAYON CORPORATION

SALES OFFICES
500 FIFTH AVENUE
NEW YORK 18, N.Y.

PLANTS
CLEVELAND, OHIO
PAINESVILLE, OHIO
COVINGTON, VIRGINIA

GENERAL OFFICES
CLEVELAND, OHIO

CHARLES W. CARVIN
VICE PRESIDENT
IN CHARGE OF SALES

Dear Mom –

I enjoyed the letters that had accumulated when I returned and I know that you enjoy letters too and I am sorry my record is so bad – I mean well, but I spell so poorly that a letter the length of mine takes me longer than your flowing talented productions.

I know a vacation is punk without an escort and I too would love to wander around Florida with you and our family – but we must eat and I am getting ready to retire – some day so the youngsters and you get a break.

Answering your questions. Collins lost his house - moved to Rye – Haven't seen Sokol but he phoned today – Brooks does not look well – was in today – has a cold, and his legs bother him again – I haven't seen a movie or show since you left.

Last Sunday Ralph McClellan and the town Club Committee met at our house and I had dinner with them at Scarsdale Club.

The show next Wed will be alrite - nothing extra – a lot of work, nice fellas so – it's worth it – my contribution.

Enjoyed talking to you but you get disappointed so easily – Buck up – I understand –

Will write tomorrow – have a rehearsal at the "fire house" at 2:30 - Writing some songs – Doin a "What Comes Naturally."

Jackson can get Joe in Citadel Greenville 1150 [so if] Joe wants to call him his home address is 101 – Argonne Drive Greenville S.C. He says he will drive Joe from Greenville to the College if Joe likes.

I took Sam to get the license this A.M. – 1000 people in line – last day. Signed the papers and left him there – wasted 1 hr – Hope he got it – will send it tomorrow –

Father Benno* coming in to see me Monday – Received a letter from Isabelle today – Enclosing it – typical – first I've heard.

Rusty leave by plane Saturday – for Hollywood Beach Hotel –

All now – 5:30 P.M. Friday – have to sign my mail – Meeting tonite Republican Club – Stassen speaks – Love to all –

The Ole Man.

---

* Presumably the Father Benno Brink who later married Stel and Frank Carmody.

Letter <u>No. 13</u>: Charles W. Carvin to Mrs. C. W. Carvin, 5901 Atlantic Ave., Ventnor, New Jersey, dated August 8, 1949.

CHARLES W. CARVIN CO., INC

450 SEVENTH AVENUE • NEW YORK 1, N.Y. • BRYAN T 9-7132

Mrs. C. W. Carvin
5901 Atlantic Ave.
Ventnor, New Jersey

August 8, 1949

Dearest Mom.

This is the first letter that you will have received dictated to the new secretary we have with us by the name of Stella Marie Carvin. It seems to me that I am always changing my plans. Phil Brown is having an outing at Winged Foot on Thursday the eleventh, and I accepted a long time ago to play with him. Therefore, I am forwarding the box and admission tickets in case anyone would like to go to the races on Thursday.

I spoke to Mr. Rogoson and he and Mrs. Rogoson have accepted my invitation to spend the weekend in Atlantic City. I plan to drive down with them early Friday morning. It is Charlie's plan to drive down with Julie and David Thursday night.

I will probably talk to you on the telephone before, but am taking this opportunity to advise you and mail you the tickets in the event you or anyone else wish to use them.

We will all be down soon, so take care of yourself and get a good rest till then.

My love,

Dad

CWC:SC
enc.
P.S. Take good care of these tickets because we will want to go to the races on Saturday.

Letter No. 14: Charles W. Carvin to Stella Marie Carvin, undated, addressed to Mrs. C. W. Carvin, c/o Ida. No postage (presumably hand delivered to Ida).

Charles W.
Carvin
Co., Inc.
649 AVENUE OF THE AMERICAS
NEW YORK 11, N. Y.

Friday Morning –

Dearest Mom –

I read your note very carefully – You know I would do anything at all to make you "Better" – So far all my attempts have failed and as has yours.

You keep tangling it up with "caring for one another" – this has nothing to do with the problem – we have always cared. I am terribly lonesome without you. I am no youngster and am not too well but I just cannot stand by and see you destroy yourself with drugs, liquor and foolish ideas, particularly when it always ends up by your stating it would have been different if only "I" had done this, that, or the other thing –

It is evident we need skilled professional help and at once – whether it be Richmond, Phila or White Plains is not important.

It is important that it be successful. I would rather avoid the responsibility of this decision. I will spend all the money we have to put you on your feet but I confess that to date my guesses as to the method have failed.

If it helps you to know that I love you – let me tell you so – I do – I always did and always will – but this alone is no cure – and I many times made the mistake of thinking it would be.

Don't talk about my forgiving you – there is nothing to forgive; you are sick – and your type of illness hurts us both – Don't think of the past, go to work on the future, the short time it will take in comparison to the reward we receive will be nothing –

I feel sure you can and will do it –

All my love –

> *Dad –*

Anything you need let Ida know – it is lonesome in the house but if progress is being made it is worth it!! Love – D –

Appendix 6

Interview of Nancy Maddux Lowrie by Charles W. Carvin

December 25, 1962

Nancy, we've been together a good many years and I'm just trying to think back to the days on Buffalo Avenue, remember?

Yeah.

And old Sam was there. Boy, we had a lot of fun in those days. Didn't we?

We sure did. Sure did. We had a lot of fun.

And remember then, you got the Cadillac car, and by gosh, nobody in the country could drive a car, and you got permission to go all the – to take it to Florida –

Yes –

And you and Ida get in the back seat and off we go to Florida.

That's right. (laughing) Didn't we have a good time?

We certainly did, and then on the road, the first day, we were stopped by the policemen and they take us in to the state cop and he won't believe that I got the owner of the car with me and he sends for – and you go in there, remember?

Yes, I do.

And yeah, we had to pay his fine, and he says, Boy, he's seen everything now. He couldn't imagine a man driving his maid to Florida – in her Cadillac – right?

Yeah, and but, he said, "It's Nancy's car?"

Yeah, that's right.

"What are you doin' with Nancy's car?" (Laughing.) And "Well, we're taking her down to Florida."

Yeah, that was really somethin'.

And then, remember when we used to… you could bake all our breads?

Oh yeah, sure did.

And those cinnamon buns. Nancy, they're something. If we could only put them in the deep freeze we'd make a lot of 'em. And save 'em –

That's right.

Well –

Old Nancy can still bake cinnamon buns. And make rolls.

Yeah.

Friday cake.

I want to tell you, your tomatoes this year were the finest tomatoes I've ever seen.

Now ain't that nice.

That was a terrible shock to Mrs. Carvin. She told the gardener to put in flowers and you told him tomato bushes.

Yeah (laughing).

All of a sudden she's looking for roses, and up come your tomatoes!

No… The rose bushes was there already anyway. My tomatoes was between the bushes.

I see.

And I certainly had nice tomatoes. And we ain't bought any this season.

That's right. Well the thing we miss mostly this year, Nancy, is the jellies that you always put up. You haven't bothered much this year about jellies.

No, we haven't made any jelly.

You used to give them to the whole neighborhood.

Yeah, givin' everybody jelly. It's a lot of trouble to make jelly anyway, and so, Ida says she's gonna make some after everything gets... kinda slow...

That's right... Well, we certainly had many nice summers together. Enjoyed it. And winters too, eh? Lots of cold winters.

Sure enough.

Remember that winter the heater blew out up there? Oh, boy.

Oh, boy.

Up in Scarsdale. That was somethin'.

Yeah, we certainly had a good time together.

And now our children are growin' up. We're just on the fence, aren't we? They're just doin' everything, and we're just watchin' 'em.

That's right.

That's the way it gets.

Tell us about your family, Nancy. How hard did you work?

Oh I worked night and day, Mr. Carvin. I'd work – sometime I'd go home at one o'clock, two o'clock, and I was back at six o'clock in the morning there to get breakfast. And I worked for many years, I had to have breakfast at six o'clock. I used to feed Mr. Straus. He'd hear me runnin' around the house. He'd jump up and try to shave and get dressed by the time I get his breakfast ready. And I'd have three fires to make, and a heater. And I'd make – I'd have those three fires made – the heater – and those three heaters – and his breakfast ready when he come sittin' at the table, and his table set... It was very nice.

How many children did you have at that time?

Oh, 'um... How many children did I have?

Yes.

I had seven children at that time.

Is that right.

I had seven children in the house.

You were support those children –

Supporting all those children myself.

Never got a penny from your husband.

Nope. Never got a penny from him and never asked him for anything. I asked him if he'd leave, if he'd leave I and my childrens alone, and I would never ask him for a penny. And I didn't. And I raised my children until they got up big enough to think they was mens, and they got up to think they was – the girls – was women. And they left, one by one, until the last one left. Then I decided I would buy me a home. I was only makin' eight dollars a week.

Isn't that amazing, and on eight dollars a week, and then gradual raises, you bought two houses in Florida.

Yeah.

You bought a house up in Newburg.

Yeah.

You bought a lot on the corner. You paid every cent of your debts every day. You never owed a dime.

Yeah, and Mr. Carvin, you know still, I been living with you and been with you a long, long time.

That's right.

I've never been any trouble and never come to you, for your assistance to help me out. I made a way some way.

That's right.

And you know that. And I'm still doin' the same thing today. Course I'm glad that the Lord opened the way, and I have a place where I can sit down now and eat and sleep. And have anything I want, and feel like I'm at home. And I can rest all I want. Get up when I get ready, and do as I please.

Nancy, in the thirty-five years we've been together, we've never had any trouble of any kind?

Never had a fuss nor quarrel. As long as I and Ida been together, we never had a fuss. Never had no misunderstanding. And so we've always gotten on alright.

That doesn't happen today very often, does it?

No, it doesn't –

See, what's going on –

It doesn't happen today.

Everybody wants the government to take care of 'em, and social security and everything else, and here, you've bought these houses clear, you own that, and you're leaving your children a lot of real estate that's gonna be marvelous, and you did it all on your own hard work.

All my own hard work. I certainly have worked hard in my life to be… eighty-four years old. Now. And I feel fine.

Of course we disagree about that eighty-four years… I think… I – [Both laughing] I think… It doesn't make any difference –

You said I was a hundred when I came.

[Still laughing] I figured it out – No, no, not when you came here, but the way it figures back, from the time in Columbus Georgia. You could remember almost, just the turn, when the slaves had just gone out, right?

No I don't remember that, Mr. Carvin, when the slaves went out. The only what I know about slaves was hearin' my parents talkin' about it.

Yeah, I said… Your parents were slaves.

My parents used – my parents was slaves and they used to talk and tell me about how they used to do. And really, they enjoyed it.

I know, yeah, that's the thing that's amazing.

Really, they enjoyed it.

I mean, you were down on the plantation where they'd been slaves; remember, you were up in the big house, weren't you?

Yeah. My mother was the cook and I was raised right up with the children there in the house.

With the white children.

With the white children there in the house.

And that's where you learned –

We all used to play together.

And you say that you had a ham house, and all –

We had a big smoke house, and had meats on one side to the other, hams and shoulders and middlins and hog jowls, salt heads, everything. Lard, and cans all around. And they had a big pantry with tobacco, hominy grits, flour, barrels of syrup, barrels of brown sugar, barrels of white sugar. I remember all of that.

And all those people, you say, were living together, and very happy.

All were happy. My people was happy as they could be, 'cause my mother and father was the first Negroes that he ever owned. And then they was made man and wife. And they lived there. And he died there.

Who was – what was his name?

Darrel Maddux. And Sarah Maddux. He give them a home there as long as they lived. He had enough ground to plant cotton. Corn. Potatoes. Have his little watermelon patch, and his garden. And he stayed there until he died. Some of his apple trees was there the last time I was down there. I saw some of them standin' there.

Was this in Columbus?

Pineville, Georgia.

Oh, Pineville,

Pineville, Georgia.

Well you didn't have much opportunity then to go to school, did you?

Not very much.

No.

No.

Course in those days, there were no roads, and no buses or anything else to take you to school.

No roads. No buses. No...

Well did they teach you on the plantation to read and write?

No, we had a school house that old Judge Bivens give them... The deeds to the... uh.. tract of land down there. And they built a church and a school house that's still there.

Is that right?

It belonged to them. No one could take it away from them. That's where I went to school.

And they ran the school themselves?

Well –

I mean, it wasn't owned by the state, then, if they owned it...

They had school teachers to come. I don't know how they did that. But I... they had... First school teacher I went to was a white man named Huffman. And the next one was King. And the next one was Smith. That was my last school teacher.

Smith?

Smith.

It's amazing that you remember the school teachers.

I remember all – I remember all the school teachers.

Well then after things began to get bad, after that happened and you were married, I remember you talking about the fact that you pushed a plow, you used to –

Oh I used to could plow. Anywhere anybody else could stick a plow in the ground, I could too. Oh, I plowed. I – that was my trouble. I always worked hard Mr. Carvin. I plowed. I hoed. I picked cotton. I could pick two hundred pound of cotton. And I'd go out and get me a big bag of chestnuts and chickp –

Is that right? Well, after you picked this cotton, would you go home and –

Go home and cook. Yeah. Sure I would.

Do you remember what they paid you for picking the cotton?

25 cents a hundred.

25! And you got 50 cents a day?

25 cents a hundred and when I picked two hundred I made 50 cents.

Imagine that.

That's the truth.

Oh, I know.

I'm tellin' the truth. Henry, he's always tellin' me about that. That's the truth, whatever I told it.

Henry, where do your parents come from?

Albany, Georgia.

Whereabouts in Georgia?

Albany, Georgia.

Albany Georgia, eh? Of course, you don't remember back that far. You see, Nancy and I disagree about her age. According to Sam, Nancy's 94. She says she's 84.

Yeah, he say I'm 94. If he say I'm 94, I'm 94.

Other Nothing in Common Books

Cage Stories: Memories of Fatherhood and Creation
by jwcarvin (2000)
ISBN 978-0-9768183-1-1

A Piece of the Pie: The Story of Customer Service at Publix
by jwcarvin (2005)
ISBN 978-0-9768183-7-3
and its 90th Anniversary Edition (2020)
ISBN 978-1-7332515-0-1

Alemeth
by jwcarvin (2017)
ISBN 978-0-9768183-8-0

Oh, Mother, That Man's Here Again!!
The Christmas Cards of Charles W. Carvin,
annotated and with an introduction by jwcarvin (2018)
ISBN 978-0-9768183-5-9

It's Been Four Billion Years:
The Story of Life on Earth a Million Years at a Time
by jwcarvin (2020)

The Rivercane Cabin Coloring Book,
by Lynda McLaughlin and Roger Fingar (2022)
ISBN 978-0-9768183-3-5

Praise for Alemeth:

Carvin masterfully brings to life a South in dramatic transition, and he avoids the binary categories of pro and con that often typify the genre… [A] thoughtful, sensitive rendering of a complex period in American history. A philosophically challenging look at the inner turmoil of the American South in the 19th century.

– Kirkus Reviews

jwcarvin can be contacted on the web at jwcarvin.com

www.ingramcontent.com/pod-product-compliance
Lightning Source LLC
Chambersburg PA
CBHW061958090426
42811CB00006B/971

9 780976 818342